SUNDAYS

AND

SEASONS

2004

Augsburg Fortress

SUNDAYS AND SEASONS
2004, Year C

RELATED RESOURCES

Icon: Visual Images for Every Sunday (AFP 0-8066-4077-4)
Worship Planning Calendar, 2004, Year C (AFP 0-8066-4545-8)
Words for Worship, 2004, Year C (AFP 0-8066-4544-X)

ACKNOWLEDGMENTS

Copyright © 2003 Augsburg Fortress. All rights reserved. Except for brief quotations in critical articles or reviews, no part of this book may be reproduced in any manner without prior written permission from the publisher. Write to: Permissions, Augsburg Fortress, Box 1209, Minneapolis, MN 55440-1209.

Scripture quotations are from the New Revised Standard Version Bible © 1989 Division of Christian Education of the National Council of the Churches of Christ in the United States of America. Used by permission.

The prayers (printed in each Sunday/festival section) may be reproduced for onetime, congregational use, provided copies are for local use only and the following copyright notice appears: From *Sundays and Seasons*, copyright © 2003 Augsburg Fortress.

Annual Materials
    The Gospel of Luke, Year C: William Heisley

Seasonal and Weekly Materials
    Images of the Season: Lynn Pagliarini (Christmas Cycle), Cathy Malotky (Easter Cycle), Brian T. Johnson (Season after Pentecost)

    Environment and Art for the Season: Scott A. Moore

    Preaching with the Season and Images for Preaching: George W. Hoyer (Christmas Cycle), Twila Schock and Bill Swanson (Easter Cycle), Robert Brusic (Summer), Frederick Niedner (Autumn, November)

    The Prayers: Timothy V. Olson (Christmas Cycle), Foy Christopherson (Easter Cycle), Rhoda Schuler (Season after Pentecost)

    Worship Matters: Timothy Keyl (Christmas Cycle), Craig Mueller (Easter Cycle)

    Let the Children Come: Mary Pechauer (Christmas Cycle, Easter Cycle), Sandra Anderson (Season after Pentecost)

Music Materials
    Assembly Song for the Season: Erik Floan; Mainstream Choral: Thomas Pavlechko; Classic Choral: Bradley Ellingboe; Children's Choral: Marilyn Comer; Keyboard/Instrumental: Janet Linker and Jane McFadden; Handbells: June Rauschnabel; Praise Ensemble: Mark Albrecht

Editors
    Norma Aamodt-Nelson, Carol Carver, Robert Buckley Farlee, Jessica Hillstrom, and Martin A. Seltz

Art and Design
    Art: Tanja Butler
    Book Design: The Kantor Group, Inc.

Manufactured in the U.S.A.   0-8066-4543-1

Introduction

Advent

Christmas

Epiphany

Lent

The Three Days

Easter

Summer

Autumn

November

Introduction

When a Christian assembly gathers together in

worship on a Sunday (or other day), it engages in much

more than just speaking and singing to God and each other.

The liturgy involves the present community, to be sure—the ministers, readers, musicians, and many others who offer their gifts in leading and enabling the assembly's central voice. The sermon has been crafted to speak to that particular group of people on that particular day. And this resource is designed to help those local leaders serve their communities of faith, providing ideas and tools that will be adapted to suit local circumstances.

A LARGER SPHERE

But the circle surrounding that congregation's worship is larger than just the people involved in that place on that day. We are blessed with people throughout the church who have shown great abilities in certain facets of the church's worship life. In *Sundays and Seasons* we try to make their gifts available to local users. In the area of preaching, for example, writers help us both with an approach for each Sunday or holy day, as well as taking a step back and providing a perspective for each season. Once again this year we are fortunate to have intriguing contributions to inspire our own creative efforts. In the Advent-Christmas-Epiphany seasons, our thoughts are led by George W. Hoyer, retired from teaching homiletics at the Pacific Lutheran School of Theology and now living in Massachusetts. Moving into the Easter cycle, we are assisted by Lutheran missionaries Twila Schock and William Swanson, a married pastoral couple currently serving in Wittenberg, Germany. Robert Brusic, seminary pastor at Luther Seminary in St. Paul, is our writer for the summer months. Finally, in the autumn and November times, our thoughts are sparked by the gifts of Frederick Niedner, professor of religion at Valparaiso University.

The prayers of the people are another area of the liturgy that requires a strong local voice, but model prayers can be helpful. This year, three writers have shaped those intercessions for us. The Christmas cycle prayers were written by Timothy V. Olson, pastor in Belvidere, Illinois. Those for the Easter cycle come to us from Foy Christopherson, general manager of ecclesiastical arts for Augsburg Fortress. And prayers for the season of the church were provided by Rhoda Schuler, currently teaching religion at Concordia College, Moorhead, Minnesota.

Two other features that appear each week are Worship Matters and Let the Children Come. The Worship Matters columns for the time after Pentecost are an assembly of some of the insights from years past. In the first half of the year, though, we are grateful for thoughts from Timothy Keyl, pastor in Nashua, New Hampshire, and Craig Mueller, pastor in Chicago. The columns that provide helps for better including children in worship are this year provided by two writers deeply involved in the topic, Mary Pechauer, a pastor in Bloomington, Minnesota, and Sandra Anderson, a director of children's ministry in Moorhead, Minnesota.

For each season, additional features assist worship planners and leaders in taking a larger view in certain areas. Assembly Song for the Season, written throughout the year by Erik Floan, a church musician in Seattle, provides ideas for strengthening and giving variety to the congregation's own song. Another regular facet is Environment and Art for the Season. This year it is written by Scott A. Moore, a pastor and graduate student currently working in Chicago. His contribution encourages a broader and longer view of the subject, moving beyond mere decoration to help us think about some basic aspects of our worship spaces.

OPENING UP TO FRESH INSIGHTS

Images are powerful things, often leading our musings to unexpected and fruitful locales that would have been overlooked in a more regimented progression. Our seasonal images have been provided by three gifted pastors. In the Christmas cycle, they come from Lynn Pagliarini, who serves as a pastor in Stillwater, Minnesota. Writing for the Easter cycle is Catherine Malotky, a pastor currently working for the ELCA Board of Pensions. For the time of the church, we have engaged Brian T. Johnson, chaplain at Gustavus Adolphus College, St. Peter, Minnesota. And providing an overview to the Gospel of Luke that serves as the central gospel for this lectionary year is William Heisley, pastor in Minneapolis.

Our local liturgies reflect gifts from outside our community, but also are enriched by contributions from many times. Besides the scripture readings and the liturgy itself, this temporal breadth is reflected in the music that weaves through our worship. On any given Sunday, we may hear music from twentieth century Zimbabwe or sixteenth century France. We are fortunate to have musicians steeped in different aspects of choral and instrumental music providing their suggestions. Among those musicians are Thomas Pavlechko from Memphis and Bradley Ellingboe from Albuquerque in adult choral, and Marilyn Comer from Mead, Oklahoma, in children's choral. Janet Linker of Columbus, Ohio, assisted by Jane McFadden helps us with suggestions for keyboard music. June Rauschnabel from Moorhead, Minnesota, provides handbell listings. And Mark Albrecht, who serves in West Allis, Wisconsin, provides ideas for praise ensemble.

As has become customary, this book also provides the features Worship Planning Checklist, Music for the Season, Shape of Worship for the Season, seasonal Alternate Worship Texts, and Seasonal Rites, as well as an extensive bibliography. Complete weekly resources are also included for those lesser festivals on the *LBW* calendar that fall on a Sunday this church year.

IN THIS BOOK AND BEYOND

Changes for this year include more references to the Renewing Worship series of volumes, produced as the process of preparing for a projected new set of primary Lutheran worship resources continues. Because a main goal of the Renewing Worship enterprise is to gather responses from congregations that are trying out new proposals, we hope that users of this volume will be active in both putting the resources through their paces and reporting their reactions and suggestions. A listing of the Renewing Worship volumes is found on page 366 of the bibliography; more up-to-date information can be found on the Web site, www.renewingworship.org. Incidentally,

note that in the hymn listings in this edition of *Sundays and Seasons*, the abbreviation for the first volume of Renewing Worship, *Congregational Song*, has changed from CS to RW1. New hymn volumes in that series are RW5 (*New Hymns and Songs*) and RWSB (*Renewing Worship Songbook*).

Responding to user requests, another tweak to *Sundays and Seasons* is an expansion in the alternate texts for the Day of Pentecost. As one of the principal festivals of the church year, it deserves the added attention.

We have also tried to indicate when an Augsburg Fortress musical resource is no longer in print. See page 16 for an explanation.

The *Sundays and Seasons* family of publications is larger than this volume. Its direct descendents include the CD-ROM *Words for Worship*, which contains electronic text and graphic files for service folders of readings, prayers, psalms with their tones, and much more. It is produced each year, as is the *Worship Planning Calendar*, spiral-bound and helpful for all worship planners. This year brings an additional member of the family, *Sundays and Seasons* Leaders Edition, containing prayers and a limited number of other seasonal and weekly texts, and designed to be used by ministers within the worship service. It is not a planning tool like this book, but rather a complement to the *LBW* altar and *WOV* leaders editions.

Other worthwhile "cousins" to *Sundays and Seasons* are *Hymns for Worship*, providing more than 1,200 hymns in electronic format to include in service folders; the entire *Life Together* series of resources based on the liturgy, including *Kids Celebrate* reproducible children's bulletins for each lectionary year; the Church Year Calendar, a one-page overview of the church year suitable for distribution to the entire congregation; and Calendar of Word and Season, a wall calendar that combines striking liturgical art with lessons and colors for the church year.

We are grateful to the users of *Sundays and Seasons*, both for their loyal readership from year to year (and their faithful service to the church), and for their suggestions for improvement. We wish the richest blessings on all whose work in the liturgy reflects the life-giving love of God in Christ.

— Robert Buckley Farlee, general editor

The Gospel *of* Luke

"Tell all the Truth but tell it slant." Thus begins

Emily Dickinson's deeply religious, deeply spiritual poem.

Barbara Brown Taylor, Episcopal priest and one of the great

preachers of the gospel, quoted this poem in a lecture on preaching. In order for the powerful truth of the good news of Jesus to be heard, she said, people have to be approached on a slant. Straight on is just too intimidating, too overwhelming. Later that day she preached a sermon on a slant and at the end, as she quoted her biblical tale for the last time, she had to stop to remind her listeners to breathe. The story, told one more time, had taken our breath away. The power of truth on the slant is beyond explanation.

St. Luke knew how to tell truth on a slant. His gospel, easily read in one sitting, provides one of the great adventures in biblical literature. From the cycle that recounts the birth of Jesus, through his life and ministry, his parables, his miracles, and his teaching, to his death and resurrection, the reader is enveloped in the powerful presence of God at work in the world. Stories of the unfathomable love of God for us and for all of creation come in a slanted profusion that brings us ever into the fold of the faithful. This is not a straightforward lecture in theology. It is, instead, an account of Jesus, incarnate in the ancient world, and now in our lives. We look at Luke's stories, and on that slant, we see the unseeable face of God.

Perhaps one of the strongest impressions given by Luke's gospel is that stories of people abound. The Jesus of Luke is one who is decidedly incarnate. This Jesus is very human, living, laughing, loving, and suffering. And this Jesus is, at the same time, God become a person, one of us. The humanity of Jesus is underlined in his constant encounters with people like his mother, Mary (as in 2:48-50); his disciples (6:1-5); the Jewish and Roman leaders of his time (11:37-54; 23:1-25); and most of all, with everyday, normal human beings like the woman who washes his feet with her tears, dries them with her hair, and anoints them with costly ointment (7:36-50); the woman who was crippled for eighteen years and is

healed (13:10-17); and Zacchaeus, the rich tax collector who repented of his abuse of others and is forgiven (19:1-10).

Luke the physician calls to our attention the fact that Jesus is regularly and deeply immersed in healing. Not only does he cure the crippled woman, but, among other miracles, he also heals the centurion's slave (7:1-10); he casts out a demon that is mute (11:14); and he relieves a man of his dropsy on the Sabbath (14:1-4). Jesus' healings reveal his deep love for people, for the weak and the lame, for those who know no other hope. And they reveal his mission to bring wholeness and compassion to all the world.

In *The Ongoing Feast: Table Fellowship and Eschatology at Emmaus* (The Liturgical Press, 1993), Arthur A. Just Jr. calls our attention to an even more profound way in which Luke's Jesus participates in and sanctifies human life: he engages in table fellowship.

Luke frequently shows Jesus in social situations, dining with friend and foe alike. Levi throws a great banquet for him and his table is crowded with tax collectors and others (5:29). The woman who bathes his feet with her tears does so at a meal in a Pharisee's house (7:36). A vast crowd of people, including five thousand men, is fed on the five loaves and two fish that Jesus blesses for their consumption (9:10-17). And he dines at the home of a leader of the Pharisees on the Sabbath (14:1).

Table fellowship can be the most intimate setting in which people engage. Jesus is deeply intimate with humanity. He shares food and drink with all who invite him. He interacts with them, challenging them to think in new ways about their present realities and about the future of the world. In doing so, he sets the course of his followers through the various hungers that mark life today.

The Day of Unleavened Bread was near. Jesus prepared for the culmination of his ministry by having his disciples arrange a banquet for them to share (22:1-23). He prepared for profound intimacy with them and with the future. They ate and drank the Passover meal together, and in and around that meal Jesus showed himself to be the ultimate food and drink for a hungry and thirsty world. "This is my body, which is given for you" (22:19). "This cup that is poured out for you is the new covenant in my blood" (22:20). In this meal, all the meals Jesus eats with his contemporaries are gathered and made into one holy meal for the future. Jesus bids farewell to his disciples with a banquet and, at the same time, promises them his continuing presence.

But there is more. The eating and drinking are not over. The intimacy for which the disciples long continues. Jesus has been killed and his body has disappeared. Going home from a failed mission, distraught disciples walk the lonely road to Emmaus (24:13-35). The banqueting has ended—or so they think. Then a stranger appears on the road. He goes home with them and teaches them, starting from the beginning: Moses, the prophets, the entire history of God's interaction with humanity—these are the subjects of his discourse. Then they eat and drink together. Bread and wine are broken and they remember: "This is my body. This is my blood." The promise of those words becomes their present reality and they rush off to tell the others. They are sent from that place back into the world in the power of the spirit of the One who has fed them and who has vanished.

The disciples are gathered to the table with Jesus. They are drawn more deeply into the mystery of his truth by the power of his words. They are fed on the eternal food that he provides. They are sent into the world, rejoicing and proclaiming the good news that the One who was dead is alive.

Arthur Just shows us that this is the ancient ordo: gathering, word, meal, sending. The disciples, met on the road and gathered together with Jesus around the table, are the church gathered at the foot of the altar. They are gathered to hear the word of God mediated through the mouth of Jesus himself and of his emissaries of truth. They are gathered to eat and drink his body and blood, launching them into the heart of Jesus' compassion, and embracing and blessing them so that they might tell the good news to others. They are sent out to bear that news, to be that news. They are sent out rejoicing, bringing delight in their new knowledge to a pain-filled, aching world.

Luke's gospel climaxes in its final chapter with this post-resurrection appearance. But it is not the simple apparition of a ghost-like Jesus. It is the church's encounter with the risen Lord in worship. It is the offering of the early church to the future church. It is the gift of a holy structure that draws us over and over into the depth of Jesus' message of hope, forgiveness, and healing.

Luke does not allow his tale to end here. Yes, it continues with his accounts of the formation of the church in the Acts of the Apostles. It also continues in the gospel itself. We read the rich history of the people Israel as it is changed forever by Jesus, one of its own. We read of meal after meal, food image after image. We see the healings and feel the embrace of compassion and comfort. We worship with the church immemorial. Then we are spun back to the beginning of the gospel. Grabbed by the power of the good news, we ask, "Isn't this the One who healed . . . who taught . . . who prophesied . . . who died? Isn't this the One?"

Luke's gospel does not necessarily let us off the hook. Instead of forcing us to turn the page to Acts, it calls us to return to its beginning. Worship inspires more learning. Deeper learning inspires deeper proclamation. Jesus' profound understanding of the sorrows and joys, the challenges and accomplishments, the sins and the repentance of humanity—Jesus' incarnational reality— teaches us to more fully respect each other and ourselves. It teaches us to celebrate our communal successes of love and acceptance. It calls us always, repeatedly, back to the table.

Luke's understanding of the table and of table fellowship cuts through all of the other stories he tells. It is at the table that the stories are told in all their power and clarity. It is at the table that the stories explain the feeding that is about to take place. It is at the table that the people become the assembly of those who know the name Jesus, and on whose brows the name is written. It is at the table that they are inspired to learn the stories, but learn them more fully. To speak about them, but more clearly; to love, but more deeply. And it is at the table that they are challenged to do it all again.

Gathering, hearing the word of God, sharing the holy meal, and being sent out to minister and to share the good news of wholeness and grace with others, this

9

liturgy is the deepest mark of Luke's gospel. All of life is gathered as a sacrifice to be placed at the foot of the table, to be brought as a gift to the One who does these things repeatedly for us, his own. Luke's stories of Jesus become the stories of our lives. Our lives become for others the waters of life flowing into the arid deserts of their pain and brokenness.

People who minister in the name of Christ during the year of Luke have a great opportunity set before them: to pair Luke's stories with our stories and to thus tell the truth on a powerful slant. More than ever, the advent of a still-new millennium calls for the church to perform such a task. As populations burgeon, as tensions between various groups multiply, as hunger grows, and as the earth itself seems to cry out for the gift of peace, the church has the opportunity and the responsibility to draw those who hunger, those who thirst, into relationship. As they are welcomed with open arms around the word read and preached, and as they gather with the assembly around the table where the word is joined to the bread and wine

of salvation, the stories become theirs. As they live in the stories, they are formed and reformed by them.

A student who expects to graduate from college in 2006 observes that about fifty percent of students who worship at his school attend the traditional liturgy, which is accompanied by the pipe organ. Fifty percent of the students attend a form of worship using guitars and other instruments in a less formal setting. But one hundred percent of the students who worship seek to be in deeper, more intimate relationships with the Lord of the church and with his people. They hunger and thirst, and they are drawn to the table for food that will make them fit for the journey ahead.

Whether you are a worship planner, a preacher, a musician, or one who assists in liturgy, use the year of Luke to draw the people of Christ deeper into the story of God's love, acceptance, and forgiveness. Walk down the road to Emmaus, listen to the story, and hear the invitation to dine on things eternal. Then, go back. Go back up the road to the rest of life. Live in hope. Tell the stories. Build relationships. Tell all the Truth but tell it slant.

Worship Planning Checklist

In order for this checklist to be most helpful, it needs to be consulted well ahead of each season. You might consider working by cycle rather than season. For example, in October the worship planners could gather and think through the entire Christmas cycle consisting of the Advent, Christmas, and Epiphany seasons. This approach helps to get everyone planning ahead, and also assists in unifying the larger divisions of the church year. One more bonus of this approach is that it may ease the Epiphany-as-afterthought syndrome.

ADVENT

- Purchase materials needed for the Advent wreath (four candles and enough greens to cover the wreath). Are any changes desired to the construction or location of the wreath? Perhaps more than one wreath will be wanted for your congregation if Sunday school students and other groups gather for

worship during the season in locations other than the sanctuary.
- Arrange for the Advent wreath to be set up one or two days before the first Sunday in Advent (November 30).

CHRISTMAS

- Arrange for purchase or donation of a Christmas tree.
- Locate any decorations that are in storage from previous years for the Christmas tree, the crèche, the chancel, and other interior or exterior areas. Repair or replace decorations as needed.

10

- Decide on a date and time for Christmas decorating, and solicit volunteer help.
- Prepare extra communion elements and communionware that may be needed for additional worshipers at Christmas services.
- Prepare a sign-up list for those who wish to sponsor additional flowers or poinsettia plants at Christmas.
- Plan for removal of Christmas decorations following the twelve days.
- If handheld candles are used by worshipers on Christmas Eve, determine how many candles and holders can be used from previous seasons and how many new candles and holders will be needed.
- Order special bulletin covers if needed for services on Christmas Eve or Christmas Day.
- Decide whether you will observe the festival of the Holy Innocents on December 28. If so, paraments will need to be changed.

EPIPHANY

- Determine what (if any) Epiphany decorations are needed.
- If incense is to be used for a service on the festival of the Epiphany, purchase a small quantity of it (along with self-lighting charcoal).
- If the Baptism of Our Lord (January 11) is to be observed as a baptismal festival, publicize the festival through congregational newsletters and bulletins; arrange for baptismal preparation sessions with parents, sponsors, and candidates; and when the day arrives set out the following:
  - Towel (baptismal napkin) for each person baptized
  - Baptismal candle for each person baptized
  - Shell (if used)
  - Oil for anointing (also a lemon wedge and a towel for removing oil from the presiding minister's hands)
  - Baptismal garment for each person baptized (if used)
  - Fresh water in a ewer (pitcher) or the font
- Will your congregation be observing the feasts of the Confession of St. Peter (January 18) and the Conversion of St. Paul (January 25), which fall on Sundays this year? Those two days, which frame the Week of Prayer for Christian Unity, make fine times

to join in worship with those of other Christian denominations. Make plans early if you want to do that, and publicize well.
- If you plan on burning last year's palms to make ashes (see below), place a notice in the bulletin on February 8 and 15 inviting members to return their palms by Transfiguration Sunday (February 22).

LENT

- If ashes are used on Ash Wednesday (February 25), arrange for someone (perhaps one or two altar guild members) to burn palms from the previous Passion Sunday. Or contact a church supply store for a supply of ashes. (A small quantity of ashes mixed with a bit of olive oil or water will go a long way.)
- Determine whether any Lenten decorations other than Lenten paraments are to be used.
- If crosses or images are draped in purple during the Lenten season, recruit volunteers to do this between the Transfiguration of Our Lord and Ash Wednesday.
- Order enough palm branches to distribute to worshipers on Passion Sunday. (Additional palm branches or plants may be used as decorations that day.) If the long individual palm fronds are used, they will need to be separated ahead of time. Make sure that they are fresh.
- Make sure worshipers know where to gather for a procession with palms liturgy. Prepare signs to direct them. Determine how those with physical disabilities will participate in the procession or be seated ahead of time.
- Reserve leftover palm branches to be burned for ashes next Ash Wednesday.
- Order worship participation leaflets if used for the Ash Wednesday liturgy or Passion Sunday processional liturgy.
- Order additional bulletin covers if needed for any special Lenten services (especially midweek liturgies).

THE THREE DAYS

- Schedule special rehearsals for the liturgies on these days. The liturgies in this week are unique, so all worship leaders, even those who have been involved in previous years, need to prepare for their roles.
- Be sure that altar guild members are well-equipped and informed about their tasks for these busy days.

11

- Locate one or more basin and pitcher sets for the Maundy Thursday liturgy. Towels are also needed for drying the feet of participants.
- Determine how participants will be recruited for the footwashing. Even if all in the congregation are invited, several people should be specifically prepared to participate.
- If the altar and the rest of the chancel is to be stripped on Maundy Thursday, recruit helpers (sacristans/altar guild members, even children) for this task.
- If you ring bells to announce services or chimes to mark times of the day, consider silencing them from the beginning of the Maundy Thursday liturgy until the hymn of praise at the Easter Vigil (or the first celebration of Easter).
- Keeping in mind that all of the liturgies of the Three Days are considered to be as one, do not plan a procession of worship leaders for Good Friday. All worship leaders simply find their own way to their respective places before the service.
- If a rite of procession and veneration of the cross is to be used on Good Friday, find or construct a rough-hewn cross, and determine how it will be placed in the chancel ahead of time or carried in procession.
- Prepare to thoroughly clean the worship space sometime between the Maundy Thursday liturgy and the Easter Vigil.
- If handheld candles are to be used by worshipers at an Easter Vigil, determine how many candles and holders can be used from previous seasons, and how many new candles and holders will need to be purchased.
- Well before the Easter Vigil, purchase a paschal candle (or arrange to make one) that will fit your congregation's stand. When the candle is received or finished, check to be sure it fits the stand snugly yet without being forced into place.
- Prepare materials needed to start a fire at the beginning of the Easter Vigil (kindling, wood, brazier, matches). Also, recruit someone to start and extinguish the fire properly.
- Prior to the Easter Vigil, place the paschal candle stand in the chancel for use throughout the fifty days of Easter.

- Make sure worshipers know where to gather for the service of light at the Easter Vigil. If you plan to gather outside, be sure to make backup plans in case you have inclement weather.
- Decide how light will be provided so assisting ministers and lectors can see to read during the Easter Vigil service. Determine what level of light is needed so all members of the congregation can participate during this liturgy. Practice setting lighting levels (at night) with the person who will be responsible for this during the vigil.
- Plan how the readings of the Easter Vigil will be proclaimed. Consider having a different person proclaim each of the readings to enliven the readings for the assembly.
- Prepare extra communion elements and communionware that may be needed for additional worshipers at Holy Week and Easter services.
- Order worship participation leaflets if used for the Maundy Thursday, Good Friday, or Easter Vigil liturgies.
- Order bulletin covers for Holy Week liturgies.
- It is helpful to prepare printed materials for worship leaders for the Three Days. Consider placing all the texts and musical resources needed by worship leaders into three-ring binders (half-inch binders purchased at an office supply store work well). Highlight speaking parts and instructions for each worship leader in individual copies.
- If the Easter Vigil (or Easter Sunday) is to be observed as a baptismal festival, see the suggestions for the Baptism of Our Lord in the Epiphany season, p. 11.

EASTER

- Determine whether special flowers are to be used on Pentecost (May 30). (Some churches order red geraniums to be placed around the church grounds or given away following Pentecost services.)
- If Pentecost is to be observed as a baptismal festival, see the suggestions for the Baptism of Our Lord in the Epiphany season, p. 11.
- On Pentecost, seven votive candles in red glass holders may be lighted and placed on or near the altar to recall the gifts of the Spirit.

- This year, in the United States, Pentecost falls on the weekend of Memorial Day. If many choir members will be absent because of that holiday, music leaders should consider whether alternate plans need to be made to provide for celebratory music on this principal festival.

SUMMER

- If the worship schedule changes, notify local newspapers and change listings on exterior signs and church answering machines.
- If your space is not air conditioned, consider ways to make worshipers cooler during warm weather.
- If the congregation worships outside one or more times during the summer, decide how worshipers will know where to gather and how they will be seated.
- This year, two lesser festivals fall on Sundays during summer: St. James the Elder on July 25 and Mary, Mother of Our Lord on August 15. Decide whether, and how, you want to observe those days. If you will celebrate them, paraments will need to be changed.

AUTUMN

- For worship schedule changes, notify local newspapers and change listings on exterior signs and church answering machines.
- If a harvest festival is scheduled, determine what (if any) additional decorations are to be used and who is to do the decorating.
- If one or more food collections are to be received, notify the congregation about them in advance, and arrange to deliver food to the appropriate agency within a day or two after the collection.

NOVEMBER

- Provide a book of remembrance or another way to collect the names of those who have died and who are to be remembered in prayers this month (or only on All Saints Sunday).
- If All Saints is to be observed as a baptismal festival, see the suggestions for the Baptism of Our Lord in the Epiphany season, p. 11.

13

Selected Publishers

AMSI
Contact the Lorenz Corp.

ABINGDON PRESS
201 8th Avenue South
PO Box 801
Nashville TN 37202-0801
800/251-3320 Customer Service
800/836-7802 Fax
permissions@abingdonpress.com

AGEHR, INC.
1055 E. Centerville Station Road
Centerville OH 45459
800/878-5459
937/438-0085
937/438-0434 Fax
office@agehr.org

ALFRED PUBLISHING CO., INC.
Box 10003
Van Nuys CA 91410-0003
818/891-5999
818/891-2369 Fax
customerservice@alfred.com

AMERICAN LUTHERAN
Publicity Bureau
PO Box 327
Delhi NY 13753-0327
607/746-7511 General

ARISTA MUSIC
PO Box 1596
Brooklyn NY 11201

AUGSBURG FORTRESS
PO Box 1209
Minneapolis MN 55440-1209
800/328-4648 Ordering
800/421-0239 Permissions
612/330-3300 General

BECKENHORST PRESS
PO Box 14273
Columbus OH 43214
614/451-6461 General
614/451-6627 Fax
www.beckenhorstpress.com

BOOSEY & HAWKES, INC.
35 East Twenty-first Street
New York NY 10010-6212
212/358-5300 General
212/358-5301 Fax
info.ny@boosey.com

BOSTON MUSIC CO.
215 Stuart Street
Boston MA 02116
800/863-5150
617/528-6100
617/426-5100 Retail
info@bostonmusiccompany.com

BOURNE COMPANY
5 West 37th Street
New York NY 10018
212/391-4300 General
212/391-4306 Fax
Bourne@bournemusic.com

BRENTWOOD-BENSON MUSIC, INC.
741 Cool Springs Blvd
Franklin, TN 37067
800/846-7664 General
615/261-3381 Fax
admin@brentwoodbenson.com

BROUDE BROTHERS LTD.
141 White Oaks Road
Williamstown MA 01267
413/458-8131
413/458-5242 Fax

BROADMAN HOLMAN GENEVOX
See LifeWay Christian Resources

C.F. PETERS CORPORATION
70-30 80th Street
Glendale NY 11385
718/416-7800 General
718/416-7805 Fax
sales@cfpeters-ny.com

CHANGING CHURCH FORUM
Prince of Peace Publishing
200 E. Nicollet Boulevard
Burnsville MN 55337
800/874-2044

CHESTER MUSIC
Contact Hal Leonard Corp-Music Dispatch

CHURCH PENSION FUND
Order from: Church Publishing Corp.
445 Fifth Avenue
New York NY 10016
800/242-1918 General
212/779-3392 Fax

CONCORDIA PUBLISHING HOUSE
3558 South Jefferson Avenue
Saint Louis MO 63118
800/325-3040 Customer Service
314/268-1329 Fax

E.C. SCHIRMER MUSIC CO.
138 Ipswich Street
Boston MA 02215-3534
617/236-1935 General
617/236-0261 Fax
office@ecspublishing.com

EUROPEAN AMERICAN MUSIC DIST.
P.O. Box 4340
15800 Northwest 48th Avenue
Miami FL 33014
305/521-1604
305/521-1638 Fax
eamdc@eamdc.com

CARL FISCHER, INC.
Order from local music store

GIA PUBLICATIONS, INC.
7404 South Mason Avenue
Chicago IL 60638
800/442-1358 General
708/496-3828 Fax
custserv@giamusic.com

GALAXY COMMUNICATIONS
Contact E. C. Schirmer Music Co

HINSHAW MUSIC CO, INC.
PO Box 470
Chapel Hill NC 27514-0470
919/933-1691 General
919/967-3399 Fax
www.hinshawmusic.com

HAL LEONARD CORP
PO Box 13819
7777 West Bluemound Road
Milwaukee WI 53213
414/774-3630 General
800/637-2852 Music Dispatch
414/774 3259 Fax
www.halleonard.com

HOPE PUBLISHING CO.
380 South Main Place
Carol Stream IL 60188
800/323-1049 General
630/665-2552 Fax
hope@hopepublishing.com

ICEL (INTERNATIONAL COMMISSION
ON ENGLISH IN THE LITURGY)
1522 K Street Northwest
Suite 1000
Washington DC 20005-1202
202/347-0800 General
202/347 1839 Fax

IONIAN ARTS, INC.
PO Box 259
Mercer Island WA 98040-0259
206/236-2210 General

LIFEWAY CHRISTIAN RESOURCES
One LifeWay Plaza
Nashville TN 37234
800/251-3225 Broadman & Holman
800/884-7712 Genevox
customerservice@lifeway.com

THE LITURGICAL CONFERENCE
8750 Georgia Ave.
Suite 123
Silver Spring MD 20910-3621
301/495 0885

THE LITURGICAL PRESS
St. John's Abbey
PO Box 7500
Collegeville MN 56321-7500
800/858-5450 General
320/363-2213 General
320/363-3299 Fax
sales@litpress.org

LITURGY TRAINING PUBLICATIONS
1800 North Hermitage Avenue
Chicago IL 60622-1101
800/933-4779 Customer Service
800/933-7094 Fax
orders@ltp.org

LIVE OAK HOUSE
6700 Piedras Blanco Drive
Austin, TX 78747-4084
512/282-3397
www.liveoakhouse.com

THE LORENZ CORPORATION
501 East Third Street
PO Box 802
Dayton OH 45401-0802
800/444-1144 General
937/223.2042 Fax
info@lorenz.com

LUDWIG MUSIC PUBLISHING CO.
557 East 140th Street
Cleveland OH 44110-1999
800/851-1150 General
216/851-1958 Fax
info@ludwigmusic.com

MARANATHA! MUSIC
205 Avenida Fabricante
San Clemente CA 92672
800/245-7664 Retail
customerservice@corinthian.com
www.maranathamusic.com

MASTERS MUSIC PUBLICATIONS
PO Box 810157
Boca Raton FL 33481-0157
800/434-6340
561/241-6169 General
561/241-6347 Fax
info@masters-music.com

MORNINGSTAR MUSIC PUBLISHERS
1727 Larkin Williams Road
Fenton MO 63026
800/647-2117 Ordering
636/305-0121 Fax
morningstar@morningstarmusic.com

MUSICA RUSSICA
27 Willow Lane
Madison CT 06443
800/326-3132
203/421-3132 Fax
rusmuscat@musicarussica.com

NEW GENERATION PUBLISHERS
Box 321
Waverly IA 50677
319/352-4396
319/352-3814
319/352-0765 Fax
fern@ylvisaker.com

NORTHWESTERN PUBLISHING
HOUSE
1250 North 113th Street
Milwaukee WI 53226-3284
800/662-6093 Customer Service
414/475-7684 Fax
www.nph.net

OREGON CATHOLIC PRESS
OCP Publications
P.O. Box 18030
Portland OR 97218-0030
800/548-8749 General
800/462-7329 Fax
liturgy@ocp.org

OXFORD UNIVERSITY PRESS
2001 Evans Road
Cary NC 27513
800/445-9714Customer Service
919/677-1303 Fax
custserv@oup-usa.org

PARACLETE PRESS
P.O. Box 1568
Orleans, MA 02653
800/451-5006 General
508/255-4685
508/255-5705 Fax
mail@paracletepress.com

PLYMOUTH MUSIC CO.
Po Box 24330
Fort Lauderdale FL 33307
954/563-1844 General
954/563-9006 Fax

RANDALL M. EGAN, PUBLISHERS
2024 Kenwood Parkway
Minneapolis MN 55405-2303
612/377-4450 General
800/269-3426 Orders
612/377-4450 + *51 Fax

SELAH PUBLISHING CO.
PO Box 3037
Kingston NY 12402
845/338 2816 General
800/852-6172 Ordering
845/338 2991 Fax
customerservice@selahpub.com

SHAWNEE PRESS
PO Box 690
49 Waring Drive
Delaware Water Gap PA 18327-1690
570/476-0550 General
570/476-5247 Fax
shawnee-info@shawneepress.com

THEODORE PRESSER CO.
588 North Gulph Road
King of Prussia PA 19406
610/525-3636
610/527-7841 Fax
www.presser.com

WARNER BROTHERS PUBLICATIONS
15800 Northwest 48th Avenue
Miami FL 33014
800/327-7643 General
305/621-4869 Fax

WESTMINSTER/JOHN KNOX PRESS
100 Witherspoon Street
Louisville KY 40202-1396
800/227-2872 Customer Service
502/569-5113 Fax

WORD MUSIC INC.
3319 West End Avenue, Suite 200
Nashville TN 37203
888/324-9673
888/324-4329 Fax
questions@wordmusic.com

WORLD LIBRARY PUBLICATIONS
3825 North Willow Road
Schiller Park IL 60176-2309
800/566-6150
888/957-3291 Fax
wlpcs@jspaluch.com

15

Key *to* Music Publishers

ABI	Abingdon		GIA	GIA Publications		MF	Mark Foster
AFP	Augsburg Fortress		GS	GlorySound		MSM	MorningStar Music
AG	Agape (Hope)		GSCH	G. Schirmer (Hal Leonard)		NOV	Novello (Shawnee)
AGEHR	AGEHR Inc.		HAL	Hal Leonard		NMP	National Music Publishers
ALF	Alfred		HIN	Hinshaw		OCP	Oregon Catholic Press
AMSI	AMSI (Lorenz)		HOP	Hope		OXF	Oxford University Press
AUR	Aureole		HWG	H. W. Gray (Warner)		PAR	Paraclete
BEC	Beckenhorst		INT	Integrity (Word)		PET	C. F. Peters
BEL	Belwin (Warner)		ION	Ionian Arts		PLY	Plymouth
B&H	Boosey & Hawkes		JEF	Jeffers		PRE	Presser
BRN	Bourne		KIR	Kirkland House		PVN	Pavane (Intrada)
CFI	Carl Fischer		KJO	Kjos		RME	Randall M. Egan
CFP	C. F. Peters		LAK	Lake State		RR	Red River
CG	Choristers Guild (Lorenz)		LAW	Lawson-Gould Publishing		SEL	Selah
CHA	Chantry (Augsburg Fortress)		LED	Leduc		SHW	Shawnee
CPH	Concordia		LEM	Lemoine (Presser)		SMP	Sacred Music Press (Lorenz)
DUR	Durand (Presser)		LIL	Lillenas (Royal Marketing)		WAL	Walton
ECS	E. C. Schirmer		LOR	Lorenz		WAR	Warner (Plymouth)
FB	Fred Bock Music Co.		LP	The Liturgical Press		WJK	Westminster John Knox
FLA	Flammer (Shawnee)		MAR	Maranatha		WLP	World Library
GAL	Galaxy		MAY	Mayhew		WRD	Word Music

16

A Note *on* Music Listings

In the seasonal and daily listings of choral and instrumental music, we have made an effort to indicate if a piece published by Augsburg Fortress is out of print as of the publication of this volume. If it is, "OP" will appear at the end of the listing.

Why do we still list it if it is out of print? Primarily because many music planners may have that piece in their files, and can consider it for use. If a planner wishes to use a piece that has gone out of print, that may still be possible. For Augsburg Fortress resources, call 800/421-0239 or email copyright@augsburgfortress.org to inquire about onetime reprint rights or to see if a piece may be available by print on demand.

Please note that there may be Augsburg Fortress resources that have gone out of print since this volume went to press, and also that we are unable to research whether musical pieces from other publishers are still available.

Music *for* Worship Key

acc	accompaniment	hc	handchimes	qrt	quartet
bar	baritone	hp	harp	rec	recorder
bng	bongos	hpd	harpsichord	sax	saxophone
bsn	bassoon	hrn	horn	sop	soprano
cant	cantor	inst	instrument	str	strings
ch	chimes	kybd	keyboard	synth	synthesizer
cl	clarinet	M	medium	tamb	tambourine
cong	congregation	MH	medium high	tba	tuba
cont	continuo	ML	medium low	tbn	trombone
cym	cymbal	mxd	mixed	timp	timpani
DB	double or string bass	narr	narrator	trbl	treble
dbl	double	ob	oboe	tri	triangle
desc	descant	oct	octave	tpt	trumpet
div	divisi	opt	optional	U	unison
drm	drum	orch	orchestra	vc	violoncello
eng hrn	English horn	org	organ	vcs	voices
fc	finger cymbals	perc	percussion	vla	viola
fl	flute	picc	piccolo	vln	violin
glock	glockenspiel	pno	piano	ww	woodwind
gtr	guitar	pt	part	xyl	xylophone
hb	handbells	qnt	quintet		

17

Key *to* Hymn *and* Psalm Collections

ASG* *As Sunshine to a Garden: Hymns and Songs of Rusty Edwards.* Mpls: Augsburg Fortress, 1999.

BC *Borning Cry: Worship for a New Generation.* Waverly, IA: New Generation Publishers, 1992.

BL* *Bread of Life: Mass and Songs for the Assembly.* Mpls: Augsburg Fortress, 2000.

CW *Christian Worship: A Lutheran Hymnal* (Wisconsin Evangelical Lutheran Synod). Milwaukee: Northwestern Publishing House, 1993.

DH* *Dancing at the Harvest: Songs of Ray Makeever.* Mpls: Augsburg Fortress, 1997.

GC *Gather Comprehensive.* Chicago: GIA Publications, 1994.

GS2* *Global Songs 2: Bread for the Journey.* Mpls: Augsburg Fortress, 1997.

H82 *The Hymnal 1982* (Episcopal). New York: The Church Pension Fund, 1985.

HFG *Hymns for the Gospels.* Chicago: GIA Publications, 2001.

HFW *Hymns for Worship.* Mpls: Augsburg Fortress, 2001.

HS98 *Hymnal Supplement 98.* St. Louis: Concordia Publishing House, 1998.

LBW* *Lutheran Book of Worship.* Mpls: Augsburg; Philadelphia: Board of Publication, LCA, 1978.

LLC* *Libro de Liturgia y Cántico.* Mpls: Augsburg Fortress, 1998.

LS* *LifeSongs.* Mpls: Augsburg Fortress, 1999.

LW *Lutheran Worship* (Lutheran Church–Missouri Synod). St. Louis: Concordia Publishing House, 1982.

NCH *The New Century Hymnal* (United Church of Christ). Cleveland: The Pilgrim Press, 1995.

OBS* *O Blessed Spring: Hymns of Susan Palo Cherwien.* Mpls: Augsburg Fortress, 1997.

PCY *Psalms for the Church Year.* 8 vol. Chicago: GIA Publications.

PH *The Presbyterian Hymnal* (PC-USA). Louisville: Westminster John Knox Press, 1990.

PsH *Psalter Hymnal.* Grand Rapids: CRC Publications, 1988.

PS *Psalm Songs.* 3 vol. Mpls: Augsburg Fortress, 1998.

PW *Psalter for Worship.* 3 vol. (Cycles A, B, C.) Mpls: Augsburg Fortress.

REJ *Rejoice in the Lord* (Reformed Church in America). Grand Rapids: William B. Eerdmans Publishing Co., 1985.

RS *RitualSong.* Chicago: GIA Publications, 1996.

RW1* Renewing Worship 1: *Congregational Song: Proposals for Renewal.* Evangelical Lutheran Church in America. Mpls: Augsburg Fortress, 2001.

RW5 Renewing Worship 5: *New Hymns and Songs.* Evangelical Lutheran Church in America. Mpls: Augsburg Fortress, 2003.

RWSB *Renewing Worship Songbook.* Evangelical Lutheran Church in America. Mpls: Augsburg Fortress, 2003.

SNC *Sing! A New Creation.* Grand Rapids: The Calvin Institute of Worship, Faith Alive Christian Resources, Reformed Church in America, 2001.

SP *The Selah Psalter.* Kingston: Selah Publishing, 2001.

STP *Singing the Psalms.* 3 vol. Portland: OCP Publications.

TFF* *This Far by Faith.* Mpls: Augsburg Fortress, 1999.

TP *The Psalter: Psalms and the Canticles for Singing.* Louisville: Westminster/John Knox Press.

TWC *The Worshiping Church.* Carol Stream, IL: Hope Publishing Company, 1990.

UMH *The United Methodist Hymnal.* Nashville: The United Methodist Publishing House, 1989.

VU *Voices United.* Ontario: The United Church Publishing House, 1996.

W3 *Worship: A Hymnal and Service Book for Roman Catholics.* Third ed. Chicago: GIA 1986.

WOV* *With One Voice.* Mpls: Augsburg Fortress, 1995.

W&P* *Worship & Praise.* Mpls: Augsburg Fortress, 1999.

* Indicates resources whose hymns are, at least in part, included in the CD-ROM resource *Hymns for Worship* (Mpls: Augsburg Fortress, 2001).

ADVENT

Learning to bask in the mystery

Images *of the* Season

There is a deep mystery to the season of Advent.

This meditative season is integrally linked to the waiting

and wondering that accompany pregnancy and birth. Just

as pregnancy gives parents-to-be time to adjust to the prospect of a new child, so this season provides opportunity for the church to step back from the surrounding busyness and breathe in the wonder, the expectation, the miracle of the coming celebration of the incarnation. Yet, for all its benefits, we eagerly rush this time of waiting to its conclusion. Few of us have learned to bask in the mystery, the sweetness of this time of gestation. We don't sufficiently appreciate the beauty in watching something grow and come to fruition. There is holiness in the time of birthing. To rush this profound gestation time of Advent to its conclusion will result in an underdeveloped, premature Christmas celebration.

A Celtic prayer seems appropriate to this time:

> In the mighty name of God,
> In the saving name of Jesus,
> In the strong name of the Spirit,
> we come
> we cry
> we watch
> we wait
> we long
> for you.

(*The Open Gate* © 1994 David Adam. Reprinted by permission of Morehouse Publishing.)

Of course, there are hints of the season to come as we walk through the season of Advent. It is not a trudge through depression and melancholy. The minor strains of the Advent hymns are punctuated by the joyful song of Mary's Magnificat, the majesty of Elizabeth's pregnancy and profession of faith, and the tenderness of Joseph's protection. The hint of evil in the background—in biblical times as well as our own—gives depth to the season. This is no fairy tale. The Advent gospel, beginning with prophecy of apocalypse, moving through the witness

of John, and ending with the excitement of Mary and Elizabeth, is a story of good and evil, tenderness and cruelty, faith and incredulity. It is a telling of signs and wonders. As the child grows and thrives in Mary's womb, so our excitement swells within our worship, prayers, and music. As the light of the candles on the Advent wreath grow brighter, so we are called to brightness of great expectations. To rush too much into Christmas music would be premature and a miscarriage of the exultation of the Christmas season itself.

The sweetness of the season of Advent is so precious to us because it is so short. It is only four weeks long! To children that may seem like an eternity. To adults it goes by in the blink of an eye. But there is sacredness to the waiting time and the preparation in this season. Preserve times in Advent simply to sit and savor the anticipation. Allow times of quiet in our worship, a rich quiet that invites deep thought and prayer. Our worship needs to create an environment—visually, liturgically, musically—that celebrates the holy waiting. The anticipation should be just as exciting and stirring as the actual event. If we can't enjoy the anticipation, we won't enjoy the event. Our waiting can be fraught with fear, boredom, restlessness, and frenetic activity and the day itself can be anticlimactic at best. But if our fears are tempered by hope, our boredom by eager anticipation, and our restlessness with purposeful preparation, then the waiting season can be meaningful and holy.

Advent, the season of waiting, watching, and wondering, is an anomaly in our frantic, fast-paced culture. Yet, God continues to call us to step out of the madness that afflicts us for a season. God calls us to pause and reflect, to wonder and hope, and to wait and savor the holy mystery of birth and new life.

20

Environment *and* Art *for the* Season

Advent is about hurrying up and waiting. It is about

living in the joy of knowing that Jesus has come, and living

in the hope of his promised return. We as worship planners

and leaders strive to capture and encourage an atmosphere of anticipation during this Advent season. It is not easy. Not everyone is interested in living in the tension of waiting to celebrate the birth of Jesus, nor is everyone interested in hurrying Jesus to come back any time soon. Our tendency is to rush Jesus' birth and hold off his return as long as possible. Knowing this about ourselves, how can our physical worship environment—that which we can see and touch and smell—support the appointed scripture and the selected hymns and music in order to help us live in the tension of Advent?

EVALUATING YOUR SPACE

The following questions are designed to help worship planners focus on elements within our worship space that might help or hinder the Advent spirit.

Does the worshiping assembly gather in one or more areas prior to entering the worship space?

Are those spaces used for other purposes (for example, a fellowship hall) or have they been established solely for the purpose of gathering before worship?

Are the gathering spaces right outside of the worship space? Or, does the community have to travel to get from one place to another?

Is there a main entrance into the worship space that most of the assembly uses? Or, do people gather from many directions?

What are the strong visual symbols, if any, in the place where the congregation gathers?

What is the most obvious thing you see in your gathering space?

Continue to reflect on your answers to these questions as we explore the season's possibilities.

So often in this Advent season preachers and worship leaders work to convey feelings and moods of tension and anticipation through the words and music that we choose. It is possible, however, to make use of the assembly's physical movement throughout the gathering

and worship spaces to convey these same moods—perhaps even to a much greater degree. In an era that is very mobile—commuting to work and traveling around the globe—we, ironically, love being sedentary. We drive in circles for quite a long time looking for the right parking space so that we can avoid walking to our final destination. We want to get there, comfortably. Once we are there, we want to stay put for as long as we can. Our worship experience is often similar. Most of us in the assembly want to hurry and get in, get our seat and settle in, standing and perhaps kneeling occasionally with one trip toward the altar for our holy meal.

What might happen if we were to delay our entrance into the worship space? We might even have pre-service music starting while we wait at the doors becoming more and more anxious to be a part of what is going on. Look for times within the worship service when we can practice waiting and practice moving.

Rearranging the objects within the worship space may also elicit a sense of expectation and tension. For example, moving an empty chair or table out into a normally open space will draw attention to the fact that something is expected to happen. The same is true if we remove something and clear a space yet wait to fill it with something new. We can apply this technique to our usual display of Christmas tree or crèche. Imagine clearing the usual space for the congregation's Christmas tree by the first Sunday in Advent and waiting to fill it. Or, to build up anticipation, build or erect the tree and maybe decorate it in stages over the four weeks of Advent. Using the crèche in the same way, make a place for it and fill in the participants slowly over the weeks, waiting until Christmas Eve for Mary, Joseph, and the infant Jesus to arrive on the scene.

Other familiar elements and suggestions about their use: *The Advent wreath* is an element of measuring the anticipation for our weekly worship. We count the weeks with our lighted candles as we look forward to the

21

Christmas celebration to come. Think about where you might place the wreath in your space, different from its placement in previous years. It might even be possible to find four distinct and progressive locations for the wreath. The wreath could physically journey from your gathering space to your chancel.

The Christmas tree is the focal point that so many people in our secularized society rely on during the weeks before and during the Christmas feast, whether they know the story of the coming of Jesus or not. Out of strong desires for our churches to feel like our homes, and out of convenience, we rob the season of Advent of its purpose when we place the very strong symbol of a Christmas tree in our worship space before the Christmas celebration begins. Would you place a birthday cake on your dining room table weeks before your child's birthday? Would you expect a new bride to walk around wearing her wedding dress weeks before the wedding? It is no wonder that we are so eager to dismantle our Christmas trees before the twelve days have past. We are not able to enjoy having them in our midst because they have been in our homes and our churches for weeks before Christmas even arrives. If time is critical for your volunteers, and your congregation uses an artificial tree (see the next paragraph), you could build it in stages, which might help the sense of building anticipation. If you use a real tree and cannot find the time or the help to erect it between the fourth Sunday in Advent and Christmas Eve, then perhaps you can compromise and erect the tree before the fourth Sunday and decorate it after.

With each of the elements listed above, it is extremely important that wherever possible, we use real, natural materials: living or freshly cut greens and wax candles, for example. Real elements change with time. Greens lose needles and candles decrease in size as they are consumed. Both of these phenomena help us to experience the passage of time in a subtle yet deep way that goes beyond simply counting the weeks or representing a place to share gifts.

ART FOR THE SEASON

There is more to art within any liturgical season than simply the color we use. Embracing the use of art within our liturgical gatherings is often difficult because true art is provocative. Art has the ability to mean many things to many people and has a deep and lasting power. Using color and some very familiar symbols and words on a banner is safe. Using art is risky. The art a worshiping community uses does not have to be permanent. Art can be borrowed or rented. You can start this process by contacting the Evangelical Lutheran Church in America. The ELCA houses many works of religious art that are available on loan to congregations. You can also contact a local gallery or your local arts council. This would help your congregation find and support local artists that might be willing to create temporary art for you. Or you can offer your space as a place for a liturgical artist to show some of his or her art for the weeks of Advent. A great resource for finding artists is CIVA (Christians in the Visual Arts—www.civa.org). Asking the children of your Sunday school to create temporary art out of materials as simple as paper and paint would be a great way to interest them in art and environment. These are often forgotten aspects to using art in your worship space. Seasonal use of powerful and provocative art is a great way to introduce a community to the benefits of making use of art in the place where they worship.

What might we want the art we use in Advent to say to us and for us? What would we want the world to know about what it means to wait for the coming of Jesus? How could art communicate that? What can art do for us in helping us focus on this Advent "hurry up and wait" experience? What would we want to tell a visitor who enters a church for the first time in their life during Advent? Where would we place the art?

We have the opportunity and the challenge to help people practice hurrying up and waiting. True, there may be some grumbling if this Advent is not like last Advent. Hold fast. If prayerful and thoughtful planning has preceded this, then the way is prepared for your congregation to experience new and exciting insights as all of us wait the return of our Lord Jesus Christ.

Preaching *with the* Season

"Advent we sing of the Lord's birth to come.

And Christmas we sing of his new life begun."

Something like that the round begins.

Even as we think "Advent," we remember that the liturgically cautious avoid celebrating a feast or a festival before it has arrived. That should be especially pertinent in the season of Advent when we remember not only that our Lord came, but that he will come again. And if in God's mercy our Lord should return in the next four weeks, surely we would not want to be found celebrating his birth with Christmas hymns and songs when the day observing his nativity has not yet arrived. As with the sale of good wine, "we observe no festival before its time."

No doubt the words in your mind as you read that are, "You can't be serious." Exactly. The proper word is "playful." Playful we are, and can be, in letting Advent be Advent and letting Christmas wait its time. After a fast, the feast is all the more festive.

That having been said, why not say some more? In the July-August 2001 issue of *Lutheran Partners*, J. Roderick Rinell Sr. argued for "bending a little." He noted, "How can we pull a charade and pretend for four weeks and Sundays that we are waiting for the birth of Christ—then spend only two Sundays celebrating it, one of which is New Year's when most of the congregation is missing?"

He counted the hymns in *Lutheran Book of Worship*—hymns 22–38 in the Advent section, a total of 17 for Advent, while hymns 39–74 total 36 for Christmas. His comment: "Twice as many hymns in Christmas as in Advent—yet we are supposed to have twice as long an Advent as Christmas." He characterized the Christmas Sundays as "two perfunctory Sundays when the people have tired of all the 'Christmas music' in the mall."

We should protest some of the premises, but later. First, how might we "bend a little"? During Advent the children are practicing for the Christmas service, singing Christmas hymns, rehearsing Christmas passages. Could that be our opening? The reasoning would be, "It's necessary for us to practice to make our Christmas celebration perfect. And Advent is a time of preparation—for

that, too. Could our Advent services not include a little practice for a Christmas celebration worthy of its importance?" Sung within that frame, that context, the Christmas hymns will serve to underscore the Advent season as a time of preparing for the Nativity.

Perhaps the Advent services could be structured something like this. As the liturgy is about to begin, the lighting of the Advent wreath candles could be quite an affair. A California congregation has mounted its wreath in such a way that it can be lowered to the height of a child, and the children gather around it for the lighting. Let all the words and music stress the Advent themes as the candles shine and the wreath is raised again to its proper height, or otherwise celebrated. Then, perhaps at the offertory, it could be said that "the children—and all of us—are preparing to celebrate our Lord's nativity and we need to practice." Then as part of the offertory action we could sing a hymn of Christmas. That might also be a way to help the congregation sing some of the Christmas hymns that are not as well known and are neglected. Could we not save the too-familiar ones for Christmas 1 and 2 and in our preparation sing some of the other worthy hymns?

Back to the problematic premises above. Take the comment that "we pretend for four weeks and Sundays that we are waiting for the birth of Christ and then spend only two Sundays celebrating it." It should be evident from our remembrances of Advent lessons in the past and from a glance at those assigned for this year that what we meditate on in Advent is theologically more all-encompassing than "waiting for the birth of Christ." Of course, Jesus had to "get borned" if he was to live for us, instruct us, give the example of a holy life for us. But he also had but one birthday and something like 33 × 365 days of living and dying and rising and ascending. All of those call for observation, instruction, and celebration. The Advent lessons touch on them all and, in addition, on the end time and Christ's glorious return.

23

The lessons assigned for this Advent in Series C of the Revised Common Lectionary help make that case. They make Advent not only a season of waiting but of theological weight. Because the mall singing of Christmas carols distorts the celebration of the Nativity and makes Christmas more a day of mirth than a meditation on God's human birth is precisely the reason we need the days of Advent for a clear gospel and a complete theology. And fewer hymns are needed in the Advent section of the hymnal because the themes of Advent draw the support of hymns from other sections.

The images for Advent Sundays in this series focus on four words: Signs, Ways, Joys, Bodies. They may serve for illustrative purposes and can provide a sense of movement through Advent.

Consider some of the profound and serious themes that sound in this year's Advent lessons. The gospel for the first Sunday in Advent with its cosmic signs alerts us to the end time. Many around us are not only unprepared for "heaven and earth to pass away" but are unbelieving. Yet it is because this Advent theme has been taken seriously over the years that "when these things begin to take place," Christians will be able to follow the directive, "Stand up and raise your heads, because your redemption is drawing near." "Even so, come, Lord Jesus"—*Christian Hope.*

The second Sunday in Advent brings John's message of repentance for forgiveness. 2 Peter 3:11-12 asks the question this Sunday answers: "What sort of persons ought you to be in leading lives of holiness and godliness, waiting for and hastening the coming of the day of God?"—*Christian Holiness.*

The third Sunday in Advent lays again the foundation for our joy in the faithfulness of God. Zechariah, Elizabeth, Mary, and Joseph testify year after year that what God promises God performs—*Christian Happiness.*

Finally, the fourth Sunday in Advent stresses the immensity of the miracle the Nicene Creed summarizes in the clause "and was made man." Mary had nine months to experience that miracle. With her we do well to ponder in our hearts "God in flesh made manifest." God has a mother. We have a Brother—*Christian Heritage.*

No wonder that in the Adventtide we need twice as many Sundays as we do for the Nativity, and many borrowed hymns!

Shape *of* Worship *for the* Season

BASIC SHAPE OF THE EUCHARISTIC RITE

* Confession and Forgiveness: see alternate worship text for Advent on page 28. In this and all of the following "alternate worship text" suggestions, it is fine to use the text in place in the worship setting. Other possibilities for confession and forgiveness are in *Holy Baptism and Related Rites*, Renewing Worship, vol. 3, pp. 87*ff.* (ELCA/Augsburg Fortress, 2002), or at www.renewingworship.org/publications/holy_baptism/index.html

GATHERING

* Greeting: see alternate worship text for Advent
* Use the Kyrie, either in the form found in the communion setting or WOV 601, 602, 604, or LBW 168.
* Omit the hymn of praise

WORD

* Use the Nicene Creed
* The prayers: see alternate forms and responses for Advent

MEAL

* Offertory prayer: see alternate worship text for Advent
* Use the proper preface for Advent
* Eucharistic prayer: in addition to the four main options in *LBW*, see "Eucharistic Prayer A: The Season of Advent" in *WOV* Leaders Edition, p. 65
* Invitation to communion: see alternate worship text for Advent

Post-communion prayer: see alternate worship text for Advent

SENDING

- Benediction: see alternate worship text for Advent
- Dismissal: see alternate worship text for Advent

OTHER SEASONAL POSSIBILITIES
BLESSING THE ADVENT WREATH

The gathering rite for either the first week or all the weeks in Advent may take the following form of lighting the Advent wreath. Following the entrance hymn and the greeting, one of the prayers of blessing in the seasonal rites section may be spoken. A candle on the wreath may then be lit during the singing of an Advent hymn, such as "Light one candle to watch for Messiah" (WOV 630). The service then continues with the prayer of the day. On the remaining Sundays in Advent, the number of candles lighted before the service would be the total number lighted the previous week. One new candle is then lighted each week during the service.

Alternatively, candles of the Advent wreath may simply be lighted before the service, without any special prayer of blessing. Candles may also be lighted during the singing of an entrance hymn, the Kyrie, or the psalm for the day, without any special accompanying prayers or music.

EVENING PRAYER FOR ADVENT

Consider holding an evening prayer service one weeknight each week throughout the Advent season. All the events might take place in a fellowship hall around tables. A possible format for the gatherings:

- Light candles placed at tables as worshipers begin singing a hymn of light ("Joyous light of glory" *LBW*, p. 143, "O Trinity, O blessed Light" LBW 275, "O Light whose splendor thrills" WOV 728, among others). Follow with a table prayer.
- Have a simple meal, perhaps consisting only of soup, bread, and a salad.
- Prepare gifts to be given to homebound people or others in need.
- Close with an abbreviated form of evening prayer:
  - a psalm (especially 141)
  - a short scripture reading (see *LBW* p. 186 for ideas)
  - the Song of Mary (Canticle 6 in *LBW*, or "My soul now magnifies the Lord" LBW 180, or "My soul proclaims your greatness" WOV 730)
  - brief prayers of intercession, perhaps from the people gathered
  - the Lord's Prayer
  - dismissal

Other possibilities for musical settings of evening prayer include *Joyous Light Evening Prayer* (Ray Makeever) and *Stay with Us, Lord* (David Cherwien).

Try to focus in these gatherings on things that people of all ages can do together, so that families are brought together during this time of year.

LECTIONARY OPPORTUNITY
FOR HEALING SERVICES

- Third Sunday in Advent (first reading)

25

Assembly Song *for the* Season

O Wisdom, Word of God most high, / embracing

all things far and nigh:/ in strength and beauty

come and stay; / teach us your will and guide our way.

("O Come, O Come, Emmanuel," RW1 55, stanza for December 17)

Amid the bustle of the retail season, the church makes a stand for Advent. While North American culture taunts us with immediate consumer pleasures, the faithful Christian assembly embraces the beautiful wisdom of waiting, patience, and hope.

GATHERING

Embody the entrance of the new church year with a procession: either a simple procession into the building, or a more complete procession with the processional cross, incense, bells, choir, and ministers weaving through every nook and cranny of the worship space, singing and ringing.

On the first Sunday of Advent utilize "An Advent Litany" by Peter Hallock for congregation, organ, bells, choirs, and cantors (Ionian Arts: CH-1041). On subsequent Sundays engage congregation, choir, bells, and organ, in Carl Crosier's setting of "Veni, Veni Emmanuel/O Come, O Come, Emmanuel" (Ionian Arts: CH-1029).

You might also utilize new and renewed translations of traditional Advent hymns: "Come, thou long-expected Jesus" (RW1 21); "O come, O come, Emmanuel" (RW1 55); "Creator of the stars of night" (RW1 22).

The Advent wreath is often lit before the liturgy begins. If you light the wreath during the opening rites, employ a song like "Light one candle to watch for Messiah" (WOV 630). Teach the song to the Sunday school or children's choirs, and have them teach it to the assembly.

WORD

Sing Advent psalms from Peter Hallock's *Ionian Psalter,* with beautifully written choral verses and accessible congregational refrains. Or, sing the psalms in alternation be-

tween psalmist and assembly by whole stanza to a simple *LBW* tone, such as tone 1 or 5, with bells sounding open fifths at the end of each verse.

The Magnificat or Song of Mary is a key Advent hymn. "A New Magnificat" by Carolyn Jennings for choir, congregation, and organ ingeniously weaves the texts of Mary and Hannah (AFP 080665255X). Two other nontraditional settings are the haunting and introspective "My Soul Magnifies the Lord" by Ben Houge (www.benhouge.com/eveningprayer.html), and "Canticle of the turning" (W&P 26) for guitar, praise band, and congregation.

A sturdy alternate gospel verse is the renewed translation of "Wake, awake, for night is flying" (RW1 82).

MEAL

If you have been singing chant this season—"O come, O come, Emmanuel" or "Creator of the stars of night"— this is a good time to use *LBW* Setting 3 for the "Holy, holy, holy" and "Lamb of God."

At communion, sing "Let all mortal flesh keep silence" (LBW 198), with a simple accompaniment of handbells ringing D and A. Hymns with refrains are effective as the assembly enters the communion procession, especially "Wait for the Lord" (Taizé: *Songs for Prayer,* p. 58, GIA G-4956) with congregational refrain and verses sung by a cantor.

SENDING

Send the assembly into the world to await the word with strong images and tunes: "Hark! the glad sound" (LBW 35); "Savior of the nations, come"(LBW 28); "Lift up your heads, ye mighty gates" (RW1 48).

Music *for the* Season

VERSE AND OFFERTORY

Cherwien, David. *Verses for the Sundays in Advent.* U, org, opt hb.
MSM 80-001.

Gospel Acclamations. Cant, choir, cong, inst. MAY 0862096324.

Haas, David. *Advent/Christmas Gospel Acclamations.* 2 pt, org, gtr, solo
inst. OCP 8732GC.

Hillert, Richard. *Verses and Offertory Sentences, Part 1: Advent through Christmas.* U, kybd. CPH 97-5509.

Krentz, Michael. *Alleluia Verses for Advent.* SAB, org. AFP 0800647041.
OP.

Schiavone, J. *Gospel Acclamation Verses for the Sundays of Advent.*
GIA G-2110.

Wetzler, Robert. *Verses and Offertories: Advent 1—Baptism of Our Lord.*
SATB, kybd. AFP 0800648994.

CHORAL

Ellingboe, Bradley. "Prepare the Royal Highway." SATB, org.
KJO 8860.

Haugen, Kyle. "Lost in the Night." SAB, pno. AFP 0800659244.

Helgen, John. "Come to Us." SATB, pno, rec, opt perc. KJO 8904.

Howells, Herbert. "Like As The Hart." SATB, org. OXF A109.

Organ, Anne Krentz. "Come My Light." 2 pt, pno.
AFP 0800675819.

Pavlechko, Thomas. "Look Toward the East." SATB, div, org.
SEL 410-511.

Petker, Allan. "Come, Thou Long-expected Jesus." SATB, kybd.
HAL JG2298.

Sirett, Mark. "Thou Shalt Know Him." SSAA. AFP 0800675304.
SATB. AFP 0800655206.

Thompson, Randall "The Best of Rooms." SATB. ECS 2672.

Thompson, Randall. "The Paper Reeds by the Brooks." SATB.
ECS 1751.

CHILDREN'S CHOIR

Currie, Randolph. "A Child's Advent Prayer." U, kybd/hb.
GIA G-2984.

Hart, Kathy Lowe. "We Wait for a Little Child." U/2 pt, kybd.
AFP 0800675975.

Keesecker, Thomas. "All Earth Is Hopeful." U, 2/3 pt trbl, pno.
AFP 0800657411.

Lindh, Jody. "An Advent Carol." U, kybd. CG CGA648.

McRae, Shirley. "The King of Glory Comes" in *Lift Up Your Voices.*
U/2 pt, Orff, perc. CG CGA622.

KEYBOARD/INSTRUMENTAL

Augsburg Organ Library: Advent. Org. AFP 0800658957.

Benson, Robert A. *A Lovely Rose.* Org. AFP 0800675711.

Oliver, Curt. *Advent Keyboard Seasons.* Pno. AFP 0800655788.

Organ, Anne Krentz. *Advent Reflections for Piano and Solo Instrument.* Kybd,
inst. AFP 0800657284.

Organ, Anne Krentz. *Global Piano Reflections for Advent.* Pno.
AFP 0800675762.

Music for Manuals: Advent. Org. MSM 10-346.

Rodriguez, Penny. "O Come, O Come, Emmanuel" in *Piano Solos for
the Christmas Season.* Pno. BEC PC12.

Wood, Dale. "Come, O Thou Traveler Unknown" in *Wood Works on International Folk Hymns.* Org. SMP 70/10705.

Wood, Dale. "People, Look East" in *Wood Works on International Folk
Hymns.* Org. SMP 70/10705.

HANDBELL

Biggs, Susan. "Come, Thou Long-Expected Jesus." 3 oct.
AFP 0800659872.

Lohr, Alan. "O Come, O Come, Emmanuel." 3-5 oct. AGEHR
AG35146.

Morris, Hart. "The Promise Fulfilled." 3-6 oct. RR HB0027.

Organ, Anne Krentz. "Three Advent Settings (Veni, Emmanuel; Puer
Nobis/Besançon; Tif in veldele)." 3 oct. AFP 080067491X.

PRAISE ENSEMBLE

Avery, Richard and Donald Marsh, arr. Jennings. "Mary, Mary." 2 pt,
kybd. KJO C8117.

Chepponis, James. "Advent Gathering Song." SATB, kybd, gtr, C inst.
GIA G-4131.

Chisum, John and George Searcy. "Come and Behold Him" in *More
Songs for Praise and Worship.* SATB. WRD 3010387016 (vocal
ed); WRD 3010186363 (pno, vcs, perc).

Damzio, Sharon. "Crown Him King of Kings" in *More Songs for Praise
and Worship.* SATB. WRD 3010387016 (vocal ed);
WRD 3010186363 (pno, vcs, perc).

Sleeth, Natalie. "Light One Candle" in *Best of the Best.*
FEL 1891062018.

Alternate Worship Texts

CONFESSION AND FORGIVENESS

In the name of the Father, and of the ✚ Son, and of the Holy
 Spirit.
Amen
Let us prepare to receive Christ by turning from our sin
and seeking God's tender mercy and compassion.

Silence for reflection and self-examination.

Almighty God,
we confess that we have sinned against you,
and against our sisters and brothers.
Our words and deeds have not proclaimed
your reign of justice and truth.
We have failed to watch and pray
for the signs of your advent among us.
Forgive our sin,
and come quickly to save us. Amen

In the advent of Christ,
the dawn from on high breaks upon us
with light and healing.
Through Jesus Christ,
God looks with favor upon you,
and forgives you all your sins.
Amen

GREETING

From the one who is and who was
and who is to come, the Almighty:
grace, light, and peace be with you all.
And also with you.

PRAYERS

As the fulfillment of our hope draws near, let us lift our voices in
prayer for the church, the world, and all according to their need.

A brief silence.

Each petition ends:
O God, whose advent is near,
hear us and renew us with your love.

Concluding petition:
Hear our prayers, mighty God,
as we rejoice in your reign already revealed,
and long for the peace, justice, and love yet to dawn,
through Jesus Christ our Lord.
Amen

OFFERTORY PRAYER

O Mighty One,
you have done great things for us,
and holy is your name.
Bless all we offer you—
our selves, our time, and our possessions—
that through us your grace and favor
may be made known to all the world;
for the sake of Jesus Christ, our redeemer. Amen

INVITATION TO COMMUNION

The door to God's banquet hall is open.
Enter into the joy of this feast.

POST-COMMUNION PRAYER

O God,
in this eucharist you give us a foretaste of that day
when all the hungry will be fed with good things.
Send us forth to make known your deeds,
and to proclaim the greatness of your name.
Grant this through the one whose advent is certain,
whose day draws near, your Son, Jesus Christ our Lord.
Amen

BLESSING

The God of hope strengthen your hearts
as you await the coming of our Lord Jesus Christ
with all the saints,
and the blessing of almighty God,
the Father, the ✚ Son, and the Holy Spirit,
be among you and remain with you always.
Amen

DISMISSAL

The coming of the Lord is near.
Go in peace. Serve the Lord.
Thanks be to God.

28

Seasonal Rites

Blessing of the Advent Wreath

FIRST SUNDAY IN ADVENT

We praise you, O God, for this evergreen crown
that marks our days of preparation for Christ's advent.
As we light the first candle on this wreath,
rouse us from sleep, that we may be ready to greet our Lord
when he comes with all the saints and angels.
Enlighten us with your grace,
and prepare our hearts to welcome him with joy.
Grant this through Christ our Lord,
whose coming is certain and whose day draws near.
Amen

Light the first candle.

SECOND SUNDAY IN ADVENT

We praise you, O God, for this circle of light
that marks our days of preparation for Christ's advent.
As we light the candles on this wreath,
kindle within us the fire of your Spirit,
that we may be light shining in the darkness.
Enlighten us with your grace,
that we may welcome others as you have welcomed us.
Grant this through Christ our Lord,
whose coming is certain and whose day draws near.
Amen

Light the second candle.

THIRD SUNDAY IN ADVENT

We praise you, O God, for this victory wreath
that marks our days of preparation for Christ's advent.
As we light the candles on this wreath,
strengthen our hearts as we await the Lord's coming in glory.
Enlighten us with your grace,
that we may serve our neighbors in need.
Grant this through Christ our Lord,
whose coming is certain and whose day draws near.
Amen

Light the third candle.

FOURTH SUNDAY IN ADVENT

We praise you, O God, for this wheel of time
that marks our days of preparation for Christ's advent.
As we light the candles on this wreath,
open our eyes to see your presence
in the lowly ones of this earth.
Enlighten us with your grace,
that we may sing of your advent among us
in the Word made flesh.
Grant this through Christ our Lord,
whose coming is certain and whose day draws near.
Amen

Light the fourth candle.

29

Lessons and Carols for Advent (based on the O Antiphons)

The O Antiphons are a set of medieval refrains originally used before and after the singing of the Magnificat. They were in use already in the eighth century. Each of them invokes the Messiah under a different title derived from the Old Testament. This title is then amplified, and followed by an appeal to "come" and save us in a particular way. Around the twelfth century, they were collected into a Latin verse hymn, which was later translated by John Mason Neale, finally becoming the beloved Advent hymn "Oh, come, oh, come, Emmanuel" (LBW 34). (The version in LBW omits two of the original seven stanzas, which are included here, in the version from Congregational Song: Proposals for Renewal, *Augsburg Fortress, 2001. Revised wording for the other stanzas is also available in that resource.) These antiphons form the structure of this service. They are pointed for chanting (LBW psalm tone 3, sung in E minor, could be used), or they may be spoken.*

30

ENTRANCE HYMN

Fling wide the door   LBW 32

DIALOGUE

Blessed is the king who comes in the name of the Lord.

Peace in heaven, and glory in the highest heaven!

I will hear what the Lord God has to say—

A voice that speaks for peace.

Peace for all faithful people

And those who turn to him in their hearts.

God's help is near for those who fear him,

That his glory may dwell in our land.

Blessed is the king who comes in the name of the Lord.

Peace in heaven, and glory in the highest heaven!

OPENING PRAYER

The Lord be with you.

And also with you.

Let us pray.

Gracious God, through the ages you have sent your promise to your people in many ways, through many voices. But in these last days, your Son has come to bring it among us in person. Through your Spirit, prepare our hearts to recognize him in his many forms, and to receive him as our Lord and Savior.

Amen

LESSONS AND CAROLS

Antiphon   *spoken or chanted*

O Wisdom,

> proceeding from the mouth of the Most High,
> pervading and permeating all creation,
> mightily order- | ing all things:
> Come and teach us the | way of prudence.

O Wisdom, Word of God   *tune: LBW 34*

> O Wisdom, Word of God most high,
> Embracing all things far and nigh:
> In strength and beauty come and stay;
> Teach us your will and guide our way.
> Rejoice! Rejoice! Emmanuel
> Shall come to you, O Israel.

From *Congregational Song: Proposals for Renewal* © 2001 Augsburg Fortress.

Lesson: Isaiah 40:3-5

Carol: Prepare the royal highway LBW 26

Antiphon

> O Adonai
> and ruler of the house of Israel,
> who appeared to Moses in the burning bush
> and gave him the | Law on Sinai:
> Come with an outstretched arm | and redeem us.

Oh, come, oh, come, great Lord of might   LBW 34, stanza 2

Lesson: Exodus 6:2–7a

Carol: My Lord, what a morning WOV 627

Antiphon

> O Root of Jesse,
> standing as an ensign before the peoples,
> before whom all kings are mute,
> to whom the nations | will do homage:
> Come quickly to de- | liver us.

Oh come, strong Branch of Jesse   LBW 34, stanza 3

Lesson: Isaiah 11:1–5, 10

Carol: Come, thou long-expected Jesus   LBW 30

Antiphon

> O Key of David and scepter of the house of Israel,
> you open and no one can close,
> you close and no | one can open:
> Come and rescue the prisoners
> who are in darkness and the sha- | dow of death.

Oh, come, O Key of David   LBW 34, stanza 5

Lesson: Isaiah 42:6–9

Carol: Hark, the glad sound!   LBW 35

Antiphon:

> O Dayspring,
>
> splendor of light | everlasting:
>
> Come and enlighten those who sit in darkness
>
> and in the sha- | dow of death.

Oh, come, blest Dayspring   LBW 34, stanza 4

Lesson: Isaiah 9:1–3a

Carol: Awake, awake, and greet the new morn   WOV 633

Antiphon:

> O King of the nations,
>
> the ruler they long for,
>
> the cornerstone unit- | ing all people:
>
> Come and save us all,
>
> whom you formed | out of clay.

O Ruler of the nations, come   *tune:* LBW 34

> O Ruler of the nations, come,
>
> O Cornerstone that binds in one:
>
> Refresh the hearts that long for you;
>
> restore the broken, make us new.
>
> Rejoice! Rejoice! Emmanuel
>
> shall come to you, O Israel.

From *Congregational Song: Proposals for Renewal* © 2001 Augsburg Fortress.

Lesson: Ephesians 2:12–18

Carol: The King shall come   LBW 33 (stanzas 1, 2, 5)

Antiphon:

> O Emmanuel,
>
> our king and our lawgiver,
>
> the anointed of the nations | and their Savior:
>
> Come and save us, | Lord our God.

Oh, come, oh, come, Emmanuel   LBW 34, stanza 1

Lesson: Isaiah 7:13–15

Carol: All earth is hopeful   WOV 629

RESPONSIVE PRAYER

Our world stumbles blindly toward chaos—

Come and be our Wisdom.

What we imagine to be strength is really weakness—

Come and be our mighty Lord.

We yearn for a standard to look up to—

Come and be our Root of Jesse.

We languish in prisons of mind and spirit—

Come and be our Key of David.

The darkness grows thick around us—

Come and be our Light of day.

We are scattered, lacking a sure leader—

Come and be our King of peace.

We need to know that God is with us—

Come and be our Emmanuel,

that we may rejoice in you. Amen

THE LORD'S PRAYER

BLESSING AND DISMISSAL

Let us bless the Lord.

Thanks be to God.

In our Savior Christ, God is with us.

Almighty God, Father, ✛ Son, and Holy Spirit,

bless you now and forever.

Amen

SENDING HYMN

I want to walk as a child of the light   WOV 649

31

November 30, 2003

First Sunday in Advent

INTRODUCTION

Like an expectant mother, the church in Advent prepares for an arrival: we anticipate the celebration of Jesus' birth and look forward to Christ's coming again at the end of history. But here and now—in scripture and preaching, in water and bread and wine—God comes to us.

PRAYER OF THE DAY

Stir up your power, O Lord, and come. Protect us by your strength and save us from the threatening dangers of our sins, for you live and reign with the Father and the Holy Spirit, one God, now and forever.

VERSE

Alleluia. Show us your mercy, O LORD, and grant us your salvation. Alleluia. (Ps. 85:7)

READINGS

Jeremiah 33:14-16

In the Hebrew scriptures, righteousness is not so much a moral virtue as the fulfillment of the responsibilities of a relationship among people or with God. God acts righteously in speaking against Israel's faithlessness and in working salvation for them. In today's reading, Jerusalem's future name—"The LORD is our righteousness"—serves as a sign that the Lord is even now working salvation for the people.

Psalm 25:1-9 (Psalm 25:1-10 NRSV)

To you, O LORD, I lift up my soul. (Ps. 25:1)

1 Thessalonians 3:9-13

From Timothy, Paul hears about the faithful congregation in Thessalonica and is moved to express his thanks to God. He prays that the congregation may grow in love and holiness until "the coming of our Lord Jesus with all the saints."

Luke 21:25-36

When God brings the creation to fulfillment, there will be dismay, perplexity, fright, and shaking heavens. But with this vision also come words of assurance: for the faithful, it will be a time not to cower in fear, but to stand boldly and receive God's promised redemption.

COLOR Blue *or* Purple

THE PRAYERS

As the fulfillment of our hope draws near, let us raise our heads and lift our voices in prayer for the church, the world, and all according to their need.

A BRIEF SILENCE.

Lord, our righteousness, we pray for your church, that we may abound in love for one another, stay alert to the dawn of your reign, and have strength to do your will. O God, whose advent is near,

hear us and renew us with your love.

Grant that amid signs of danger and violence, leaders of nations will hunger for the peace and justice that will dawn with your Son's coming. Overcome all hatred and malice with your persistent love. O God, whose advent is near,

hear us and renew us with your love.

Lift up the souls of all those who suffer illness or any need *(especially)*, that they may be sustained as they wait for wholeness and healing, and make us signs for them of your coming. O God, whose advent is near,

hear us and renew us with your love.

Be present with those who struggle with addictions, and help them to fight off that which is unhealthy. Give those who love them the courage to take the hard steps that will lead to their well-being. O God, whose advent is near,

hear us and renew us with your love.

Lead this congregation in ways that are right, and teach us your way. Give us courage to wait in patience and yet to work diligently for the spread of the gospel. O God, whose advent is near,

hear us and renew us with your love.

HERE OTHER INTERCESSIONS MAY BE OFFERED.

Unite us with the apostle Andrew, *(other names)*, and all your saints whose hope is now certain, that we may all stand before you in praise and worship when your kingdom comes in its fullness. O God, whose advent is near,

hear us and renew us with your love.

Hear our prayers, mighty God, as we rejoice in your reign already revealed, and long for the peace, justice, and love yet to dawn, through Jesus Christ our Lord.

Amen

IMAGES FOR PREACHING

Drivers encounter all kinds of signs. Some are simple kindergarten-level drawings: a squiggly arrow means curves ahead, and we hold the wheel more firmly, sharpen our gaze. An odd cross consisting of a vertical with two arms coming off at different points represents two side streets, one left, one right. What appears to be a real cross warns of an intersection ahead. We prepare to slow down. We obey. We understand and we *do*.

The dictionary explains that a sign is something indicating the existence of something else. Jesus reminded the disciples that the fig tree sprouting leaves is a sign that summer is already near. The real "something else" we should know about is that "the kingdom of God is near." We are to understand and do. And we should understand that "hearts weighed down with dissipation and drunkenness and the worries of this life" (Luke 21:34) are also a sign—a sign, perhaps, that we do *not* understand—even worse, a sign that although we *do* understand, we *don't* do.

Advent itself is a sign. Christ is coming soon. This Sunday's signs are very clear. One would hope that of all the signs that surround us, the ones from God would receive our most earnest attention. And what good signs they are. We do well to go back to the simplest sign, the sign of an intersection—God's intersection with us—our Lord's cross. And then to look ahead. The best sign on our travels, at journey's end, is our own street sign, our own house number, our home. We will see the Son of Man coming with power and great glory, some of us rising from graves, some standing on our front porch, all of us realizing our redemption is here.

Even so, come, Lord Jesus!

WORSHIP MATTERS

Oremus! "Let us pray," the deacon said. In the ancient church, one of the primary roles for the deacon was to draw the assembly's attention to prayer. In our celebrations, it is the assisting minister who marks times for prayer in the singing of the Kyrie, and during intercessory prayer, the offertory prayer, and the post-communion prayer.

There are many ways to get people's attention. Because worship is meant to engage all the senses, consider how your congregation might be invited into the communal activity of prayer. Make eye contact as the words "let us pray" are spoken. Allow spaces of silence to let others listen and reflect. Try the use of uplifted hands when inviting prayer, and closed hands when concluding prayer. Know that verbal and nonverbal elements cue the rest of the praying community, and keep the assembly at prayer alerted to God's presence.

LET THE CHILDREN COME

Advent is the season of getting ready: setting the stage for the story of Jesus' birth and preparing for his second coming. Our culture uses sights, smells, and sounds to prepare people for the season. Encourage people to live with eyes of faith and to get ready for the Lord's coming. Choose one thing people encounter daily (suggestions: a smell—evergreen; sight—wreath; sound—a bell/phone ringing) and invite children to take a moment each time they encounter it to pray for God's Spirit to come into their hearts. Is there a way to include this same sound, smell, or sight in your worship space this season?

33

HYMNS FOR WORSHIP

GATHERING

Rejoice, rejoice, believers   LBW 25
Blessed be the God of Israel   WOV 725
Let justice roll like a river   W&P 85

HYMN OF THE DAY

People, look east   WOV 626

ALTERNATE HYMN OF THE DAY

Wake, awake, for night is flying   LBW 31, RWSB
My Lord, what a morning   WOV 627, TFF 40

COMMUNION

As the grains of wheat   WOV 705
Come, O precious ransom   LBW 24

SENDING

Once he came in blessing   LBW 312
Soon and very soon   WOV 744, TFF 38

ADDITIONAL HYMNS AND SONGS

I want to be ready   TFF 41
Stir up your power   ASG 38
Come now, O prince of peace   RWSB, LS 13
The King of glory   RWSB, W&P 136

MUSIC FOR THE DAY

PSALMODY

Artman, Ruth. "Psalm 25" in Sing Out! A Children's Psalter.
WLP 7191.

Balhoff, M., G. Daigle, and D. Ducote. "Psalm 25" in PCY, vol. 6.

Haas, David. "To You, O Lord" in PCY, vol. 9.

Jennings, Carolyn. PW, Cycle C.

"Psalm 25: To You, O Lord" in Forty-one Grail Gelineau Psalms.
GIA G-4402.

Soper, Scott. "Psalm 25: To You, O Lord" in STP, vol. 1.
See Proper 10.

CHORAL

Bach, J.S. "Savior of the Nations, Come" in Bach for All Seasons. SATB.
AFP 080065854X.

Distler, Hugo. "Lo! How a Rose E'er Blooming" in Chantry Choirbook.
SATB. AFP 0800657772.

Howells, Herbert. "A Spotless Rose." SATB, T/B solo. GAL 1.5014.

Nelson, Bradley. "Lo, How A Rose E'er Blooming." SATB, org,
french hrn. KJO 8879.

Sedio, Mark. "Once He Came in Blessing" in The Augsburg Easy Choirbook. 2 pt mxd, org, fl. AFP 0800676025.

CHILDREN'S CHOIR

Clemens, Jim. "Sing and Rejoice with Heart and Voice." U/2 pt,
kybd. CG CGA799.

Helgen, John. "Something Special." U, kybd. AFP 0800675320.

Shute, Linda Cable. "Stir Up Your Power." 2 pt, kybd, opt cong.
AFP 0800675274.

KEYBOARD/INSTRUMENTAL

Kerr, J. Wayne. "Besançon" in Christ Is Born: Carols for Organ. Org.
AFP 0800658981.

Mann, Adrian. "Besançon" in 'Tis the Season: Preludes for Treble Instrument and Keyboard. Kybd, inst. AFP 0800659848.

Wold, Wayne L. "Besançon" in Augsburg Organ Library: Advent. Org.
AFP 0800658957.

Wood, Dale. "Prepare the Way, O Zion" in Wood Works, Book 2. Org.
SMP KK 400.

HANDBELL

Behnke, John A. "My Lord, What a Morning." 3-5 oct. AG 1877.

Larson, Katherine Jordahl. "Wake, Awake, For Night Is Flying." 4-5
oct. AFP 0800655109.

PRAISE ENSEMBLE

Del Hierro, Jude. "More Love, More Power" in Best of the Best.
FEL 1891062018.

Smith, Bessie and Steven Curtis Chapman, arr. Allen. "Our God Is
With Us." SATB, pno, orch. GVX 0-7673-9676-6.

Monday, December 1

ST. ANDREW, APOSTLE (TRANSFERRED)

Andrew was the first of the twelve. He is known as a fisherman who left his net to follow Jesus. As a part of his calling, he brought outher people including Simon Peter to meet Jesus. The Byzantine church honors Andrew as its patron and points out that because he was the first of Jesus' followers he was, in the words of John Chrysostom, "the Peter before Peter." Together with Philip, Andrew leads a number of Greeks to speak with Jesus. It is Andrew who shows Jesus a boy with five barley loaves and two fish. Andrew is said to have died on a cross saltire, an "X" shaped cross.

We too are called to invite others to the life of Christ that we celebrate during Advent and Christmas. In what ways will the hope that people have in these weeks be found in the church that bears the light of Christ?

Wednesday, December 3

FRANCIS XAVIER, MISSIONARY TO ASIA, 1552

Francis Xavier was born in the Basque region of northern Spain. Francis's native Basque language is unrelated to any other, and Francis admitted that learning languages was difficult for him. Despite this obstacle he became a missionary to India, Southeast Asia, Japan, and the Philippines. At each point he learned the local language and, like Martin Luther, wrote catechisms for the instruction of new converts. Another obstacle Francis overcame to accomplish his mission work was a propensity to seasickness. All his travels to the Far East were by boat. Together with Ignatius Loyola and five others, Francis formed the Society of Jesus (Jesuits). Francis spoke out against the Spanish and Portuguese colonists when he discovered their oppression of the indigenous people to whom he was sent as a missionary.

34

Pray for churches and missionaries in Asia, spiritual heirs to Francis Xavier. Consider singing "Lord your hands have formed" (WOV 727, Philippine traditional) to honor the work of Francis.

Saturday, December 6

NICHOLAS, BISHOP OF MYRA, C. 342

Though Nicholas is one of the church's most beloved saints, little is known about his life. In the fourth century he was a bishop in what is now Turkey. Legends that surround Nicholas tell of his love for God and neighbor, especially the poor. One famous story tells of Nicholas secretly giving bags of gold to the three daughters of a father who was going to sell them into prostitution because he could not provide dowries for them. Nicholas has become a symbol of anonymous gift giving.

In some countries gifts are given on this day, and may include a visit from Nicholas himself. One of the ways Nicholas can be remembered is to have the congregation or families within it gather to prepare gifts that will be given anonymously as a way to remind us of the tradition of giving gifts as a sign of God's love given freely to all.

December 7, 2003

Second Sunday in Advent

INTRODUCTION

During this second week of Advent, John the Baptist walks onto the stage and calls people to a new beginning. Our baptism is also a new beginning. Day after day, as we are renewed in our baptism, God who began a good work in us continues to prepare us for the day of Jesus Christ.

Today the church commemorates Ambrose, bishop of Milan in the fourth century. He is remembered for his preaching, for having been instrumental in the conversion of St. Augustine, and for writing hymns still sung today.

PRAYER OF THE DAY

Stir up our hearts, O Lord, to prepare the way for your only Son. By his coming give us strength in our conflicts and shed light on our path through the darkness of this world; through your Son, Jesus Christ our Lord, who lives and reigns with you and the Holy Spirit, one God, now and forever.

VERSE

Alleluia. Prepare the way of the Lord, make his paths straight; all flesh shall see the salvation of our God. Alleluia. (Luke 3:4, 6)

READINGS

Malachi 3:1-4

The Lord announces a covenant with Israel. A messenger like Malachi (his name means "my messenger") shall prepare a way for the sudden coming of the Lord, who will purify and refine God's people for the offering of pleasing sacrifices.

or Baruch 5:1-9

A poem of hope from the school of the prophet Jeremiah speaks of the return of scattered Israel from Babylon, but also looks beyond that to the end times when God's kingdom will be established.

Luke 1:68-79

In the tender compassion of our God, the dawn from on high shall break upon us. (Luke 1:78)

Philippians 1:3-11

Paul exhorts Christians to experience love that grows "richer in knowledge and insight of every kind" until the day of Christ Jesus. On that day, the good work begun in them will be flawless, a "full harvest of righteousness."

Luke 3:1-6

Luke takes care to place John in secular history. Yet John's arrival also heralds a new age of salvation. John refers to the words of the prophets, but with a vigorous immediacy: Now is the time to prepare for Christ through a "baptism of repentance for the forgiveness of sins."

COLOR   Blue *or* Purple

THE PRAYERS

As the fulfillment of our hope draws near, let us raise our heads and lift our voices in prayer for the church, the world, and all according to their need.
A BRIEF SILENCE.

Most Merciful God, awaken your church from complacency and drive us to share your abundant grace with the lost and forsaken. O God, whose advent is near,
hear us, and renew us with your love.

Overwhelm the world's destructive powers with a flood of righteousness, bringing forth new life for all people and the whole creation. O God, whose advent is near,
hear us and renew us with your love.

Make the rough ways smooth, gracious God, for those who have been exiled from their homes because of warfare and political unrest. Use us to help them find refuge and safe homes. O God, whose advent is near,
hear us and renew us with your love.

Give your radiant light to all those who sit in the darkness of grief, shame, and sickness *(especially)*. Guide the feet of your people to bear your tender mercy to all those in need. O God, whose advent is near,
hear us and renew us with your love.

Strengthen the resolve of this congregation to become the body of Christ in this place, confident that you have begun a good work in us and you will not fail to bring it to completion through Christ. O God, whose advent is near,
hear us and renew us with your love.
HERE OTHER INTERCESSIONS MAY BE OFFERED.

Bind us together with the saints of all times and places, with Ambrose, bishop and renewer of the church, and all those who have spread your gospel, that we may stand together, pure and blameless in the day of Jesus Christ. O God, whose advent is near,
hear us and renew us with your love.

Hear our prayers, mighty God, as we rejoice in your reign already revealed, and long for the peace, justice, and love yet to dawn, through Jesus Christ our Lord.
Amen

IMAGES FOR PREACHING

"Prepare the way"? Perhaps the *ways*. Prepare the *ways* of the Lord.

We are to prepare the way for the Lord to get to us. That's one way. Then, each one of us should undertake to become a way for others "to be gotten" by our Lord. That's a second way—and it takes some preparation, a wilderness of preparation, as John the Baptist discovered.

What clears the way for the Lord's coming, straightens his path, fills valleys, lowers mountains, straightens the crooked and smooths the rough paths? John proclaimed "a baptism of repentance for the forgiveness of sins." Paul wrote to the Philippians, "All of you share in God's grace with me" (1:7). And that's what prepares the way for the Lord to get to us—God's grace. God prepares God's way to us. God refines, soaps, purifies and makes a way to us. Don't be in the way—make way. Accept forgiveness. Be on the way. God is the way ahead, and we are invited to join God and become the way—be the way for others to be begotten.

True, we are not mighty prophets like Isaiah and John. The thought of us being part of such a large task may seem overwhelming. But mighty road construction projects, employing massive machinery and millions of dollars, still require someone with a paint can to mark where digging will take place. They require back-in-the-garage workers to oil, maintain, and repair those mighty machines. So "in many and various ways" God uses us to help prepare the way.

Make way for the Lord who comes. Be on the way the Lord has made. Be the way the Lord will come. This is the way the Lord has planned it. Let us rejoice and be glad in it!

WORSHIP MATTERS

John the Baptist prepared the way for Christ. His work was in one sense a rehearsal for the ministry of the Savior.

Planning and rehearsal enable the assembly to be at its best each week in worship. Those who prepare the altar are to be aware of little things like candle wicks as well as the placement of communion vessels. Acolytes benefit from finding their places, spending time outside of worship practicing processing together while carrying cross and book. Ushers are to ensure that lighting is adequate and worship books and leaflets are in order. Pastors, readers, and assisting ministers do well to read the

36

texts aloud in advance. All worship participants may gather for prayer prior to the assembly's gathering.

For worship to be done well and received well, time spent in preparation and practice allow the main event in Jesus to be front and center.

LET THE CHILDREN COME

Many people come to worship expecting to get something out of it. Do any come expecting to encounter the living Christ? He promises to be wherever two or more are gathered in his name. Few people understand that if anyone is the "audience" during worship, it is God, not the congregation. Take a moment to teach children (and adults!) that worship happens when people gather together and bring their joy, concerns, cares, needs, and prayers to God. What is something they could bring to God in worship? Hearts ready to love? Ears open to listen? Spirits eager to serve?

HYMNS FOR WORSHIP

GATHERING
The advent of our God   LBW 22
Light one candle to watch for Messiah   WOV 630

HYMN OF THE DAY
Comfort, comfort now my people   LBW 29

ALTERNATE HYMN OF THE DAY
On Jordan's banks the Baptist's cry   LBW 36
Prepare the royal highway   LBW 26

COMMUNION
Soul, adorn yourself with gladness   LBW 224
Father, we thank you   WOV 704

SENDING
Hark, the glad sound!   LBW 35
All earth is hopeful   WOV 629, TFF 47
Let justice roll like a river   W&P 85

ADDITIONAL HYMNS AND SONGS
There's a voice in the wilderness   RWSB
Freedom is coming   TFF 46
He who began a good work in you   W&P 56
Wild and lone the prophet's voice   PH 409

MUSIC FOR THE DAY

PSALMODY
Jennings, Carolyn. PW , Cycle C.
Makeever, Ray. "Blessed Are You, Lord" in DH.
LBW 2; WOV 725; W&P 20; RS 7.

CHORAL
Ferguson, John. "Comfort, Comfort." SATB, opt picc, 2 cl, tamb/opt kybd. AFP 0800646355.
Handel, G. F. "And He Shall Purify" in Messiah. SATB, kybd. Various ed.
Handel, G. F. "But Who May Abide" in Messiah. A/B solo, kybd. Various ed.
Helgen, John. "Prepare the Royal Highway." SATB, pno. AFP 0800674227.
Manz, Paul. "E'en So, Lord Jesus, Quickly Come." SATB. MSM 50-0001.

CHILDREN'S CHOIR
Bostrom, Sandra. "Christ Is Coming." U/2 pt, kybd. CG CGA691.
Hart, Kathy Lowe. "We Wait for a Little Child." U/2 pt, kybd. AFP 0800675975.
Hopson, Hal H. "Prepare Ye the Way." U/2 pt, kybd. AFP 0800675258.

KEYBOARD/INSTRUMENTAL
Albrecht, Timothy. "Comfort, Comfort Ye My People" in Grace Notes II. Org. AFP 080065305X.
Böhm, Georg. "Freu dich sehr" (Variations) in Orgelwerke. Org/kybd. Breitkopf ed.
Dahl, David P. "Puer Nobis" in Hymn Interpretations for Organ. Org. AFP 0800658248.
Hamilton, Gregory. "Veni, Emmanuel" in As the Grains of Wheat. Pno. AFP 0800675770.
Hovhaness, Alan. "Dawn." Org. PET 6488.

HANDBELL
Afdahl, Lee J. "Prepare the Royal Highway." 3-5 oct. AFP 080065577X.
Lamb, Linda R. "Celtic Farewell." 3-5 oct, opt fl. AGEHR AG35210.
Lamb, Linda R. "People, Look East." 2-3 oct. AG 2139.

PRAISE ENSEMBLE
Collins, Dori Erwin. "A Story for All People" in W&P.
Helgen, John. "Prepare The Royal Highway." SATB, pno. AFP 0800674227.
Mohr, John. "He Who Began a Good Work in You" in W&P.

37

Sunday, December 7

AMBROSE, BISHOP OF MILAN, 397

Ambrose was a governor of northern Italy and a catechumen when he was elected bishop of Milan. He was baptized, ordained, and consecrated a bishop all on the same day. While bishop he gave away his wealth and lived in simplicity. He was a famous preacher and is largely responsible for the conversion of St. Augustine.

He is also well known for writing hymns. On one occasion, Ambrose led people in a hymn he wrote while the church in which they were secluded was threatened by attack from Gothic soldiers. The soldiers turned away, unwilling to attack a congregation that was singing a hymn. Ambrose's hymn "Savior of the nations, come" (LBW 28) could be sung during these first weeks in Advent when the apocalyptic readings on Sundays encourage believers to stand firm in their faith.

Thursday, December 11

LARS OLSEN SKREFSRUD, MISSIONARY TO INDIA, 1910

Lars Olsen Skrefsrud was born in Norway in 1840. When he was nineteen years old, he and some friends robbed a bank. In prison he began to read religious books. Visits with a pastor who came to the prison revived Skrefsrud's earlier desire to become a pastor. In 1863 he began work among the Santals of northern India. His work among them included providing a written language, translating the gospels and the Small Catechism, and writing hymns in that language. He also taught agriculture and carpentry methods to raise the Santal's standard of living. The Christian community he founded there continues to flourish.

Consider ways in which Skrefsrud's life echoes the prophetic work of Isaiah and John the Baptist, who prepared the way of the Lord. In what ways can a congregation's proclamation of the gospel and its work for justice point the way to the coming Christ?

December 14, 2003

Third Sunday in Advent

INTRODUCTION

The arrival is fast approaching; the light from the Advent wreath is growing. How shall we prepare for God's coming among us? With joy! With resolute action! With prayer and thanksgiving! The Lord is near.

John of the Cross and his mentor, Teresa of Avila, are commemorated today. Both were sixteenth-century mystical writers and reformers of the church who belonged to the Carmelite order in Spain.

PRAYER OF THE DAY

Almighty God, you once called John the Baptist to give witness to the coming of your Son and to prepare his way. Grant us, your people, the wisdom to see your purpose today and the openness to hear your will, that we may witness to Christ's coming and so prepare his way; through Jesus Christ our Lord, who lives and reigns with you and the Holy Spirit, one God, now and forever.

or

Lord, hear our prayers and come to us, bringing light into the darkness of our hearts; for you live and reign with the Father and the Holy Spirit, one God, now and forever.

VERSE

Alleluia. See, I am sending my messenger ahead of you, who will prepare your way before you. Alleluia. (Matt. 11:10)

READINGS

Zephaniah 3:14-20

The prophet Zephaniah's message is mostly one of judgment for sin. This reading, however, which comes from the conclusion of the book, pictures the new people of God (3:12-13). Judgment has brought repentance and salvation, and now is the time of celebration.

Isaiah 12:2-6

In your midst is the Holy One of Israel. (Isa. 12:6)

Philippians 4:4-7

The theme of joy sounded in the first reading continues in Paul's confident words to the Philippians. Although he writes from prison, Paul finds hope in the assurance that hearts and minds are guarded securely by the peace of God.

Luke 3:7-18

Before he begins his account of Jesus' ministry, Luke describes the work of John the Baptist, who proclaimed the good news in startling images. Radical generosity and faithfulness in vocation are among the fruits of repentance John identifies.

COLOR   Blue *or* Purple

THE PRAYERS

As the fulfillment of our hope draws near, let us raise our heads and lift our voices in prayer for the church, the world, and all according to their need.

A BRIEF SILENCE.

God our salvation, fill the hearts of all the baptized with thanksgiving, that we may make known your mighty deeds and proclaim your exalted name with voices that never waver and hands that never grow tired. O God, whose advent is near,

hear us, and renew us with your love.

Help us to repent of smugness, leaving behind the attitude that we are better than others by virtue of our religion, nationality, or social standing. Bring us instead to rely only on you, and to open ourselves to works of charity. O God, whose advent is near,

hear us and renew us with your love.

Guide the nations of the earth toward the fulfillment of your will, that all people may enjoy peace, justice, and daily bread. Put an end to the violence and warfare, and overcome the powers that advance evil in your creation. O God, whose advent is near,

hear us and renew us with your love.

Give your peace, which surpasses all understanding, to all those who suffer from illness of mind, body, or spirit *(especially)*. Fill our hearts with compassion that we may be the hands and feet of Christ to all who long for healing. O God, whose advent is near,

hear us and renew us with your love.

Shape the mission and ministry of this parish, that bearing fruits worthy of repentance we may give clothing to those in need of it, food to the hungry, and hope to all who come searching for peace. O God, whose advent is near,

hear us and renew us with your love.

HERE OTHER INTERCESSIONS MAY BE OFFERED.

Gather all your saints as wheat into the granary, where we may join with John of the Cross and Teresa of Avila, renewers of the church, *(others)*, and all who have lived lives of faith knowing that the Lord is coming soon. O God, whose advent is near,

hear us and renew us with your love.

Hear our prayers, mighty God, as we rejoice in your reign already revealed, and long for the peace, justice, and love yet to dawn, through Jesus Christ our Lord.

Amen

IMAGES FOR PREACHING

After Advent's first sign urging us to "obey" and its second stress on the "way," we come to the exhortation of this third Sunday: "Rejoice!"

John rebuked and exhorted, but also "proclaimed the good news." We have learned more of that good news than John knew and it fills our Advent. First and foremost, the joy set before us is that Jesus endured the cross "and has taken his seat at the right hand of the throne of God" (Heb. 12:2). And secondly, the joy the Holy Spirit's baptism has given us is to possess "the peace of God which surpasses all understanding" (Phil. 4:7).

An old carol asks *"Ubi sunt gaudia?"*—where do we find joy? Scan the first reading, Zephaniah 3:14-20— "Sing aloud. . . . Rejoice and exult with all your heart. . . . The LORD, your God, is in your midst . . . he will rejoice over you with gladness." God has brought us home! Certainly that is the foundation of our joy.

Beyond that, what makes you glad? Compare it with John's answers to the crowd's questioning, "What then should we do?" Consider contrasting reasons for joy—"I have two coats! Isn't that great?" or "I can share my coats with you! Here, take one!" Another example: "I have so much food I will buy a bigger freezer to store it all!" or "Spare a buck? I can spring for dinner!" One more: "I had to bend a few rules, but I made a pile on a sharp deal" or "I am content with my honest wages."

Seldom is our joy unselfish, but the first reading un-

39

derlines our true reason for joy: "The LORD has taken away the judgments against you" (v. 15). We repent our selfishness, and forgiveness awaits us—reason indeed for joy!

"Rejoice! Again I will say, Rejoice!" Advent's best reason for joy: "The Lord is near!"

WORSHIP MATTERS

Someone once said that the church has an obligation to lift up in particular the poor, the lonely, the sick, and the oppressed in prayer because no one else will. As we consider the needs of the community and the world, think of prayer on behalf of others in concentric circles, beginning around the earth and moving in to your local community. Strive for balance in the crafting of prayers, so that you don't forget the world "out there," nor omit naming the problems in your own backyard.

In the same way, be attentive to prayer that is lived in the actions of those "called and empowered by the triune God." How is the ministry of your congregation shaped by prayer? How is prayer in your congregation shaped by ministry?

LET THE CHILDREN COME

Invite two or three children (different ages, could be of the same family, perhaps also one adult and one child) to write or lead the prayers of the church for today. Include in the bulletin an insert of prayer prompters that people can take and use at home once a day until Christmas. Some examples of prayer prompters would be: "Lord, be with us this year as we . . ." or "O God, forgive us for . . ." or "Dear Jesus, help us to . . ." Include one prompter per day for the rest of the season.

HYMNS FOR WORSHIP
GATHERING

Awake, awake, and greet the new morn   WOV 633
Comfort, comfort now my people   LBW 29

HYMN OF THE DAY

Fling wide the door   LBW 32

ALTERNATE HYMN OF THE DAY

Surely it is God who saves me   WOV 635
Lift up your heads   W&P 88

COMMUNION

Rejoice, rejoice, believers   LBW 25
Eat this bread, drink this cup   WOV 706

SENDING

Hark! A thrilling voice is sounding!   LBW 37
To God be the glory   TFF 264

ADDITIONAL HYMNS AND SONGS

Lord, my strength   W&P 93
I've got the joy, joy, joy   TFF 257
Make me a channel of your peace   W&P 95, RWSB

MUSIC FOR THE DAY
PSALMODY

Haugen, Marty. "With Joy You Shall Draw Water" (Isaiah 12) in PCY, vol. 2.
Lindh, Jody. "Behold, God Is My Salvation." U. CPH 98-3193.
Mealy, Norman. "Canticle of Thanksgiving" in TP.
White, Jack Noble. "The First Song of Isaiah." SATB, cong, kybd, opt gtr, opt hb, opt perc, opt dance. HWG CMR 3347.
Surely it is God who saves me   WOV 635

CHORAL

Crotch, William. "Be Peace on Earth" in *The Oxford Easy Anthem Book.* SA, org. OXF 3533219.
Erickson, Richard. "Light One Candle to Watch for Messiah." SATB, org. AFP 0800657519.
Jacob, Gordon. "O Lord I Will Praise Thee" in *The Oxford Easy Anthem Book.* SATB, org. OXF 3533219.
Jennings, Carolyn. "Climb to the Top of the Highest Mountain." SATB, opt children's choir. KJO C8118.
Organ, Anne Krentz. "Come, My Light." 2 pt, pno. AFP 0800675819.
Purcell, Henry. "Rejoice in the Lord Always." SATB, ATB soli, opt str, org. CPH 97-6344.
Robinson, Marc. "Prepare Ye." SATB, solo, perc. KJO 8830.

CHILDREN'S CHOIR

Shute, Linda Cable. "Stir Up Your Power." 2 pt, kybd, opt cong. AFP 0800675274.
Ziegenhals, Harriet Ilse. "Sing, Dance, Clap Your Hands." (Isaiah 12:6) U, opt desc, kybd. CG CGA625.

KEYBOARD/INSTRUMENTAL

Burkhardt, Michael. "Come, Thou Long-Expected Jesus" in *Five Christmas Hymn Improvisations, Set II.* Org. MSM 10-121.

Cherwien, David. "Awake, O Spirit of the Watchman" in *Evening and Morning: Hymn Settings for Organ.* Org. AFP 080067572X.

Farlee, Robert Buckley. "Macht hoch die Tür" in *Many and Great.* Org. AFP 0800658949.

Manz, Paul. "Rejoice, Rejoice, Believers" (Haf trones lampa färdig) in *Six Advent Improvisations.* Org. MSM 10-002.

Mason, Monte. "Posadas" in *Organ Music for the Seasons,* vol. 3. Org. AFP 0800675649.

HANDBELL

Dicke, Martin. "Rondo for Bells." (Phil. 4:6-7) 2 oct. AFP 0800659945.

Kinyon, Barbara Baltzer. "Let All Mortal Flesh Keep Silence." 2 oct. AG 1659.

Sherman, Arnold B. "Come, Thou Long-Expected Jesus." 3-5 oct. LOR 20/1062L.

PRAISE ENSEMBLE

Nelson, Jeff. "Purify My Heart" in *Best of the Best.* FEL 1891062018.

Robinson, Marc. "Prepare Ye." SATB, perc, opt. pno. KJO 8830.

Sunday, December 14

JOHN OF THE CROSS, RENEWER OF THE CHURCH, 1591
TERESA OF AVILA, RENEWER OF THE CHURCH, 1582

John and Teresa were both members of the Carmelite religious order. John met Teresa when she was working to reform the Carmelite Order and return it to a stricter observance of its rules, from which she believed its members had departed. John followed Teresa's lead and encouraged others to follow her reform. He was imprisoned when he encountered opposition to the reform. Both John and Teresa's writings reflect a deep interest in mystical thought and meditation. Their emphasis on contemplation can guide us in our Advent worship as we watch for the coming Christ.

Both John and Teresa believed that authentic prayer leads to greater love of neighbor and service to those in need. Teresa wrote, "Christ has no body now but yours . . . yours are the eyes through which he looks in compassion on the world." In one of John's poems, "The Spiritual Canticle," he cried, "Oh, that my griefs would end! Come, grant me thy fruition full and free!"

Tuesday, December 16

LAS POSADAS

Las Posadas, "lodgings," is celebrated in homes of Mexican heritage and is becoming a popular parish practice as well. Families or groups of people wander through the neighborhood to mark the journey of Mary and Joseph to Bethlehem. They knock on doors, asking to come in, but a rude voice says that there is no room. The visitors either respond that Mary is about to give birth to the king of heaven, or they sing an Advent carol foretelling his birth. Eventually the door is opened, and everyone is welcomed into a great party of traditional Mexican holiday food and singing.

The traditional songs of this celebration are included in *Libro de Liturgia y Cántico* (284–86). Prepare a special package or offering for a shelter or halfway house. Las Posadas can be a strong reminder of Christ's humble birth among the poor and the importance of extending hospitality.

41

December 21, 2003

Fourth Sunday in Advent

INTRODUCTION

We come to the threshold of the celebration. The time is right; the place, Bethlehem of Judah, is identified; Mary's song announces the great things God is doing. A new day is being birthed into existence, and we are meant to be a part of it. These final few days of preparation lead to the darkness of Christmas Eve and the dawn of the festival of our Lord's nativity, where the mystery unfolds again.

PRAYER OF THE DAY

Stir up your power, O Lord, and come. Take away the hindrance of our sins and make us ready for the celebration of your birth, that we may receive you in joy and serve you always; for you live and reign with the Father and the Holy Spirit, now and forever.

VERSE

Alleluia. The virgin shall conceive and bear a son, and they shall name him Emmanuel. Alleluia. (Matt. 1:23)

READINGS

Micah 5:2-5a

Many years before the time of Micah, God promised David that his dynasty would last forever. Although prophets such as Micah warned that judgment would come from unfaithfulness, Micah foresees a restoration beyond that judgment.

Luke 1:47-55

The LORD has lifted up the lowly. (Luke 1:52)

or Psalm 80:1-7

Show the light of your countenance and we shall be saved. (Ps. 80:7)

Hebrews 10:5-10

The author of Hebrews uses the image of religious sacrifice to convey the significance of Christ's coming. Through obedient acceptance of God's will, Christ allows his own body to become the greatest sacrifice of all, one through which we are made a holy people.

Luke 1:39-45 [46-55]

Luke presents Elizabeth, the mother of John the Baptist, and Mary, the mother of Jesus, as women who are filled with the Holy Spirit and with faith. We hear Elizabeth's inspired greeting and Mary's song of praise: God is among the lowly and the hungry.

COLOR   Blue or Purple

THE PRAYERS

As the fulfillment of our hope draws near, let us raise our heads and lift our voices in prayer for the church, the world, and all according to their need.

A BRIEF SILENCE.

Mighty One, whose name is holy, fill your church in all places with wonder at your mighty deeds, that we may practice your will, sing your praise, and answer your constant calling. O God, whose advent is near,

hear us, and renew us with your love.

Humble the nations with the compassion you show to the poor and lowly, that with softened hearts, world leaders may turn from war and embrace the way of justice you have shown in Jesus Christ. O God, whose advent is near,

hear us and renew us with your love.

Give peace to those who are too busy, who are hurting emotionally, who are unable to hear your message of hope. Embrace us, and love us. O God, whose advent is near,

hear us and renew us with your love.

Speak a word of hope to those who suffer the pain of abuse, and those who are burdened by illness *(especially)*. Use us to lift up the lowly and proclaim a song of hope to all in need. O God, whose advent is near,

hear us and renew us with your love.

Build up your people in this parish for the work of ministry, that the hearts of all the baptized will be moved to witness to your power in the world. O God, whose advent is near,

hear us and renew us with your love.

HERE OTHER INTERCESSIONS MAY BE OFFERED.

Prepare our hearts to join the eternal voices of the apostle Thomas, *(other names)*, and all the faithful who have died in you. May we draw strength from their lives, and join them in singing of your wondrous acts of salvation. O God, whose advent is near,

hear us and renew us with your love.

Hear our prayers, mighty God, as we rejoice in your reign already revealed, and long for the peace, justice, and love yet to dawn, through Jesus Christ our Lord.

Amen

IMAGES FOR PREACHING

Today we are invited to think of human bodies. In today's second reading, the author of the book of Hebrews cites the words of Psalm 40 (in the Greek version) as if Jesus himself were speaking them to God the Father. "When Christ came into the world, he said, '. . . a body you have prepared for me.' " Ordinarily, we don't think of bodies being *prepared* by God (except for Adam and Eve, of course). But the two Advent 4 baby boys, John and Jesus, are not ordinary children. Consider how the bodies of these boys were extraordinary.

Look to the mothers. In John's case, Zechariah put it mildly: "My wife is getting on in years" (Luke 1:18). This child was custom-built by God—"even before his birth, he will be filled with the Holy Spirit" (Luke 1:15). When Mary arrived carrying Jesus in her womb, John, in the womb of Elizabeth, leaped for joy (Luke 1:44). Think of God's knowing the hands of this baby would have to grasp the bars of a prison cell. Or think of that baby's neck and Herod's henchmen . . .

Think of Mary, the mother of Jesus . . . the annunciation . . . the stable birth of the child. How true that the boy Jesus could have grown up to say, "A body you have prepared for me." That body had to be strong, healthy, with muscular legs to walk all over Palestine, to walk to Golgotha—a body to last thirty-three years, until, legs unbroken, it was laid to rest in a tomb—only to get up again on the third day. That body prepared for him he voluntarily and obediently offered for us and for our salvation.

A third special Advent body to consider—yours. "Present your bodies as a living sacrifice, holy and acceptable to God" (Rom. 12:1). As we await the celebration of God's incarnation, we already celebrate the ways God uses bodies—including our own!

WORSHIP MATTERS

In the three-year lectionary cycle, the fourth Sunday in Advent always lifts up Mary, the mother of Jesus. Today we hear of Mary's joyful meeting with Elizabeth, and we hear Mary's song. And just as the Sunday cycle of readings has its own annual rhythm of marking Mary's role as faithful mother, so too those that gather for daily prayer point to Mary as an example of righteousness. In Evening Prayer, Mary's Magnificat is sung as the gospel canticle.

What is it about Mary and her song, that they mark and inform the day's end for so many praying Christians? An ordinary person until chosen by God, she lives with hope for God's promises to come. She sings of God's great reversal, as the powerful are brought down and the lowly lifted up. Praying Christians everywhere may sing her song and remember her witness, and ask God in Christ to redeem the day, and the world.

LET THE CHILDREN COME

Mary is a wonderful role model for us all. She sang a song of faith even though the news of God's plans came as a complete surprise and did not coincide with the life plans she must already have made. She trusted in the goodness of God and was ready and willing to serve her Lord. Challenge children to look for one new way to intentionally serve God this week. It's always amazing to see what God can accomplish through willing servants.

HYMNS FOR WORSHIP

GATHERING

Oh, come, oh, come, Emmanuel   LBW 34

O little town of Bethlehem   LBW 41

A story for all people   W&P 2

HYMN OF THE DAY

The only Son from heaven   LBW 86

ALTERNATE HYMN OF THE DAY

My soul proclaims your greatness   WOV 730

The angel Gabriel from heaven came   WOV 632

COMMUNION

Let all mortal flesh keep silence   LBW 198

43

Creator of the stars of night   RWSB, RWI 22
(or O Lord of light, who made the stars   LBW 323)

SENDING

Joy to the world   LBW 39
Canticle of the turning   W&P 26

ADDITIONAL HYMNS AND SONGS

That boy-child of Mary   TFF 54
Emmanuel W&P 36
Unexpected and mysterious   RWSB
Little Bethlehem of Judah   PsH 204

MUSIC FOR THE DAY

PSALMODY

LUKE 1:47-55

Haugen, Marty. "My Soul Proclaims Your Greatness" in PCY, vol. 2.
Jennings, Carolyn. PW , Cycle C.
LBW 6; LBW 180; TFF 168; WOV 730; W&P 26; RWSB.

PSALM 80:1-7

Callahan, Mary David. PW , Cycle B.
Cox, Joe. "Restore Us, O God" in *Psalms for the People of God.*
    SMP 45/1037 S.
Haugen, Marty. "Lord, Make Us Turn to You" in PCY, vol. 2.
Kogut, Malcolm. "Lord, Make Us Turn to You" in PCY, vol. 10.
Schoenbachler, Tim. "Psalm 80/85: Maranatha" in STP, vol. I.

CHORAL

Benson, Robert A. "Gabriel's Message." SATB, kybd.
    AFP 0800675134.
Carter, Andrew. "Mary's Magnificat." SATB, org. OXF X299.
Jennings, Carolyn. "A New Magnificat." SATB, org, SA soli, opt cong.
    AFP 080065255X. Also in *The Augsburg Choirbook.*
    AFP 0800656784.
Rachmaninoff, Sergei. "Ave Maria" from *All Night Vigil* in *Songs of the
    Church.* SATB, div. HWG GB 640.
Rachmaninoff, Sergei. "Magnificat" from *All Night Vigil* in *Songs of the
    Church.* SATB, div. HWG GB 640.
Schütz, Heinrich, arr. Robert Buckley Farlee. "My Soul Exalts Your
    Name, O Lord." SATB, kybd. AFP 080067524X.

CHILDREN'S CHOIR

Rotermund, Donald. "A Responsorial Magnificat." U, org, 2 oct hb,
    cong. CPH 98-3576.

Sleeth, Natalie. "O Come, O Come Immanuel." (Ps. 80:2) U, opt
    desc, kybd. CG CGA273.

KEYBOARD/INSTRUMENTAL

Bach, J.S. "Wachet auf, ruft uns die Stimme" in *Six Schübler Chorales.*
    Org. Various ed.
Buxtehude, Dietrich, Johann Pachelbel, H. Scheidemann, J. S. Bach,
    and others. *Magnificat settings and fugues.* Org. Various ed.
Gant, Andrew. "A Virgin Most Pure" in *Augsburg Organ Library: Christ-
    mas.* Org. AFP 080065935X.
Manz, Paul. "Prepare the Royal Highway" (Bereden väg för Herran)
    in *Six Advent Improvisations.* Org. MSM 10-002.

HANDBELL

McChesney, Kevin. "Joseph and Mary." 3-5 oct. ALF 19004.
Moklebust, Cathy. "Come, Thou Long-Expected Jesus." 2-3 oct, perc.
    CG CGB266.

PRAISE ENSEMBLE

Cain, Patricia. "Jesus, Name above All Names" in W&P.
Griepentrog, Maureen. "Light the Candle" in Best of the Best.
    FEL 1891062018.

Monday, December 22

ST. THOMAS, APOSTLE (TRANSFERRED)

Thomas is perhaps best remembered as "Doubting
Thomas." But alongside this doubt, the gospel of John
shows Thomas as fiercely loyal: "Let us also go, that we
may die with him" (John 11:16). And John's gospel
shows Thomas moving from doubt to deep faith.
Thomas makes one of the strongest confessions of faith
in the New Testament, "My Lord and my God!" (John
20:28). From this confession of faith, ancient stories tell
of Thomas's missionary work to India where Christian
communities were flourishing a thousand years before
the arrival of sixteenth-century missionaries.

Though we hear about Thomas each year on the
second Sunday of Easter, Thomas can also serve as an
Advent saint. He watched for the risen Christ and
looked for the signs of Christ's incarnation. In Advent
we, too, watch. We look for the coming of Christ in our
lives, his risen presence in the sacraments, and his incarnation soon to be celebrated at Christmas.

CHRISTMAS

We celebrate Christ born anew

into our hearts and lives

Images *of the* Season

Christmas is a time of vivid images, many of them

so familiar as to have nearly worn out their power.

Among them are the manger, angels, shepherds, Christmas

tree, wrapped gifts, and children's shining faces. A Celtic prayer, though not particular to the nativity, suggests some alternate words, different lenses to focus our thinking in this time.

> Come, my Lord,
> My light, my way;
> Come, my lantern
> Night and day;
> Come, my healer,
> Make me whole;
> Come, my Saviour,
> Protect my soul;
> Come, my King,
> Enter my heart;
> Come, Prince of Peace,
> And never depart.
>
> (*The Open Gate* © 1994 David Adam. Reprinted by permission of Morehouse Publishing.)

God-with-us: a lantern in our dark world, a healer who knows our trials intimately, a Savior, a sovereign, the source of peace.

The Christmas season is even shorter than the Advent season, and its burden of emotions and high expectations can be overwhelming. We all know how easy it is to lose sight of the season's center, to forget that it isn't an event—Christmas—that comes, but Jesus Christ who comes! Amid all the trappings, the frivolity and foolishness, the whole point of this celebration is that Christ comes—God has become one of us. The birthing season, the groaning, the waiting is over. We celebrate in order to bring Christ anew into our hearts and lives.

Those who lead worship face the annual challenge of presenting in a fresh way a truth that is at the same time so familiar and so foreign. Christmas is a comfort zone for most people in our society—but often for reasons that pull them away from, rather than toward, the miracle of the incarnation. How then can we, in terms

that are graspable by the child (in age or Christian maturity), proclaim the gospel of the Christmas season? We might begin with a few more of those lenses.

Christmas is a season of welcoming—a time to welcome the stranger, welcome the newborn, welcome the lost sheep, welcome the near and dear. Yearly, we invite Christ to come fresh into our hearts, to lighten our darkness, heal our wounds, and restore our souls. Our worship needs to reflect this welcoming attitude for it is the attitude of grace. Now is not the time to scold, but to enfold all into the family gathered around the manger.

Christmas is a season of gifts, both given and received. We are profoundly gifted by the presence of Christ in our midst. It is a precious gift intended to make us whole and holy. Freely we have been given this gift, freely we receive this gift with joy. Frequently we respond in this season by giving gifts to each other. Besides trinkets and toys, we are invited to give the gifts of welcome, friendship, peace, patience, blessing, and love. Freely we have been given, freely we give. We need not always bemoan materialism. Rather, begin with the grace from God that allows us to give, and then move into how we can model our gift giving after God's. How can our gifts, like those God gives us, lift up and truly enrich those who receive them?

Christmas is a season of healing: the binding up of the fresh wounds and the final closure on the old wounds. The Christ touch heals our brokenness and gives us the power to heal relationships. We receive the ability to reconcile with each other. In Christ's coming we are empowered to look beyond our current petty grudges and our deep-seated resentments to a time when lion and lamb can lie down together. Christ shows us how the world can look if we put aside our differences to look for those things that bring us together. A service of healing during the season of Christmas provides that ritual time when we are touched by a loving healing hand and prayed for with sighs too deep for words. It can be a time when tears fall like rain, but these tears detoxify us of the pains that have poisoned our spirits. Christmas is a sacred time of weeping and laughter.

Finally, Christmas is a season of joy and celebration.

It is a time when we lay aside our daily work and concerns. It is a time that God calls us to dance, play, love, laugh, eat, enjoy, and celebrate with each other and God. Rejoice: Christ has come!

Environment *and* Art *for the* Season

Christmas is about being in the moment in the world—here and now. Christmas is our celebration of God becoming human in the person of Jesus Christ. The

incarnation ("becoming flesh") is the joining of the mystical and the real, the merging of heaven and earth. The text for Christmas Eve from Luke's gospel is the memorable story of the birth of Jesus Christ where heavenly beings meet earthly beings to proclaim the coming of one promised of old. Ordinary people like Mary and Joseph and individual angels or a multitude of angels are all engaged as eternal God enters earthly time. The text for Christmas Day from the Gospel of John is the theological explanation of those same events. "The Word became flesh and lived among us, . . . full of grace and truth" (John 1:14). A light in the darkness. A light for us. God in the here and now.

EVALUATING YOUR SPACE

How well do we see in the worship space? Have people complained about not being able to read during evening services? Is it hard to read even sometimes during daytime worship? What is the prevailing mood of the worship space? Is it one that is light or dark?

Use of good materials is important in building a place for worship. However, some of the choices our forebears made did not reflect sufficiently on how we would see in worship or on the effect many dark surfaces might have. Dark stone, dark wood or paneling, and darker shades of carpeting all have an impact with regard to ambient light.

Are there pockets of light and dark in the seating area of the assembly?

You can find this out by turning on the overhead lights some evening and looking at the empty seats. You

can also take a book or bulletin around with you to all the possible places and check to see where, if any, the dim places are.

Are there times throughout the day where the sun comes through windows in a brilliant or blinding way? (Remember that this will change throughout the year.) How much candlelight is currently used in worship? Are there other places where candles could be used either as a particular focus or to increase the light throughout the space?

Another evaluation experiment would be to test and see what different combinations you could achieve during daylight and evening hours with your current lighting system and candlelight. (You can borrow candles from other churches if you don't want to invest in enough candles for this experiment.) Think about the answers to these questions as you reflect on the use of light within your worship space.

It is rare that any of us, even worship leaders and planners, ever think about the varying effects of light on our mood during worship. We tend to think about light in purely pragmatic ways: can we see the preacher, can we see where we are walking, can we read our bulletin? If we notice the light in worship at all, we most likely only think of the Sunday morning worship time. But even the patterns on any given Sunday change as the sun rises higher, as clouds come and go, and so forth. Medieval church builders went to great extremes to make use of the available natural light. Light was one of the most important elements of the period of architecture known as Gothic (Notre Dame Cathedral in Paris is a well-known example). Builders in that time developed wider and

47

taller spaces in order to have more and more glass so they could make use of light in both its natural form and through the colorful array of stained glass. The Christmas season gives us a wonderful opportunity to focus on and reflect the amazing light that has come into the world.

The interplay between light and darkness, both subtle and extreme, creates contrast. Without light, there can be no shadow. Without the contrast of darkness or shadow, there is no full understanding of the power and magnitude of the light. In the Christmas season, there are opportunities to create an environment that makes creative use of both artificial and natural light. Christmas Eve may have multiple services: earlier family services can be well-lit to be able to see children in costumes and later evening services can be held in dimmer light so that worshipers can light candles in the dark and sing "Silent Night." After these liturgies that touch on our sentimental selves, we are blessed again as we celebrate the mystery of God's incarnation Christmas morning with ample daylight pouring through our windows and doors. Establishing what we are going to do within the liturgy and at which of the services our congregation celebrates is a challenge. If we are going to make use of the power of light and contrast, then we must use what we have learned about our worship space to focus, rearrange, and structure our worship environment so that we may get the most out of what our space has to offer.

The darkest place in the worship space during this season could be some corner or place somewhere on Christmas Eve. That location could receive the focus as a place for a lesson or the proclamation of the birth of Christ delivered by the light of the Christ candle. The brightest place may be the location for the gospel reading or the sermon the following morning. Shifting from darkness to light or vice versa at certain points within the liturgy may evoke strong responses from the worshiping assembly.

Whatever is done with regard to lighting during the liturgy, two rules of thumb will be helpful: 1) Less is more. Don't let the power of an effect become the focus of the experience. If it is not supporting the proclamation of the gospel in word and action, then it is simply bad theater. The light is a supporting actor for the star of the show, which is the gospel proclamation and enactment in the sacrament. 2) Every lighting decision should still provide for all members of the assembly to do what they need to do to make the liturgy happen. If we need to listen and not read, then we don't need as much light. If we need to see in order to move safely, then we need more light. Always practice and run through light choices and settings at the same time of day as you will be doing it in worship. Don't assume that an usher will be able to follow some notes in the bulletin about when to switch which lights on and off. If your church doesn't have a sophisticated lighting system complete with dimmers, experiment with using only some of the lighting circuits or with auxiliary lighting. You might even consider judiciously using strings of white or colored Christmas lights. The more time you spend in evaluation and preparation, the better the worship environment will be.

ART DURING THE SEASON

This wonderful season that is so full of rich imagery is too short. That is part of what leads us to wanting to stretch it out and take over the preceding season of Advent. Because we reach a liturgical climax on Christmas Eve and Christmas Day, afterwards we often are ready to relax and settle back into our pre-Advent routine. But this twelve-day Christmas season is full of opportunities for reflection on the incarnation. We have twelve days to flesh out what this gift of grace in Jesus Christ is all about. A great advantage of the first week or so of the Christmas season is that children are off from school and many people take some time to slow down. The festival days that start off this season can be visually overwhelming: manger scenes, pageants, trees with decorations, many familiar and unfamiliar faces, and so forth. The days following could be the perfect time to use the worship space and gathering areas as a place of quiet reflection on the mystery of the incarnation. Turn your worship space into a quiet prayer space. Make use of the art and artists you have contacted in the previous season (see Advent for suggestions) to provide for places of meditation with art as a focus. Give those interested something else to look at besides the images they see every year. Or perhaps set up a theme with art from different times or cultures addressing that theme. The church has been a major patron of the arts for many years. Maybe your congregation can do the same thing this season. You can take the lead. You can be a witness to the light of Christ to your neighborhood.

Preaching *with the* Season

There is probably more Christmas preaching

going on during the Advent days than during the

actual season of Christmas. The carols and hymns preach

on radio, TV, and wherever recordings play—in elevators, department stores, and over the vegetables, meats, and groceries. What is not happening enough is the *hearing*; the failure is in the receiving. "Joy to the world! The Lord is come"—true. "Let earth receive its King"—not so true.

In the Revised Standard Version, the admonition to Timothy was "Preach the word, be urgent in season and out of season." We could add the word "Christmas" to "season." The NRSV translates, "Proclaim the message; be persistent whether the time is favorable or unfavorable." Christmas programs are favorable times for the message in spite of the elements of unfavorableness—the children receive the oohs and ahs and the preacher is a necessary good. So we give it our best, trying to "convince, rebuke, and encourage, with the utmost patience in teaching" (2 Tim. 4:2). Two things might help us in that task: to lift up the word "Savior" and synonyms, and to avoid any overdose of sentiment. Remember, the Word was made flesh to save the world and we translate the Word into words that we might save some. By proclaiming the liberating Word without too many flights of fancy, we give room to the incarnation. We allow people to see and encounter for themselves that simple yet profound miracle when the Word lived among us, and died, and arose.

If our preaching avoids the trap of sentimentality, it doesn't mean it should be prosaic. Remember *awesome*? In late years that word was used by young people to characterize almost anything. Will we not, should we not in some way say "awesome" about everything Christmas? About the lessons? And about the liturgies? If we believe and would confess Jesus Christ, his being in the beginning with God, his birth from the Virgin Mary, his life and death and resurrection, and his living now—will we not, should we not, exclaim about all of that, *"Awesome!"*

There is a word *aweless*, you know—"feeling no awe." People today would be more likely to put it in phrases

such as "That was nice." And some will depart from the Christmas services, smiling and saying, "Nice!" We—never mind others at this point—strive to realize our worship at Christmas as being more than nice, in fact *distinctly awesome*—awe full! That best comes to pass not when we tack spectacular accoutrements onto our liturgies, but when the grace-filled truth within is allowed to shine forth.

Remember, not all of the original Christmas participants were immediately bowled over. Some things take a while to sink in. Mary bought into Gabriel's announcement with only a perplexed, "How?" She said, "Here am I, the servant of the Lord; let it be with me according to your word" (Luke 1:38). And when the shepherds came, words tumbling out all over about what they had seen and heard, she still had to treasure and ponder in her heart what it all would mean.

After some years, however, many had got it right. John began at the beginning—The Word was, the Word became, the Word comes to us. And the writer to the Hebrews could sum it all up "in these last days." He wrote of this Son, "He is the reflection of God's glory and the exact imprint of God's very being. . . . When he had made purification for sins, he sat down at the right hand of the Majesty on high" (Heb. 1:3).

What about Joseph? The evangelist put a song in Mary's mouth—or maybe it was Elizabeth's. A duet? In any case, magnificent! Zechariah, newly voiced, sang the *Benedictus*. What about Joseph? Perhaps he didn't sing very well? Imagine this:

Mary and Joseph were required by the Emperor Augustus to register at Bethlehem. While they were there, Jesus was born. That birth was much more important than registering, surely. So it might have been quite some time before they took care of the registration. Imagine, then, the three of them, Joseph and Mary and the babe in her arms, coming up to the desk where the registrar was sitting with the official record book open before him.

49

"Your name?"

"Joseph, from the house and family of David."

"And you?"

Did Joseph speak for her? "Her name is Mary."

"And the kid?"

This time, surely, Joseph sang out, "He is named Wonderful Counselor, Mighty God, Everlasting Father, Prince of Peace!"

When Ted Williams died at 83, the *Boston Globe* came out with a two-inch headline:

ADIEU, KID

When this kid, Jesus, died at 33, there was no headline. But then, again, he did not stay dead.

AWESOME!

Shape *of* Worship *for the* Season

BASIC SHAPE OF THE EUCHARISTIC RITE

- Confession and Forgiveness: see alternate worship text for Christmas on page 53 as an option to the form in the liturgy setting. Other possibilities for confession and forgiveness are in *Holy Baptism and Related Rites*, Renewing Worship, vol. 3, pp. 87*ff.* (ELCA/Augsburg Fortress, 2002), or at www.renewingworship.org/publications/holy_baptism/index.html

GATHERING

- Greeting: see alternate worship text for Christmas
- Use the Kyrie, particularly for the most festive liturgies during this season
- Use the hymn of praise ("Glory to God")

WORD

- Use the Nicene Creed
- The prayers: see alternate forms and responses for Christmas

MEAL

- Offertory prayer: see alternate worship text for Christmas
- Use the proper preface for Christmas (this would also be recommended for use on the festival of the Holy Innocents, Martyrs)
- Eucharistic prayer: in addition to the four main options in *LBW*, see "Eucharistic Prayer B: The Season of Christmas" in *WOV* Leaders Edition, p. 66. An option for use on the festival of the Holy Innocents, Martyrs would be "Eucharistic Prayer I: November" in *WOV* Leaders Edition, p. 73
- Invitation to communion: see alternate worship text for Christmas

- Post-communion prayer: see alternate worship text for Christmas

SENDING

- Benediction: see alternate worship text for Christmas
- Dismissal: see alternate worship text for Christmas

OTHER SEASONAL POSSIBILITIES

PROCLAMATION OF THE BIRTH OF CHRIST

The services on Christmas Eve may begin with the proclamation of the birth of Christ (see text in the seasonal rites section), taken from the ancient martyrology. The proclamation should be understood as the announcement of the incarnation within human history rather than a literal counting of years. The lights may be turned down, and, following a period of silence, the proclamation may be read or sung on one note by a leader standing at the entrance to the church. Following the proclamation, the lights are turned on as the entrance hymn is begun.

CANDLE LIGHTING OPTIONS FOR CHRISTMAS EVE

OPTION 1

- The liturgy may begin with a service of light as at evening prayer. The congregation may face the entrance to the church, and handheld candles may be lighted. As the procession passes during the Christmas versicles, all turn to face forward.
- Christmas versicles (*LBW*, p. 175)

- Hymn of light (LBW 45, 56, or WOV 638)
- Thanksgiving for light (*LBW*, p. 144)
- The service may then continue with the greeting, followed by the hymn of praise and the prayer of the day.

OPTION 2

Light handheld candles at the reading of the gospel. A hymn, such as "The first Noel" (LBW 56) or "Angels, from the realms of glory" (LBW 50), may be sung as handheld candles are lighted. The gospel may be read from the midst of the people. "Silent night, holy night!" (LBW 65) may be sung following the gospel, after which handheld candles are extinguished.

OPTION 3

- Light handheld candles at the close of the service. Following the post-communion canticle (or at a service without communion, following the offering and the prayers), handheld candles are lighted. Instrumental or choral music may accompany the candle lighting.
- Hymn: "Silent night, holy night!" (LBW 65:1–2; or another hymn of light, as listed in option I)
- Reading from John 1:1-14. A gospel procession may move to the midst of the assembly.
- LBW 65:3 (or the final stanza of another hymn of light)
- Benediction and dismissal

Assembly Song *for the* Season

Welcome to earth, O noble Guest, / through whom

this sinful world is blest! / You turned not from our

needs away; / how can our thanks such love repay?

("From heaven above" RW1 30, stanza 3)

The Christmas narratives give us examples of how to adore, how to enter the faith journey: angels sing, shepherds quake, and magi traverse great distances to greet the Christ child. Even as a baby, Christ causes complete strangers to embark on a journey in faith, like the journey to and from the baptismal waters. Indeed, how can our thanks such great love repay?

GATHERING

For the prelude, let loose with all those Christmas carols the faithful assembly waited for all Advent with a lively carol sing.

Make the angelic Christmas connection by singing a "Glory to God in the highest" setting of the hymn of praise, such as the thoughtful "Christmas Gloria" setting by Daniel Laginya (GIA G-2971) for cantors, congregation, and organ, which quotes the popular refrain of "Angels we have heard on high" (LBW 71).

WORD

Try singing a Christmas hymn between the second reading and the gospel. Two appropriate options are "Good Christian friends, rejoice!" (LBW 55), or "From heaven above" (LBW 51, RW1 30), sung in alternation between choir or cantors and congregation.

MEAL

If you've been using Setting 3 in Advent, continue its use now and strengthen the connection between the seasons of the Christmas cycle.

Two good carols for offertory or at communion are "What feast of love" (WOV 701) and "Oh, come, all ye faithful" (LBW 45).

SENDING

Reinforce incarnational themes with a setting of "Lord, now you let your servant go in peace" (Nunc dimittis), or the chant setting from Prayer at the Close of Day (*LBW*, p. 159).

51

Music *for the* Season

VERSES AND OFFERTORIES

Boehnke, Paul. *Festive Verse Settings for Christmas, Epiphany, and Transfiguration.* SATB, opt kybd. MSM 80-100.

Haas, David. *Advent/Christmas Gospel Acclamations.* 2 pt, org, gtr, solo inst. OCP 8732GC.

Hillert, Richard. *Verses and Offertory Sentences, Part 1: Advent through Christmas.* U, kybd. CPH 97-5509.

Schiavone, J. *Gospel Acclamation Verses for the Christmas Season.* GIA G-2111.

Wetzler, Robert. *Verses and Offertories: Advent 1—Baptism of Our Lord.* SATB, kybd. AFP 0800648994.

CHORAL

Bach, J.S. "From Heaven Above to Earth I Come" in *Bach for All Seasons.* SATB. AFP 080065854X.

Britten, Benjamin. "A Hymn to the Virgin." SATB, SATB soli. B&H 1856.

Ellingboe, Bradley. "In the Bleak Midwinter." 2 pt mxd, SAB/SATB, kybd. KJO 8947.

Jennings, Carolyn. "Go Tell It On the Mountain." SATB. MF 554.

Kern, Philip. "Glory Hallelujah to the Newborn King." SATB, pno. AFP 0800675169.

Lauridsen, Morton. "O Magnum Mysterium." SATB. Peer Music 61860-121.

Pavlechko, Thomas. "Sleep, Holy Child." SATB, org. SEL 405-274.

Schein, Johann. "From Heav'n Above." SSB, org. GIA G-3008.

Scholz, Robert. "Come to the Cradle." SATB, kybd/orch. AFP 0800675363.

CHILDREN'S CHOIR

Gibson, Colin, and John Ferguson. "Carol Our Christmas." U/2 pt, org. CG CGA925.

Leavitt, John. "Witness to the Nativity." U/2 pt, pno. CPH 98-3693.

Pote, Allen. "Hurry to Bethlehem." U/2 pt, pno. CG CGA858.

Rocherolle, Eugenie R. "Savior Child." U/3 pt trbl, pno. CG CGA922.

KEYBOARD/INSTRUMENTAL

Augsburg Organ Library: Christmas. Org. AFP 080065935X.

Bach, J. S. "In dulci jubilo." Org. Various ed.

Carter, John. "He Is Born" in *Five Piano Duets.* Pno. BEC PC11.

Carter, John. "There's A Star in the East." Pno. BEC PC9.

Cherwien, David. *Carol Vignettes for Christmas.* Org. LOR 70/14005-16.

Daquin, Louis-Claude. *Noels for the Organ.* Org. Kalmus 3368.

Hobby, Robert A. *Three Christmas Preludes, Set 2.* Org. MSM 10-150.

Kerr, J. Wayne. "On This Day Earth Shall Ring; Rock-a-bye, My Dear Little Boy; He Is Born" in *Sing We Now of Christmas.* Org. AFP 0800675029.

Lochstampfer, Mark. *Carols for Christmas.* Org. AFP 0800674979.

Music With Minimal Pedal - Christmas. Org. MSM 10-149.

Rodriguez, Penny. *Portraits of Christmas I and II.* Pno. BEC PC1 and PC5.

HANDBELL

Edwards, Dan R. "Variations on a French Carol." 2 oct. CG CGB246.

Geschke, Susan. "O Come, Little Children." 2-3 oct. AGEHR AG23018.

Helman, Michael. "Christmas Meditation." 3-5 oct. AGEHR AG35126.

McChesney, Kevin. "Angel Glory." 3-5 oct. AFP 0800653955.

McChesney, Kevin. "'Twas in the Moon of Wintertime." 3-5 oct. ALF 16467.

Wagner, Douglas E. "O Come, All Ye Faithful." 3-5 oct. AG 1262.

PRAISE ENSEMBLE

Beech, Jay. "We Welcome You" in *Everyone Who Is Thirsty, Come!* Baytone Music 821103010013.

LeBlanc, Lenny, arr. Greer. "Come and See." SATB, kybd. WRD 3010898169.

McGee, Bob. "Emmanuel" in W&P.

Rice, Chris, arr. Hart. "Welcome to Our World." SATB, kybd. WRD 080689320279.

Smith, Michael W. and Amy Grant. "Christmas Hymn" in *Amy Grant's Greatest Hits.* HAL HL00359067.

Alternate Worship Texts

CONFESSION AND FORGIVENESS

In the name of the Father, and of the ✢ Son,
and of the Holy Spirit.
Amen

Amid the shadows of this world, let us confess our sin
and welcome the light of God's forgiveness.

Silence for reflection and self-examination.

God of grace and truth,
in Christ Jesus you come among us
as light shining in the darkness.
We confess that we have not welcomed the light,
nor trusted the good news of great joy.
Forgive us and renew our hope,
so that we may live in the fullness of your love,
trusting in the grace of Christ our Lord. Amen

The angel said, You shall call his name Jesus
for he will save his people from their sins.
With great joy, I announce to you
the entire forgiveness of your sins,
in the name of the Father, and of the ✢ Son,
and of the Holy Spirit.
Amen

GREETING

The grace and lovingkindness of our Savior Jesus Christ,
Word made flesh, born of the virgin Mary,
be with you all.
And also with you.

PRAYERS

Filled with joy at the birth of the one sent to save us,
let us offer our prayers to God who gives us peace and hope.

A brief silence.

Each petition ends:

God of our salvation,
have mercy and hear us.

Concluding petition:

Grant us these prayers, almighty Father,
in the name of your Word made flesh dwelling among us,
Jesus Christ our Lord.
Amen

OFFERTORY PRAYER

Eternal God,
with Mary we treasure the gift of your Son,
and in our hearts we ponder the mystery of his birth.
Receive these offerings,
that our lives may declare the wonders of your love
in Jesus Christ our Lord. Amen

INVITATION TO COMMUNION

In this holy sacrament God makes a home with us.
Let us approach in wonder at all that God has done.

POST-COMMUNION PRAYER

God of light,
with our eyes we have seen your salvation
in this holy feast you have prepared for us.
Send us forth into the world to be your holy people,
revealing your glory made known to us
in Jesus Christ our Lord.
Amen

BLESSING

May Christ, born into time to bring endless peace,
guide your days and years in righteousness
from this time onward and forevermore.
The Lord bless you and keep you.
The Lord's face shine on you with grace and mercy.
The Lord look upon you with favor and ✢ give you peace.
Amen

DISMISSAL

Filled with the joy of Christ's birth,
go in peace to love and serve the Lord.
Thanks be to God.

53

Seasonal Rites

Blessing of the Nativity Scene

This blessing may be used after the sermon or after the communion of the people on Christmas Eve.

O Lord our God, with Mary and Joseph, angels and shepherds, and the animals in the stable, we gather around your Son, born for us. Bless us with your holy presence, and inspire us to help those who have no place to dwell. Be with us that we might share Christ's love with all the world, for he is our light and salvation. Glory in heaven and peace on earth, now and forever. **Amen**

Proclamation of the Birth of Christ

Today, the twenty-fifth day of December,
unknown ages from the time when God created the heavens
and the earth and then formed man
and woman in his own image.

Several thousand years after the flood,
when God made the rainbow shine forth
as a sign of the covenant.
Twenty-one centuries from the time of Abraham and Sarah;
thirteen centuries after Moses led the people of Israel out of
    Egypt.

Eleven hundred years from the time of Ruth and the Judges;
one thousand years from the anointing of David as king;
in the sixty-fifth week according to the prophecy of Daniel.

In the one hundred and ninety-fourth Olympiad;
the seven hundred and fifty-second year from the foundation
of the city of Rome.

The forty-second year of the reign of Octavian Augustus;
the whole world being at peace,
Jesus Christ, the eternal God and Son of the eternal Father,
desiring to sanctify the world by his most merciful coming,
being conceived by the Holy Spirit,
and nine months having passed since his conception,
was born in Bethlehem of Judea of the Virgin Mary.

Today is the nativity of our Lord Jesus Christ according to
    the flesh.

Lessons and Carols for Christmas

This service may be used during the twelve days of Christmas.

ENTRANCE HYMN
Oh, come, all ye faithful   LBW 45
Once in royal David's city   WOV 643
Jesus, the Light of the world   TFF 59

DIALOG
The people who walked in darkness have seen a great light.
The light shines in the darkness,
and the darkness has not overcome it.
Those who dwelt in the land of deep darkness,
on them light has shined.
We have beheld Christ's glory,
glory as of the only Son from the Father.
To us a child is born, to us a Son is given.
In him was life, and the life was the light of all people.

OPENING PRAYER
The Lord be with you.
And also with you.
Let us pray.
Almighty God, you have filled us with the new light of the Word who became flesh and lived among us. Let the light of our faith shine in all we do; through your Son, Jesus Christ our Lord, who lives and reigns with you and the Holy Spirit, one God, now and forever.
Amen

LESSONS AND CAROLS
First Reading: Isaiah 9:2-7
Lo, how a rose is growing   LBW 58
Emmanuel   TFF 45, W&P 36
Lo, how a rose e'er blooming   RW1

Second Reading: Micah 5:2-5a
O little town of Bethlehem   LBW 41, HFW (FOREST GREEN)
There's a star in the East   WOV 645, TFF 58

Third Reading: Luke 1:26-35, 38
What child is this   LBW 40
Sing of Mary, pure and lowly   WOV 634
Jesus, what a wonderful child   TFF 51, RWSB

54

Fourth Reading: Luke 2:1-7
Away in a manger   LBW 67, WOV 644
I wonder as I wander   WOV 642, TFF 50
The virgin Mary had a baby boy   TFF 53

Fifth Reading: Luke 2:8-16
Infant holy, infant lowly   LBW 44
On Christmas night   RWSB
Mary had a baby   TFF 55

Sixth Reading: Luke 2:21-36
In his temple now behold him   LBW 184; RW1
That boy-child of Mary   TFF 54

Seventh Reading: Matthew 2:1-11
The first Noel   LBW 56
We three kings of Orient are   WOV 646
Sister Mary   TFF 60

Eighth Reading: Matthew 2:13-18
Oh, sleep now, holy baby   WOV 639
Oh, Mary, gentle poor Mary (María, pobre María)   LLC 310

Ninth Reading: John 1:1-14
Of the Father's love begotten   LBW 42
Let our gladness have no end   LBW 57
He came down   TFF 37

RESPONSIVE PRAYER

Glory to God in the highest,
and peace to God's people on earth.
Blessed are you, Prince of peace.
You rule the earth with truth and justice.
Send your gift of peace to all nations of the world.
Blessed are you, Son of Mary. You share our humanity.
Have mercy on the sick, the dying,
and all who suffer this day.
Blessed are you, Son of God.
You dwell among us as the Word made flesh.
Reveal yourself to us in word and sacrament
that we may bear your light to all the world.

THE LORD'S PRAYER

BLESSING AND DISMISSAL
Let us bless the Lord.
Thanks be to God.   55
May you be filled with the wonder of Mary, the obedience of
Joseph, the joy of the angels, the eagerness of the shepherds,
the determination of the magi, and the peace of the Christ child.
Almighty God, Father, ☩ Son, and Holy Spirit bless you now and
forever.
Amen

SENDING HYMN
Hark! The herald angels sing   LBW 60
Jesus, the Light of the world   TFF 59

December 24, 2003

The Nativity of Our Lord
Christmas Eve

INTRODUCTION

The miracle happens in the dark. A cold stable, inky night, and tired shepherds—all is jolted to a new awakening when God comes among us! We, too, are greeted with angel song as Christ makes his way among us in an old story, in miracles of bread and wine, in the wondrous fellowship of flesh-and-blood people called together to be a body for Christ.

PRAYER OF THE DAY

Almighty God, you made this holy night shine with the brightness of the true Light. Grant that here on earth we may walk in the light of Jesus' presence and in the last day wake to the brightness of his glory; through your only Son, Jesus Christ our Lord, who lives and reigns with you and the Holy Spirit, one God, now and forever.

VERSE

Alleluia. To you is born this day a Savior, who is the Messiah, the Lord. Alleluia. (Luke 2:11)

READINGS

Isaiah 9:2-7

Originally this poem was written to celebrate either the birth or the coronation of a new king in David's line. After the fall of Jerusalem, the passage came to be viewed as an expression of the hope that eventually God would raise up a new ruler who would possess the qualities described in the text.

Psalm 96

Let the heavens rejoice and the earth be glad. (Ps. 96:11)

Titus 2:11-14

The appearance of God's grace is an invitation for God's people to live a life worthy of the new age inaugurated in Jesus.

Luke 2:1-14 [15-20]

Luke tells the story of Jesus' birth with reference to rulers of the world because his birth has significance for the whole earth, conveying a divine offering of peace.

COLOR   White

THE PRAYERS

Filled with joy at the birth of the one sent to save us, let us offer our prayers to God who gives us peace and hope.

A BRIEF SILENCE.

We give you thanks for the good news of great joy you have once again announced to your people. Send us on our way glorifying and praising you for all the good news that we hear and see. God of our salvation,

have mercy and hear us.

Pierce the darkness of our world. Draw the nations to your brilliant light, that justice and peace may flourish, the rod of oppressors may be broken, and the tools of warfare may be destroyed. God of our salvation,

have mercy and hear us.

Change us, gracious God, through the salvation you have sent. Turn us from the ways of this world and lead us into lives that are self-controlled, upright, and godly. God of our salvation,

have mercy and hear us.

Hold gently in your arms all those who long for wholeness and healing in their lives *(especially)*. Grant that they may receive good news of great joy in the coming of the Savior and through the care and compassion we offer them in his name. God of our salvation,

have mercy and hear us.

Bless the people of this congregation. Bind the wounds that divide us. Sanctify us with the presence of the one born to us in the city of David, that we may announce your salvation to friend and stranger. God of our salvation,

have mercy and hear us.

HERE OTHER INTERCESSIONS MAY BE OFFERED.

Unite us with your holy angels and with the saints who have died in the light of your salvation, that we may stand with them before you as your light banishes all remaining darkness. God of our salvation,

have mercy and hear us.

Grant us these prayers, almighty Father, in the name of your Word made flesh dwelling among us, Jesus Christ our Lord.

Amen

IMAGES FOR PREACHING

In the readings of Christmas Eve the shepherds are the only ones pictured who seem to react as normal humans— "they were terrified." "But the angel said to them, 'Do not be afraid; for see—I am bringing you good news of great joy for all the people'" (Luke 2:10). So they weren't! They went to see, and to believe, and to worship. Thus it can be for all people, including the people who come to church this night to hear again of "this thing that has taken place, which the Lord has made known to us."

The situation has changed since the angels first declared the birth, and perhaps terror is no longer the reaction to the divine, which is experienced by what we call "normal humans." Ought there not be some talk of fear as well this night?

Not the made-up kind in which we feel a bit sorry for little Lord Jesus—when "the cattle are lowing," he wakes. "Poor baby!" Then Jesus, stiff upper lip, "no crying he makes." Rather, find wake-up words for all of us in the readings. "To you is born . . . a Savior, who is the Messiah, the Lord" (Luke 2:11). "The grace of God has appeared, bringing salvation to all" (Titus 2:11). "He it is who gave himself for us that he might redeem us from all iniquity and purify for himself a people of his own" (Titus 2:14).

All the "Don't be afraids" in the world cannot remove the cause for our fear—the sin that won't let us go. It is only because of the grace of God that we are not to be afraid, the grace that is "bringing salvation to all." That grace is "training us to renounce impiety and worldly passions, and in the present age to live lives that are self-controlled, upright, and godly" (Titus 2:11-12). Declare these things as well.

WORSHIP MATTERS

Did you ever sit next to someone in worship or in a choir whose singing supported your own singing, and even made your voice sound better? At Christmas as at no other time, the church's song is carried as congregations and choirs sing familiar carols.

Think of this: your song on this night joins the angelic choir. Your singing, your voice this night is carried by the hosts of heaven! The sound that results is most glorious because of the good news that God has come in Jesus, born in Bethlehem!

This night, this Christmas Eve, sing the "Glory to God in the highest" like you're part of the choir, the angels' choir. Add some ringing bells to make a joyful noise. Engage brass musicians to play along. Pull out all the stops, as with angels and archangels and all the company of heaven together we sing and praise God, going from glory to *glory!*

LET THE CHILDREN COME

Reserve front pews for families with young children. Remind them about the difference it makes in worship when we can see what is going on. The same is true in life. We are people who walk in darkness but we have seen a great light. God sent Jesus into the world to save us and so we rejoice with the angels and praise God's holy name. Consider a verse or other worship element with a response that can easily be repeated by the children. Invite older children to process in with candles during the opening hymn.

HYMNS FOR WORSHIP

57

GATHERING

Angels, from the realms of glory   LBW 50
Once in royal David's city   WOV 643

HYMN OF THE DAY

Let all together praise our God   LBW 47

ALTERNATE HYMN OF THE DAY

O little town of Bethlehem   LBW 41
Once again my heart rejoices   LBW 46

COMMUNION

Before the marvel of this night   WOV 636
I am so glad each Christmas Eve   LBW 69
A stable lamp is lighted   RWI 6, LBW 74

SENDING

Good Christian friends, rejoice   LBW 55
Silent night, holy night!   LBW 65
Night of silence   W&P 101

ADDITIONAL HYMNS AND SONGS

Midnight stars make bright the sky   RWSB
Hush, little Jesus boy   TFF 56
Hear the angels   W&P 57
One sacred moment   ASG 32

MUSIC FOR THE DAY

PSALMODY

Christopherson, Dorothy. "The Lord Is King." U, opt cong, kybd.
AFP 0800650611. OP.

Daw Jr., Carl P. and Kevin R. Hackett. *A Hymn Tune Psalter, Book One.*
Church Publishing, Inc. 0898692709.

Haugen, Marty. "Today Is Born Our Savior" in PCY, vol. 2.

Hobby, Robert A. PW , Cycle C.

Inwood, Paul. "Psalm 96: Today Is Born Our Savior" in STP, vol. I.

Marchionda, James V. *Psalms for the Cantor,* vol. III. WLP 2504.

Let the heavens rejoice   TFF 10

CHORAL

Benson, Robert A. "From Heaven Above to Earth I Come." SATB,
org. AFP 0800675851.

Christiansen, F. Melius. "Lullaby on Christmas Eve." SATB.
AFP 0800645103.

Fedak, Alfred V. "The Shepherds Were Not Waiting." SATB, kybd.
AFP 0800675290.

Gardner, John. "Tomorrow Shall Be My Dancing Day." SATB, perc.
OXF X356.

Poulenc, Francis. "O Magnum Mysterium." SATB. Salalbert Editions, R.L. 12525.

Rachmaninoff, Sergei. "O Come, Let Us Worship" from *All Night Vigil*
in *Songs of the Church.* SATB, div. HWG GB 640.

CHILDREN'S CHOIR

Collins, Dori Erwin. "Hurry to the Stable." U, kybd.
AFP 0800674154.

Ford, Sandra T. "Once on a Quiet Night." U/2 pt, kybd.
ABI 081246.

Rameau, J. Philippe, arr. Ronald A. Nelson. "Wake, O Shepherds." U,
kybd, C inst. AFP 0800675967.

Schalk, Carl. "A Christmas Slumber Song." U/2 pt, org.
AFP 0800675908.

KEYBOARD/INSTRUMENTAL

Gabrielsen, Stephen. "Jeg er saa glad" in *Augsburg Organ Library: Christmas.* Org. AFP 080065935X.

Leavitt, John. "Silent Night" in *Christmas Suite.* Org.
AFP 0800657217.

Linker, Janet. "Away in a Manger" in *Carols of the Christ Child.* Org.
BEC OC8.

Milford, Robin. "Sussex Carol" in *Augsburg Organ Library: Christmas.*
Org. AFP 080065935X.

Pachelbel, Johann. "Vom Himmel hoch" in *The Oxford Book of Christmas
Organ Music.* Org. OXF 0193751240.

HANDBELL

Buckwalter, Karen. "In the Bleak Midwinter." 3-5 oct. FLA HP5317.

Garee, Betty. "Stille Nacht." 4-5 oct. SHW HP5096.

Rogers, Sharon Elery. "Infant Holy in a Manger." 2-3 oct, opt hc.
AFP 0800674871.

PRAISE ENSEMBLE

Beech, Jay. "All Is Ready Now" in W&P.

Chisum, John and George Searcy. "Come and Behold Him" in *More
Songs for Praise and Worship.* SATB. WRD 3010387016 (vocal
ed); WRD 3010186363 (pno, vcs, perc).

Kantor, Daniel. "Night of Silence." U, kybd. GIA G-2760.

Wimber, John. "Isn't He?" in *Best of the Best.* FEL 1891062018.

December 25, 2003

The Nativity of Our Lord
Christmas Dawn

INTRODUCTION

The miracle happens in the dawn. "Glory to God in the highest!" the angels sing. We echo their song in our hymn of praise. The light that springs upon us at God's arrival invites us to greet this new day with joy. Christ the Savior is born—and in baptism we too are born into eternal life.

PRAYER OF THE DAY

Almighty God, you have made yourself known in your Son, Jesus, redeemer of the world. We pray that his birth as a human child will set us free from the old slavery of our sin; through Jesus Christ our Lord, who lives and reigns with you and the Holy Spirit, one God, now and forever.

VERSE

Alleluia. The LORD said to me, You are my son; this day have I begotten you. Alleluia. (Ps. 2:7)

READINGS

Isaiah 62:6-12

When Israel returned from exile and Jerusalem still lay in ruins, the prophet invited God's people to imagine the city's restoration.

Psalm 97

Light has sprung up for the righteous. (Ps. 97:11)

Titus 3:4-7

Salvation is a free and gracious gift from God. In baptism, God's people have a new birth with Christ.

Luke 2:[1-7] 8-20

The darkness of the world is shattered by the light of God's new day. Shepherds not only come to the manger to see what has happened; they also return to share the good news with others.

COLOR White

THE PRAYERS

Filled with joy at the birth of the one sent to save us, let us offer our prayers to God who gives us peace and hope.
A BRIEF SILENCE.

Open the hearts of your people, the church. Inspire us to prepare a path for all people, clear the stones that hinder hospitality, and raise a banner to guide the lost and forsaken. God of our salvation,
have mercy and hear us.

Fill us with gratitude for the miracle of the birth in Bethlehem. Help us to live lives that continually announce the grace shown when Christ was born as one of us. God of our salvation,
have mercy and hear us.

Guide the hearts and minds of leaders in all nations, that they might love justice and be swayed to your course of peace and compassion. God of our salvation,
have mercy and hear us.

Announce to all those who suffer sickness of mind, spirit, or body the good news of your coming. *(We especially pray for . . .)* Send us as your messengers of salvation and hope to those who long to be made whole. God of our salvation,
have mercy and hear us.

Pour out your Spirit upon this congregation, that we may give witness to our neighbors of all we have heard and seen. God of our salvation,
have mercy and hear us.

HERE OTHER INTERCESSIONS MAY BE OFFERED.

Gather together all your people of all times, that we may at last join the angels in singing "Glory to God in the highest" around your throne. God of our salvation,
have mercy and hear us.

Grant us these prayers, almighty Father, in the name of your Word made flesh dwelling among us, Jesus Christ our Lord.
Amen

IMAGES FOR PREACHING

The Christmas hymn begins, "Of the Father's love begotten ere the worlds began to be." That begetting was beyond our human knowing. It was eternally before the Bethlehem birth—"that birth forever blessed, when the virgin, full of grace, by the Holy Ghost conceiving, bore the Savior of our race." We celebrate both begettings today.

In the Nicene Creed we confess that Jesus was "eternally begotten of the Father." The word "begotten" is familiar to many who know the King James version of John 3:16 by heart. That quaint-sounding word remains in Psalm 2:7, quoted in Acts 13:33 and in Hebrews 1:5 and 5:5—"You are my Son; today I have begotten you."

Are there troubled days in which you confess, "You are God's Son, all right," only to go on, "but today you have forgotten me"? Isaiah in the first lesson calls the sentinels on the walls of Jerusalem those "who remind the Lord." They are told to "take no rest, and give him no rest until he establishes Jerusalem." Do you sometimes feel God needs to be reminded about you and your problems?

Remember Luther's suggestion for times of discouragement. Say to yourself, "I am baptized!" Today's second lesson brings Christian joy and baptism's assurance together: "When the goodness and loving kindness of God our Savior appeared, he saved us, not because of any works of righteousness that we had done, but according to his mercy, through the water of rebirth and renewal by the Holy Spirit. This Spirit he poured out on us richly through Jesus Christ our Savior" (Titus 3:4-6).

W. B. Yeats in *Sailing to Byzantium* connects two other words to "begotten":

> Fish, flesh, or fowl, commend all summer long
> Whatever is begotten, born, and dies.

And we add more words when we worship at the manger—"begotten, born, dies, rises, ascends, and will come again!"

WORSHIP MATTERS

In the story of Jesus' birth, the shepherds encountered angels and the glory of the Lord while at their workplace, in the fields. The good news was told to them as they were doing their jobs. They went and saw Jesus in the manger, and then went home to tell others what they had heard and seen.

That good news connects to the real lives of shepherds. That good news connects to real lives of those at work and at home today. What we hear and see in our worship celebrations spills over into the conversations we have with family and friends, neighbors and coworkers.

Consider all that you have heard and seen, as Christ

born for us is proclaimed in word and sacrament. As you are sent on your way, bring that good news back into the places where you return to, into your life.

LET THE CHILDREN COME

When the shepherds first heard the news, they were afraid, but the angels convinced them that the news was good. Indeed it was! After seeing Jesus, the shepherds returned home to share the good news with others. We too are called to share God's good news with others, but it's not always easy to do in this era of sensitivity to other cultures and beliefs. Put an invitation in the bulletin today that includes information about worship times or the life of your congregation and encourage children to give it to a friend in their neighborhood or school.

HYMNS FOR WORSHIP
GATHERING
Come rejoicing, praises voicing   LBW 66
Rejoice, rejoice this happy morn   LBW 43
Jesus, the Light of the world   TFF 59

HYMN OF THE DAY
Go tell it on the mountain   LBW 70, TFF 52

ALTERNATE HYMN OF THE DAY
Once in royal David's city   WOV 643
Jesus, the Light of the world   TFF 59

COMMUNION
What child is this   LBW 40
Your little ones, dear Lord   LBW 52
Holy Child within the manger   WOV 638

SENDING
Joy to the world   LBW 39
Once again my heart rejoices   LBW 46
There's a star in the east   WOV 645

ADDITIONAL HYMNS AND SONGS
Break forth, O beauteous heavenly light   RWSB
Jesus, what a wonderful child   TFF 51, RWSB
Christians, awake, salute the happy morn   H82 106

60

MUSIC FOR THE DAY
PSALMODY

Black, George. "Light Dawns for the Righteous" in SP.

Cooney, Rory. "The Lord Is King" in STP, vol. 4.

Haas, David. "Psalm 97: Our God Is Here" in PCY, vol. 9.

Hobby, Robert A. PW, Cycle C.

Hopson, Hal H. "Psalm 97" in *Psalm Refrains and Tones for the Common Lectionary.* HOP 425.

Marcus, Mary. "The Nativity of Our Lord/Christmas Day" in *Psalm Antiphons 2.* MSM 80-722.

CHORAL

Bach, J.S. "Break Forth, O Beauteous Heavenly Light" in *Bach for All Seasons.* SATB, kybd. AFP 080065854X.

Burt, Alfred. "All On A Christmas Morning" in *The Alfred Burt Carols, Set 1.* SATB/solo, kybd. SHW A-449.

Ellingboe, Bradley. "Jesus, Jesus, Rest Your Head." SATB. AFP 0800655796. Also in *The Augsburg Choirbook.* AFP 0800656784.

Morton, Graeme. "In the Splendor of the Dawn." SATB. AFP 0800675312.

CHILDREN'S CHOIR

Bedford, Michael. " 'Twas in the Moon of Wintertime." U/2 pt trbl, kybd/trbl rec/fl, hand drum. AFP 0800674316.

Horman, John. "To Us Emmanuel." U, kybd. HOP A605.

Mitchell, Tom. "Hydom, Hydom." U, kybd. CG CGA787.

KEYBOARD/INSTRUMENTAL

Benson, Robert A. "Es ist ein Ros' " in *A Lovely Rose.* Org. AFP 080065854X.

Brahms, Johannes. "Es ist ein Ros' entsprungen" in *Eleven Chorale Preludes.* Kybd/org. Mercury or various ed.

Koch, Lynn Arthur. "Vom Himmel hoch" in *From Heaven Above.* Org. AFP 0800675746.

Rodriguez, Penny. "It Came Upon a Midnight Clear" in *Midnight Clear.* Pno. BEC PC12.

Rowley, Alex. "Benedictus" in *Augsburg Organ Library: Advent.* Org. AFP 0800658957.

HANDBELL

Afdahl, Lee J. "Once in Royal David's City." 3-5 oct. AFP 0800658892.

Larson, Katherine Jordahl. "When Christmas Morn Is Dawning." 3-5 oct. AFP 0800653580.

PRAISE ENSEMBLE

McGee, Bob. "Emmanuel" in W&P.

Moody, Dave. "All Hail, King Jesus" in W&P.

61

December 25, 2003

The Nativity of Our Lord
Christmas Day

INTRODUCTION

The miracle happens in the bright light of day. Where God is, it is day. The light shining in the darkness is a sign of new creation, and the Word that is flesh is among us also in bread and wine and even in our own humanity born anew from God.

PRAYER OF THE DAY

Almighty God, you wonderfully created and yet more wonderfully restored the dignity of human nature. In your mercy, let us share the divine life of Jesus Christ who came to share our humanity, and who now lives and reigns with you and the Holy Spirit, one God, now and forever.

VERSE

Alleluia. When the fullness of time had come, God sent his Son. Alleluia. (Gal. 4:4)

READINGS

Isaiah 52:7-10

Changing events in Babylon inspire this announcement of hope and joy to the people of Judah near the end of their exile. "Your God reigns," says the prophet. It is not some Babylonian god who rules. It is the dawn of comfort, redemption, and the salvation of our God.

Psalm 98

All the ends of the earth have seen the victory of our God. (Ps. 98:4)

Hebrews 1:1-4 [5-12]

The letter to the Hebrews begins with a strong affirmation of Jesus as the Son of God. To call Jesus God's Son is to recognize that he is superior even to prophets and angels.

John 1:1-14

The poetic opening words of John's gospel refer to Jesus as the Word that became flesh—that is, the one whose human existence incorporates God's very self.

COLOR   White

THE PRAYERS

Filled with joy at the birth of the one sent to save us, let us offer our prayers to God who gives us peace and hope.

A BRIEF SILENCE.

Place a new song upon the hearts and lips of your people the church, that we may testify to the light that shines in the darkness. God of our salvation,

have mercy and hear us.

Fill the hearts of nations and their leaders with the gift of peace born in Jesus, that they may embrace justice and put an end to all that scars the goodness you have created. God of our salvation,

have mercy and hear us.

Comfort and refresh with your light and life all those who live in the darkness brought upon by loneliness, grief, sickness, and death *(especially)*. Send us to bring your glad tidings to all in need. God of our salvation,

have mercy and hear us.

Speak your word powerfully to this congregation in these last days, that we rise from the manger and go into our community as messengers announcing peace, bringing good news, and proclaiming your salvation in word and deed. God of our salvation,

have mercy and hear us.

HERE OTHER INTERCESSIONS MAY BE OFFERED.

Inspire us through the lives of all the saints who have gone before us that, along with all creation, we may join them in singing a new song of joy to you. God of our salvation,

have mercy and hear us.

Grant us these prayers, almighty Father, in the name of your Word made flesh dwelling among us, Jesus Christ our Lord.

Amen

IMAGES FOR PREACHING

See double images today in the lessons and in the contemplation of the birth of Jesus, our Savior.

Begin with Mary. The first image: On Christmas we see her in the stable where she "brought forth" her firstborn

62

son. She is "treasuring" the shepherds' report of their angelic vision and pondering it in her heart.

Now the second, the double of the vision:

> At the cross, her station keeping,
> Stood the mournful mother weeping,
> Close to Jesus to the last.
> Through her heart, his sorrow sharing,
> All his bitter anguish bearing,
> Now at length the sword had passed.
> (LBW 110)

Then consider Jesus. He "became flesh." See the fair little Lord Jesus, swaddled, in the straw and hay of the manger. See his glory, "the glory of an only Son coming from the Father, filled with enduring love" (John 1:14, translated by Raymond E. Brown in *The Gospel According to John*). "He is the reflection of God's glory and the exact imprint of God's very being" (Heb. 1:3).

Now, the double of that image: See him at Pilate's judgment hall. See that once fair face bloodied from the crown of thorns; that head, bowed. Dead.

Now see ourselves, united with our risen Lord. Know that his right hand and his left hand and his holy arms have gotten him the victory. He has forever changed "this sorry Scheme of Things entire." See us, then, each of us, with our child Jesus, our risen Savior, continuing God's redeeming, remolding work.

> Ah Love! Could you and I with Him conspire
> To grasp this sorry Scheme of Things entire,
> Would not we shatter it to bits—and then
> Re-mold it nearer to the Heart's Desire!
> (From the *Rubáiyát* of Omar Khayyám, translated by Edward FitzGerald, 4th ed.)

WORSHIP MATTERS

When listening to words, one must weigh both the medium and the message. When your life partner says, "I love you," it could also mean "Don't be mad at me!" When your child says, "I love you," it could also mean "You're a great mom."

Today we also hear of love from the voice of God. The ELCA's *Principles for Worship* affirm that God's word from all times and places speaks also today: "God, who spoke at creation, through the incarnate Word, through the prophets and apostles, continues to speak into our times and places" (Principle P-14).

The prologue to John's gospel waxes poetic about the Word being there from the beginning. There also, however, we discover God finding a place in history as the "Word became flesh" in Jesus. The word that is spoken becomes a living being, for us. Jesus is God's Word, in person, because God so loved the world.

LET THE CHILDREN COME

God's greatest gift to us came in the form of a baby. Celebrate the amazing gifts that come to us through children today. There is nothing quite like the sound of a child singing praises to God. Many children know the refrains of our Christmas hymns well. Be sure to find ways to include their voices in worship by inviting just the children to sing on some of the well-known hymn refrains for the day. Have a child design a bulletin cover and use it for today's service.

HYMNS FOR WORSHIP

GATHERING

Angels we have heard on high   LBW 71
Oh, come, all ye faithful   LBW 45
Hear the angels   W&P 57

HYMN OF THE DAY

Of the Father's love begotten   LBW 42

ALTERNATE HYMN OF THE DAY

Hark! The herald angels sing   LBW 60
All praise to you, eternal Lord   LBW 48

COMMUNION

From east to west   LBW 64
(May be sung to HER KOMMER DINE ARME SMAA,
   LBW 52)
The bells of Christmas   LBW 62
What feast of love   WOV 701

SENDING

Let all together praise our God   LBW 47
The virgin Mary had a baby boy   TFF 53

ADDITIONAL HYMNS AND SONGS

Glory in the highest   LLC 297
The trees of the field   W&P 138
Love has come!   RWSB

63

MUSIC FOR THE DAY
PSALMODY

Colgan, Tobias. "Psalm 98: Joyfully Give Praise to God" in STP, vol. 2.

Haugen, Marty. "All the Ends of the Earth" in PCY, vol. 1.

Hobby, Robert A. PW , Cycle C.

Hruby, Dolores. *Seasonal Psalms for Children with Optional Orff.* WLP 7102.

Hurd, David. "Cantate Domino: Psalm 98." SATB. AFP 0800650468. OP.

Smith, Timothy R. "Psalm 98: The Lord Has Revealed" in STP, vol. 4.

Joy to the world   LBW 39

CHORAL

Bach, J.S. "Gloria In Excelsis Deo" in *Bach for All Seasons.* SATB, kybd. AFP 080065854X.

Cool, Jayne Southwick. "Gentle Mary Laid Her Child." 2 pt mxd, pno. AFP 0800675142.

Ferguson, John. "In the Beginning." SATB, org, opt ob. KJO 8885.

Kern, Philip. "Glory Hallelujah to the Newborn King." SATB, pno. AFP 0800675169.

Morton, Graeme. "Ring Glad Bells." SATB, org/pno. AFP 0800675894.

Sweelinck, J.P. "Hodie Christus Natus Est." SSATB. HWG GCMR01855.

Thomas, André. "Here's a Pretty Little Baby." SATB, solo, synth, opt DB. Earthsongs S-80.

CHILDREN'S CHOIR

Bedford, Michael. "Cantate Domino." (Ps. 98) U/2 pt, kybd. CG CGA689.

Blanck, Dana and Bill Peterson. "Power in the Children" in *Welcome the Child.* U, solo, gtr, pno, hb. GIA G-3812.

Collins, Dori Erwin. "Hurry to the Stable." U, kybd. AFP 0800674154.

KEYBOARD/INSTRUMENTAL

Albrecht, Timothy. "Angels We Have Heard on High" in *Grace Notes II.* Org. AFP 080065305X.

Guilmant, Alexander. "Offertoire sur Deux Noels" in *The Oxford Book of Christmas Organ Music.* Org. OXF 0193751240.

Johnson, Edwin C. "Angels, from the Realms of Glory" in *Organ Music for the Seasons,* vol. 2. Org. AFP 0800658779.

Uehlein, Christopher. "God Rest You Merry" in *A Blue Cloud Abbey Christmas Organ Book.* Org. AFP 0800659791.

HANDBELL

Kinyon, Barbara Baltzer. "What Child Is This?" 2-3 oct, opt hc. AG 1765.

Morris, Hart. "On This Day Earth Shall Ring." 3-5 oct. CPH 97-6681.

PRAISE ENSEMBLE

Carey, Mariah, arr. Emerson. "Jesus Born On This Day." SATB, kybd. HAL 08200309.

Hearn, Naida. "Jesus, Name Above all Names" in W&P.

Vogels, Joseph. "Victory Chant" in *Best of the Best.* FEL 1891062018.

The virgin Mary had a baby boy.   TFF 53.

Friday, December 26
ST. STEPHEN, DEACON AND MARTYR

St. Stephen was a deacon and the first martyr of the church. He was one of those seven upon whom the apostles laid hands after they had been chosen to serve widows and others in need. Later, Stephen's preaching angered the temple authorities, and they ordered him to be put to death by stoning.

The Christmas song "Good King Wenceslas" takes place on the feast of Stephen. The king sees a peasant gathering wood near the forest and sends his page to invite the peasant to a feast. The song, with its theme of charity to the poor, can be a way to remember St. Stephen, who cared for widows and those in need. Congregations and families within them can be invited to include gifts to charitable organizations during these days of Christmas in honor of St. Stephen.

Saturday, December 27
ST. JOHN, APOSTLE AND EVANGELIST

John, the son of Zebedee, was a fisherman and one of the twelve. John, his brother James, and Peter were the three who witnessed the light of the Transfiguration. John and James once made known their desire to hold positions of power in the kingdom of God. Jesus' response showed them that service to others was the sign of God's reign in the world. Though authorship of the gospel and the three epistles bearing his name has often been attributed to the apostle John, this tradition cannot be proven from scriptural evidence.

John is a saint for Christmas through his proclamation that the Word became flesh and dwelt among us, that the light of God shines in the darkness, and that we are called to love one another as Christ has loved us. According to an early story about John, his enemies once tried to murder him with poisoned wine. On this day, many Christians in Europe will toast one another with the words "I drink to the love of John."

December 28, 2003

The Holy Innocents, Martyrs

INTRODUCTION

Already today we are reminded of the need for Christ's birth among us, into this world ruled by sin and sorrow. A jealous ruler tried to end this child's life before his work even got underway. Though Jesus' life was wonderfully spared, other children, the poignantly named Holy Innocents, died. We are impelled already to look ahead to the culmination of Jesus' life, when he died and rose again to bring life to all.

PRAYER OF THE DAY

We remember today, O God, the slaughter of the holy innocents of Bethlehem by order of King Herod. Receive, we pray, into the arms of your mercy all innocent victims, and by your great might frustrate the designs of evil tyrants and establish your rule of justice, love, and peace; through Jesus Christ our Lord, who lives and reigns with you and the Holy Sprit, one God, now and forever.

VERSE

Alleluia. Blessed are those who are persecuted for righteousness' sake, for theirs is the kingdom of heaven. Alleluia. (Matt. 5:10)

READINGS

Jeremiah 31:15-17

Jeremiah is primarily concerned with Judah, yet these verses are a lament on the defeat and exile of the Northern Kingdom. The oldest tradition located the tomb of Rachel, mother of Joseph and Benjamin, in Ramah, north of Jerusalem. The later tradition followed by the author of Matthew placed it near Bethlehem.

Psalm 124

We have escaped like a bird from the snare of the fowler. (Ps. 124:7)

1 Peter 4:12-19

In this letter the writer is encouraging early Christians who were facing persecution for their beliefs. Though life is sometimes hard for the faithful, they are advised to rejoice as they share Christ's sufferings.

Matthew 2:13-18

Whether or not the slaughter of the Bethlehem children is a historical event, the story's inclusion in Matthew's gospel makes the point that Jesus was God's chosen leader of the Jewish people as well as of the Gentiles represented by the magi. Herod's fury over the birth underscores the claim.

COLOR Red

THE PRAYERS

Filled with joy at the birth of the one sent to save us, let us offer our prayers to God who gives us peace and hope.

A BRIEF SILENCE.

We pray for those who weep over their children, for those who face persecution because of their beliefs, and for all who courageously witness to their faith in Christ. Lead us to stand with them and for them. God of our salvation,

have mercy and hear us.

We pray for the nations of the world and all their leaders, that softening the hearts of those who destroy the innocent, you would draw them into your reign of peace. God of our salvation,

have mercy and hear us.

65

We pray for all who seek healing and wholeness in their lives *(especially)*, that they may draw strength and hope from the suffering of the Savior and may be sustained by the hands and voices of your people. God of our salvation, **have mercy and hear us.**

We pray for this congregation. Strengthen our resolve to be faithful in adversity and to endure suffering in your name, knowing that your Spirit rests upon us. God of our salvation,

have mercy and hear us.

HERE OTHER INTERCESSIONS MAY BE OFFERED.

We remember before you the holy innocents of Bethlehem, and all the saints whose blood was spilled in the name of the Lord. Inspired by their sacrifice, may we lead holy lives and at last join with them in your holy presence. God of our salvation,

have mercy and hear us.

Grant us these prayers, almighty Father, in the name of your Word made flesh dwelling among us, Jesus Christ our Lord.

Amen

IMAGES FOR PREACHING

Suffering is never enjoyable, but is there a suffering more endurable than the usual? The 1 Peter lesson urges its readers to rejoice in their suffering "insofar as you are sharing Christ's sufferings." Few of us in a country where freedom of religion is a given have that "opportunity" to rejoice. Who would seek suffering? It is always thrust upon us. Certainly that was true for the children who felt the swords of the killers Herod sent. Even more true for their parents—the Rachels as well as the fathers who also wept for their children.

Could those bereft parents comfort themselves with the knowledge they were sharing Christ's suffering? More difficult still, could they go along with the words "suffering in accordance with God's will"?

We find a bit of wisdom and some help in "entrusting ourselves to a faithful Creator" by considering how that faithful Creator went about saving his world. God did not will that the Savior enter the world with power and great glory and simply overwhelm all people into believing and obedience. Clearly, God wants to let mortals be the way they were created, with wills that are free, able to choose. And so God decided that what's good for the child Savior is good for all the saved.

And the faithful Creator also declared through Paul: "We know that all things work together for good for those who love God" (Rom. 8:28). According to God's ultimate will, the final outcome of all our suffering will be lives as good or better than if there had been no suffering. It may take a while, but "what's a heaven for?"

Rachel and spouse, while you keep on weeping over lost hopes "because they are no more," think on these things, and be consoled.

WORSHIP MATTERS

The feast day today commemorates the silent witness of children. How do we honor the gifts that youth bring to our worshiping communities? Are there ways to engage young readers in proclaiming Scripture for the assembly regularly? Do children's choirs lead portions of the liturgy, in addition to singing anthems? Might intercessory prayer be led on this day by the youth, bringing to light issues of innocence lost?

Another way to lift up the ministry of children is to honor those who serve at the altar, acolytes. See if all of your acolyte crews can don vestments on this day, and pray publicly for this ministry of worship (see "Recognition of Ministries," pp. 143–46, in *Occasional Services*). Identify the ministries of children, and name them in thanksgiving. Make it a day to honor today's Holy Innocents.

LET THE CHILDREN COME

We live in a war-torn world in which many suffer because of injustice and poverty. We are called to be seekers and keepers of peace. Our first step must be to always call upon the name of our Lord to make us instruments of his peace. Psalm 124 reads "Our help is in the name of the Lord, the maker of heaven and earth." Consider having children speak the first phrase and adults speak the second phrase following each petition of prayer in today's service.

HYMNS FOR WORSHIP
GATHERING

What child is this   LBW 40
It came upon the midnight clear   LBW 54

HYMN OF THE DAY

A stable lamp is lighted   RW1 6, LBW 74

66

ALTERNATE HYMN OF THE DAY

When Christ's appearing was made known   LBW 85
By all your saints in warfare   LBW 177 (1, 9, 3)

COMMUNION

Children of the heavenly Father   LBW 474
Oh, sleep now, holy baby   WOV 639

SENDING

The hills are bare at Bethlehem   LBW 61
Sister Mary   TFF 60

ADDITIONAL HYMNS AND SONGS

Lully, lullay, thou little tiny child   H82 247
You who dwell in the shelter of the Lord   WOV 779
How long, O God   RWSB

MUSIC FOR THE DAY

PSALMODY

Haas, David. "Our Soul Has Escaped" in PCY, vol. 9.
Hallock, Peter. "Psalm 124" in TP.
Hopson, Hal H. "Psalm 124" in *Psalm Refrains and Tones.* HOP 425.
Pavlechko, Thomas. PW , Cycle C.
If God the LORD were not our constant help PsH 124

CHORAL

Erickson, Richard. "'Twas in the Moon of Wintertime." SATB, hp/pno. AFP 0800675959.
Kopylow, A. "Heavenly Light." SATB. CFI CM 497.
Petker, Allan. "I Will Follow Your Call." SATB hp/pno. PVN P1203.

Shaw, Martin. "Coventry Carol" in *100 Carols for Choirs.* SATB. OXF 3532271.

CHILDREN'S CHOIR

Cherwien, David. "Your Little Ones, Dear Lord." U/2 pt, fl, org. CPH 98-3356.
Hopson, Hal H. "Oh, Sleep Now, Holy Baby." U/2 pt, kybd, opt C inst. MSM 50-1203.
Schultz, Donna Gartman. "Cold December's Winds Were Stilled." 2 pt trbl, pno. AFP 0800675916.

KEYBOARD/INSTRUMENTAL

Farlee, Robert Buckley. "A Stable Lamp Is Lighted" in *Carols for Organ and Oboe.* Org, inst. AFP 0800657292.
Haan, Raymond. "In the Bleak Midwinter" in *Organ Reflections for Advent, Christmas and Epiphany.* Org. SMP KK 311.
Thomas, David Evan. "I Wonder" in *Early American Tunes for Organ.* Org. AFP 0800674804.
Wold, Wayne L. "Once in Royal David's City" in *God With Us.* Org. AFP 0800658213.

HANDBELL

Dobrinski, Cynthia. "Coventry Carol." 3-5 oct. AG 1537.
Piercy, Noel A. "Coventry Carol." 2 oct. AG 1163.

PRAISE ENSEMBLE

Gay, Robert. "No Other Name" in *Best of the Best.* FEL 1891062018.
Krippaehne, Dean. "Lord, My Strength" in W&P.
Smith, Martin. "Shout to the North" in *Best of the Best.* FEL 1891062018.

67

December 28, 2003

First Sunday after Christmas

INTRODUCTION

During Christmastide, our attention is drawn to the holy family: Jesus, Mary, and Joseph. We, too, are God's children and part of a holy family, set apart through the baptismal waters in which we have been washed. As we end one year and begin another, we ask how God's likeness in Christ may become more visible in us, God's new offspring.

PRAYER OF THE DAY

Almighty God, you have made yourself known in your Son, Jesus, redeemer of the world. We pray that his birth as a human child will set us free from the old slavery of our sin; through Jesus Christ our Lord, who lives and reigns with you and the Holy Spirit, one God, now and forever.

or

Almighty God, you wonderfully created and yet more wonderfully restored the dignity of human nature. In your mercy, let us share the divine life of Jesus Christ who came to share our humanity, and who now lives and reigns with you and the Holy Spirit, one God, now and forever.

VERSE

Alleluia. Let the peace of Christ rule in your hearts. Alleluia. (Col. 3:15)

READINGS

1 Samuel 2:18-20, 26

Like Mary and Joseph in the gospel text, Hannah and Elkanah were faithful parents. At the time of their annual pilgrimage to visit their son, the high priest blesses them with a prayer for more children in return for the dedication of Samuel.

Psalm 148

The splendor of the LORD is over earth and heaven. (Ps. 148:13)

Colossians 3:12-17

Just as newly baptized Christians in the early church were clothed with white robes upon arising from the baptismal waters, so all who have received God's gift of life in Jesus Christ are clothed with those qualities that reflect the Lord's presence.

Luke 2:41-52

Jesus grew up in a family that went to the Passover festival each year. Their faithful adherence to the law provided a healthy environment for the young Jesus to grow into spiritual maturity.

COLOR   White

THE PRAYERS

Filled with joy at the birth of the one sent to save us, let us offer our prayers to God who gives us peace and hope.

A BRIEF SILENCE.

We pray for your church around the world as it gathers to worship and is sent to serve, that you would clothe us with your compassion, kindness, humility, meekness, and patience, and bind us together with your love. God of our salvation,

have mercy and hear us.

We pray for the world suffering under the darkness of sin and death, that you would guide leaders and all citizens of this earth to bring healing and redemption to the whole creation. God of our salvation,

have mercy and hear us.

We pray for all who read and study the Bible, seeking to know your will and your love. Guide their efforts and give them wise teachers and families that support their faith. God of our salvation,

have mercy and hear us.

We pray for all who are in need of comfort, peace, hope, and healing *(especially)*. Let your word soothe body, mind, and spirit, and make us, in part, the answer to their prayer. God of our salvation,

have mercy and hear us.

We pray for the ministries of this congregation and all those who serve with glad and thankful hearts. Place your love within our hearts, that we may find delight in our Father's house and desire to serve you all our days.

68

God of our salvation,
have mercy and hear us.

HERE OTHER INTERCESSIONS MAY BE OFFERED.

We thank you for the Holy Innocents, martyrs in Bethlehem, *(other names)* and all the saints who let the peace of Christ rule their hearts. Help us to see in them a glimpse of the faith-filled joy that frees us to sing and to serve. God of our salvation,
have mercy and hear us.

Grant us these prayers, almighty Father, in the name of your Word made flesh dwelling among us, Jesus Christ our Lord.
Amen

IMAGES FOR PREACHING

Today's lessons make this a "children's day." Samuel and Jesus are the children. What we learn from them can help us in being children again, children of God.

"The boy Samuel continued to grow both in stature and in favor with the Lord and with the people" (1 Sam. 2:26). "Jesus increased in wisdom and in years, and in divine and human favor" (Luke 2:52). That's more than assimilating food and letting metabolism do the rest. They had to do things that God and fellow humans favored. So it is with us as well, including those who have completed our growing up. Just as some of us are still growing out and putting on weight, so we need as well to be putting on virtues that God favors.

Samuel grew in favor. Jesus got into trouble. Not bad trouble—really more of a miscommunication based on a lack of understanding on Mary and Joseph's part. Mary had complained, "Your father and I . . . great anxiety!" He said, "My *Father's* house—*this* house—*My* Father, not *this* father." Joseph didn't seem to feel hurt. He, and Mary, just did not understand.

To be the children of God we need to know *our* Father, which is why it is so great that our Father has introduced himself to us and made us part of the family. After Jesus' rebuke to his parents, he went down to Nazareth "and was obedient to them." Now it is our turn to obey.

Samuel and Jesus, Hannah and Elkanah, Eli, Mary and Joseph—they were, and now we are, "God's chosen ones, holy and beloved."

One of children's first accomplishments is to put on their own clothes. Paul tells the Colossians and us to clothe ourselves "with compassion, kindness, humility, meekness, and patience . . . Above all, clothe yourselves with love" (Col. 3:12, 14).

Put on the new nature. It fits best at Christmastime.

WORSHIP MATTERS

Martin Luther called mothers and fathers the "pastors" of the household. Even when we are at home, we continue to be "the church." Consider how praying at home can be a kind of "mini-church." Is there a central place for household prayer, even if it is at the kitchen table? How can that space be set apart, perhaps with candles? A crèche, artwork, or a craft depicting the Christ child can be a focus of prayer and devotion.

Jesus at age twelve was found by his parents in the temple conversing with teachers. Set aside regular times to read aloud from the Bible as a family, and allow conversation, questions, and comments to bubble up from children. Bring the hymns and the prayers from your assembly for use at home. Make church not something that you go to, but something that you are.

LET THE CHILDREN COME

Jesus grew up and was nurtured in a family that was faithful in their relationship with God. The family continues to play a critical role for nurturing children in the faith today. As the saying goes, faith is caught, not taught. Provide a list of devotional resources for families and encourage them to find opportunities to read and learn from God's word together.

HYMNS FOR WORSHIP
GATHERING

Good Christian friends, rejoice   LBW 55
Your little ones, dear Lord   LBW 52

HYMN OF THE DAY

Cold December flies away   LBW 53

ALTERNATE HYMN OF THE DAY

Holy child within the manger   WOV 638
In a lowly manger born   LBW 417

COMMUNION

I wonder as I wander   WOV 642
Good Christian friends, rejoice   LBW 55

69

SENDING

The first Noel   LBW 56

Greet now the swiftly changing year   LBW 181

That boy-child of Mary   TFF 54

ADDITIONAL HYMNS AND SONGS

Come and go with me to my Father's house   TFF 141

Lo, how a rose e'er blooming   RWSB, RWI 49

From God the Father, virgin-born   RWI 29, LBW 83

MUSIC FOR THE DAY

PSALMODY

Gelineau, Joseph. "Psalm 148." 2 pt mxd, cant, cong. GIA G-2245.

Haas, David. "Praise in the Heights" in PCY, vol. 9.

Hobby, Robert A. PW, Cycle C.

Hopson, Hal H. "Praise the Lord." SAB, kybd. AFP 0800674626.

Marcus, Mary. "First Sunday after Christmas" in *Psalm Antiphons-2.*
MSM 80-722.

"Psalm 148." (refrain based on "Lasst uns erfreuen") UMH p. 861.

Schaap, David P. "Praise the God of Heaven" in SP.
LBW 242; LBW 540; LBW 541.

CHORAL

Berger, Jean. "O Give Thanks unto the Lord." SATB. AFP 11-1982.
OP.

Carnahan, Craig. "The Christ-Child Lay on Mary's Lap." SATB,
pno/hp. AFP 0800659260.

Ellingboe, Bradley. "Teach Each Other in Wisdom." SATB, org.
KJO 8986.

Vaughan Williams, Ralph. "The Blessed Son of God" in *Two Chorals
from the Cantata 'This Day' (Hodie).* SATB. OXF 43.929. Also in
Carols for Choirs 1. OXF 3532220.

CHILDREN'S CHOIR

Heim, Bret. "All Glory Be to God Alone." U, kybd. CPH 98-3619.

Horman, John. "When Jesus Was a Growing Lad." (Luke 2:41-52)
U/2 pt, pno. CG CGA772.

KEYBOARD/INSTRUMENTAL

Carlson, J. Bert. "Jeg er saa glad" in *Carols from Many Lands.* Pno.
AFP 0800659767.

Hudson, Richard. "He Is Born!" in *Augsburg Organ Library: Christmas.*
Org. AFP 080065935X.

Lochstampfor, Mark. "He Is Born" in *Carols for Christmas.* Org.
AFP 0800674979.

Moore, David W. *Three Carols for Piano and Solo Instrument.* Pno, inst.
AFP 0800659082.

HANDBELL

Buckwalter, Karen Lakey. "I Wonder as I Wander." 3-5 oct.
SHW HP5323.

Sherman, Arnold B. "Christmastide, A Medley of Six Carols." 2-3
oct. RR HB0024A; 4-5 oct. RR HB0024B.

PRAISE ENSEMBLE

Temple, Sebastian. "Make Me a Channel of Your Peace" in W&P.

Watts, Isaac and G.F. Handel, arr. Sterling. "Joy to the World." SATB,
pno. WRD 00689453274.

Sunday, December 28

THE HOLY INNOCENTS, MARTYRS

See pages 65–67.

Thursday, January 1

THE NAME OF JESUS

The observance of the octave (eighth day) of Christmas
has roots in the sixth century. Until the recent past,
Lutheran calendars called this day "The Circumcision
and Name of Jesus." The emphasis on circumcision is
the older emphasis. Every Jewish boy was circumcised
and formally named on the eighth day of his life. Already
in his youth, Jesus bears the mark of a covenant that he
makes new through the shedding of his blood, now and
on the cross. That covenant, like Jesus' name, is a gift to
us and marks us as children of God. Baptized into
Christ, we begin this new year in Jesus' name. Sustained
by the gift of his body and blood, we will find that this
year, too, we will be sustained by the gift of Christ's
body and the new covenant in Christ's blood.

Friday, January 2

JOHANN KONRAD WILHELM LOEHE, PASTOR, 1872

Loehe was a pastor in nineteenth-century Germany.
From the small town of Neuendettelsau he sent pastors
to North America, Australia, New Guinea, Brazil, and
the Ukraine. His work for a clear confessional basis
within the Bavarian church sometimes led to conflict
with the ecclesiastical bureaucracy. Loehe's chief concern

was that a parish finds its life in the eucharist, and from that source evangelism and social ministries would flow. Many Lutheran congregations in Michigan, Ohio, and Iowa were either founded or influenced by missionaries sent by Loehe, and the chapel at Wartburg Theological

Seminary is named in his honor.

Loehe's vision to see the eucharist at the center of parish life can lead us on to think about ways that the incarnate presence of Christ in holy communion sends us out in a life of ministry and mission.

January 4, 2004

Second Sunday after Christmas

INTRODUCTION

During the twelve days of Christmas we continue to sing and be radiant over the goodness of God. We celebrate the light that the darkness has not overcome, Jesus Christ our Lord. That light is made known to us in the incarnation, God sharing our humanity in the Word made flesh. In communion, the Word is made flesh in us as well, that we may go forth from worship to share the light of Christ in our daily lives.

PRAYER OF THE DAY

Almighty God, you have filled us with the new light of the Word who became flesh and lived among us. Let the light of our faith shine in all that we do; through your Son, Jesus Christ our Lord, who lives and reigns with you and the Holy Spirit, one God, now and forever.

VERSE

Alleluia. All the ends of the earth have seen the victory of our God. Alleluia. (Ps. 98:4)

READINGS

Jeremiah 31:7-14

Like the prophets who announce homecoming and salvation in the book of Isaiah, Jeremiah announces the wondrous homecoming of God's people from exile. Once again the Lord enters in human history to fulfill the covenantal promise made during the exodus from Egypt so long ago: "I will be your God, and you will be my people."

or Sirach (Ecclesiasticus) 24:1-12

In the intertestamental writing, Wisdom is identified as

the first of God's creations and is later identified with the Torah, the center of Hebrew scriptures. This passage helps set the stage for the prologue to John's gospel.

Psalm 147:13-21 (Psalm 147:12-20 NRSV)

Worship the LORD, O Jerusalem; praise your God, O Zion. (Ps. 147:13)

or Wisdom of Solomon 10:15-21

We sing, O Lord, to your holy name; we praise with one accord your defending hand. (Wis. 10:20)

Ephesians 1:3-14

The letter to the Ephesians addresses the church concerning God's plans and purpose for the world. It begins with a prayer thanking God for the blessings that already belong to us in Christ and for the yet more glorious future that awaits us.

John 1:[1-9] 10-18

John's gospel presents Jesus as the full embodiment of God's grace and truth, as the one who reveals God's love for the whole creation.

COLOR   White

THE PRAYERS

Filled with joy at the birth of the one sent to save us, let us offer our prayers to God who gives us peace and hope.
A BRIEF SILENCE.

Merciful giver, as you lavishly pour upon us the riches of your grace, cause us to overflow in thanks, offering hope to a world caught in the clutches of sin and death. God of our salvation,

have mercy and hear us.

We pray for the world and its peoples, that this new year

71

may be one of greater prosperity for those who are poor, increased justice for those who lack it, and a full measure of peace for all. God of our salvation,

have mercy and hear us.

We pray for all who journey in the wilderness of grief, despair, and sickness *(especially)*. Transform their mourning to dancing, give them gladness for their sorrow, and guide us in ministering to those who call upon you. God of our salvation,

have mercy and hear us.

We pray for this congregation, your adopted sons and daughters in this place who have been marked with the seal of the Holy Spirit in baptism. Help us find strength to give up worldly desires for the sake of all whom you love. God of our salvation,

have mercy and hear us.

HERE OTHER INTERCESSIONS MAY BE OFFERED.

We bless you for the saints who set their hope on you and now rest in your loving arms *(especially)*. May their witness lead us also to live and die for the praise of your glory. God of our salvation,

have mercy and hear us.

Grant us these prayers, almighty Father, in the name of your Word made flesh dwelling among us, Jesus Christ our Lord.

Amen

IMAGES FOR PREACHING

What and how does God speak? The psalm for today describes a lowercase *word*. The gospel deals with an uppercase *Word*. The lowercase *word* "runs swiftly," melts snow and frost and hail. More is implied in verse 19: "He declares his word to Jacob." But the gospel gets very personal with its uppercase *Word*. "The Word was God." And then "the Word" becomes *he*—"He was in the beginning with God." He was God. He was with God. He was God *acting*. "The Word became flesh and lived among us."

In the Christmastide we celebrate that "God-in-action" took on our human nature so that "in him we have redemption through his blood, the forgiveness of our trespasses" (Eph. 1:7). We bless "the God and Father of our Lord Jesus Christ," and give God thanks that "when [we] heard the word of truth, the gospel of our salvation, and believed in him, [we] were marked with the seal of the promised Holy Spirit" (Eph. 1:13).

When a child falls from a trike and badly skins her knees, no philosophical explanation is necessary before a mother's hug is claimed for healing comfort. All who believe in this Word-made-flesh have become children of God and know God's healing hug.

Remember the story of the little girl who declared, "I'm going to draw a picture of God." Her smart brother quoted John 1, "No one has ever seen God," and added, "No one knows what God looks like." To which his sister replied, "They will once I've finished my picture."

That is how people will know something of what God is like. In us "who have received from his fullness grace upon grace" they will see a reflection of God's graciousness. Our living will testify to the true light that has come into the world, which enlightens everyone, and who has come into our hearts.

WORSHIP MATTERS

Dancing is a biblical art form that has a place in the church. The ELCA's statement on worship practices, *The Use of the Means of Grace*, states that "the arts serve the Word."

During Christmas we are drawn to the image of the "Word made flesh," in awe and wonder of God incarnate in Christ, in the flesh. Perhaps we might consider using dance, the art form of body movement, in worship today. A local dance group might be honored to try something in a place of worship, during the singing of a hymn or the reading of the hymn-like prologue to John. A single dancer may dance while carrying the lectionary book during an extended gospel acclamation. Rhythm instruments may also accompany song or reading this day, to encourage those playing and listening to embody the gospel.

LET THE CHILDREN COME

"God is light, and in him there is no darkness at all" (1 John 1:5). Use this verse as an introductory sentence for today's worship, and, if possible, begin the service in the dark or with the lights turned down low. The congregation could sing "This little light of mine" as an opening hymn while the lights come on in the sanctuary. There is darkness all around us but as followers of Jesus we are people who walk in light. We have been promised that as we live in God, so God will live in and through us.

HYMNS FOR WORSHIP
GATHERING

Angels, from the realms of glory   LBW 50

Word of God, come down on earth   WOV 716

HYMN OF THE DAY

Let our gladness have no end   LBW 57

ALTERNATE HYMN OF THE DAY

From east to west   LBW 64

Praise to you, O Christ, our Savior   WOV 614, W&P 118

COMMUNION

Away in a manger   WOV 644, LBW 67

In the bleak midwinter   RW1 45

Peace came to earth   WOV 641

SENDING

Hark! The herald angels sing   LBW 60

Holy Child within the manger   WOV 638

ADDITIONAL HYMNS AND SONGS

Light shines in darkness   RWSB

My light and my salvation   ASG 25

O splendor of God's glory bright   HFW

MUSIC FOR THE DAY
PSALMODY

Black, George. "Jerusalem, Give Glory!" in SP.

Folkening, John. "Psalm 147" in *Six Psalm Settings with Antiphons*. SATB, cong, opt kybd. MSM 80-700.

Guimont, Michel. "Psalm 147: Praise the Lord" in RS.

Hobby, Robert A. PW , Cycle C.

Marcus, Mary. "Second Sunday after Christmas" in *Psalm Antiphons-2*. MSM 80-722.

Phillips, J. Gerald. *Psalms for the Cantor*, vol. III. WLP 2504.

CHORAL

Bach, J. S. "O Jesus Christ, My Light, My Life" in *Bach for All Seasons*. SATB, org. AFP 080065854X.

Gardner, John. "Tomorrow Shall Be My Dancing Day." SATB, kybd, perc. OXF 40.107.

Kallman, Dan. "Walk As Children of Light." SATB, org. MSM 50-9047.

Roberts, Paul. "The Word Became Flesh." SATB, fl. AFP 0800657659.

Willcocks, David. "Of the Father's Heart Begotten" in *100 Carols for Choirs*. SATB div, org. OXF 3532271.

CHILDREN'S CHOIR

Bågenfelt, Susanne. "There's a Light in the World." U/2 pt, kybd. AFP 0800674286.

Christopherson, Dorothy. "God of the Universe." (John 1:4-5) 2 pt, fl, perc, pno/Orff. CG CGA821.

KEYBOARD/INSTRUMENTAL

Ashdown, Franklin D. *Triptych on an English Noel*. Org. AFP 0800675002.

Cherwien, David. "Hark! The Herald Angels Sing" in *Carol Vignettes for Organ*. Org. SMP 70/1400S.

Held, Wilbur. *Two Traditional Carols for Organ and C Instrument*. Org, inst. AFP 0800645537.

Linker, Janet. Variations on "Hark! The Herald Angels Sing" in *Carols of the Christ Child*. Org. BEC OC8.

Lochstampfor, Mark. "O Come, All Ye Faithful" in *Carols for Christmas*. Org. AFP 0800674979.

HANDBELL

McChesney, Kevin. "Joy to the World." 3-5 oct. AFP 0800653602. OP.

McChesney, Kevin. "Rise Up, Shepherds, and Follow." 3-5 oct. BEC HB178.

PRAISE ENSEMBLE

Altrogge, Mark. "I'm Forever Grateful" in *Best of the Best*. FEL 1891062018.

Kendrick, Graham. "Amazing Love" in W&P.

Monday, January 5

KAJ MUNK, MARTYR, 1944

Munk, a Danish Lutheran pastor and playwright, was an outspoken critic of the Nazis who occupied Denmark during the Second World War. His plays frequently highlighted the eventual victory of the Christian faith despite the church's weak and ineffective witness. The Nazis feared Munk because his sermons and articles helped to strengthen the Danish resistance movement. In one of his sermons for New Year's Day he wrote, "The cross characterizes the flags of the North [Nordic countries]. . . . Lead us, thou cross in

73

our flag, lead us into that Nordic struggle where shackled Norway and bleeding Finland fight against an idea which is directly opposed to all our ideals" (*Four Sermons*, trans., J. M. Jensen. Blair, Neb: Lutheran Publishing House, 1944).

Munk's life and death invite us to ponder the power of the gospel in the midst of social and political conflicts. Offer prayers for those who face persecution and for those who resist and challenge tyranny.

74

EPIPHANY

We are invited to welcome the light

Images *of the* Season

As we fumble our way out of bed in a winter

morning that seems more like night, Isaiah's words

"Arise, shine for your light has come!" may sound ironic,

even sardonic. Still, we know that the prophet's words have no connection at all to the changing seasons. No, they come to us in the context of our Lord's revelation as the beacon of salvation for the whole world. In response, the Epiphany season calls us, entices us, *commands* us to rise up, to leap out of those places where we live in spiritual dimness. God calls us to polish our glasses, clean our windows to be able to see with clarity this new thing that has happened. Arise! Shine! We are invited to greet and welcome the light—a luminescence that shines with such magnitude that it melts the icy coldness of our hearts. Epiphany is no wimpy one-candle-in-the-darkness deal, but rather a blast of brightness heretofore unseen. Get up and see it! Bask in its brightness! Behold the light that shines upon us, scattering the darkness of our minds so that we may walk as children of the light.

> Creator of light,
> the blessing of light be upon us,
> the blessing of day light
> the blessing of sunlight
> the blessing of Christ light.
> Scatter the darkness from before us
> That we may walk as children of light.
> (*The Open Gate* © 1994 David Adam. Reprinted by permission of Morehouse Publishing.)

The light is Christ. Any spiritual light that we have is his, shining in and through us. Indeed, so great is the grace that shines upon us that it seems that our faces, like Moses', should be glowing with reflected glory. At the very least, our way of living surely will catch the light of Christ's love and shine it on those around us. Such is the extroverted, mission nature of this season.

Although the people are the church and thus will be the primary light-givers in this season, our centers of worship, too, should glow with the light. Don't let Epiphany be wimpy. Let everything associated with our worship shine in celebration that the light of our lives is living within us. Polish the metals in the worship center

till they gleam. Light those candles. Let the light shine full blast. Our places of worship should be beacons, searchlights, calling out to all those who labor in spiritual darkness.

Epiphany begins at Bethlehem, but it deserves to be more than a half-baked rerun of Christmas—it has much to offer of its own. The magi followed an unmistakably bright star previously unknown, a luminous sign from God to pay attention. During the season of Epiphany we also celebrate the baptism of Jesus, introducing the one who will baptize with the Holy Spirit and fire. A liturgy that includes the affirmation of our baptism certainly has a place on that day. Let it be a time to celebrate the brightness of being a child of God. Be washed in the bright waters of baptism, burn again with the fire of the Holy Spirit.

The brightness carries on through the season. At Cana, Jesus does the first of his signs, revealing his glory. (Or, alternatively, Peter demonstrates that his receptors have caught at least one beam of the light, as he confesses that Jesus is the Messiah.) The rabbi Jesus proclaims the recovery of sight for the blind. (Or the lesser festival in which Saul is blinded by the light of Christ, then becomes the great apostle Paul.) Jesus' is a light seemingly too intense for some in his hometown. He invites others into the circle of his light, inviting fisherfolk to pull in people. Christ is a light that shines where none has before, blessing the poor, the hungry, the sorrowful. Finally comes the dazzling light of the transfigured Lord.

This light is for all people: "a light to reveal you to the nations and the glory of your people Israel" in the words of Simeon. This light and fire of God shines like a therapeutic laser right into the places where it is most needed. This cleansing light sears away the scales on our eyes, cauterizes the seeping wounds of sin, and halts the gnawing darkness of anxiety. This is a healing light, a refining light, a burnishing light, and a purifying light. This light is like no other. This light has the power to save.

Environment *and* Art *for the* Season

Epiphany is the time when God's glory in Jesus

Christ is increasingly revealed to us. The Word is being

heard and felt in profound ways. We have waited for the

Christ to be with us, and celebrated his arrival in the birth of Jesus. Now we begin our journey with the promised one. The texts in this season give us glimpses into who this Jesus is—God's beloved child. In Jesus' baptism and transfiguration, the liturgical bookends of this season, God's heavenly voice speaks of Jesus' identity. The world is starting to see and hear the power of God that is manifest in Jesus Christ. God the Father's voice is not the only one heard in this season. Jesus begins his ministry—a ministry of calling disciples and preaching and teaching to the crowds in the temple and on the open plain. Jesus puts himself in our midst so that his healing word can be heard.

EVALUATING YOUR SPACE

What is the sound like in your worship space? Is it a "dead" space, one with no echo or reverberation? Or is it a "live" space, one with lots of echo and reverberation where sounds bounce around and linger? Can everybody hear the spoken word clearly? What about music? Is one clear and the other difficult to make out?

Live spaces are wonderful for singing and playing music. When you can hear others singing around you as well as yourself, the singing of the entire assembly improves. But most people have experienced the difficulty of hearing someone clearly in a large, reverberant space. The echo distorts the clarity of the consonants in the speaker's words, making communication a challenge.

Dead spaces are better for hearing the spoken word clearly. There is no echo or reverb. However, if all you can hear is yourself singing, the chances are greater that you won't sing out. Acoustic music must then battle to be heard and choirs often resort to being amplified in order to be understood. This can take something away from the natural beauty of the human voice and risk overamplification. However, amplified instrumental music tends to come across better in "dry" spaces.

Modern technology can help bridge the gap between acoustics and needs, enabling sound to carry well throughout your space. It is easier to compensate for the spoken word and "plugged in" music in a live space than to compensate for acoustic music and congregational singing in a dead space.

Where are the first and second readings proclaimed? From where is the psalm led? Where is the gospel read and from where is the sermon preached?

Christian tradition started with one single place to proclaim the word of God, but then developed two places of proclamation: one place for the laity—the lectern—and one, higher up in many cases, for the "more important" proclamation—the pulpit. Now, though, worshiping assemblies throughout the church are returning to one central place (often called an *ambo*) for the reading and proclaiming of the word. This may include the leading of the psalm because it, too, is the word of God. Different people may share responsibilities but they are all ministers of the word with specific roles in the liturgical assembly.

HEARING THE WORD

We are present in worship for many reasons, but for hearing people, all of them are somehow incomplete without the power of the spoken word. The Bible readings, the sermon, the praying, the speaking of peace—all are, for most of us, oral. We teach that the sacraments are not simply water or bread and wine, but those common elements connected to the word of God. We do not do any of these things of our faith without the word, or at the very least the memory of it.

Weekly, we are hoping that God will speak to us a word of grace in the midst of our confusion, isolation, and brokenness. We are anxious to actually hear the words of forgiveness, of communion, of peace. We want to hear the prayers of the church. We want to hear the word of God read in our midst clearly so that it may speak to us. We want to hear the words that our preacher has carefully selected in order to help us understand God's word.

It is essential that the words of those leading worship be heard clearly if we are to continue to have the fullness of meaning that our liturgy deserves. What good is proclaiming a word of grace if no one can hear it or some only hear part of it? The acoustics of any space where communication is expected to take place are critical.

ART FOR THE SEASON

In the season of Epiphany, images of light continue to be central as we proclaim that the Light has come into the world for good. The continued presence of light in your worship and gathering spaces witnesses to the reality that even after the Christmas tree and Advent wreath have been taken down, the light of the promised one still shines in our midst.

Many modern artists have experimented with combining sights and sounds, primarily in the form of both standing and hanging sculpture. Artwork has been created with materials that make different sounds either when blown by the wind or air, or when struck. The use of sound-producing art in the worship space can be a

powerful reminder of the ability of sounds to reveal another reality to us. You might make use of something like wind chimes fashioned to evoke a visual idea of light yet also capture attention through a unique sound. Depending on the types of sounds that the art makes, you could use them as transitional sounds between elements of worship. In coordination with your parish musicians, you might use them with some appropriate music. You could use them to produce a background that would support certain parts of the liturgy. For example, a delicate wind chime—or a piece of art made from metal or paper that makes enough noise to carry lightly through the worship assembly—could be used whenever the name of Jesus is spoken or sung. It might serve as an audible reminder that Jesus Christ is the Light of the world.

Remember that the visual or audible nature of this art should always enhance worship in part and in whole—it should never be something that distracts us from hearing the word in our midst. Those of us who engage our worshiping communities with new ideas concerning art and environment have a responsibility to create an atmosphere where the word of God can be heard with clarity and without distraction.

Preaching *with the* Season

The children of Israel look to Abraham's day

for their special calling. Those of us who have been

grafted into the tree of life might well look to Epiphany as

the most significant day in history. In the second lesson for the Feast of the Epiphany, St. Paul makes that point as he writes of his "understanding of the mystery of Christ." "The Gentiles have become fellow heirs, members of the same body, and sharers in the promise in Christ Jesus through the gospel" (Eph. 3:6).

St. Augustine in the fifth century agreed:

Only a few days ago we celebrated the Lord's birthday. Today we are celebrating with equal solemnity, as is proper, his Epiphany, in which he began to manifest himself

to the Gentiles. On the one day the Jewish shepherds saw him when he was born; on this day the magi coming from the east adored him. Now, he had been born that cornerstone, the peace of the two walls coming from very different directions, from circumcision and uncircumcision. Thus they could be united in him who had been made our peace, and "who has made both one. . ." Let us, therefore, with joy of the spirit hold dear these two days, the Nativity and the Manifestation of our Lord.

(Quoted in *A Christmas Sourcebook*, edited by Mary Ann Simcoe. Liturgy Training Publications, Chicago, 1984, p. 113)

A splendid celebration of Epiphany can be the antidote to post-Christmas apathy. *Apathy*—it's the fatigue that descends on those who have permitted Christmas shopping and Christmas singing to invade and dominate Advent. When the Red-Nosed Reindeer is stabled and post-Christmas sales seem to conclude the season of the Nativity, what is needed is another festivity! Epiphany is a possibility.

Epiphaneia—Greek for "manifestation" or "revelation." For us today the force of "epiphany" might better be defined as "to show" or "to make known." For all of us who have been shown, who have come to know, it might well be best to define epiphany with a word describing our reaction to the revealing of God-in-Christ born for us. Try, *Aha!* Epiphany is an *Aha!* experience. We realize anew that the Light of the World is for all the world, not only for the *first-chosen*, but also for the *second-chosen*. The Gentiles, too, come to that Light. Every member of the chosen race has reason for celebrating the arrival of the long-promised Messiah, and every Gentile has reason for celebrating the revelation of the mystery of Christ to all second-choice peoples.

Just as the birth day of our Lord has an anticipatory Eve to begin the celebration, so Epiphany has Twelfth Night as its introduction vigil, on the evening of January 5. Gertrud Mueller Nelson's book *To Dance With God* (New York: Mahwah Paulist Press, 1986) is a splendid source for "family ritual and community celebration." Some of her suggestions for a celebratory sequence in the home could be adapted for a Twelfth Night service that would excite both children and older worshipers. It could easily develop into a festival that would rival Christmas Eve for popularity.

Preparation for this *Aha!* service could well begin in Advent. The children could people the Christmas crèche Sunday by Sunday, the manger and the straw first, then the animals, and even the innkeeper if his figure could be found. Finally, Mary and Joseph and the child arrive on Christmas. The magi should be visible somewhere in the church during the twelve days of Christmas, moving day by day closer, but their arrival to pay homage to the Christ child is scheduled for Twelfth Night. Mueller Nelson suggests that "brass candlesticks and a bit of velvet" can change the manger into the appearance of a royal throne from which the newborn king can welcome the magi.

In the tradition of Twelfth Night we will surely want something of a party after the Eucharist. A special Twelfth Night cake could be served, and every household receive chalk for marking their home's doorway. Mueller Nelson's book can tell you all about it.

The *Aha!* experiences in the Epiphany lessons could tie the services together in the season right up to the Sunday before Lent when the three disciples see the Lord transfigured.

- The magi had the Aha! of the star.
- A more theological Aha! at the Lord's baptism as he steps into Jordan and into his redeemer role.
- Peter sharing his Aha! at his confession of Jesus as the Son of the Living God.
- Or the Aha! of the sign of the wine revealing the glory of Christ.
- Saul's Aha! which altered his name and his mission.
- Or the Aha! of the word as Jesus reveals that he is its fulfillment.
- The dreadful Aha! warning that unbelief is least desirable—or the Aha! telling that the greatest of all gifts is love.
- The disciples' Aha! as they catch on they are to catch people.
- The Aha! of two resurrections—his and ours.
- The transfiguring of the Lord. Aha! for him and for the three disciples and for us, and the beginning of his transfiguring passion.

All of it pointing to the last Aha!, to which we all look eagerly.

79

Shape *of* Worship *for the* Season

BASIC SHAPE OF THE EUCHARISTIC RITE

- Confession and Forgiveness: see alternate worship text for Epiphany on page 85 as an option to the form in the liturgy setting. Other possibilities for confession and forgiveness are in *Holy Baptism and Related Rites*, Renewing Worship, vol. 3, pp. 87*ff.* (ELCA/Augsburg Fortress, 2002), or at www.renewing worship.org/publications/holy_baptism/index.html

GATHERING

- Greeting: see alternate worship text for Epiphany
- Consider omitting the Kyrie on the nonfestival Sundays after the Epiphany, but use the Kyrie on the festivals of the Epiphany, the Baptism of Our Lord, and the Transfiguration of Our Lord, as well as on the Confession of St. Peter and the Conversion of St. Paul, if observed.
- Use the hymn of praise "Glory to God" throughout Epiphany

WORD

- Use the Nicene Creed for festival days and Sundays in this season; use the Apostles' Creed for the "green" Sundays after the Epiphany
- The prayers: see alternate forms and responses for Epiphany

BAPTISM

- Consider having a baptismal festival on the Baptism of Our Lord (January 11)
- If there are no baptisms, use the Remembrance of Baptism from *Holy Baptism and Related Rites*, pp. 101*ff*, eithe rat the profession of faith or as part of the gathering rite

MEAL

- Offertory prayer: see alternate worship text for Epiphany
- Use the proper preface for Epiphany
- Eucharistic prayer: in addition to the four main options in *LBW*, see "Eucharistic Prayer C: The Season of Epiphany" in *WOV* Leaders Edition, p. 67
- Invitation to communion: see alternate worship text for Epiphany
- Post-communion prayer: see alternate worship text

SENDING

- Benediction: see alternate worship text for Epiphany
- Dismissal: see alternate worship text for Epiphany

OTHER SEASONAL POSSIBILITIES

- The festival of the Epiphany of Our Lord (January 6) is a fitting occasion to use incense. *Worship Wordbook* (pp. 103–104), *Manual on the Liturgy* (pp. 279–82), and *Altar Guild and Sacristy Handbook* (p. 81) are three resources to consult for instructions on using incense.
- If you are making the Baptism of Our Lord (January 11) a baptismal festival, resources in *Holy Baptism and Related Rites* could be helpful. See especially pp. 1–20 and 51–68.
- This year, the Confession of St. Peter and the Conversion of St. Paul fall on Sundays (Jan. 18 and 25), framing the Week of Prayer for Christian Unity. Either of those days would be ideal for an emphasis on ecumenical relationships, perhaps including representatives from a nearby congregation of a different denomination.

Assembly Song *for the* Season

When Christ's appearing was made known, /

King Herod trembled for his throne; / but he who

offers heavenly birth / seeks not the kingdoms of this earth.

("When Christ's appearing was made known" RW1 87, stanza 1)

Christ's appearance surprises: in the temple and syna-gogue, at a wedding banquet, at the bed of a crippled person, on a mountain. In all places Christ calls us to offer healing and be light to the world. The world's rulers rightly tremble, for when Christ is made known, peace and freedom are never far behind.

GATHERING

The season calls for images of light, baptismal rebirth, and transformation. Good opening hymns are "As with gladness men of old" (LBW 82), or "We are marching in the light of God/Siyahamba" (WOV 650, TFF 63, W&P 148), and "In the morning" (W&P 75). Children's choirs can lead the congregation in "I want to walk as a child of the light" (WOV 649) and "This little light of mine" (TFF 65).

Emphasize the baptismal imagery with a sprinkling rite (sprinkling the congregation with water from the font, using an evergreen branch) as the congregation sings a "Glory to God in the highest" setting from *LBW* or *WOV*, or "Oh, come, let us sing" (W&P 107), a jaunty setting of Psalm 95 for piano and congregation. Alternately, sing "Song over the waters" (W&P 127).

WORD

Catch the assembly's ear before the gospel with "Listen, God is calling" (WOV 712, TFF 130), using creative solo techniques on the "Listen" parts: vary the dynamics, timing, even the pitches. One could even have the leader parts sung from different spots in the worship space.

Highlight the mystical body of Christ through his church throughout the world by singing "Nasadiki" (TFF 204), a delightful setting of the Apostles' Creed, led *a cappella* by a soloist in a call and response setting, perhaps with a simple drum, shakers, or even a couple small stones knocked together on the strong beats.

Though not difficult, both of these pieces call for

rehearsal with the congregation before the service, and would lend themselves to use throughout the Epiphany season. By the end, even the initial skeptics will likely be enjoying the African touch!

MEAL

The season of Epiphany, and in particular the Week of Prayer for Christian Unity (January 18–25), is a good time to highlight and strengthen ecumenical ties. Learn a sung setting of the ecumenical version of the Lord's Prayer (*LBW*, p. 112).

Have the congregation continue singing the unison setting of "Holy, holy, holy" and "Lamb of God" from *LBW* Setting 3. Or try the four-part *a cappella* setting at TFF 32.

SENDING

As a post-communion canticle, affirm the experience of Simeon and Anna in the temple with a setting of "Lord, now you let your servant go in peace" (*LBW*, pp. 73, 93–94, 116), or the hymn setting "O Lord, now let your servant" (LBW 339). Alternately, let the cross lead the closing procession as everyone sings the repetitive South African hymn "Send Me, Jesus" (WOV 773, TFF 244/245).

On Transfiguration, the last Sunday after the Epiphany, sing lots of alleluias, then banish "alleluia" from the congregation's lips until Easter. In the weeks leading to Transfiguration, teach the Sunday School a simple alleluia, such as W&P 6, and sing it today. At the close of the Transfiguration liturgy, say farewell to the alleluia by singing "Alleluia, song of gladness" (WOV 654) as children escort an alleluia banner from the church, and "bury" it until the Easter vigil. It may be hidden away, or you might build a small, simple wooden casket for it. On Easter Sunday, the alleluia banner can "rise from the dead" as did Christ.

81

Music *for the* Season

VERSE AND OFFERTORY

Boehnke, Paul. *Festive Verse Settings for Christmas, Epiphany, and Transfiguration.*
SATB, opt kybd. MSM 80-100.

Cherwien, David. *Verses for the Epiphany Season.* U, opt hb, org.
MSM 80-200.

Johnson, David N. *Verses and Offertories for Epiphany 2 through Transfiguration.*
U, kybd. AFP 0800649028.

Verse and Offertory Sentences, Part II: Epiphany through Transfiguration.
CPH 97-5502.

CHORAL

Bach, J. S. "O Morning Star, How Fair and Bright" in *Bach for All Seasons.* SATB. AFP 080065754X.

Bach, J. S. "The Only Son from Heaven" (alt. text for "Bring Low
Our Ancient Adam") in *Bach for All Seasons.* SATB, kybd.
AFP 080065854X.

Christianson, F. Melius. "Beautiful Savior." SATB. AFP
0800652584. Also in *The Augsburg Choirbook.* AFP 0800676025.

Christiansen, Olaf C. "Light Everlasting." SATB. KJO 5110.

Erickson, Richard. "I Want to Walk As a Child of the Light." SATB,
org, fl. AFP 0800658396.

Fleming, Larry. "Humble Service." SATB. AFP 0800646223.

Helgen, John. "Brighter Than the Sun." SATB, pno.
AFP 0800659155.

CHILDREN'S CHOIR

Helgen, John. "This Little Light of Mine." U/2 pt, pno.
AFP 0800675932.

Hopson, Hal H. "We are the Children of Light." U, kybd, opt desc,
tamb, hb. HOP C5080.

Howell, Robert. "Shine, Children, Shine." U/2 pt, kybd. Triune
Music 10/1873K.

Shields, Valerie. "Let Your Light So Brightly Shine." 2 pt, org, opt
hb. MSM 50-8410.

Westendorf, Craig. "Lord, Now You Let Your Servant Go in Peace."
U, org. CG CGA911.

KEYBOARD/INSTRUMENTAL

Augsburg Organ Library: Epiphany. Org. AFP 0800659341.

Behnke, John A. Partita on "I Want to Walk As a Child of the
Light." Org. CPH 97-6595.

Held, Wilbur. *Music for the New Year.* Org. MSM 10-199.

Hobby, Robert A. *Three Epiphany Preludes.* Org. MSM 10-208.

Linker, Janet. *Three Epiphany Pieces.* Org. AFP 0800658221.

Music With Minimal Pedal - Advent and Epiphany. Org. MSM 10-207.

HANDBELL

Gramann, Fred. "Lumière." 3-5 oct. AGEHR AG35174.

Honoré, Jeffrey. "The Epiphany of Our God." 3-5 oct. LOR
20/1005.

Kinyon, Barbara Baltzer. "Brightest and Best (of the Stars)." 2-3 oct,
hb, hc. CPH 97-6709.

Linker, Janet and Jane McFadden. "Rise, Shine, You People." 3-5 oct,
org, tpt. AFP 0800655052 (handbell part); AFP 0800655044
(full score). OP.

Moklebust, Cathy. "Light Eternal." 3-5 oct. LOR 20/1188L.

PRAISE ENSEMBLE

Davis, Holland. "Let It Rise" in *More Songs for Praise and Worship.*
SATB. WRD 3010387016 (vocal ed); WRD 3010186363
(pno, vcs, perc).

DeShazo, Lynn. "Worthy of Praises" in *More Songs for Praise and Worship.*
SATB. WRD 3010387016 (vocal ed); WRD 3010186363
(pno, vcs, perc).

Kendrick, Graham, arr. Schrader. "Shine, Jesus, Shine." SATB, kybd.
HOP GC 937.

Paris, Twila, arr. Kirkland. "Honor and Praise." SATB, kybd. Allegis
AG-1017.

Smith, Michael W. "How Majestic is Your Name" in W&P.

Alternate Worship Texts

CONFESSION AND FORGIVENESS

In the name of the Father, and of the ✛ Son,
and of the Holy Spirit.
Amen

Through water and the Spirit God gives us new life.
Let us confess our sin
that we may be renewed in the covenant of baptism.

Silence for reflection and self-examination.

Strong and faithful God,
we confess that we have not lived
as the body of Christ in the world.
We have veiled our hearts from your light.
We have resisted your call to follow.
We have failed to exercise your gift of love.
Forgive us for the sake of Christ,
heal us with your abundant grace,
and help us walk as children of light. Amen

In the mercy of almighty God,
Jesus Christ came among us
to proclaim release to the captives,
to let the oppressed go free.
Today the promise is fulfilled:
God forgives you all your sins.
May the Holy Spirit strengthen you
to follow Christ in newness of life.
Amen

GREETING

The light and love of God
who wonderfully made you,
who graciously redeemed you,
who calls you each by name,
be with you all.
And also with you.

PRAYERS

Encouraged by the radiant light of God
revealed to us in Jesus Christ,
let us pray with boldness and confidence.

A brief silence.

Each petition ends:
Let us pray to the Lord:
Hear us, O God, and show us your glory.

Concluding petition:
Into your hands, great God of heaven, we lay our prayers,
trusting in your mercy through the one who showed us your face,
Jesus Christ, our Lord.
Amen

OFFERTORY PRAYER

God of all creation,
all you have made is good,
and your love endures forever.
You bring forth bread from the earth
and fruit from the vine.
Nourish us with these gifts,
that we might be for the world
signs of your gracious presence
in Jesus Christ our Lord. Amen

INVITATION TO COMMUNION

Come, eat and drink,
that you may know yourselves as Christ's own.

POST-COMMUNION PRAYER

Holy God,
in this eucharist you reveal your faithfulness
to us, your beloved children.
Anoint us with your Spirit,
that we may be signs of your grace
and compassion for the world.
Grant this through Christ our Lord.
Amen

BLESSING

May Christ, whose epiphany
revealed God's glory to the world,
deepen your faith and make your hearts glad.
Almighty God, Father, ✛ Son, and Holy Spirit,
bless you now and forever.
Amen

DISMISSAL

The joy of the Lord is your strength.
Go in peace. Serve the Lord.
Thanks be to God.

83

Seasonal Rites

Lessons and Carols for Epiphany

ENTRANCE HYMN
Good Christian friends, rejoice LBW 55
The first Noel LBW 56

DIALOG
The people who walked in darkness have seen a great light.
The light shines in the darkness,
and the darkness has not overcome it.
Those who dwelt in the land of deep darkness,
on them light has shined.
We have beheld Christ's glory,
glory as of the only Son from the Father.
For to us a child is born, to us a Son is given.
In him was life, and the life was the light of all people.

OPENING PRAYER

See the prayer of the day for Epiphany.

LESSONS AND CAROLS
First Reading: John 1:1-14
Of the Father's love begotten LBW 42
A Light shines in darkness RWSB
He came down TFF 37

Second Reading: John 1:18-25
Infant holy, infant lowly LBW 44
Away in a manger LBW 67, WOV 644
Jesus, the light of the world TFF 59

Third Reading: Matthew 2:1-12
Bright and glorious is the sky LBW 75
We three kings of Orient are WOV 646
The magi who to Bethlehem did go RWSB, LLC 317
Sister Mary TFF 60

Fourth Reading: Matthew 2:13-23
By all your saints in warfare (st. 9) LBW 177
Oh, sleep now, holy baby WOV 639
Oh, Mary, gentle poor Mary LLC 310

Fifth Reading: Luke 2:41-51
In a lowly manger born LBW 417
Once in royal David's city WOV 643
The virgin Mary had a baby boy TFF 53

Sixth Reading: Matthew 3:13-17
When Christ's appearing was made known LBW 85
When Jesus came to Jordan WOV 647
Wade in the water TFF 114

Seventh Reading: John 2:1-11
Now the silence LBW 205
Jesus, come! for we invite you WOV 648

RESPONSIVE PRAYER
Glory to God in the highest,
and peace to God's people on earth.
Blessed are you, Prince of Peace.
You rule the earth with truth and justice.
Send your gift of peace to all nations of the world.
Blessed are you, Son of Mary. You share our humanity.
Have mercy on those who are sick, dying,
and all who suffer this day.
Blessed are you, Son of God.
You dwell among us as the Word made flesh.
Reveal yourself to us in word and sacrament,
that we may bear your light to all the world.

THE LORD'S PRAYER

BLESSING AND DISMISSAL
Let us bless the Lord.
Thanks be to God.
May you be filled with the wonder of Mary, the obedience of
Joseph, the joy of the angels, the eagerness of the shepherds,
the determination of the magi, and the peace of the Christ child.
Almighty God, Father, ✝ Son, and Holy Spirit bless you now and
forever.
Amen

SENDING HYMN
Songs of thankfulness and praise LBW 90
The Lord is my light RWSB, TFF 61

Blessing of the Home at Epiphany

Matthew writes that when the magi saw the shining star stop overhead, they were filled with joy. "On entering the house, they saw the child with Mary his mother" (2:10-11). In the home, Christ is met in family and friends, in visitors and strangers. In the home, faith is shared, nurtured, and put into action. In the home, Christ is welcome.

Twelfth Night (January 5) or another day during the season of Epiphany offers an occasion for gathering with friends and family members for a blessing of the home, using the following as a model. Someone may lead the greeting and blessing, while another person may read the scripture passage. Following an eastern European tradition, a visual blessing may be inscribed with white chalk above the main door; for example, 20 + C M B + 04. The numbers change with each new year. The three letters stand for either the ancient Latin blessing Christe mansionem benedica, *which means "Christ, bless this house," or the legendary names of the magi (Caspar, Melchior, and Balthasar).*

GREETING

May peace be to this house and to all who enter here. By wisdom a house is built and through understanding it is established; through knowledge its rooms are filled with rare and beautiful treasures.

See Proverbs 24:3-4.

READING

As we prepare to ask God's blessing on this household, let us listen to the words of scripture.
In the beginning was the Word, and the Word was with God, and the Word was God. He was in the beginning with God. All things came into being through him, and without him not one thing came into being. What has come into being in him was life, and the life was the light of all people. The Word became flesh and lived among us, and we have seen his glory, the glory as of a father's only son, full of grace and truth. From his fullness we have all received, grace upon grace.

See John 1:1-4, 14, 16.

INSCRIPTION

This inscription may be made with chalk above the entrance:

20 + C M B + 04
The magi of old, known as
C Caspar,
M Melchior, and
B Balthasar
    followed the star of God's Son who came to dwell among us
20 two thousand
04 and four years ago.
+ Christ, bless this house,
+ and remain with us throughout the new year.

PRAYER

O God, you revealed your Son to all people by the shining light of a star. We pray that you bless this home and all who live here with your gracious presence. May your love be our inspiration, your wisdom our guide, your truth our light, and your peace our benediction; through Christ our Lord. Amen

Then everyone may walk from room to room, blessing the house with incense or by sprinkling with water, perhaps using a branch from the Christmas tree.

Adapted from *Come, Lord Jesus: Devotions for the Home* (Augsburg Fortress, 1996).

85

Ecumenical Service during the Week of Prayer for Christian Unity

CONFESSION AND FORGIVENESS

We gather as the people of God
to offer our repentance and praise,
to pray for the unity of the church
and the renewal of our common life.
Trusting in God's mercy and compassion,
let us ask for the forgiveness of our sins.

Silence for reflection and self-examination.

Lord Jesus, you came to reconcile us
to one another and to the Father:
Lord, have mercy on us.
Lord, have mercy on us.

Lord Jesus, you heal the wounds
of pride and intolerance.
Christ, have mercy on us.
Christ, have mercy on us.

Lord Jesus, you pardon the sinner
and welcome the repentant.
Lord, have mercy on us.
Lord, have mercy on us.

May almighty God grant us pardon and peace,
strengthen us in faith,
and make us witnesses to Christ's love.
Amen

HYMN OF PRAISE

PRAYER OF THE DAY

God our Father, your Son Jesus prayed that his followers might
be one. Make all Christians one with him as he is one with you,
so that in peace and concord we may carry to the world the
message of your love; through your Son, Jesus Christ our Lord,
who lives and reigns with you and the Holy Spirit, one God, now
and forever.
Amen

READINGS

Isaiah 2:2-4
Psalm 133
Ephesians 4:1-6
John 17:15-23

SERMON

HYMN OF THE DAY

THANKSGIVING FOR BAPTISM

*The people remain standing after the hymn as the minister(s)
gather at the font. After the prayer, the people may be sprinkled
with water from the font. Or, at the conclusion of the service,
they may be invited to dip their hands in the font and trace the
sign of the cross over themselves.*

The Lord be with you.
And also with you.
Let us give thanks to the Lord our God.

It is right to give our thanks and praise.
Holy God and mighty Lord, we give you thanks,
for you nourish and sustain us and all living things
with the gift of water.
In the beginning your Spirit moved over the waters,
and you created heaven and earth.
By the waters of the flood you saved Noah and his family.
You led Israel through the sea out of slavery
into the promised land.
In the waters of the Jordan
your Son was baptized by John and anointed with the Spirit.
By the baptism of his death and resurrection
your Son set us free from sin and death
and opened the way to everlasting life.
We give you thanks, O God,
that you have given us new life in the water of baptism.
Buried with Christ in his death,
you raise us to share in his resurrection
by the power of the Holy Spirit.
May all who have passed through the water of baptism
continue in the risen life of our Savior.
To you be all honor and glory, now and forever.
Amen

CONFESSION OF FAITH

There is one Lord, one faith, and one baptism.
United in Christ, let us confess the faith we hold in common.

The people recite the Apostles' Creed.

THE PRAYERS

At the conclusion, the people pray the Lord's Prayer.

GREETING OF PEACE

The Lord Jesus prayed for the unity of his disciples.
We look for the day when the church will shine forth
in unity at his holy supper.
The peace of the Lord be with you always.
And also with you.

The people exchange a sign of Christ's peace.

BLESSING AND DISMISSAL

SENDING HYMN

86

January 6, 2004

The Epiphany of Our Lord

INTRODUCTION

The Epiphany of Our Lord brings the twelve days of Christmas to an end and begins a season that will focus on God's revelation in Jesus. The day is filled with surprises, mysterious visitors, and exotic gifts. God's story leads us through unexpected twists and turns, and the mission of God's people introduces us to faith partners we have never expected.

PRAYER OF THE DAY

Lord God, on this day you revealed your Son to the nations by the leading of a star. Lead us now by faith to know your presence in our lives, and bring us at last to the full vision of your glory, through your Son, Jesus Christ our Lord, who lives and reigns with you and the Holy Spirit, one God, now and forever.

VERSE

Alleluia. We observed his star in the East, and have come to pay him homage. Alleluia. (Matt. 2:2)

READINGS

Isaiah 60:1-6

The long years of darkness are over. The prophet announces the end of exile in Babylon and looks forward to the restoration of the city of Jerusalem. God's light, reflected in Israel, will draw caravans bearing treasure from all the nations who freely come to praise the Lord.

Psalm 72:1-7, 10-14

All kings shall bow down before him. (Ps. 72:11)

Ephesians 3:1-12

Though it had been hidden for years, Paul now reveals the secret that has shaped his apostolic witness: in Jesus Christ, God's salvation extends beyond the Jews to include all people. The light of Christ shines upon Jew and Gentile alike.

Matthew 2:1-12

The rich symbolism of this story—the magi, a star in the East, Herod's plots—announces the prophetic hope for an epiphany, the revelation that God has entered into our history as one of us.

COLOR White

THE PRAYERS

Encouraged by the radiant light of God revealed to us in Jesus Christ, let us pray with boldness and confidence.

A BRIEF SILENCE.

For all who are on a journey to find the source of grace and forgiveness, that like the magi they may be led to Christ and freely offer him their gifts, let us pray to the Lord:

Hear us, O God, and show us your glory.

For the mission of the church that, like the holy star of Bethlehem, we may be a beacon of hope, safety, and love for all who are seeking your face, let us pray to the Lord:

Hear us, O God, and show us your glory.

For the people of the world, that the poor and needy be sustained and victims of violence and oppression be restored, let us pray to the Lord:

Hear us, O God, and show us your glory.

For those who bear the burden of illness and long for healing (*especially*), that their health may be renewed, and that they may see God's holy light in our compassion and love, let us pray to the Lord:

Hear us, O God, and show us your glory.

For the people of this congregation, that we may continue to be fed by God's Spirit and may lay the offerings of our lives before the one born to save us, let us pray to the Lord.

Hear us, O God, and show us your glory.

HERE OTHER INTERCESSIONS MAY BE OFFERED.

In thanksgiving for all those who bore Christ's light, revealing his glory, and who now rest in God's eternal peace, that we may follow their course until the day we stand with them as one holy people, let us pray to the Lord:

Hear us, O God, and show us your glory.

Into your hands, great God of heaven, we lay our prayers, trusting in your mercy through the one who showed us your face, Jesus Christ, our Lord.

Amen

87

IMAGES FOR PREACHING

Robert Frost wrote, "Two roads diverged in a wood." The magi, those wise people of old, traveled two roads—one to go to Bethlehem and one to get out of Bethlehem, away from Herod's evil. Which road made all the difference for the magi? Certainly it was the road that took them to the Savior, the road to Jesus' epiphany! For us, too, the road to the Christ child makes all the difference.

What is the most significant day in human history, the one that has made the greatest difference? For those of us who are not of the originally chosen race, is it not the day of the revelation of "the mystery of Christ"? Because of that revelation, "the Gentiles have become fellow heirs, members of the same body, and sharers in the promise in Christ Jesus through the gospel" (Eph. 3:4, 6). On this day we celebrate that time when we too joined the heirs—and we call that day "the Epiphany."

How God-in-Christ made all the difference should never be forgotten. The Isaiah lesson speaks of kings coming with gold and frankincense. Matthew tells us that the wise men also brought myrrh, the precursor of death.

Dying, our Lord's dying, was the beginning. But remember the final lines of the familiar carol for the triumphant ending that has made all the difference! "Glorious now behold him arise, / King and God and Sacrifice!" (WOV 646).

The star that stopped overwhelmed the wise men with joy. Now they knew where the child was to be found. Today we use the words of Herod as God would change them into a directive for us: "Seek diligently for the child so that you also may pay him homage." When we worship him also, each time, it is our epiphany.

WORSHIP MATTERS

Second only to Easter, Epiphany has been a time for baptismal renewal in the church. The *illuminandi*, "the enlightened ones," is an ancient name for the baptized. Light is associated with the presence of God, with images from the burning bush in the desert, the pillar of fire through the Red Sea, to the glory in the heavens at Jesus' birth.

That sense of God's presence is conveyed through the burning of candles in our worship spaces. One of the ways the newly baptized are welcomed is through the presentation of a candle that is a miniature version of the paschal candle. The resurrected life of Jesus is passed on to the newly enlightened, even as they rub shoulders with the rest of the illuminandi. "Let your light shine before others, so that they may see your good works and give glory to your Father in heaven" (Matt. 5:16).

LET THE CHILDREN COME

The magi bring gifts as a sign of their adoration and love. Include in the bulletin pieces of blank paper and invite children (and everyone) to write down or draw a picture of the gifts they could share for God's glory (care for others, welcome, carpentry skills, and so forth). Collect the papers in the offering baskets when you collect the offering for the day. Include in the prayers a prayer for all to have courage to share the gifts we've been given so that others see the love of Christ at work in our world.

HYMNS FOR WORSHIP
GATHERING

As with gladness men of old   LBW 82
Christ, whose glory fills the skies   LBW 265
We three kings of Orient are   WOV 646

HYMN OF THE DAY

O Morning Star, how fair and bright!   LBW 76

ALTERNATE HYMN OF THE DAY

I want to walk as a child of the light   WOV 649
Jesus, the Light of the world   TFF 59

COMMUNION

Beautiful Savior   LBW 518
Jesus, come! for we invite you   WOV 648

SENDING

The first Noel   LBW 56
We are marching in the light of God   WOV 650, TFF 63

ADDITIONAL HYMNS AND SONGS

The magi who to Bethlehem did go   LLC 317, RWSB
Sister Mary   TFF 60
Christ, be our light   RWSB
Wise men, they came to look for wisdom   TWC 186

88

MUSIC FOR THE DAY
PSALMODY

Daw Jr., Carl P. and Kevin R. Hackett. *A Hymn Tune Psalter.* Church Publishing Inc.

Haugen, Marty. "Every Nation on Earth Will Adore You" in PCY, vol 1.

Hobby, Robert A. PW, Cycle C.

Patterson, Joy F. "O God, in Christ We Meet the King" in SP.

Schoenbachler, Tim. "Psalm 72: Justice Shall Flourish" in STP, vol. 3.

Hail to the Lord's anointed   LBW 87

Jesus shall reign   LBW 530

CHORAL

Bach, J. S. "O Morning Star, How Fair and Bright" in *Bach for All Seasons.* SATB, opt fl. AFP 080065854X.

Ellingboe, Bradley. "How Far Is the Star?" SATB, pno. KJO 8936.

Keesecker, Thomas. "The Silent Stars Shine Down on Us" in *Augsburg Easy Choirbook.* 2 pt mxd, pno, fc. AFP 0800676025.

Martinson, Joel. "Arise, Shine." SATB, org. AFP 0800652401. OP.

Willan, Healey. "Arise, Shine." SATB, org. CPH 98-1508.

Willan, Healey. "The Three Kings." SSATBB. OXF OCS 718.

CHILDREN'S CHOIR

Christopherson, Dorothy. "The Night of the Star." U/2 pt, opt desc, fl, perc, pno. AFP 0800657543.

Miller, Jeff. "Star Shine Bright." U, kybd, opt C inst. CG CGA759.

KEYBOARD/INSTRUMENTAL

Buxtehude, Dietrich. "Wie schön leuchtet der Morgenstern" in *Chorale Preludes.* Org. PET 4457 or other ed.

Drischner, Max. "Wie schön leuchtet der Morgenstern" in *Augsburg Organ Library: Epiphany.* Org. AFP 0800659341.

Leupold, Anton Wilhelm. "Marsch der heil'gen drei Könige" in *Augsburg Organ Library: Epiphany.* Org. AFP 0800659341.

Linker, Janet. "We Three Kings" in *Three Epiphany Pieces.* Org. AFP 0800658221.

HANDBELL

Dobrinski, Cynthia. "We Three Kings." 3-5 oct. AG 1390.

Helman, Michael. "From a Distant Home." 3-5 oct, opt hc. CG CGB272.

PRAISE ENSEMBLE

Bancroft, Charity Lees, arr Vikki Cook. "Before the Throne of God" in *Worship Leader's Song Discovery,* vol. 28. WLP 2001-09-LS.

Kendrick, Graham. "Shine, Jesus, Shine" in W&P.

Moody, Dave. "All Hail, King Jesus" in W&P.

Friday, January 9

ADRIAN OF CANTERBURY, TEACHER, C. 710

African by birth, Adrian (or Hadrian) worked with Theodore, archbishop of Canterbury, in developing the church in England, particularly through his direction of an influential school where many church leaders were instructed.

The growing awareness of the multicultural life of the church leads many to discover surprises in the church's history; for example, that an African missionary such as Adrian would have been influential in the development of the church in England, a church sometimes perceived only as Western and European in its history. Within parish groups, use the example of Adrian to explore the cross-cultural influence within the ancient church.

89

January 11, 2004

The Baptism of Our Lord

INTRODUCTION

Baptism is the beginning of a new story. It was for Jesus; it is for us. God claims us as sons and daughters, fills us with the Holy Spirit, and promises to travel the path with us—a path that will bring us home.

PRAYER OF THE DAY

Father in heaven, at the baptism of Jesus in the River Jordan you proclaimed him your beloved Son and anointed him with the Holy Spirit. Make all who are baptized into Christ faithful in their calling to be your children and inheritors with him of everlasting life; through your Son, Jesus Christ our Lord, who lives and reigns with you and the Holy Spirit, one God, now and forever.

VERSE

Alleluia. You are my Son, the Beloved; with you I am well pleased. Alleluia. (Mark 1:11)

READINGS

Isaiah 43:1-7

Near the end of Israel's exile in Babylon, God promises to bring them home. They need no longer fear, because the one who formed, created, and called them by name now claims and redeems them.

Psalm 29

The voice of the LORD is upon the waters. (Ps. 29:3)

Acts 8:14-17

Peter and John are sent by the church to the Christians in Samaria, a group that had been converted through the preaching of Philip. Here the Samaritans received the gift of the Holy Spirit in the laying on of hands.

Luke 3:15-17, 21-22

The last of the prophets of Israel, John the Baptist points ahead to "the one mightier than I [who] is coming." Although John baptizes with water, Jesus will baptize with the Spirit and fire. In Luke's version of this story, the focus is not on John, however. God is the actor, causing the Spirit to descend upon Jesus and inaugurating his mission with the proclamation that he is the "beloved Son."

COLOR White

THE PRAYERS

Encouraged by the radiant light of God revealed to us in Jesus Christ, let us pray with boldness and confidence.

A BRIEF SILENCE.

For the baptized throughout the world, that having been called by name, we will be renewed in our calling to make Christ known to the nations, let us pray to the Lord:

Hear us, O God, and show us your glory.

For those throughout the world who lack clean water, that our intelligence and resources may be brought to bear on the crisis, and that we may live in a compassionate manner, let us pray to the Lord:

Hear us, O God, and show us your glory.

For those who thirst for healing *(especially)*, that the strength and comfort of God and the compassion of God's people wash over them, granting relief and refreshment, let us pray to the Lord:

Hear us, O God, and show us your glory.

For this congregation, that as we are continually cleansed, so through the gift of the Holy Spirit we may share God's cleansing word of grace with all who are burdened by sin, let us pray to the Lord:

Hear us, O God, and show us your glory.

HERE OTHER INTERCESSIONS MAY BE OFFERED.

That we may remember the baptized of all times and places who have died and await the resurrection feast *(especially)*, and that we may be strengthened by their faith until we join them in the age to come, let us pray to the Lord:

Hear us, O God, and show us your glory.

Into your hands, great God of heaven, we lay our prayers, trusting in your mercy through the one who showed us your face, Jesus Christ, our Lord.

Amen

IMAGES FOR PREACHING

By now a goodly number of Christmas gifts and toys have been shown to be too fragile for the real world—or

90

perhaps the recipients weren't sufficiently careful, not "goodly" enough. How about the gift of the Holy Spirit? Surely it is not too fragile for the real world. We have received the Spirit at our baptism. Are we taking good care, making good use of that Spirit?

When Jesus presented himself to John for baptism, John was astonished. "I need to be baptized by you, and do you come to me?" Did John fully understand Jesus' reply? "Let it be so now; for it is proper for us in this way to fulfill all righteousness" (Matt. 3:14, 15). John and the people gathered around Jordan could see Jesus stepping into the river's water, but they could not realize he was stepping into his offered life as the representative of all the people of the world. He, sinless, offered himself as the sin bearer for all sinners. He, the Lamb of God, began the living and the dying that would take away the sin of the world.

And then, it was as if God couldn't stand it—all this significant beginning and the people saying only, "That's Jesus stepping into Jordan." And so God opened the heavens, the Holy Spirit assumed the bodily form of a dove, and God himself used words to make the case: "You are my Son, the Beloved, with you I am well pleased" (Luke 3:22).

That was already an indication of what we humbly believe, that the Father accepts this Savior's sacrifice for us all, has raised the Savior from the dead, and will raise to everlasting life all who believe this gospel. In the meantime, we have the wonderful gift of the Spirit to care for, as the Spirit cares for us.

WORSHIP MATTERS

Naming one's child is an important decision for parents. That name will accompany that son or daughter throughout life, giving him or her a handle on a personal identity. Children eagerly listen to stories of how their names were chosen, so that they can know their place in the world and in their family. "You were named after your aunt Elizabeth." "You were named after Saint Philip, because you were born on his day."

At baptisms, the entire worshiping assembly hears the candidates' names announced as sponsors present them. For many who are worshiping, they hear this name for the first time, especially if those who are baptized are young children. At the time the candidates are washed with water, their names are forever linked with the triune God, Father, Son, and Holy Spirit, and their identity is tied to Jesus, who is called God's Son, the Beloved.

LET THE CHILDREN COME

With the story of Jesus' baptism we are reminded of God's great gift of love given to us in our own baptism. In baptism we become God's children and are inheritors of eternal life. Send a small candle home with the children or, if possible, with all those who worship today. Encourage them to light it every day this week and to remember the light of Christ that shines in and through them.

HYMNS FOR WORSHIP
GATHERING

Oh, love, how deep   LBW 88
When Jesus came to Jordan   WOV 647

HYMN OF THE DAY

When Christ's appearing was made known   LBW 85

ALTERNATE HYMN OF THE DAY

To Jordan came the Christ, our Lord   LBW 79
Wash, O God, our sons and daughters   WOV 697, TFF 112

COMMUNION

Welcome table   TFF 263, RWSB
Spirit of God, descend upon my heart   LBW 486

SENDING

Let all things now living   LBW 557
Go, my children, with my blessing   WOV 721
Baptized and set free   W&P 14

ADDITIONAL HYMNS AND SONGS

Healing river   RWSB
I'm going on a journey   TFF 115, RWSB
Christ, when for us you were baptized   H82 121
When Jesus comes to be baptized   VU 100

MUSIC FOR THE DAY
PSALMODY

Black, George. "Worship the Lord in the Beauty of Holiness" in SP.
Haas, David. "The Lord Will Bless All People" in PCY, vol. 8.
Hobby, Robert A. PW, Cycle C.
Marshall, Jane. *Psalms Together*, vol. 2. CG CGC-21.
Psalms for the Cantor, vol. III. WLP 2504.

91

CHORAL

Cleobury, Stephen. "Joys Seven" in *100 Carols for Choirs*. SATB, org. OXF 3532271.

Helman, Michael. "Christ, When for Us You Were Baptized." SAB, kybd. AFP 800674057.

Hogan, Moses. "I'm Gonna' Sing 'Til the Spirit Moves In My Heart." SATB, solo. HAL 08740284.

Jennings, Kenneth. "Spirit of God, Descend Upon My Heart." SATB. AFP 6000098332. OP.

Vaughan Williams, Ralph. "The Blessed Son of God" in *Two Chorals from Hodie*. SATB. OXF 43.929.

CHILDREN'S CHOIR

Helman, Michael. "Jesus, We Want to Meet." U, hb, perc. AFP 0800655885.

Nelson, Ronald A. "Gather Together!" U/2 pt, kybd, opt cong, fl, vc. MSM 50-9450.

KEYBOARD/INSTRUMENTAL

Barr, John. "On the Wings of a Dove" (Veni Creator) in *Church Windows*. Org. HWG GBM0105.

Burkhardt, Michael. "Hail to the Lord's Anointed" in *Five Christmas Hymn Improvisations*. Org. MSM 10-111.

Neswick, Bruce. *Partita on Winchester New* (On Jordan's Banks the Baptist's Cry). Org. AFP 0800674995.

Sedio, Mark. "Wo Gott zum Haus" in *Augsburg Organ Library: Epiphany*. Org. AFP 0800659341.

Young, Jeremy. "O Come Divine Messiah" in *Gathering Music for Advent*. Kybd, inst. AFP 0800656598.

HANDBELL

Matheny, Gary. "Puer nobis." 3 oct. AMSI HB3.

Sherman, Arnold B. "In the Beauty of Holiness." 3-6 oct. RR HB0038.

Stephenson, Valerie. "Waters in the Wilderness." 4-5 oct. Gentry JG0707.

PRAISE ENSEMBLE

Barnett, John. "Holy and Anointed One" in *Best of the Best*. FEL 1891062018.

Hanson, Handt. "Waterlife" in *Spirit Calls . . . Rejoice*. SATB. CCF 0933173393 (pew ed); CCF 0933173385 (acc ed).

Haugen, Marty. "He Came Down." SATB, pno, gtr. GIA G-3808.

Makeever, Ray, arr. Helgen. "Brighter Than the Sun." SATB, pno. AFP 0800659155.

92

Tuesday, January 13

GEORGE FOX, RENEWER OF SOCIETY, 1691

Fox severed his ties among family and friends in search of enlightenment. He found no comfort in the traditional church, and he became an itinerant preacher. His preaching emphasized the abiding inward light given by God to believers as the real source of comfort and authority. His preaching led to the establishment of preaching bands of women and men known as the "Publishers of the Truth." In time, these preachers established local communities that came to be known as the Society of Friends, or Quakers. During visits to the Caribbean and North America, Fox witnessed the evil of the slave trade, and he founded the abolitionist movement in England.

Quakers are known for the long period of silence in their meetings. Consider growing into the practice of silence in worship. Be mindful of the ways that silence breaks the hectic pace of life and leads us to attend to the wisdom of God in spoken word and through service to others.

Wednesday, January 14

EIVIND JOSEF BERGGRAV, BISHOP OF OSLO, 1959

In 1937, Berggrav was elected bishop of Oslo and primate of Norway. In 1940, he was asked to negotiate with the Nazi regime in order to ascertain its intentions regarding the social and religious life of the Norwegian people. Rejecting any compromise with the occupation forces, he left the negotiations and demanded that the Nazis recognize the rights of the Jews and the autonomy of the church. Deprived of his episcopal title in 1943, he was placed under arrest, only to escape and remain in hiding in Oslo until the end of the war.

During the season of Epiphany, the life of Berggrav is another witness to the light of Christ. His life raises questions for believers today about the readiness to risk title, power, and prestige to speak for victims of injustice and seek truth in the midst of evils that face us in the world.

Thursday, January 15

MARTIN LUTHER KING JR.,
RENEWER OF SOCIETY, MARTYR, 1968

Martin Luther King Jr. is remembered as an American prophet of justice among races and nations, a Christian whose faith undergirded his advocacy of vigorous yet nonviolent action for racial equality. A pastor of churches in Montgomery, Alabama, and Atlanta, Georgia, his witness was taken to the streets in such other places as Birmingham, Alabama, where he was arrested and jailed while protesting against segregation. He preached nonviolence and demanded that love be returned for hate. Awarded the Nobel Peace Prize in 1964, he was killed by an assassin on April 4, 1968.

Congregations may choose to remember King by singing "We shall overcome" (TFF 213) or "Holy God, you raise up prophets" (TFF 299).

Saturday, January 17

ANTONY OF EGYPT, RENEWER OF THE CHURCH, C. 356

Antony was born in Qemen-al-Arous, Upper Egypt, and was one of the earliest Egyptian desert fathers. Born to Christian parents from whom he inherited a large estate, he took personally Jesus' message to sell all that you have, give to the poor, and follow Christ. After making arrangements to provide for the care of his sister, he gave away his inheritance and became a hermit. Later, he became the head of a group of monks that lived in a cluster of huts and devoted themselves to communal prayer, worship, and manual labor under Antony's direction. The money they earned from their work was distributed as alms. Antony and his monks also preached and counseled those who sought them out.

Antony and the desert fathers serve as a reminder that certain times and circumstances call Christians to stand apart from the surrounding culture and renounce the world in service to Christ.

93

January 18, 2004

The Confession of St. Peter

INTRODUCTION

On the rock of Peter's confession of faith, said Jesus, he would build his church. That apostle's simple yet world-shaking proclamation is the basis for all Christian unity. No matter what our differences (and we pray that they might diminish), we proclaim that Jesus is "the Messiah, the Son of the living God."

PRAYER OF THE DAY

Almighty God, you inspired Simon Peter to confess Jesus as the Messiah and Son of the living God. Keep your Church firm on the rock of this faith, that in unity and peace it may proclaim one truth and follow one Lord, your Son, our Savior Jesus Christ, who lives and reigns with you and the Holy Spirit, one God, now and forever.

VERSE

Alleluia. You will be my witnesses in Jerusalem, in all

Judea and Samaria, and to the ends of the earth. Alleluia. (Acts 1:8)

READINGS

Acts 4:8-13

Peter, though an uneducated fisherman, is given the gift of the Spirit enabling him to proclaim to the Jewish leaders that the crucified Jesus has become the risen Savior.

Psalm 18:1-7, 17-20 (Psalm 18:1-6, 16-19 NRSV)

My God, my rock, you are worthy of praise. (Ps. 18:2)

1 Corinthians 10:1-5

In this part of the letter, Paul is establishing a comparison between the events following the exodus from Egypt and the Christian church. Passing through the sea equates to baptism, manna and water from the rock to the eucharist. Jesus, then, is the new Moses.

Matthew 16:13-19

Jesus had been teaching, healing, working miracles, and generating opposition. But did his closest followers understand who he was? Peter, under the guidance of the Spirit, spoke his great confession of faith, one that continues to define our understanding of Christ.

COLOR   White

THE PRAYERS

Encouraged by the radiant light of God revealed to us in Jesus Christ, let us pray with boldness and confidence.
A BRIEF SILENCE.

For the church of Christ in all its denominations, that all may boldly confess Jesus as Messiah and Lord and find in that confession the cornerstone for increased unity, let us pray to the Lord:
Hear us, O God, and show us your glory.
For all who serve the church as leaders, that their confession may be true and their leadership compassionate, let us pray to the Lord:
Hear us, O God, and show us your glory.
For nations that are torn by religious wars and conflicts, that a mutual respect may be established, trust strengthened, and peace regained, let us pray to the Lord:
Hear us, O God, and show us your glory.
For all who suffer brokenness of spirit, mind, or body (*especially*), that they may be lifted up by the hands of gifted caregivers and returned to health, let us pray to the Lord:
Hear us, O God, and show us your glory.
For this congregation, that filled with the Spirit of boldness and power, we will be driven to proclaim Christ crucified and raised from the dead, bringing new life to both friend and stranger, let us pray to the Lord:
Hear us, O God, and show us your glory.
HERE OTHER INTERCESSIONS MAY BE OFFERED.

That we may imitate the strong confession and sacrifice of Peter and all those who have borne the name of Jesus to the world, and may be united with them at the day of resurrection, let us pray to the Lord:
Hear us, O God, and show us your glory.
Into your hands, great God of heaven, we lay our prayers, trusting in your mercy through the one who showed us your face, Jesus Christ, our Lord.
Amen

94

IMAGES FOR PREACHING

Given the disciples' frequent lack of understanding, Jesus must have crossed his fingers when he asked it: "Who do people say, who do you say, that I am?" How he must have rejoiced that finally someone got it right. Peter answered the Lord's "Who am I?" question with the confession, "You are the Messiah, the Son of the living God!" "About time!" Jesus might have thought. At last, one of them had got it right! Who he was. Is! "From that time on, Jesus began to show his disciples that he must go to Jerusalem and undergo great suffering . . . and be killed, and on the third day be raised" (Matt. 16:21). And from that time on whoever confessed him would not, will not, perish but have everlasting life.

From our vantage point all these centuries later, we would echo Peter's confession. Take care, though—like the apostle, we can quickly slip from faith to foolishness, to failure. When Jesus began to tell them how God would make our forgiveness possible—by the Son's suffering and death—Peter said, "God forbid it, Lord! This must never happen to you!" "You are Peter," Jesus might well have repeated, but changed the meaning. "That means stumbling block!" He adds for us all, "To be a follower you must take up your cross. And that means a cross like mine. Not just your average pain and woe, not just your arthritis or even your loneliness and sorrow, but like my cross—doing the will of the Father, mine, yours."

Years later Peter and John were arrested. And Peter, this time unafraid, produced a clear second confession, read in today's first reading. "The healing? Jesus did it. The crucifixion? You did it. The resurrection? God did it. Salvation? God will do it. The church? God builds it. We have the keys. By no other name, only the name of Jesus, must we be saved."

WORSHIP MATTERS

Peter is remembered today for his insight into Jesus' identity. He names Jesus as the Christ, "the Messiah, the Son of the living God." One of the earliest creedal statements emerging from the ancient church is "Jesus Christ is Lord." We celebrate Peter's bold confession, and mirror that in our assembly's profession of the creed.

At baptismal celebrations, the candidates and the assembly are invited to name God-in-Three by reciting the creed. During these times, the recitation of the Apostles'

Creed is preceded by three questions: "Do you believe in God the Father?" "Do you believe in Jesus Christ, the Son of God?" "Do you believe in God the Holy Spirit?"

As we remember Peter's response to Jesus' question, we might recite the creed preceded by the three questions, that, together with Peter and others who have confessed Jesus as Lord, we might be numbered among the blessed.

LET THE CHILDREN COME

After Peter makes his confession, Jesus calls this faith the rock upon which the church will be built. Have blank paper available for children to make cards for another congregation of another denomination in the community. The cards should be pictures or words that express how thankful we are to have one another as sisters and brothers in Christ. There may be differences in how we interpret certain things but the truth is that we all believe Jesus is the Messiah, the Son of the living God. We are one in Christ. Arrange to have the cards delivered in the coming week.

HYMNS FOR WORSHIP

GATHERING

Built on a rock   LBW 365
Each morning brings us   WOV 800

HYMN OF THE DAY

Christ is made the sure foundation   WOV 747, LBW 367

ALTERNATE HYMN OF THE DAY

Built on a rock   LBW 365
O God of light   LBW 237

COMMUNION

Grains of wheat   WOV 708
Blest be the tie that binds   LBW 370

SENDING

Jesus shall reign   LBW 530
Praise to you, O God of mercy   WOV 790

ADDITIONAL HYMNS AND SONGS

The church song   W&P 135

In Christ there is no east or west   TFF 214
We are all one in Christ   LS 130, LLC 470, TFF 221

MUSIC FOR THE DAY
PSALMODY

Guilmont, Michel. "Psalm 18: I Love You, Lord, My Strength" in RS.
Pavlechko, Thomas. PW , Cycle C.
"Psalm 17 (18)" in *The Grail Gelineau Psalter*. GIA G-1703.
How I love you, LORD my God   PsH 18
Thee will I love, my strength   LBW 502

CHORAL

Beck, John Ness. "Upon This Rock." SATB, org, opt brass. HAL 11467.
Ellingboe, Bradley. "You Are Peter!" SATB. MF 2109.
Schutte, David L., arr. Ovid Young. "Here I Am, Lord." SATB, pno. AFP 0800656059.
Wells, Dana F. "The Lord Is My Rock" in *Four Modern Anthems*. SATB, pno. ABI APM-619.

CHILDREN'S CHOIR

Lord, Suzanne. "Faith That's Sure." U, kybd. CG CGA695 and LS.
Sleeth, Natalie. "Everywhere I Go." U/2 pt, kybd. CG CGA171.

KEYBOARD/INSTRUMENTAL

Carlson, J. Bert. "Christe sanctorum" in *Augsburg Organ Library: Epiphany*. Org. AFP 0800659341.
Johnson, David N. "Deus tuorum militum" in *Hymn Settings for Organ*. Org. AFP 0800674987.
Mulet, Henri. "Tu es Petra." (Thou Art the Rock) Org. LED AL 21309.
Rodriguez, Penny. "What Can I Give Him?" in *Twelve Piano Solos for the Christmas Season*. Pno. BEC PC12.

HANDBELL

Helman, Michael. "Built on a Rock." 3-5 oct. ALF 19006.
Page, Anna Laura. "Foundation." 3-5 oct. ALF 20205.

PRAISE ENSEMBLE

Baloche, Rita. "Rock of Ages" in *Best of the Best*. FEL 1891062018.
Beaker. "Step by Step" in W&P.
DeShazo, Lynn. "Worthy of Praises." 3 pt trbl. *Sing for Joy Songbook Hosanna!* HOS 21377.

95

January 18, 2004

Second Sunday after the Epiphany

INTRODUCTION

Scenes from familiar life and landscapes of disappointment become the setting where God intends to perform miracles. A wedding is about to happen between God and people, joining the predictable with the extraordinary. And the light of Jesus' glory begins to shine from within his actions. Today is the beginning of the week of prayer for Christian unity.

PRAYER OF THE DAY

Lord God, you showed your glory and led many to faith by the works of your Son. As he brought gladness and healing to his people, grant us these same gifts and lead us also to perfect faith in him, Jesus Christ our Lord.

VERSE

Alleluia. The LORD said to me: You are my servant in whom I will be glorified. Alleluia. (Isa. 49:3)

READINGS

Isaiah 62:1-5

The people's return to their homeland after the exile was not the glorious event announced earlier by the prophet. Nevertheless, the prophet declares hope. Jerusalem receives a new name as it becomes God's bride; the people are called to the celebration.

Psalm 36:5-10

We feast on the abundance of your house, O Lord. (Ps. 36:8)

1 Corinthians 12:1-11

The Corinthian congregation experienced division as various factions each claimed to have superior spiritual gifts. Paul invites this fractured community to discover a deeper unity from the Spirit who binds us together.

John 2:1-11

John's gospel describes Jesus' first miracle as an epiphany, a "sign" that reveals God's presence and power in and through Jesus.

COLOR   Green

THE PRAYERS

Encouraged by the radiant light of God revealed to us in Jesus Christ, let us pray with boldness and confidence.
A BRIEF SILENCE.

For the body of Christ, that the gifts of all God's people may be joined in the unity that is Christ's gift, let us pray to the Lord:

Hear us, O God, and show us your glory.

For all who enjoy this life's pleasures, that we may also taste of the wine offered by Christ and know the incomparable riches of heaven, let us pray to the Lord:

Hear us, O God, and show us your glory.

For the world scarred by warfare and plunder, that all people may work to preserve the Creator's gifts, and that by God's power the land shall no more be called desolate, let us pray to the Lord:

Hear us, O God, and show us your glory.

For all who call upon the Lord for healing and health *(especially)*, that they may be filled with hope and restored to wholeness through the work of caregivers and the healing hand of God, let us pray to the Lord:

Hear us, O God, and show us your glory.

For this congregation as it gathers around word and sacraments, that as we have been invited as guests to the great wedding feast of Christ, we may invite others into our midst with joy and thanksgiving, let us pray to the Lord:

Hear us, O God, and show us your glory.

HERE OTHER INTERCESSIONS MAY BE OFFERED.

In gratitude for the saints of all times and places who have lived and died in the faith *(especially)*, that we may be inspired by their faithfulness and join them at the great feast that has no end, let us pray to the Lord:

Hear us, O God, and show us your glory.

Into your hands, great God of heaven, we lay our prayers, trusting in your mercy through the one who showed us your face, Jesus Christ, our Lord.

Amen

IMAGES FOR PREACHING

Now Jesus gets into the act. "Jesus did this"—the changing of the water into wine—"and revealed his glory." Think about that glory. Up to this point in Jesus' life, it could have been seen only with the eyes of faith. The shepherds were notified by angels reflecting "the glory of the Lord," but probably the best they got from Jesus was a baby smile. The magi "knelt down and paid him homage"—but they and their gifts probably outshone in glory this newborn king of the Jews. The Spirit voiced Jesus' glory after his baptism. Now, at last, Jesus himself shows a bit of glory. The head waiter recognized that the wine was the finest. The servants who had drawn the water knew where it came from. The word must certainly have spread quickly—"Jesus did this!" It was the first of his signs. He revealed his glory, a bit of it, "and his disciples believed in him."

This wine sign seems almost just "tossed off." The head waiter didn't know that anything special had occurred, but "the servants who had drawn the water knew." They were just servants, and like us, they probably didn't think they ranked high in the "varieties of gifts" mentioned in today's second reading. Yet they were able to discern that Jesus had done something miraculous, and passed that message on to the head waiter. Just so, when we say in words or acts "Jesus is Lord," the Spirit is speaking, and when we and the Spirit reveal a bit of his glory, disciples believe in him. To each of us has been given some "manifestation of the Spirit for the common good" (1 Cor. 12:7). In that Spirit, heed the words Mary said to the servants, "Do whatever he tells you." For in that path lies glory—"the glory as of a father's only son, full of grace and truth" (John 1:14).

WORSHIP MATTERS

In our regular gatherings around word and sacrament, many ingredients come together to give a sense of the whole. Each week, we are fed and nourished with God's grace. Each week, we are washed over with the abundance of God's mercy. Each week, we discover in Jesus the newness of God breaking in.

As the wine steward in John's gospel was impressed by the taste of the water now become wine, we might, upon reflection, marvel at all that we receive as a worshiping community. We share the peace of Christ with our neighbor. We sing a hymn that echoes in our head as we walk around the neighborhood. We are thrilled to process to the table to receive Christ's body and blood in bread and wine. We, like the stone jars at the wedding in Cana, are filled to the brim as these glories are revealed.

LET THE CHILDREN COME

At the wedding in Cana the people were in need of wine. They came to Jesus and Jesus gave them what they needed. We too are in need—of healing, forgiveness, God's grace, mercy, and love. When we gather in the name of Jesus Christ for worship, God promises us that we will receive all that we need. God is generous. Encourage the children to look for signs of God's generosity as they worship today—at the communion table, the baptismal font, the pulpit, and at the cross.

HYMNS FOR WORSHIP

GATHERING

Songs of thankfulness and praise   LBW 90
God, whose giving knows no ending   LBW 408
We are called   W&P 147, RWSB

HYMN OF THE DAY

Soul, adorn yourself with gladness   LBW 224, RWSB

ALTERNATE HYMN OF THE DAY

Jesus, come! for we invite you   WOV 648
What feast of love   WOV 701

COMMUNION

Now the silence   LBW 205
Now the feast and celebration   WOV 789

SENDING

Lord of glory, you have bought us   LBW 424
We all are one in mission   WOV 755

ADDITIONAL HYMNS AND SONGS

All praise to you, O Lord   HFW
Just as Jesus told us   DH 29
All are welcome   RWSB
Come, join in Cana's feast   HS98 817

MUSIC FOR THE DAY

PSALMODY

"Psalm 35 (36)" in *The Grail Gelineau Psalter*. GIA G-1703.

Black, George. "Your Steadfast Love, O Lord" in SP.

Haas, David. "The Fountain of All Life" in PCY, vol. 9.

Hopson, Hal H. *Psalm Refrains and Tones*. HOP 425.

Isele, David Clark. TP.

Kallman, Daniel. PW , Cycle C.

CHORAL

Byrd, William. "Surge illuminare." NOV TM 6.

Edwards, Paul. "Thy Mercy O Lord Reacheth unto the Heavens."
    SATB, org. RSCM A.404.

Ellingboe, Bradley. "Soul Adorn Yourself with Gladness." SATB.
    AFP 0800658477.

Handel, G.F. "All My Spirit Longs to Savor" in *Chantry Choirbook*.
    SATB, org. AFP 0800657772.

Mozart, W.A. "Laudate Dominum." SATB, S solo, org.
    GSCH 51165.

CHILDREN'S CHOIR

LeDoux, Joanne Brown. "Let the Whole Creation Cry Alleluia!" U/2
    pt, kybd. Triune Music K128.

Marshall, Jane. "Gifts." (1 Cor. 12:4-6) U/2 pt, kybd. CG CGA803.

KEYBOARD/INSTRUMENTAL

Linker, Janet. "Dix" in *Three Epiphany Pieces*. Org. AFP 0800658221.

Wold, Wayne L. "Houston" in *Child of the Light*. Org.
    AFP 0800657993.

Wold, Wayne L. "Soul, Adorn Yourself with Gladness" (Schmücke
    dich) in *Songs of Thankfulness and Praise, Set I*. Org. MSM 10-711.

HANDBELL

Geisler, Herb. "Now the Silence." 3-5 oct. CPH 97-6732.

Sherman, Arnold B. "Bind Us Together." 3-5 oct. AG 2185.

PRAISE ENSEMBLE

Sedio, Mark. "Take My Life That I May Be." SATB, pno, fl, opt gtr.
    AFP 0800658299.

Willard, Kelly and Paul Baloche. "Most Holy One" in *Praise Hymns
    and Choruses, 4th ed.* MAR 3010130368.

Zschech, Darlene. "The Potter's Hand" in *Best of the Best*.
    FEL 1891062018.

Sunday, January 18

WEEK OF PRAYER FOR CHRISTIAN UNITY BEGINS
THE CONFESSION OF ST. PETER

See pages 93–95.

Monday, January 19

HENRY, BISHOP OF UPPSALA,
MISSIONARY TO FINLAND, MARTYR, 1156

Henry, an Englishman, became bishop of Uppsala, Sweden, in 1152 and is regarded as the patron of Finland. He traveled to Finland with the king of Sweden on a mission trip and remained there to organize the church. He was murdered in Finland by a man whom he had rebuked and who was disciplined by the church. Henry's burial place became a center of pilgrimage. His popularity as a saint is strong in both Sweden and Finland.

Today is an appropriate day to celebrate the Finnish presence in the Lutheran church. Consider singing "Lost in the night" (LBW 394), which uses a Finnish folk tune. During Epiphany we celebrate the light of Christ revealed to the nations, and martyrs such as Henry continue to reveal that light through their witness to faith.

January 25, 2004

The Conversion of St. Paul

INTRODUCTION

Within the season of Epiphany, a time of light and mission emphases, we lift up today the moment when Saul was blinded by the light of Christ and directed onto the path that would make him Paul, the great apostle to the Gentiles. Christ has promised to give us, like Paul, words and a wisdom to testify to him. Fittingly, this festival marks the conclusion of the week of prayer for Christian unity that was begun with Peter's confession.

PRAYER OF THE DAY

Lord God, through the preaching of your apostle Paul, you established one Church from among the nations. As we celebrate his conversion, we pray that we may follow his example and be witnesses to the truth in your Son, Jesus Christ our Lord, who lives and reigns with you and the Holy Spirit, one God, now and forever.

VERSE

Alleluia. This Jesus God raised up, and of that all of us are witnesses. Alleluia. (Acts 2:32)

READINGS

Acts 9:1-22

Three times the book of Acts describes Paul's conversion. This telling, coming between Philip with the Ethiopian and Cornelius's conversion, sets the stage for extending the gospel to the Gentiles.

Psalm 67

Let all the peoples praise you, O God. (Ps. 67:3)

Galatians 1:11-24

Here Paul himself tells of the prologue to his becoming the great apostle to the Gentiles. He admits his former blindness, seeing the contrast as an avenue for the greater glory of God.

Luke 21:10-19

The third gospel contains several short apocalyptic passages, which helped to encourage readers who, in the decades after the resurrection, were experiencing persecution for their faith. Paul had found himself on both sides of such persecution.

COLOR   White

THE PRAYERS

Encouraged by the radiant light of God revealed to us in Jesus Christ, let us pray with boldness and confidence.

A BRIEF SILENCE.

For all who call upon Christ, that divisions among the faithful may be overcome and that the unity that comes from the Spirit may be a sign of reconciliation and peace to the world, let us pray to the Lord:

Hear us, O God, and show us your glory.

For the nations of the world, that the ears and eyes of all people be fixed on you so that your way and your saving power may be known throughout the world, let us pray to the Lord:

Hear us, O God, and show us your glory.

For all people who are looked down upon as of lesser worth, lower class, or unclean, that they may be lifted up by God and in the eyes of those around them, let us pray to the Lord:

Hear us, O God, and show us your glory.

For those who are close to death and all the sick *(especially)*, that as God's face shines upon them they may receive hope, healing, and the mercies rendered by God's people, let us pray to the Lord:

Hear us, O God, and show us your glory.

For the people of this congregation, that as we are strengthened by the presence of Christ we will find courage to face whatever may come when we are faithful to God's gracious call, let us pray to the Lord:

Hear us, O God, and show us your glory.

HERE OTHER INTERCESSIONS MAY BE OFFERED.

Remembering Paul and all the faithful witnesses who suffered to spread God's word, that we also may run the race until the day we will stand together around the heavenly throne, let us pray to the Lord:

Hear us, O God, and show us your glory.

Into your hands, great God of heaven, we lay our prayers, trusting in your mercy through the one who showed us your face, Jesus Christ, our Lord.

Amen

IMAGES FOR PREACHING

God doesn't give everyone a Damascus vision and directive. But we all need to seek God's will for us, even if the answer is not always clear. Probably throughout his life Saul thought he was doing exactly what God wanted him to do. As a youth he tried to be the best of the Chosen, "far more zealous for the traditions of my ancestors" (Gal. 1:14). Was God pleased with him then?

Afterwards, he became Saul the persecutor, "breathing threats and murder against the disciples of the Lord" (Acts 9:1), trying to destroy those who followed the Risen One—and all the time Saul thought he was doing exactly what God wanted him to do. Could God have been pleased with him then?

Finally it was as if God had had enough. "Saul, Saul!" the voice of Jesus came to him, "Why do you persecute me?" God had set Paul apart for special service before he was born. "He is an instrument," Ananias was told, "whom I have chosen to bring my name before Gentiles and kings and before the people of Israel" (Acts 9:15). God finally made Paul see the light. As he wrote to the Galatians, "God . . . was pleased to reveal his Son to me, so that I might proclaim him among the Gentiles" (Gal. 1:15-16). God was surely pleased with him then!

Can God say of you, "In you I am well pleased"? What if you are set apart and are not doing your part? We can hardly all demand a personal epiphany visit. The epiphany of the Son of God was for all the world, and continues for us in our world and time in sacrament and scripture.

This may be the first and best thing that we can do—join in the prayer, "Lord, what will you have me do?"

WORSHIP MATTERS

During Paul's conversion process and in his subsequent ministry he worked to understand and clarify faith in Christ with others. In the book of Acts he encounters the disciple Ananias, who is sent to help Saul (later named Paul) regain his sight. Paul then spends time with the other followers of Jesus in Damascus. In the letter to the Galatians, Paul mentions his conference with the early church leaders in Jerusalem, including Cephas (also known as Peter) and James, the brother of Jesus. Today is the conclusion of the week of prayer for Christian unity. We might ask, how is the gospel of Jesus Christ being shared by other Christian partner churches? What beliefs and practices do we have in common? Where can there be ongoing conversation on issues that divide us? What may we celebrate in worship that demonstrates our unity in Christ?

LET THE CHILDREN COME

Today's reading from Acts can easily be brought to life through a dramatic reading. Assign a confirmation-aged youth to each role: narrator, Saul, Jesus, and Ananias. If you want to involve a variety of ages and make it even more engaging for children, recruit people to prepare a drama for worship using the lesson as their script.

HYMNS FOR WORSHIP
GATHERING

Holy God, we praise your name   LBW 535
Shall we gather at the river   WOV 690

HYMN OF THE DAY

Shout for joy loud and long   WOV 793

ALTERNATE HYMN OF THE DAY

O Spirit of the living God   LBW 388
(May be sung to O Jesu Christe, wahres Licht, LBW 380)
By all your saints in warfare   LBW 177 (I, II, 3)

COMMUNION

We who once were dead   LBW 207
One bread, one body   WOV 710

SENDING

Lord, keep us steadfast in your word   LBW 230
Glory to God, we give you thanks   WOV 787
I shall not be moved   TFF 147

ADDITIONAL HYMNS AND SONGS

We all are one in mission   WOV 755
Heaven is singing for joy / El cielo canta   RWSB
Rise, O Sun of righteousness   RWSB
Oh, let the Son of God enfold you   TFF 105

MUSIC FOR THE DAY
PSALMODY

Batastini, Robert J. "Psalm 67: May God Bless Us in His Mercy" in RS.

Brown, Teresa. "O God Be Gracious" in PS I.

Burns, James M. *Psalms for the Cantor,* vol. III. WLP 2504.

Gieseke, Thomas. "May the People Praise You, O God." U.
CPH 98-2929.

Makeever, Ray. "Let All the People Praise" in DH.

Pavlechko, Thomas. PW , Cycle C.

May God bestow on us his grace   LBW 335

CHORAL

Hein, David. "Lord I Want to Be a Christian." SATB. KJO 8828.

Halloran, Jack. "Witness." SSAATTBB. HAL JG2010.

Martinson, Joel. "By All Your Saints." 2 pt mxd, org.
AFP 080065160X.

Mueller, Carl F. "Grace Be to You and Peace." SATB, kybd.
CFI CM-6715.

White, David Ashley. "O Jesus, I Have Promised." SATB, kybd.
MSM 50-9055.

CHILDREN'S CHOIR

Bedford, Michael. "Let All the Peoples Praise You, O God." 2 pt, fl,
pno. CG CG A933.

Bouman, Paul. "God Be Merciful." (Ps. 67) 2 pt, kybd.
MSM 50-7039.

Marshall, Jane. "Psalm 67" in *Psalms Together II.* U, kybd. CG CGC21.

KEYBOARD/INSTRUMENTAL

Hassell, Michael. "This Little Light of Mine" in *Jazz Sunday Morning.*
Pno. AFP 0800655400.

Johnson, David N. "Salzburg" in *Hymn Settings for Organ.* Org.
AFP 0800674987.

Kerr, J. Wayne. "On This Day Earth Shall Ring/Shout for Joy" in *Sing
We Now of Christmas.* Org. AFP 0800675029.

Sedio, Mark. "O Zion, Haste" in *Augsburg Organ Library: Epiphany.* Org.
AFP 0800659341.

HANDBELL

Behnke, John A. "I Want to Walk as a Child of the Light." 3-5 oct.
CPH 97-6611.

Tucker, Sondra K. "I Want to Walk as a Child of the Light." 3-5 oct.
AFP 0800658868.

PRAISE ENSEMBLE

Espinosa, Eddie. "Change My Heart, O God" in W&P.

Founds, Rick. "Jesus, Draw Me Close" in *Best of the Best.* FEL
1891062018.

Park, Andy. "In the Secret" in *More Songs for Praise and Worship.* SATB.
WRD 3010387016 (vocal ed); WRD 3010186363 (pno,
vcs, perc).

101

January 25, 2004

Third Sunday after the Epiphany

INTRODUCTION

Preaching is powerful, and the power is in the word of God. That word can convict us of sin and raise us to new life. That word can heal divisions in Christ's body and help us appreciate the gifts of others. And that Word has become flesh in Jesus of Nazareth. As we conclude the week of prayer for Christian unity, we join with other Christians to pray that we can come together in Christ.

PRAYER OF THE DAY

Almighty God, you sent your Son to proclaim your kingdom and to teach with authority. Anoint us with the power of your Spirit, that we, too, may bring good news to the afflicted, bind up the brokenhearted, and proclaim liberty to the captive; through your Son, Jesus Christ our Lord.

VERSE

Alleluia. Jesus went throughout Galilee, teaching, proclaiming the good news, and curing every disease. Alleluia. (Matt. 4:23)

READINGS

Nehemiah 8:1-3, 5-6, 8-10

The exiles have returned. Under Nehemiah they have rebuilt the city of Jerusalem and its walls. Now the people ask Ezra, the priest, to read the law of Moses to them in the public square. When they hear it they weep for their sins, for the long years in exile, and for the joy of the Lord that was their strength.

Psalm 19

The law of the LORD revives the soul. (Ps. 19:7)

1 Corinthians 12:12-31a

Paul writes to the divided congregation in Corinth to tell them what it means for the church to be the one body of Christ.

Luke 4:14-21

Near the beginning of Jesus' public ministry, he visits his hometown of Nazareth. In the words of Isaiah, he clearly states his purpose and mission.

COLOR   Green

THE PRAYERS

Encouraged by the radiant light of God revealed to us in Jesus Christ, let us pray with boldness and confidence.
A BRIEF SILENCE.

For all people who call upon the name of Christ, that we may be renewed and united in our call to bring good news to the hungry, captive, and oppressed people of the world, let us pray to the Lord:
Hear us, O God, and show us your glory.

For the world pulled apart by destructive powers and people, that all creation may be knit together and healed by the power of the word of God and the witness of God's people, let us pray to the Lord:
Hear us, O God, and show us your glory.

For those who live with disabilities and who struggle with barriers that most of us are not aware of, that they may witness the Lord's favor in their lives and may be given honor within the body of Christ, let us pray to the Lord:
Hear us, O God, and show us your glory.

For those who are ill, who are weak, who face surgery *(especially)*, that they may be filled with patience, strength and courage from the hand of God, and may be restored to health, let us pray to the Lord:
Hear us, O God, and show us your glory.

For the people of this congregation, that all may discover the generosity of God and respond eagerly to the call to be members of Christ's body in the world, let us pray to the Lord:
Hear us, O God, and show us your glory.

HERE OTHER INTERCESSIONS MAY BE OFFERED.

In thanksgiving for the members of the body of Christ who have played their part and now rest from their labors, that we may honor their lives with our own and join them in the age to come, let us pray to the Lord:
Hear us, O God, and show us your glory.

Into your hands, great God of heaven, we lay our prayers, trusting in your mercy through the one who showed us your face, Jesus Christ, our Lord.
Amen

102

IMAGES FOR PREACHING

The scripture reveals the Lord. Out of the scriptures comes his epiphany. Call it the *Word* epiphany. Jesus' scripture reading in the synagogue set the stage. When Jesus said, "This is about me!" then the epiphany—the great *Aha!*—began. It took the next years before those who saw him could know the whole salvation story. Now we search the scriptures to learn and know, for "it is they that testify on my behalf" (John 5:39).

The lesson from Nehemiah suggests another epiphany, an epiphany we experience. For the exiles who had returned it was a law of Moses epiphany. For us, Sunday after Sunday, call it the liturgy epiphany.

The assembly, "all who could hear with understanding," gathered, as we do on a Sunday. There are some among us who can't yet understand, some who sleep. But for those who understand, a marvelous thing is happening. In the lesson, Ezra read from scriptures "and the ears of all the people were attentive to the book of the law" (Neh. 8:3). When Ezra opened the book "all the people stood up" as we do today when the gospel is announced. Then "they read from the book, from the law of God, with interpretation." Like a sermon? "They gave the sense, so that the people understood the reading" (v. 8).

Is there a parallel in our services to the way the people reacted? "All the people wept when they heard the words of the law" (v. 9). They shed tears over their captivity and tears of joy at their return to their land. We rejoice at the presence of the Lord where we two or three are gathered together. Ours is a eucharist, a giving of thanks, as our Lord says again, "This is my body given for you" and "This is my blood shed for you and for many." We give thanks, we remember, and we experience epiphany.

WORSHIP MATTERS

Reminiscent of the passage from Isaiah read by Jesus, an African hymn called "Good News" has this refrain: "To bring good news to needy / to make the blind to see / the broken hearts filled again / to set the captives free."

When coming from our daily lives into worship, we open our ears for the good news from God's word. Our pattern is not that different from the Sabbath synagogue worship that Jesus attended. Someone stands up to read in public. People are attentive, because they are yearning to discover God's promises proclaimed for a world in need. The weekly proclamation of scripture is an oral event. Honor the reading by having a substantial book. Honor the word by finding readers who speak clearly and with appropriate inflection. Honor the word by listening with all ears. Acclaim the good news by assenting, "The word of the Lord. Thanks be to God!"

LET THE CHILDREN COME

God's word is good news and everyone needs to hear it! It is a source of strength, healing, and comfort. God's word can be spoken or sung. Invite children to sing the first verse of "Jesus loves me" as a gospel response today. The sermon could include a section about how we respond to God's word with thankfulness and praise for God's amazing love revealed to us in Jesus Christ.

HYMNS FOR WORSHIP
GATHERING
Oh, for a thousand tongues to sing   LBW 559
Oh, sing to the Lord   WOV 795
I will enter his gates   TFF 291

HYMN OF THE DAY
We all are one in mission   WOV 755

ALTERNATE HYMN OF THE DAY
Hail to the Lord's anointed   LBW 87
O Spirit of life   WOV 680

COMMUNION
Lord Jesus Christ, we humbly pray   LBW 225
Word of God, come down on earth   WOV 716

SENDING
Hark, the glad sound!   LBW 35
The Spirit sends us forth to serve   WOV 723

ADDITIONAL HYMNS AND SONGS
Let justice roll like a river   W&P 85, RWSB
Oh sing a song of Bethlehem   RWSB
Jesus has come and brings pleasure eternal   LW 78
What a mighty word God gives   W&P 155

MUSIC FOR THE DAY
PSALMODY

Cox, Joe. "The Heavens Are Telling the Glory of God" in *Psalms for the People of God.* SMP 45/1037 S.

Haas, David. "Lord, You Have the Words" in PCY.

Hruby, Dolores. *Seasonal Psalms for Children with Optional Orff Instruments.* WLP 7102.

Inwood, Paul. "Psalm 19: You, Lord, Have the Message" in STP, vol. 2.

Kallman, Daniel. PW , Cycle C.

"Your Law, O Lord, Is Perfect" in SP.

CHORAL

Bach, J.S. "All Who Believe and are Baptized" in *Bach for All Seasons.* SATB, kybd. AFP 080065854X.

Elgar, Edward. "The Spirit of the Lord Is Upon Me." SATB, org. NOV Chor. 805.

Helgen, John. "Good News." SATB, solo, pno. KJO 8937.

Helgen, John. "We Are God's People." SATB, pno, rec. KJO 8935.

CHILDREN'S CHOIR

Cool, Jayne Southwick. "With the Help of the Spirit of the Lord." (Luke 4:18-19) U/2 pt, kybd. CG CGA508.

Helgen, John. "This Little Light of Mine." U/2 pt, pno. AFP 0800675932.

Tucker, Margaret. "Christ's Own Body." (1 Cor. 12:12-14) U/2 pt, kybd, opt 2 oct hb. CG CGA801.

KEYBOARD/INSTRUMENTAL

Carter, John. "Thy Word" in *Today's Hymns and Songs for Piano.* Kybd. HOP 244.

Cherwien, David. "Kuortane" in *Organ Plus One.* Org, inst. AFP 0800656180.

Fleischer, Heinrich. "O God, Our Help in Ages Past" in *Wedding Music, Part II.* CPH 97-1370.

HANDBELL

Afdahl, Lee J. "Abbot's Leigh." 3-5 oct. AG 2103.

Helman, Michael. "Let Us Talents and Tongues Employ." 2-3 oct, opt perc. AFP 0800659937.

PRAISE ENSEMBLE

Gibbons, Lana. "Renew Me" in *Best of the Best.* FEL 1891062018.

Foley, John. "One Bread, One Body." SATB, kybd, gtr, opt cong. OCP 9494.

Batstone, Bill, John Barbour, and Anne Barbour. "Let the Walls Fall Down" in *Best of the Best.* FEL 1891062018.

104

Sunday, January 25
WEEK OF PRAYER FOR CHRISTIAN UNITY ENDS
THE CONVERSION OF SAINT PAUL
See pages 99–101.

Monday, January 26
TIMOTHY, TITUS, AND SILAS

Following the celebration of the Conversion of Paul, we remember his companions. Today, we remember Timothy, Titus, and Silas. They were missionary coworkers with Paul. Timothy accompanied Paul on his second missionary journey and was commissioned by Paul to go to Ephesus, where he served as bishop and overseer of the church. Titus was a traveling companion of Paul, accompanied him on the trip to the council of Jerusalem, and became the first bishop of Crete. Silas traveled with Paul through Asia Minor and Greece, and was imprisoned with him at Philippi, where they were delivered by an earthquake.

This festival invites the church to remember Christian leaders, bishops, pastors, and teachers—both men and women—who have been influential in the lives of individual members as gospel signs of the light of Epiphany.

Tuesday, January 27
LYDIA, DORCAS, AND PHOEBE

Today we remember three women in the early church who were companions in Paul's ministry. Lydia was Paul's first convert at Philippi in Macedonia. She was a merchant of purple-dyed goods, and because purple dye was extremely expensive, it is likely that Lydia was a woman of some wealth. Lydia and her household were baptized by Paul, and for a time her home was a base for Paul's missionary work. Dorcas is remembered for her charitable works, particularly making clothing for needy widows. Phoebe was a diakonos, a deacon in the church at Cenchreae, near Corinth. Paul praises her as one who, through her service, looked after many people.

Today provides an opportunity for congregations to reflect the ministry of women, ordained and lay, wealthy and poor, who have given of themselves in service to the church and to the ministry of the gospel in their congregations.

February 1, 2004

Fourth Sunday after the Epiphany

INTRODUCTION

An epiphany ought to be a surprise. The prophet Jeremiah is surprised that God would call a youth, but Jeremiah has been in God's sight for a long, long time. Jesus is popular in many places but maybe not at home. Love, which seems so familiar, is really a radical invitation to care for others on their terms. How will love surprise us this day?

PRAYER OF THE DAY

O God, you know that we cannot withstand the dangers which surround us. Strengthen us in body and spirit so that, with your help, we may be able to overcome the weakness that our sin has brought upon us; through Jesus Christ, your Son our Lord.

VERSE

Alleluia. The Spirit of the Lord is upon me, because he has anointed me to bring good news to the poor. Alleluia. (Luke 4:18)

READINGS

Jeremiah 1:4-10

Today's reading relates Jeremiah's call and commission as a prophet in the years before the Babylonian exile. His task was to preach God's word in the midst of the difficult political realities of the time. He was to make God known, not just among the Israelites, but also among the nations.

Psalm 71:1-6

From my mother's womb you have been my strength. (Ps. 71:6)

1 Corinthians 13:1-13

Some at Corinth prided themselves on their spiritual gifts. Paul reminds them that God gives us many gifts through the Holy Spirit, but the most important of these is love, the kind of love that allows us to live and work in cooperation with one another, the kind of love that God showed us particularly in Christ.

Luke 4:21-30

People in Jesus' hometown are initially pleased when he says that God will free the oppressed. Their pleasure turns to rage, however, when he reminds them that prophets often bring God's blessings to those who are regarded as outsiders.

COLOR   Green

THE PRAYERS

Encouraged by the radiant light of God revealed to us in Jesus Christ, let us pray with boldness and confidence.
A BRIEF SILENCE.

For pardon at those times when we refuse to acknowledge Jesus as Lord of our lives, that in forgiveness we may be turned from selfishness and restored to faith, let us pray to the Lord:

Hear us, O God, and show us your glory.

For the leaders of the church, that they embrace the word of God, faithfully proclaim it to all, and humbly guide the people with integrity and vigor, let us pray to the Lord:

Hear us, O God, and show us your glory.

For the world's diverse cultures, that they may celebrate and uphold their unique heritages and build upon all that is good in them, while showing tolerance for other ways of life, let us pray to the Lord:

Hear us, O God, and show us your glory.

For those whose lives are touched by despair, grief, pain, or illness *(especially)*, that God restore them to wholeness and provide them sustaining love through our ministry, let us pray to the Lord:

Hear us, O God, and show us your glory.

For this congregation, that our life and mission may be governed by love for God, love for our neighbor, and love for one another, let us pray to the Lord:

Hear us, O God, and show us your glory.
HERE OTHER INTERCESSIONS MAY BE OFFERED.

In remembrance of all the beloved saints who have lived and died in faith, that we may be instructed by their example and united with them in the love that will not let us go, let us pray to the Lord:

Hear us, O God, and show us your glory.

105

Into your hands, great God of heaven, we lay our prayers, trusting in your mercy through the one who showed us your face, Jesus Christ, our Lord.
Amen

IMAGES FOR PREACHING

Jesus stands in the synagogue in his hometown, reading the scripture. Then he sits down, as was the custom, to interpret—to preach. He is surrounded by kinfolk, neighbors, friends. Surely this is a loving assembly, as when one of our own goes to seminary and returns to preach among us. And at first "all spoke well of him" and were properly impressed at his gracious words.

This reception was less than it seemed. Quibbles arose: "Is not this Joseph's son?" Just a carpenter, a common man. Rumors had returned here of Jesus' healings in Capernaum. Some who knew him thought he should heal himself, others wanted to see the show. There is nothing here reflecting the sort of encouragement God showed to Jeremiah.

Proclamation of the gospel, as Jesus will make clear in parables, is a two-way street. The word must be lovingly proclaimed, and it must be lovingly received. Paul lays out memorably the parameters of love in today's second reading. In fact, it takes little effort to alter Paul's words to fit the hearing assembly: "If one speaks in tongues of mortals and of angels, but does not have love, it will sound like a noisy gong or a clanging cymbal." The original wording, of course, applies to the preacher; the responsibility lies on both parties.

The gospel flourishes in the matrix of love. It has amazing power in itself, but it cannot do its work where it is strangled by an absence of love. Every congregation wants to be a gathering of loving people nourishing all that is good. But we need to be reminded now and then of the hard truth that warm, fuzzy thoughts are not enough. The gospel calls from us loving action—patient, kind, not envious or arrogant—in response to the proclamation.

WORSHIP MATTERS

A Greek word from the early church for the sacraments is *mysteria*, "the holy mysteries." Rituals in our worship, as in our daily lives, invite us to explore their depths, mysterious and wonderful. We may have been taught as children to fold our hands so that we would keep them still. Now, folding hands fosters our openness to being in God's presence. We may have been taught from a young age to shake hands as a gesture of welcome. Now, extending hands to others may give us a sense of Christ's peace as we have been shaped by that weekly Sunday ritual. Little by little, week by week, over time, we will become more of what we are, in faith, hope, and love.

LET THE CHILDREN COME

Even adults don't understand everything that goes on during worship, much less the children. Take time just before the liturgy to invite children to ask a few questions that they have about worship. If you don't know the answer, admit that, but promise to print answers in next week's bulletin. Use this exercise as a teaching tool. We don't have to understand everything we do in worship, but we still worship to give our thanks and praise to God.

HYMNS FOR WORSHIP
GATHERING

Hail to the Lord's anointed   LBW 87
Lord, you give the great commission   WOV 756

HYMN OF THE DAY

O God of light   LBW 237

ALTERNATE HYMN OF THE DAY

He comes to us as one unknown   WOV 768
O Zion, haste   LBW 397

COMMUNION

Take my life, that I may be   LBW 406
I received the living God   WOV 700

SENDING

Let all things now living   LBW 557
Shine, Jesus, shine   WOV 651, TFF 64, W&P 123
Step by step   W&P 132

ADDITIONAL HYMNS AND SONGS

Stand in the congregation   W&P 131, RWSB
Rock of my salvation   W&P 161
Love is never-ending   LS 117, HFW
Sing of the Lord's goodness   RWSB

106

MUSIC FOR THE DAY

PSALMODY

Barrett, James, Hal H. Hopson. TP.

Black, George. "Incline Your Ear to Me" in SP.

Currie, Randolph. "Psalm 71: I Will Sing" in RS.

Haas, David. "I Will Sing" in PCY, vol. 3.

Kallman, Daniel. PW , Cycle C.

CHORAL

Bairstow, Edward. "I Sat Down Under His Shadow." SATB.
OXF 43.002.

Hopp, Roy. "God of Grace and God of Laughter." SATB, kybd.
AFP 0800659570.

Hopson, Hal H. "I Am the Light of Nations." SATB, pno, opt fl,
perc. AFP 080067586X.

McKie, William. "We Wait for Thy Loving Kindness, O God." SATB,
solo, org. OXF 42.081.

Pavlechko, Thomas. "The Greatest Gift." 2 pt, kybd. SEL 420-561.

Titcomb, Everett. "Jesus, Name of Wondrous Love." SATB, org.
WAR 44-669.

CHILDREN'S CHOIR

McRae, Shirley. "Your Trusting Child." (Ps. 71:5) U, kybd, sg, fl, fc.
CG CGA614.

Pethel, Stan. "Give Us Love." (I Cor. 13:4-13) U/2 pt, kybd.
CG CGA728.

KEYBOARD/INSTRUMENTAL

Cherwien, David. "Divinum mysterium" in Gotta Toccata. Org.
AFP 0800658752.

Organ, Anne Krentz. "He Comes to Us" in Come to Us, Creative Spirit.
Pno. AFP 080065904X.

Rinehart, Marilyn. "I Want Jesus to Walk with Me" in Spirituals and
More for Organ. Org. FLA HF521.

Wold, Wayne L. "Suite on Bright and Glorious is the Sky." Org.
AFP 0800659023.

HANDBELL

Burroughs, Bob. "Fanfare on O Zion Haste." 3-5 oct. ALF 18566.

Kinyon, Barbara Baltzer. "O Morning Star, How Fair and Bright."
3 oct. AG 1690.

PRAISE ENSEMBLE

Likens, Jim. "God Knew Your Name" in Best of the Best.
FEL 1891062018.

Walker, Tommy. "He Knows My Name." 3 pt trbl. Never Gonna Stop
Songbook. HOS 18467.

Monday, February 2

THE PRESENTATION OF OUR LORD

Forty days after the birth of Christ we mark the day
Mary and Joseph presented him in the temple in accordance with Jewish law. There in the temple, a prophet
named Anna began to speak of the redemption of Israel
when she saw the young child. Simeon also greeted Mary
and Joseph. He responded to the presence of the consolation of Israel in this child with the words of the
Nunc dimittis. His song described Jesus as a "light for
the nations."

Because of the link between Jesus as the light for the
nations, and because an old reading for this festival contains a line from the prophet Zephaniah, "I will search
Jerusalem with candles," the day is also known as Can-
dlemas, a day when candles are blessed for the coming
year. If no service is planned to celebrate this day in the
congregation, be sure to read the story about the presentation when congregational groups meet and include a setting of the Song of Simeon (such as LBW 339 or 349).

107

Tuesday, February 3

ANSGAR, ARCHBISHOP OF HAMBURG,
MISSIONARY TO DENMARK AND SWEDEN, 865

A traditional emphasis during the weeks of Epiphany
has been the mission of the church. Ansgar was a monk
who led a mission to Denmark and then later to Sweden,
where he built the first church. His work ran into difficulties with the rulers of the day, and he was forced to
withdraw into Germany, where he served as a bishop in
Hamburg. Despite his difficulties in Sweden, he persisted
in his mission work and later helped consecrate Goth-
bert as the first bishop of Sweden. Ansgar also had a
deep love for the poor. He would wash their feet and
serve them food provided by the parish.

Ansgar is particularly honored by Scandinavian
Lutherans. The Church of Sweden honors him as an
apostle. His persistence in mission and his care for the
poor invite congregations to reflect on their own ministry of bearing the light of Christ during the days of
Epiphany.

Thursday, February 5

THE MARTYRS OF JAPAN, 1597

In the sixteenth century, Jesuit missionaries, followed by Franciscans, introduced the Christian faith in Japan. A promising beginning to those missions—there were perhaps as many as 300,000 Christians by the end of the sixteenth century—met complications from competition between the missionary groups, political difficulty between Spain and Portugal, and factions within the government of Japan. Christianity was suppressed. By 1630, Christianity was driven underground.

Today we commemorate the first martyrs of Japan, twenty-six missionaries and converts, who were killed by crucifixion. Two hundred and fifty years later, when Christian missionaries returned to Japan, they found a community of Japanese Christians that had survived underground. The Martyrs of Japan are a somber reminder of the cost of Christianity and discipleship. Their witness invites us to pray for the church's own witness to the gospel and encourages us to trust that the church is sustained in times of persecution.

February 8, 2004

Fifth Sunday after the Epiphany

INTRODUCTION

We are part of God's epiphany. In baptism God calls us. In the eucharist Christ feeds us and sends us to the world—just as God called Isaiah, and just as Jesus sent Simon, James, and John. The good news handed down to us is meant to be passed on to others.

PRAYER OF THE DAY

Almighty God, you sent your only Son as the Word of life for our eyes to see and our ears to hear. Help us to believe with joy what the Scriptures proclaim, through Jesus Christ our Lord.

VERSE

Alleluia. Jesus said: I am the light of the world. Whoever follows me will never walk in darkness but will have the light of life. Alleluia. (John 8:12)

READINGS

Isaiah 6:1-8 [9-13]

Today's reading recounts Isaiah's commission as a prophet in Jerusalem during the second half of the eighth century B.C. Isaiah's intense experiences were part of his credentials to announce God's judgment and warn God's people.

Psalm 138

I will bow down toward your holy temple. (Ps. 138:2)

1 Corinthians 15:1-11

Paul stresses that the proclamation of the resurrection is not a novelty. Along with the story of Jesus' crucifixion and burial, this resurrection witness has shaped the whole church from the time of the apostles to the present. The Christian church is solidly founded upon this good news.

Luke 5:1-11

Near the beginning of Jesus' ministry, his words and signs have powerful and surprising effects: crowds press upon him, a great and unexpected number of fish fill the nets, and a fisherman becomes an apostle.

COLOR   Green

THE PRAYERS

Encouraged by the radiant light of God revealed to us in Jesus Christ, let us pray with boldness and confidence.

A BRIEF SILENCE.

For the people of God bound together in baptism, that the glory of the Lord continually humble us, cleanse us, and compel us to cry "Here I am, send me!" let us pray to the Lord:

Hear us, O God, and show us your glory.

For God's good creation, tainted by overuse and abuse, that all people and nations become stewards of the grace and goodness God has given, let us pray to the Lord:

Hear us, O God, and show us your glory.

For those who make their living on the sea, that they may prosper while protecting that resource, may be guarded from danger, and may be welcomed at voyage's end, let us pray to the Lord:

Hear us, O God, and show us your glory.

For all who suffer in mind, body, or spirit *(especially)*, that God grant them healing and hope, let us pray to the Lord:

Hear us, O God, and show us your glory.

For the mission of this congregation, that as the disciples left behind their nets to spread the good news, we might leave behind all that hinders us from our call to mission, let us pray to the Lord:

Hear us, O God, and show us your glory.

HERE OTHER INTERCESSIONS MAY BE OFFERED.

In the memory of all who answered God's call and followed until death, that their lives may inform our own and that we may stand with them around the heavenly throne, let us pray to the Lord:

Hear us, O God, and show us your glory.

Into your hands, great God of heaven, we lay our prayers, trusting in your mercy through the one who showed us your face, Jesus Christ, our Lord.

Amen

IMAGES FOR PREACHING

A song from a musical asserts, "Anything you can do I can do better!" In today's lessons people are outdoing one another in humbleness. The prophet Isaiah moans, "Woe is me! I am lost, for I am a man of unclean lips . . . yet my eyes have seen the King, the Lord of hosts!" Simon Peter cries out, "Go away from me, Lord, for I am a sinful man!" St. Paul describes himself as "the least of the apostles, unfit to be called an apostle."

These are not cases of pride at being humble, but honesty. We may never experience an epiphany like Isaiah's who saw the Lord high and lifted up, but we know our Lord made low in the manger, we know our Lord lifted up on the cross, we know him arisen. Such a magnificent epiphany "demands my soul, my life, my all!"

The disciples were not always so humble. They were known at times to have argued about their just rewards. They could have compared all they had given up to follow Jesus. Simon and James and John: "Two boats full—I mean full to overflowing—full of fish. We left it all

and followed him." Or Matthew, "I had it made—a job as a tax collector. But when he said, 'Follow me,' I left it all, everything, and just got up and followed him."

No, if ever we brag, let's brag about what God has done for us. Isaiah could say, "The seraph touched my lips with the live coal and now my sin is blotted out." Peter would have to admit, "Three times I denied, but the angel at his empty grave said to the women, 'Go tell his disciples and Peter . . . !' " And Paul could say, "By the grace of God I am what I am."

Say it this way: "I am what I am because God is how God is—forgiving!"

WORSHIP MATTERS

Some worshipers don't realize that most of the texts in our liturgy are biblical. "Glory to God in the highest" is the song of the angels heard by shepherds at Jesus' birth from Luke 2. "This is the feast" uses a compilation of texts from the book of Revelation.

As we sing the words of the Sanctus, "Holy, holy, holy Lord" we recall the encounter Isaiah had with angels filling the temple with fire and smoke, and the glory of God from Isaiah 6.

As the preface for communion concludes "and so with the Church on earth and hosts of heaven, we . . . join their unending hymn," imagine your song joining a choir of angels. Recall that this celebration is in continuity with glorious worship of past, present, and future. And lift up your hearts and voices!

LET THE CHILDREN COME

In today's first reading we hear the story of Isaiah's commission and his amazing vision of the angels singing "Holy, holy, holy Lord" to proclaim God's glory. When we celebrate communion we recognize God's presence among us as we echo this song during the great thanksgiving. Worship is not all serious business. Make sure the children know that there are times when sounds of joy and celebration are appropriate during worship—the Sanctus is one of those times when we make a joyful noise unto the Lord!

HYMNS FOR WORSHIP
GATHERING

My God, how wonderful thou art   LBW 524

Lift up your heads, O gates   WOV 631

Holy, holy   TFF 289

HYMN OF THE DAY

The Son of God, our Christ   LBW 434

ALTERNATE HYMN OF THE DAY

You have come down to the lakeshore   WOV 784
Rejoice in the mission   W&P 120

COMMUNION

Hail to the Lord's anointed   LBW 87
Come, let us eat   LBW 214

SENDING

O Jesus, I have promised   LBW 503
I, the Lord of sea and sky   WOV 752
The summons   W&P 137, RWSB

ADDITIONAL HYMNS AND SONGS

Rejoice in the mission   W&P 120
Send me, Jesus (I am willing)   TFF 245, RWSB
They cast their nets   RWI 80, LBW 449
In Christ called to baptize   RWSB

MUSIC FOR THE DAY

PSALMODY

Cooney, Rory. "On the Day I Called" in STP, vol. 4.
Haas, David. "The Fragrance of Christ" in PCY, vol. 3.
Kallman, Daniel. PW , Cycle C.
Stewart, Roy James. "Lord, Your Love Is Eternal" in PCY, vol. 5.
See Proper 12.

CHORAL

Cherwien, David. "Come, Beloved of the Maker." SATB, org, fl, opt
cong. AFP 0800675150.
Holst, Gustav. "Let All Mortal Flesh." SATB, opt orch, org.
PRE 392-03013.
Schutte, David L., arr. Ovid Young. "Here I Am, Lord." SATB, pno.
AFP 0800656059.
Williams, David McK. "In the Year King Uzziah Died." SATB, org.
HWG 1356.

CHILDREN'S CHOIR

Dietterich, Philip. "Come One, Come All, Come Follow." (Luke
5:11) U, kybd. CG CGA553.
Lindh, Jody. "I Give You Thanks." (Ps. 138) U, pno, perc, opt brass
and synth. CG CGA561.

Patterson, Mark. "Let Praise Be the First Word." U/2 pt, kybd.
AFP 0800675347.

KEYBOARD/INSTRUMENTAL

Farlee, Robert Buckley. "Pescador de Hombres" in *Many and Great.*
Org. AFP 0800658949.
Linker, Janet. "Here I Am, Lord." Org/pno, opt inst. CPH 97-6803.
Manz, Paul. "Let Us Ever Walk with Jesus" in *Five Hymn Improvisations
for Weddings and General Use.* Org. MSM 10-850.

HANDBELL

Afdahl, Lee J. "You Have Come Down to the Lakeshore" in *Two Spanish Tunes for Handbells.* 3-5 oct, opt perc. AFP 0800657381.
Tucker, Sondra K. "Here I Am, Lord." 3-5 oct. CPH 97-6756.

PRAISE ENSEMBLE

Gordon, Nancy and Jamie Harvill. "Because We Believe" in *More Songs
for Praise and Worship.* SATB. WRD 3010387016 (vocal ed);
WRD 3010186363 (pno, vcs, perc).
Sadler, Gary and Jamie Harvill. "Ancient of Days" in *More Songs for
Praise and Worship.* SATB. WRD 3010387016 (vocal ed); WRD
3010186363 (pno, vcs, perc).
Schutte, Dan, arr. Craig Courtney. "Here I Am, Lord" (Isaiah 6).
SATB, kybd. BEC BP1403.

Saturday, February 14

CYRIL, MONK, 869; METHODIUS, BISHOP, 885;
MISSIONARIES TO THE SLAVS

These two brothers from a noble family in Thessalonika
in northeastern Greece were priests and missionaries.
After some early initial missionary work by Cyril among
the Arabs, the brothers retired to a monastery. They were
later sent to work among the Slavs, the missionary work
for which they are most known. Because Slavonic had no
written form at the time, the brothers established a written language with the Greek alphabet as its basis. They
translated the scriptures and the liturgy using this Cyril-
lic alphabet. The Czechs, Serbs, Croats, Slovaks, and
Bulgars regard the brothers as the founders of Slavic literature. The brothers' work in preaching and worshiping
in the language of the people are honored by Christians
in both East and West.

February 15, 2004

Sixth Sunday after the Epiphany

INTRODUCTION

A fundamental decision is placed before us this day: Will we choose the way of blessing or the way of woe? The death and resurrection of Jesus is the pivot on which the decision turns. To be in Christ means that we get planted by streams of water and are rooted among those who thirst for God's reign. The eucharistic acclamation points the path to life: "Christ has died. Christ is risen. Christ will come again."

PRAYER OF THE DAY

Lord God, mercifully receive the prayers of your people. Help us to see and understand the things we ought to do, and give us grace and power to do them; through your Son, Jesus Christ our Lord.

VERSE

Alleluia. Lord, to whom shall we go? You have the words of eternal life. Alleluia. (John 6:68)

READINGS

Jeremiah 17:5-10

These verses compose a poem that is part of a larger collection of wisdom sayings contrasting two ways of life. Life with God brings blessing; the power and vitality of God is active in our life. Life without God brings a curse, the power of death.

Psalm 1

They are like trees planted by streams of water. (Ps. 1:3)

1 Corinthians 15:12-20

For Paul, the resurrection of Christ is the basis for Christian hope. Because Christ has been raised, those who are in Christ know that they too will be raised to a new life beyond death.

Luke 6:17-26

After choosing his twelve apostles, Jesus teaches a crowd of followers about the nature and demands of discipleship. He begins his great sermon with surprising statements about who is truly blessed in the eyes of God.

COLOR   Green

THE PRAYERS

Encouraged by the radiant light of God revealed to us in Jesus Christ, let us pray with boldness and confidence.

A BRIEF SILENCE.

For the church in all the earth, that filled with the light of the resurrection, we may proclaim the blessing of God upon all who hunger, thirst, and suffer, and may work to ease their misery, let us pray to the Lord:

Hear us, O God, and show us your glory.

For the nations distressed by war and famine, violence and oppression, that illumined by the light of God, they may be drawn into God's reign of peace and justice, let us pray to the Lord:

Hear us, O God, and show us your glory.

For people who suffer from loneliness and isolation, that a door may be opened to companionship and human warmth, let us pray to the Lord:

Hear us, O God, and show us your glory.

For the hungry, poor, grieving, and sick *(especially)*, that they may enjoy the embrace of God's blessings, be restored to wholeness, and be comforted by God's people, let us pray to the Lord:

Hear us, O God, and show us your glory.

For the people of God in this place, that we may trust in the Lord and bloom like a tree planted by water, giving comfort and life to our neighbors, let us pray to the Lord:

Hear us, O God, and show us your glory.

HERE OTHER INTERCESSIONS MAY BE OFFERED.

In gratitude for those who have died in Christ *(especially)*, that we find inspiration from their lives and join with them in your resurrection to new life, let us pray to the Lord:

Hear us, O God, and show us your glory.

Into your hands, great God of heaven, we lay our prayers, trusting in your mercy through the one who showed us your face, Jesus Christ, our Lord.

Amen

IMAGES FOR PREACHING

Many would say that nothing is more inevitable than

111

death. But St. Paul contends that the *resurrection* from death is equally certain. The greatest epiphany is the resurrection of our Lord. Perhaps the next best will be our own—or that of a loved one.

The lack of such hope is, for Christians, unthinkable. As Paul said, "If for this life only we have hoped in Christ, we are of all people most to be pitied. But in fact . . ." (1 Cor. 15:19). In fact, as Jesus himself promised, "Blessed are you who weep now, for you will laugh" (Luke 6:21).

The resurrection from the dead, wonderful as it is and will be, does not stand alone. It represents the ultimate point in the life of faith, a life that is summarized in Jesus' beatitudes. "Blessed are you who are poor, . . . who are hungry now." God's people are continually being raised from such little deaths and reassured of their citizenship in the kingdom of God.

If we fail to pay enough attention to such words of blessing, perhaps it is because we are aware of the associated woes, "Woe to you who are rich, . . . who are full now." Those bring God's care for the poor into sharp relief. Or perhaps, childishly, we simply want to wish away realities like poverty, hunger, death. As poet Edna St. Vincent Millay put it,

> Childhood is not from birth to a certain age and at a
>   certain age
> The child is grown, and puts away childish things.
> Childhood is the kingdom where nobody dies.
> Nobody that matters, that is.
> (From "Childhood Is the Kingdom Where Nobody Dies")

But people do die, and suffer from poverty and hunger. In faith we look to the final resurrection that will end all such sorrow. Until then, we "who trust in the Lord . . . shall be like a tree . . . [that] does not cease to bear fruit" (Jer. 17:7-8).

WORSHIP MATTERS

In showing great appreciation for the soprano's aria, the audience rises for a standing ovation. As the bases are loaded with two outs, the fans rise to their feet to cheer on their team. When an esteemed guest enters the room, you get up from your chair to greet her.

We stand in worship, too. Yes, it is a sign of appreciation and respect. But more than that, it is a symbol of the life in Christ we share. It is an active gesture, moving up from sitting or kneeling. It signals that we are ready to sing, to pray, and to hear the gospel. As we get up

onto our feet, we may bring to mind the hope of the resurrected Christ. While we rise, we are modeling the Christian journey from sin to freedom, from despair to hope, from death to life.

LET THE CHILDREN COME

Worship involves listening and speaking, singing and praying, standing and sitting. We often stand to hear the word of God. When we stand we are also reminded that we are raised to a new life in Jesus Christ. Begin the service by inviting children to stand as soon as they think of some way in which Jesus makes a difference in their life. Extend the invitation to all who are worshiping. When everyone stands take a moment to have them share the peace, love, joy, and hope that we all have in Jesus Christ.

HYMNS FOR WORSHIP
GATHERING

Sing praise to God, the highest good   LBW 542
Shout for joy loud and long   WOV 793

HYMN OF THE DAY

Your Word, O Lord, is gentle dew   LBW 232

ALTERNATE HYMN OF THE DAY

Lift every voice and sing   LBW 562
Let justice flow like streams   WOV 763, TFF 48

COMMUNION

Jesus, the very thought of you   LBW 316
There in God's garden   WOV 668

SENDING

God of grace and God of glory   LBW 415
All my hope on God is founded   WOV 783

ADDITIONAL HYMNS AND SONGS

Blessed are you   DH 86
I shall not be moved   TFF 147
Come to the feast   RWSB
When the poor ones   RWSB, LLC 508

MUSIC FOR THE DAY
PSALMODY

Haas, David. "Happy Are They" in PCY, vol. 3.

Howard, Julie, arr. Vera Lyons. "Like a Tree" in LS.

Kallman, Daniel. PW , Cycle C.

Kline, Patsy Hilton. "Psalm 1: Planted by the Waters" in *Renew*. HOP 1997.

Schoenbachler, Tim. "Psalm 1: Happy Are They" in STP, vol. 2. See Proper 18.

CHORAL

Ashdown, Franklin D. "Jesus, the Very Thought of Thee." SATB, org, opt C inst. AFP 0800657500.

Carter, John and Mary Kay Beall. "Blessed Are They Who Walk in the Pathways of Peace." SAB, pno. AFP 080067510X.

Cool, Jayne Southwick. "As Trees By the Waters." SAB, 4 hb, kybd, opt cong. AFP 080067507X.

Handel, G.F. "I Know That My Redeemer Liveth" in *Messiah*. S solo, kybd. Various ed.

Noble, T. Tertius. "The Risen Christ." SATB, org. HWG 383.

Petker, Allan. "Grace Above All." SATB, pno. HAL HL08301589.

Rachmaninoff, Sergei. "Blessed Is the Man" from *All Night Vigil* in *Songs of the Church*. SATB div. HWG GB640

Wilkinson, Scott. "Blessed Are They." SATB, org. CFI ZCM-105.

CHILDREN'S CHOIR

Howard, Julie. "Like a Tree" (Ps. 1) in LS. U, kybd, opt hb/fl.

Mayo, Becki. "A Child's Beatitudes." 2 pt, pno. ABI 0687051959.

KEYBOARD/INSTRUMENTAL

Bach, J.S. "In dir ist Freude" in *Orgelbüchlein*. Org. CPH 97-5774 or other ed.

Biery, James. "Salzburg" in *Augsburg Organ Library: Epiphany*. Org. AFP 0800659341.

Langlois, Kristina. "Cantad al Señor" in *Five Hymns of Praise*. Org. MSM 10-722.

Wold, Wayne L. "Salzburg" in *Songs of Thankfulness and Praise, Set I*. Org. MSM 10-711.

HANDBELL

Kerr, J. Wayne. "There in God's Garden." 3-5 oct. MSM 30-820.

Kinyon, Barbara Baltzer. "The Ash Grove." 2 oct. CG CGB132.

Page, Anna Laura. "The Ash Grove." 3-5 oct. ALF 17557.

PRAISE ENSEMBLE

Espinosa, Eddie. "Change My Heart, O God" in RWSB.

Willard, Kelly. "Cares Chorus" in W&P.

Wednesday, February 18
MARTIN LUTHER, RENEWER OF THE CHURCH, 1546

For those in the habit of remembering the work of Martin Luther on Reformation Day, this commemoration may seem out of place. It is a custom, however, to remember saints on the day of their death, their "heavenly birthday." On this day Luther died at the age of 62. For a time, he was an Augustinian monk, but it is his work as a biblical scholar, translator of the Bible, reformer of the liturgy, theologian, educator, and father of German vernacular literature, which holds him in our remembrance. In Luther's own judgment, the greatest of all of his works was his catechism written to instruct people in the basics of faith. It was his baptism that sustained him in his trials as a reformer.

If a congregation has catechumens who will be baptized at the Easter Vigil, they might receive the catechism during the Enrollment of Candidates on the first Sunday in Lent. If there are no catechumens, a congregation might study the catechism during Lent to renew its own baptismal faith.

113

Friday, February 20
RASMUS JENSEN, THE FIRST LUTHERAN PASTOR IN NORTH AMERICA, 1620

Jensen came to North America in 1619 with an expedition sent by King Christian IV of Denmark and Norway. The expedition took possession of the Hudson Bay area, naming it Nova Dania. Within months of their arrival, most of the members of the expedition died, including Jensen. After this expedition, much Danish missionary activity was concentrated in India and the Virgin Islands.

Today would be an appropriate time to give thanks for the church in Canada, which flourished even after its early struggles. It would also be an opportunity to pray for missionaries who face difficulty in their tasks.

February 22, 2004

The Transfiguration of Our Lord

INTRODUCTION

Things are not always what they seem! Bread and wine can become a place where we meet God. We, too, are changed in our encounter with grace. When Moses came back from speaking with God, no one could look at him the same. How will we reflect our Lord's glory as we begin our Lenten walk?

PRAYER OF THE DAY

Almighty God, on the mountain you showed your glory in the transfiguration of your Son. Give us the vision to see beyond the turmoil of our world and to behold the king in all his glory; through your Son, Jesus Christ our Lord, who lives and reigns with you and the Holy Spirit, one God, now and forever.

or

O God, in the transfiguration of your Son you confirmed the mysteries of the faith by the witness of Moses and Elijah, and in the voice from the bright cloud you foreshadowed our adoption as your children. Make us with the king heirs of your glory, and bring us to enjoy its fullness, through Jesus Christ our Lord, who lives and reigns with you and the Holy Spirit, one God, now and forever.

VERSE

Alleluia. You are the fairest of men; grace flows from your lips. Alleluia. (Ps. 45:2)

READINGS

Exodus 34:29-35

Moses' face shone with the reflected glory of God after he received the Ten Commandments. The sight caused the Israelites to be afraid. Moses wore a veil to mask the radiance of God's glory while allowing direct communication with the people.

Psalm 99

Proclaim the greatness of the LORD; worship upon God's holy hill. (Ps. 99:9)

2 Corinthians 3:12—4:2

In his debates with the Corinthians, Paul contrasts the glory of Moses with the glory of Christ. The Israelites could not see Moses' face because of the veil. But in Christ we see the unveiled glory of God and are transformed into his likeness.

Luke 9:28-36 [37-43]

Today's reading offers a remarkable conclusion to the Epiphany season and turns us toward Lent. The transfiguration of Jesus is itself a great epiphany or manifestation. In the very midst of this event is talk of what will happen in Jerusalem, where Jesus must suffer and die.

COLOR White

THE PRAYERS

Encouraged by the radiant light of God revealed to us in Jesus Christ, let us pray with boldness and confidence.
A BRIEF SILENCE.

For the church, that we may gather with reverence in the presence of the Lord and be sent into the world to serve with hearts full of faith and love, let us pray to the Lord:
Hear us, O God, and show us your glory.

For the nations and world leaders, that they may serve in humility and be driven by God's mighty hand to act with justice and righteousness on behalf of the whole creation, let us pray to the Lord:
Hear us, O God, and show us your glory.

For those who long for wholeness and health *(especially)* that they may look to Christ the healer for hope and to his people for daily comfort, let us pray to the Lord:
Hear us, O God, and show us your glory.

For the ministries of this congregation, that our worship of God and our service to our neighbors and one another may be fervent and faithful, let us pray to the Lord:
Hear us, O God, and show us your glory.

HERE OTHER INTERCESSIONS MAY BE OFFERED.

Remembering all the saints who have reflected God's glory, that we may see the hand of God in their lives and join them on the mountain of the Lord when all has come to pass, let us pray to the Lord:
Hear us, O God, and show us your glory.

114

Into your hands, great God of heaven, we lay our prayers, trusting in your mercy through the one who showed us your face, Jesus Christ, our Lord.
Amen

IMAGES FOR PREACHING

Wouldn't you be self-conscious if you were suddenly aware that your face was shining with a glory-of-God shine? The first time Moses knew about it was when "Aaron and all the Israelites . . . were afraid to come near him." He couldn't check it in a mirror, but he must have been able to imagine how his face looked by the looks on their faces.

Moses' self-consciousness and his others-consciousness then dictated his procedure. He worked up a veil with which to hide the glory when it was too overwhelming. He would remove the veil in the presence of God. Then he would let the people see his shining face reflecting God's glory as he reported what God had revealed to him. Afterwards he would cover his face with the veil once more to "keep the people of Israel from gazing at the end of the glory" (2 Cor. 3:13).

Image may not be everything, but it would be a help if every good sermon were matched with a glory face on the part of the preacher. What if, when the worshipers really were in conversation with God during the liturgy, their faces would reflect the glory! Or if, when the parishioners were leaving the church, some had glory faces and some had not. And if the glory faded through the week, wouldn't we all be eager to make it to church the next Sunday for a glory polishing?

It's happening!

"In the beauty of the lilies Christ was born across the sea, / With a glory in his bosom that transfigures you and me." (LBW 332)

It's happening!

"All of us, with unveiled faces, seeing the glory of the Lord as though reflected in a mirror, are being transformed into the same image from one degree of glory to another; for this comes from the Lord, the Spirit!" (2 Cor. 3:18).

It's happening!

It's a repeated epiphany!

IMAGES FOR PREACHING

For the last few weeks we have been living with green on our altar paraments, and on the worship leaders' stoles and chasubles. Today they are transformed into sparkling new white!

Moses' face gleamed with the reflection of God. On the day of his transfiguration, Jesus' own face shone like the sun. His clothes became white as he was filled with glory and shared the stage with God's ancient leaders Moses and Elijah.

As we live with this in-between feast, after Epiphany and before Lent, how does it look on your mountain? Are you rubbing shoulders with others washed white in baptism? Is glory weighing you down, or lifting you up? Can you see your way to the next mountain, as Jesus is lifted up on the cross, and after three days is raised? How can our worship be transfigured this day as we hail the crucified and risen Jesus as God's Son?

LET THE CHILDREN COME

Pass out white ribbons to the children today or, if possible, to the entire congregation. Suggest that they pin this to their clothing or place it somewhere in their home to remind them of their life in Christ. White is a color that is clean and bright. When something is white it looks new—exactly what we are when we live our lives in Christ. We make mistakes. We sin. But we are cleansed of sin and made new in Christ. We are forgiven and free to begin again.

HYMNS FOR WORSHIP
GATHERING
Christ, whose glory fills the skies   LBW 265
Alleluia, song of gladness   WOV 654

HYMN OF THE DAY
Renew me, O eternal Light   LBW 511

ALTERNATE HYMN OF THE DAY
Oh, wondrous type! Oh, vision fair   LBW 80
Love divine, all loves excelling   LBW 315

COMMUNION
Shine, Jesus, shine   WOV 651
The Lord is my light   TFF 61, RWSB

SENDING
Beautiful Savior   LBW 518
Shine, Jesus, shine   WOV 651, W&P 123, TFF 64

ADDITIONAL HYMNS AND SONGS
Christ, be our light   RWSB

115

Come to the mountain   W&P 32

We have come, at Christ's own bidding   VU 104

O Morning Star, how fair and bright   LBW 76

MUSIC FOR THE DAY

PSALMODY

Hobby, Robert A. PW , Cycle C.

Hopson, Hal H. TP.

Bow down before the holy mountain of God   TFF 11

The Lord God reigns in majesty   PsH 99

CHORAL

Bach, J.S. "Alleluia" in *Bach for All Seasons*. SATB, kybd.
AFP 080065854X.

Cherwien, David. "Beautiful Savior." SATB. Org, cong, opt fl.
AFP 0800675088.

Farlee, Robert Buckley. "Farewell to Alleluia." U, org, opt tpt.
AFP 0800649486.

Helman, Michael. "Go Up to the Mountain of God." SATB, pno,
opt fl. AFP 0800658353.

Hobby, Robert A. "Offertory for the Transfiguration of Our Lord."
2 pt mxd, org, hb. MSM 80-225.

Scholz, Robert. "O Wondrous Type, O Vision Fair." SATB, hb.
MSM 50-2600.

Tallis, Thomas. "O Nata Lux." SATTB. OXF 43.228.

CHILDREN'S CHOIR

Behnke, John A. "The Lord Is King" in *Three Psalms for Unison Choir*.
(Ps. 99:1-3) U, kybd. CPH 98-3578.

Bisbee, B. Wayne. "O Splendor of God's Glory Bright." 2 pt
trbl/mxd, pno. AFP 0800659252.

Crutchfield, Jonathan. "Fairest Lord Jesus." U, desc, kybd.
CG CGA743.

Hughes, Pamela. "Come to the Mountain" in LS. U, kybd.

KEYBOARD/INSTRUMENTAL

David, Anne Marie. "Beautiful Savior" in *Here I Am, Lord: Piano Stylings*.
Pno. AFP 0800675665.

Hamilton, Gregory. "Beautiful Savior" in *Augsburg Organ Library:
Epiphany*. Org. AFP 0800659341.

Hobby, Robert A. Partita on "Praise My Soul, the King of Heaven."
Org. CPH 97-6082.

Young, Gordon. "Fairest Lord Jesus" in *Chorale Preludes on Seven Hymn
Tunes*. Org. FLA 3762.

HANDBELL

Afdahl, Lee J. "Thaxted / O God Beyond All Praising." 3-5 oct, opt
brass. AFP 0800658140.

Bettcher, Peggy. "Shine Jesus Shine." 2-3 oct. AG 2069.

PRAISE ENSEMBLE

Smiley, Bill, Mark Gersmehl, and Bob Farrell. "Shine Down" in
Hosanna! Music, #3. INT.

Smith, Michael W. and Deborah D. Smith. "Great is the Lord" in
W&P.

Tunseth, Scott and Kathy Donlan Tunseth. "Come to the Mountain"
in W&P.

Monday, February 23

POLYCARP, BISHOP OF SMYRNA, MARTYR, 156

Polycarp was bishop of Smyrna and a link between the
apostolic age and the church at the end of the second
century. He is said to have been known by John, the author of Revelation. In turn he was known by the Irenaeus, bishop of Lyon in France, and Ignatius of Antioch. At the age of eighty-six was martyred for his faith.
When urged to save his life and renounce his faith, Polycarp replied, "Eighty-six years I have served him, and he
never did me any wrong. How can I blaspheme my king
who saved me?" The magistrate who made the offer was
reluctant to kill a gentle old man, but he had no choice.
Polycarp was burned at the stake.

In church gatherings, one might use the example of
Polycarp to underscore what Paul is saying in 2
Corinthians: "Therefore, since it is by God's mercy that
we are engaged in this ministry, we do not lose heart."

Monday, February 23

BARTHOLOMAEUS ZIEGENBALG,
MISSIONARY TO INDIA, 1719

Bartholomaeus Ziegenbalg was a missionary to the
Tamils of Tranquebar on the southeast coast of India.
The first convert to Christianity was baptized about ten
months after Ziegenbalg began preaching. His missionary work was opposed both by the local Hindus and also
by Danish authorities in that same area. Ziegenbalg was
imprisoned for his work on a charge of converting the

natives. The Copenhagen Mission Society that opposed him wanted an indigenous church that did not reflect European patterns or show concern for matters other than the gospel. Ziegenbalg, in contrast, argued that concern for the welfare of others is a matter of the gospel. Today, the Tamil Evangelical Lutheran Church carries on his work.

With Ash Wednesday this same week, consider Isaiah 58:1-12 for the first reading, "Is not this the fast that I choose . . . to share your bread with the hungry." Ziegenbalg's missionary work can lead us into Lent with the reminder that we are called to live in service to others.

Tuesday, February 24

ST. MATTHIAS, APOSTLE

After Christ's ascension, the apostles met in Jerusalem to choose a replacement for Judas. Matthias was chosen over Joseph Justus by the casting of lots. Little is known about Matthias, and little is reported about him in the account of his election in Acts 1:15-26. Matthias had traveled among the disciples from the time of Jesus' baptism until his ascension. His task, after he was enrolled among the eleven remaining disciples, was to bear witness to the resurrection.

During the weeks of Lent, congregations with catechumens will have a chance to learn stories of how people have been called, some in unusual ways like Matthias.

117

LENT

Begin again the journey toward life

Images *of the* Season

When Christianity was new, still resonating with its

Jewish roots, the year revolved around a Passover retuned

by the resurrection. The history of God's saving ways, the

ancient story of the release and rescue from Egypt was infused with this new chapter of God's saving intervention in Jesus, the long-promised Messiah. The tempo and flow of the annual holy days carried over easily.

So Lent became the time of preparation for the greatest holy day of all—Easter. New believers were prepared in the weeks preceding the celebration of the resurrection to enter into the community of faith. Lent was a time, therefore, of awakening and emerging. In the Northern Hemisphere, the seasons of creation undergirded this deep metaphor. Spring slowly unfolded during Lent, buds gathered strength and winter's dormancy eased as the weeks went by.

Lent has become a time to face the truth of our humanity, our utter inability to be God, and our inability to believe that God is. Our human limitations get us into all kinds of trouble, seizing up our relationships with ourselves, with each other, and with the earth itself. In our desperate attempts to measure up to what we imagine we ought to be or in our fatalistic abandonment of the gifts God has given us, we deny our limitations and/or the miracle we are. Unable to hold these two polarities in tension, we wreak havoc in our relationships and on the earth.

It is for this we need salvation by the one who is without limits and who also loves us beyond measure.

Ash Wednesday begins Lent by forcing our eyes open to our failings. Whose interest do we really serve? Do we loose the bonds of injustice? Undo the thongs of the yoke? Let the oppressed go free? Share our bread with the hungry? Bring the homeless poor into our homes? Cover the naked? If not, we do not offer the worship God most welcomes and values. If not, we serve our own interests, not God's. Because we do not, our churches are bare; our vestments are black. If we are to begin the journey toward life and be able to welcome the Messiah, we must begin in this place, clear about how far God must come to meet us. The smear of ashes borne on

our foreheads speaks of our mortality, our frailty, and our own undoing. Our forebears remembered Yom Kippur, the Day of Atonement. It was the one day the Hebrew high priest could enter the temple's Holy of Holies, bearing in his body the repentance of the nation. It was the day to stand before God, vulnerable and stripped of pretense. It is how we begin Lent, the season of awakening.

The coming Sundays will walk us along the path to Easter. First, we must remember our story, the history of our salvation. We can confess with our forebears that we come from the same wandering Aramean who first heard God's call. The story traces God's faithfulness. We are reminded that the righteous flourish and will not be shamed. We are called to keep our eyes and ears tuned to God, not the many temptations that surround us.

We acknowledge on the second Sunday that we live in a state of promise—"now" and "not yet" simultaneously. We are people in a covenant with God, who does and will transform us. Even as Jesus wept over Jerusalem and predicted his passion, he said they would one day call him blessed. This is where we live too, sustained by the washing we received in baptism and the nourishment of the holy meal, leaning toward the day we, too, will call God blessed.

We who thirst for God are invited, on the third Sunday, to drink from God's waters. God's invitation is not without some expectation, however. God looks for lives that reflect the loving care God gives. There is great mercy, but God expects fruit. We can learn from our past, and God promises to sustain us.

On the fourth Sunday, we stand on the threshold of the promised land. When the people of Israel finished their wilderness wanderings, they celebrated the Passover using the fruits of the land they had been given. They did not need manna anymore. God releases us from the bondage of our past and makes us into a new creation.

God gives us the gift of reconciliation and welcomes all prodigal children home.

By the fifth Sunday in Lent, we can almost smell the passion ahead of us, and we recall the irony of death as an ember for life. The desert, dry and barren, needs only water to awaken it, to break open the seed and refresh the land. Jesus will die and be buried. Mary's tears and costly anointing pointed to this truth, but in his death, he will bring sweet water to our wilderness.

The Sunday of the Passion is rife with contrast.

Jesus is the King, but he rides on a donkey. Jesus is the Son of God, but he is mocked and humiliated. Jesus brings life, but he must die. His utter defeat is also his glory. The procession of palms waving, the reading of the passion, the immediacy of the holy meal—we can smell and taste what is coming, but we will not go there quite yet. This Sunday leaves us hanging on the edge of the tomb. We will revisit the details soon, but we will have to wait just a little longer for the promise to be fulfilled.

Environment *and* Art *for the* Season

These great forty days of Lent serve as a time of

preparation for the paschal feast. They have also

traditionally been connected to the preparation of

121

the catechumenate (those preparing for baptism at the Easter Vigil), and present an opportunity for the assembly to remind themselves of their baptism and incorporation into the body of Christ. The season of Lent, with its focus on self-reflection and spiritual discipline, draws the worshiping assembly into the journey of our Lord on the way toward the triumph of cross and resurrection. This passionate journey is one of sacrifice: almsgiving, prayer, fasting, and repentance. These are some of the outward actions of our inward desire for reconciliation with God, and between the rest of creation and us. The Lenten lengthening of days moves us toward the ultimate goal of the church year, the Three Days.

The restrained mood of the season of Lent encourages the worshiping community to zero in on a growing awareness of mystery and passion of God in Jesus Christ. We engage in liturgical sobriety, limiting our decorations just as many limit ourselves through our spiritual disciplines. This holding back of excess helps direct our focus upon our renewed attention to sacrificial giving and prayer. The people who gather and the furnishings we use can become the hallmark of the environment and art for this season. There will be time in several weeks to pull out all the stops with your visual environment and

art. The simplicity of Lent can set up the drama of the Three Days and the Easter season.

EVALUATING THE SPACE

What do you currently do to change the environment during Lent?

Think about previous years and make a list. Consult the altar guild if you have not already done so. They, too, are an integral part of the ministry of art and environment. It is important to bring them along on the journey of discovery. The more people are a part of the learning process, the easier the change over the long run.

Do you make a distinction between midweek services and the Sunday liturgy with regard to your appointments or decorations?

If your congregation has special midweek services (healing services, services of word and prayer, preaching services) that are different in structure and emphasis from your usual weekend eucharist experience, you might want to consider a different location within your church. Simple changes to your paraments might also help the assembly shift their attention from one service to the other. For example, if your midweek service is not a service of Holy Communion, you could remove colored paraments from the altar, saving them for Sundays. (But they could be kept on locations related to the word.) Not lighting the altar candles during those services where the eucharist is not being celebrated would also be appropriate. Why dress and light the altar if it is not used during the liturgy? It then becomes merely decoration and can distract us from the places where liturgical action is taking place.

Does the congregation do special things for those preparing for their upcoming baptisms, especially if they are older catechumens?

Where we sit can be very influential to our sense of participation in the assembly's liturgy. In some churches, those adolescents and adults who are preparing for Easter Vigil baptism sit together in an area set aside for them where they have "front row" seats to hear the preaching and see everything that is going on in the liturgy. It is seen as a place of honor. Instituting a practice such as this would take patience and education maybe spanning several years. It is good to note at this point that the best place for young children and families is also toward the front of the assembly. This is especially the case if your nave is long and narrow and there is a lot of distance between what happens up front and where people in the back are sitting. Many families with young children want to sit in the back, thinking that they are less disturbing there. The reality is that noise from the back can be more distracting, even causing one to turn around and see what it is. Besides, the better a child can hear and see, the more likely that child will participate in the liturgy.

Where is your baptismal font located currently? Is it fixed in place or movable? Has your congregation experimented with moving the font for liturgical reasons in the past?

Two issues can arise here. First, the font may be movable, but due to a congregation's desire for permanence, the font may be virtually fixed to a spot that doesn't allow it to speak well to the fullness of our baptismal theology—in a corner of the nave, for instance. Conversely, sometimes a congregation has a notion that the baptismal font is like a folding chair: move it if it is in the way, then move it back when you are done. As a primary visual symbol, the font deserves a place of some permanence, at least within a season. That location can itself speak eloquently, as we will see.

Baptismal fonts are not mere containers for water;

rather, they can symbolize the things we profess about the sacrament itself. We say that in baptism we die and are raised up to new life. We say it is a washing of our sins. We say it is the sacrament that serves as the entrance into membership in the body of Christ. For generations in the more recent history of the western church, we have reduced the size of our fonts and made them visually trivial. In recent years, though, more congregations are building baptismal fonts that reflect more of baptism's importance. Many fonts now being created have enough volume that a child or an adult can be immersed or submersed, physically and visually experiencing washing, confronting the potential that they could die in this water and instead are given new life in Christ. Fonts of this size are being placed at the entryway in the worship space as a powerful reminder that it is through the flowing waters of baptism that we become part of the body of Christ.

If your font is located up front in the chancel and is movable, consider bringing it to the place in your worship space just inside the main entryway. Some churches already do this and they leave the font open with fresh water in it so the assembly can remind themselves of their baptism when they touch the water upon entering. Alternatively, for Lent, consider leaving the font open but without water. Let the empty font serve as a reminder of the baptismal season that is to come. Another way to draw attention to the font, wherever it is located, is to have wide bands of some light fabric in the color of the season placed so they appear to be flowing out of a dry, open font.

ART FOR THE SEASON

In this time of baptismal preparation, a focus on instruction might be in order. Displays including images of texts from throughout the history of Christianity would be an interesting visual focus on our call to constant learning as disciples. You might find in the library or from members of the congregations old catechisms that you could borrow and put out in the gathering space. They could serve as a visual reminder of the tradition in which we stand. Another suggestion might be to find a creative way to display images of the members of the congregation along with their names and their dates of baptism. This might also encourage people to investigate their own baptismal date, which is a wonderful way to connect them with their journey as a baptized child of God.

The use of color in the space should be noticeable yet at the same time should emphasize the beauty of your space and the furnishings of altar, font, and ambo/pulpit/lectern. You might also use the purple color of the season in a few choice places outside the worship space: on your sign or property to indicate that

we are in this Lenten season, along the entryway and maybe even in certain areas throughout the building. Whatever you choose to do, try to employ the limited use of color in such a way as to draw people's attention to the sparsely adorned building and furnishings and the people that worship there.

Preaching *with the* Season

Deliverance to dust. Dust to dust. Dust to

deliverance. Dust and deliverance succeed one

another in this remarkable—if rather unmarketable—

season of the church year. Last year's Palm Sunday branches have all but crumbled in our offices and living rooms. We are glad to give them new purpose as we return them to the community for burning. Yet, the space that they occupied on our walls leaves a certain emptiness in our spirits, despite the fact that they had, in recent months, become only a shadow of last spring's succulent symbols of our hoped-for Messiah.

Our sin has delivered us to dust, and so we paint our destiny on our foreheads; and so we willingly follow Christ into the dry and dusty deserts of our lives. "Deliverance to dust" we regret as we once again acknowledge that no mere human can die our death for us; that our destiny is ours, and ours alone. "Deliverance to dust" we dread as we step out into the wilderness where angels minister to us in the face of the wild beasts and where, ironically, we hope once again to find rehydration— life-giving waters, succulent plants.

Our dusty journey begins as a seemingly solitary one as each of us individually receives the dirty cross. Yet one must ask: Is Lent truly about solitude? About the individual? Our strongly individualistic culture would push us in that direction. Further, Lent has, in the history of the church, been a period of preparation for individuals, baptismal candidates, to enter the church. But to what end has this formation been directed? For nothing other than life in community.

So, yes, our dusty journey begins with an acknowledgment of the destiny of the solitary individual. But the first readings of this year's Lent invite us to arrange a meeting place with the community of Israel as it, too, treks through the dust.

Already on Ash Wednesday, the communal nature of the coming Lenten fast is lifted up by Isaiah. Serving "your own interest on your fast day," Isaiah says, "will not make your voice heard on high." Rather, he propels the individualist outward with a fast for the world with a challenge "to loose the bonds of injustice, to undo the thongs of the yoke, to let the oppressed go free . . . to share your bread with the hungry, and bring the homeless poor into your house; when you see the naked, to cover them."

The first Sunday in Lent allows the individual who has just entered the desert to ask, "Who am I?" No sooner is the question uttered, however, than we find ourselves inserted in the story of salvation history. The Deuteronomist reminds us of our humble, wandering community of origin, and of the required response, "first fruits giving," as our sacrifice of thanksgiving. Celebration is in order, says the Deuteronomist, but not just for those "in the club." The "aliens who reside among us" are also to be on the guest list.

The second Sunday in Lent continues this theme of identity as God and Abram write out the family will for,

123

as yet, nonexistent heirs. "Who will the heirs be?" we ask. "What is our family of origin? What and where is our inheritance? What is our true relationship to the land in which we live? With which soil will our mortal dust ultimately be mingled?"

After three weeks in the dusty desert, the language of the third Sunday in Lent allows us to acknowledge our hunger and thirst. Parallel to that, however, Isaiah reminds us that we, along with the people of David, will indeed "eat what is good and delight ourselves in rich food." Come back! "Return to the Lord," says Isaiah to the wandering people! The desert is easier with travel companions; let us join the Israelites as they "seek the Lord."

On the fourth Sunday in Lent we can almost hear the Israelites rejoicing, "At last! Homegrown tomatoes!" After forty years of whining about their wilderness diet, they have finally tasted the produce of the promised land. Let us, as prodigals returning to a family celebration, join them on the day after the Passover feast and contemplate the deep satisfaction of our own communal food—the cup of salvation; the bread of life.

"Are we almost there yet?! I'm thirsty!" we grumble as the novelty of the journey has long worn off. The fifth Sunday in Lent brings the promise of refreshing water to the community of Israel. "I am about to do a new thing," quotes Isaiah, "now it springs forth. . . . I will make a way in the wilderness, and rivers in the desert." Our fortunes will be restored, says our psalmist, "like the watercourses of the Negeb" (43:19). The promise to our travel companions is ours as well as we now begin to glimpse the promised pool of baptism in the coming Easter feast.

At last! Dust to deliverance. On Passion Sunday, we've found our way out of the dusty desert and have been delivered back into civilization. We've come full circle. We've been handed our new, green palm branches and stand in the midst of the Jerusalem crowd of strangers. Our Messiah is coming! Our deliverance is at hand! The community on this day quickly moves from deafening accolades to deathly silence. Where has the silence of our community found us guilty? And yet, "It is the Lord GOD who helps me [us!]; who will declare me guilty?"

124

Shape *of* Worship *for the* Season

BASIC SHAPE OF THE EUCHARISTIC RITE

- Confession and Forgiveness: see alternate worship text for Lent on page 130 as an option to the form in the liturgy setting. Other possibilities for confession and forgiveness are in *Holy Baptism and Related Rites*, Renewing Worship, vol. 3, pp. 87*ff.* (ELCA/Augsburg Fortress, 2002), or at www.renewing worship.org/publications/ holy_baptism/index.html

GATHERING

- Greeting: see alternate worship text for Lent
- Use the Kyrie during Lent
- Omit the hymn of praise during Lent

WORD

- For dramatic readings based on lectionary passages, use *Scripture Out Loud!* (AFP 0806639644) for Ash Wednesday and the First Sunday in Lent
- For contemporary dramas based on lectionary passages, use *Can These Bones Live?* (AFP 0806639652) for Ash Wednesday, the First Sunday in Lent, and Sunday of the Passion
- Use the Nicene Creed
- The prayers: see the prayers for Ash Wednesday and each Sunday

MEAL

- Offertory prayer: see alternate worship text for Lent
- Use the proper preface for Lent
- Use the proper preface for Passion beginning with Sunday of the Passion
- Eucharistic prayer: in addition to four main options in *LBW*, see "Eucharistic Prayer D: The Season of Lent" in *WOV* Leaders Edition, p. 68
- Invitation to communion: see alternate worship text for Lent
- Post-communion prayer: see alternate worship text for Lent

SENDING

- Benediction: see alternate worship text for Lent
- Dismissal: see alternate worship text for Lent

OTHER SEASONAL POSSIBILITIES

- Ash Wednesday liturgy: see *LBW* Ministers Edition, pp. 129–31; congregational leaflets available from Augsburg Fortress (AFP 080660574X)
- Enrollment of Candidates for Baptism (for First Sunday in Lent): see *Welcome to Christ: Lutheran Rites for the Catechumenate*, pp. 18–21; or *Holy Baptism and Related Rites*, pp. 30–33
- Midweek Lenten worship: see order for evening prayer services in seasonal rites section
- Many congregations include a Service of Healing during Lent. Resources for that can be found in *Occasional Services*, pp. 89–98; and *Life Passages: Marriage, Healing, Funeral*, pp. 23–39
- Blessing of Candidates for Baptism (for Third, Fourth, and Fifth Sundays in Lent): see *Welcome to Christ: Lutheran Rites for the Catechumenate*, pp. 22–34; and *Holy Baptism and Related Rites*, pp. 34–47
- Procession with Palms liturgy for Sunday of the Passion: see *LBW* Ministers Edition, pp. 134–35; congregational leaflets available from Augsburg Fortress (AFP 0806605766)
- Blessing of oil: This could be done as a synod or other group of congregations wishing to celebrate this order; see Dedication of Worship Furnishings in *Occasional Services*, pp. 176–77

125

Assembly Song *for the* Season

The forty-day Lenten pilgrimage takes us on a

marvelous and hopeful journey. The gospel stories

call us to press toward the promised land, and encourage

us to cleanse our hearts, renew our faith, and restore grace and balance to our lives. Through baptismal waters we are restored, cleansed, and renewed.

GATHERING

Encourage Lenten contemplation by choosing quieter, simpler music for assembly and choirs. Embrace silence: perhaps omit prelude and postlude altogether, or at least abstain from loud percussion, brass, and organ reeds and mixtures. If *a cappella* singing (unison or multipart) is not a tradition in the congregation, Lent is a good time to introduce the concept.

Signal Lent's start with a solemn procession while singing a setting of The Litany (*LBW*, p. 168), using simple keyboard accompaniment, handbell cues for petitions, or even a cappella. If you have more substantial choral forces, try Carl Crosier's fine setting of "The Great Litany" for cantor and congregation with SATB choral fauxbourdons and optional handbell peals by Peter Hallock (Ionian Arts CH-1013).

The Kyrie is a logical Lenten choice. In addition to those in *LBW, WOV,* and *This Far by Faith,* alternate and interesting settings are "Have mercy on us, Lord (Kyrie)" (RW1 36), and "Kyrie" (WOV 601, TFF 20).

Two good entrance hymns are "O Christ, our king, creator, Lord" (LBW 101) and "As the deer" (W&P 9), a quiet and simple setting of Psalm 42, led by guitar or piano.

WORD

Lent is a good time to reinforce the rich tradition of psalmody. Sing verses in alternation by whole verse between psalmist and cantor using *LBW* pointed psalms to tone 5 or tone 2. Choirs and congregations will also enjoy the haunting settings of Peter Hallock's *Ionian Psalter* (Ionian Arts), with beautifully written choral verses and accessible congregational refrains.

With "alleluia" banished from our lips, use "Return to the Lord, your God" for the verse, or use proper verses, such as David Cherwien's *Verses for the Sundays in Lent,* for unison or two-part choir, and organ (MorningStar MSM 80-300).

As the assembly prepares to welcome catechumens through the Rite of Welcome and Rite of Enrollment, baptismal acclamations such as "Praise to you, O Christ," and "God calls you" may be found in Welcome to Christ: Lutheran Rites for the Catechumenate (AFP 0806633956).

Highlight the intercessory prayers with a sung prayer response, such as the Taizé refrain "O Lord, hear my prayer" (WOV 772).

MEAL

Both *With One Voice* and *This Far by Faith* offer quiet settings of the major sung liturgical texts surrounding the eucharist. At the offertory, sing "Create in me a clean heart" (WOV 732) or "Give me a clean heart" (TFF 216). Congregations with a tradition of multipart choral singing will enjoy settings of Schubert's "Holy, holy, holy, Lord" and "Amen" (WOV 617a, 617b). Accompany them with string or wind quartet (parts available from GIA: G-2848A, G-2848B). Teach and have the children's choir lead the simple chant setting of "Agnus Dei" (WOV 620). At communion use repetitive refrains like "Eat this bread" (WOV 709, TFF 125). The hymn calls for solo verses, which are short and especially suitable for children.

SENDING

Remind the assembly of its Lenten journey by sending them into the world singing "O Lord, throughout these forty days" (LBW 99), or "Jesus, remember me" (WOV 740, W&P 78). If the congregation holds midweek evening services, "Now the day has drawn to a close" (W&P 105) is an excellent choice for beginning or ending the liturgy.

Music *for the* Season

VERSE AND OFFERTORY

Busarow, Donald. *Verses and Offertories, Part III—Ash Wednesday through Maundy Thursday.* SATB, org.   CPH 97-5503.

Cherwien, David. *Verses for the Sundays in Lent.* U/2 pt, org.
MSM 80-300.

Farlee, Robert Buckley. *Verses and Offertories for Lent.* U/SATB.
AFP 0800649494.

Gospel Acclamations. Cant, choir, cong, inst.   MAY 0862096324.

Schalk, Carl. "Return to the Lord, Your God." SATB, opt kybd.
MSM 50-3033.

Schiavone, J. *Gospel Acclamation Verses for the Sundays of Lent.* GIA G-2160.

Schramm, Charles. *Verses for the Lenten Season.* SATB, opt org.
MSM 80-301.

CHORAL

Brahms, Johannes. "Let Nothing Ever Grieve Thee." SATB, org.
PET 6093.

Chilcott, Robert. "God So Loved the World." SATB, S solo.
OXF BC29.

Christiansen, F. Melius. "Lamb of God." SATB. AFP 0800652592.
Also in *The Augsburg Choirbook.* AFP 0800656784.

Dirkson, Richard Wayne. "Humbly I Adore Thee." SATB, org.
Trinitas 4538.

Ellingboe, Bradley. "The Lord's My Shepherd." SATB, opt. pno.
KJO 8956.

Goss, John. "God So Loved the World." SATB. AMC AE539.

Ireland, John. "Greater Love Hath No Man." SATB, org.
GAL 1.5030.

McKie, William. "We Wait for Thy Loving Kindness, O God." SATB,
solo, org. OXF 42.081.

Sateren, Leland. "Two Folksongs for Lent." SATB. KJO 8824.

CHILDREN'S CHOIR

Burkhardt, Michael. "Agnus Dei." U, C inst, org. MSM 50-3752.

Croft, William. "Forgive Our Sins" in LS. U, kybd.

Hopson, Hal H. "I Want Jesus to Walk with Me." 2 pt, kybd.
CG CGA701.

Sleeth, Natalie. "Fear Not for Tomorrow" in LS. U, kybd.

Wold, Wayne L. "Kyrie Eleison: Lord, Have Mercy." U, kybd.
MSM 80-303.

KEYBOARD/INSTRUMENTAL

Augsburg Organ Library: Lent. Org. AFP 0800658973.

Burkhardt, Michael. *Five Lenten Improvisations.* Org. MSM 10-309.

Linker, Janet. *Hymns of the Cross.* BEC OC4.

Music for Manuals: Lent, Easter, Pentecost. Org. MSM 10-346.

Rodriguez, Penny. *Portraits of the Cross.* Pno. BEC PC3.

HANDBELL

Behnke, John A. "Jesus, Priceless Treasure." 3-5 oct. CPH 97-6683.

Mathis, William H. "Pie Jesu." 3-5 oct. H.T. FitzSimons FB F0703.

Merrett, Fred A. "My Jesus! Oh, What Anguish." 3-5 oct.
Composers Music HY0774.

Moklebust, Cathy. "Thee We Adore" and "Lamb of God, Most
Holy" in *Thee We Adore.* 2 oct. CG CGB166.

Payn, William A. "O God, beneath Your Guiding Hand." 3-5 oct.
NMP 118.

Rogers, Sharon Elery. "Nearer to the Cross." 2-3 oct. MSM 30-301.

PRAISE ENSEMBLE

Carter, John. "For Love of You." SATB, kybd. HOP JC293.

Espinosa, Eddie. "Change My Heart, O God" in W&P.

Getty, Keith. "O, for a Closer Walk with God" in *New Songs 2003/03.*
Kingsway.

Leblanc, Lenny, and Paul Baloche. "Above All" in *Best of the Best.*
FEL 1891062018.

Alternate Worship Texts

CONFESSION AND FORGIVENESS

In the name of the Father, and of the ✝ Son,
and of the Holy Spirit.
Amen
Trusting in the steadfast, sure love of God,
let us return to the Lord, confessing our sins.

Silence for reflection and self-examination.

God of all mercy,
we confess that we have sinned against you,
opposing your will in our lives.
We have denied your goodness in each other,
in ourselves, and in the world you have created.
We repent of the evil that enslaves us,
the evil we have done,
and the evil done on our behalf.
Forgive, restore, and strengthen us
through our Savior Jesus Christ,
that we may abide in your love and serve only your will.
Amen

God is generous to all who ask for help.
Almighty God have mercy on you,
forgive you all your sins
through the grace of ✝ Jesus Christ,
strengthen you in all goodness,
and by the power of the Holy Spirit
keep you in eternal life.
Amen

GREETING

From our God who loves us with an everlasting love,
who brings forth a new creation in Christ,
who leads us by the Spirit in the wilderness:
Grace and abundant mercy be with you all.
And also with you.

PRAYERS

As we seek in this Lenten time to grow in our faith, let us pray
for the life of the world.

A brief silence.

Each petition ends:

Let us pray to the Lord.
Lord, have mercy.

Concluding petition:

Grant these prayers, merciful God, and all that we need,
as we eagerly await the Easter feast; through Jesus Christ our
Lord.
Amen

OFFERTORY PRAYER

God our Redeemer,
receive all we bring to you this day—
these gifts and the offering of our lives.
Refresh us with this holy food and drink
that we may reach the promised land,
the Easter feast of victory in Christ our Lord. Amen

INVITATION TO COMMUNION

All who are hungry, come and eat the bread of life.
All who are thirsty, come and drink the cup of salvation.

POST-COMMUNION PRAYER

Compassionate God,
your Son welcomed sinners and ate with them.
We give you thanks for the forgiveness and grace
we have received in this meal.
Make us signs of your love,
that all the world may know your mercy and blessing;
through Jesus Christ our Lord.
Amen

BLESSING

The God who formed us in love,
who renews us through grace,
and who will transform us into glory,
✝ bless you this day and always.
Amen

DISMISSAL

Reconciled to God through Christ,
go in peace to love and serve the Lord.
Thanks be to God.

128

Seasonal Rites

Service of the Word for Healing in Lent

In addition to the liturgy in Renewing Worship 4: Life Passages, an order for Service of the Word for Healing is presented in this volume with the seasonal materials for autumn. It may also be adapted for use during Lent in the following ways:

DIALOG

Behold, now is the acceptable time;
now is the day of salvation.
Return to the Lord, your God,
who is gracious and merciful, slow to anger,
and abounding in steadfast love.
God forgives you all your sins
and heals all your infirmities.
God redeems your life from the grave
and crowns you with mercy and lovingkindness.
God satisfies you with good things,
and your youth is renewed like an eagle's.
Bless the Lord, O my soul,
and all that is within me bless God's holy name.

FIRST READING: Isaiah 53:3-5
PSALM: Psalm 138
GOSPEL: Matthew 8:1-3, 5-8, 13-17

THE PRAYERS

HYMNS

Either of these hymns may be used when the Service of the
Word for Healing occurs during Lent:
Jesus, refuge of the weary LBW 93
In the cross of Christ I glory LBW 104

Midweek Evening Prayer for Lent

This flexible order of evening prayer may be celebrated as a midweek service during Lent. It is an adaptable form of vespers with readings and music that highlight five of the readings from the Easter Vigil. These stories are among the most prominent of passages that announced hope and salvation to the ancient Hebrew people. For Christians these readings are regarded as "types" of the salvation brought to us through the death and resurrection of Christ. Because of their traditional use in the Easter Vigil, the primary liturgy for baptism, these readings also have a strong baptismal association for Christians.

Contemporary dramatizations of these same five readings are available in Can These Bones Live? Contemporary Dramas for Lent and Easter *by David Kehret (AFP 0806639652).*

129

OVERVIEW: MIDWEEK THEMES BASED ON READINGS FROM THE EASTER VIGIL

FIRST WEEK
Genesis 1:1—2:4a
Creation

SECOND WEEK
Genesis 7:1-5, 11-18; 8:6-18; 9:8-13
The Flood

THIRD WEEK
Genesis 22:1-18
The Testing of Abraham

FOURTH WEEK
Exodus 14:10-31; 15:20-21
Israel's Deliverance

FIFTH WEEK
Ezekiel 37:1-14
The Valley of the Dry Bones

Service of Light

A lighted vesper candle may be carried in procession during the following versicles and placed in its stand near the altar.

These versicles may be sung to the tones given in Evening Prayer, LBW, p. 142.

Behold, now is the accept- | able time;
now is the day of sal- | vation.
Turn us again, O God of | our salvation,
that the light of your face may shine on | us.
May your justice shine | like the sun;
and may the poor be lifted | up.

HYMN OF LIGHT

One of the following hymns may be sung.

Dearest Jesus, at your word LBW 248
O Light whose splendor thrills WOV 728
Christ, mighty Savior WOV 729, RW1 19
I heard the voice of Jesus say LBW 497, RW1: 39

THANKSGIVING FOR LIGHT

This is set to music in LBW, p. 144.

The Lord be with you.
And also with you.
Let us give thanks to the Lord our God.
It is right to give our thanks and praise.
Blessed are you, O Lord our God, king of the universe,
who led your people Israel by a pillar of cloud by day
and a pillar of fire by night:
Enlighten our darkness by the light of your Christ;
may his Word be a lamp to our feet and a light to our path;
for you are merciful, and you love your whole creation,
and we, your creatures, glorify you, Father, Son, and Holy Spirit.
Amen

PSALMODY

The first psalm may be Psalm 141, as printed in LBW, pp. 145–46; or another setting of this psalm may be used.

130

An additional psalm or canticle may be used for each of the weeks during Lent (see Psalter for Worship):

FIRST WEEK
Ps. 136:1-9, 23-26
SECOND WEEK
Ps. 46
THIRD WEEK
Ps. 16
FOURTH WEEK
Exodus 15:1b-13, 17-18 (Song of Moses and Miriam)
FIFTH WEEK
Ps. 143

HYMN

Possibilities for hymns related to the readings for each of the weeks follow.

FIRST WEEK
How marvelous God's greatness LBW 515
When long before time WOV 799
God the sculptor of the mountains TFF 222

SECOND WEEK
Oh, happy day when we shall stand LBW 351
Thy holy wings WOV 741
'Tis the old ship of Zion TFF 199

THIRD WEEK
A multitude comes from the east and the west LBW 313
Day by day WOV 746
God has smiled on me TFF 190

FOURTH WEEK
When Israel was in Egypt's land WOV 670
Glories of your name are spoken LBW 358
Wade in the water TFF 114, RWSB

FIFTH WEEK
Love divine, all loves excelling LBW 315
The Word of God is source and seed WOV 658
Jesus, keep me near the cross TFF 73, RWSB

OTHER HYMN OPTIONS INCLUDE:

All who believe and are baptized LBW 194

Lord, thee I love with all my heart LBW 325

Peace, to soothe our bitter woes LBW 338

We were baptized in Christ Jesus WOV 698

O blessed spring WOV 695

A wonderful Savior is Jesus TFF 260

Song over the waters RWSB

READINGS FOR EACH OF THE WEEKS OF LENT

FIRST WEEK

Genesis 1:1—2:4a

SECOND WEEK

Genesis 7:1-5, 11-18; 8:6-18; 9:8-13

THIRD WEEK

Genesis 22:1-18

FOURTH WEEK

Exodus 14:10-31; 15:20-21

FIFTH WEEK

Ezekiel 37:1-14

A homily or meditation may follow the reading.

Silence is kept by all.

The silence concludes:

Long ago, in many and various ways,

God spoke to our ancestors by the prophets;

but in these last days God has spoken to us by the Son.

GOSPEL CANTICLE

My soul now magnifies the Lord LBW 180

My soul proclaims your greatness WOV 730

My soul does magnify the Lord TFF 168

Magnificat RWSB

LITANY

The music for the litany in LBW, p. 148, may be used with the following.

In peace, let us pray to the Lord.

Lord, have mercy.

For the peace from above, let us pray to the Lord.

Lord, have mercy.

For the peace of the whole world, for the well-being of the church of God, and for the unity of all, let us pray to the Lord.

Lord, have mercy.

For those who are preparing for the Easter sacraments, let us pray to the Lord.

Lord, have mercy.

For the baptized people of God and for their varied ministries, let us pray to the Lord.

Lord, have mercy.

For those who are poor, hungry, homeless, or sick, let us pray to the Lord.

Lord, have mercy.

Help, save, comfort, and defend us, gracious Lord.

Silence is kept by all.

Rejoicing in the fellowship of all the saints, let us commend ourselves, one another, and our whole life to Christ, our Lord.

To you, O Lord.

PRAYER OF THE DAY

From the previous Sunday if a service is held during the week.

THE LORD'S PRAYER

BLESSING

For a musical setting, see LBW, p. 152.

Let us bless the Lord.

Thanks be to God.

The almighty and merciful Lord, the Father, the ✚ Son, and the Holy Spirit, bless and preserve us.

Amen

131

February 25, 2004

Ash Wednesday

INTRODUCTION

Ash Wednesday marks the beginning of Lent with ash on our foreheads. This cross echoes our baptismal anointing, when we were buried with Christ. The ash is a chilling reminder of our mortality, but because our death is now in Christ, our endings are beginnings. The Lenten disciplines of acts of kindness, prayer, and fasting are tools of discipleship that can lead us to renewal as we bury all that is holding us back from being truly alive.

PRAYER OF THE DAY

Almighty and ever-living God, you hate nothing you have made and you forgive the sins of all who are penitent. Create in us new and honest hearts, so that, truly repenting of our sins, we may obtain from you, the God of all mercy, full pardon and forgiveness; through your Son, Jesus Christ our Lord, who lives and reigns with you and the Holy Spirit, one God, now and forever.

VERSE

Return to the LORD, your God, who is gracious and merciful, slow to anger, and abounding in steadfast love. (Joel 2:13)

READINGS

Joel 2:1-2, 12-17

The context of this reading is a community liturgy of sorrow over sin. The prophet has called the people to mourn a devastating plague and to announce a day of darkness, the day of the Lord. The people are called to repent and to return to God, who is gracious and merciful.

or Isaiah 58:1-12

The fast that God chooses is not merely outward, but one that gives evidence of repentance through works of mercy.

Psalm 51:1-18 (Psalm 51:1-17 NRSV)

Have mercy on me, O God, according to your lovingkindness. (Ps. 51:1)

2 Corinthians 5:20b—6:10

Out of love for humankind, Christ experienced sin and

suffering, so that the saving power of God could penetrate the most forbidding and tragic depths of human experience. No aspect of human life is ignored by the presence of God's grace. Because of this, Paul announces that this day is a day of God's grace, an acceptable time to turn toward God's mercy.

Matthew 6:1-6, 16-21

In this passage Matthew sets forth a vision of genuine righteousness illustrated by three basic acts of Jewish devotion: almsgiving, prayer, and fasting. Jesus does not denounce these acts—in the New Testament they are signs of singular devotion to God. Rather, he criticizes those who perform them in order to have a sense of self-satisfaction or to gain public approval. Care for the poor, intense prayer, and fasting with a joyous countenance are signs of loving dedication to God.

COLOR   Black *or* Purple

THE PRAYERS

As we seek in this Lenten time to grow in our faith, let us pray for the life of the world.

A BRIEF SILENCE.

For our Lenten journey, that the clouds and thick darkness of our sin might give way to Easter's rising light, and that through humble almsgiving, prayer, and fasting our lives would breathe in and out God's constant love, let us pray to the Lord.

Lord, have mercy.

For those whose brows are marked on this day, that the reminder of mortality might lead them closer to the one who has overcome death for all, let us pray to the Lord.

Lord, have mercy.

For those preparing for Easter baptism, that this Lent may be for them a watered garden that nurtures faith, let us pray to the Lord.

Lord, have mercy.

For the world, that conflicts might cease, disaster be averted, hatred transformed, and peace be found, through the One who is slow to anger and abounding in love, let us pray to the Lord.

Lord, have mercy.

For the church, that we may be humble in our serving, giving food to the hungry, shelter to the homeless poor, comfort to the afflicted (*especially*), let us pray to the Lord.

Lord, have mercy.

HERE OTHER INTERCESSIONS MAY BE OFFERED.

In remembrance of those who have died and have found their rest in you, that we, having nothing, may join with them in possessing everything, let us pray to the Lord.

Lord, have mercy.

Grant these prayers, merciful God, and all that we need, as we eagerly await the Easter feast; through Jesus Christ our Lord.

Amen

IMAGES FOR PREACHING

Discerning the heart and quality of a watermelon is not an easy task. Near the supermarket melon display, one hears self-proclaimed experts analyze anything from the depth of the melon's stripes, to its shape, to the ever-popular quality of its "thunk" when snapped by the thumb and index finger. On the other hand, one also overhears those less confident—but perhaps more truthful—who observe, "You never really know the heart of a melon until you slice it open."

The task of the Ash Wednesday preacher is not unlike discerning the heart of a melon. The outward signs of a penitent heart are not easily discerned; they are even less easily described or proclaimed.

Ash Wednesday scripture lifts up the tension that accompanies the Lenten discipline of discerning and rending the heart. "Blow the trumpet," says Joel. "Sanctify the fast."

Matthew, on the other hand, exhorts, "So whenever you give alms, do not sound a trumpet before you, as the hypocrites do in the synagogues and in the streets." Piety practiced before others in order to be seen is condemned. "In secret" is the operative word for piety.

Yet, if "in secret" is the operative word of Matthew, "in public" is that of Isaiah. "Shout out, do not hold back! Lift up your voice like a trumpet!" Fasting? Of course! Not as a private, pious deed; but rather, fasting as a public witness. Free the oppressed; feed the hungry; house the homeless; clothe the naked.

The Lenten heart is both condemned and extolled by its public acts, and difficulty of discernment might soon become despair until we are reminded of the psalmist's words. Indeed, it is God who creates clean hearts; it is God who renews our spirits; it is God who gifts us with saving help; it is God who opens our lips and fills our words and deeds with rightful praise.

WORSHIP MATTERS

Earth to earth, ashes to ashes, dust to dust. We recall those words as ashes are placed on our heads and we are vividly reminded that we are dust and to dust we shall return. Ash Wednesday can sometimes feel like a heavy, even morbid day. It is an intense experience for pastors to put ashes on the heads of infants and young children, the elderly, and those with terminal illnesses. Yet the beginning of Lent is an invitation to a journey that will lead to the new life and resurrection of Easter. Though Ash Wednesday is one of the most solemn and serious liturgies of the year it is also filled with great promise. Through the language of sermons, prayers, and hymn texts (such as WOV 659, 662) the congregation can make the connection that from the earth will come spring and rebirth.

LET THE CHILDREN COME

In baptism the pastor proclaims that the baptized are sealed by the Holy Spirit and marked with the cross of Christ forever. The ashes on our foreheads remind us that we are children of God and disciples of Christ. As we die with Christ so too will we be raised with Christ. Encourage adults (parents, grandparents, godparents, aunts, and uncles) to begin a daily ritual of making a sign of the cross on their children's foreheads while saying: "You are a child of God. Jesus loves you." Children reciprocate to the adults. Through this daily ritual the family of God more easily remembers who they are and to whom they belong.

HYMNS FOR WORSHIP

GATHERING

Savior, when in dust to you   LBW 91
I want Jesus to walk with me   WOV 660, TFF 66

HYMN OF THE DAY

Just as I am, without one plea   LBW 296

133

ALTERNATE HYMN OF THE DAY

Out of the depths I cry to you   LBW 295

O Sun of justice   WOV 659

(May be sung to TALLIS' CANON, LBW 278)

COMMUNION

Our Father, we have wandered   WOV 733

Jesus, your blood and righteousness   LBW 302

SENDING

O Lord, throughout these forty days   LBW 99

Be thou my vision   WOV 776

ADDITIONAL HYMNS AND SONGS

Create in me a clean heart   LLC 442

Restore in us, O God   RWSB, WOV 662, RWI 60, 61

Dust and ashes touch our face   NCH 186

Give me a clean heart   TFF 216

MUSIC FOR THE DAY

PSALMODY

Cox, Joe. "Create in Me a Clean Heart, O God" in *Psalms for the People of God.* SMP 45/1037S.

Hurd, David. "Psalm 51: Create in Me" in STP, vol. I.

Kogut, Malcolm. "Psalm 51: Create in Me a Clean Heart" in PCY, vol. 10.

Kreutz, Robert. *Psalms and Selected Canticles.* OCP TM-8311.

Makeever, Ray. "Be Merciful, O God" in DH.

Schwarz, May. PW , Cycle C.

See Proper 19.

CHORAL

Allegri, Gregorio. "Miserere mei, Deus." SSATB. CHE CH55059.

Bach, J.S. "Jesu, meine Freude" in *Bach for All Seasons.* SATB, opt kybd. AFP 080065854X.

Nelson, Ronald A. "Create in Me a Clean Heart." SATB. KJO 8808.

Schalk, Carl. "Have Mercy on Me, O God." SATB. AFP 0800657845.

Schütz, Heinrich. "Out of the Depths We Cry, Lord." SATB. AFP 11-1546. OP.

Scott, K. Lee. "Out of the Depths I Cry to Thee." 2 pt mxd, kybd. AFP 0800647327.

CHILDREN'S CHOIR

Horman, John. "Faith Is Believing." U, opt desc, pno, opt fl, perc. ABI 0687051851.

Marshall, Jane. "Create In Me, O God." U, kybd. CG CGA750. And in *Psalms Together II.* CG CGC21.

KEYBOARD/INSTRUMENTAL

Bach, J.S. "Herzlich tut mich verlangen." (O Sacred Head, Now Wounded). Org. Various ed.

Brahms, Johannes. "Herzliebster Jesu" (Ah, Holy Jesus) in *Eleven Chorale Preludes.* Org. Mercury or various ed.

Harbach, Barbara. "Rhapsody on Aus tiefer Not" in *Suite on German Chorales.* Org. AFP 0800675010.

Honoré, Jeffrey. "Ashes" in *Contemporary Classics: OCP Organ Series Anthology,* vol. 3. Org. OCP 6837118130.

HANDBELL

Afdahl, Lee J. "Psalm 51." 3-5 oct, opt marimba. AFP 0800675061.

Linker, Janet and Jane McFadden. "Reflection on Aberystwyth." 3-5 oct, org. CPH 97-6759; CPH 97-6758 (full score).

PRAISE ENSEMBLE

Getty, Keith. "O, for a Closer Walk with God" in *New Songs 2003/03.* Kingsway.

Park, Andy. "In the Secret" in *More Songs for Praise and Worship.* SATB. WRD 3010387016 (vocal ed); WRD 3010186363 (pno, vcs, perc).

Wednesday, February 25

ELIZABETH FEDDE, DEACONESS, 1921

Fedde was born in Norway and trained as a deaconess. In 1882, at the age of thirty-two, she was asked to come to New York to minister to the poor and to Norwegian seamen. Her influence was wide ranging, and she established the Deaconess House in Brooklyn and the Deaconess House and Hospital of the Lutheran Free Church in Minneapolis. She returned home to Norway in 1895 and died there.

Fedde was an example of selfless service to those in need. How does your congregation reach out to those who are sick, in need, or forgotten? Perhaps ways to reach out that have been overlooked can easily be incorporated in your congregation's ministry.

February 29, 2004

First Sunday in Lent

INTRODUCTION

The Lenten discipline is a spiritual struggle. In the confession of sins we acknowledge that we struggle and seek God's strength. Jesus struggles with us, and so we are sustained. Help is as close as a prayer and a confession that we cannot do it on our own. God gives life and its fruit, and so all we offer in worship is giving back what was first given us by grace.

PRAYER OF THE DAY

Lord God, you led your ancient people through the wilderness and brought them to the promised land. Guide now the people of your Church, that, following our Savior, we may walk through the wilderness of this world toward the glory of the world to come; through your Son, Jesus Christ our Lord, who lives and reigns with you and the Holy Spirit, one God, now and forever.
or
Lord God, our strength, the battle of good and evil rages within and around us, and our ancient foe tempts us with his deceits and empty promises. Keep us steadfast in your Word and, when we fall, raise us again and restore us through your Son, Jesus Christ our Lord, who lives and reigns with you and the Holy Spirit, one God, now and forever.

VERSE

One does not live by bread alone, but by every word that comes from the mouth of God. (Matt. 4:4)

READINGS

Deuteronomy 26:1-11

The annual harvest festival called the feast of Weeks provides the setting for this reading. This festival celebrates the first fruits of the produce of the land offered back to God in thanks. In this text, worshipers announce God's gracious acts on behalf of Israel.

Psalm 91:1-2, 9-16

God shall charge the angels to keep you in all your ways. (Ps. 91:11)

Romans 10:8b-13

Paul reminds the Christians at Rome of the foundational affirmation of those who are saved: the confession of faith in the risen Jesus as Lord.

Luke 4:1-13

After being filled with the Holy Spirit at his baptism, Jesus is tempted by the devil and defines what it means to be called "the Son of God."

COLOR   Purple

THE PRAYERS

As we seek in this Lenten time to grow in our faith, let us pray for the life of the world.
A BRIEF SILENCE.
That all fertile lands be tended with care, that crops be successfully planted and that the coming growing season might yield abundant harvests and all the bounty needed to feed this hungry world, let us pray to the Lord.
Lord, have mercy.
That the church be strengthened in its forty-day Lenten journey, be delivered from all temptation and harm, and be found faithful on the day of Christ's coming, let us pray to the Lord.
Lord, have mercy.
That by grace, those preparing for baptism and those who will affirm their baptisms may confess with their lips that Jesus is Lord, let us pray to the Lord.
Lord, have mercy.
That those people who lack a home and wander in our modern wilderness might be helped to find a permanent place of welcome, let us pray to the Lord.
Lord, have mercy.
That those who are ill or in any need *(especially)* may find comfort and deliverance in the generosity of the Lord of all, let us pray to the Lord.
Lord, have mercy.
That this community through Lenten almsgiving might find joy in returning the firstfruits of their labors, let us pray to the Lord.
Lord, have mercy.

135

HERE OTHER INTERCESSIONS MAY BE OFFERED.

That the witness of the faithful departed (*especially*) may strengthen us in our journey, and that we be joined with them by the power of our baptism into Christ, let us pray to the Lord.

Lord, have mercy.

Grant these prayers, merciful God, and all that we need, as we eagerly await the Easter feast; through Jesus Christ our Lord.

Amen

IMAGES FOR PREACHING

"I know a hot piece of real estate in Florida" or "I've got a bridge I could sell you." We are teased with this quip when we realize that we've been duped; when we've succumbed to temptation and have sold out to an empty promise. We sense these words lurking about the devil who, with a "*deceptive* hand and an outstretched arm," met Jesus in the wilderness and taunted him with the kingdoms of the world.

Clearly, Jesus' response indicates it is not the promise of real estate that can cause him to stumble; nonetheless, it may be the wisdom of the real estate agent that enlightens our reading of today's texts.

"Location! Location! Location!" is the motto of today's property peddler; what one has and where one has it not only defines our property value, but often our worth as human beings. People living in "high density districts" in Zimbabwe are accorded shorter—if any—newspaper obituaries when they die; in the eyes of society, where one has lived determines whether one's life and death is worthy of note.

Indeed, careful attention to prepositions—the "where" words—lifts up both the tension and release of today's lessons. If only we can position ourselves correctly, we will not be duped! We must go "through the wilderness" implies Luke. We must come "out of Egypt," and "into the land which the Lord our God has given" according to the Deuteronomist, in order to dwell, according to the psalmist, "in the shelter of the Most High" and abide "under the shadow of the Almighty."

However, in our quest to locate ourselves well, we must not forget that which first locates itself in us. Paul reminds us today, quoting Deuteronomy, the word is "near you, on your lips, in your heart." Despite our best efforts to position ourselves, it is here where the word of grace is found. "For one believes with the heart and so is justified, and one confesses with the mouth and so is saved."

WORSHIP MATTERS

Lent is a time for simplicity and sparseness. Some congregations may choose to not have processions during Lent, or to have additional times of silence in the liturgy. As we return to our baptism we confront the sinfulness and brokenness in our lives and long for the healing waters of Easter. Certainly every Sunday is a celebration of the resurrection, but the Sundays of Lent may have a certain sense of restraint and introspection. That doesn't mean the liturgy should be a "downer"; the Lenten proper preface bids us to cleanse our hearts and "prepare with joy for the paschal feast."

LET THE CHILDREN COME

Lent begins with the story of Jesus' temptation. As Christians we are also tempted by the ways of this world. To resist temptation we must seek God's word and will. In the Lord's Prayer we pray to be saved from trial and temptation, and delivered from evil. We pray seeking God's will and to have God's glory revealed to us. Invite Sunday school children to pray the Lord's Prayer in worship today. Younger children could draw a picture on poster-sized board for each petition and hold it up for the rest of the congregation to see while older children pray the prayer.

HYMNS FOR WORSHIP
GATHERING

If you but trust in God to guide you   LBW 453
He leadeth me   TFF 151
The glory of these forty days   WOV 657

HYMN OF THE DAY

Jesus, still lead on   LBW 341

ALTERNATE HYMN OF THE DAY

I want Jesus to walk with me   WOV 660, TFF 66
God, with a mighty hand / *Tú diste a Israel*   LLC 476

COMMUNION

Lord Jesus Christ, we humbly pray   LBW 225
Bind us together   WOV 748

SENDING

Lift every voice and sing   LBW 562, TFF 296
Lead me, guide me   TFF 70
The summons   W&P 137, RWSB

ADDITIONAL HYMNS AND SONGS

I must tell Jesus   TFF 183
Bless now, O God, the journey   RWSB
Out in the wilderness   W&P 115
Jesus, tempted in the desert   RS 548

MUSIC FOR THE DAY

PSALMODY

Haas, David. "Lord, Be with Me" in PCY, vol. 9.
Joncas, Michael. "Psalm 91: Be with Me, Lord" in STP, vol. 1.
Keesecker, Thomas. PW , Cycle C.
On Eagle's Wings   WOV 779, W&P 110.

CHORAL

Adelmann, Dale. "Swing Low." SATTBB. PAR PPM 09522.
Busarow, Donald. "The Provençal Carol." SATB, kybd.
    CPH 98-3221.
Hopson, Hal H. "Psalm of Confession." SATB. AFP 080065952X.
Rowan, William P. "With the Lord, There is Mercy." SATB, kybd.
    AFP 0800675584.
Sitton, Michael. "Tantum ergo." U, org. PAR PPM 09111.
Ylvisaker, John. "Lord, Keep Us Steadfast in Your Word." SATB,
    kybd, opt perc, DB. KJO 8864.

CHILDREN'S CHOIR

Marshall, Jane. "Psalm 91:1-4" in *Psalms Together II.* U, kybd.
    CG CGC21.
Powell, Robert. "A Lenten Prayer." (Luke 4:1) U, fl, org.
    CG CGA159.

KEYBOARD/INSTRUMENTAL

Albrecht, Mark. "Sojourner" in *Meditations of Faith for Woodwinds and
    Keyboard.* Kybd, inst. AFP 0800659414.
Cherwien, David. "Sojourner" in *Groundings.* Org. AFP 0800659805.
Drischner, Max. "Aus tiefer Not" in *Augsburg Organ Library: Lent.* Org.
    AFP 0800658973.
Manz, Paul. "Seelenbräutigam" in *Augsburg Organ Library: Lent.* Org.
    AFP 0800658973.

HANDBELL

Berns, Susan Ullom. "Psalm 91." 3 oct. Thomas House 1H708952.
Rogers, Sharon Elery. "A Lenten Bell Meditation." 3-5 oct.
    LOR 20/1087L.

PRAISE ENSEMBLE

Hooker, John Leon. "Now Let Us All with One Accord" in *Gather.*
    GIA.
Jerrigan, Dennis. "You Are My All in All" in *Best of the Best.*
    FEL 1891062018.
Zschech, Darlene. "Shout to the Lord" in W&P.

Monday, March 1

GEORGE HERBERT, PRIEST, 1633

As a student at Trinity College, Cambridge, George Herbert excelled in languages and music. He went to college with the intention of becoming a priest, but his scholarship attracted the attention of King James I. Herbert served in parliament for two years. After the death of King James and under the influence of a friend, Herbert's interest in ordained ministry was renewed. He was ordained a priest in 1630 and served the little parish of St. Andrew, Bremerton, until his death. He was noted for unfailing care for his parishioners, bringing the sacraments to them when they were ill, and providing food and clothing for those in need.

Herbert was also a poet and hymnwriter. One of his hymns, "Come, my way, my truth, my life" (LBW 513), invites an intimate encounter with Christ through a feast that "mends in length."

Tuesday, March 2

JOHN WESLEY, 1791; CHARLES WESLEY, 1788; RENEWERS OF THE CHURCH

The Wesleys were leaders of a revival in the Church of England. Their spiritual discipline of frequent communion, fasting, and advocacy for the poor earned them the name "Methodists." The Wesleys were missionaries in the American colony of Georgia for a time but returned to England discouraged. Following a conversion experience while reading Luther's Preface to the Epistle to the Ro-

137

mans, John was perhaps the greatest force in eighteenth-century revival. Their desire was that the Methodist Societies would be a movement for renewal in the Church of England, but after their deaths the societies developed a separate status.

Charles wrote more than six hundred hymns, twelve of which are in *Lutheran Book of Worship* and one of which is in *With One Voice*. Three of Charles's hymns are especially appropriate for Lent: "Christ, whose glory fills the skies" (LBW 265), "Love divine, all loves excelling" (LBW 315), and "Forth in thy name, O Lord, I go" (LBW 505).

March 7, 2004

Second Sunday in Lent

INTRODUCTION

Baptism is the compass that guides us through life. Lent is a season for immersing ourselves in a new identity—reminding us who we are and calling us to what we are to be doing. The miracle of grace is as amazing as starting a family in your old age, as Abraham and Sarah did, or being reminded that our true citizenship lies beyond this world.

Today the church remembers Perpetua, Felicity, and their companions, early Christians who were martyred when they refused to renounce their faith, as well as Thomas Aquinas, one of the great theologians in the history of the church.

PRAYER OF THE DAY

Eternal God, it is your glory always to have mercy. Bring back all who have erred and strayed from your ways; lead them again to embrace in faith the truth of your Word and to hold it fast; through Jesus Christ your Son our Lord, who lives and reigns with you and the Holy Spirit, one God, now and forever.

VERSE

God so loved the world that he gave his only Son, so that everyone who believes in him may not perish but may have eternal life. (John 3:16)

READINGS

Genesis 15:1-12, 17-18

God promises a childless and doubting Abram that he will have a son, that his descendants will be as numerous as the stars, and that the land will be their inheritance. Abram's trust in God's promise is sealed with a covenant-making ritual, a sign of God's promise.

Psalm 27

In the day of trouble, the Lord shall keep me safe. (Ps. 27:7)

Philippians 3:17—4:1

Although Paul's devotion to Christ has caused him to be persecuted, he does not regret the course he has taken. Writing from prison, he expresses confidence in a glorious future and encourages other Christians to follow in his footsteps.

Luke 13:31-35

Jesus likens the tyrant Herod to a murderous fox. He speaks of himself as a mother hen who would sacrifice her own life to shield her children from danger.

COLOR Purple

THE PRAYERS

As we seek in this Lenten time to grow in our faith, let us pray for the life of the world.

A BRIEF SILENCE.

That the whole church may return to the font this Lent and through the promises of baptism be found faithful to our citizenship that is in heaven, let us pray to the Lord.

Lord, have mercy.

That those preparing for Easter baptism will discover God's ever-widening covenant embrace, let us pray to the Lord.

Lord, have mercy.

138

That the nations find peace this season, that trust be rebuilt and enemies become neighbors, and for the peace of Jerusalem, let us pray to the Lord.

Lord, have mercy.

That all exiles and refugees find comfort and welcome in the kind embrace of others, let us pray to the Lord.

Lord, have mercy.

That those who suffer illness of body or mind *(especially)* may receive God's gracious healing, let us pray to the Lord.

Lord, have mercy.

That the leaders of this congregation may serve in imitation of Christ and faithfully guide us, let us pray to the Lord.

Lord, have mercy.

HERE OTHER INTERCESSIONS MAY BE OFFERED.

That together with Perpetua, Felicity, and their martyred companions, Thomas Aquinas, teacher, *(other names)*, and all the faithful departed, we may at last find a home in the heavenly Jerusalem, let us pray to the Lord.

Lord, have mercy.

Grant these prayers, merciful God, and all that we need, as we eagerly await the Easter feast; through Jesus Christ our Lord.

Amen

IMAGES FOR PREACHING

"Jerusalem, my happy home, when shall I come to thee?" we sing. "When shall my sorrows have an end? Thy joys when shall I see?" (LBW 331).

What sharp contrast Jesus brings to this image when he mourns, "Jerusalem, Jerusalem, the city that kills the prophets and stones those who are sent to it! How often have I desired to gather your children together as a hen gathers her brood under her wings, and you were not willing!"

For perhaps the past five decades, it is the latter of these images which more fully describes our contemporary image of Jerusalem. The "happy harbor of the saints" has become the harbor for centuries-old grudges. The "sweet and pleasant soil" has been soaked with the blood of battle.

This reality, a shattered terrestrial counterpart of the heavenly Jerusalem, is not inconsistent with the words of scripture assigned for today. The temporal nature of all of earthly life is lifted up. "Know this for certain," said the Lord to Abram, "that your offspring shall be aliens in a land that is not theirs" for four hundred years. As history bears out, even after Abraham's descendents return to the awaited land of promise, they discover it to be flawed—pre-owned and still claimed.

Further, even family values have their limitations, implies the psalmist: "Though my father and my mother forsake me, the Lord will sustain me."

"Once again we are reminded that we have no abiding city on this earth." How often clergy have prefaced the announcement of death with these words. It is in this face of the temporal that Paul reminds us of the permanent; in the face of our status as earthly refugees that we are granted eternal citizenship; in the face of frail deteriorating bodies that we glimpse our body of his glory. "Our citizenship is in heaven, it is from there that we are expecting a Savior, the Lord Jesus Christ."

"Wait patiently for the Lord," says the psalmist.

WORSHIP MATTERS

Absence makes the heart grow fonder. Traditionally the word "alleluia" isn't sung during Lent, and flowers are often not used. In some places the font is closed and sealed, suggesting our wilderness exile and our thirst for the baptismal waters of Easter. If crosses are veiled it is helpful to make the point that we aren't mourning Jesus' death for forty days, but the veiling suggests a sense of penitence and sorrow for sin and injustice in the world. On Easter Day the chancel will be filled with spring flowers, the font filled with fresh water, and the cross of victory will lead us in procession.

LET THE CHILDREN COME

There is no place that feels safe in our world today. Schools, churches, homes, and office buildings are all vulnerable. Adults and, to an extent, even children are aware of life's uncertainties. For that reason the image Jesus uses in the gospel today should be highlighted. The only place to know the comfort and strength of always feeling safe is in the arms of Jesus. Just as a mother hen protects her chicks, Jesus protects us by having died for us and giving us the promise and hope of everlasting life.

139

HYMNS FOR WORSHIP

GATHERING

Beneath the cross of Jesus   LBW 107

Blessed be the God of Israel   WOV 725

HYMN OF THE DAY

Around you, O Lord Jesus   LBW 496

ALTERNATE HYMN OF THE DAY

Lord Christ, when first you came to earth   LBW 421

When twilight comes   WOV 663

COMMUNION

Draw near and take the body of the Lord   LBW 226

By your hand you feed your people   RWSB

SENDING

There's a wideness in God's mercy   LBW 290, RWI 76, 77

Thy holy wings   WOV 741

ADDITIONAL HYMNS AND SONGS

A song of unity (As a mother hen)   W&P 1

Eternal Lord of love, behold your church   RWSB

God is my strong salvation   PH 179

MUSIC FOR THE DAY

PSALMODY

DeBruyn, Randall. "The Lord Is My Light" in STP, vol. 4.

Howard, Julie. *Sing for Joy: Psalm Settings for God's Children.*
LP 0814620787.

Keesecker, Thomas. PW , Cycle C.

Kreutz, Robert. *Psalms and Selected Canticles.* OCP TM-8311.

Zimmerman, Heinz Werner. "The Lord Is My Light." SATB, org.
CPH 98-2174.

CHORAL

Bach, J.S. "Lord, Thee I Love" in *Bach for all Seasons.* SATB, kybd.
AFP 080065854X.

Ellingboe, Bradley. "Thy Holy Wings." SATB. KJO C9001.

Farlee, Robert Buckley. "When Twilight Comes." 2 pt mxd, pno.
AFP 0800675576.

Hopp, Roy. "May I Love You Lord." SATB, kybd.
AFP 080067541X.

Mendelssohn, Felix. "Jerusalem, Jerusalem." in St. Paul. S solo, kybd.
Various ed.

Sateren, Leland. "Jerusalem, My Happy Home." SATB.
AFP 6000101627. OP.

Vierne, Louis. "Benedictus" in *Solemn Mass.* SATB, org. MF MF190.

CHILDREN'S CHOIR

Bedford, Michael. "The Lord is My Light." (Ps. 27) U/2 pt, fl, kybd.
CG CGA878.

Horman, John. "God So Loved the World." (John 3:16, Verse) U/2
pt, kybd, opt fl/vln.   CG CGA447.

KEYBOARD/INSTRUMENTAL

Burkhardt, Michael. "O Sacred Head, Now Wounded" in *Five Lenten
Hymn Improvisations.* Org. MSM 10-309.

Gabrielsen, Stephen. "O Jesu, an de Dina" in *We Are Your Own Forever.*
Org. AFP 0800652517. OP.

Reuss, Jon. "Around You, O Lord Jesus" in *Organ Music for the Seasons,*
vol. 3. Org.   AFP 0800675649.

Walther, Johann. "Jesus, Priceless Treasure" (Jesu, meine Freude) in
Choralvorspiele alter Meister. Org. PET 3048.

HANDBELL

McFadden, Jane. "Thy Holy Wings" in *Two More Swedish Melodies for
Handbells* (Day By Day; Thy Holy Wings) 3-4 oct, opt hc.
AFP 0800657357.

Wagner, Douglas E. "Rhosymedre." 3–4 oct. AG 1318.

PRAISE ENSEMBLE

Mohr, Jon. "Find Us Faithful" in *Best of the Best.* FEL 1891062018.

Schutte, Daniel. "Here I Am, Lord" in W&P.

Sunday, March 7

PERPETUA AND FELICITY AND COMPANIONS, MARTYRS AT CARTHAGE, 202

In the year 202 the emperor Septimius Severus forbade conversions to Christianity. Perpetua, a noblewoman, Felicity, a slave, and other companions were all catechumens at Carthage in North Africa. They were imprisoned and sentenced to death. Perpetua's father, who was not a Christian, visited her in prison and begged her to lay aside her Christian convictions in order to spare her life and spare the family from scorn. Perpetua responded and told her father, "We know that we are not placed in own power but in that of God."

140

During the weeks of Lent, congregations that do not have catechumens can pray for those who do as they approach their own death and rebirth in the waters of baptism at the Easter Vigil and are clothed with the new life of Christ.

Sunday, March 7

THOMAS AQUINAS, TEACHER, 1274

Thomas Aquinas was a brilliant and creative theologian of the thirteenth century. He was first and foremost a student of the Bible and profoundly concerned with the theological formation of the church's ordained ministers. As a member of the Order of Preachers (Dominicans), he worked to correlate scripture with the philosophy of Aristotle, which was having a renaissance in Aquinas's day. Some students of Aristotle's philosophy found in it an alternative to Christianity. But Aquinas immersed himself in the thought of Aristotle and worked to explain Christian beliefs in the philosophical culture of the day. The contemporary worship cultural studies done by the Lutheran World Federation resonate with Aquinas's method.

Aquinas was also a hymnwriter. His hymn "Thee we adore, O hidden Savior" (LBW 199) is traditionally sung on Maundy Thursday.

Friday, March 12

GREGORY THE GREAT, BISHOP OF ROME, 604

Gregory was born into a politically influential family. At one time he held political office, and at another time he lived as a monk, all before he was elected to the papacy. Gregory's work was extensive. He influenced public worship through the establishment of a lectionary and prayers to correlate with the readings. He established a school to train church musicians, and Gregorian chant is named in his honor. He wrote a treatise underscoring what is required of a parish pastor serving a congregation. He sent missionaries to preach to the Anglo-Saxons who had invaded England. At one time he even organized distribution of grain during a shortage of food in Rome.

Gregory's life serves as an example of the link between liturgy and social justice. His Lenten hymn, "O Christ, our king, creator, Lord" (LBW 101), sings of God's grace flowing out from the cross to all creation.

141

March 14, 2004

Third Sunday in Lent

INTRODUCTION

Can we take the news to heart? Each story we encounter in this season is really about us. Lent began as we were reminded by an ashen cross that we are mortal; death awaits us. The clock is ticking; the forty days are unwinding. We have now! If we take this day seriously, we may discover that our deepest hungers can be filled. When we know that we are heading toward a forgiving God, the news becomes good news.

PRAYER OF THE DAY

Eternal Lord, your kingdom has broken into our troubled world through the life, death, and resurrection of your Son. Help us to hear your Word and obey it, so that we become instruments of your redeeming love; through your Son, Jesus Christ our Lord, who lives and reigns with you and the Holy Spirit, one God, now and forever.

VERSE

Jesus humbled himself and became obedient to the point of death—even death on a cross. (Phil. 2:8)

READINGS

Isaiah 55:1-9

To those who have experienced long years in exile, the return to their native land seems like an unbelievable promise of free food and drink for all who come to the celebration. What is more, those who return to the Lord also enjoy new life and forgiveness, because God's ways are not our ways.

Psalm 63:1-8

O God, eagerly I seek you; my soul thirsts for you. (Ps. 63:1)

1 Corinthians 10:1-13

Paul uses images from Hebrew story and prophecy to speak the truth of Jesus Christ: He is our rock, our water, our food, and our drink. Christ is the living sign of God's faithfulness.

Luke 13:1-9

Jesus addresses the age-old question of whether people deserve the seemingly random calamities that happen to them. The short answer is no, but the key to our peace is using the present moment to throw ourselves upon God's grace.

COLOR Purple

THE PRAYERS

As we seek in this Lenten time to grow in our faith, let us pray for the life of the world.
A BRIEF SILENCE.

That the whole church might in this Lent return to the Lord, abundant in mercy and pardon, let us pray to the Lord.

Lord, have mercy.

That those preparing for baptism this season might quench their thirst in the waters of life and eat what is good at the table of the Lord, let us pray to the Lord.

Lord, have mercy.

That the leaders of the nations of the world may walk in the way of the Lord, let us pray to the Lord.

Lord, have mercy.

That those whose spirit is fragile find courage in the rock that is Christ and not be tested beyond their strength, let us pray to the Lord.

Lord, have mercy.

That all who are ill or face surgery *(especially)* may be given comfort and healing, let us pray to the Lord.

Lord, have mercy.

That this congregation might bear good fruit worthy of its calling and be a beacon of hope in this community; let us pray to the Lord.

Lord, have mercy.

HERE OTHER INTERCESSIONS MAY BE OFFERED.

That we with all the saints *(especially)* may at length eat and drink at the promised feast of the covenant; let us pray to the Lord.

Lord, have mercy.

Grant these prayers, merciful God, and all that we need, as we eagerly await the Easter feast; through Jesus Christ our Lord.

Amen

IMAGES FOR PREACHING

"Look, Mom! No hands!" shrieks the little boy, gaining premature confidence on his bicycle. One no sooner hears these words than one anticipates the sound of a falling bicycle and the subsequent wailing.

"Falling" and "felling" seem to be standard fare for the day as we are reminded of the false confidence of our ancestors. Paul reminds the Corinthians that, despite their consumption of spiritual food and spiritual drink from the spiritual rock, God was not pleased with the Israelites, "and they were struck down in the wilderness." He becomes yet more explicit when he calls to mind that "twenty-three thousand fell in one day" as a result of their sexual exploits.

"Beware false confidence and putting Christ to the test" seems to be the caution of Paul. "If you think you are standing, watch out that you do not fall."

Jesus, however, seems to be addressing false confidence of another sort among his hearers. "Beware of interpreting the fall of others as the judgment of God on them," he seems to say. When the tower of Siloam fell and eighteen were killed, "do you think that they were worse offenders than all the others living in Jerusalem?" he chides.

He points to the contrary. At the "near felling" of the unproductive fig tree, he recalls the intervention of the merciful gardener, who urges the tree owner to let it stand until he has nurtured it fully.

The prayer of the day reminds us of the one who has intervened on our behalf—who has "broken into our troubled world"—so that we might be bearers of fruit and avoid the fall of the falsely confident.

WORSHIP MATTERS

Lent exists only in relation to the great feast of Easter. We need not pretend that we don't know what is coming, and not mention the resurrection. Liturgy isn't a passion play; rather we enter fully into the mystery of the unitive event of Jesus' death and resurrection. Use the season of Lent to prepare the congregation for the Three Days (from Maundy Thursday evening through Easter Day). Through bulletins, newsletters, sermons, and parish announcements, invite people to participate fully in the Three Days. As there are usually always some new members in a congregation, each year continue to offer insight into the meaning of the central symbols and rituals of Holy Week and Easter. The more the word is out, the more the congregation will not want to miss these once-a-year liturgies!

LET THE CHILDREN COME

Isaiah invites all who are thirsty to come and for those without money, to buy and eat! Jesus has commanded his followers, similarly, to be baptized and eat the bread and drink the wine in remembrance of him. Invite families with children of different ages to bring the elements forward today. Or invite children to come to the font to be reminded of their baptism. Remind all who gather that we need food and water to live. God promises to give us at the baptismal font and at the communion table all that we need to live a life of faith.

HYMNS FOR WORSHIP

GATHERING

O Master, let me walk with you   LBW 492

Oh, praise the gracious power   WOV 750

HYMN OF THE DAY

Guide me ever, great Redeemer   LBW 343

ALTERNATE HYMN OF THE DAY

Restore in us, O God   WOV 662

I heard the voice of Jesus say   LBW 497

(May be sung to KINGSFOLD, as in RWSB)

COMMUNION

O living Bread from heaven   LBW 197

This is my body   WOV 707

SENDING

The Spirit sends us forth to serve   WOV 723

Glories of your name are spoken   LBW 358

ADDITIONAL HYMNS AND SONGS

As the deer runs to the river   RWSB

How can I be free from sin?   W&P 65

Praised be the Rock   TFF 290

In suffering love the thread of life   RWSB

MUSIC FOR THE DAY

PSALMODY

Haugen, Marty. "Your Love Is Finer Than Life" in PCY, vol. I.

143

Keesecker, Thomas. PW , Cycle C.

Psalms for All Seasons: An ICEL Collection. OCP 6111.

Schutte, Daniel. "My Soul Thirsts" in STP, vol. 4.

Walker, Christopher. "Psalm 63: O Lord, I Will Sing" in STP, vol. 2.

CHORAL

Dowland, John. "He That Is Down Need Fear No Fall" in *Oxford Book of Easy Anthems.* SATB. OXF 3533219.

Halloran, Jack. "Witness." SSAATTBB. HAL JG2010.

Moore, Philip. "He That Is Down Need Fear No Fall." SATB, org. RME.

Paulus, Stephen. "Built on a Rock." SATB. WAR 1408152.

White, David Ashley. "Come, Ye Sinners." 2 pt, kybd, ob/C inst. AFP 0800653246.

CHILDREN'S CHOIR

Handel, G.F., arr. Stephen Roddy. "Almighty Father, Hear Me." U, kybd. Gentry JG2247.

Pethel, Stan. "Give Us Love." U/2 pt, kybd. CG CGA728.

144

KEYBOARD/INSTRUMENTAL

David, Anne Marie. "By the Babylonian Rivers" in *Here I Am, Lord: Piano Stylings.* Kybd. AFP 0800675665.

Hanff, Johann. "In God, My Faithful God" *(Auf meinem lieben Gott)* in *Choralvorspiele alter Meister.* Org. PET 3048.

Manz, Paul. "Cwm Rhondda" in *A New Liturgical Year.* Org. AFP 0800656717.

Organ, Anne Krentz. "Cwm Rhondda" in *Piano Reflections for the Church Year.* Pno. AFP 080067474X.

HANDBELL

Honoré, Jeffrey. "What Wondrous Love is This." 3-5 oct. CPH 97-6926.

Larson, Lloyd. "What Wondrous Love is This." 3-5 oct. BEC HB150.

Sherman, Arnold B. "What Wondrous Love is This." 2-3 oct, opt hc. RR HB0020A; 4-5 oct, opt hc. RR HB0020B.

PRAISE ENSEMBLE

Founds, Rick. "Jesus, Draw Me Close" in *Praise Hymns and Choruses,* 4th ed. MAR 3010130368.

Harris, Don and Martin J. Nystrom. "A Broken Spirit" in *Best of the Best.* FEL 1891062018.

Wednesday, March 17

PATRICK, BISHOP, MISSIONARY TO IRELAND, 461

At sixteen, Patrick was kidnapped by Irish pirates and sold into slavery in Ireland. He himself admitted that up to this point he cared little for God. He escaped after six years, returned to his family in southwest Britain, and began to prepare for ordained ministry. He later returned to Ireland, this time to serve as a bishop and missionary. He made his base in the north of Ireland and from there made many missionary journeys with much success. In his autobiography he denounced the slave trade, perhaps from his own experience as a slave.

Patrick's famous baptismal hymn to the Trinity, "I bind unto myself today" (LBW 188), can be used as a meditation on Lent's call to return to our baptism.

Friday, March 19

JOSEPH, GUARDIAN OF OUR LORD

The gospels are silent about much of Joseph's life. We know that he was a carpenter or builder by trade. The gospel of Luke shows him acting in accordance with both civil and religious law by returning to Bethlehem for the census and by presenting the child Jesus in the temple on the fortieth day after his birth. The gospel of Matthew tells of Joseph's trust in God, who led him through visionary dreams. Because Joseph is not mentioned after the story of a young Jesus teaching in the temple, it is assumed that he died before Jesus reached adulthood.

Congregations might consider a Sicilian tradition to commemorate Joseph that combines the three Lenten disciplines of fasting, almsgiving, and prayer. The poor are invited to a festive buffet called "St. Joseph's Table." Lenten prayers and songs interrupt the course of the meal. What other ways can a congregation's almsgiving and charity be increased during Lent?

March 21, 2004

Fourth Sunday in Lent

INTRODUCTION

Lent is the time for coming home. In the ancient church it was the season for reconciling lapsed Christians to the community of the faithful. Today's readings provide images of homecoming—Israel's entry into the land of promise, a prodigal son who returned to his waiting father.

PRAYER OF THE DAY

God of all mercy, by your power to heal and to forgive, graciously cleanse us from all sin and make us strong; through your Son, Jesus Christ our Lord, who lives and reigns with you and the Holy Spirit, one God, now and forever.

VERSE

Just as Moses lifted up the serpent in the wilderness, so must the Son of Man be lifted up, that whoever believes in him may have eternal life. (John 3:14-15)

READINGS

Joshua 5:9-12

By celebrating the Passover and eating the produce of the promised land instead of the miraculous manna that had sustained them in the desert, the Israelites symbolically bring their forty years of wilderness wandering to an end at Gilgal.

Psalm 32

Be glad, you righteous, and rejoice in the Lord.
(Ps. 32:12)

2 Corinthians 5:16-21

In Jesus' death on the cross, God works to persuade us of divine love, so that we might be reconciled to God. As part of God's new creation, we are challenged to share with others the good news of our reconciled relationship to God.

Luke 15:1-3, 11b-32

Jesus tells a story about a son who discovers his father's love only when he walks away from it. But the father's grace is also a crisis for an older brother, who thought that by his obedience he had earned a place in the father's home.

COLOR   Purple

THE PRAYERS

As we seek in this Lenten time to grow in our faith, let us pray for the life of the world.
A BRIEF SILENCE.
That the church in every place work faithfully in its ministry of reconciliation, as ambassadors for Christ, let us pray to the Lord.
Lord, have mercy.
That those preparing for baptism be welcomed like the prodigal, with celebration and rejoicing for the forgiveness and new life, let us pray to the Lord.
Lord, have mercy.
That the governments of the world may be just and fair, from presidents to tax collectors, from ambassadors to civil servants, let us pray to the Lord.
Lord, have mercy.
That those who are estranged might find reconciliation through Christ and that we might be generous toward them with our inheritance from God, let us pray to the Lord.
Lord, have mercy.
That God's wings of healing might hover over those who are weak and ill *(especially)*, let us pray to the Lord.
Lord, have mercy.
That this congregation might be like manna in the land, providing relief for those in need, let us pray to the Lord.
Lord, have mercy.
HERE OTHER INTERCESSIONS MAY BE OFFERED.
That we together with all the faithful departed *(especially)* might celebrate the new creation that is ours in Christ Jesus, let us pray to the Lord.
Lord, have mercy.
Grant these prayers, merciful God, and all that we need, as we eagerly await the Easter feast; through Jesus Christ our Lord.
Amen

145

IMAGES FOR PREACHING

*Our Father, we have wandered and hidden from your face; in foolish-
ness have squandered your legacy of grace* (WOV 733).

Waywardness and wandering form the backdrop for
our readings today. At long last, the Israelites have a
change of diet; forty years of manna are replaced by the
produce of the promised land. Yet, these images of unleavened cakes and parched grain are seen in the context
of a previously itinerant, nomadic, and undoubtedly
tiring existence.

Wandering and squandering also characterize the
wayward son who demands his inheritance—an action
which in this culture implies that his father is dead. He
wastes it away, and finds himself wallowing with the
hogs.

*In haste you come to meet us and home rejoicing bring, in glad-
ness there to greet us with calf and robe and ring.*

Yet, equally as powerful as the backdrop of wandering is the image of welcome. "Welcome home!" we say
to those who have trekked far off.

"Welcome home," indeed, as the palmist speaks of
the mercy that "embraces those who trust the Lord."

"Welcome home," we hear as the father, earlier
treated by his son as dead, now embraces the son, once
spiritually dead, as living! "For this son of mine was
dead and is alive again; he was lost and is found!" rejoices the father.

*Grant now that our transgressing, our faithlessness may cease.
Stretch out your hand in blessing, in pardon, and in peace.*

Something new is now warranted. Something new is
granted. Paul reminds us, "If anyone is in Christ, there is
a new creation." Everything old—waywardness and wandering; wandering and squandering—has passed away.
"See, everything has become new!"

WORSHIP MATTERS

Lent used to feel like a whole season of Good Friday
with hymns, sermons, and midweek services focusing on
the passion of Christ. In the past several decades nearly
all denominations have returned to the ancient practice
of observing Lent as a spiritual time to prepare catechumens for baptism and the assembly for the renewal of
baptismal vows at Easter. Consider how your congregation observes Lent. Take a look at the hymns, prayers,
sermons, art, vestments and other symbols in your setting. Consider Holy Week as the time for intense

meditation on the passion of Christ and keep the focus
of Lent on baptism and spiritual renewal. Because people
are hungering for a deeper sense of spirituality in their
lives, Lent is a wonderful time to lead them to word of
life and the bread and cup of salvation.

LET THE CHILDREN COME

At the communion table we eat and drink with all the
company of heaven! We receive a foretaste of the feast
to come. All who are baptized are welcome at the
Lord's table. Is this true in your particular congregation? Perhaps Lent is an appropriate season to have
conversation about how all people of faith—regardless
of age—are in need of the gifts our Lord gives at the
table. Find a time, separate from worship to invite
questions and conversation about the history of how
communion has been practiced as well as possibilities
for practice in the future.

HYMNS FOR WORSHIP
GATHERING

Come, thou Fount of every blessing   LBW 499
By grace we have been saved   W&P 25

HYMN OF THE DAY

Our Father, we have wandered   WOV 733

ALTERNATE HYMN OF THE DAY

Today your mercy calls us   LBW 304
Amazing grace, how sweet the sound   LBW 448

COMMUNION

One there is, above all others   LBW 298
Softly and tenderly Jesus is calling   WOV 734

SENDING

Give to our God immortal praise!   LBW 520
Bind us together   WOV 748
Beauty for brokenness   W&P 17

ADDITIONAL HYMNS AND SONGS

Just a closer walk with thee   TFF 253, RWSB
Like a little child   RWSB
You are my hiding place   W&P 160
Far from home we run rebellious   HFG 86

146

MUSIC FOR THE DAY
PSALMODY

Cooney, Rory. "I Turn to You" in PCY, vol. 4.

"How Blessed Are Those" in SP.

Howard, Julie. "Psalm 32" in *Sing for Joy: Psalm Settings for God's Children.*
LP 0814620787.

Isele, David Clark. TP.

Keesecker, Thomas. PW , Cycle C.

See Proper 6 and Proper 26.

CHORAL

Bach, J.S. "O Bread of Life from Heaven" in *Bach for All Seasons.* SATB.
AFP 080065854X.

Bertalot, John. "Amazing Grace." SATB, pno. AFP 0800649141. *The Augsburg Choirbook.* AFP 0800656784.

Furnivall, Anthony C. "Amazing Grace." SATB div, org, opt brass, timp. HIN HMC-255.

Mendelssohn, Felix. "So We Are Ambassadors" in *St. Paul.* TB duet, org. Various ed.

Nelson, Ronald A. "Create In Me a Clean Heart." SATB. KJO 8808.

Purcell, Henry. "Thou Knowest, Lord, the Secrets of Our Hearts." SATB, opt kybd. CPH 98-2321.

CHILDREN'S CHOIR

Johnson, Ralph. "As Moses Lifted Up." (Verse) U, fl, org.
CG CGA550.

Ziegenhals, Harriet Ilse. "Sing, Dance, Clap Your Hands." (Ps. 32:11) U, opt desc, kybd. CG CGA625.

KEYBOARD/INSTRUMENTAL

Brahms, Johannes. "Herzlich tut mich verlangen" in *Eleven Chorale Preludes.* Org. Mercury or various ed.

Carlson, J. Bert. "Southwell" in *Augsburg Organ Library: Lent.* Org.
AFP 0800658973.

Dahl, David P. "Nordic Aria" in *Organ Music for the Seasons,* vol. 3. Org.
AFP 0800675649.

Farlee, Robert Buckley. "Just as I Am" in *Deep Waters.* Org, sax.
AFP 0800656539. OP.

HANDBELL

Dobrinski, Cynthia. "Come, Thou Fount of Every Blessing." 3-5 oct.
AG 1832.

Starks, Howard F. "God's Amazing Grace." 3-5 oct. FLA HP5370.

Wagner, Douglas E. "Near the Cross." 2-3 oct. LOR 20/1045L.

PRAISE ENSEMBLE

Adler, Dan, arr. Dan Goeller. "Make Me an Answer to Prayer." SAB, pno, 1/2 C inst, opt cong. AFP 0800674405.

Landry, Carey. "Come Home" in *Glory and Praise.* OCP 5205.

Tikka, Kari. "For by Grace You Have Been Saved" in RWSB.

Monday, March 22

JONATHAN EDWARDS, TEACHER,
MISSIONARY TO THE AMERICAN INDIANS, 1758

Edwards was a minister in Connecticut and has been described as the greatest of the New England Puritan preachers. One of Edwards's most notable sermons has found its way into contemporary anthologies of literature. In this sermon, "Sinners in the Hands of an Angry God," he spoke at length about hell. Throughout the rest of his works and his preaching, however, he had more to say about God's love than God's wrath. His personal experience of conversion came when he felt overwhelmed with a sense of God's majesty and grandeur rather than a fear of hell. Edwards served a Puritan congregation. He believed that only those who had been fully converted ought to receive communion; his congregation thought otherwise. Edwards left that congregation and carried out mission work among the Housatonic Indians of Massachusetts. He became president of the College of New Jersey, later to be known as Princeton.

Wednesday, March 24

OSCAR ARNULFO ROMERO, BISHOP OF EL SALVADOR, MARTYR, 1980

Romero is remembered for his advocacy on behalf of the poor in El Salvador, though it was not a characteristic of his early priesthood. After being appointed as bishop he preached against the political repression in his country. He and other priests and church workers were considered traitors for their bold stand for justice, especially defending the rights of the poor. After several years of threats to his life, Romero was assassinated while presiding at the eucharist. During the 1980s thousands died in El Salvador during political unrest.

Romero is remembered as a martyr who gave his life

147

in behalf of the powerless in his country. Our Lenten journey of conversion calls us to be bold in our witness to Christ, work on behalf of the powerless, and speak on behalf of justice and equality for all people, who are created in the image of God.

Thursday, March 25

THE ANNUNCIATION OF OUR LORD

Nine months before Christmas we celebrate the annunciation. In Luke we hear how the angel Gabriel announced to Mary that she would give birth to the Son of God

and she responded, "Here am I, the servant of the Lord." Ancient scholars believed that March 25 was also the day on which creation began and the date of Jesus' death on the cross. Thus from the sixth to eighth centuries, March 25 was observed as New Year's Day in much of Christian Europe.

Set within Lent, Mary's openness to the will of God is an example of faithful discipleship and leads us to the work of God in our own lives. In worship today, sing "The angel Gabriel from heaven came" (WOV 632). Or, as a canticle after communion, sing a setting of the Magnificat, such as the paraphrase "My soul proclaims your greatness" (WOV 730).

March 28, 2004

Fifth Sunday in Lent

INTRODUCTION

The Lenten preparation is almost at an end. Something new is about to happen! Mary's act of anointing Jesus is extravagant, but when we know that grace has come to us, it is time for lavishness. Our old values get rearranged when we realize how deeply we are loved.

PRAYER OF THE DAY

Almighty God, our redeemer, in our weakness we have failed to be your messengers of forgiveness and hope in the world. Renew us by your Holy Spirit, that we may follow your commands and proclaim your reign of love; through your Son, Jesus Christ our Lord, who lives and reigns with you and the Holy Spirit, one God, now and forever.

VERSE

The Son of Man came not to be served but to serve, and to give his life as a ransom for many. (Mark 10:45)

READINGS

Isaiah 43:16-21

This prophet of the exile declares that long ago the Lord performed mighty deeds and delivered Israel from

Egyptian bondage. Now, the Lord is about to perform another act of deliverance. This salvation leads the people to praise God.

Psalm 126

Those who sowed with tears will reap with songs of joy. (Ps. 126:6)

Philippians 3:4b-14

Writing to Christians in Philippi, Paul admits that his heritage and reputation could give him more reason than most people to place confidence in his spiritual pedigree. But the overwhelming grace of God in Jesus calls Paul to a new set of values.

John 12:1-8

Judas misunderstands Mary's extravagant act of anointing Jesus' feet with a costly perfume. Jesus recognizes the true significance of her beautiful expression of love and commitment as an anticipation of his burial.

COLOR Purple

THE PRAYERS

As we seek in this Lenten time to grow in our faith, let us pray for the life of the world.

A BRIEF SILENCE.

That the church might always be watchful for God's love that is always new, and might be found faithful on the day of resurrection, let us pray to the Lord.

Lord, have mercy.

That throughout the world, nations and peoples might experience peace, justice, and beauty, let us pray to the Lord.

Lord, have mercy.

That those preparing for baptism might find in those waters springs of new life, rivers in the desert, and mighty seas of deliverance, let us pray to the Lord.

Lord, have mercy.

That our stewardship of the creation be faithful, and that animals and plants, waters and seas, desert and wilderness might declare their Creator's praise, let us pray to the Lord.

Lord, have mercy.

That those in need: the sick, the grieving, the poor, the dying, *(especially)*, be cared for as Christ, and receive God's care; let us pray to the Lord.

Lord, have mercy.

That this congregation, like Mary, Martha, and Lazarus, may always be ready to receive the Lord at table, let us pray to the Lord.

Lord, have mercy.

HERE OTHER INTERCESSIONS MAY BE OFFERED.

That we might press on toward the goal, and together with *(names, and)* all the saints, attain the resurrection from the dead through Christ Jesus, let us pray to the Lord.

Lord, have mercy.

Grant these prayers, merciful God, and all that we need, as we eagerly await the Easter feast; through Jesus Christ our Lord.

Amen

IMAGES FOR PREACHING

Having not yet rid ourselves of the sharp stench of Lazarus's death (the background of today's gospel), we now find ourselves sitting in his home filled with the "fragrance of the perfume" of Christ's upcoming death.

Anticipation is written all over the texts for this day; something is about to happen, which will reorder all previously known priorities. "I am about to do a new thing . . . do you not perceive it?" says Isaiah. Can't you feel it? It's almost palpable!

"You always have the poor with you, but you do not always have me," anticipates Jesus. Judas, as reported by John, "is about to betray him."

Our first reading and psalm are rife with future tense: "I will make a way in the wilderness and rivers in the desert. The wild animals will honor me." "Those who sowed with tears will reap with songs of joy. Those who go out weeping . . . will come again with joy."

Our culture does not condition us to savor anticipation. Our gift has been, rather, to bring about immediate success, to seek results. We're good at that! Yet Paul, who by his own account has been an overachiever of the right bloodline, turns these priorities on their head. "Yet whatever gains I have, these I have come to regard as loss because of Christ."

Paul, too, has begun to find his strength in anticipation. Having found "surpassing value" in the knowledge of Christ Jesus his Lord, he now "presses on" and "strains forward" to what lies ahead. We, in the assembly, are called to join him in anticipating—in pressing on "toward the goal for the prize of the heavenly call of God in Christ Jesus."

WORSHIP MATTERS

During Holy Week your congregation will participate in several once-a-year liturgies, each with its own rituals, music, and many details to coordinate. When carefully planned, rehearsed, and led, these liturgies have the potential to profoundly touch and draw the assembly into the paschal mystery. Sometimes pastors and worship leaders fail to adequately rehearse or go over the various actions of these liturgies. Stage directions and instructions whispered during the actual liturgy can be distracting for worshipers. The rituals of the palm procession, footwashing, stripping of the altar, and the whole Easter Vigil require great attention to detail. Consider writing out the instructions for those leading the service and actually rehearsing elements that need a walk-through. Everyone—leaders and assembly—will then be more relaxed in the actual liturgy.

LET THE CHILDREN COME

In the gospel story Mary is preparing Jesus for his death. Anointing his feet with expensive perfume is an extravagant sign of her love. In these next weeks the church also prepares for a funeral but the journey does

149

not end with death. Jesus lives! God's extravagant gift of Christ calls us to give of ourselves extravagantly. Perhaps the children could challenge the congregation to participate in a food/clothes/school supply drive. Invite them to share with others as a way to respond to the amazing love of Jesus Christ.

HYMNS FOR WORSHIP
GATHERING

Once he came in blessing   LBW 312

Come to Calvary's holy mountain   LBW 301

Come, ye disconsolate   TFF 186

HYMN OF THE DAY

Jesus, thy boundless love to me   LBW 336

ALTERNATE HYMN OF THE DAY

When I survey the wondrous cross   LBW 482, RWI 88

As the sun with longer journey   WOV 655

COMMUNION

Jesus, the very thought of you   LBW 316

Beneath the cross of Jesus   LBW 107

SENDING

We sing the praise of him who died   LBW 344

Come, we that love the Lord   WOV 742

Rejoice in the mission   W&P 120

ADDITIONAL HYMNS AND SONGS

Give thanks   W&P 41

Holy woman, graceful giver   OBS 100

Lamb of God   RWSB

Holy God, holy and glorious   RWSB

MUSIC FOR THE DAY
PSALMODY

Busarow, Donald. "When the Lord Restored Our Fortunes" in SP.

Haugen, Marty. "God Has Done Great Things for Us" in PCY, vol. 2.

Keesecker, Thomas. PW, Cycle C.

Roff, Joseph. Psalms for the Cantor, vol. III. WLP 2504.

Stewart, Roy James. "The Lord Has Done Great Things" in PCY, vol. 5.

CHORAL

Ashdown, Franklin D. "Jesus, the Very Thought of Thee." SATB, org, opt inst. AFP 0800657500.

Fleming, Larry L. "Humble Service." SATB. AFP 0800646223.

Gibbs, C. Armstrong. "Bless the Lord O My Soul" in Oxford Book of Easy Anthems. 2 pt ST, AB, org. OXF 3533219.

Nelson, Ronald A. "Whoever Would Be Great Among You." SAB gtr/kybd. AFP 0800645804. Also in The Augsburg Choirbook. AFP 0800656784.

Walton, William. "A Litany" ("Drop slow tears") in Anthems for Choirs IV. SATB. OXF 353018X.

CHILDREN'S CHOIR

Sleeth, Natalie. "Prayer." U/2 pt, kybd, opt C inst. CG CGA565.

Summers, Roger. "Take My Heart." U/2 pt, kybd. Triune Music 10/2771K.

KEYBOARD/INSTRUMENTAL

Johnson, David N. "Erhalt uns, Herr" in Hymn Settings for Organ. Org. AFP 0800674987.

Martin, Gilbert. "When I Survey the Wondrous Cross." Org. PRE 113-40037.

Sowash, Bradley. "Kum ba Yah/Were You There?" in We Gather Together, vol. 2. Pno. AFP 0800675630.

Wood, Dale. "Savior, Like a Shepherd Lead Us" in Softly and Tenderly. Org. SMP KK505.

HANDBELL

Sherman, Arnold B. "Beneath the Cross of Jesus." 3-5 oct. LOR 20/1052L.

Sherman, Arnold B. "When I Survey the Wondrous Cross." 2-3 oct. RR HB00010A; 4-5 oct. Red River HB00010B.

PRAISE ENSEMBLE

Brown, Clint. "You Are" in Dwell in The House Songbook. HOS 19357.

DeShazo, Lynn. "More Precious than Silver" in Best of the Best. FEL 1891062018.

Sims, Randy, arr. Dan Goeller. "You Are the Lord of Me." SAB, pno, opt C inst, cong. AFP 0800674421.

Monday, March 29

HANS NIELSEN HAUGE, RENEWER OF THE CHURCH, 1824

Hans Nielsen Hauge was a layperson who began preaching about "the living faith" in Norway and Denmark after a mystical experience that he believed called him to share the assurance of salvation with others. At the time itinerant preaching and religious gatherings held without the supervision of a pastor were illegal, and Hauge was arrested several times. He also faced great personal suffering: his first wife died, and three of his four children died in infancy.

Some might remember Hauge by singing the Norwegian hymn "My heart is longing" (LBW 326), with its devotional response to the death of Christ.

Wednesday, March 31

JOHN DONNE, PRIEST, 1631

This priest of the Church of England is commemorated

for his poetry and spiritual writing. Most of his poetry was written before his ordination and is sacred and secular, intellectual and sensuous. He saw in his wife, Anne—a marriage that resulted in his imprisonment—glimpses of the glory of God and a human revelation of divine love. In 1615 he was ordained, and seven years later he was named dean of St. Paul's Cathedral in London. By that time his reputation as a preacher was firmly in place.

In his poem "Good Friday, 1613. Riding westward" he speaks of Jesus' death on the cross: "Who sees God's face, that is self life, must die; What a death were it then to see God die?"

April 4, 2004

Sunday of the Passion
Palm Sunday

INTRODUCTION

The procession with palms brings us into Holy Week and the celebration of the mystery of our salvation. We enter the week by hearing the story of Jesus' passion—his suffering and death. In baptism we have been fused to this story; in Holy Week we make our way through it again, because it brings us to life with Christ.

Today the church remembers Benedict the African, who went from slavery in Sicily to become a Franciscan monk and confessor in the sixteenth century.

PRAYER OF THE DAY

Almighty God, you sent your Son, our Savior Jesus Christ, to take our flesh upon him and to suffer death on the cross. Grant that we may share in his obedience to your will and in the glorious victory of his resurrection; through your Son, Jesus Christ our Lord, who lives and reigns with you and the Holy Spirit, one God, now and forever.

VERSE

The hour has come for the Son of Man to be glorified. (John 12:23)

READINGS FOR PROCESSION WITH PALMS

Luke 19:28-40

Psalm 118:1-2, 19-29

Blessed is he who comes in the name of the LORD. (Ps. 118:26)

READINGS FOR LITURGY OF THE PASSION

Isaiah 50:4-9a

This text, the third of the Servant Songs that arose in the last years of Israel's exile in Babylon, speaks of the servant's obedience in the midst of persecution. Though the servant has been variously understood as the prophet himself or a remnant of faithful Israel, Christians have often recognized the figure of Christ in these poems.

Psalm 31:9-16

Into your hands, O LORD, I commend my spirit. (Ps. 31:5)

Philippians 2:5-11

Paul quotes from an early Christian hymn that describes Jesus' humble obedience, even to death, and his exaltation as Lord of all.

Luke 22:14—23:56 or Luke 23:1-49

The passion story in Luke's gospel is filled with human

and cosmic images of what God is doing through the death of Jesus: restoring all creation to the grace and peace of paradise.

COLOR   Scarlet *or* Purple

THE PRAYERS

As we seek in this Lenten time to grow in our faith, let us pray for the life of the world.

A BRIEF SILENCE.

For the whole church, that the love of God shown in Christ's passion may be reflected in its words and deeds, let us pray to the Lord.

Lord, have mercy.

For those preparing for baptism and those who will affirm their baptisms, that in every tongue and nation the confession of Jesus Christ as Lord be heard anew, let us pray to the Lord.

Lord, have mercy.

For peace and harmony among the religions and nations of the world, that celebrations of Passover and Easter be delivered from bloodshed, let us pray to the Lord.

Lord, have mercy.

For those in any need during this holy week *(especially)*, that they may find comfort and relief from God and from those who follow in the way of the cross, let us pray to the Lord.

Lord, have mercy.

For this congregation, that through the celebration of Christ's passion our ministry might be renewed and our faith restored; let us pray to the Lord.

Lord, have mercy.

HERE OTHER INTERCESSIONS MAY BE OFFERED.

Remembering Benedict the African, monk, and all the faithful departed *(especially)*, that we may at length celebrate with them at the unending feast of the Paschal Lamb, let us pray to the Lord.

Lord, have mercy.

Grant these prayers, merciful God, and all that we need, as we eagerly await the Easter feast; through Jesus Christ our Lord.

Amen

IMAGES FOR PREACHING

"Why didn't you say something?" the silent bystanders of Nazi Germany are often asked. "How could you sell out so badly?" a contemporary missionary pastor is asked when, in order to be allowed to offer a Christian presence in a country still hostile toward Christianity, she voluntarily vowed not to baptize anyone. The answers to these questions are bleak at best. "What could we do?" reply the former. "I did what I could," shrugs the missionary.

"What would I have done?" the hearer of today's passion reading is compelled to ask, afraid of already knowing the answer. "What do I do in the face of world hunger, the threat of war, the plight of the homeless?" Indeed, today's reading confronts each of us with the pervasive and damning power of silence. Herod questions Jesus at some length; Jesus gives him no answer. Lots are cast to divide Jesus' clothes; "the people stood by, watching." Jesus breathes his last; "but all his acquaintances, including the women who had followed him from Galilee, stood at a distance, watching these things."

Indeed, "too little, too late" is the judgment when the silent bystanders, at last, take action. The damage is done already when Joseph, who at least had the courage to disagree with his fellow council members, wraps the body in grave clothes; when the bystanding centurion announces Christ's innocence; when the women who followed him from Galilee prepare spices and ointments.

Yet, we are not, like the silent crowd, sent home today "beating our breasts." For the gospel cannot be contained by human silence. The good news today has come through the stones. In our processional gospel, Jesus declares that if his disciples were silenced, "the stones would shout out." Better yet, absolution is declared even before the threefold sin of denial, when Jesus counsels Simon "the Rock" Peter: "after you have turned back, strengthen your brothers."

It is both our indictment and our hope when we, today, with the crowds cry out, "Hosanna! Save us Lord!" For he has come for this very purpose.

WORSHIP MATTERS

Why read a passion account on this day and also on Good Friday? First, our lectionary joins us to Christians around the world observing Holy Week in this manner. Second, because Lent is no longer seen as an extended meditation on the passion, it is appropriate to have two liturgies during Holy Week with this important focus. Finally, the passion accounts from Matthew, Mark, or

Luke read on Sunday of the Passion differ greatly from John's version read on Good Friday. For example, this year in Luke's passion Jesus responds with compassion and words of forgiveness even to those who harm him. In John, Jesus is the king who reigns from the cross and even his final words ("It is finished") are filled with triumph. Worship planners, musicians, and preachers can assist parishoners to experience how different Luke's passion is from John's account.

LET THE CHILDREN COME

This Sunday is usually characterized with the people standing and singing praises to our King: "Hosanna!" and "Blessed be the one who comes in the name of the Lord!" Lots of fanfare occurs with trumpets playing and palms waving, and "the lips of children" can take a lead in the praise. Let's not forget, though, that this week Jesus reveals his ultimate obedience to his Father in heaven. Invite all ages to kneel (or sit if kneeling is impossible) while the congregation prays the Lord's Prayer. Remind the congregation that just as Jesus was obedient to God's will we too are called to be obedient to our Creator, Redeemer, and Sustainer.

HYMNS FOR WORSHIP
GATHERING

Ride on, ride on in majesty   LBW 121, RWI 62
Lift up your heads, O gates   WOV 631
Ride on, King Jesus   TFF 182

HYMN OF THE DAY

My song is love unknown   LBW 94

ALTERNATE HYMN OF THE DAY

A lamb goes uncomplaining forth   LBW 105
Of the glorious body telling   LBW 120
(May be sung to PICARDY, LBW 198)

COMMUNION

Jesus, remember me   WOV 740, W&P 78
In the quiet consecration   LBW 223

SENDING

Jesus, I will ponder now   LBW 115
Ah, holy Jesus   LBW 123, RWI 7

ADDITIONAL HYMNS AND SONGS

On a hill far away (The old rugged cross)   TFF 77
Filled with excitement / *Mantos y palmas*   LLC 333, RWSB
Jesus, keep me near the cross   TFF 73, RWSB
Now we remain   W&P 106

MUSIC FOR THE DAY
PSALMODY
PSALM 118:1-2, 19-29 (PROCESSION)

Hommerding, Alan J. "Psalm 118" in *Sing Out! A Children's Psalter.* WLP 7191.
Hopson, Hal H. "Praise the Lord: Service Music." U, opt inst. CG CGA 530.
Hruby, Dolores. *Seasonal Psalms for Children with Optional Orff.* WLP 7102.
Smith, Timothy R. "Give Thanks to the Lord" in STP, vol. 4.

PSALM 31:9-16

DeBruyn, Randall. "Father, I Put My Life in Your Hands" in STP, vol. 4.
Farlee, Robert Buckley. PW , Cycle C.

CHORAL

Benson, Robert A. "Ride On! Ride On in Majesty." SATB, org, opt cong. AFP 0800674634.
Carter, John. "Blessed Is He Who Comes in the Name of the Lord." SATB/U (children's), kybd. AFP 0800674510
Casals, Pablo. "O Vos Omnes." SSAATTBB. Broude AB 128.
Gibbons, Orlando. "Hosanna to the Son of David." SSAATB. BEL 64024.
Mathias, William. "Lift Up Your Heads, O Ye Gates." SATB, org. OXF 42.380.
Petrich, Roger T. "Ah, Holy Jesus" in *Anthems for Choirs IV.* SSATB. OXF 353018X.
Proulx, Richard. "We Adore You O Christ." SATB. PAR PPM09836.

CHILDREN'S CHOIR

Lindh, Jody. "Hosanna to the Son." U, kybd, opt 3-4 oct. CG CGA606.
Taranto, A. Steven. "Into Jerusalem." U, kybd, opt Orff. CG CGA735.
Tunseth, Kathleen. "Hosanna! This Is a Special Day" in LS. (Luke 19:37-38).

153

KEYBOARD/INSTRUMENTAL

Albrecht, Mark. "Valet will ich dir geben" in *Festive Processionals for Organ and Trumpet.* Org, tpt. AFP 0800657985.

Johnson, David N. "Trumpet Tune in B-flat" in *Trumpet Tunes for Organ.* Org. AFP 0800674820.

Linker, Janet. "All Glory, Laud and Honor" in *Suite for Holy Week.* Org. BEC OC5.

Manz, Paul. "All Glory, Laud and Honor" in *Improvisations for the Lenten Season,* Set I. Org. MSM 10-300.

Vaughan Williams, Ralph. "Rhosymedre" in *Augsburg Organ Library: Lent.* Org. AFP 0800658973.

HANDBELL

Gramann, Fred. "Prelude on Herzliebster Jesu." 4-7 oct. AGEHR AG47002.

Kerr, J. Wayne. "There in God's Garden." 3-5 oct. MSM 30-820.

Kinyon, Barbara Baltzer. "All Glory, Laud and Honor" in *Eastertide Bells.* 2-3 oct. AG 1342.

Moklebust, Cathy. "My Song Is Love Unknown." 3-5 oct. CG CGB203.

PRAISE ENSEMBLE

Berthier, Jacques. "Jesus, Remember Me" in W&P.

Hanson, Handt. "Broken in Love" in *Spirit Calls . . . Rejoice.* SATB. CCF 0933173393 (pew ed); CCF 0933173385 (acc ed).

Pote, Allen. "Hosanna." SATB, kybd. CG CGA596.

Sunday, April 4

BENEDICT THE AFRICAN, CONFESSOR, 1589

Born a slave on the island of Sicily, Benedict first lived as a hermit and labored as a plowman after he was freed.

When the bishop of Rome ordered all hermits to attach themselves to a religious community, Benedict joined the Franciscans, where he served as a cook. Although he was illiterate, his fame as a confessor brought many visitors to the humble and holy cook, and he was eventually named superior of the community. A patron saint of blacks in the United States, Benedict is remembered for his patience and understanding when confronted with racial prejudice and taunts.

Use the story of Benedict's ministry as a confessor to revisit Martin Luther's advocacy of mutual consolation and conversation among the community.

Tuesday, April 6

ALBRECHT DÜRER, PAINTER, 1528; MICHELANGELO BUONARROTI, ARTIST, 1564

These two great artists revealed through their work the mystery of salvation and the wonder of creation. Dürer's work reflected the apocalyptic spirit of his time, when famine, plague, and social and religious upheaval were common. He was sympathetic to the reform work of Luther but remained Roman Catholic. At his death, Luther wrote to a friend, "Affection bids us mourn for one who was the best." Michelangelo was a sculptor, painter, poet, and architect. His works such as the carving of the Pietà and the statue of David reveal both the tenderness and the grandeur of humanity.

With Good Friday three days away, consider the ways in which the art of these two people might highlight the church's celebration of the mystery of Christ's passion.

April 5, 2003

MONDAY IN HOLY WEEK

INTRODUCTION

Monday, Tuesday, and Wednesday in Holy Week focus on the events of the last week of Jesus' earthly life. Rather than trying to "walk where Jesus walked," the church uses these days to view Christ more particularly in our lives today. Jesus comes to us in our day through the reading of scripture, through preaching, through the water of baptism, through the bread and wine of communion, and through the prayers.

Be open to the surprising ways in which Christ is made known to you this week. Also look for opportunities to share the gift of his life with others.

This week concludes with the Three Days: Maundy Thursday, Good Friday, and the Resurrection of Our Lord.

PRAYER OF THE DAY

O God, your Son chose the path that led to pain before joy and the cross before glory. Plant his cross in our hearts, so that in its power and love we may come at last to joy and glory; through your Son, Jesus Christ our Lord.

VERSE (MONDAY, TUESDAY, AND WEDNESDAY)

May I never boast of anything except the cross of our Lord Jesus Christ. (Gal. 6:14)

READINGS

Isaiah 42:1-9
    The servant brings forth justice.
Psalm 36:5-11
    Your people take refuge under the shadow of your wings. (Ps. 36:7)
Hebrews 9:11-15
    The blood of Christ redeems for eternal life.
John 12:1-11
    Mary anoints the feet of Jesus with costly perfume.

COLOR Scarlet *or* Purple (Monday, Tuesday, and Wednesday)

April 6, 2004

TUESDAY IN HOLY WEEK

PRAYER OF THE DAY

Lord Jesus, you have called us to follow you. Grant that our love may not grow cold in your service, and that we may not fail or deny you in the hour of trial.

READINGS

Isaiah 49:1-7
    The servant brings salvation to earth's ends.
Psalm 71:1-14
    From my mother's womb you have been my strength. (Ps. 71:6)
1 Corinthians 1:18-31
    The cross of Christ reveals God's power and wisdom.
John 12:20-36
    The hour comes for the Son of Man to be glorified.

155

April 7, 2004

WEDNESDAY IN HOLY WEEK

PRAYER OF THE DAY

Almighty God, your Son our Savior suffered at human hands and endured the shame of the cross. Grant that we may walk in the way of his cross and find it the way of life and peace; through your Son, Jesus Christ our Lord.

READINGS

Isaiah 50:4-9a
    The servant is vindicated by God.
Psalm 70
    Be pleased, O God, to deliver me. (Ps. 70:1)
Hebrews 12:1-3
    Look to Jesus, who endured the cross and sits at the right hand of God.
John 13:21-32
    Judas, who is later to betray Jesus, departs from the last supper.

THE THREE DAYS

We encounter the center of our life

Images *of the* Season

You can tell when the climax of a story is near. Time

slows down so we can take it all in and feel the full effect.

This mimics our own lives. When we are in the midst

of a liminal moment, our bodies seem to slow. Our senses are heightened as we attempt to integrate what is happening.

The Three Days, or Triduum, slows down time as we move through the climax of the story of faith, Jesus' betrayal, death, and resurrection. Worship throughout the rest of the year skims the surface in some ways, whisking us through the story of Jesus' life. But in these three days, we linger. There is so much centered here. We have to take our time to be able to receive it.

Worship over these three days will cover it all—creation and redemption, death and life, fire and water, desolation and celebration. These days enact the great Christian drama, and the worship services are, in many ways, dramas that embody the story, the tensions, and the teachings of the very core of our faith.

On Maundy Thursday evening (liturgically, the beginning of Good Friday), we reach back to the beginning of Lent to recall the confession we made on Ash Wednesday. The service is mixed up—not the normal order—because we are both continuing and beginning an extraordinary worship experience. We will be touched and hear words of forgiveness. It is only with a clear knowledge of being forgiven that we can engage the rest of the story.

Forgiven, we learn of God's new commandment. Foot washing, so intimate that it's embarrassing in our culture, is the image Jesus chose to demonstrate the servant nature of our calling. We watch and we eat a last supper with Jesus. We hear him offer all of himself to us, even his body and blood.

With the taste of wine still fresh in our mouths, the altar is stripped bare. It will be the consequence of Jesus' love for us. He gives us all of himself. Judas slips out to meet his conspirators. As adornment after adornment leaves the sanctuary, as the words of the psalm drift through the air, we are reminded of what this love will cost Jesus, our Lord. We leave, the service lingering. It is holy time.

GOOD FRIDAY

When we return to the sanctuary, hours have passed. We hear about Jesus' betrayal, capture, and trial. We hear of his humiliation, his interrogation. We know the night was long for him, and lonely. Our visual center is the cross. There is nothing else to distract us. The pace is slow, as those final hours must have been for him. We move, relentlessly, toward the end.

At this time, when he is near to breathing his last, we read Pilate's mocking sign, "Jesus of Nazareth, King of the Jews." Because we believe it is true, we pray, interceding for all the world around us, for our church, and for ourselves. We are reminded that Jesus' death was, paradoxically, the moment of his triumph. Through his death he defeated death. In gratitude we may spend a few private moments in adoration of the crucified one.

We confess that this death is God's glory, but it is also silent between now and tomorrow. Deadly silent. Our hope and his promise will sustain us.

THE VIGIL OF EASTER

Now we are almost there, almost at the hour when Jesus' death itself was overcome, the death become life—the victory we so need. Now time stands still for us to remember all that has gone before. No other service is so full of the heritage of faith; at no other time in the church year do we gather together all of the richest metaphors and symbols of our faith.

We gather around new fire, itself a sign of creation renewed. From it we light the paschal candle to illumine our way. Like the pillar of fire led the people of Israel in the wilderness, so the paschal candle will lead us to Easter—the light of Christ our beacon. In the silence from Good Friday, the light is rekindled.

Gathered around the light, we wrap the great stories of faith like a blanket around ourselves. We recall our ancestors and God's saving work among us throughout the ages—creation from a word, the earth washed clean in the flood, the deliverance at the Red Sea, dry bones given

158

life again, the miracle in the fiery furnace, and others.

The font beckons us to affirm our baptisms, to re-member and confess our welcome into the community of faith, and maybe to welcome others newborn into the faith. We may be sprinkled with the baptismal water as a reminder of our own beginnings and the miracle of "God with us."

The gospel reading draws us out of our holy recol-lections and into the events of the story again. Now we are prepared. We know where we have come from before we peek into the tomb with the women and Peter. When we hear the angel say, "He is not here, but has risen," we know again that life is always God's way with us. Death

is defeated. We can dance through the holy meal, now, each one confessing the truth of the story. Light the church! Shout Alleluia! Celebrate with high praise! He is risen!

THE RESURRECTION OF OUR LORD

Now we feast with abandon. He who was dead lives. The promise has been fulfilled. Flowers, which begin again the cycle of life, surround us. The aroma of bread and wine reminds us that the holy meal is a celebration this day, for in it we confess that life is stronger than death under God's reign and we have seen it with our own eyes. Christ is risen! Alleluia!

Environment *and* Art *for the* Season

The Three Days (Triduum) is the central liturgy in the

church year. It is a liturgy so full of symbol and ritual

action that is has been stretched out over the centuries

159

to become three separate liturgies on three successive days. Here the mysterious drama unfolds before our watchful eyes. We are drawn into participating in this drama along with Christians from around the world and throughout time. Each of the three services is now experienced by the entire community as a separate in-stallment with a break in between. The demands and the possibilities for the environment and the art are so great and so many and the time is so short that many congre-gations balk at the challenge. It takes a lot of work to create one environment for the season, let alone three separate environments in three days. The three acts of this cosmic drama have distinct themes: Thursday's man-date to love one another as Christ has loved us symboli-cally portrayed in the washing of feet; Friday's reconcili-ation between God and the world shown in the reflection on the mystery of the crucifixion and the historic Bid-ding Prayer; Saturday's liturgies of light, readings, bap-tism, and meal shape the climax of these three days. That central liturgy comes to a conclusion, but the celebration is just beginning as the Three Days jubilantly end with a grand eucharistic feast on Easter Sunday, and perhaps a liturgy that evening that serves as a benediction to the time.

EVALUATING YOUR SPACE

Which of the following parts of the Triduum liturgies does your con-gregation currently practice? If you need clarification on any of the elements mentioned here (except stations of the cross), consult *LBW* Minister's Desk Edition, pp. 137f.

MAUNDY THURSDAY

- The sermon and confession and forgiveness at the beginning of worship
- The foot washing
- The eucharist
- The stripping of the altar

GOOD FRIDAY DAY

- The stations of the cross

GOOD FRIDAY EVENING

- The reading of the Passion according to St. John
- The Bidding Prayer
- The procession and meditation on the cross

EASTER VIGIL

- Gathering around the fire

- Procession of the paschal candle
- The Service of Light
- The Service of Readings (at least 4; better 7 or 12)
- The Service of Baptism or Affirmation of Baptism
- The eucharistic meal

EASTER SUNDAY

- Full celebration of gathering, word, meal, and sending

EASTER EVENING

- Quieter eucharistic celebration

Where do these parts currently take place? Or, where could you imagine these separate rites taking place if you are going to introduce them for the first time?

Visualize the location of each element by drawing it on a floor plan of the worship space and surrounding areas.

The varying liturgies beg for certain settings and furnishings from bowls and ewers (pitchers) for foot washing on Maundy Thursday, to a large wooden cross for the Good Friday liturgy, to a fire pit or fireplace and large paschal candle for the Easter Vigil. Not only do these liturgies require spaces and objects but they allow for many different participants. The cast of people that might be involved in leading these Three Days could be numerous. Here, those worship planners concerned with the environment and art for the season have an opportunity to involve many individuals from the congregation who normally do not take a leadership role. The Triduum liturgy is one to be acted out by many, not by a mere few.

If you are taking a planning role for these services, it is important to plan out step-by-step what will happen and when and who is responsible. There are some who feel comfortable "winging it" during worship. These important liturgies should be talked through and walked through. It will not diminish the spirit of the worship if everyone knows exactly what he or she is doing. Even for those who have done this before, it has probably been at least one year since the last time and there is likely to be something that is different. It is better to see how each liturgy works best in your space. Not all liturgies can be staged the same way in different worship spaces. Your worship space has certain strengths and weaknesses. Thorough planning will help you see what those strengths and weaknesses are. If you find that there is a particular element of the liturgy that feels awkward or

160

does not flow the way you imagine it, check with other congregations who have a similar shape and floor plan and see how they do that part of the liturgy. You can use the drawings you made earlier to help in this staging and planning work.

ART FOR THE SEASON
MAUNDY THURSDAY

This would be a good opportunity to find and use art that shows acts of love, compassion, and charity. Perhaps in preparation for this day, during the weeks of Lent you could send groups of people out with cameras to take pictures of people engaged in ministry or places and people in need of our love and compassion. Displaying these photographs would be a powerful addition to the liturgy of foot washing. Taking pictures is also something people of all ages can do.

GOOD FRIDAY

One of the traditional expressions of art for this day is the Stations of the Cross—different scenes depicting the various stages of Jesus on the way from questioning to Calvary. This parish pilgrimage was a way for everyone to be able to walk the "Way of the Cross" as Jesus did without going to Jerusalem to do it. There are many different renderings of the Stations of the Cross in the form of paintings, sculpture, and stained glass. Your congregation can purchase, borrow, or rent stations to put up along the walls in the worship space. If you decide to use the Stations of the Cross, you should make sure that individuals are able to walk or travel from scene to scene easily. You might also want to consider whether to omit the non-biblical stations (numbers 3, 4, 6, 7, and 9 in the traditional listing). Prepare a handout that explains where you start and what each scene means. You can let this be an individual experience or you can ritualize it by having people move together in groups while singing the verses of an appropriate hymn or by having music that aids in the meditation on the stations. *This Far By Faith* has a powerful version of the "Way of the Cross." In one option, the community walks the stations throughout their neighborhood stopping at each "station" where violence has occurred.

For Good Friday evening, let the starkness of the unadorned and stripped church stand as an appropriate setting for the service of the cross.

EASTER VIGIL

If there is ever a time for "party decorations," this is it. The white and gold banners and paraments along with living plants and flowers are just a start. Other cloth or paper hangings in white and gold can be used throughout the space. Lots of light will be needed because this service takes place after sunset. You can ask members in the congregation if they have icons or other images of the resurrection. You could prepare them to be installed in the gathering space or in the fellowship areas, extending the artistic environment throughout your entire building.

Depending on how the lighting works in your space, Easter hangings and flowers might be in place before the liturgy and just not visible in the darkness, or they may be brought in as the hymn of praise is sung.

EASTER SUNDAY

The adornments from the Vigil may just be carried over, but it might serve well to add even more to emphasize the joy of this day of days. Just make sure that the central focuses of font, ambo (or pulpit and lectern), and table are not obscured or overshadowed.

Preaching *with the* Season

"The use of white space," a graphic artist will say,

"is every bit as important as the use of word, color,

or image. White becomes a color in its own right."

"Musical rests," musicians will agree, "speak every bit as loudly as the notes that lie between them."

"Silence—its amount and quality," the communications instructor advises, "has much to say about the words actually uttered."

White space.

Rests.

Silence.

If there is one time of the church year above all else in which white space, rests, and silence add texture to the depth of liturgical action, the richness of the readings, and the sounds and smells that surround the assembly, it is the Triduum. If there is a point when words should be measured, weighed, and only added when necessary, it is at this time.

It is in these three days in which things ultimate are addressed. It is in the Three Days when preaching, if it is not attuned to the liturgies and scripture that surround and inform it, can rob the day of its simple eloquence.

Perhaps the role of preaching in this period can best be likened to the role of words, both scripted and spoken, in a visit to Auschwitz. Auschwitz, the largest Nazi extermination camp in Poland, has come to represent evil and is often referred to as "the graveyard of the nations."

A visit to Auschwitz is all but devoid of words. Only at the gate is the visitor greeted with a brief spoken or written introduction. Then the silent walk begins. At one station, the visitor stands in a room filled to the ceiling with only human hair. The text is spartan . . . one sentence . . . enough for the sojourner to understand that this hair once bounced on the heads of innocent children giggling on a playground.

The visitor walks on. At the next station, the visitor stands in a room filled with a mountain of worn shoes. The text? Another sentence only . . . enough to remind the visitor that these shoes hobbled elderly women toward their yet premature deaths at the crematorium.

The walk continues. Next the visitor stands in a room of only artificial limbs. . . .

Words cannot describe the horror, nor should they try to. But select words focus the experience. Words, like careful lighting in a museum, bring out the essence of the experience.

Such is the power that the preached word may have during the Three Days. Our words would do well to allow the action to speak for itself. Our words will do very well if we use them, like a spotlight, to focus our attention on particular images of the day.

On Maundy Thursday, the sermon is situated early in the liturgy; it functions as both a conclusion to Lent and a beginning of a three-day odyssey. What words can both return us to Ash Wednesday and prepare us for Jerusalem? What language can invite us to participate fully in the three-day journey before us? What phrases can compel us to remove our Nikes and allow others to see our dirty feet? What urging will remind us that we need this breaking of bread, this flowing of wine?

Good Friday is a celebration of the triumph of the cross. The full passion narrative is heard; one need say little more. What few words can pull this event up from the past into the present? What phrases can transform the day's timbre from tragedy to triumph? What reflections can portray the progression of God from powerful to willfully powerless?

The Vigil of Easter already provides a rich multi-sensory feast of narrative, sound, smell, and taste. What words can sharpen our senses? What language can fuse us with fire, water, beeswax, speech, oil, bread, and wine? What images can lift up the paradox of meeting in darkness to praise the light? What metaphors can unite tonight's ancient symbols with today's certainties? Perhaps simply a few words around the fire, the font, the table?

It is at this point—at the Easter conclusion of the Three Days—that the balance and quality of language may shift. The community has now entered a new season.

Easter Sunday juxtaposes a festive liturgy with a variety of cultural and situational challenges. While a traditional sermon is appropriate, the task is complex. There will be visitors. There will be those present for whom this day is the community's one opportunity this year to show hospitality. There will be family meal preparations and other distractions to occupy the minds of some. There will be those who have recently stood at the open grave of a loved one and who are, on this day, grappling with the true feasibility of open tombs and empty graves. And, there will be the many images of the day—an empty tomb, a baptismal pool, unused spices, a Messiah mistaken as a gardener, angels, tears, joys, and fears.

If there is a time for several well-chosen words, this is the week. If there is a point at which the preacher feels drawn to "say it all," this is the week. If there is a week in which the preacher has little time to choose words, this is the week.

What simple words are potent enough to speak in such a richly layered time? What particularities can we hold up in order for others to glimpse the universal? What curiosity can be aroused to invite the occasional worshiper to come and see what the full Fifty Days hold? What gentle words can impart hope for the grieving man who has not yet seen the stone move from his wife's tomb? What spirit of contagion can we inspire in the faithful to leave this feast and proclaim, "I have seen the Lord"?

Finally, Easter Evening might easily be perceived as a graduation, an end to a rich array of liturgies. Instead, it is like a service of commencement—a beginning of a new life of witness. How can the hearts of the faithful be ignited tonight as we interpret the scripture? What metaphors can reconcile our invitation to Christ to "stay" with his command to "go"? What impulses can we give to turn the assembly outward in mission?

162

Shape *of* Worship *for the* Season

BASIC SHAPE OF THE MAUNDY THURSDAY LITURGY

- See Maundy Thursday liturgy in *LBW Ministers Edition*, pp. 137–38; also available as a congregational leaflet from Augsburg Fortress (AFP 0806605758)

GATHERING

- The sermon may begin the liturgy
- An order for corporate confession and forgiveness may be used (*LBW*, pp. 193–94, or *RW3: Holy Baptism and Related Rites*, pp. 93–96)
- The sharing of the peace follows the order for confession and forgiveness

WORD

- The washing of feet may follow the reading of the gospel
- For a dramatic reading based on the gospel use *Scripture Out Loud!* (AFP 0806639644)
- For a contemporary drama based on the second reading, use *Can These Bones Live?* (AFP 0806639652)
- No creed is used on Maundy Thursday
- The prayers: see the prayers for Maundy Thursday on pages 171–72

MEAL

- Offertory prayer: see alternate worship text for Maundy Thursday on page 169 as an option to the ones provided in the liturgy setting
- Use the proper preface for Passion
- Eucharistic prayer: in addition to the four main options in *LBW*, see "Eucharistic Prayer D: The Season of Lent" in *WOV* Leaders Edition, p. 68
- Invitation to communion: see alternate worship text for Maundy Thursday
- Post-communion prayer: see alternate worship text for Maundy Thursday
- No post-communion canticle
- Stripping of the altar, accompanied by singing of Psalm 22, follows post-communion prayer
- No benediction on Maundy Thursday
- No dismissal on Maundy Thursday

BASIC SHAPE OF THE GOOD FRIDAY LITURGY

- See Good Friday liturgy in *LBW* Ministers Edition,

pp. 139–43; also available as a congregational leaflet from Augsburg Fortress (AFP 0806605774)

WORD

- The Passion according to St. John is read; a version involving readers and congregation may be used (AFP 0806605707)
- For a reading based on the passion interspersed with choral music, use *St. John Passion* (AFP 0800658582) or a similar setting
- The bidding prayer for Good Friday may be used (*LBW* Ministers Edition, pp. 139–42)
- Adoration of the Crucified may be used (*LBW* Ministers Edition, p. 142)
- No communion for Good Friday
- No benediction for Good Friday
- No dismissal for Good Friday

BASIC SHAPE OF THE RITE FOR THE EASTER VIGIL

- See Vigil of Easter in *LBW* Ministers Edition, pp. 143–53; *WOV* Leaders Edition, pp. 88–89; *Vigil of Easter—Music Edition* (AFP 0806605782); also see congregational leaflet from Augsburg Fortress (AFP 0806605790)

LIGHT

- The service of light may begin outside at the lighting of a new fire
- The congregation processes into the darkened nave following the lighted paschal candle
- A cantor sings the Easter proclamation (*Exsultet*)

WORD

- Twelve readings appointed for the Easter Vigil (each of which may be followed by a sung response and a prayer) are listed in *WOV* Leaders Edition, pp. 88–89. All or some of them may be used, but the first and fourth should always be read
- Psalm responses to the readings may be found in *Psalter for Worship, Cycle C*, pp. 39–51

163

- Canticle of the Sun (RWI 8, LBW 527) may conclude the service of readings as an alternative to the Song of the Three Young Men
- For dramatic readings based on two of the appointed passages, see *Scripture Out Loud!* (AFP 0806639644)
- For contemporary dramas based on five of the passages, see *Can These Bones Live?* (AFP 0806639652)

BAPTISM

- If no candidates will be baptized, a congregational renewal of baptism may be used; see *Holy Baptism and Related Rites*, pp. 65–68.

MEAL

- During the movement from font to the place of the meal, a litany may be sung. Options include the Litany of the Saints in the seasonal rites section (a setting may be found in *Welcome to Christ: Lutheran Rites for the Catechumenate* [AFP 0806633956], pp. 70-71), the Litany in *Manual on the Liturgy: Lutheran Book of Worship*, pp. 336-37, or the Kyrie from settings one, two, or three in *LBW.*
- The hymn of praise (traditionally "Glory to God") is sung
- During the hymn of praise, lights may be turned on, accompanied by the ringing of bells
- The prayers: see the prayers for Vigil of Easter in *Sundays and Seasons*
- Offertory prayer: see alternate worship text for Easter Vigil/Day, p. 169
- Use the proper preface for Easter
- Eucharistic prayer: in addition to four main options in *LBW*, see "Eucharistic Prayer E: The Season of Easter" in *WOV* Leaders Edition, p. 69
- Invitation to communion: see alternate worship text for Easter Vigil/Day
- Post-communion prayer: see alternate worship text for Easter Vigil/Day
- Benediction: see alternate worship text for Easter Vigil/Day
- Dismissal: see alternate worship text for Easter Vigil/Day

BASIC SHAPE OF THE RITE FOR EASTER DAY

- Confession and Forgiveness: see alternate worship text for the Easter season

GATHERING

- Greeting: see alternate worship text for Easter Vigil/Day, page 169
- Use the Kyrie
- Use the hymn of praise ("This is the feast of victory")

WORD

- For a dramatic reading based on the Easter gospel from John, use *Scripture Out Loud!* (AFP 0806639644)
- Use the Nicene Creed
- The prayers: see the prayers for Easter Day, pp. 182–83

MEAL

- Offertory prayer: see alternate worship text for Easter Vigil/Day
- Use the proper preface for Easter
- Eucharistic prayer: in addition to four main options in *LBW*, see "Eucharistic Prayer E: The Season of Easter" in *WOV* Leaders Edition, p. 69
- Invitation to communion: see alternate worship text for Easter Vigil/Day
- Post-communion prayer: see alternate worship text for Easter Vigil/Day

SENDING

- Benediction: see alternate worship text for Easter Vigil/Day
- Dismissal: see alternate worship text for Easter Vigil/Day

OTHER SEASONAL POSSIBILITIES
PASCHAL VESPERS

- If you are able to gather for worship on Easter Evening, a festival form of evening prayer may be desired. Although it is printed as a part of morning prayer, consider appending the paschal blessing to evening prayer (*LBW*, pp. 138–41) anytime in the Easter season. See notes for this order in *LBW* Ministers Edition, p. 16, and *Manual on the Liturgy*, pp. 294–95. A hymn, such as "We know that Christ is raised" (LBW 189), "I bind unto myself today" (LBW 188), or "O blessed spring" (WOV 695), may replace the canticle "Te Deum," which is customarily associated with morning prayer.

Assembly Song *for the* Season

Christ calls us to stay and keep watch through Holy

Week and the Great Three Days. Busy and unbalanced

lives often leave us weary, and we do little better than

the disciples staying awake at Gethsemane's garden. Still, with Christ always with us, we can remain and readily await the Easter dawn.

MAUNDY THURSDAY

This evening's liturgy is a subdued one. Reinforce the servant themes of Maundy Thursday with the simple chant "Where true charity and love abide" (RWI 90). Another option is "Ubi caritas et amor"(WOV 665), a refrain from Taizé with solo verse sung over the last half of the refrain. Either of these can be done during foot washing or communion. During the stripping of the altar, Psalm 22 might be chanted by several singers in different spots around the congregation.

GOOD FRIDAY

Consider renewed settings of time-honored hymns such as "O sacred head, now wounded" (RWI 54), sung in a four-part setting by J. S. Bach, or the textually updated "Ah, holy Jesus"(RWI 7). During the meditation on the cross, all or part of the "Solemn Reproaches of the Cross" (setting by Robert Buckley Farlee, AFP 0806674723) could be presented. The refrain is simple enough that the congregation might be able to sing it with the choir.

VIGIL OF EASTER

In addition to the stories of faith, baptism and affirmation of baptism are key elements of the Easter Vigil. Baptismal acclamations such as "Springs of water, bless the Lord," may be found in *Welcome to Christ: Lutheran Rites for the Catechumenate* (AFP 0806633956).

The hymn of praise is the turning point in the Easter Vigil, where the stories of redemption and baptismal covenant turn toward resurrection. Have children bring bells from home, and ring them during the hymn

of praise and every time the word "alleluia" sounds. In addition to the hymns of praise in LBW , WOV, and TFF, consider the lively "The trumpets sound, the angels sing" (W&P 139), for organ, piano, brass, or band.

EASTER MORNING
GATHERING

Easter Sunday calls for sturdy opening hymns, such as "Jesus Christ is risen today" (LBW 151), or "Christ the Lord is risen today; Alleluia!" (LBW 128). Introduce the hymn of praise with a handbell peal or a brassy introduction, such as John Ferguson's *Festival Setting of the Communion Liturgy* (*LBW* Setting 2) for congregation, organ, choir, brass, and timpani (CPH 97-6127).

WORD

On Easter morning encourage children of all ages to bring bells and ring at every alleluia, especially the Great Alleluia, found in several sources, including at number 826 in *Worship: Third Edition* (GIA). Sing this alleluia three times, cantor then all, rising a musical step each time.

MEAL

Don't let the high point of the Sanctus be overshadowed by all the other festive music. Provide a festive "Holy, holy, holy" and "Lamb of God" using John Ferguson's *Festival Setting of Holy Communion* (*LBW* Setting 2) for congregation, organ, choir, brass, and timpani.

SENDING

In addition to "Thank the Lord" from *LBW* Setting 2, enjoy festive, renewed hymns such as "Christ is risen! Shout hosanna" (RWI 16), or "The day of resurrection!" (RWI 74, 75).

165

Music *for the* Season

See the Easter section for additional music appropriate for the Resurrection of Our Lord.

CHORAL

Byrd, William. "Ave verum." SATB, opt org. OXF 43.323.

Byrd, William. "The Passion according to St. John." SAB, soli. CPH 97-4868.

Copland, Aaron. "Help Us, Lord." SATB. B&H 6018.

Elgar, Edward. "Ave verum corpus" in *The New Church Anthem Book.* SATB, opt S solo, kybd. OXF 0-19-353109-7. Also octavo HWG GCMR 00039.

Fauré, Gabriel. "Ave Verum." SA, org. ECS 860.

Proulx, Richard. "Were You There?" in *The Augsburg Choirbook.* SATB. AFP 0800656784.

Victoria, Tomás Luis de. "The Passion According to St. John." SATB, soli. CPH 97-5430.

CHILDREN'S CHOIR

Anderson, Norma. "The Walk to Calvary." U, kybd. CG CGA739.

Hopson, Hal H. "A Lenten Walk: Jesus Walked this Lonesome Valley." 2 pt mxd, org, opt solo, opt timp, hb. AFP 080065448X.

Kemp, Helen. "A Lenten Love Song." U, kybd. CG CGA486.

KEYBOARD/INSTRUMENTAL

Augsburg Organ Library: Lent. Org. AFP 0800658973.

Linker, Janet. *Suite for Holy Week.* Org. BEC OC5.

Mendelssohn, Felix. "Adagio" from *Sonata I* in *Six Sonatas for the Organ.* Org. Various ed.

Wood, Dale. *Wood Works for Lent and Easter.* Org. SMP 70/13185.

Young, Jeremy. *At the Foot of the Cross.* Pno. AFP 0800655397.

HANDBELL

Kinyon, Barbara Baltzer. "Lenten Bells" ("Beneath the Cross of Jesus" and "Go to Dark Gethsemane") 2-3 oct. AG 1423.

Kinyon, Barbara Baltzer. "Throned upon That Awful Tree." 3 oct. BEC HB143.

Smoke, Gary R. "O Sacred Head, Now Wounded." 3-4 oct. High Meadow HM-01-004.

Thompson, Martha Lynn. "O Sacred Head, Now Wounded." 3-5 oct. MSM 30-303.

PRAISE ENSEMBLE

Dearman, Kirk and Deby Dearman. "I Will Glory in the Cross" in *Best of the Best.* FEL 1891062018.

Founds, Rick. "Jesus, Draw Me Close" in *More Songs for Praise and Worship.* SATB. WRD 3010387016 (vocal ed); WRD 3010186363 (pno, vcs, perc).

Founds, Rick. "We Remember You" in *W&P.*

Helgen, John. "That Priceless Grace." SATB, pno. AFP 0800658590.

Paris, Twila, arr. Rhodes. "Lamb of God." SATB, pno. WRD 30109246X.

Alternate Worship Texts

GREETING (EASTER DAY)

Alleluia! Christ is risen!

Christ is risen indeed! Alleluia!

The grace and peace of Jesus Christ,
who was raised from the dead to bring everlasting hope,
be with you all.
And also with you.

OFFERTORY PRAYER
(MAUNDY THURSDAY, EASTER VIGIL/DAY)

God of glory,
receive these gifts and the offering of our lives.
As Jesus was lifted up from the earth,
draw us to your heart in the midst of this world,
that all creation may be brought from bondage to freedom,
from darkness to light, and from death to life;
through Jesus Christ our Lord. Amen

INVITATION TO COMMUNION
(MAUNDY THURSDAY)

This is the food and drink of remembrance.
Let all who hunger for grace come and eat.
Let all who thirst for salvation take the cup.

INVITATION TO COMMUNION (EASTER VIGIL/DAY)

Christ our passover is sacrificed for us.
Therefore let us keep the feast. Alleluia!

POST-COMMUNION PRAYER (MAUNDY THURSDAY)

Lord God, in a wonderful sacrament
you have left us a memorial of your suffering and death.
May this sacrament of your body and blood
so work in us that the way we live
will proclaim the redemption you have brought;
for you live and reign with the Father and the Holy Spirit,
one God, now and forever.
Amen

POST-COMMUNION PRAYER (EASTER VIGIL/DAY)

God, our strength and salvation,
in this eucharistic feast
we have entered a paradise
of sweet honey and flowing milk,
where death no longer has dominion.
Empower us to tell the good news of the risen Christ,
through whom we praise you now and forever.
Amen

BLESSING (EASTER VIGIL/DAY)

Alleluia! Christ is risen!

Christ is risen indeed! Alleluia!

Almighty God, Father, ✛ Son, and Holy Spirit,
bless you and raise you to newness of life,
now and forever.
Amen

DISMISSAL (EASTER VIGIL/DAY)

Go in peace. Serve the risen Christ.

Thanks be to God. Alleluia, alleluia!

167

Seasonal Rites

Litany of the Saints

This may be used in the Easter Vigil as the transition from the Service of Holy Baptism to the Service of Holy Communion. A musical setting is available in Welcome to Christ: Lutheran Rites for the Catechumenate *(Augsburg Fortress, 1997), p. 70.*

Lord, have mercy.
Lord, have mercy.
Christ, have mercy.
Christ, have mercy.
Lord, have mercy.
Lord, have mercy.

Be gracious to us.
Hear us, O God.
Deliver your people.
Hear us, O God.
You loved us before the world was made:
Hear us, O God.
You rescued the people of your promise:
Hear us, O God.
You spoke through your prophets:
Hear us, O God.
You gave your only Son for the life of the world:
Hear us, O God.

For us and for our salvation he came down from heaven:
Great is your love.
And was born of the virgin Mary:
Great is your love.
Who by his cross and suffering has redeemed the world:
Great is your love.
And has washed us from our sins:
Great is your love.
Who on the third day rose from the dead:
Great is your love.
And has given us the victory:
Great is your love.
Who ascended on high:
Great is your love.
And intercedes for us at the right hand of God:
Great is your love.

For the gift of the Holy Spirit:
Thanks be to God.
For the one, holy, catholic, and apostolic church:
Thanks be to God.
For the great cloud of witnesses into which we are baptized:
Thanks be to God.

For Sarah and Abraham, Isaac and Rebekah:
Thanks be to God.
For Gideon and Deborah, David and Esther:
Thanks be to God.
For Moses and Isaiah, Jeremiah and Daniel:
Thanks be to God.
For Miriam and Rahab, Abigail and Ruth:
Thanks be to God.
For Mary, mother of our Lord:
Thanks be to God.
For John, who baptized in the Jordan:
Thanks be to God.
For Mary Magdalene and Joanna, Mary and Martha:
Thanks be to God.
For James and John, Peter and Andrew:
Thanks be to God.
For Paul and Apollos, Stephen and Phoebe:
Thanks be to God.
Other names may be added.
For all holy men and women, our mothers and fathers in faith:
Thanks be to God.
For the noble band of the prophets:
Thanks be to God.
For the glorious company of the apostles:
Thanks be to God.
For the white-robed army of martyrs:
Thanks be to God.
For the cherubim and seraphim, Michael and the holy angels:
Thanks be to God.

Be gracious to us.
Hear us, O God.
Deliver your people.
Hear us, O God.
Give new life to these chosen ones by the grace of baptism:
Hear us, O God.
Strengthen all who bear the sign of the cross:
Hear us, O God.
Clothe us in compassion and love:
Hear us, O God.
Bring us with all your saints to the river of life:
Hear us, O God.

Lord, have mercy.
Lord, have mercy.
Christ, have mercy.
Christ, have mercy.
Lord, have mercy.
Lord, have mercy.

168

April 8, 2004

Maundy Thursday

INTRODUCTION

Maundy Thursday is the beginning of the Three Days—the ancient observance of the mystery of our salvation, which plunges the faithful into the death of Jesus and brings them with him to resurrection life. The Three Days begin with one liturgy extending from Thursday evening through the Easter Vigil.

The Maundy Thursday liturgy focuses on three significant actions. First, the confession of sins and announcement of forgiveness brings to a conclusion the Lenten discipline of repentance that began on Ash Wednesday. Second, the church obeys Jesus' command (in Latin, *mandatum*, from which this day receives its name) to follow his example and wash each other's feet. Third, we celebrate our meal of deliverance, taking our place at the supper Jesus shared with his disciples on this night.

PRAYER OF THE DAY

Holy God, source of all love, on the night of his betrayal, Jesus gave his disciples a new commandment: To love one another as he had loved them. By your Holy Spirit write this commandment in our hearts; through your Son, Jesus Christ our Lord, who lives and reigns with you and the Holy Spirit, one God, now and forever.
or
Lord God, in a wonderful Sacrament you have left us a memorial of your suffering and death. May this Sacrament of your body and blood so work in us that the way we live will proclaim the redemption you have brought; for you live and reign with the Father and the Holy Spirit, one God, now and forever.

VERSE

As often as you eat this bread and drink the cup, you proclaim the Lord's death until he comes. (I Cor. 11:26)

READINGS

Exodus 12:1-4 [5-10] 11-14

Israel celebrated its deliverance from slavery in Egypt by keeping the festival of Passover. This festival included the slaughter, preparation, and eating of the Passover lamb, whose blood was used to protect God's people from the threat of death. The early church described the Lord's supper using imagery from the Passover, especially in portraying Jesus as the lamb who delivers God's people from sin and death.

Psalm 116:1, 10-17 (Psalm 116:1-2, 12-19 NRSV)

I will take the cup of salvation and call on the name of the LORD. (Ps. 116:11)

1 Corinthians 11:23-26

In all of Paul's letters, the only story from the life of Jesus that he recounts in detail is this report of the last supper. His words to the Christians at Corinth are reflected today in the liturgies of churches throughout the world.

John 13:1-17, 31b-35

The story of the last supper in John's gospel presents a remarkable event not mentioned elsewhere. Jesus performs the duty of a slave, washing the feet of his disciples and urging them to do the same for each other.

COLOR   Scarlet *or* White

THE PRAYERS

As we begin these holy Three Days, let us offer our prayer for the life of the world.
A BRIEF SILENCE.

For the whole church, that obeying the Lord's command that we love one another, we might serve one another as Christ, let us pray to the Lord:
Lord, have mercy.

For those preparing for Easter baptism, that as they make final preparations to cross through the waters and join us at the table of the Lord, they might find peace, courage, and joy, let us pray to the Lord.
Lord, have mercy.

For the strife-torn regions of the world, that war might cease and love prevail, let us pray to the Lord.
Lord, have mercy.

For those who are ill or weak in body, mind, or spirit *(especially)*, that they might receive God's strength and healing, let us pray to the Lord.
Lord, have mercy.

169

For those in any need, for prisoners and the condemned, for the homeless and the hungry, for the lost and alone, let us pray to the Lord.

Lord, have mercy.

For our congregation, that strengthened by the Lord's supper, we might make Christ visible through our own humble service, let us pray to the Lord.

Lord, have mercy.

HERE OTHER INTERCESSIONS MAY BE OFFERED.

Remembering those who have died in faith, that we with them might find our place at the table of the Lord, let us pray to the Lord.

Lord, have mercy.

Grant these prayers, merciful God, and all that we need, as we eagerly await the Easter feast; through Jesus Christ our Lord.

Amen

IMAGES FOR PREACHING

"I know Jesus because of my 'stara matka,' " said Lenka, a twenty-year-old Slovak woman. Lenka's grandmother, a victim of forty years of Communist party oppression, snuck Lenka to a neighboring village in the dark of night to have her baptized and instructed in the Christian faith. Party officials would not, in the end, pass over her "stara matka's" house without punishment, but the knowledge and remembrance of Jesus had been preserved for yet another generation in Lenka.

Remembrance. Knowing. Passing on. Passing over. Such are the images of Maundy Thursday.

In Exodus, the passover story becomes a "day of remembrance . . . throughout the generations" to be "observed as a perpetual ordinance."

The passing on of tradition is also central in Paul's letter to the community at Corinth as he both hands on what he has received, and recounts the *anamnesis*, the "remembrance" in the words of institution.

Knowing and understanding are pivotal in John's gospel as Jesus "knew that his hour had come to depart." He acted, "knowing that the Father had given all things into his hands." He chides Peter, "You do not now know what I am doing." He "knew who was to betray him." After the foot washing, he questions his disciples, "Do you know what I have done to you?" He challenges them to act on the basis of their understanding: "If you know these things you are blessed if you do them."

Indeed, passing over, remembrance, passing on, and knowledge are all bound together in his Maundy Thursday mandate: "By this everyone will know that you are my disciples, if you have love for one another."

"Write this commandment in our hearts," we pray in the prayer of the day. Amen. May it become a part of our permanent memory.

WORSHIP MATTERS

If your congregation has never participated in a foot-washing ritual on Maundy Thursday, consider ways to introduce this significant part of the liturgy for the day. Because the washing of feet is no longer a gesture of hospitality as it was in biblical times, it is unlikely that everyone in the congregation will want to participate in the ritual. Through newsletters, bulletins, and preaching, make the connections between ritual foot-washing, Jesus' example of servanthood, and our baptismal call. Though a congregation may want to invite any members of the assembly to come forward for footwashing, it would be wise to ask six or more persons to volunteer prior to the service. One possible model for the ritual is to have the presiding minister wash the feet of the first person who then washes the feet of the next person, and so on.

LET THE CHILDREN COME

When we receive communion we remember Jesus' last supper with his disciples, Christ's saving death, and the passover in Egypt. We celebrate communion because Jesus commanded us to "do this in remembrance of me." Do children truly understand the miracle of this meal? Of course not—none of us do. But even children can trust that God's promise is true and that in the eating of the bread and drinking of the wine Christ is present and he gives us what we need to feed our faith.

HYMNS FOR WORSHIP
GATHERING

Around you, O Lord Jesus   LBW 496

Great God, your love has called us   WOV 666

HYMN OF THE DAY

You satisfy the hungry heart   WOV 711

ALTERNATE HYMN OF THE DAY

Lord, who the night you were betrayed   LBW 206

Where charity and love prevail   LBW 126

COMMUNION

Thee we adore, O hidden Savior   LBW 199

SENDING

None

ADDITIONAL HYMNS AND SONGS

Take off your shoes   DH 62
Jesus is a rock in a weary land   RWSB
Jesus took a towel   RS 566
We have been told   SNC 136

MUSIC FOR THE DAY

PSALMODY

Farlee, Robert Buckley. PW , Cycle C.

Haas, David. "Psalm 116: The Name of God" in PCY, vol. 3.

Joncas, Michael. "Psalm 116: Our Blessing Cup" in STP, vol. 2.

Kendzia, Tom. "In the Presence of God" in STP, vol. 4.

Schalk, Carl. "Now I Will Walk at Your Side" in *Sing Out! A Children's Psalter.* WLP 7191.

CHORAL

Christiansen, F. Melius. "Lamb of God." SATB. AFP 0800652592.
    Also in The Augsburg Choirbook. AFP 0800656784.

de Lienas, Juan. "Coenantibus autem illis." SATB. KJO 8820.

Duruflé, Maurice. "Ubi caritas." SATB. PRE 312-41253.

Hopson, Hal H. "Canticle of Love." SATB, org. AFP 0800657799.

Moore, Philip. "O sacrum convivium." SATB, A solo.
    MAY 5101193M.

Walton, William. "A Litany." ("Drop Slow Tears") SATB.
    OXF 43.349.

CHILDREN'S CHOIR

Adams, Aaron. "Remember Me." (I Cor. 11:23-26) U/2 pt, kybd.
    Triune Music 10.2459K.

Hopson, Hal H. "Love One Another." (John 13-34-35) U, kybd.
    CG CGA741.

KEYBOARD/INSTRUMENTAL

Biery, Marilyn. "Ubi caritas" in *Augsburg Organ Library: Lent.* Org.
    AFP 0800658973.

Cherwien, David. "Song 1" in *Evening and Morning: Hymn Settings for Organ.* Org.   AFP 080067572X.

Honoré, Jeffrey. "Bicentennial" in *Contemporary Hymn Settings for Organ.*
    Org. AFP 0800674782.

Organ, Anne Krentz. "Shades Mountain" in *Woven Together.* Pno, inst.
    AFP 0800658167.

Pethel, James. "Go to Dark Gethsemane" in *Twelve Hymn Preludes for Organ.* Org. BEL EL03930.

HANDBELL

Honoré, Jeffrey. "Adoro te devote." 3-5 oct. CPH 97-6693.

Sherman, Arnold B. "Ah, Holy Jesus." 3-5 oct. AG 1612.

PRAISE ENSEMBLE

Adkins, Donna. "Glorify Thy Name" in W&P.

Chisum, John and Nancy Gordon, arr. Greer. "Come Expecting Jesus." SATB, pno. Allegis AG-1024

Willard, Kelly. "Make Me a Servant" in W&P.

171

April 9, 2004

Good Friday

INTRODUCTION

This day is the second portion of the liturgy of the Three Days, which extends from Maundy Thursday through the Easter Vigil. As the church gathers to re-member the death of Jesus, we focus not only upon the agony of the cross but especially upon God's victory through the crucified. Even more, we "lift high the cross" as the sign of God's triumph over sin, death, and evil.

PRAYER OF THE DAY

Almighty God, we ask you to look with mercy on your family, for whom our Lord Jesus Christ was willing to be betrayed and to be given over to the hands of sinners and to suffer death on the cross; who now lives and reigns with you and the Holy Spirit, one God, forever and ever.

or

Lord Jesus, you carried our sins in your own body on the tree so that we might have life. May we and all who re-member this day find new life in you now and in the world to come, where you live and reign with the Father and the Holy Spirit, now and forever.

READINGS

Isaiah 52:13—53:12

The prophet weaves a vision of the suffering servant, whose agony is not a sign of God's rejection, but points to the God who brings healing out of suffering.

Psalm 22

My God, my God, why have you forsaken me? (Ps. 22:1)

Hebrews 10:16-25

The writer to the Hebrews uses the Hebrew scriptures to understand the meaning of Christ's death on the cross. Like a great priest, Jesus offered his own blood as a sacri-fice for our sins, so that now we can worship God with confidence and hope.

or Hebrews 4:14-16; 5:7-9

Jesus is our merciful high priest.

John 18:1—19:42

On Good Friday, the story of Jesus' passion—from his

arrest to his burial—is read in its entirety from the gospel of John. For John, the death of Jesus is the sign of God's victory, and the cross is the throne from which the new king reigns.

THE PRAYERS

On Good Friday, the church's ancient Bidding Prayer is said or sung. See *LBW* Ministers Edition, pp. 139-42; or *Book of Common Worship*, pp. 283-86.

IMAGES FOR PREACHING

The sheer volume of words in today's readings, not to mention their weight, may be enough for the assembly. The preacher may do well to follow one church tradition of silence for meditation in lieu of a sermon on this day.

Yet, if commentary is warranted, perhaps this very image of "weight" might be lifted up. In our prayer of the day, we acknowledge that Christ carried the weight of our sins in his body. The suffering servant of Isaiah is nearly flattened beneath the load, as "he has borne our infirmities and carried our diseases . . . was crushed for our iniquities; upon him was the punishment that made us whole." Indeed, "it was the will of the Lord to crush him with pain" as he "bore the sin of many." This crush-ing weight comes to a culmination in the passion in which Jesus "carrying the cross by himself" went to the place of crucifixion.

How have we contributed to the weight of the cross as individuals? As a church? As a nation? Yet, even on this Good Friday, we sense that the load is about to lighten, that the scale has begun to tip in the opposite direction. As the cross is lifted, the burden is subsumed. "See, my servant shall prosper; he shall be exalted and lifted up, and shall be very high," says Isaiah.

Our alternate reading from the Hebrews further in-dicates a levity—almost a weightlessness—that accom-panies the release of the burden: "We have a great high priest who has passed through the heavens."

Regardless of what we have contributed to the bur-den of the cross, we glimpse on this day that, thanks to Christ's sacrificial triumph, we will be able to "approach

172

with a true heart in full assurance of faith, with our hearts sprinkled clean from an evil conscience and our bodies washed with pure water."

WORSHIP MATTERS

The veneration of the cross is an ancient tradition that is becoming meaningful to contemporary congregations. Since the Good Friday liturgy doesn't usually include Holy Communion and is therefore rather sparse in ritual actions, the veneration offers a way for worshipers to offer a nonverbal sign of reverence to Christ and the cross of our salvation. After a large wooden cross is carried in procession, those in the assembly who choose may come forward and pause briefly before the cross, touch the wood, bow or kneel. (This may also be done at the end of the liturgy.) Though the ritual is unfamiliar to many, with appropriate pastoral preparation and music the veneration of the cross can be one of the high points of Holy Week.

LET THE CHILDREN COME

On this night we gather to hear the story of Jesus' arrest, trial, crucifixion, and death. Jesus' full humanity is revealed to us. He suffered unimaginably, but he remained obedient to the will of God. Consider having a child read poetry in addition to the assigned readings for this service. The work of Mattie Stepanek, an eleven-year-old, is a potential resource. He has written many poems (published by Hyperion) and touched the lives of thousands of people. He writes movingly and courageously about life and death, love and loss, faith and hope.

HYMNS FOR WORSHIP

GATHERING

None

HYMN OF THE DAY

Sing, my tongue   LBW 118

ALTERNATE HYMN OF THE DAY

Were you there   LBW 92
There in God's garden   WOV 668

COMMUNION

None

SENDING

None

ADDITIONAL HYMNS AND SONGS

Calvary   TFF 85, RWSB
At the foot of the cross   W&P 11
Son of God, by God forsaken   HFG 38

MUSIC FOR THE DAY

PSALMODY

Farlee, Robert Buckley. PW , Cycle C.
Haugen, Marty. "My God, My God" in PCY, vol. 1.
Kogut, Malcolm. "I Will Praise You, Lord" in PCY, vol. 10.
"Psalm 22." SNC 142.
Schiavone, John. "Psalm 22: My God, My God, Why Have You Abandoned Me" in STP, vol. 3.

CHORAL

Burleigh, H.T. "Were You There?" SSATTBB. Ricordi NY 423.
Casals, Pablo. "O vos omnes." SSAATTBB. Broude AB 128.
Ellingboe, Bradley. "There Is A Green Hill Far Away." 2 pt mxd, pno. KJO 5765.
Farlee, Robert Buckley. "Solemn Reproaches of the Cross." SATB, solo, pno. AFP 0800674723.
Ferguson, John. "Ah, Holy Jesus." SATB, org, opt cong. AFP 0800654528. Also in *The Augsburg Choirbook*. AFP 0800656784.
Proulx, Richard. "We Adore You O Christ." SATB. PAR PPM09836.
Shute, Linda Cable. "Thirty Years Among Us." SATB, org. AFP 0800658647.

CHILDREN'S CHOIR

Christopherson, Dorothy. "There Was a Man." U, pno, ob. AFP 0800657047.
Fauré, Gabriel, arr. John Leavitt. "Pie Jesu" in *Requiem*. U, pno. HAL 08551530.
Jennings, Carolyn. "Ah, Holy Jesus." SA, vc. AFP 0800645154.

KEYBOARD/INSTRUMENTAL

Bach, J. S. "O Man, Bewail Thy Grievous Fall" (O Mensch, bewein dein Sünde gross) in *Orgelbüchlein*. Org. CPH 97-5774 or other ed.
Cherwien, David. "Go to Dark Gethsemane" in *Augsburg Organ Library: Lent*. Org. AFP 0800658973.
Young, Jeremy. "Were You There" in *At the Foot of the Cross*. Pno. AFP 0800655397.

173

HANDBELL

Eithun, Sandra. "Gethsemane's Prayer." 3 oct. JEF JH S9281.

Hascall, Nancy. "Gethsemane." 3-5 oct. Red River BL5022.

PRAISE ENSEMBLE

Barbour, Anne and Barbara Skidmore, arr. Wyrtzen. "The Holy Heart." SATB, pno. WRD 3010838166.

Leblanc, Lenny and Paul Baloche. "Above All" in *Best of the Best.* FEL 1891062018.

Paris, Twila. "Lamb of God." RWSB.

Webber, Andrew Lloyd, arr. Leavitt. "Pie Jesu." SATB, kybd. HAL 086 03519.

"When I Survey the Wondrous Cross" in *Best of the Best.* FEL 1891062018.

174

Friday, April 9

DIETRICH BONHOEFFER, TEACHER, 1945

Bonhoeffer was a German theologian who, at the age of twenty-five, became a lecturer in systematic theology at the University of Berlin. In 1933, and with Hitler's rise to power, Bonhoeffer became a leading spokesman for the confessing church, a resistance movement against the Nazis. He was arrested in 1943. He was linked to a failed attempt on Hitler's life and sent to Buchenwald, then later to Schoenberg prison. After leading a worship service on April 8, 1945, at Schoenberg, he was taken away to be hanged the next day. His last words as he left were, "This is the end, but for me the beginning of life."

A hymn written by Bonhoeffer shortly before his death includes the line, "By gracious powers so wonderfully sheltered, and confidently waiting come what may, we know that God is with us night and morning, and never fails to greet us each new day" (WOV 736). Bonhoeffer's courage is a bold witness to the paschal mystery of Christ's dying and rising celebrated on this and following days.

April 10, 2004

The Resurrection of Our Lord
Vigil of Easter

INTRODUCTION

The Easter Vigil is the ancient and powerful celebration
of the new creation that springs from Jesus' open tomb.
The striking of the Easter fire; the lighting of the
paschal candle; the singing of the ancient Easter proclamation, which calls the faithful to join the universe in
new creation; the baptismal washing that buries us with
Christ and raises us to life—all these powerful actions
draw us into the wonder of resurrection. The church
gathers to hear the whole story, from creation through
exodus and the prophets, ending the liturgy with the first
taste of the resurrection celebration.

PRAYER OF THE DAY

O God, who made this most holy night to shine with the
glory of the Lord's resurrection: Stir up in your Church
that Spirit of adoption which is given to us in Baptism,
that we, being renewed both in body and mind, may
worship you in sincerity and truth; through Jesus Christ
our Lord, who lives and reigns with you, in the unity of
the Holy Spirit, one God, now and forever.

VERSE

Alleluia. Christ being raised from the dead will never die
again; death has no more dominion over him. Alleluia.
Let us sing to the LORD who has triumphed gloriously.
Alleluia. (Rom. 6:9; Exod. 15:1)

READINGS

Creation: Genesis 1:1—2:4a

Response: Psalm 136:1-9, 23-36

God's mercy endures forever. (Ps. 136:1b)

The Flood: Genesis 7:1-5, 11-18; 8:6-18; 9:8-13

Response: Psalm 46

The LORD of hosts is with us; the God of Jacob is our
stronghold. (Ps. 46:4)

The Testing of Abraham: Genesis 22:1-18

Response: Psalm 16

You will show me the path of life. (Ps. 16:11)

Israel's Deliverance at the Red Sea: Exodus 14:10-31; 15:20-21

Response: Exodus 15:1b-13, 17-18

I will sing to the LORD who has triumphed gloriously.
(Exod. 15:1)

Salvation Freely Offered to All: Isaiah 55:1-11

Response: Isaiah 12:2-6

With joy you will draw water from the wells of salvation. (Isa. 12:3)

The Wisdom of God: Proverbs 8:1-8, 19-21; 9:4b-6

or Baruch 3:9-15, 32—4:4

Response: Psalm 19

The statutes of the LORD are just and rejoice the heart.
(Ps. 19:8)

A New Heart and a New Spirit: Ezekiel 36:24-28

Response: Psalm 42 and Psalm 43

My soul is athirst for the living God. (Ps. 42:2)

The Valley of the Dry Bones: Ezekiel 37:1-14

Response: Psalm 143

Revive me, O LORD, for your name's sake. (Ps. 143:11)

The Gathering of God's People: Zephaniah 3:14-20

Response: Psalm 98

Lift up your voice, rejoice and sing. (Ps. 98:5)

The Call of Jonah: Jonah 3:1-10

Response: Jonah 2:1-3 [4-6] 7-9

Deliverance belongs to the LORD. (Jonah 2:9)

The Song of Moses: Deuteronomy 31:19-30

Response: Deuteronomy 32:1-4, 7, 36a, 43a

The LORD will give his people justice. (Deut. 32:36)

The Fiery Furnace: Daniel 3:1-29

Response: Song of the Three Young Men 35-65

Sing praise to the LORD and highly exalt him forever.
(Song of Thr. 35b)

NEW TESTAMENT READING

Romans 6:3-11

Christians are baptized into the death of Christ and are
also joined to Christ's resurrection.

Response: Psalm 114

Tremble, O earth, at the presence of the LORD.
(Ps. 114:7)

175

GOSPEL

Luke 24:1-12

The women who followed Jesus take the lead in proclaiming the resurrection.

COLOR   White *or* Gold

THE PRAYERS

Rejoicing in the resurrection, let us remember in prayer the church, the world, and all those in need.

A BRIEF SILENCE.

Blessed are you, almighty God, for you created the universe and gave it life. Preserve your creation, maintain its abundance, and inspire its stewardship among your people. For this we pray:

Hear us, living God.

Blessed are you, for you created a holy people and call them your own. Continue to preserve, protect and deliver your children. For this we pray:

Hear us, living God.

Blessed are you, for you have made us a new creation through Christ Jesus. Continue to bless your church, and especially all those baptized this holy night, that we might bring your creative and redeeming word to all the world. For this we pray:

Hear us, living God.

Blessed are you, for you have the power to bring life from death. Humble any in this world who would wield tyrannical power and by the power of the resurrection establish justice throughout the earth. For this we pray:

Hear us, living God.

Blessed are you, for you continually care for your people. Deliver all those in need from affliction and pain, from grief and despair, from poverty and homelessness, from hunger and want, from loneliness and abuse, *(especially).* For this we pray:

Hear us, living God.

Blessed are you, for by the power of the resurrection you make all things new. Renew this congregation that we may live abundantly in Easter joy. For this we pray:

Hear us, living God.

HERE OTHER INTERCESSIONS MAY BE OFFERED.

Blessed are you, for you have enfolded our lives in Christ Jesus. Give us hope, that together with the saints and all the witnesses of the resurrection we may appear with you in glory. For this we pray:

Hear us, living God.

With alleluias in our hearts and on our lips we commend to your care all for whom we pray, trusting in your mercy; through your Son, Jesus Christ our Lord.

Amen

IMAGES FOR PREACHING

"It began around a charcoal grill and ended in a blaze of light," said Ernie, always the skeptical one, who had been co-opted into attending "that long service" by being assigned as a lector. "And it was amazing!"

Like Peter, we—still in a state of denial—gather around the fire on this night to warm ourselves. We will need this fire tonight. It only gets darker as we follow it into the tomb of the church; as we follow it, in the reading of the creation story, to the beginning of time, when there was no light; as, perhaps, we go deep into the dark belly of the whale with Jonah.

Abraham, too, greets us with fire on this evening, as he prepares for the thwarted sacrifice of his son Isaac. And fire takes us through the wilderness as we follow its nighttime blaze, which protects the Israelites from the Egyptians.

We feel the heat being turned up as we enter the fiery furnace with Shadrach, Meshach, and Abednego.

We rejoice in this fire tonight, even as we heard in the Easter Proclamation:

Exult, also, O earth, enlightened with such radiance; and, made brilliant by the splendor of the eternal King, know that the ancient darkness has been banished from all the world. Be glad also, O mother Church, clothed with the brightness of such a light. . . . This, indeed, is the night in which the darkness of sin has been purged away by the rising brightness.

Like Peter, we gather around the fire to warm ourselves. With Peter, we can on this night, having glimpsed the brilliant light of our salvation, leave "amazed at what has happened."

WORSHIP MATTERS

The Easter Vigil is a time for baptisms, especially the baptism of adults! Whenever you schedule baptisms always start by suggesting the Vigil and explain that the Easter Vigil developed during the early centuries of Christianity as a time when adults were baptized into the

Christian faith. A community's experience of Easter is deepened when Lent has been a journey with persons preparing to be plunged into the font and the mystery of Christ's death and resurrection. Because many have not previously attended a Vigil, it is important to approach the liturgy pastorally. It may mean the service needs to be held (after dusk) at a time when the most number of people are likely to attend. Some attention needs to be given to length and flow of the service, especially for those new to the service. A congregation can provide information about the symbols and meaning of the Vigil in bulletins, newsletters, handouts, classes, and sermons.

LET THE CHILDREN COME

Though the Vigil sometimes gets late for young children, there is plenty to appeal to them. The fire, the candles, the movement, great stories, baptism, and communion—all these attract interest. If worship planners view the service through children's eyes, looking for elements that might cause them to tune out, the liturgy can be strengthened for all. In particular, pay attention to the way the readings are presented. They can be just a lot of words, or a high point of the evening.

HYMNS FOR WORSHIP
GATHERING
None

HYMN OF THE DAY
We know that Christ is raised   LBW 189

ALTERNATE HYMN OF THE DAY
At the Lamb's high feast we sing   LBW 210
Brighter than the sun   DH 64

COMMUNION
Come away to the skies   WOV 669
Come, you faithful, raise the strain   LBW 132

SENDING
This joyful Eastertide   LBW 149, WOV 676
All creatures of our God and King   LBW 527
Up from the grave he arose   TFF 94, RWSB

ADDITIONAL HYMNS AND SONGS
Rise, O church, like Christ arisen   RWSB, RWI 63

At the font we start our journey   NCH 308
Blessing, honor, and glory   W&P 21

MUSIC FOR THE DAY
AROUND THE GREAT FIRE
Berthier, Jacques. "Within Our Darkest Night" in *Songs and Prayers from Taizé*. GIA G-3719.
Biery, James. "Easter Sequence." U, brass qrt, org. MSM 80-404.
Schutte, Dan. "Holy Darkness." Cong, kybd, gtr, vln, vla, vc, hrn. OCP 9906CC.

AROUND THE LIGHT OF CHRIST
Batastini, Robert. "Exsultet." (Easter Proclamation) U chant. GIA G-2351.
"Rejoice Now, All Heavenly Choirs" in *Music for the Vigil of Easter*. Cant, cong. AFP 0806605790.
Tamblyn. "Lumen Christi." Presider, cant, SATB, org, perc. OCP 7235CC.
"The Exsultet" in TP.

AROUND THE READINGS
Responses to all readings in PW , Cycle C.
Trapp, Lynn. "Responses for the Triduum." Cant, cong, kybd, opt solo, C inst. MSM 80-305.
FIRST READING
Carmona, Paul. "A Canticle of Creation." U/cant, desc, org, tpt. OCP 9973.
Erickson, Richard. "When Long Before Time." SATB, org. AFP 0800656768.
Hopson, Hal H. "O Praise the Lord Who Made All Beauty." U, kybd. CG CGA143.
Reeves, Jeff. "In the Beginning." U, perc, Orff/pno. CG CGA929.
Smith, Alan. "God's Love Is Forever!" in PS 2.
SECOND READING
Cherwien, David. "God Is Our Refuge and Strength." U, org. MSM 80-800.
Harbor, Rawn. "The Lord of Hosts Is with Us." TFF 6.
Rock of my salvation W&P 161
THIRD READING
Inwood, Paul. "Centre of My Life" in PS 2.
Trinkley, Bruce. "I Want Jesus to Walk with Me." SATB, pno. AFP 0800657071.
When we are living / *Pues si vivimos* RWSB, LLC 462
FOURTH READING
Barker, Michael. "Miriam's Song." U, kybd, opt tamb. CG CGA740.
Cherwien, David. "Go Down, Moses." U, kybd. AMSI AM 3010.

177

Daw Jr., Carl P. "Metrical Canticles 25 and 26" in *To Sing God's Praise.* Cong, kybd. HOP 921.

Gibbons, John. "Canticle of Moses" in PS 2.

FIFTH READING

DeLong, Richard. "Seek Ye the Lord" in *Five Sacred Songs.* Solo, kybd. ECS 4759.

Lindh, Jody. "Behold, God Is My Salvation." U/2 pt, org. CPH 98-3193.

Rusbridge, Barbara. "Sing a Song to the Lord" in PS 1.

Surely it is God who saves me WOV 635

SIXTH READING

Cox, Joe. "Psalm 19" in *Psalms for the People of God.* Cant, choir, cong, kybd. SMP 45/1037S.

Ogden, David. "You, Lord, Have the Message of Eternal Life" in PS 2.

SEVENTH READING

Hopson, Hal H. "Let All the Gates Be Opened Wide." U/2 pt, kybd. CG CGA736.

Howells, Herbert. "Like as the Hart." SATB, org. OXF 42.066.

Hurd, Bob. "As the Deer Longs" in PS 2.

As pants the hart for cooling streams LBW 452

As the deer RWSB, W&P 9

NINTH READING

Johnson, Alan. "All the Ends of the Earth" in PS 1.

Jothen, Michael. "O Sing Ye!" U, kybd. BEC BP1128.

Martinson, Joel. "Psalm 98." SATB, cong, tpt, org. CPH 98-3225.

TENTH READING

I, the Lord of sea and sky WOV 752, TFF 230

TWELFTH READING

Daw Jr., Carl P. "Metrical Canticles 13 and 14" in *To Sing God's Praise.* Cong, kybd. HOP 921.

Proulx, Richard. "Song of the Three Children." U/2 pt, cant, cong, perc, org. GIA G-1863.

Let all creation bless the Lord SNC 34

AROUND THE FONT

"A Litany of the Saints" and "Springs of Water, Bless the Lord" in *Welcome to Christ: Lutheran Rites for the Catechumenate.* AFP 0806633956.

Cherwien, David and Susan Palo Cherwien. "Life Tree." SAB, org, opt fl. CPH 98-3190.

Cooney, Rory, arr. Gary Daigle. "Glory to God/Sprinkling Rite." Choir, cong, gtr, kybd, fl. GIA G-4020.

Farlee, Robert Buckley. "O Blessed Spring." SATB, ob, org, opt cong. AFP 0800654242.

Keesecker, Thomas. "Washed Anew." SAB/SATB, opt 2 oct hb, opt cong. AFP 6000001355.

Palmer, Nicholas. "Cleanse Us, O Lord: Sprinkling Rite." Cant, SATB, cong, gtr, org, opt inst. GIA G-4064.

Taylor-Howell, Susan. "You Have Put on Christ." U/3 pt, opt Orff. CG CGA 325.

Trapp, Lynn. "Music for the Rite of Sprinkling." SATB, org. MSM 80-901.

You have put on Christ WOV 694

PSALMODY

Farlee, Robert Buckley. PW, Cycle C.

Hopson, Hal H. *Psalm Refrains and Tones.* HOP 425.

The Psalter—Psalms and Canticles for Singing. WJK 0664254454.

CHORAL

Frese, Everett. "Exsultet." SATB, kybd. OCP 11659.

Grieg, Edvard. "Pentecost Hymn." SATB. KJO 8825.

Jennings, Kenneth. "All You Works of the Lord, Bless the Lord" in *The Augsburg Choirbook.* SATB, org. AFP 0800656784.

Leavitt, John. "Begin the Song of Glory Now." SATB, org, perc. AFP 6000001258. OP.

CHILDREN'S CHOIR

Krape, William. "O Praise Him!" U, org. Gentry JG2263.

Layton, James. "They Rolled the Stone Away." SAB, kybd. MSM-50-4036.

Lindner, Jane. "Christ is Risen." (Luke 24:1-9) U, kybd, opt 2 oct hb. CG CGA767.

Reilly, Dadie. "Resurrection." 2 pt, kybd, opt rhythm bells. AFP 0800646312.

KEYBOARD/INSTRUMENTAL

Hyslop, Scott. "Noel Nouvelet" in *Six Chorale Fantasias for Solo Instrument and Piano.* Pno, sax. AFP 0800656601.

Lasky, David. "Variations on 'O filii et filiae' " in *Trilogy for Holy Week.* Org. HWG GB00676.

Wood, Dale. "Were You There" in *Wood Works for Organ, Book I.* Org. SMP KK 357.

HANDBELL

Sherman, Arnold B. "The Strife is O'er." 3-5 oct. AG 1847.

Smith, Vicki. "Gaudeamus." (Let Us Rejoice) 4-5 oct. CPH 97-6104.

PRAISE ENSEMBLE

Haugen, Marty. "All You Works of God." U/SATB, kybd, opt gtr, perc, electric bass, children, cong. GIA 3481.

Kogut, Malcolm. "Like a Deer That Longs for Flowing Streams" in PCY, vol. 10. U, kybd, solo, opt cong, gtr.

Saturday, April 10
MIKAEL AGRICOLA, BISHOP OF TURKU, 1557

Agricola was consecrated as the bishop of Turku in 1554 without papal approval. As a result, he began a re-form of the Finnish church along Lutheran lines. He translated the New Testament, the prayerbook, hymns, and the mass into Finnish and through this work set the rules of orthography that are the basis of modern

Finnish spelling. His thoroughgoing work is particularly remarkable in that he accomplished it in only three years. He died suddenly on a return trip after negotiating a treaty with the Russians.

In the coming weeks of Easter, the hymn "Arise, my soul, arise!" (LBW 516), with a Finnish tune, can be sung at parish gatherings. In text and melody, it encourages us to rise as Christ has risen.

April 11, 2004

The Resurrection of Our Lord
Easter Day

INTRODUCTION

The Lord is risen indeed! The open tomb of Jesus is the door to a new way of being in the world. Easter is not one day but fifty. For a week of weeks—fifty days—the church will explore the dimensions of this new life and raise a joyful alleluia!

PRAYER OF THE DAY

O God, you gave your only Son to suffer death on the cross for our redemption, and by his glorious resurrection you delivered us from the power of death. Make us die every day to sin, so that we may live with him forever in the joy of the resurrection; through Jesus Christ our Lord, who lives and reigns with you and the Holy Spirit, one God, now and forever.

or

Almighty God, through your only Son you overcame death and opened for us the gate of everlasting life. Give us your continual help; put good desires into our minds and bring them to full effect; through Jesus Christ our Lord, who lives and reigns with you and the Holy Spirit, one God, now and forever.

VERSE

Alleluia. Christ being raised from the dead will never die again; death no longer has dominion over him. Alleluia. On this day the LORD has acted; we will rejoice and be glad in it. Alleluia. (Rom. 6:9; Ps. 118:24)

READINGS

Acts 10:34-43

179

Peter's sermon, delivered at the home of Cornelius, a Roman army officer, is a summary of the essential message of Christianity. Everyone who believes in Jesus, whose life, death, and resurrection fulfilled the words of the prophets, receives forgiveness of sins through his name.

or Isaiah 65:17-25

God promises a new heaven and a new earth.

Psalm 118:1-2, 14-24

On this day the LORD has acted; we will rejoice and be glad in it. (Ps. 118:24)

1 Corinthians 15:19-26

Paul describes the consequences of the resurrection, including the promise of new life in Christ to a world that has been in bondage to death. He celebrates the destruction of the forces of evil and the establishment of God's victorious rule over all.

or Acts 10:34-43

See above.

John 20:1-18

Easter morning began with confusion: the stone was moved and the tomb was empty. Disciples arrive, then angels, and finally Jesus himself. Out of the confusion, hope emerges, and a weeping woman becomes the first to confess her faith in the risen Lord.

or Luke 24:1-12

The women who followed Jesus take the lead in proclaiming the resurrection.

COLOR White *or* Gold

THE PRAYERS

Rejoicing in the resurrection, let us remember in prayer the church, the world, and all those in need.

A BRIEF SILENCE.

Blessed are you, holy God, for you call us together in your name and join us to Christ's resurrection through Holy Baptism. Bless the newly baptized everywhere and bring aid to all who seek to bear one another's burdens. For this we pray:

Hear us, living God.

Blessed are you, for you continue to create, to liberate, to judge, to love, to suffer, and to give peace in our troubled world. Inspire the nations of the world by the power of the resurrection, that your name might be glorified and proclaimed by all people. For this we pray:

Hear us, living God.

Blessed are you, for you extend the power of the resurrection to those who are broken in body, mind, or spirit. Be with those who are sick and in need *(especially)*, and give again your generous help and healing. For this we pray:

Hear us, living God.

Blessed are you, for by the power of the resurrection you make all things new. Renew this congregation, that we may live abundantly in Easter joy. For this we pray:

Hear us, living God.

Blessed are you, for you have restored our joy. Help us to extend this celebration beyond these walls, that everyone may know the joyful news and share in the new life you offer. For this we pray:

Hear us, living God.

HERE OTHER INTERCESSIONS MAY BE OFFERED.

Blessed are you, for you are the hope of all who have died in faith. Renew our hope, that with Mary Magdalene, the disciples, and all the saints we may see and worship you in glory. For this we pray:

Hear us, living God.

With alleluias in our hearts and on our lips we commend to your care all for whom we pray, trusting in your mercy; through your Son, Jesus Christ our Lord.

Amen

IMAGES FOR PREACHING

Water shows no partiality. Anyone who has lived through a flood knows that water will go where it can flow, sweeping along everything in its path and drowning all living things it subsumes. The Easter liturgies and today's lessons take us to the edge of the font, where we see the impartiality—the rippling and sweeping, drowning and delivering power—of water.

God, like the waters of the flood, "shows no partiality," says Peter in the book of Acts, "but in every nation anyone who fears him and does what is right is acceptable to him." Indeed, the texts for today are swollen with images of the gospel rippling outward—sweeping along all those it encounters.

Mary, upon encountering the risen Christ, is commanded to go to the disciples and bear witness to what she has seen. She announces, "I have seen the Lord." These simple words set the waters in motion.

This message of the rippling, sweeping impartiality of God, according to Peter in Acts, was sent to the people of Israel and spread throughout Judea. "We are witnesses to all that he did in Judea. . . . He commanded us to preach to the people."

Paul describes to the community at Corinth the "theological ripple" ordering both resurrection and death: "All will be made alive in Christ. But each in his own order: Christ the first fruits, then at his coming those who belong to Christ. Then comes the end, when he hands over the kingdom. . . ." As in a flood, death itself is swept along in the ordering flow "after he has destroyed every ruler and every authority and power. For he must reign until he has put all his enemies under his feet. The last enemy to be destroyed is death."

This is our death of which he speaks. This is our life.

WORSHIP MATTERS

Easter is about the resurrection. It is also about hospitality. Many of our churches will be filled to capacity and will include persons estranged from the church, or who attend infrequently, or who are unfamiliar with the liturgy and rituals of our faith. On one hand, a congregation may not wish to change its liturgy to suit the needs of those who come but one or two times a year. On the other hand, there are ways to express the gospel through a spirit of hospitality and welcoming. Perhaps more of the liturgy and hymns need to be printed in the service folder. Are instructions for communion clear? Are we genuinely glad to have many guests who have the opportunity to experience the presence of the risen Christ, or are we somewhat put off by CEOs (those who come on Christmas, Easter, and "other occasions")? Ushers, greeters, ministers, and other leaders of the liturgy will all set the tone. Sometimes it is hard to get new persons inside our churches. May Easter be a day when we give thanks for the opportunity to celebrate the heart of our faith with a full church!

LET THE CHILDREN COME

This is the day that the Lord has made. Let us rejoice and be glad in it! The Easter story is for all people at all times! Invite children to participate in many ways during today's worship. Older children could process in with the paschal candle. A younger child could lead the congregation in the Easter greeting. Someone from junior high could read one of the lessons. The good news of Christ's resurrection is for all ages. Make sure all ages are represented among your worship leaders this morning.

HYMNS FOR WORSHIP
GATHERING

Jesus Christ is risen today   LBW 151
Christ has arisen, alleluia   WOV 678, TFF 96

HYMN OF THE DAY

This joyful Eastertide   WOV 676

ALTERNATE HYMN OF THE DAY

Awake, my heart, with gladness   LBW 129
The strife is o'er, the battle done   LBW 135

COMMUNION

I know that my Redeemer lives!   LBW 352
The day of resurrection   RWI 74, 75
We who once were dead   LBW 207

SENDING

Christ is risen! Alleluia!   LBW 131
Alleluia, alleluia, give thanks   WOV 671
We will glorify   W&P 154

ADDITIONAL HYMNS AND SONGS

Alleluia! Christ is arisen/¡Aleluya! Cristo resucitó   RWSB
Christ the Lord is risen   RS 600
He Is Lord   LS 63
Good news, alleluia!   DH 65

MUSIC FOR THE DAY
PSALMODY

Haas, David. "Alleluia! Let Us Rejoice!" in PCY, vol. 3.
Roth, John. "Give Thanks Unto the Lord." CPH 98-3277.
Schalk, Carl. PW , Cycle C.
Shields, Valerie. "Psalm for Easter." MSM 80-405.
Smith, Timothy R. "Give Thanks to the Lord" in STP, vol. 4.
Soper, Scott. "Psalm 118: This Is the Day" in STP, vol. 2.

CHORAL

Handel, G.F. "Since By Man Came Death" in *Messiah.* SATB, org. Various ed.
Hayes, Mark. "Alleluia, Christ Is Risen." SATB, kybd, opt 2 tpt. AFP 0800659538.
Johnson, Carolyn. "Now the Green Blade Rises." SATB, kybd, tpt. AFP 0800675428.
MacFarlane, Will C. "Christ Our Passover." SATB, org. PRE 322.35139.
Nygard, Carl J. "Resurrection Hymn." SATB, org, opt brass qrt. AFP 0800675509.
Peeters, Flor. "Entrata Festiva." U, org, opt brass. PET 6159.
Petker, Allan. "Canon of Praise for Easter Morning." SATB, opt brass. FB BG2106.
Rachmaninoff, Sergei. "Today Hath Salvation Come" from *All Night Vigil* in *Songs of the Church.* SATB div. HWG GB640.
Rachmaninoff, Sergei. "When Thou, O Lord, Hadst Arisen." from *All Night Vigil* in *Songs of the Church.* SATB div. HWG GB 640.

CHILDREN'S CHOIR

Horman, John. "Mary Told the Good News." U/2 pt, kybd, opt hb, Orff. ABI 07225-5.
Lau, Robert. "This Is the Day." (Ps. 118:24) U, kybd, opt fl. CG CGA552.
Page, Anna Laura. "A New Song." 2 pt trbl, kybd, opt fl. AFP 0800674499.

KEYBOARD/INSTRUMENTAL

Albrecht, Mark. "Easter Hymn" in *Festive Processionals.* Org, tpt. AFP 0800657985.
Goemanne, Noël. "Easter Hymn" in *Augsburg Organ Library: Easter.* Org. AFP 0800659368.

181

Johnson, David N. and Bert Landman, arr. Douglas Henderson. *Brass Processionals: Trumpet Tunes in D for Brass.* Org, brass. AFP 0800675045.

Kerr, J. Wayne. "Truro" in *Augsburg Organ Library: Easter.* Org. AFP 0800659368.

Kolander, Keith. "Easter Hymn" in *All Things Are Thine.* Org. AFP 0800658000.

Webster, Richard. *Paschal Suite for Organ and Trumpet.* Org, tpt. AFP 080065692X.

HANDBELL

Afdahl, Lee J. "Jesus Christ Is Risen Today." 3-5 oct. AFP 0800659899.

Ingram, Bill. "Thine Is the Glory." 2-3 oct. Ring Out! RO 0502.

McChesney, Kevin. "Jesus Christ Is Risen Today." 3 oct. LOR 20/1073L.

Sherman, Arnold B. "Gaudeamus." 3-5 oct. AG 1764.

PRAISE ENSEMBLE

Card, Michael, arr. Wolaver. "Love Crucified Arose." SATB, pno. BNT SP6107.

Crouch, Andrae, arr. Bolks. "The Blood Will Never Lose Its Power." SATB, pno, opt. gtr, bass. BEL LOC 06048X.

Founds, Rick. "Lord, I Lift Your Name on High" in W&P.

Smith, Martin. "Did You Feel the Mountains Tremble?" in *Best of the Best.* FEL 1891062018.

182

April 11, 2004

The Resurrection of Our Lord
Easter Evening

INTRODUCTION

The excitement of Easter morning has ended, but the adventure of the resurrection is only beginning. In the twilight of that hectic day, weary disciples try to piece the chaos together. We, too, pause to reflect on the magnitude of the events we have celebrated this day.

PRAYER OF THE DAY

Almighty God, you give us the joy of celebrating our Lord's resurrection. Give us also the joys of life in your service, and bring us at last to the full joy of life eternal; through your Son, Jesus Christ our Lord, who lives and reigns with you and the Holy Spirit, one God, now and forever.

VERSE

Alleluia. Christ being raised from the dead will never die again; death no longer has dominion over him. Alleluia. Beginning with Moses and all the prophets, Jesus interpreted the things about himself in all the scriptures. Alleluia. (Rom. 6:9; Luke 24:27)

READINGS

Isaiah 25:6-9

This section of Isaiah seems to come from a time after the exile. The prophet looks forward to a day beyond death. Israel's pagan neighbors knew a god of death whose mouth was an open grave. The prophet knows that God will one day swallow death.

Psalm 114

Hallelujah. (Ps. 114:1)

1 Corinthians 5:6b-8

Paul discerns the implications of Jesus' resurrection. There is an interesting similarity between bread and Easter people: both rise!

Luke 24:13-49

Luke tells a story about distraught disciples who cannot piece together the puzzle of this new day. A stranger consoles them and begins to unlock the mystery.

COLOR White

THE PRAYERS

Rejoicing in the resurrection, let us remember in prayer the church, the world, and all those in need.

A BRIEF SILENCE.

Blessed are you, for through the power of the resurrection we have been joined as the church. Bless the newly baptized everywhere and make them with us to be leaven in the loaf, bringing word of your salvation to all the world. For this we pray:

Hear us, living God.

Blessed are you, for you are Lord of every village, town, and city, of every farm, ranch, and county. Guide our local leaders in good stewardship, just lawmaking, and compassionate community service. For this we pray:

Hear us, living God.

Blessed are you, for you walk with us in the way of life. Walk tonight with those in any need *(especially)* and deliver them from all their affliction. For this we pray:

Hear us, living God.

Blessed are you, for our hearts burn within us by the power of your presence in the breaking of the bread. Through the power of the resurrection make this congregation ever more faithful in its proclamation and celebration of the sacraments. For this we pray:

Hear us, living God.

HERE OTHER INTERCESSIONS MAY BE OFFERED.

Blessed are you, for you have promised always to be with us. At the last, gather us up with all the faithful departed that we may rest in you. For this we pray:

Hear us, living God.

With alleluias in our hearts and on our lips we commend to your care all for whom we pray, trusting in your mercy; through your Son, Jesus Christ our Lord.

Amen

IMAGES FOR PREACHING

"It's always interesting to join my spouse on congregational visits," said the workshop leader. "I love to see how congregations worship and how they live out their callings. And it's of particular interest to see how they respond to me as a visitor—both before and after they recognize that I'm married to the bishop."

"Their eyes were kept from recognizing him," writes Luke, our evangelist for today. Recognition and response are evident in today's readings. Indeed, the clarity of the response seems to correspond with the clarity of the recognition.

"What ailed you?" asks the psalmist, baffled by the response of nature, which can, at best, be described as unnatural. In the face of full recognition of the God of Jacob, nature becomes unbridled, undone, untied. The sea fled; the Jordan turned back. Mountains skipped like rams; little hills like sheep. Glorious disorder abounds!

Not so in the Lukan account. Reason tempers both recognition and response.

"Why are you frightened?" asks Jesus of the eleven. In the natural world, fear is an authentic response. Yet, human reason delays, and almost blocks, recognition on both the road to Emmaus, and later among the eleven. In this encounter with the holy, recognition is more like a slow sunrise that finally begins to dawn on the disciples.

To the same degree that recognition is tempered by reason, the response is reasoned, restrained, and reserved. Luke writes, "In their joy they were disbelieving and still wondering." No reversal of rivers or prancing peaks here. Rather, life as usual is the order of the day; the disciples broil Jesus some fish.

But such is this lifetime. Our prayer of the day reminds us that there is joy (singular) in the present-day celebration, there are joys (plural) in the present-day life of service, but there is *full joy* only in life eternal.

WORSHIP MATTERS

The gospel for Easter evening is the Emmaus story with the news of the resurrection burning in the hearts of the two walkers and Jesus being made known in the breaking of the bread. Holy Communion, then, is a natural liturgy for use this evening. However, the familiar line, "Stay with us, because it is almost evening and the day is now nearly over," makes evening prayer also an appropriate liturgy. If it doesn't seem feasible to add another service to a very busy week, consider using evening prayer at another time in the Easter season, or at any time, for that matter. There are a variety of settings available and the texts and images of evening prayer (or vespers) are cherished by many congregations. With the eucharist being celebrated more frequently, parishes need to be creative in finding other occasions to use morning or evening prayer.

183

LET THE CHILDREN COME

The gospel reads: "Their eyes were opened and they recognized him." We often take the sounds and sights of the gospel for granted—especially in our worship space. Have blindfolds available in the pews for tonight. When it comes time for the gospel to be read, ask children—or everyone!—to put on their blindfolds. Listen to the gospel blindfolded. Before the congregation sings the gospel response allow time for them to remove the blindfolds and look for signs of Christ in the worship space and in the people around them.

HYMNS FOR WORSHIP

GATHERING

Alleluia! Jesus is risen   WOV 674

HYMN OF THE DAY

That Easter day with joy was bright   LBW 154

COMMUNION

Stay with us   WOV 743

SENDING

Abide with us, our Savior   LBW 263

ADDITIONAL HYMNS AND SONGS

Day of arising   RWSB
Open our eyes, Lord   TFF 98
Come to us, beloved stranger   SNC 153
As I walked home to Emmaus / *El peregrino de Emaús*
LLC 362

MUSIC FOR THE DAY

SERVICE MUSIC

For a musical setting of the eucharistic liturgy especially suited to evening and to the Easter cycle of the church year, consider Stay with Us, Lord, *with music by David Cherwien and hymn texts by Susan Palo Cherwien. AFP 0800674839 (full music ed); AFP 0800674847 (cong pt).*

CHORAL

Dirksen, Richard. "Christ Our Passover." SATB, brass qrt, timp, org. HWG GCMR 02874.

Hovland, Egil. "Stay With Us." SATB, kybd. AFP 0800658825.

Phillips, Craig. "On This Bright Easter Morn." SATB, org. OCP 10258.

Sirett, Mark. "Thou Shalt Know Him." SATB. AFP 0800655206.

Vulpius, Melchior. "Arisen Is Our Blessed Lord" in *Chantry Choirbook*. SATB dbl chorus, inst. AFP 0800657772.

CHILDREN'S CHOIR

Hopson, Hal H. "Luke 24:34" in *Praise the Lord: Service Music*. U/2 pt, kybd. CG CGA530.

Schalk, Carl. "The Whole Bright World Rejoices Now." U, org, opt fl, hb (1 oct 5 bells). CG CGA560.

KEYBOARD/INSTRUMENTAL

Cherwien, David. "Now the Green Blade Rises" in *Interpretations*. Org. AMSI OR-1.

Keesecker, Thomas. "Middlebury" in *Come Away to the Skies*. Pno. AFP 0800656555.

Raney, Joel. "Christ the Lord is Risen Today." Pno and org duet, opt cong. HOP 8045.

Thomas, David Evan. "Middlebury" in *Early American Tunes for Organ*. Org. AFP 0800674804.

HANDBELL

Kinyon, Barbara Baltzer. "Jesus Christ Is Risen Today" in *Eastertide Bells*. 2-3 oct. AG 1342.

Sherman, Arnold B. "Risen Today, Alleluia!" FLA HP5289 (2-3 oct); FLA HP5334 (4-5 oct).

PRAISE ENSEMBLE

Oliver, Gary. "Celebrate Jesus" in *Best of the Best*. FEL 1891062018.

Smith, Martin. "Shout to the North" in *More Songs for Praise and Worship*. SATB. WRD 3010387016 (vocal ed); WRD 3010186363 (pno, vcs, perc).

EASTER

Called to claim and proclaim the resurrection

Images *of the* Season

On Easter Day, we stand gaping at the open and

empty tomb. Though we have had centuries to get used

to the idea, if we think about it at all, it is dumbfounding.

He is risen? Really?

On that first evening, Jesus' followers, understandably more flummoxed than we, found what they thought would be a safe place and hid there. When Jesus appeared among them, he began the process of drawing them away from the graveyard and into the land of the living. The season of Easter does the same for us. We need not linger at the tomb. Because he is risen indeed, we must discern how we shall live.

White Easter paraments set off the beauty of our emerging understanding, like the dormant plants now stirring outdoors. The fresh colors of spring, buds swelling and then releasing the pent-up leaves and flowers, all shine vividly after the sparsity of the Lenten season. We can sing Alleluia again!

Easter is the morning of faith. The air is fresh and new. The sun is not too harsh. If Lent was the night of waiting, Easter is the dawn of hope, not yet tarnished by discouragement or impatience. The texts for the third Sunday of Easter work this theme. We could not see in the night, but in the morning, we can recognize that it is Jesus who feeds us and calls us to feed others.

During the Easter season, the raw fear and confusion of the hours surrounding Jesus' death and resurrection slowly gives way to a growing awareness that we are called out of our comfort zones to claim and proclaim the power of the resurrection. Faced with this new identity, we need assurances, much like a child who is learning to walk. No longer immobile or a crawler, a walking child gains a certain independence and is faced with the responsibility and risk inherent in it. The fourth Sunday reminds us that God is still in charge and will use the power of the resurrection to bring life to others and to us. Dorcas, who had done much good, was raised to life again. We shall not want, the psalmist confesses. Jesus, with a view of the Mount of Olives where he prayed so earnestly before his death, asserts that no one can snatch his sheep from his hand. We are encouraged to venture

forth, people of the resurrection. We can boldly claim the bloom that is ours.

Assured of God's steadfastness, we are invited into the visions of what this resurrection faith looks like. Peter's dream vision expanded his view of salvation to include the Gentiles, an unthinkable option before the resurrection. All people and all creation praise God's goodness in this new world—it is truly a new heaven and a new earth, a place where death will be no more and the spring of the water of life flows freely for all. Jesus offered the new commandment at the last supper: "Love one another." This will be the mark of our new identity, that we love one another.

The visions play out even more in the following weeks. Paul is drawn to Macedonia and the faith of Lydia, ever farther from the temporal city of Jerusalem. The new Jerusalem, though, is filled with God. No temple is needed, nor sun, nor moon. From the throne flows the river of the water of life, which nourishes the tree of life, whose leaves are for the healing of the nations.

This vision is what the resurrection has broken open for us. Our thirst for wholeness and holiness is slaked in this river. Our need for cleansing is satisfied in this river. From this river of life flows the baptismal water that has made each of us, and all of creation, God's chosen. Ours is not a God of modest means, but one of poignant purpose. God's power is for the sake of the well-being of all of God's creatures. Anyone who wishes may take the water of life.

In the season of Easter, we are called beyond our fears and confusion and into the light of day. We are offered a vision of the power of God's abundant, steadfast, and irrepressible love. We see a God who is truly the beginning and the end, calling us to live in love and unity with each other in a world made radically new by the resurrection of Jesus. Death defeated, we can live lives of new possibility, fashion a world of peace and hope, and cherish each other as the gifts we are.

Environment *and* Art *for the* Season

Our Lord has come, has suffered, has died, and has

been raised. The gospel preachers share with us

a new reality: a Christ, bodily raised from the dead,

who transcends the limitations of the physical world to be with his disciples. Jesus' two appearances among the disciples in the locked upper room, the appearance and mysterious disappearance in Emmaus, the appearance on the shore to the fishing disciples to share a word and a meal, all point to this post-resurrection Christ who desires to be in fellowship with his disciples. This is a fellowship of teaching and sharing and breaking of the bread.

This Easter season is a week's worth of Sundays: seven weeks for us to celebrate Christ's real presence among us. This true presence of Christ in our assemblies happens most profoundly in our family meal, the Holy Eucharist (which means thanksgiving). Here, around the table, we celebrate the mystical yet real presence in, with, and under the simple elements of bread and wine. It is not a show. It is not something for a worthy few. It is rather a life-giving meal of Christ's body and blood for all baptized believers. This Easter season, this week of Easter Sundays is our opportunity to reflect on the amazing and mysterious presence of Christ among the believers in the church.

ANALYZING YOUR SPACE

Take a fresh look at the floor plan or setup of your worship space. What is the shape of your space? Long and narrow? Shallow and wide? Do all of the seats face in the same direction? Is the chancel area "set off" by rising steps? Do you have a communion rail that is a separation between where the pastor and assisting ministers lead from and where the rest of the assembly sits, stands, or kneels? Is your altar fixed to the wall? Has it been pulled out from the wall where the ministers preside from behind it facing the people? Could anybody regardless of her or his ability to walk reach the altar area without having to be carried or helped up?

Until recent decades most of our worship spaces were designed with a floor plan in the shape of the cross with the head of the cross being the chancel/altar area. Some of our churches are wider with developed "arms" of the cross pattern. Others have shortened arms or none at all. Often, these worship spaces also have steps climbing up into the raised chancel area with some higher up than others. This is often coupled with altars that may still be attached to the wall, leaving our pastors two choices: either keep their backs turned away from the assembly during the liturgy of the meal, or turn back and forth with their backs to the altar when they address the congregation. Even the second solution still keeps them placed between the elements of the meal and the assembly until the time of distribution. Add to that the visual and tangible "fence" of a communion rail, and we have a physical environment that speaks (at best) of a place for communion (and much of the rest of the liturgy) that is set apart from the community.

The developed tradition that contributed to these architectural arrangements served us well for hundreds of years. Still, we must ask ourselves: Do we want a liturgical experience where word and sacrament, particularly eucharist, is literally celebrated in our midst? Or are we going to remain content with a more mystical communion experience that happens "up there" with us watching from afar, waiting for our Lord to be brought to us from across a dividing line?

Recognize that the way those questions are answered bears practical implications. If it is part of your worshiping community's piety to kneel at communion, would that be possible with no dividing rail? If you took to heart some of these challenges and wanted to make changes to your current architecture in order to have an environment that "speaks" theologically in a more current way, that would likely take time and money to achieve. You may have an historic building with structural limitations. You may not want to disturb the "look" your worship space currently has.

There are many ways to address the varying issues that each particular worship space has. And, there may be simple adjustments you can make. Perhaps the altar could be moved off the wall so the ministers could stand behind it. Perhaps your community does not kneel at

187

communion and therefore doesn't need the communion rail as a support. If you didn't want to remove your rail permanently, you could see if you could adjust it so it could be removable. If your altar is already off of the wall, maybe it could come out further into the assembly.

Perhaps you could temporarily experiment with some of these challenging ideas. Your congregation may already have flexible seating in the worship space but you have not yet experimented with seating plans that are more in the round or plans that place the altar more centrally. If such is the case, you have a great advantage. If your seating is fixed pew seating (which is the case in most congregations), you will have to be a little more creative at this point. For example, if you have another area in your church building (older worship space, fellowship hall, and so forth), you might set up a temporary worship environment with flexible seating so you can try how it feels to be worshiping with the altar and place for the word more in the midst of the assembly.

188

The last six of the seven Sundays of Easter is a short enough period of time to try something new with a definite end in sight. The Easter season is also long enough to actually see for a few weeks what a different setup might look like. The great advantage to this kind of experiment is that the worshiping community does not have to commit to a long-term change and can go into it with an open mind. This attempt should be considered and planned with all parties included in the conversation. You will need the support of the assembly's musicians for this kind of experiment to be a success. If you have an organ or other large instruments or sound systems, you will have to make temporary accommodations. If the Easter season does not appear to be the best time, you can certainly postpone this until the summer months.

ART FOR THE SEASON

The resurrected Christ is a Christ who challenges our preconceptions. The Easter season is an appropriate time not only for radical ideas in the environment but in the art we use as well. Liturgical art can be much more than recognizable representations of biblical scenes. Our churches are inundated with the same or similar pictures of Jesus at a traditional last supper, praying in the garden, or with a group of children around him. While these images are often beloved and speak to us about a very real and human Jesus, celebrating the resurrected Christ is mysterious and dynamic. This new reality cannot be fully captured by representational art: art that represents something that we can see. Often, when we think of art that is not representational, we think of abstract art—something that has to be explained in order for us to have any hopes of understanding what the artist was trying to communicate. But there are many ways that biblical and theological realities can be expressed through art. The challenge is to find art that is neither a painting of a scene that tries to define visually how it may have "really" been, nor is an image or sculpture so abstract that only a few understand.

An anecdote relating to representational art: On a train, Pablo Picasso met a man who announced with some disgust that Picasso's paintings didn't look anything like real people. Picasso asked the man to show him something that did look like a real person, and the man pulled out a photograph of his wife. Picasso studied the photograph for a moment and said, "She's awfully small, isn't she?"

Many modern artists have rendered provocative (in the best sense) depictions of Christ both crucified and raised—images that give us insights beyond even what a photograph would reveal. Check out the library or the Internet for these artists and their creations. You might be able to find a poster version of a challenging depiction for display in your space.

Preaching *with the* Season

"An elephant is like a hose pipe!" announced one

of six blind men attempting to discern the essence

of 'elephant-ness.' He was clinging to its trunk. The one

under the big flapping ear corrected, "No! I've got it! It's like a big flag." "Not so! It's like a thick pillar," asserted the one who was hugging a leg.

So the popular Hindu tale goes. The six bring their sightless, but tangible, experience to bear upon their understanding of this sacred creature. This creature, the living incarnation of Ganesh, an elephant-headed Hindu deity who rides atop a mouse, is the symbol of the one who beholds the future and recognizes truth. This symbol is invoked at the beginning of any new creation or endeavor.

How clear-sighted are we as we stand at the cusp of a new creation—something which we both await and are already a part of? What are our symbols? What tangible, if necessarily incomplete, description can we bring to the church as we depict the already-not-yet quality of life in the Easter world and the celebration of these fifty days? What images can we invoke as we attempt to describe the sacred, yet secular, time in which we live? What senses have we engaged in an attempt to experience and describe the new creation of which we are a part?

We have touched water. We have tasted wine and bread. We have smelled the scented oil. We have sung the liturgy. We have heard the witness of the community. We have beheld the cross.

These images are sacred and powerful for us. In our human frailty, though, we must still acknowledge that we are, at best, like near-sighted creatures attempting to describe the sacred from a distance. We must bring a sixth sense to understanding this new life in which we live. The witness of scripture must be allowed to shape our imaging. These fifty days offer us unique scriptural vistas of Easter community.

The Revelation to John provides us with a series of verbal snapshots that lend color and texture to the already-not-yet era in which we live. John's Revelation sequence begins like the projection of the first slide in a slide show; with each touch of the focus button, the image sharpens.

The second Sunday of Easter is an image of an other-worldly kingdom, the details of which are, as yet, hazy; clarity comes only with the Almighty's announcement, "I am the Alpha and the Omega." Easter Three sharpens the image enough for us to glimpse the Lamb on the throne, surrounded by a swirl of angels, elders, myriads of myriads, thousands of thousands—indeed, every creature—singing "Worthy is the Lamb!"

In the fourth week, color, depth, and graphic detail enliven the image as white robes, palms, and people from every tribe and nation join the heavenly throng. Easter Five clarifies that which has not been perceptible until now: God is among these people, all of whom dwell in the New Jerusalem. Easter Six causes us to question whether this is, indeed, a slide at all. Or is it, perhaps, a hologram? We virtually gasp at the details as we are taken on a virtual tour of the New Jerusalem, a visit that culminates in a glimpse of the Lamb's face.

Finally, the seventh Sunday of Easter brings the image full-circle. "I am the Alpha and the Omega," Jesus says once again. Now that we have seen the fullness of the new creation, we, too, are invited into the picture as we, along with all who thirst, are urged to "Come! . . . Come!"

If the Revelation to John provides us with a heavenly image, the Acts of the Apostles offers us a more down-to-earth picture of the Spirit's power to advance the Easter community in this lifetime. Like a tidal wave, the Spirit advances outward from Jerusalem, impartially sweeping humankind in its flow, striking down every barrier humans can erect. It is these broken barriers that give us a glimpse of the "already" of Easter in this lifetime.

Temporal powers are overcome on the second Sunday of Easter as Peter, forbidden to preach, thumbs his nose at the authority of the Jerusalem council. Human will and obstinacy are routed out on Easter Three as Saul, in an about-face, becomes an instrument of the gospel to the Gentiles. Death provides no obstacle on the fourth week as Dorcas is raised by Peter; further,

189

the power of resuscitation is no longer limited to Jesus' invocation.

Religious mores are struck down on Easter Five as even Gentiles receive the baptism of the Spirit via Peter's witness. Cultural barriers and sheer physical distance cannot contain the church as Paul, on Easter's sixth Sunday, hazards far outward to Philippi where Lydia and her household are baptized and receive their place in the new community. Indeed, on Easter Seven, not even Roman maximum-security prisons and jailers are strong enough as prison walls tumble and the jailer and his family are captured by the Spirit's saving grace. And on the Day of Pentecost, we are reminded how, and by whose windy work, this growth began.

And so, in the end, we find ourselves back at the beginning. Indeed, we may find ourselves, like the disciples at Bethany, gazing upward into the sky, wondering "What was that all about?" When all is said and done, we see that our vision is still impaired and our proclamations are as complete as "An elephant is like a hose pipe!"

But, perhaps, herein lies the good news. We have not yet joined the swirling throng surrounding the Lamb. The barriers of our lives have not yet been decisively demolished. Despite that, the gift of the Spirit has been given. The Pentecost has ensured that the images of these fifty days have been given a lifetime—indeed, an eternity—in which to come into focus through our lives in Easter community.

Shape *of* Worship *for the* Season

190

BASIC SHAPE OF THE EUCHARISTIC RITE

- Confession and Forgiveness: see alternate worship text for Easter, page 198, as an option to the text in the liturgy setting.
- Or, use Remembrance of Baptism with sprinkling from the seasonal rites section

GATHERING

- Greeting: see alternate worship text
- Use the Kyrie throughout Easter
- As the hymn of praise, use "This is the feast of victory"

WORD

- For dramatic readings based on lectionary passages, use *Scripture Out Loud!* (AFP 0806639644) for the second Sunday of Easter and Pentecost Day
- For contemporary dramas based on lectionary passages, use *Can These Bones Live?* (AFP 0806639652) for the second and fourth Sundays of Easter and Pentecost Day
- Use the Nicene Creed

BAPTISM

- Consider observing Pentecost Day (May 30) as a baptismal festival

MEAL

- Offertory prayer: see alternate worship text for Easter
- Use the proper preface for Easter; use the proper preface for Pentecost on the Vigil of Pentecost and Pentecost Day
- Eucharistic Prayer: in addition to four main options in *LBW*, see "Eucharistic Prayer E: The Season of Easter" in *WOV* Leaders Edition, p. 69; and "Eucharistic Prayer F: The Day of Pentecost" in *WOV* Leaders Edition, p. 70
- Invitation to communion: see appropriate alternate worship text for Easter 2–7 and for Pentecost
- Post-communion prayer: see appropriate alternate worship text for Easter 2–7 and for Pentecost

SENDING

- Benediction: see alternate worship text for Easter
- Dismissal: see alternate worship text for Easter

OTHER SEASONAL POSSIBILITIES
ROGATION BLESSING

- See seasonal rites section; may be used to conclude

worship on the sixth Sunday of Easter (traditionally, rogation days are the Monday, Tuesday, and Wednesday before Ascension of Our Lord) or at another time when such a blessing is appropriate

VIGIL OF PENTECOST

- A celebration for this evening could be modeled on the Vigil of Easter, but using these elements:
  - Service of Light (from *LBW*, pp. 142–44)

- Service of Word (eucharistic rite, from the prayer of the day through the hymn of the day)
- Service of Baptismal Affirmation (from *LBW*, pp. 199–201, with the congregation gathering around the font, space permitting; water may be sprinkled from the font during the recitation of the creed)
- Service of Communion (from the offering through the dismissal)

Assembly Song *for the* Season

Trumpets, bells, pipes, drums, alleluias galore!

The noise of our Easter celebrations can shake

the rafters of our buildings, and bring us great joy.

191

Do these sounds also shake justice free to spill over the earth? This is the hope of all who sing the resurrection song.

The week of weeks that is Easter can be one of those ideas that works better in theory than in practice, as the weeks move on toward summer and the memory of Easter Sunday fades. While this phenomenon is, to an extent, inevitable, the use of unifying factors through the season can lessen its impact. Find a good, joyful way to do the gospel acclamation, offertory, or post-communion song, and keep it going (though perhaps with some internal variations) throughout the season. On the other side of the coin, don't be afraid to let the anticipation of the Day of Pentecost increasingly color the liturgy as we approach that festival.

GATHERING

After the Easter Sunday festival, it can be difficult to sustain the Easter message in succeeding Sundays, so remind the assembly of the season with sturdy opening hymns. Use a setting of "This is the feast/Worthy is Christ" as the hymn of praise, either an *LBW* setting or the high-energy WOV 608 for congregation, band, and soloists. As an alternative introit or hymn of praise, explore "Surrexit Christus (The Lord is risen)" in *Taizé: Songs for Prayer*, p. 44 (GIA G-4956). This setting has a

refrain and short solos especially suitable for children, sung between two parts of the refrain.

WORD

For seasonal psalmody, encourage congregational singing of *LBW* pointed psalms to tones 1, 3, and 8. Begin and end the psalm with choral antiphons based on familiar alleluia refrains, like LBW 135 or LBW 139. On the fourth Sunday of Easter, introduce the renewed setting of the psalm paraphrase "My Shepherd, you supply my need" (RW1 50, 51) in unison or harmony.

In place of standard alleluia verses, extract hymn refrains from popular Eastertide hymns like "The strife is o'er, the battle done" (LBW 135) and "O sons and daughters of the King" (LBW 139). Another festive option for choir and congregation is an "An Alleluia Canon for Easter" by David Hurd (GIA G-3227)

For the Day of Pentecost, sing the Taizé setting of "Veni Sancte Spiritus/Come Holy Spirit" (WOV 686) in place of the gospel verse, using soloists singing the stanzas in a variety of languages.

MEAL

Throughout Easter utilize a strong setting of the "Holy, holy, holy" and "Lamb of God," such as *LBW* Setting 2. If you used congregational bell-ringing to punctuate high moments in the Easter Vigil, you might continue the practice for the Sanctus during Easter.

Communion hymns such as "Alleluia, alleluia, give thanks" (WOV 671) and "I am the Bread of life" (WOV 702) provide a quieter take on the season's joy.

SENDING

The Easter season is a great time to learn challenging hymns. Try "This joyful Eastertide" (WOV 676) as a post-communion hymn, and encourage its singing in harmony. If you use a closing hymn, "Christ is risen! Alleluia!"(LBW 131) is a delightful choral romp, which is best done at a good clip with solid organ accompaniment, and complete choral forces present—especially sopranos with a high F. Try it several Sundays in a row to help the assembly get the hang of it.

Music *for the* Season

VERSE AND OFFERTORY

Cherwien, David. *Verses for the Sundays of Easter.* U, org. MSM 80-400.

Farrell, Bernadette. "Eastertide Gospel Acclamation." OCP 7172CC.

Gospel Acclamations. Cant, choir, cong, inst. MAY 0862096324.

Pelz, Walter L. *Verses and Offertories: Easter—The Holy Trinity.* SATB, org. AFP 0800649044.

Schalk, Carl. *Verses and Offertory Sentences: Part IV, Easter Day through Easter 7.* CPH 97-5504.

Willan, Healey, arr. Guenther. *Verses for the Easter Season.* SATB, kybd. CPH 98-3057.

CHORAL

Crüger, Johann. "Awake, My Heart, with Gladness" in *Chantry Choirbook.* SATB, C inst, org. AFP 0800657772.

Harris, William H. "This Joyful Eastertide." SATB, org. NOV 29 0151.

Jennings, Kenneth. "With a Voice of Singing." SATB. AFP 0800645669.

Schütz, Heinrich. "I Am the Resurrection." SATB dbl chorus. PET 6591.

Stanford, Charles Villiers. "Ye Choirs of New Jerusalem" in *Anthems for Choirs I.* SATB, org. OXF 353214X.

CHILDREN'S CHOIR

Bertalot, John. "When Jesus Came Down to Earth." U, kybd. CG CGA909.

Burkhardt, Michael. "Alleluia." U, 2 C inst, kybd. MSM 50-7500.

McRae, Shirley. "Now the Green Blade Rises" in LS. U, kybd.

Running, Joseph. "An Easter Carol." U, kybd. MSM 50-4751.

KEYBOARD/INSTRUMENTAL

Augsburg Organ Library: Easter. Org. AFP 0800659368.

Busarow, Donald. "Processional on 'Lift High the Cross.'" Org. CPH 97-5442.

Mathias, William. "Processional" and others in *Modern Organ Music, Bk. I.* OXF 0-19-3751410.

Organ, Anne Krentz. "Crown Him With Many Crowns" in *Piano Reflections for the Church Year.* Pno. AFP 080067474X.

Rodriguez, Penny. "Christ the Lord is Risen Today" in *Portraits of the Cross.* Pno. BEC PC3.

HANDBELL

Gramann, Fred. "Festive Praises." 4-5 oct. AGEHR AG45043.

Moklebust, Cathy. "Ring to the Lord a New Song." AFP 0800657874 (4 oct) OP; AFP 0800658914 (4-6 oct).

Stephenson, Valerie W. "Gaudio Exultans." 3-5 oct. AGEHR AG35208.

Young, Philip. "Good Christian Friends, Rejoice and Sing!" and "This Joyful Eastertide." 2-3 oct. AFP 080065627X.

PRAISE ENSEMBLE

Davis, Holland. "Let It Rise" in *More Songs for Praise and Worship.* SATB. WRD 3010387016 (vocal ed); WRD 3010186363 (pno, vcs, perc).

Morgan, Reuben. "Hear Our Praises." *Worship Leader's Song Discovery,* vol. 13. Worship Leader 1999-03-LS.

Morgan, Reuben, arr. Mark Cole. "My Redeemer Lives." 3 pt, kybd, gtr, orch. *By Your Side.* Hillsongs/Integrity.

Alternate Worship Texts

CONFESSION AND FORGIVENESS

In the name of the Father, and of the ✝ Son,
and of the Holy Spirit.
Amen

Rejoicing in the resurrection,
let us seek God's forgiveness,
that dying to sin, we may walk in newness of life.

Silence for reflection and self-examination.

Faithful God,
**we confess that we have tried
to live by our own poor strength,
shunning the earth-shaking power of the resurrection.
We have doubted your promises.
We have failed to recognize you in the poor and needy.
Have mercy on us, forgive us our sin,
and restore to us the joy of your salvation
through Jesus Christ our Lord. Amen**

Christ died to sin once for all,
and now, victorious, lives to God.
Our Savior has delivered you from the power of darkness
and welcomed you into the realm of light.
For his sake God grants you pardon and peace,
the remission of all your sins.
Amen

GREETING

Alleluia! Christ is risen!
Christ is risen indeed! Alleluia!
The grace and peace of Jesus Christ,
who was raised from the dead to bring everlasting hope,
be with you all.
And also with you.

PRAYERS

Rejoicing in the resurrection,
let us remember in prayer the church, the world,
and all those in need.

A brief silence.

Each petition ends:

For this we pray:
Hear us, living God.

Concluding petition:

With alleluias in our hearts and on our lips
we commend to your care all for whom we pray,
trusting in your mercy; through your Son, Jesus Christ our Lord.
Amen

OFFERTORY PRAYER

God of blessing and glory,
**with people of every language and nation
we bring the first fruits of our labor.
Let the sharing of these gifts
proclaim our joyful hope in Jesus Christ,
the first fruits of the resurrection.
Thanksgiving and honor be to you, O God,
forever and ever. Amen**

INVITATION TO COMMUNION (EASTER 2–7)

Christ our Passover is sacrificed for us.
Therefore let us keep the feast. Alleluia!

INVITATION TO COMMUNION (PENTECOST)

Be filled with the Spirit;
receive and become the body of Christ.

POST-COMMUNION PRAYER (EASTER 2–7)

Living God,
**as the disciples ate and drank with the risen Lord,
we have been nourished with the very presence of Christ.
Through this meal may we be strengthened to keep your word
and to proclaim the power of your saving love
in Jesus Christ our Lord.
Amen**

POST-COMMUNION PRAYER (PENTECOST)

Almighty and most merciful God,
**as we have been nourished by this holy sacrament,
grant that by the indwelling of the Holy Spirit
we may be enlightened and strengthened for your service;
through your Son, Jesus Christ our Lord.
Amen**

193

BLESSING

The God of life,
who raised Jesus from the bonds of death,
who sends forth the Spirit to renew the face of the earth,
be merciful to you and ✛ bless you, now and forever.
Amen

DISMISSAL

Rejoicing in the power of the Spirit,
go in peace to love and serve the Lord.
Thanks be to God.

194

Seasonal Rites

Remembrance of Baptism with Sprinkling

See also Renewing Worship 7: Holy Communion.

The order may be used before or after the entrance hymn. People are invited to turn and face the baptismal font or the place where the sprinkling bowl is located. All stand.

GREETING

The grace and peace of Jesus Christ,
who was raised from the dead
to bring everlasting hope,
be with you all.
And also with you.

THANKSGIVING FOR WATER

In the waters of holy baptism
God liberates us from the power of sin and death,
forever joining us to the death and resurrection
of our Lord Jesus Christ.
May God's promise of everlasting life
be renewed in us as we remember our baptism.

Blessed are you, O God of grace.
From age to age you made water a sign
of your presence among us.
In the beginning your Spirit brooded over the waters
and you created the world by your word,
calling forth life in which you took delight.
You led Israel safely through the Red Sea
into the land of promise,
and in the waters of the Jordan,
you proclaimed Jesus your beloved one.
By water and the Spirit you adopted us
as your daughters and sons,
making us heirs of the promise and servants of God.
Through this water remind us of our baptism.
Shower us with your Spirit,
that your forgiveness, grace, and love
may be renewed in our lives,
To you be given honor and praise through Jesus Christ our Lord
in the unity of the Holy Spirit, now and forever.
Amen.

BAPTISMAL REMEMBRANCE

The presiding minister sprinkles the people with water in silence, during the entrance hymn (in procession), or during the hymn of praise. Musical suggestions are provided in Holy Baptism and Related Rites, *pp. 101-11. After the sprinkling, the liturgy continues with the prayer of the day.*

Adapted from *Holy Baptism and Related Rites,* Renewing Worship, vol. 3.

Rogation Blessing

PRAYER FOR SEEDS

Hold seeds aloft.

Creating God, you have given seed to the sower and bread to the people. Nourish, protect, and bless the seeds which your people have sown in hope. By your loving and bountiful giving, may they bring forth their fruit in due season, through Jesus Christ our Lord. Amen

PRAYER FOR THE SOIL

Hold soil aloft.

Giver of life, we give you thanks that in the richness of the soil, nature awakens to your call of spring. We praise you for the smell of freshly tilled earth, the beauty of a cleanly cut furrow, and a well-plowed field. We ask that you help us to be good stewards of this land. In the name of the one who gives us new life, Jesus Christ our Lord. Amen

PRAYER FOR WATER AND RAIN

Hold water aloft.

Sustaining God, we receive the fruits of the earth from you. We give you thanks for the smell of the earth after rain, for its welcome cooling, and its necessary hydration for the land. We ask that the rain come as often as it is needed so that the crops may flourish and the coming harvest be indeed bountiful. Amen

From *Worship from the Ground Up: A Worship Resource for Town and Country Congregations.* Dubuque, Iowa: Center for Theology and Land, University of Dubuque and Wartburg Theological Seminaries, 1995. Contact 563/589-3117 for reprint permission.

195

April 18, 2004

Second Sunday of Easter

INTRODUCTION

These first weeks of Easter focus our attention on appearances of the risen Lord. It is not always easy to see Jesus after his resurrection. The gospel will remind us that Jesus has a new body in which he now lives: As we gather this day to greet each other and share the peace of the Lord, may our eyes be opened to discern that we are looking at the risen body of Christ!

PRAYER OF THE DAY

Almighty God, with joy we celebrate the festival of our Lord's resurrection. Graciously help us to show the power of the resurrection in all that we say and do; through your Son, Jesus Christ our Lord, who lives and reigns with you and the Holy Spirit, one God, now and forever.

VERSE

Alleluia. Christ being raised from the dead will never die again; death no longer has dominion over him. Alleluia. Blessed are those who have not seen and yet have come to believe. Alleluia. (Rom. 6:9; John 20:29)

READINGS

Acts 5:27-32

Peter has been arrested for proclaiming the good news of Jesus' death and resurrection. His response to the charges of the high priest summarizes the early church's proclamation of forgiveness of sin through repentance.

Psalm 118:14-29

This is the LORD's doing and it is marvelous in our eyes. (Ps. 118:23)

or Psalm 150

Let everything that has breath praise the LORD. (Ps. 150:6)

Revelation 1:4-8

The book of Revelation recounts a vision of the risen Christ experienced by a Christian prophet named John. Here he describes Christ as the faithful witness, or martyr; firstborn of the dead; ruler in a kingdom of priests; the one who comes; the beginning and the end of all time.

John 20:19-31

The proclamation of Easter continues in John's gospel as Jesus appears to his disciples. Jesus' words to Thomas assure us that the blessings of the resurrection are also for those who "have not seen and yet believe."

COLOR   White

THE PRAYERS

Rejoicing in the resurrection, let us remember in prayer the church, the world, and all those in need.
A BRIEF SILENCE.

Blessed are you, O Lord our God, for you brought us to yourself through our baptism into the Easter mystery. Now deliver your church from all doubt, fear, and inaction, that together with your apostles we might be witnesses to the power of your resurrection. For this we pray:
Hear us, living God.

Blessed are you, for you are over all the rulers of the earth. Humble all who are in positions of authority. Raise up justice-seekers and peacemakers and protect all peoples from abuse of power. For this we pray:
Hear us, living God.

Blessed are you, for you have freed us from sin by the blood of the Lamb. Loose the bonds of all those whose sin imprisons them. Free all who unjustly suffer. Deliver those broken in mind, body, or spirit (*especially*), and by your love bring abundant life to us all. For this we pray:
Hear us, living God.

Blessed are you, for you move beyond closed doors, enfolding all into your love. Look kindly upon those young people who worship you, giving them a rich measure of your Spirit and your peace. For this we pray:
Hear us, living God.

Blessed are you, for you promise life to those who have not seen and yet have come to believe. Build up the faith of this congregation, that through our celebration of the passion and resurrection we may be renewed in our witness and service. For this we pray:
Hear us, living God.

HERE OTHER INTERCESSIONS MAY BE OFFERED.

Blessed are you, for in Christ Jesus we have known the firstborn of the dead. Bring us, together with (*names*, and) all your saints, to resurrection life. For this we pray: **Hear us, living God.**

With alleluias in our hearts and on our lips we commend to your care all for whom we pray, trusting in your mercy; through your Son, Jesus Christ our Lord. **Amen**

IMAGES FOR PREACHING

"Now Jesus did many other signs in the presence of his disciples which are not written in this book." This phrase has been bothersome for those seeking to defend the Christian faith to the skeptical. Certainly John, if he were serious about making his case to the doubting, would have provided all of the admissible evidence.

Evidence. Witnesses. Judgment. Punishment. Legal language and courtroom imagery abound today. "I need evidence!" we hear Thomas say to the disciples. "Unless I can verify your claim, I will not believe." Jesus is on trial once again, this time to prove the authenticity of his resurrection.

Yet, can the authenticity of the resurrection be proven? Faith must pick up where certainty leaves off. In *Glimpses of Grace* (Crosswicks, 1996), Madeleine L'Engle writes, "The Resurrection . . . is beyond the realm of fact (Do you believe in the literal fact of the Resurrection? No! I believe in the Resurrection!) and bursts into the realm of love, of truth, for in Jesus, truth and love are one and the same."

Indeed, the proof is provided by powerful witnesses! In Acts we read, "we are witnesses to these things, and so is the Holy Spirit whom God has given to those who obey him." What, then, is the function of the witness? To persuade with facts? Or, rather, to be a character witness—to witness with one's life?

In fact, a life-changing event has taken place. The very use of the book of Revelation alerts the worshiper that a judgment of eschatological proportion is about to be issued. The psalmist, too, alerts us to the justice of God, which will prevail. "The right hand of the Lord has triumphed! The right hand of the Lord is exalted!" And the psalmist rejoices that he has not received the sentence of death: "The Lord has punished me sorely, but he did not hand me over to death."

We, with the psalmist, can rejoice. A "life sentence" has been issued. May we, as the prayer of the day asks, provide the ultimate witness and "show the power of the resurrection in all that we say and do."

WORSHIP MATTERS

The renewal of baptismal vows is an integral part of the Easter Vigil, but don't limit it to that night. Consider using a "Remembrance of Baptism" rite at one or even every liturgy during the Fifty Days of Easter. (For help, see pp. 100–105 in *Renewing Worship 3: Holy Baptism and Related Rites.*) The baptismal remembrance could be used in place of confession and forgiveness, at the gathering rite, or at the profession of faith. The ministers would gather around the font and during the hymn of praise (or another hymn or piece of liturgical music) the assembly may be sprinkled with water from the font. If the assembly is small in number, individual worshipers may approach the font, touch the water, and trace a cross upon themselves.

LET THE CHILDREN COME

Sharing the peace is an important part of our identity as Christians. After his resurrection Jesus appeared to his disciples who hovered in fear and gathered behind locked doors. Jesus spoke the words "Peace be with you!" This greeting became part of another of Jesus' miracles. His words eventually changed their doubting minds and fearful hearts into faithful disciples who would go and share the news of God's love. Because of the movement and touching inherent in sharing Christ's peace in the assembly, it is naturally attractive to children. Make sure to include them in your greeting, and encourage people to take extra time in sharing this life-giving form of greeting.

HYMNS FOR WORSHIP
GATHERING

The strife is o'er, the battle done   LBW 135

Christ is risen! Shout hosanna!   WOV 672, RWSB

That Easter day with joy was bright   RWI 71, RWSB,
   LBW 154

HYMN OF THE DAY

We walk by faith and not by sight   WOV 675

ALTERNATE HYMN OF THE DAY

Thine is the glory   LBW 145

197

The first day of the week   LBW 246

COMMUNION

Dona nobis pacem   WOV 774

Here, O my Lord, I see thee   LBW 211

SENDING

Christ is arisen   LBW 136

Go, my children, with my blessing   WOV 721

Go in peace and serve the Lord   W&P 46

ADDITIONAL HYMNS AND SONGS

The risen Christ   RWSB

O sons and daughters of the King   LBW 139

Open our eyes, Lord   W&P 113

Show me your hands, your feet, your side   HFG 109

MUSIC FOR THE DAY

PSALMODY

PSALM 118:14-29

Hruby, Dolores. *Psalms for All Seasons: An ICEL Collection.* OCP 6111.

Kreutz, Robert. *Psalms and Selected Canticles.* OCP 8311.

Shields, Valerie. "Psalm for Easter." MSM 80-405.

Smith, Timothy R. "Give Thanks to the Lord" in STP, vol. 4.

Walker, Christopher. "Psalm 118: This Day Was Made by the Lord" in STP, vol. 3.

PSALM 150

Dexter, Noel. "O Praise Ye the Lord" in *Let the Peoples Sing, Vol. 1: Sacred Music of the Caribbean,* SATB, kybd, opt perc. AFP 0800675398.

Haas, David. "Singing Praise to God." PCY, vol. 9.

Hopson, Hal H. "Psalm 150" in TP.

Schalk, Carl. PW , Cycle C.

Young, Jeremy. "Praise God with the Trumpet." 2 pt mxd, kybd, opt brass. AFP 0800657586 (choral score); AFP 0800657748 (complete score, brass pt). OP.

CHORAL

Christiansen, Paul J. "Easter Morning." SATB, opt solo. AFP 080064557X. Also in *The Augsburg Choirbook.* AFP 0800656784.

Hassler, Hans L. "Quia vidisti me, Thoma" (Because Thou Hast Seen Me, Thomas) SATB. CPH 98-1741.

Helman, Michael. "We Walk By Faith." SATB, pno, opt 4 oct hb, fl. AFP 0800659759.

Johnson, Carolyn. "Now the Green Blade Rises." SATB, kybd, tpt. AFP 0800675428.

Manz, Paul. "E'en So, Lord Jesus, Quickly Come." SATB. MSM 50-0001.

Noble, T. Tertius. "Grieve Not the Holy Spirit." SATB, T solo, org. HWG GCMR 00409.

Pelz, Walter L. "Peace I Leave With You." SATB. AFP 0800645650. Also in *The Augsburg Choirbook.* AFP 0800656784.

Toppenberg, Edouard, arr. Rufo Odon. "Hallelu, Let the People All Sing!" in *Let the Peoples Sing, Vol. 1: Sacred Music of the Caribbean.* SATB, kybd, opt perc. AFP 0800675398.

CHILDREN'S CHOIR

Bågenfelt, Susanne. "For a Sunrise in the Morning." U/2 pt, pno, opt perc. AFP 0800675517.

Ferguson, John. "Hallelujah, Praise the Lord." (Ps. 150) U/2 pt, fl, Orff/kybd. SEL 241-189.

Lindh, Jody and Joe Cox. "Jesus, Son of God Most High." (John 20:31) U, opt desc, pno, fl, gtr, opt bass. CG CGA377.

KEYBOARD/INSTRUMENTAL

Blersch, Jeffrey. "Crown Him With Many Crowns" in *Laudate!* vol. 4. Org. CPH 97-6665.

Hamilton, Gregory. "Victory" in *As the Grains of Wheat.* Pno. AFP 0800675770.

Mann, Adrian. "This Joyful Eastertide" in *Arise and Rejoice! Preludes for Treble Instrument and Keyboard.* Kybd, inst. AFP 0800674960.

HANDBELL

McChesney, Kevin. "Now the Green Blade Riseth." 3-6 oct. AG 1892.

Moklebust, Cathy and David Moklebust. "Praise to the Lord, the Almighty." 4-5 oct, org, opt cong. AFP 0800658906 (hb score); AFP 0800659333 (full score).

PRAISE ENSEMBLE

Horley, Doug. "We Want to See Jesus Lifted High" in *More Songs for Praise and Worship.* SATB. WRD 3010387016 (vocal ed); WRD 3010186363 (pno, vcs, perc).

Iverson, Daniel. "Spirit of the Living God" in W&P.

Ruis, David. "You Are Worthy of My Praise" in *More Songs for Praise and Worship 2.* SATB. WRD 080689351174 (vocal ed); WRD 080689314186 (pno, vcs, perc).

Monday, April 19

OLAVUS PETRI, PRIEST, 1552;
LAURENTIUS PETRI, ARCHBISHOP OF UPPSALA, 1573;
RENEWERS OF THE CHURCH

These two brothers are commemorated for their intro-duction of the Lutheran movement to the Church of Sweden after studying at the University of Wittenberg. They returned home and, through the support of King Gustavus Vasa, began their work. Olavus published a cat-echism, hymnal, and a Swedish version of the mass. He resisted attempts by the king to gain royal control of the church. Laurentius was a professor at the university in Uppsala. When the king wanted to abolish the ministry of bishops, Laurentius persuaded him otherwise, and the historic episcopate continues in Sweden to this day. To-gether the brothers published a complete Bible in Swedish and a revised liturgy in 1541.

This week the Church of Sweden can be remem-bered in prayer. The Easter hymn "Praise the Savior, now and ever" (LBW 155) uses a Swedish folk tune and can be sung to commemorate the contributions of the Petris and the Swedish church to our worship life.

Wednesday, April 21

ANSELM, ARCHBISHOP OF CANTERBURY, 1109

This eleventh-century Benedictine monk stands out as one of the greatest theologians between Augustine and Thomas Aquinas. He is counted among the medieval mystics who emphasized the maternal aspects of God. Of Jesus Anselm says, "In sickness you nurse us and with pure milk you feed us." He is perhaps best known for his theory of atonement, the "satisfaction" theory. In this theory he argued that human rebellion against God demands a payment, but because humanity is fallen, it is incapable of making that satisfaction. Therefore, God

takes on human nature in Jesus Christ in order to make the perfect payment for sin.

In preaching this Sunday, Anselm's theory of atone-ment may be used to underscore the message of the sec-ond reading, which describes Jesus as one "who loves us and freed us from our sins by his blood."

Thursday, April 22

DAY OF THE CREATION (EARTH DAY)

This day calls us to attend to the glories of creation that surround us. Especially in the Northern Hemisphere, creation springs green again after the death of winter, and we are mindful of our stewardship of the earth as our God-given home. The great hymn of Francis of Assisi, "Canticle of the Sun" (see LBW 527 or RWI 8), might be sung today both for its Easter alleluias and its rejoicing in the gift of creation.

199

Friday, April 23

TOYOHIKO KAGAWA, RENEWER OF SOCIETY, 1960

Toyohiko Kagawa was born in 1888 in Kobe, Japan. Or-phaned early, he was disowned by his remaining extended family when he became a Christian. Kagawa wrote, spoke, and worked at length on ways to employ Christ-ian principles in the ordering of society. His vocation to help the poor led him to live among them. He estab-lished schools, hospitals, and churches. He also worked for peace and established the Anti-War League. He was arrested for his efforts to reconcile Japan and China after the Japanese attack of 1940.

In celebration of his witness, recognize those people in your parish who work on behalf of the poor and op-pressed and who, through their work, reveal the peace of Christ that is a gift of the resurrection.

April 25, 2004

Third Sunday of Easter

INTRODUCTION

Resurrection also means reconciliation. In today's gospel, Peter's denials are trumped by a threefold commissioning from Jesus. We, too, are reconciled to one another and to God as we join in the hymn of all creation with angels and archangels and all the company of heaven: "Worthy is the Lamb who was slain!" Normally the church would celebrate the feast of St. Mark on this date, but since nothing displaces a Sunday of Easter, his festival is transferred to tomorrow.

PRAYER OF THE DAY

O God, by the humiliation of your Son you lifted up this fallen world, rescuing us from the hopelessness of death. Grant your faithful people a share in the joys that are eternal; through your Son, Jesus Christ our Lord, who lives and reigns with you and the Holy Spirit, one God, now and forever.

VERSE

Alleluia. Christ being raised from the dead will never die again; death no longer has dominion over him. Alleluia. Our hearts burn within us while he opens to us the scriptures. (Rom. 6:9; Luke 24:32)

READINGS

Acts 9:1-6 [7-20]

Saul (later called Paul) appears for the first time in Acts at the stoning of Stephen. He becomes an ardent persecutor of the Christian church. This reading recounts his blinding and conversion experiences on the way to Damascus.

Psalm 30

You have turned my wailing into dancing. (Ps. 30:12)

Revelation 5:11-14

The vision of John recorded in Revelation offers a glimpse of cosmic worship on the Lord's Day. At its center is "the Lamb who was slain."

John 21:1-19

The risen Christ blesses his followers, especially Peter, and welcomes them to a meal of fellowship and forgiveness.

COLOR White

THE PRAYERS

Rejoicing in the resurrection, let us remember in prayer the church, the world, and all those in need.

A BRIEF SILENCE.

Blessed are you, for you are the source of every gift for ministry. Bless the work of leaders in your church and all who respond to your call. Give them confidence that with your call comes every necessary tool and talent. For this we pray:

Hear us, living God.

Blessed are you, for you are the joy of every creature of your making. Preserve your creation from all harm and guide our stewardship of the earth. For this we pray:

Hear us, living God.

Blessed are you, for you promise to be always with us. Deliver those in any need *(especially)*, and those who suffer alone, who are homebound, lonely, or depressed. Encourage them by the ministry and consolation of this community. For this we pray:

Hear us, living God.

Blessed are you, for you inspire angel choirs in glory. Bless the work of those who make music and art in this congregation that through their witness your name may be glorified. For this we pray:

Hear us, living God.

Blessed are you, for you always richly feed your followers. Give this congregation both the will and the gifts to extend that nourishment to many in our community. For this we pray:

Hear us, living God.

HERE OTHER INTERCESSIONS MAY BE OFFERED.

Blessed are you, for you sent Christ to be the way, the truth, and the life. Deliver us from every adversity and at the last bring us, together with Mark, the apostle and evangelist *(other names)*, and all your saints, to your feast of victory. For this we pray:

Hear us, living God.

With alleluias in our hearts and on our lips we commend to your care all for whom we pray, trusting in your mercy; through your Son, Jesus Christ our Lord.

Amen

IMAGES FOR PREACHING

Spiritual gifts assessments can be useful tools for helping Christians to discern vocation, their call in the church. Yet, these calculated and quantifiable means of assessing spiritual suitability, for all of their usefulness, may fly in the face of this day's calling of both Simon Peter and Saul.

"You've got the job!" says God to each.

"He's totally unqualified!" assess the onlookers.

"Noted," says God. "Oh, and by the way . . . this will not be easy."

Who is called? Today's texts make it clear that God's criteria in assessing spiritual gifts challenge our own.

Position: Model Missionary to the Gentiles. Appointee: Saul. Previous work history: Hunter, of Christians. Personal attributes: Tenacious. Well-connected.

Position: Shepherd of Jesus' Sheep. Appointee: Simon Peter. Previous work history: Fisherman, none too successful. Personal attributes: Cowardice. Modesty.

The bad news in today's texts is that our reliable tools of measuring spiritual suitability, as well as our own preconceptions, are called into question. The good news is that we clearly see, in light of God's seemingly illogical assessment standards, that we too have a place in God's work force. It is not our worthiness that readies us for the call; it is God's pronouncement.

Yet, if we are called to that for which we are unqualified, what are we to be doing? Perhaps the task performed is secondary to the message conveyed with our lives. What shall this message be?

"See!" our lives announce, "In our very unworthiness, you are seeing in your midst the saving and redeeming grace of God. To the one seated on the throne and to the Lamb be blessing and honor and glory and might forever and ever!"

WORSHIP MATTERS

During this Easter season our second readings are from the book of Revelation. Today's reading includes the great throng in heaven singing with full voice: "Worthy is the Lamb . . . to receive power and wealth and wisdom and might and honor and glory and blessing!" As we hear those words we are reminded how much of our liturgy is from the Bible. The canticle we know as "This is the feast" is a favorite of many congregations and helps connect the eucharistic celebration to the Easter feast of victory. This Easter, pay attention to the readings from Revelation and use *Indexes for Worship Planning* to notice, plan, and sing the many hymns that were inspired by these passages. Among them are "Blessing and honor," "Alabaré," "Come away to the skies," "Who is this host arrayed in white," "Shall we gather at the river," and many more!

LET THE CHILDREN COME

"Alleluia! Christ is risen! Christ is risen indeed!" So goes the Christian greeting during this Easter season. It is our "pep" song—our cheer for the good news that Jesus lives. It is a song of victory! Invite the children to practice this greeting with joy and enthusiasm. Provide opportunities for them to say it throughout the service. Encourage everyone to use this greeting outside of worship too. Greet fellow Christians with this Easter proclamation instead of our traditional cultural greeting of "Hi, how are you? . . . Just fine" and they just might find their day taking on a fresh meaning!

HYMNS FOR WORSHIP   201

GATHERING

All creatures of our God and King   LBW 527
All creatures, worship God most high!   RWI 8
When long before time   WOV 799

HYMN OF THE DAY

The Church of Christ, in every age   LBW 433

ALTERNATE HYMN OF THE DAY

That Easter day with joy was bright   LBW 154
Alabaré   WOV 791

COMMUNION

What wondrous love is this   LBW 385
Thine the amen, thine the praise   WOV 801

SENDING

Jesus shall reign   LBW 530
Let us talents and tongues employ   WOV 754
The Lamb   TFF 89

ADDITIONAL HYMNS AND SONGS

Holy, holy   W&P 60
Feed my lambs   ASG 8
Rise, O church, like Christ arisen   RWSB
Let all that is within me cry, "Holy!"   TFF 282

MUSIC FOR THE DAY

PSALMODY

Daigle, Gary. "I Will Praise You, Lord" in PCY, vol. 4.

Haas, David. "I Will Praise You, Lord" in PCY, vol. 3.

Ridge, M.D. "Psalm 30: I Will Praise You, Lord" in STP, vol. 3.

Schalk, Carl. PW , Cycle C.

Mourning into dancing W&P 99

CHORAL

Bertalot, John. "Come, Risen Lord" in *The Augsburg Choirbook*. SATB, org. AFP 0800656784.

Carter, John. "We Sing Your Mighty Power, O God." SATB, kybd. AFP 0800675568.

Ellingboe, Bradley. "The Chief Cornerstone" in *The Augsburg Easy Choirbook*. 2 pt mxd, kybd. AFP 0800676025.

Handel, G.F. "Worthy Is the Lamb, Blessing and Honor, Amen" in *Messiah*. SATB, org. Various ed.

Hovland, Egil. "Saul." SATB, narr, org. WAL 08500232.

Sweelinck, Jan Pieterszoon. "Sing to the Lord, New Songs, Be Raising" in *Chantry Choirbook*. SATB. AFP 0800657772.

CHILDREN'S CHOIR

Folkening, John. "Feed Us, Jesus" in LS. U, kybd.

Shute, Linda Cable. "Feed My Lambs." U, kybd, opt desc, perc. AFP 0800674111.

Sleeth, Natalie. "Feed My Lambs." U, kybd, 2 fl. CFI CM7777.

KEYBOARD/INSTRUMENTAL

Albrecht, Mark. "Alleluia! Jesus Is Risen" in *Timeless Tunes for Flute and Piano*. Pno, inst. AFP 0800659074.

Held, Wilbur. "Come, Ye Faithful, Raise the Strain." (Gaudeamus pariter) in *Six Preludes on Easter Hymns*. Org. CPH 97-5330.

Osterland, Karl. "Gaudeamus Domino" in *Lift One Voice*. Org. AFP 0800659007.

Widor, Charles Marie. "Toccata" in *Symphony V.* Various ed.

HANDBELL

Bock II, Almon C. "This Joyful Eastertide." 2 oct. AFP 0800652053. OP.

Morris, Hart. "Canticle of Creation." 3-5 oct. RR HB0023.

PRAISE ENSEMBLE

Getty, Keith. "O, for a Closer Walk with God" in *New Songs 2003/03*. Kingsway.

Hayford, Jack. "Majesty" in W&P.

Park, Andy. "The River Is Here" in *More Songs for Praise and Worship*.

SATB. WRD 3010387016 (vocal ed); WRD 3010186363 (pno, vcs, perc).

Monday, April 26

ST. MARK, EVANGELIST (TRANSFERRED)

Though Mark himself was not an apostle, it is likely that he was a member of one of the early Christian communities. The gospel attributed to him is brief and direct. It is considered by many to be the earliest gospel. Tradition has it that Mark went to preach in Alexandria, Egypt, where he was martyred.

Mark's story of the resurrection ends with women at the tomb, who say nothing to anyone because of their fear. Though their witness faltered, the good news of the resurrection, the good news of these fifty days, has reached out to include us.

Thursday, April 29

CATHERINE OF SIENA, TEACHER, 1380

Catherine of Siena was a member of the Order of Preachers (Dominicans), and among Roman Catholics she was the first woman to receive the title Doctor of the Church. She was a contemplative and is known for her mystical visions of Jesus. Catherine was a humanitarian who worked to alleviate the suffering of the poor and imprisoned. She was also a renewer of church and society and advised both popes and any uncertain persons who told her their problems.

Catherine's life is a reminder that prayer and activism belong together and that the glorious vision in today's second reading from Revelation can lead to Jesus' commission to Peter in the gospel, "Feed my sheep."

Saturday, May 1

ST. PHILIP AND ST. JAMES, APOSTLES

Philip, one of the first disciples of Jesus, after following Jesus invited Nathanael to "come and see." According to tradition, he preached in Asia Minor and died as a martyr in Phrygia. James, the son of Alphaeus, is called "the less" to distinguish him from another apostle named

James, commemorated July 25. Philip and James are commemorated together because the remains of these two saints were placed in the Church of the Apostles in Rome on this day in 561.

During these fifty days of Easter, how can your community invite others to come and see the new life of Christ?

May 2, 2004

Fourth Sunday of Easter

INTRODUCTION

With the fourth Sunday of Easter the gospel readings turn away from resurrection appearances of Jesus and begin to focus on echoes of Jesus' earlier words that had pointed toward his death and resurrection during his ministry. He meant to go this path all along. As we listen to Jesus' words from the tenth chapter of John's gospel, we learn that Jesus is both shepherd as well as the victorious Lamb. Peter is a shepherd like Jesus as he leads one of Jesus' sheep from death to life. Another shepherd, a few generations after Peter, was Bishop Athanasius of Alexandria, a defender of the faith whom the church remembers today.

PRAYER OF THE DAY

God of all power, you called from death our Lord Jesus, the great shepherd of the sheep. Send us as shepherds to rescue the lost, to heal the injured, and to feed one another with knowledge and understanding; through your Son, Jesus Christ our Lord, who lives and reigns with you and the Holy Spirit, one God, now and forever.

or

Almighty God, you show the light of your truth to those in darkness, to lead them into the way of righteousness. Give strength to all who are joined in the family of the Church, so that they will resolutely reject what erodes their faith and firmly follow what faith requires; through your Son, Jesus Christ our Lord, who lives and reigns with you and the Holy Spirit, one God, now and forever.

VERSE

Alleluia. Christ being raised from the dead will never die again; death no longer has dominion over him. Alleluia.

I am the good shepherd. I know my own and my own know me. Alleluia. (Rom. 6:9; John 10:14)

READINGS

Acts 9:36-43

When Dorcas, faithful minister to the widows of Joppa, fell ill and died, Peter raised her back to life through the power of prayer.

Psalm 23

The LORD is my shepherd; I shall not be in want. (Ps. 23:1)

Revelation 7:9-17

Christ is the shepherd who leads his faithful to springs of the water of life. Christ is also the lamb who vanquishes sin and suffering, in whose blood the saints have washed their robes and made them white.

John 10:22-30

Three times Jesus says that his sheep are secure; no one will snatch them from Jesus' or the Father's hands. The sheep have eternal life and so shall never perish.

COLOR   White

THE PRAYERS

Rejoicing in the resurrection, let us remember in prayer the church, the world, and all those in need.

A BRIEF SILENCE.

Blessed are you, for you are the Lamb who has become our Shepherd. Through death and resurrection, you wash your whole church clean and nurture us to greater faithfulness to follow your voice. For this we pray:

Hear us, living God.

Blessed are you, for you have caused your name to be

203

proclaimed to all nations. Shepherd the nations of the world in your ways of peace. For this we pray:

Hear us, living God.

Blessed are you, for you are the good shepherd. Preserve those in your flock who are in any need *(especially)*, bear up those who grieve, and walk with the dying through the shadow of death. For this we pray:

Hear us, living God.

Blessed are you, for you are the hope of your disciples Peter and Tabitha, and all who look for your help. Inspire this congregation by their good works and acts of charity to further ministry among the poor. For this we pray:

Hear us, living God.

HERE OTHER INTERCESSIONS MAY BE OFFERED.

Blessed are you, for you offer the gift of eternal life. Bring us together with Athanasius, bishop and renewer of the church, *(other names)*, and all the saints at last before the throne of grace, that we may join with them and the heavenly choirs to praise your name. For this we pray:

Hear us, living God.

With alleluias in our hearts and on our lips we commend to your care all for whom we pray, trusting in your mercy; through your Son, Jesus Christ our Lord.

Amen

IMAGES FOR PREACHING

What is it about "Good Shepherd Sunday" that wins the hearts and worship attendance of so many Christians? What draws so many technological, fast-paced, nonpastoral types to shepherd and sheep imagery, today only truly relevant to a few rural types (who may, in truth, find the imagery to be more odoriferous than charming)? Are we longing for an escape? Are we retreating to a Saturday afternoon movie where we can convince ourselves, if for only a moment, that everyone lives happily ever after after all? Is it a visit to "First Century Land" in which we assure ourselves that there is a place where security, lavish tables, and quiet green pastures really do exist? Perhaps this momentary escape can indeed help us to face our lives. If so, how does this escape prepare us for the wolves in our concrete jungles and on our asphalt pathways?

What about the wolves? They don't go away. Where and who are our wolves today? How do they threaten us? How does the Good Shepherd protect us? And those wolves—are they all really wolves? Or are some just misguided sheep (sheep in wolves' clothing?) who need to be brought into the fold with us?

Go back to the Shepherd. Given our contemporary wolves and their sophisticated communications media, how do we today hear the voice of the Shepherd? In a generation of secularized sound bites in which many of the sheep have left for "greener pastures," what does the Good Shepherd's voice sound like? How can we learn to voice the Shepherd's call so that those who have not yet experienced the security of the fold can know it?

WORSHIP MATTERS

Easter is fifty days long, but it is often hard to keep the festive spirit and energy alive for the entire Easter season. With the onset of spring, attendance often drops in the weeks following Easter Sunday. What are some ways to mark the season as a fifty-day celebration of Easter? Since lilies and other special Easter flowers only last three or four weeks, consider allocating money for spring flowers during the second half of the season. Through the use of processions, banners, and music, continue to treat each Sunday of Easter as a festival. Keep the paschal candle lit during the entire Fifty Days as well. Consider using a liturgy of baptismal remembrance each Sunday of Easter, adding a special ritual element to the service. Remind the assembly that the season of Easter rejoicing continues!

LET THE CHILDREN COME

Not many in our country know a lot about sheep. But many, including children, do know how a pet clearly responds to the voice of its owner. Mothers and fathers know the cry of their own child. Children know the voice of their parents. Make the point with children that to be able to hear the voice of God we need to spend time getting to know God. That means we must spend time praying, reading and hearing scripture, and worshiping God. Through Jesus we are able to learn all we need to know about God. When we know God, we know God's peace and love.

HYMNS FOR WORSHIP
GATHERING

Glories of your name are spoken   LBW 358
At the Lamb's high feast we sing   LBW 210
Majesty   W&P 94

HYMN OF THE DAY

In thee is gladness   LBW 552

204

ALTERNATE HYMN OF THE DAY

I'm so glad Jesus lifted me   WOV 673

The King of love my shepherd is   LBW 456

COMMUNION

Have no fear, little flock   LBW 476

You satisfy the hungry heart   WOV 711

SENDING

With God as our friend   LBW 371

Praise to you, O God of mercy   WOV 790

ADDITIONAL HYMNS AND SONGS

Our God reigns   TFF 99

Be bold, be strong   W&P 15

You, Lord, are both lamb and shepherd   RS 699, SNC 182

Oh, when the saints go marching in   TFF 180

MUSIC FOR THE DAY

PSALMODY

Haas, David. "You Are My Shepherd" in PCY, vol. 9.

Schalk, Carl. PW, Cycle C.

Smith, Timothy R. "The Lord Is My Shepherd" in STP, vol. 4.

Young, Jeremy. PW , Cycle B.

Shepherd me, O God   RWSB

The Lord's my shepherd   LBW 451

CHORAL

Ellingboe, Bradley. "Jesus, Good Shepherd." SATB, pno.
AFP 0800658272.

Frahm, Frederick. "My Shepherd Will Supply My Need." SAB, pno.
AFP 0800675533.

Goodall, Howard. "The Lord Is My Shepherd." SATB, org.   NOV 29
0680.

Handel, G.F. "Worthy Is the Lamb, Blessing and Honor, Amen" in
Messiah. SATB, org.   Various ed.

Rutter, John. "The Lord Is My Shepherd." SATB, ob, org. OXF 94.216.

CHILDREN'S CHOIR

Cherwien, David. "Psalm 23." U, org.   MSM 80-840.

Lord, Suzanne. "Do You Know Your Shepherd's Voice?" 2 pt, kybd.
CG CGA673.

KEYBOARD/INSTRUMENTAL

Albrecht, Mark. "Softly and Tenderly Jesus Is Calling" in Timeless Tunes
for Piano and Solo Instrument, vol. 3. Pno, inst. AFP 0800675037.

Bach, J. S. "Sheep May Safely Graze." Org/kybd, inst. Various ed.

Harbach, Barbara. "Crimond" in Augsburg Organ Library: Easter. Org.
AFP 0800659368.

Wood, Dale. "Brother James' Air" in Wood Works for Organ, Book 1. Org.
SMP KK 357.

HANDBELL

Kinyon, Barbara Baltzer. "My Shepherd Will Supply My Need." 3-5
oct, opt 2-3 oct hc.   BEC HB200.

Starks, Howard F. "Beside Still Waters." 3 oct. AG 1047.

PRAISE ENSEMBLE

Smith, Martin. "Shout to the North" in More Songs for Praise and Worship. SATB. WRD 3010387016 (vocal ed);   WRD
3010186363 (pno, vcs, perc).

Zuziak, Kathy. "You Make Me Lie Down in Green Pastures" in Best of
the Best. FEL 1891062018.

Sunday, May 2

ATHANASIUS, BISHOP OF ALEXANDRIA, 373

Athanasius attended the Council of Nicea in 325 as a
deacon and secretary to the bishop of Alexandria. At the
council and when he himself served as bishop of
Alexandria, he defended the full divinity of Christ
against the Arian position held by emperors, magistrates,
and theologians. Because of his defense of the divinity
of Christ he was considered a troublemaker and was
banished from Alexandria on five separate occasions.

Athanasius is an appropriate saint to be remembered
during Easter. His name means "deathless one," though
he himself lived in threat of death because of his theological stands. We are made in God's likeness, Athanasius
affirmed. By the resurrection we are remade in the likeness of the Son, who has conquered death.

Tuesday, May 4

MONICA, MOTHER OF AUGUSTINE, 387

Monica was married to a pagan husband who was ill-
tempered and unfaithful. She rejoiced greatly when both
her husband and his mother became Christian. She is
best known because she is the mother of Augustine.
Monica had been a disciple of Ambrose, and eventually

205

Augustine came under his influence. Almost everything we know about Monica comes from Augustine's Confessions, his autobiography. Her dying wish was that her son remember her at the altar of the Lord, wherever he was.

Monica's life bore witness to the vital role that parents play in the faith formation of their children. Consider how the church supports parents in that task.

Saturday, May 8

VICTOR THE MOOR, MARTYR, 303

Known also as Victor Marus, this native of the African country of Mauritania was a Christian from his youth. He served as a soldier in the Praetorian Guard. Under the persecution of Maximian, Victor died for his faith at Milan. Few details are known about his life, but many churches in the diocese of Milan are dedicated to him.

May 9, 2004

Fifth Sunday of Easter

INTRODUCTION

Visions of the end time work their way into our Easter worship. A strange and wondrous vision from God instructs Peter about how wide the new fellowship in Christ might be. John's vision of a new Jerusalem suggests that beginnings and endings are tied to Jesus. In the gospel, Jesus begins to prepare his disciples for his departure. We, too, gather this day as Jesus' end-time community, with one foot planted in this world and the other in the world to come.

PRAYER OF THE DAY

O God, form the minds of your faithful people into a single will. Make us love what you command and desire what you promise, that, amid all the changes of this world, our hearts may be fixed where true joy is found; through your Son, Jesus Christ our Lord, who lives and reigns with you and the Holy Spirit, one God, now and forever.

VERSE

Alleluia. Christ being raised from the dead will never die again; death no longer has dominion over him. Jesus said, I am the way, and the truth, and the life. Alleluia. (Rom. 6:9; John 14:6)

READINGS

Acts 11:1-18

In defense of his earlier baptism of pagan believers,

Peter demonstrates to the members of the Jerusalem church that God's intention to save Gentiles as well as Jews is revealed in Jesus' own testimony. In this way the mission to the Gentiles is officially authorized.

Psalm 148

The splendor of the LORD is over earth and heaven. (Ps. 148:13)

Revelation 21:1-6

John's vision shows us that in the resurrection the new age has dawned; God dwells with us already. Yet we wait for the time when the tears that cloud our vision will be wiped away. Then we will see the new heaven, new earth, and new Jerusalem.

John 13:31-35

Jesus speaks of his glorification on the cross. As Jesus loves, even to death on the cross, so ought his disciples love one another. Indeed, love will be the distinctive mark of Jesus' community.

COLOR White

THE PRAYERS

Rejoicing in the resurrection, let us remember in prayer the church, the world, and all those in need.

A BRIEF SILENCE.

Blessed are you, for you give the gift of faith. Through the ministries of your whole church, extend the promise of your covenant to all peoples. For this we pray:

Hear us, living God.

Blessed are you, for you are the Alpha and Omega, the beginning and the end. Extend your reign over the nations of the world and conform this weary world to your will. For this we pray:

Hear us, living God.

Blessed are you, for in Christ you have conquered death. Give peace and comfort to those in pain, illness, or mourning *(especially)*, assuring them of the promise of resurrection for all of our lives. For this we pray:

Hear us, living God.

Blessed are you, for your Son gave a new commandment to love one another. Grant that this congregation may be found faithful to this commandment, serving one another as Christ. For this we pray:

Hear us, living God.

Blessed are you, for your own love is reflected within loving families. Bless all mothers, and all who serve a mothering role towards those in their care. Give them joy in their relationships. For this we pray:

Hear us, living God.

HERE OTHER INTERCESSIONS MAY BE OFFERED.

Blessed are you, for through the resurrection we see the promise of a new heaven and new earth. Bring us together with all your saints into the New Jerusalem. For this we pray:

Hear us, living God.

With alleluias in our hearts and on our lips we commend to your care all for whom we pray, trusting in your mercy; through your Son, Jesus Christ our Lord.

Amen

IMAGES FOR PREACHING

In the reunified Germany, there is a poster: 1 + 1 = Eins. It translates well into English: 1 + 1 = One. The sum of two digits makes a new whole, qualitatively different from the old parts. A word is different from a digit. The sum of the former two nations now reunited is a new creation. Bringing this concept closer to home, the Great Seal on the U.S. dollar bears the motto E Pluribus Unum—"of the many, one." Gestalt Therapy puts it this way: The whole is greater than the sum of its parts.

Unity of voice. Unity of purpose. Unity of mind. Complete at-*one*-ment is evident in all of today's readings. Peter, criticized by the circumcised for fraternizing with the unclean, explains how unity of community is made by baptism with the Holy Spirit. His critics rejoice,

"Then God has given even to the Gentiles the repentance that leads to life." The psalmist gives us a glimpse of a cosmic chorus that unites all beings—maidens and monsters, hills and hail, fire and fruit trees, even the fog!—to sing with one voice. In the Revelation of John, all of time collapses into one as the one seated on the throne announces a new creation in which "It is done!" The Alpha, the Omega, the beginning, the end are joined into one heavenly being, God, whose home is now among mortals.

Our prayer of the way reminds us of the purpose of this unity. As our minds are formed into a single will, we are to "love what is commanded and desire what is promised." Indeed, says our evangelist for the day, it is our love for one another that will bear witness to the Son of Man who has been glorified and in whom God has been glorified.

WORSHIP MATTERS

A tradition for Easter Day is to wear something new, a sign of the new life we receive through the resurrection of Christ. Today's scripture readings are filled with "new" images. Jesus gives the "new commandment" to love one another, and the Revelation reading refers to the vision of a "new heaven and a new earth" in which the one seated on the throne says: "I will make all things new." Though our liturgy is filled with treasures from the church's tradition, it always finds new expression in each place and time. Does your congregation continue to learn new hymns and settings of the liturgy? Are you open to new ways to express the gospel through words, music, and art? Are you always seeking new ways to be welcoming and hospitable to guests? Each Easter season is a new opportunity to witness to the resurrection and the heart of our faith.

LET THE CHILDREN COME

When we pray "Our Father in heaven," we claim our common identity as children of God. As children with the same heavenly Father we are the family of God, called to love one another as God loves us. Send home small heart stickers with everyone today and ask them to put it someplace where they will see it every day: a watch, a mirror, a window, a book, a seat belt, etc. Every time they see the heart may they be reminded of the love Jesus asks us to share with one another.

207

HYMNS FOR WORSHIP

GATHERING

We know that Christ is raised   LBW 189

Alleluia! Jesus is risen   WOV 674, TFF 91

HYMN OF THE DAY

Great God, your love has called us   WOV 666

ALTERNATE HYMN OF THE DAY

Christ is alive! Let Christians sing   LBW 363, RWI 15

Broken in love   W&P 24

COMMUNION

A new commandment   WOV 664

May we your precepts, Lord, fulfill   LBW 353

SENDING

My God, how wonderful thou art   LBW 524

Blessed assurance   WOV 699

ADDITIONAL HYMNS AND SONGS

Beloved, God's chosen   RWSB

We will glorify   W&P 154

Who are these like stars appearing   H82 286

Lord, help us walk your servant way   HFG 150

MUSIC FOR THE DAY

PSALMODY

Hopson, Hal H. TP.

Schalk, Carl. PW , Cycle C.

Smith, J. "Let All Praise the Name of the Lord." GIA G-2989.

Praise the Lord! O heavens   LBW 540

Praise the Lord of heaven!   LBW 541

See First Sunday after Christmas.

CHORAL

Bainton, Edgar L. "And I Saw a New Heaven." SATB, org. NOV 29 0342 03.

Berger, Jean. "Glorify the Lord With Me." SATB. John Sheppard Music 1007.

Cool, Jayne Southwick. "The Life, the Truth, the Way." U/2 pt, kybd. AFP 0800674677.

Schalk, Carl. "I Saw a New Heaven and Earth." SATB. AFP 0800656644. Also in *The Augsburg Choirbook.* AFP 0800656784.

Tallis, Thomas. "If Ye Love Me." SATB. OXF 42.60.

Vaughan Williams, Ralph. "O How Amiable." SATB, org. OXF 42.056.

Vaughan Williams, Ralph. "O Taste and See." SATB, org. OXF 44.415.

Vaughan Williams, Ralph. "The Call" in *Five Mystical Songs.* B solo, kybd. GAL I.5038.

CHILDREN'S CHOIR

Burkhardt, Michael. "Praise the Lord! O Heavens Adore Him." (Ps. 148) U, trbl inst, kybd. MSM 50-9305.

Hopson, Hal H. "Love One Another." (John 13:34-35) U/2 pt, kybd. CG CGA741.

KEYBOARD/INSTRUMENTAL

Albrecht, Timothy. "Llanfair" in *Grace Notes,* vol. 3. Org. AFP 0800653505.

Kerr, J. Wayne. "Open Now Thy Gates of Beauty" in *Nine Easy Preludes on Familiar Hymn Tunes.* Org. FLA HF-5169.

Kerr, J. Wayne. "The Strife is O'er" in *Christ Is Alive.* Org. AFP 0800658027.

Lovinfosse, Dennis. "Victory" in *A New Liturgical Year.* Org. AFP 0800656717.

HANDBELL

Hopson, Hal H. "The Gift of Love." 3-5 oct. AG 1419.

Lamb, Linda R. "Alleluia." 3-5 oct, opt hc. AGEHR AG35177.

PRAISE ENSEMBLE

Adkins, Donna. "Glorify Thy Name" in W&P.

Haugen, Marty. "Gathered in the Love of Christ." 2 pt, solo, cong, gtr, kybd, opt fl, ob, vc. GIA G-5066.

Zschech, Darlene, "Shout to the Lord" in W&P.

Friday, May 14

PACHOMIUS, RENEWER OF THE CHURCH, 346

Pachomius was born in Egypt about 290. He became a Christian during his service as a soldier. In 320 he went to live as a hermit in Upper Egypt, where other hermits lived nearby. Pachomius organized them into a religious community in which the members prayed together and held their goods in common. His rule for monasteries influenced both Eastern and Western monasticism through the Rule of Basil and the Rule of Benedict, respectively.

The Egyptian (Coptic) church may be unfamiliar to many Western Christians. Use the commemoration of Pachomius to teach about the Egyptian church at parish gatherings this week.

May 16, 2004

Sixth Sunday of Easter

INTRODUCTION

Visions are the distinctive mark of this day. Paul receives a vision from God telling him that he needs to leap from one continent to another to take the good news abroad. John the Seer shares his vision of the new Jerusalem—an image of what it means to live with God. Jesus is the reflection of God's plan for the world and for our lives.

PRAYER OF THE DAY

O God, from whom all good things come: Lead us by the inspiration of your Spirit to think those things which are right, and by your goodness help us to do them; through your Son, Jesus Christ our Lord, who lives and reigns with you and the Holy Spirit, one God, now and forever.

VERSE

Alleluia. Christ being raised from the dead will never die again; death no longer has dominion over him. Alleluia. Those who love me will keep my word, and my Father will love them, and we will come to them and make our home with them. Alleluia. (Rom 6:9; John 14:23)

READINGS

Acts 16:9-15

A vision compels Paul to move his ministry into Greece. There he meets Lydia, an important person in the business community, whose heart has been opened by God to receive the gospel. Her conversion and baptism provide the impetus for the founding of the church at Philippi.

Psalm 67

Let the nations be glad and sing for joy. (Ps. 67:4)

Revelation 21:10, 22—22:5

John's vision of a new Jerusalem coming out of heaven provides continuity with God's past actions. Yet in this new city, God's presence replaces the temple, and the glory of God and the Lamb supplant sun and moon.

John 14:23-29

Jesus promises to send the Advocate to teach and remind us of all Jesus taught. Under this Spirit's guidance, we shall gain a deepened understanding of what Jesus has told us, and we shall experience Jesus' gift of peace that overcomes fear.

or John 5:1-9

Jesus heals on the Sabbath.

COLOR White

THE PRAYERS

Rejoicing in the resurrection, let us remember in prayer the church, the world, and all those in need.

A BRIEF SILENCE.

Blessed are you, for you are the river and tree of life. Preserve your whole church, sending the promised advocate, your Holy Spirit, that we may faithfully keep your word. For this we pray:

Hear us, living God.

Blessed are you, for you are the glory and honor of the nations. Grant peace and unity in our world and encourage all those who would be peacemakers. For this we pray:

Hear us, living God.

Blessed are you, for you heal those who are ill. Restore wholeness to all who are in any need *(especially)*. For this we pray:

Hear us, living God.

Blessed are you, for you were the hope of Lydia, your disciple. Inspire this congregation by her witness and make us, like her, willing servants of the gospel. For this we pray:

Hear us, living God.

Blessed are you, for the power of the resurrection extends through all of life. Bless and guide all merchants and those who work for them, that their dealings may be honest and profitable, and that they may find joy in service. For this we pray:

Hear us, living God.

HERE OTHER INTERCESSIONS MAY BE OFFERED.

Blessed are you, for you write our names in the Lamb's book of life. At the last, bring us and all the faithful departed into that heavenly Jerusalem where there will be no more night and where your presence is the light of all. For this we pray:

Hear us, living God.

With alleluias in our hearts and on our lips we commend to your care all for whom we pray, trusting in your mercy; through your Son, Jesus Christ our Lord.
Amen

IMAGES FOR PREACHING

Water attracts life. Water gives life. The Tigris and Euphrates Rivers both cradled and gave life to the dawn of civilization. Rivers, lakes, streams, and bodies of water have throughout time been the gathering and settling points for communities. Look at a map; population density increases near large bodies of water. Some native African religions have declared sites near water to be sacred places for worship, focal points for human interaction with the divine.

Such is the supposition in today's reading from Acts. Paul reports that he and his companions on the Sabbath went "outside the gate by the river, where we supposed there was a place of prayer." Indeed, this was a holy place as Lydia and her household were soon to be baptized there.

The river of the water of life, "bright as crystal" according to the Revelation to John, is not just any river. It comes, flowing through the middle of the street of the city, surrounded by the multiple-fruited tree of life, through which will come the healing of the nations. "How can water do such great things?" we ask. We must consider the source. This river flows "from the throne of God and of the Lamb."

"How can water do such great things?" asks Martin Luther in his Small Catechism. "Clearly, water does not do it, but the Word of God, which is with and alongside the water, and faith, which trusts this Word of God in the water." The water carries the word and is a vehicle for the promised Advocate, the Holy Spirit, to come to us with strength and teaching.

The distinction between water and word becomes clear in our alternate reading from John. The healing of the sick man happens by the waters of Beth-zatha, but he never enters the water. It is the word of Jesus beside the waters that brings healing and wholeness.

WORSHIP MATTERS

If you haven't reviewed the liturgies of Holy Week and Easter, do so while it's fresh in your mind! Gather key persons responsible for worship in your congregation and discuss what worked and didn't work in these services. Include things such as bulletin format, music, and actions. Do you need to order more or fewer palms? Do you need to rethink the way you do the palm procession, foot-washing, or entry into the church at the Easter Vigil? Because these liturgies only occur once a year, you will need to rely on these notes when planning the services next year. Don't stop there, though. Remember to review Sunday services by listening to a tape or getting feedback from others.

LET THE CHILDREN COME

Brand names are a big deal, for children as for adults. We often judge others by what kinds of clothes they wear or cars they drive. Still, we already have a label, and it's unlike anything else in the world. In baptism we received the mark of the cross of Christ. No other brand makes a greater difference in our life. Various dramas are available that speak to the tension that exists between our culture's definition of "cool" and the Christian community's call to commitment. Have some young people present a drama during worship today that speaks to this topic.

HYMNS FOR WORSHIP
GATHERING

Rise, shine, you people!   LBW 393
Shout for joy loud and long   WOV 793

HYMN OF THE DAY

Peace, to soothe our bitter woes   LBW 338

ALTERNATE HYMN OF THE DAY

All glory be to God on high   LBW 166
Alleluia! Jesus is risen   WOV 674, TFF 91

COMMUNION

Come down, O love divine   LBW 508
Awake, O sleeper   WOV 745

SENDING

Savior, again to your dear name   LBW 262
I want to walk as a child of the light   WOV 649
We are called   W&P 147, RWSB

ADDITIONAL HYMNS AND SONGS

I've got peace like a river   TFF 258

Christ is risen! Shout hosanna   RWSB, WOV 672
When the morning stars together   PH 486

MUSIC FOR THE DAY
PSALMODY
Gieseke, Richard. "May the People Praise You, O God." CPH 98-3428.
Haas, David. "May God Bless Us with Mercy" in PCY, vol. 8.
Kogut, Malcolm. "May God Bless Us in His Mercy" in PCY, vol. 10.
Makeever, Ray. "Let All the People Praise You" in DH.
Schalk, Carl. PW , Cycle C.
May God bestow on us his grace   LBW 335

CHORAL
Boyle, Malcolm. "Thou O God Art Praised in Sion." SATB, org.
PAR PPM 08618.
Erickson, Richard. "Come Away to the Skies." SATB, fl, perc. AFP
0800656776. Also in *The Augsburg Choirbook.* AFP 0800656784.
Harris, William H. "Faire Is the Heaven." in *Anthems for Choirs IV.*
SATB dbl chorus.   OXF 353018X.
Nystedt, Knut. "Peace I Leave with You." SATB. AFP 0800652673.
Wilby, Philip. "If Ye Love Me." SSATB, org.   PVN 8300561.
Manz, Paul. "E'en So, Lord Jesus, Quickly Come." SATB.
MSM 50-0001.

CHILDREN'S CHOIR
Bedford, Michael. "Let All the People's Praise You, O God." (Ps. 67)
2 pt, pno, fl.
CG CGA933.
Exner, Max. "Wade in the Water." (John 5:1-9) U, kybd.
CG CGA572.

KEYBOARD/INSTRUMENTAL
Albrecht, Mark. "Heaven Is My Home" in *Timeless Tunes for Solo Instru-
ment and Piano,* vol. 3. Pno, inst. AFP 0800675037.
Callahan, Charles. "Jerusalem, My Happy Home" in *American Folk
Hymn Suite.* Pno.   CPH 97-6972.
Ferguson, John. "Thy Holy Wings" in *Thy Holy Wings.* Org.
AFP 0800647955.
Miller, Aaron David. "Morgenlied" in *Triptych for Lent and Easter.* Org.
AFP 0800659457.

HANDBELL
McChesney, Kevin. "Visions." 2 oct. LAK HB93031.
Starks, Howard F. "My Peace I Leave with You." 3-5 oct. AG 1775.

PRAISE ENSEMBLE
Haas, David. "Peace I Leave with You." SAB, kybd, opt cong, gtr.
GIA G-4869.
Hanson, Handt. "Be My Home" in W&P.
Park, Andy. "The River Is Here" in *Best of the Best.* FEL 1891062018.

Tuesday, May 18
ERIK, KING OF SWEDEN, MARTYR, 1160
Erik, long considered the patron saint of Sweden, ruled
there from 1150 to 1160. He is honored for efforts to
bring peace to the nearby pagan kingdoms and for his cru-
sades to spread the Christian faith in Scandinavia. He established a protected Christian mission in Finland that
was led by Henry of Uppsala. As king, Erik was noted for
his desire to establish fair laws and courts and for his concern for those who were poor or sick. Erik was killed by a
Danish army that approached him at worship on the day
after the Ascension. He is reported to have said to them,
"Let us at least finish the sacrifice. The rest of the feast I
shall keep elsewhere." As he left worship he was killed.

The commemoration of Erik could be the beginning of a discussion on the relationship between civil
rule and the place of faith in the public sphere.

Monday, May 19
DUNSTAN, ARCHBISHOP OF CANTERBURY, 988
By Dunstan's time, Viking invaders had wiped out English monasticism. Dunstan played an important role in
its restoration. He was commissioned by King Edmund
to reestablish monastic life at Glastonbury, which became a center for monasticism and learning. He was exiled by a later king, Edwy, whom he had publicly rebuked. After Edwy's death Dunstan was made Archbishop
of Canterbury and carried out a reform of church and
state. He corrected abuses by the clery, encouraged laity
in their devotional life, and was committed to concerns
of justice. He was also well known as a musician and for
his painting and metal work.

211

May 20, 2004

The Ascension of Our Lord

INTRODUCTION

Why did Jesus leave just when the disciples were beginning to understand his resurrection? The readings for this day point us toward an answer: Jesus' visible absence makes possible a new way for him to be in the world through his Spirit. Christ is with us through the community that gathers around the baptismal washing, the table of grace, and the living word of his forgiving and empowering love.

PRAYER OF THE DAY

Almighty God, your only Son was taken up into heaven and in power intercedes for us. May we also come into your presence and live forever in your glory; through your Son, Jesus Christ our Lord, who lives and reigns with you and the Holy Spirit, one God, now and forever.

VERSE

Alleluia. Christ being raised from the dead will never die again; death no longer has dominion over him. Alleluia. I am with you always, to the end of the age. Alleluia. (Rom. 6:9; Matt. 28:20)

READINGS

Acts 1:1-11

Before he ascends into heaven, Jesus promises that the missionary work of the disciples will spread from Jerusalem to all the world. Jesus' words provide an outline of the book of Acts.

Psalm 47

God has gone up with a shout. (Ps. 47:5)

or Psalm 93

Ever since the world began, your throne has been established. (Ps. 93:3)

Ephesians 1:15-23

After giving thanks for the faith of the Ephesians, Paul prays that they might also see the power of God, who in the ascension has now enthroned Christ as head of the church, his body.

Luke 24:44-53

At the time of his ascension, Jesus leaves the disciples with the promise of the Holy Spirit and an instruction that they should await the Spirit's descent.

COLOR White

THE PRAYERS

Rejoicing in the resurrection, let us remember in prayer the church, the world, and all those in need.
A BRIEF SILENCE.

Blessed are you, for you have given us cause for great joy through the passion, resurrection, and ascension of Christ Jesus. Inspire your whole church to joyful witness to the ends of the earth. For this we pray:
Hear us, living God.

Blessed are you, for you have caused your name to be proclaimed to all nations. Shepherd the nations of the world in your ways of peace. For this we pray:
Hear us, living God.

Blessed are you, for the fullness of your glory fills all in all. Comfort those in any need *(especially)*, and those in the throes of confusion and stress of transition. For this we pray:
Hear us, living God.

Blessed are you, for you have made Christ the head of the whole church. Enliven this congregation, part of his body, that we might do marvelous acts in his name. For this we pray:
Here us, living God.

HERE OTHER INTERCESSIONS MAY BE OFFERED.

Blessed are you, for you are the hope of the ages. Clothe with power all who have trusted in you and bring us together with them into your heavenly reign. For this we pray:
Here us, living God.

With alleluias in our hearts and on our lips we commend to your care all for whom we pray, trusting in your mercy; through your Son, Jesus Christ our Lord.
Amen

IMAGES FOR PREACHING

Power ties. Power lunches. PowerPoint. Power seems to be an adjective of choice in recent years. Wouldn't it

212

seem absurd to market a "weakness tie"? Host a lowliness luncheon? Give a "delicate point" presentation? Yet, despite our best efforts to grasp or create power, or at least the impression thereof, we may still get laid off while wearing our ties. We often gain only pounds at our heavyweight lunches. And why is it that people still miss the point in our presentations?

Power rears its head repeatedly in today's readings, but it does not stand alone. It is coupled with inheritance. Power and receiving. Not power and grasping. Not power and earning. Power and inheritance.

Jesus says, in Acts, "But you will receive power when the Holy Spirit has come upon you; and you will be my witnesses in Jerusalem, in all Judea and Samaria, and to the ends of the earth."

Our psalmist tells us that the one who empowers us, "who subdues the peoples under us, and the nations under our feet," is the one who chooses our inheritance. Whatever capacity or status we may receive is not our own doing.

Paul reminds the community at Ephesus of that which they have to look forward to—"His glorious inheritance among the saints . . . and the immeasurable greatness of his power for us who believe." Yet, he reminds them that all this is done according to the working of God's great power; not ours. And the most potent use of that power is the resurrection of Christ.

In the end, in Luke, it is the resurrected Christ's final blessing to share what God has promised—the clothing of "power from on high."

WORSHIP MATTERS

Occasionally, someone will say that Ascension is a festival with no relevance to our world today. Yet Jesus' ascension reminds us that Jesus is no longer physically on earth and urges us to consider the means of his presence today. When we gather in sacred space we declare that Christ is present in word and sacrament. *Renewing Worship 2: Principles for Worship* has a whole section entitled "Worship Space and the Christian Assembly." Our various worship spaces assist in the "formation of those called to be Christ's body in the world, proclaiming the word through nonverbal means, teaching the faith through image and symbol, and offering their own witness to the gospel" (*Principles for Worship*, Application S-2E, p. 69). Ascension helps us to remember that worship is connected to mission. We are now the body of Christ in the world!

LET THE CHILDREN COME

"They were continually in the temple blessing God" (Luke 24:53). Invite the children to trace their hands on a blank piece of paper. Have the congregation brainstorm five different ways that all of us, of any age, could bless the Lord. With the help of an adult if necessary, have the children write or draw a picture in each finger of the different ways the congregation suggests. Then encourage the children to remember all the different ways they can bless God every time they look at their hand.

HYMNS FOR WORSHIP
GATHERING
Give to our God immortal praise!   LBW 520
All hail the power of Jesus' name   TFF 267

HYMN OF THE DAY
Alleluia! Sing to Jesus   LBW 158

ALTERNATE HYMN OF THE DAY
Lord, you give the great commission   WOV 756
Up through endless ranks of angels   LBW 159

COMMUNION
Come away to the skies   WOV 669
O Christ, our hope   LBW 300

SENDING
Beautiful Savior   LBW 518
Immortal, invisible, God only wise   LBW 526
He is exalted   W&P 55

ADDITIONAL HYMNS AND SONGS
Christ is the king!   RWSB, LBW 386
He is exalted   W&P 55
Clap your hands, all you people   LS 182

MUSIC FOR THE DAY
PSALMODY
Bell, John L. "Clap your hands all you nations" in *Psalms of Patience, Protest and Praise.* GIA G-4047.

Hopson, Hal H. *Psalms for All Seasons: An ICEL Collection.* NMP.

Howard, Julie. *Sing for Joy: Psalm Settings for God's Children.* LP 0814620787.

Pelz, Walter L. PW , Cycle C.

Sterk, Valerie Stegink. "Psalm for Ascension." Cong, choir, org, tamb. SEL 24-1047.

213

CHORAL

Cherwien, David. "Up Through Endless Ranks of Angels." SAB, org, opt tpt, cong. AFP 0800658817.

Farlee, Robert Buckley. "The Lightener of the Stars" in *To God Will I Sing.* AFP 0800674332 (MH voice); AFP 0800674340 (ML voice).

Gallus, Jacobus. "Ascendit Deus." SATBB. Associated A-83.

Mathias, William. "Lift Up Your Heads" in *Anthems for Choirs 1.* SATB, org. OXF 353214X.

Moore, Philip. "The Ascension" (Lift Up Your Heads) SATB, org. PVN 1006.

Riegel, Friedrich Samuel. "See God to Heaven Ascending" in *Chantry Choirbook.* SATB. AFP 0800657772.

Titcomb, Everett. "I Will Not Leave You Comfortless." SATB, org. CFI CM 441.

Vaughan Williams, Ralph. "O Clap Your Hands." SSATTBB, brass, org, perc (orch pts available on rental). ECS 1-5000.

CHILDREN'S CHOIR

Butler, Donna. "Sing to God." (Ps. 47:1-2) 2 pt, pno, opt 2 oct hc/hb, Orff. CG CGA607.

Tucker, Margaret. "Christ's Own Body." (Ephesians 1:22-23) U/2 pt, kybd, opt 2 oct hb, opt cong. CG CGA801.

KEYBOARD/INSTRUMENTAL

Burkhardt, Michael. "Look, Ye Saints, the Sight Is Glorious" in *Five Easter Hymn Improvisations, Set II.* Org. MSM 10-412.

Ferguson, John. "Dundee" in *Three Psalm Preludes.* Org. AFP 0800656849.

Haller, William. "Look, the Sight Is Glorious" in *Augsburg Organ Library: Easter.* Org. AFP 0800659368.

Helvey, Howard. "St. Denio" in *Hymns from Around the World.* Pno. BEC PC6.

HANDBELL

Afdahl, Lee J. "Abbot's Leigh." 3-5 oct. AG 2103.

Wagner, Douglas E. "Crown Him with Many Crowns." 2-4 oct. AG 1268.

PRAISE ENSEMBLE

Baloche, Paul. "Open the Eyes of My Heart" in RW5.

Horley, Doug. "We Want to See Jesus Lifted High" in *More Songs for Praise and Worship 2.* SATB. WRD 080689351174 (vocal ed); WRD 080689314186 (pno, vcs, perc).

Friday, May 21

JOHN ELIOT, MISSIONARY TO THE AMERICAN INDIANS, 1690

John Eliot was born in England, and his first career was as a schoolteacher. In 1631 he came to New England to preach to the Puritan settlers. In New England he developed an interest in the Algonkian Indians and learned their language and customs. He published a catechism in 1654 and in 1658 translated the scriptures into Algonkian, preparing the first complete Bible printed in the colonies. Eliot also established towns for Indians who had converted to Christianity. These towns were away from Puritan colonies and were established so that the Algonkians could preserve their own culture and live according to their own laws. Eliot also trained indigenous leaders to serve as missionaries to their own people.

As we pray for greater respect and justice for indigenous peoples, use this commemoration as an opportunity to learn of various Native American and Alaskan native tribal spiritualities and traditions.

May 23, 2004

Seventh Sunday of Easter

INTRODUCTION

"Come, Lord Jesus!" John the Seer shares the ancient prayer of the early church in today's second reading. Echoes of the prayer occur as the church gathers for the eucharist, and some of us use those ancient words at our own dinner tables. The "threefold truth" propels us into this day: "Christ has died. Christ is risen. Christ will come again."

Today the church commemorates Ludwig Nommensen, a pioneering nineteenth-century missionary among the Batak people of Sumatra.

PRAYER OF THE DAY

Almighty and eternal God, your Son our Savior is with you in eternal glory. Give us faith to see that, true to his promise, he is among us still, and will be with us to the end of time; who lives and reigns with you and the Holy Spirit, one God, now and forever.

or

God, our creator and redeemer, your Son Jesus prayed that his followers might be one. Make all Christians one with him as he is one with you, so that in peace and concord we may carry to the world the message of your love; through Jesus Christ our Lord, who lives and reigns with you and the Holy Spirit, one God, now and forever.

VERSE

Alleluia. Christ being raised from the dead will never die again; death no longer has dominion over him. Alleluia. I will not leave you orphaned; I am coming to you. Alleluia. (Rom. 6:9; John 14:18)

READINGS

Acts 16:16-34

The owners of a young woman who used her powers to tell fortunes threw Paul and Silas into jail for "healing" her and consequently ruining their business. God then used their imprisonment to bring the jailer and his family to Christ.

Psalm 97

Rejoice in the LORD, you righteous. (Ps. 97:12)

Revelation 22:12-14, 16-17, 20-21

The ascended Christ, hidden from our sight, promises to come again. We eagerly pray, "Come, Lord Jesus," with all who respond to this invitation.

John 17:20-26

In the life of the church is a unity of mission: to proclaim in word and deed that God loves all people. The unity of this mission finds its source in our union with Christ through word and meal.

COLOR White

THE PRAYERS

Rejoicing in the resurrection, let us remember in prayer the church, the world, and all those in need.

A BRIEF SILENCE.

Blessed are you, for you are love itself, and Christ is the morning star. Abundantly bless your whole church in witness and service, in faith and joy, in love and compassion. For this we pray:

Hear us, living God.

Blessed are you, for the whole world is yours. Help those who are oppressed to find peaceful paths to justice, that all may live in peace and prosperity. For this we pray:

Hear us, living God.

Blessed are you, for you are the tree of life. Shelter those in any need, especially widows and orphans, the dying and the grieving, and those who are ill *(especially)*. For this we pray:

Hear us, living God.

Blessed are you, for you are the water of life and the hope of Paul and Silas. Inspire this parish by their witness that through our own witness many more may be baptized and come to faith. For this we pray:

Hear us, living God.

Blessed are you, our guardian and judge. Guide the minds and hearts of police officers, prison guards, and all who work to enforce our laws, that they may be just and compassionate; and keep them in safety. For this we pray:

Hear us, living God.

HERE OTHER INTERCESSIONS MAY BE OFFERED.

215

Blessed are you, for you are host at the heavenly marriage feast. Come and gather the church together with Ludwig Nommensen, missionary, *(other names)*, and all the saints, that at the last we may dine with you in the banquet hall. For this we pray:
Hear us, living God.
With alleluias in our hearts and on our lips we commend to your care all for whom we pray, trusting in your mercy; through your Son, Jesus Christ our Lord.
Amen

IMAGES FOR PREACHING

Oops!? Just three days ago we celebrated Christ's ascension, and today we find ourselves celebrating Easter as if nothing out of the ordinary has occurred, as if Christ were still among us, as if he had never left. Is it a flaw in the church year? A liturgical hiccough? Or is it an intentional twist of events?

Imagine how the followers of Jesus felt after Christ was taken into heaven. "Now what?" we almost hear them ask of one another. "Who's in charge?" "We need to organize." "I feel as if I'm in the dark. What comes next?" Perhaps this last burst of Easter is intended to shed some light on our darkness as well.

"Someone turn on some lights," yells the jailer, fearing that Paul and Silas have escaped their maximum-security confines. Indeed, the light comes on as he and his household hear the word and are baptized that very evening. He washes their wounds; his wounds are healed.

Clouds and darkness are round about, says our psalmist. Yet, it is in this murky darkness that "his lightnings light up the world." Indeed, as a fire goes before him, burning up enemies, "light has sprung up for the righteous" as they are delivered from the hand of the wicked.

"I am the bright morning star," says Jesus in the Revelation to John. The morning star, the herald of daylight, lends clarity to our sight as we hear the Spirit's urging to "Come!" Heeding, we join all the thirsty and, indeed, come.

On this day, the light has shone, and we see with clarity the unity of all creation—the Alpha and Omega; the Father and Son bound together as one, as we are with them; the voice of all creation bound together in praise.

Christ is ascended; but today the light has shone, and we see that we are not alone.

WORSHIP MATTERS

The days between Ascension and Pentecost have a feeling of Advent waiting and anticipation. As the disciples and Mary awaited the promised Holy Spirit, we open our hearts and minds to a new outpouring of the Spirit in our day and time. These days remind us that we experience both the absence of Christ and longing for his return, as well as his presence among us in word, meal, and the community of faith. Not only on the Day of Pentecost can we include hymns and prayers for the coming of the Spirit. As we pray "Come, Holy Spirit" during the final Sundays of the Easter season, we build to a climax at Pentecost.

LET THE CHILDREN COME

We often conclude prayers with "in Jesus' name." Much like parents who do not hesitate to be advocates for their children, Jesus speaks on our behalf. He is the one who makes our simple prayers worthy to God. There are many ways to pray, but all prayers should be in the name of Jesus. Send home a baggie of different colored Skittles candies with each child today. Teach them that the different colored Skittles are reminders of the different ways that we can pray: red for confession; green for prayers for other people; orange for prayers for peace; and yellow for prayers of thanksgiving. Each time they eat a Skittle they should remember to pray a particular prayer.

HYMNS FOR WORSHIP
GATHERING

Alleluia! Sing to Jesus   LBW 158
Now the feast and celebration   WOV 789

HYMN OF THE DAY

Son of God, eternal Savior   LBW 364

ALTERNATE HYMN OF THE DAY

Thine the amen, thine the praise   WOV 801
O Morning Star, how fair and bright   LBW 76

COMMUNION

Lord Jesus Christ, we humbly pray   LBW 225
O blessed spring   WOV 695

216

SENDING

The Church's one foundation   LBW 369
Oh, praise the gracious power   WOV 750

ADDITIONAL HYMNS AND SONGS

To God be the glory   TFF 264
Glory and praise to our God   RWSB, W&P 43
Soli Deo gloria   RWSB
O Christ Jesus, sent from heaven   NCH 47

MUSIC FOR THE DAY
PSALMODY

Cooney, Rory. "The Lord Is King" in STP, vol. 4.

Haas, David. "Our God Is Here/The Lord Rules Above" in PCY, vol. 9.

Schalk, Carl. PW, Cycle C.

See Christmas Dawn.

CHORAL

Farlee, Robert Buckley. "O Blessed Spring." SATB, org, ob. AFP 0800654242. Also in *The Augsburg Choirbook.* AFP 0800656784.

Haugen, Kyle. "Lost in the Night." SAB, pno. AFP 0800659244.

Poole, David. "Somebody's Knockin' at Your Door." SATB, pno. KJO 8949.

Scott, K. Lee. "Thy Perfect Love" in *Sing Forth God's Praise.* AFP 0800675266 (MH voice); AFP 080067538X (ML voice).

Wilby, Philip. "If Ye Love Me." SSATB, org. Banks ECS 191.

CHILDREN'S CHOIR

Delmonte, Pauline. "O Bright and Morning Star." (Rev. 22:16) U, kybd, opt desc. CG CGA697.

Sleeth, Natalie. "In the Bulb There Is a Flower" in LS. AFP 0806642718 (Song Book); AFP 080664270X (Leader Book).

KEYBOARD/INSTRUMENTAL

Bach, J. S., arr. E. Power Biggs. "My Spirit Be Joyful." (Wie will ich mich freuen) Org, 2 tpt. Mercury.

Childs, Edwin T. "Alleluia! Sing to Jesus" in *Organ Music for the Seasons,* vol. 3. Org. AFP 0800675649.

Vogt, Emanuel. "Mfurahini, haleluya" in *Augsburg Organ Library: Easter.* Org. AFP 0800659368.

Willan, Healey. "Good Christian Friends, Rejoice" in *Organ Works of Healey Willan.* Org. CPH 97-6676.

HANDBELL

Afdahl, Lee J. "Abbot's Leigh." 3-5 oct. AG 2103.

Wagner, H. Dean. "Fantasy on 'Kingsfold.'" 3-5 oct hb, opt hc. AG 2134.

PRAISE ENSEMBLE

Brown, Brenton. "Lord, Reign in Me" in *Come, Now is the Time to Worship Songbook.* Vineyard Music VMB9347.

DeShazo, Lynn and Gary Sadler. "Be unto Your Name" in *Worship Leader's Song Discovery,* vol. 18. Worship Leader 2000-01-LS.

Sunday, May 23

LUDWIG NOMMENSEN, MISSIONARY TO SUMATRA, 1918

Ludwig Ingwer Nommensen was born in Schleswig-Holstein, Germany. In the early 1860s he went to Sumatra to serve as a Lutheran missionary. His work was among the Batak people, who had previously not seen Christian missionaries. Though he encountered some initial difficulties, the missions began to succeed following the conversion of several tribal chiefs. Nommensen translated the scriptures into Batak while honoring much of the native culture and did not seek to replace it with a European one. At the time of World War II all missionaries were driven out, and the Batak people took over leadership of their own church.

217

Monday, May 24

NICOLAUS COPERNICUS, 1543;
LEONHARD EULER, 1783; TEACHERS

Scientists such as Copernicus and Euler invite us to ponder the mysteries of the universe and the grandeur of God's creation. Copernicus is an example of a renaissance person. He formally studied astronomy, mathematics, Greek, Plato, law, medicine, and canon law. He also had interests in theology, poetry, and the natural and social sciences. Copernicus is chiefly remembered for his work as an astronomer and his idea that the sun, not the earth, is the center of the solar system. Euler is regarded as one of the founders of the science of pure mathematics and made important contributions to mechanics, hydrodynamics, astronomy, optics, and acoustics.

Thursday, May 27

JOHN CALVIN, RENEWER OF THE CHURCH, 1564

John Calvin began his studies in theology at the University of Paris when he was fourteen. In his mid-twenties he experienced a conversion that led him to embrace the views of the Reformation. His theological ideas are systematically laid out in his Institutes of the Christian Religion. He is also well known for his commentaries on scripture. He was a preacher in Geneva, was banished once, and then later returned to reform the city with a rigid, theocratic discipline.

Calvin is considered the father of the Reformed churches. It would be fitting on this day to hold up the ecumenical agreement the Evangelical Lutheran Church in America shares with churches of the Reformed tradition as an example of the unity we share in Christ.

May 29, 2004

Vigil of Pentecost

INTRODUCTION

All three major festivals of the Christian year—Christmas, Easter, and Pentecost—are accompanied by vigils on the night before. Even though the Holy Spirit has already come among us, the church always eagerly awaits and anticipates further outpouring of the Spirit's power. God is not done with us yet!

PRAYER OF THE DAY

Almighty and ever-living God, you fulfilled the promise of Easter by sending your Holy Spirit to unite the races and nations on earth and thus to proclaim your glory. Look upon your people gathered in prayer, open to receive the Spirit's flame. May it come to rest in our hearts and heal the divisions of word and tongue, that with one voice and one song we may praise your name in joy and thanksgiving; through your Son, Jesus Christ our Lord, who lives and reigns with you and the Holy Spirit, one God, now and forever.

VERSE

Alleluia. Come, Holy Spirit, fill the hearts of your faithful people; set them on fire with your love. Alleluia.

READINGS

Exodus 19:1-9

After having escaped the Egyptian armies at the Red Sea, Israel gathers at the base of Mount Sinai, and Moses climbs the peak to meet God. God's word is clear and stirring: "You are my people! I am coming to you!"

or Acts 2:1-11

The disciples are filled with the Spirit to tell God's deeds.

Psalm 33:12-22

The LORD is our help and our shield. (Ps. 33:20)

or Psalm 130

There is forgiveness with you. (Ps. 130:3)

Romans 8:14-17, 22-27

Paul says even though we are God's people and led by God's Spirit, we do not always know how to express this reality in words. The apostle reminds us, however, that this struggle for speech is really part of an entire universe groaning in labor as it awaits God's redemption.

John 7:37-39

Jesus says that our ultimate thirst will be quenched by streams of water that flow from human hearts. The Holy Spirit, poured into God's people, is the source of that stream.

COLOR Red

THE PRAYERS

Rejoicing in the resurrection, let us remember in prayer the church, the world, and all those in need.

A BRIEF SILENCE.

Come, Holy Spirit, with sighs of intercession too deep for words on behalf of the whole church. Inspire us to faithfulness in the way of truth. For this we pray:
Hear us, living God.

218

Come, Holy Spirit, to all the nations of the world. Inspire them to creative and beneficial solutions to the problems that face them. For this we pray:

Hear us, living God.

Come, Holy Spirit, bear up those in need as on eagles' wings. Comfort the hurting, give hope to the hopeless, peace to the grieving, and healing to those who are ill (*especially*). For this we pray:

Hear us, living God.

Come, Holy Spirit, to inspire this congregation in its mission in this community. Give our leaders courage and our members the confidence of your presence. For this we pray:

Hear us, living God.

HERE OTHER INTERCESSIONS MAY BE OFFERED.

Come, Holy Spirit, and at the last join us with all the faithful departed at the river of living water that is Christ Jesus. For this we pray:

Hear us, living God.

With alleluias in our hearts and on our lips we commend to your care all for whom we pray, trusting in your mercy; through Jesus Christ our Lord.

Amen

IMAGES FOR PREACHING

"Paní Kovacová vari na stroji," wrote the missionary in his first Slovak class on office and home equipment. "Impossible!" replied the teacher. "It cannot be done!" This became clear to the student when he realized his sentence read, "Mrs. Kovac cooks in her typewriter."

Despite our sincere attempts at communicating, we often fail miserably. In a world of diverse cultures and subcultures, good communication can mean the difference between war and peace, embargo and embrace, AIDS and aid.

Today's readings point out exactly how effective (or ineffective) words can be, even when accompanied by great sound effects and visuals. God speaks to the Israelites, via Moses, in a voice from the mountain. In an unusual departure from the wilderness tradition, the Israelites reply with one voice. "A cloud is what I'll use in the future," says God, "so you can eavesdrop on my conversations with Moses." As history bears out, the communications honeymoon was short-lived.

A few centuries later, communications techniques had become more sophisticated. Visitors to Jerusalem were amazed to hear Galileans speaking in everyone else's native language. Yet, as we all know, such miraculous communication is the exception.

Paul points out the truth of the predicament in which we humans live. Creation, too, communicates. It groans! And we groan with it as we await our redemption. But Paul brings hope as he reminds us that, through the Holy Spirit, we have been moved out of the realm of words. "The Spirit helps us in our weakness" when our words, our prayers, even our groans fail. "The Spirit intercedes with sighs too deep for words."

John anticipates the day when we are moved from the realm of the spoken word into a relationship with the Spirit. We look forward to a time when words will make way for "rivers of living water" flowing from the believer's heart.

WORSHIP MATTERS

If you already have a Christmas Eve liturgy, and an Easter Vigil, consider adding a vigil for Pentecost, the third great festival of the church year. The main theme of the vigil is prayer for the Holy Spirit, following the example of the apostles, disciples, and Mary, who persevered in prayer as they awaited the gift of the Spirit at Pentecost. Begin with a simple Service of Light such as the one in evening prayer. If you want additional readings, consider these from the Roman rite: Genesis 11:1-9, Ezekiel 37:1-14, and Joel 2:28-32. For a baptismal remembrance, use a thanksgiving prayer with a Pentecost theme (*Holy Baptism*, RW3, p. 17). Finally, conclude with the eucharist. The service may only attract a small group at first, but those who attend will likely find it very spirited!

LET THE CHILDREN COME

Many times we long for God to hear our thoughts, concerns, cares, and joys, but words seem inadequate. And, of course, children don't have the benefit (or disadvantage?) of long exposure to formal models of prayer. In the second reading, Paul writes that the Spirit intercedes with sighs too deep for words. We can let go of our worry about praying in just the right way and instead embrace the wonderful gift of just being in God's presence. In the prayers tonight, intersperse moments of quiet, instrumental music and have the congregation focus on being in God's presence and inviting the Spirit to intercede for us. You could also set up fans throughout

219

the sanctuary as a reminder of how the Spirit of God blows in, through, and around us.

HYMNS FOR WORSHIP

GATHERING

O day full of grace   LBW 161
Veni Sancte Spiritus   WOV 686

HYMN OF THE DAY

Come, Holy Ghost, our souls inspire   LBW 473

COMMUNION

Come down, O love divine   LBW 508
Baptized in water   WOV 693

SENDING

Holy Spirit, ever dwelling   LBW 523
Holy Spirit, light divine   TFF 104

ADDITIONAL HYMNS AND SONGS

Send down the fire   RWSB
Holy Spirit, our font of love   LLC 370
Spirit of the living God   TFF 101
Song over the waters   W&P 127

MUSIC FOR THE DAY

PSALMODY

Farlee, Robert Buckley. PW , Cycle C.
Foley, John. "Psalm 33: God, Let Your Mercy" in PCY, vol. 7.

CHORAL

Manalo, Ricky. "By the Waking of Our Hearts." U, cong, desc, kybd, gtr, C inst. OCP 10981.
Schalk, Carl. "O Day Full of Grace." SATB, org, 2 tpt, 2 tbn, opt cong. AFP 0800645928.
Scott, K. Lee. "Gracious Spirit, Dwell with Me" in *The Augsburg Easy Choirbook.* 2 pt mxd, org. AFP 0800676025. Also in *The Augsburg Choirbook.* AFP 0800656784.
Tallis, Thomas. "If Ye Love Me." SATB. OXF 42.60.

CHILDREN'S CHOIR

Horman, John. "God Called Moses." (Exodus 19) U, pno, opt desc, vc/fl. CG CGA907.

Kemp, Helen. "Psalm 33:20-22" in *Sing and Speak of God's Glory.* U/2 pt, kybd, opt inst. CG CGA563.

KEYBOARD/INSTRUMENTAL

Biery, James. "Bridegroom" in *Tree of Life.* Org. AFP 0800655370.
Leavitt, John. "Komm, Gott Schöpfer" in *Hymn Preludes for the Church Year.* Org. AFP 0800650328.
Sedio, Mark. "Come Down, O Love Divine" in *Augsburg Organ Library: Easter.* Org. AFP 0800659368.

HANDBELL

Afdahl, Lee J. "Spirit in the Wind." 3-5 oct. AFP 0800655443.
McChesney, Kevin. "Song of the Spirit." 3-7 oct. Ringing Word 8138.

PRAISE ENSEMBLE

Bullock, Goeff. "Refresh My Heart" in *More Songs for Praise and Worship.* SATB. WRD 3010387016 (vocal ed); WRD 3010186363 (pno, vcs, perc).
Davis, Holland. "Let It Rise" in *More Songs for Praise and Worship.* SATB. WRD 3010387016 (vocal ed); WRD 3010186363 (pno, vcs, perc).

Saturday, May 29

JIRI TRANOVSKY, HYMNWRITER, 1637

Tranovský is considered the "Luther of the Slavs" and the father of Slovak hymnody. Trained at the University of Wittenberg in the early seventeenth century, Tranovský was ordained in 1616 and spent his life preaching and teaching in Prague, Silesia, and finally Slovakia. He produced a translation of the Augsburg Confession and published his hymn collection Cithara Sanctorum (Lyre of the Saints), the foundation of Slovak Lutheran hymnody.

Use the commemoration to pray for the Slovak church and to give thanks for the gifts of church musicians. Sing Tranovský's Easter hymn, "Make songs of joy" (LBW 150), at parish gatherings today.

May 30, 2004

The Day of Pentecost

INTRODUCTION

An ancient Hebrew harvest festival that came to be associated with the giving of God's law at Mount Sinai, Pentecost became for Christians the occasion for the gift of the Holy Spirit to the church. The Spirit is the power of the resurrected Jesus in our midst, claiming us in baptism, feeding us at the eucharist, and sending us into the world to be bearers of that divine word that can raise the dead to new life.

PRAYER OF THE DAY

God, the Father of our Lord Jesus Christ, as you sent upon the disciples the promised gift of the Holy Spirit, look upon your Church and open our hearts to the power of the Spirit. Kindle in us the fire of your love, and strengthen our lives for service in your kingdom; through your Son, Jesus Christ our Lord, who lives and reigns with you in the unity of the Holy Spirit, one God, now and forever.

or

God our creator, earth has many languages, but your Gospel announces your love to all nations in one heavenly speech. Make us messengers of the good news that, through the power of your Spirit, everyone everywhere may unite in one song of praise; through your Son, Jesus Christ our Lord, who lives and reigns with you in the unity of the Holy Spirit, one God, now and forever.

VERSE

Alleluia. Come, Holy Spirit, fill the hearts of your faithful people; set them on fire with your love. Alleluia.

READINGS

Acts 2:1-21

Before Jesus ascended into heaven, he told his disciples they would be filled with the Holy Spirit and become witnesses for him to the ends of the earth. As the people spoke in many languages, the all-encompassing nature of the church and its mission were revealed.

or Genesis 11:1-9

God scatters those who were building the tower of Babel.

Psalm 104:25-35, 37 (Psalm 104:24-34, 35b NRSV)

Alleluia,

or Send forth your Spirit and renew the face of the earth. (Ps. 104:31)

Romans 8:14-17

Here Paul speaks about the mystery of baptism: through the Spirit we are adopted, gathered, and welcomed into Christ's body, the church. And we receive new names: brother, sister, child of God.

or Acts 2:1-21

See above.

John 14:8-17 [25-27]

On the night he was betrayed, in his final address to his disciples, Jesus promises that though he must now leave them, they will soon receive the presence of an Advocate, the Spirit of truth, whom God will send to comfort and enlighten them.

COLOR   Red

THE PRAYERS

Rejoicing in the resurrection, let us remember in prayer the church, the world, and all those in need.

A BRIEF SILENCE.

Come, Holy Spirit, poured out upon the whole church. Inspire us to prophecy, witness, and service, to new visions and dreams, that through our ministry the world might know of your love. For this we pray:

Hear us, living God.

Come, Holy Spirit, to all the nations of the world. Inspire them to peace and to justice for their own citizens and for their enemies. For this we pray:

Hear us, living God.

Come, Holy Spirit, bring peace to those in need, comfort to those who grieve, courage to the hopeless, and healing to those who are ill *(especially)*. For this we pray:

Hear us, living God.

Come, Holy Spirit, and inspire this congregation to the ministry of peacemaking in this community, that through our ministry reconciliation may be found. For this we pray:

221

Hear us, living God.

Come, Holy Spirit, and inspire us in remembrance of those who gave their lives on battlefields for the sake of freedom. Lead us all to be generous with our lives for the sake of others. For this we pray:

Hear us, living God.

Come, Holy Spirit, and at the last bring us together with (*names,* and) all the faithful departed into the warm embrace of your presence. For this we pray:

Hear us, living God.

HERE OTHER INTERCESSIONS MAY BE OFFERED.

With alleluias in our hearts and on our lips we commend to your care all for whom we pray, trusting in your mercy; through Jesus Christ our Lord.

Amen

IMAGES FOR PREACHING

"What do you want for your birthday?" An innocent question. Well-intended. Practical. What may lie behind the question is, "I don't want to waste money on something you don't like, or can't use, or would store in the back of your closet." The question is sometimes replaced with, "Here's a check. Please buy something you'd really like."

What we don't receive when we place our own gift orders or when we choose our own gift is the perception and wisdom of the giver. We do not receive that which the giver saw us as needing, that which the giver guessed we would like, that which the giver's imagination chose. We miss the opportunity to receive a delightfully odd gift.

Odd gifts. "I do not give to you as the world gives," says Jesus. On this day, often referred to as the founding—a birthday of sorts—of the church, humanity received a gift it did not request, and would not have, quite likely, placed on its gift registry.

Philip placed his order. "Lord, show us the Father, and we will be satisfied." Give us something tangible and concrete. Jesus essentially tells him, "I've been trying. You've been missing the obvious. Now it's my turn to decide." An odd gift indeed! Philip requests the tangible; the gift is quite the opposite—"the Spirit of truth, whom the world cannot receive, because it neither sees him nor knows him."

Paul describes today's gift in another way. We have received a "spirit of adoption," which makes us joint

heirs with Christ. No longer do we need to join the builders of Babel, seeking to memorialize ourselves in the history of the world. Our legacy has been granted. Our gift has been chosen for us.

WORSHIP MATTERS

Pentecost is a wonderful day to witness to both the catholicity and the diversity of the church. The reading from Acts mentions persons hearing in their own languages the mighty works of God. You may want to consider ways to celebrate the diversity of tongues and cultures of the universal church. One or more of the readings could be read in another language, or during a portion of the Acts reading a variety of persons could simultaneously read in several languages, replicating in a small way the Jerusalem experience. Each prayer petition could be read in a different language with the translation in the bulletin. Music and hymns can be chosen from around the world as well. *With One Voice,* Setting 6 (p. 42) is called *All Times and Places* and lists a variety of service music that could be used as a kind of "global mass."

LET THE CHILDREN COME

One of the miracles of Pentecost is that even though we all pray and sing to God in many languages, God understands us all. It is important that a variety of voices be heard today. Make arrangements ahead of time for people from within your congregation to read a portion of the readings in another language. Make sure you include men and women, young and old. Today is an event worth celebrating in the life of the church. Fill the sanctuary with red helium balloons and invite each child to take one home after the service.

HYMNS FOR WORSHIP
GATHERING

O day full of grace   LBW 161
Holy Spirit, truth divine   LBW 257

HYMN OF THE DAY

Gracious Spirit, heed our pleading   WOV 687. TFF 103

ALTERNATE HYMN OF THE DAY

Creator Spirit, heavenly dove   LBW 284
Song over the waters   W&P 127, RWSB

COMMUNION

O Spirit of life   WOV 680

Creator Spirit, by whose aid   LBW 164

SENDING

Spread, oh, spread, almighty word   LBW 379

Blest be the tie that binds   LBW 370

Oh, let the Son of God enfold you   TFF 105, W&P 130

ADDITIONAL HYMNS AND SONGS

Fire of God, undying flame   RWSB

Holy Spirit, our font of love /

Santo Espíritu, plenitud pascual   LLC 370

Holy Spirit, light divine   TFF 104

Wind of the Spirit   W&P 157

MUSIC FOR THE DAY

PSALMODY

Haugen, Marty. "Lord, Send Out Your Spirit" in PCY, vol. 1.

Hunnicutt, Judy. "Lord, Send Out Your Spirit" in Sing Out! A Children's Psalter. WLP 7191.

Makeever, Ray. "When You Send Forth Your Spirit" in DH.

Schalk, Carl. PW , Cycle C.

Schoenbachler, Tim. "Psalm 104: Send Out Your Spirit" in STP, vol. 2.

Oh, worship the King   LBW 548

CHORAL

Bach, J. S. "Dona nobis pacem" in Bach for All Seasons. SATB, kybd. AFP 080065854X.

Berger, Jean. "The Eyes of All Wait upon Thee." SATB. AFP 0800645596.

Dawson, William. "Ev'ry Time I Feel the Spirit." SATB. KJO T117.

Teleman, G. P. "Make Me Pure, O Sacred Spirit" in To God Will I Sing. AFP 0800674332 (MH voice); AFP 0800674340 (ML voice).

Wilby, Philip. "If Ye Love Me." SSATB, org. Banks ECS 191.

CHILDREN'S CHOIR

Cool, Jayne Southwick. "Pentecost Fire." (Acts 2) U, kybd. CG CGA502.

Jothen, Michael. "We Are Children of Our God." (Rom. 8:14-17) U/2 pt, kybd, opt fl, opt 3-4 oct hb, opt cong. CG CGA731.

KEYBOARD/INSTRUMENTAL

Duruflé, Maurice. "Prélude, Adagio et Choral varié sur le thème du Veni Creator Spiritus." Org. DUR.

Folkening, John. Two Brass Fanfares. Brass. AFP 0800674944.

McCabe, Michael. "Come, Holy Ghost, Our Souls Inspire" (Veni Creator Spiritus) in Hymn Voluntaries for the Church Year. Org. SMP 70-12425.

Wold, Wayne L. "Suite on 'O Day Full of Grace.'" Org. AFP 0800656881. Also in Augsburg Organ Library: Easter. AFP 0800659368.

HANDBELL

Bartsch, Jr., John T. "Spirit Wind." 3-5 oct. FB BG0858.

Moklebust, Cathy. "Windscape." 3-5 oct. CPH 97-6833.

PRAISE ENSEMBLE

Adler, Dan, arr. Greer. "Right Here, Right Now." SATB, kybd. WRD 080689397271.

Haugen, Marty. "Send Down the Fire." SATB, pno, gtr, opt. perc. GIA G-3915.

Iverson, Daniel. "Spirit of the Living God" in W&P.

Wimber, John. "Spirit Song" in W&P.

223

Monday, May 31

THE VISITATION

The Visitation marks the occasion of Mary visiting her cousin Elizabeth. Elizabeth greeted Mary with the words, "Blessed are you among women," and Mary responded with her famous song, the Magnificat. Luke tells us that even John the Baptist rejoiced and leapt in his mother's womb when Elizabeth heard Mary's greeting. Today we are shown two women: one too old to have a child bears the last prophet of the old covenant, and the other, still quite young, bears the incarnate Word and the new covenant.

In what ways does the church bear the good news of Christ to others and remain faithful to God's call?

Tuesday, June 1

JUSTIN, MARTYR AT ROME, C. 165

Justin was born of pagan parents. At Ephesus he was moved by stories of early Christian martyrs and came under the influence of an elderly Christian man he had met there. Justin described his conversion by saying, "Straightway a flame was kindled in my soul and a love of the prophets and those who are friends of Christ possessed me." Justin was a teacher of philosophy and engaged in debates about the truth of Christian faith. He was arrested and jailed for practicing an unauthorized religion. He refused to renounce his faith and he and six of his students, one of them a woman, were beheaded.

Justin's description of early Christian worship around the year 150 is the foundation of the church's pattern of worship, East and West. His description of it is in *With One Voice* (p. 6) and helps reveal the deep roots our contemporary shape of the liturgy has in the ancient worship of the church.

Thursday, June 3

JOHN XXIII, BISHOP OF ROME, 1963

In his ministry as a bishop of Venice, John was well loved by his people. He visited parishes and established new ones. He had warm affection for the working class—he himself was the child of Italian peasants—and he worked at developing social action ministries. At age seventy-seven he was elected bishop of Rome. Despite the expectation that he would be a transitional pope, he

had great energy and spirit. He convened the Second Vatican Council in order to open the windows of the church and "let in the fresh air of the modern world." The council brought about great changes in the church's worship, changes that have influenced Lutherans and many other Protestant churches as well.

Saturday, June 5

BONIFACE, ARCHBISHOP OF MAINZ,
MISSIONARY TO GERMANY, MARTYR, 754

Boniface (his name means "good deeds") was born Wynfrith in Devonshire, England. He was a Benedictine monk who at the age of thirty was called to missionary work among the Vandal tribes in Germany. He led large numbers of Benedictine monks and nuns in establishing churches, schools, and seminaries. Boniface was also a reformer. He persuaded two rulers to call synods to put an end to the practice of selling church offices to the highest bidder. Boniface was preparing a group for confirmation on the eve of Pentecost when he and the others were killed by Vandal warriors.

224

SUMMER

The Holy One speaks to the gathered community

Images *of the* Season

In the fourteenth and fifteenth centuries, artists

created countless works focusing on the Christ story.

As we look back at these works, we are staggered

by the breadth and depth of the early church's commitment to artistic expression.

One large grouping of works focuses on Jesus and Mary in the center of a painting or fresco, with individuals gathered around them who depict saints, biblical characters, or donors. Some freestanding paintings are in triptych form with outer panels folding to cover the central image. Other paintings were intended for use above altars or were converted to stained glass. The paintings express a wide variety of emotions. Some images include characters that are engaging in quiet prayer and devotion, eyes cast down with bodies still and silent. In many of these instances, the setting is that of a church or monastic cloister. In the latter part of the fifteenth century, the characters move from a more staid and meditative placement to being engaged in laughter and emotion, in activity and expression. Musicians and teachers, poets and clergy are often included in these later depictions. Settings for the art works range from homes and sitting rooms to classrooms and halls. Though each work is different, they usually share a common title, "sacra conversazione"—the sacred conversation.

During the season following Pentecost, the church looks back at the fasting of Lent and the feast of the Resurrection by recounting the important conversations that occur as the church emerges and evolves into a community. As it moves from a loose band of followers to a recognized gathering of Christians, biblical conversations between Jesus and those he meets deepen the ensuing transformation. The church needs to retell these stories for its life to be sustained. The image of a sacred conversation grounds God and the human story in a partnership in which revelation grows out of relationship.

Whenever two or three gather, the liturgy becomes the setting for this sacred conversation to occur among the faithful. Whenever the liturgy happens, a conversation about things sacred takes place. Summer liturgy encourages sacred conversation.

Sometimes the conversation, like the paintings, is vigorous and engaging. The biblical narratives may be emotion-filled dialogues with a disciple or a challenger, a seeker or a nay-saying doubter. Sometimes, the conversation seems more one-sided, as in a proclamation, a saying, or a parable. Sometimes silence and withdrawal mark the sacred time. Yet even quiet and reflection become critical and essential so that in the inner silence, dialogue can happen.

A posture of prayer, a gesture of grace, a home for heart and spirit—these are the unspoken languages of the sacred conversation. Subtle and striking, these signs are important, too, for they mask yet another level of encounter. Touching the mind, the heart, and the body by the power of the Holy Spirit, God reaches humanity in unassuming and personal ways. This is what liturgy provides, a way for that which is wholly "Other" to meet us.

In the midst of all that happens in worship, as a community dwells in and witnesses to word and sign, the Holy One of Israel speaks. The assembly listens and a dialogue ensues, but *our* words ought not to be confused with the *living* Word. This is an important distinction to be aware of: sacred buildings and liturgies are bound by time and place, yet it is the Holy One who intercedes within the human and ordinary in sighs too deep for words by bringing the eternity into the present. The divine and living Word breaks into our existence.

The summer Sundays of the Pentecost season look back to the central feast of the church year, the Resurrection of Our Lord. All of time is measured by this transforming moment. By the time the great fiftieth day of Pentecost is reached, the church has moved from its Lenten fast, past its Easter feast, to a time of rejoicing in feasting with the Spirit—a time for telling and retelling the movable feast of redemption. It is at the eucharist table that God speaks the transforming words "given and shed." Returning to this table where all are welcome and where every person finds a place is the lasting reminder that God is always seeking and engaging individuals and communities in dialogue.

In one Sunday conversation, Jesus is talking and eating with the Pharisees while being anointed; in another conversation, he is meeting and healing the Gerasene man possessed by a demon. Sometimes he is arguing with the disciples. At other times he is sending out the seventy as witnesses. All of these encounters depend on the give and take involved in relationship, the interaction necessary for any important and life-changing conversation. All feature the enlightening power of the Spirit making us holy as well.

As important as the strong truths inherent in these stories is the value of having sacred conversations across generations of faithful people. Both society and the church tend toward homogeneity—listening only to one's own voice or perspective. This tendency is sometimes defended by the argument that the church must be contemporary and relevant; in society, we hear a constant yearning for self-fulfillment, recognition, and actualization. Although this cannot be ignored or discounted (worship should indeed in some way be relevant and fulfilling!), it is important to reinforce that worship does not exist in a vacuum. Voices from all times and places are added to the mere present, and the continuing conversation that is the church of Jesus Christ continues to expand.

The Pentecost conversation takes today's local church beyond itself. This spirited conversation has many languages and perspectives, all within the context of a diverse and equalized community. It is only in the sacred conversation of the liturgy that the church welcomes the voices that are no longer alive. To be a whole and universal church, the faithful disciples of this day need the voices of the church throughout the ages and across the continents.

In this summer time, partners in the conversation include Basil and Gregory, Melanchthon and Irenaeus, Peter and Paul. We hear from Catherine Winkworth and Birgitta, Mary, Martha, and Lazarus. Hymnwriters and poets from every time are involved, the theologians and scholars across a wide spectrum of belief are heard, and because of this, the great conversation has profound breadth and depth. It is through these conversations that the faithful are sent to bring this same word to a hungry world.

Summertime is looked forward to, yet the church, during this season, is also looking back by returning to sacred texts, sacred music, and sacred rites. These human expressions allow the Holy Spirit to intercede, to break into, and to transform the here and now by a sacred conversation with the Holy One of Israel.

227

Environment *and* Art *for the* Season

The Sundays after Pentecost comprise that time

in the church year devoted to focusing on the church itself.

We shift our attention from the time of Christ to the time

when we see how the Holy Spirit continues Christ's ministry through us. It is a time to dwell on the ministry of Jesus and how the encounter of Christ in the world matters to us in the church today. We investigate and live into our role as the body of Christ in the world. We strive to understand what it means to be church: how we do ministry, how we pray, how we worship.

ANALYZING YOUR SPACE

This season can seem like one long green season, especially for those of us who spend our time and energy on the seasonal changes and the environment in which we worship. It would be easy for us to slow down our efforts and take a break from all of the challenging work in which we have been engaged over the past six months. Fortunately, the season requires no major thematic changes. This luxury allows us the opportunity to expand our understanding as the church. We can use this time to reflect on our worship space by looking at the spaces of other worshiping communities. The summer months are the natural time for many people in our congregations to travel. Because of the less-scheduled nature for many this time of the year, we can also take advantage of an occasional Sunday to visit another congregation individually or as a group to see their environment and art.

CHURCH VISIT QUESTIONNAIRE

The following list of questions can help your congregational members think critically about the churches they visit. You can distribute them as a complete list for the vacationers, or you can make use of them in sections if you go to visit other congregations in groups. Encourage people to take extra paper with them in order to sketch or write down ideas. Follow-up is extremely important in this process. Take plenty of time to help participants reflect on their church visit. Maybe they took pictures for the group to look at. Give them a chance to

tell the story of what they experienced. Visiting and consciously reflecting on other worship spaces is a great way to develop the critical skills that can be applied to one's own space.

APPROACHING THE CHURCH BUILDING

- How far away from the church were you before you could see it?
- Could you tell from the outside that it was a church?
- Were there clear signs telling you where to park or did the layout of the property make that clear?
- From your parking space, was it obvious to you in which direction you should go to get to the main entrance of the church?
- Was the way from the place you parked to the entrance to the church well taken care of, landscaped? Were there any places to stop along the way? Were there any outdoor works of art?
- Did the entrance of the church look like what you think a church entrance should look like? (Elaborate on what this means.)

ENTRANCE TO THE CHURCH

- What does the entrance to the church remind you of? (Grocery store, ancient church, public office building, etc.)
- What are the elements that make you think that? (Style, doors, signs)
- Is there any art indicating that this entrance is the entrance to a place of worship?
- How large is the entrance to the church? How many doors? Were all of them open or unlocked? (You may check to find out.)
- Upon entering the church, is it clear that you are now in the gathering space or do you have to go someplace else to get there? (Through office space, classroom space, and so forth)

GATHERING SPACE

- Does the gathering space appear to be used for this purpose only?
- Is there liturgical art in the gathering space?
- Is it cluttered with bulletin boards and/or coats, chairs, tables, or anything else?
- Does it feel inviting? Why or why not?
- Can you see the worship space from the gathering space?
- Is the gathering space noticeably a different space from the worship space?
- Are people actually gathering here?
- What other elements are in this gathering space? (Information booth, hospitality booth, signs to re-strooms, etc.)
- Is the baptismal font located in the gathering space?

WORSHIP SPACE

- What is the very first thing that you notice when you walk into the worship space? (It can be a sight, sound, smell, or physical feeling like temperature or humidity or blowing air.)
- Where are you entering the worship space? (From the side, the back, the front?)
- Is this the only entrance into the worship space?
- If it is not the only entrance, which entrance appears to be used the most? Why do you think this is the case? (You can even ask a member of the church why they think it is the case.)
- Is the worship space dark or bright?
- What colors are used in the space? Do they work together?
- Does it appear that moving around the space is easy or cumbersome? Are there lots of aisles?
- What is the layout or floor plan of the worship space? (Sketch it if you can.)
- Where is the altar? The font? The pulpit and lectern? Or is there only one place for the reading of the word such as an ambo?
- Are the liturgical furnishings appropriate for the size of the space? Do they look too large or too small compared to the people using them?
- Is there one primary symbol that you notice or are more than one "competing" for your attention? What are those symbols? (There might be only one or even none.)

- Is there a cross in the space? If so, is it a cross with or without a corpus (body of Christ)? If there is a corpus, is it a crucified Christ or a depiction of Christ as king or a victorious Christ?
- Is there a communion rail around the altar area? Do people stand or kneel at the rail or is communion distributed elsewhere?
- Can you hear the music? What instruments are used to lead the worship? If a choir or soloist is singing, can you understand the words they are singing? How does the music sound? Is there reverberation? Are the worship leaders amplified?
- Can you understand the spoken word, the readings, the sermon?
- Is the space accessible enough that someone in a wheelchair would be able to get around well enough to serve in a leadership capacity?

ART IN THE WORSHIP SPACE

- What kind of art is in the worship space? Is it permanent? Temporary?
- What does the art portray?
- What kinds of feelings does the art evoke in you?
- Is it at all disturbing? Does it make you think?
- Did the art have a lasting effect on you?

THE EXPERIENCE OF THE LITURGY IN THE SPACE

- Did it seem like the liturgy "worked" in the space?
- Were there any moments when you thought the liturgy could have been more powerful or complete if it were going on in a different space?
- How could you imagine various liturgies working in this space? Funerals? Weddings? Easter Vigil? Christmas Eve?
- Did you enjoy worship here? Why or why not? How did or could the worship space have enriched that experience for you?

FINAL REFLECTION QUESTIONS

- In your opinion, what was the strongest feature in the worship space? Why?
- If you could take one element with you from this space back to your church, what would it be? Are there more elements you would take? What are they?
- Is there anything in this space that reminded you of your church? Was it used differently? More effectively? Less effectively? How so?

229

ART FOR THE SEASON

The summer months in most parts of the country are a time when people can spend a lot more time outdoors. If you are fortunate to live in a climate that allows for much more time outdoors during most of the year, feel free to make use of these ideas for other seasons as well. Outdoor art is a way for a congregation to witness to the beauty and mystery of the faith to others aside from those who come to our churches. It is art that engages people as they walk or drive by when they are least expecting faith-inspired art in their lives. Art of this kind can be commissioned just like art for inside your church. It can be permanent or temporary. You can erect a large canvas or use wall space to create a mural. You can make an artistic statement with your landscaping. You can solicit your congregation or just the young people to make a sidewalk mural using sidewalk chalk. If you are in a context where there are already graffiti artists, you might consider connecting with your community and sponsoring a liturgical graffiti-style art exposition where you can showcase the talents of people in your neighborhood. You have different opportunities when you take your art outdoors. It is not only the public spaces like city squares and town halls that can use art to beautify or make a statement. At many different times in history the church has taken on that same role. You can still do that today.

Preaching *with the* Season

Good preaching is always sensitive to the assembly's

context. If a child in the congregation died recently,

a sermon would take the community's grief into account.

In times of economic hardship, the pastor might find a way to bring such real-life struggles into the faith question. If the youth group is heading off on a service journey, that event provides some sermon material as well.

Context can also go beyond such current specific events. Sermons can work with a national or worldwide mood (anxious? confident? pensive?), a seasonal approach (the more laid-back attitude of summer), even—carefully—such unliturgical aspects as national holidays or sports stories.

The challenge is to not let the context *become* the sermon. This may be a greater difficulty for the veteran pastor. If you have dealt with the sending out of the seventy already in three or four sermons over the years, bringing in the other lessons as you could, the temptation may be strong to base the sermon more on an anecdote or current event than on the gospel. And because everyone loves a good story, such an approach may win the preacher plaudits.

We are called to preach the gospel. Of course, that means the good news of Jesus Christ, not necessarily the appointed gospel for the day. However, Lutherans and other liturgical churches have willingly accepted the discipline of the lectionary as a prod to preach the *whole* story of Christ, the *whole* interaction of God with humanity, not just whatever is most convenient. We should not be too ready to throw out that approach when it poses difficulties.

By all means, let today's outside world into the sermon—that helps provide a crucial point of engagement for the listener. In reality, though, the underlying factors of the human condition haven't changed all that much from Christ's time to ours. Look for the points of congruence between the newspaper and the lectionary. That youth group heading out for service—are they like Proper 9's disciples being sent out like lambs into the midst of wolves? Are those wolves more real or imagined? In Proper 13, an anecdote about corporate greed and corruption could link nicely with Jesus' parable. A series might even be built around today's troublesome attitudes—but instead of being an independent, topical series, it could be developed beginning with the lectionary gospels. For example, a series for the Sundays of August could look like this:

230

August 1: The Problem of Greed
August 8: The Problem of Apathy
August 15: The Problem of Comfort
August 22: The Problem of Piety
August 29: The Problem of Pride

Granted, that isn't a highly original list, and you may want to come up with catchier titles. But such a sequence, if publicized, might be enough to pique extra interest, especially since those ancient problems are also very current ones. Of course, you would want to move clearly from problem to the saving power we find ultimately in the gospel of Jesus Christ.

Note especially August 15, because it has two possible sets of lessons, which highlights another aspect of context. The gospel hasn't traveled through a vacuum as it made its way from Jesus to us. In between it interacted with saints of previous eras, and they provided their own stories that can add richness to our own gospel encounters. Note the lesser festivals and commemorations that fall on Sundays in this season. On July 11, we remember Benedict of Nursia, the founder of the Benedictine order and indeed of all Western monasticism, driven to that by the licentiousness of society. July 25 brings us the feast of St. James the Elder, one of the "sons of thunder" and the only apostle whose death is recorded in the Bible. Another monastic founder, Dominic, was added to our calendar after *Lutheran Book of Worship*; his commemoration falls on August 8. He battled heretics and founded the Dominicans who would sponsor the Inquisition, yet he favored kindness and gentle argument. On August 15, we celebrate the saint most revered by all Christians (including Martin Luther): Mary, Mother of Our Lord. What can her example of courageous submission say to us?

In the end, the context for the gospel is as broad and deep as all of humanity—encompassing deep and shameful sinfulness, heroic and inspired saintliness, and every possible gradient between. Make the connection between people past and present and the good news of God in Christ, and watch the glorious sparks fly!

231

Shape *of* Worship *for the* Season

BASIC SHAPE OF THE EUCHARISTIC RITE

- Confession and Forgiveness: see alternate worship text for summer on page 243 as an option to the form in the liturgy setting

GATHERING

- Greeting: see alternate worship text for summer
- Omit the Kyrie during the summer (except on the festival of the Holy Trinity and perhaps St. James the Elder and Mary, Mother of Our Lord)
- Omit or use the hymn of praise during the summer (use for the festival of the Holy Trinity and saints' days)

WORD

- Use the Nicene Creed for Holy Trinity and saints' days; use the Apostles' Creed for remaining Sundays in this season
- The prayers: see the prayers for each Sunday in the summer section

MEAL

- Offertory prayer: see alternate worship text for summer
- Use the proper preface for Holy Trinity on the festival of the Holy Trinity, the proper preface for Apostles on the festival of St. James, and the proper preface for All Saints on the festival of Mary, Mother of Our Lord; use the proper preface for Sundays after Pentecost for the remainder of the season

- Eucharistic prayer: in addition to four main options in *LBW*, see "Eucharistic Prayer G: Summer" in *WOV* Leaders Edition, p. 71
- Invitation to communion: see alternate worship text for summer
- Post-communion prayer: see alternate worship text for summer

SENDING

- Benediction: see alternate worship text for summer
- Dismissal: see alternate worship text for summer

OTHER SEASONAL POSSIBILITIES

BLESSING FOR TRAVELERS

- Use the prayer "Before Travel" in *LBW*, p. 167, before the benediction whenever groups from the congregation set out to travel. The names of those traveling may be inserted in the prayer.

FAREWELL AND GODSPEED

- See *Occasional Services*, pp. 151–52, for an order that is appropriate whenever people are transferring out of the congregation; it may be used either after the prayers or following the post-communion prayer.

232

Assembly Song *for the* Season

Summer's long weeks, even with less-active choral

and vocal forces, can be a marvelous time to

bolster congregational singing. Take time to explore

old-fashioned and refashioned psalms, hymns, and songs, especially those from *Renewing Worship 1: Congregational Song* (RW1) and the *Renewing Worship Songbook.*

GATHERING

During the "green season," assemblies need not sing both Kyrie and hymn of praise, so you have a good opportunity to focus on some new pieces for one or the other of those spots. For instance, try a new Kyrie setting, such as "Señor, ten piedad" (WOV 605, TFF 23), accompanied by guitar, autoharp, or piano, or "Lord, Have Mercy/Nkosi, Nkosi" (TFF 22) sung a cappella.

For the hymn of praise, explore a gospel-style setting of "Glory to God in the highest" at WOV 606, using piano and a small acoustic band. Alternate with "This is the feast of victory" (WOV 608). Offer solo sections to the vocal team, and encourage vocal improvisation, while the assembly sings the refrain, accompanied by keyboard and plucked bass.

WORD

In addition to singing the psalms to pointed *LBW* tones such as 1, 3, and 8, summer is a good time to sing metrical settings of the psalms. One good source is *A New Metrical Psalter* by Christopher L. Webber (Church Hymnal Corporation, 1986).

At the verse, sing one of the standards found in *LBW*, *WOV*, and *TFF*, or the chant "Alleluia" (WOV 611a). Another interesting option is to sing "Heleluyan" (WOV 609) as a round, led by a strong vocal leader with perhaps a single drum beat or one stomp of the foot per measure.

MEAL

At the offertory try a new text on an old tune, "Oh, what shall I render" (RW1 56). Sing simple hymn settings of "Holy, Holy, Holy, Lord" and "Lamb of God" (WOV 616a, 616b) using piano or small acoustic ensemble, or even a cappella. Also consider "O Lamb of God, you bear the sin" (RW1 53). At communion sing "Cup of blessing that we share" (RW1 23).

SENDING

Explore a renewed text with a familiar tune in "Thank the Lord, your voices raise" (RW1 70). Two other effective post-communion songs are "Now, Lord, you let your servant go in peace" (WOV 624); use with piano, guitar, and light trap set. Another option is "In the Lord I'll be ever thankful" (*Taizé: Songs for Prayer*, p. 20, GIA G-4956) with congregational ostinato refrain, solo verses sung over the refrain, and simple accompaniment, such as guitar, piano, organ.

233

Music *for the* Season

VERSE AND OFFERTORY

Cherwien, David. *Verses for the Season of Pentecost, Set 1.* U, kybd.
MSM 80-541.

Gospel Acclamations. Cant, choir, cong, inst. MAY 0862096324.

Powell, Robert. *Verses and Offertory Sentences,* Part VI (Pentecost 10–18).
CPH 97-5506.

Schiavone, J. *Gospel Acclamation Verses for Sundays of the Year,* I, II, III.
GIA G-2495, 2496, 2497.

Verses and Offertory Sentences, Part V (Pentecost 2–9). U/SATB, kybd.
CPH 97-5505.

CHORAL

Ahlen, Waldemar. "The Earth Adorned." SATB. WAL WH-126.

Fauré, Gabriel. "Vocalise" in *To God Will I Sing.* AFP 0800674332
(MH voice); AFP 0800674340 (ML voice).

Hopson, Hal H. "Praise the Lord." SAB, kybd. AFP 0800674626.

Mendelssohn, Felix. "They That Shall Endure to the End" in *Chantry
Choirbook.* SATB. AFP 0800657772.

Rutter, John. "For the Beauty of the Earth." SATB, kybd.
HIN HMC-550.

Schütz, Heinrich. "Sing to the Lord" in *Chantry Choirbook.* SATB,
kybd. AFP 0800657772.

Scott, K. Lee. "Thy Perfect Love" in *Sing Forth God's Praise.* AFP
0800675266 (MH voice); AFP 080067538X (ML voice).

Stearns, M.B. *Lift Up Your Voice.* M voice solo, kybd. PRE 491-00002.

The Augsburg Easy Choirbook. AFP 0800676025.

Walters, Richard. *The Oratorio Anthology.* Four vols. for S, A, T, B solo
vcs, kybd. HAL 00747058 (S); HAL 00747059 (A);
HAL 00747060 (T); HAL 00747061 (B).

CHILDREN'S CHOIR

Bågenfelt, Susanne. "For a Sunrise in the Morning." U/2 pt, pno, opt
perc. AFP 0800675517.

Cool, Jayne Southwick. "Make Your Life a Song to God." U/2 pt,
pno, opt perc. CG CGA809.

Hopson, Hal H. "O Praise the Lord, Who Made All Beauty." U,
kybd. CG CGA143.

King, Gordon. "Come and Sing." U, kybd, opt 12 hb, 3 oct range.
GIA G-5255.

Paige, Jon. "There Is a New Song." 2 pt, kybd. FLA EA5133.

KEYBOARD/INSTRUMENTAL

Carter, John. "Hymn of Promise" in *Today's Hymns and Songs for Organ.*
Org. HOP 8066. Also under same title for piano.

Franck, César. "Cantabile" in *Selected Works for Organ.* Org. Schirmer ed.

Young, Gordon. "Hymn to Joy; Mercy; Dominus Regit Me; Cru-
sader's Hymn" in *Chorale Preludes on Seven Hymn Tunes.* Org.
FLA 3762.

HANDBELL

Afdahl, Lee J. "Round Me Rings." 3-5 oct, fl. LOR 20/1221L.

Behnke, John A. "When Morning Gilds the Skies." 3-5 oct.
AFP 0800674863.

Edwards, Dan R. "Arise and Praise." 3-4 oct. CG CGB181.

McFadden, Jane. "All Things Bright and Beautiful." 3-5 oct.
BEC HB164.

PRAISE ENSEMBLE

Morgan, Reuben. "What the Lord Has Done in Me." *Worship Leader's
Song Discovery,* vol. 29. Worship Leader 2001-11-LS.

Paris, Twila. "He is Exalted" in W&P.

Sims, Randy, arr. Dan Goeller. "You Are the Lord of Me." SAB,
opt C inst, cong. AFP 0800674421.

Smith, Martin. "Shout to the North" in *Best of the Best.*
FEL 1891062018.

Smith, Michael W. and Deborah D. Smith. "Great Is the Lord" in
W&P.

234

Alternate Worship Texts

CONFESSION AND FORGIVENESS

In the name of the Father, and of the ✛ Son,
and of the Holy Spirit.
Amen

God, whose love is everlasting,
welcomes sinners to the table of mercy.
Let us confess our sin, confident in God's forgiveness.

Silence for reflection and self-examination.

Gracious God,
have mercy on us.
In your gracious compassion forgive us our sins,
both known and unknown,
things done and left undone.
Uphold us by your Spirit
so that we may serve you in newness of life,
to the honor and glory of your holy name,
through Jesus Christ our Lord. Amen

Since we are justified by God's grace through faith,
we have peace with God through our Lord Jesus Christ.
Almighty God has mercy on you,
forgives you all your sins,
and will bring you to life everlasting.
Amen

GREETING

Sisters and brothers, called to freedom in Christ:
Grace, mercy, and peace be with you all.
And also with you.

PRAYERS

Confident in God's steadfast love through Jesus Christ
and guided by the Holy Spirit, let us pray for the church,
the world, and all people according to their needs.

A brief silence.

Each petition ends:

God of grace,
let our prayer come before you.

Concluding petition:

Teach us to pray, O God,
and grant to all for whom we pray
the good gifts that you have promised,
through Jesus Christ our Lord.
Amen

OFFERTORY PRAYER

Gracious God,
you open your hand,
filling our lives with all good things
and renewing the face of the earth.
We offer these gifts in thanksgiving
for all that we have received from your bounty.
Accept them for the sake of him
who offered his life for us,
Jesus Christ our Lord. Amen

INVITATION TO COMMUNION

Come, all has been prepared;
eat and drink with delight, and be satisfied.

POST-COMMUNION PRAYER

God our creator,
at this table you have satisfied us
with the good things of your grace.
Fix our hearts on your mercy and truth,
that our lives may reflect your love for all creation;
through Jesus Christ our Lord.
Amen

BLESSING

Continue to walk in Christ Jesus,
rooted and built up in him.
Almighty God, Father, ✛ Son, and Holy Spirit,
bless you now and forever.
Amen

DISMISSAL

Go in peace to bear Christ's love to the world.
Thanks be to God.

235

June 6, 2004

The Holy Trinity

INTRODUCTION

Early Christians began to speak of the one God in three persons in order to describe more fully the wonder of salvation. God is above us, beside us, within us. God is our loving Father, our savior Jesus, our companion Spirit. To be baptized in this name is to enter into God's community.

PRAYER OF THE DAY

Almighty God our Father, dwelling in majesty and mystery, renewing and fulfilling creation by your eternal Spirit, and revealing your glory through our Lord, Jesus Christ: Cleanse us from doubt and fear, and enable us to worship you, with your Son and the Holy Spirit, one God, living and reigning, now and forever.

or

Almighty and ever-living God, you have given us grace, by the confession of the true faith, to acknowledge the glory of the eternal Trinity and, in the power of your divine majesty, to worship the unity. Keep us steadfast in this faith and worship, and bring us at last to see you in your eternal glory, one God, now and forever.

VERSE

Alleluia. Holy, holy, holy is the Lord of hosts; the whole earth is full of his glory. Alleluia. (Isa. 6:3)

READINGS

Proverbs 8:1-4, 22-31

In the Bible, wisdom has many faces. It is portrayed in terms sometimes human and sometimes divine. Often, it is personified as feminine. In this passage, wisdom is depicted not only as a creation of God, but also as part of God's creative activity.

Psalm 8

Your majesty is praised above the heavens. (Ps. 8:2)

Romans 5:1-5

Paul describes the life of faith with reference to God, Jesus, and the Holy Spirit. Even now, we have peace with God through Jesus, and our hope for the future is grounded in the love of God that we experience through the Spirit.

John 16:12-15

The Spirit, sent by the Father, reveals God's truth by glorifying the Son and making him known.

COLOR   White

THE PRAYERS

Confident in God's steadfast love through Jesus Christ and guided by the Holy Spirit, let us pray for the church, the world, and all people according to their needs.
A BRIEF SILENCE.

God of wisdom, guide your church into all truth, that we may profess before the world your majesty, mystery, and delight in all of humanity. God of grace,
let our prayer come before you.

God of all the living, implant in the hearts of all people a sense of awe for your creation, that the nations and peoples of the world may become better stewards and caretakers of the earth. God of grace,
let our prayer come before you.

God of truth, empower and strengthen those who struggle to live with dignity: those who are poor, homeless, abused, and refugees, that they may know that you have crowned them with glory and honor. God of grace,
let our prayer come before you.

God of love, lift up all those suffering from illness and grief *(especially)*, and strengthen them with the hope that does not disappoint those who belong to you. God of grace,
let our prayer come before you.

HERE OTHER INTERCESSIONS MAY BE OFFERED.

God and Father, dwelling in community with the Son and Holy Spirit, bring us with *(names,* and) all your saints and martyrs to share in full communion with you in heaven. God of grace,
let our prayer come before you.

Teach us to pray, O God, and grant to all for whom we pray the good gifts that you have promised, through Jesus Christ our Lord.
Amen

236

IMAGES FOR PREACHING

Returning from foreign travel, U.S. citizens are obliged to declare their purchases. Travelers make a final inventory of what they have acquired and come clean.

Making declarations happens in other areas of life too. Lovers declare their affection for one another, which may lead to a further declaration of love and fidelity in marriage. In early July, Americans celebrate the ratification of the ground-breaking Declaration of Independence, acknowledging and declaring that "we hold these truths to be self-evident. . . ."

In the midst of John's lengthy narrative of Jesus' final meal with his disciples—it goes on for five chapters—Jesus declares certain things to and for them. He declares that the Spirit of truth will come and guide them into all the truth, a declaration both profound and provocative. For one thing, it continues the conversation begun last week in chapter 14 when Jesus anticipated the Advocate, the Holy Spirit sent by the Father. Further, this Spirit talk anticipates Jesus' breathing on the disciples after his resurrection in chapter 20 with the declaration, "Receive the Holy Spirit." The sound waves of this proclamation energized the lives of the disciples, for upon receiving the Spirit, they went forth to witness to the world.

The long season of the church before us presents ample opportunity for *us* also to breathe in the Spirit and exhale the truth of the triune God. Our redemptive "declaration of dependence" begins when we allow the Spirit of truth to guide us into all the truth. The Spirit bears fruit in lives that follow where the Spirit leads. The catechism reminds us that the Holy Spirit calls us, forgives all sins, and raises us from the dead.

This enlivening Spirit supplies the breath for our proclamation and the steam for service every day and in every place. The Spirit sustains us in our sufferings and provides the buoyancy for our hope, as Paul says in Romans 5. Called and sent by the Spirit of truth, we have much to declare.

WORSHIP MATTERS

Have you ever heard someone say, "Oh, that pastor has a pulpit voice"? Usually such comments are not intended as compliments. The listener has concluded that there is one "voice" for worship or preaching and another "voice" for the coffee hour or casual conversation. For many people, such vocal changes signal a separation between worship and daily life. Or they suggest that the pastor as presiding minister is a performer rather than a leader of the assembly's prayer and praise.

Leading worship and preaching are ordinary acts of communication. They no more require a special voice than a Bible requires colorful inks or special illustrations. Of course, one of the easiest and most difficult ways to assess vocal communication is to have oneself video- (or at least audio-) taped throughout the entire service. Review the tape and listen for different "voices." When do they speak and how do they influence what listeners hear?

LET THE CHILDREN COME

When we are baptized, we are marked with the cross of Christ forever. Today teach the children (and the congregation) to make the sign of the cross in celebration of the triune God: God who dwells throughout creation, God who dwells in our midst, and God who dwells within us.

God be in my head. (Touch forehead.)
God be in my heart. (Touch chest.)
God be on my left. (Touch left shoulder.)
God be on my right. (Touch right shoulder.)

HYMNS FOR WORSHIP
GATHERING

Holy God, we praise your name   LBW 535
Glory to God, we give you thanks   WOV 787
In the name of the Father   TFF 142

HYMN OF THE DAY

Creator Spirit, by whose aid   LBW 164

ALTERNATE HYMN OF THE DAY

Father most holy   LBW 169
My Lord of light   WOV 796

COMMUNION

Now the silence   LBW 205
Gracious Spirit, heed our pleading   WOV 687, TFF 103

SENDING

Now thank we all our God   LBW 533, 534
On our way rejoicing   LBW 260
Holy, holy   W&P 60

ADDITIONAL HYMNS AND SONGS

Come, join the dance of Trinity   RWSB

Holy, holy   W&P 60, RWSB

O Trinity, O Trinity   HS98 836

I believe in God   TFF 204

MUSIC FOR THE DAY

PSALMODY

Cooney, Rory. "How Glorious Is Your Name" in PCY, vol. 4.

Cox, Joe. "O Lord, Our Lord, How Majestic Is Your Name" in *Psalms for the People of God.* SMP 45/1037S.

Hanson, Handt. "Psalm 8" in *Spirit Touching Spirit.* CCF.

Hopson, Hal H. "Psalm 8" in *TP.*

Shields, Valerie. PW , Cycle C.

CHORAL

Ellingboe, Bradley. "The Holy Trinity." 2 pt mxd, pno. KJO 6298.

Haydn, F.J. "Achieved Is the Glorious Work" in *The Creation.* SATB, org. Gsch S-003-02358-00.

Nygard, Jr., Carl J. "Resurrection Hymn." SATB, org, opt brass. AFP 0800675509.

Scott, K. Lee. "Trinitarian Blessings" in *Sing Forth God's Praise.* AFP 0800675266 (MH voice); AFP 080067538X (ML voice).

Turner, C. Kenneth. "O Trinity Most Blessed Light" in *Anthems for Choirs 1.* SATB div, org. OXF 353214X.

Willan, Healey. "Holy, Holy, Holy Is the Lord." SATB, org. CPH 98-1553.

CHILDREN'S CHOIR

Hopson, Hal H. "Lord, O Lord, Your Name is Wonderful." (Ps. 8) U, kybd, opt 6 hb. CG CGA762.

Perry, Dave and Jean Perry. "Praise Canon." 2 pt, kybd, opt 2 oct hb. Triune Music 10/2710K.

KEYBOARD/INSTRUMENTAL

David, Anne Marie. "Holy, Holy, Holy" in *Here I Am, Lord:* Piano Stylings. Pno. AFP 0800675665.

Farlee, Robert Buckley. "Nicaea" in *Gaudeamus!* Org. AFP 0800655389.

Honoré, Jeffrey. "Send Us Your Spirit" in *Contemporary Classics: OCP Organ Series Anthology,* vol. 3. Org. OCP 6837118130.

Post, Piet. "Fantasy on the Hymn 'Holy, Holy, Holy.' " Org. Ars Nova NR 493.

HANDBELL

Helman, Michael. "Holy, Holy, Holy." 3-5 oct, opt hc. LOR 20/1192L.

McChesney, Kevin. "Immortal, Invisible, God Only Wise." 2-3 oct. ALF 8629.

McChesney, Kevin. "Immortal, Invisible, God Only Wise." 3-5 oct. CPH 97-6559.

PRAISE ENSEMBLE

Baloche, Rita. "But for Your Grace" in *God of Wonders Songbook.* 2 pt trbl. HOS 20567.

Hayford, Jack. "Majesty" in W&P.

Zschech, Darlene. "The Potter's Hand" in *Best of the Best.* FEL 1891062018.

Monday, June 7

SEATTLE, CHIEF OF THE DUWAMISH CONFEDERACY, 1866

Noah Seattle was chief of the Suquamish tribe and later became chief of the Duwamish Confederacy, a tribal alliance. When the tribes were faced with an increase in white settlers, Seattle chose to live and work peacefully with them rather than engage in wars. After Seattle became a Roman Catholic, he began the practice of morning and evening prayer in the tribe, a practice that continued after his death. On the centennial of his birth, the city of Seattle—named for him against his wishes— erected a monument over his grave.

When parish groups gather today, remember Chief Seattle and his work as a peacemaker. Consider beginning or ending parish events with a simple form of morning or evening prayer, not only today, but as a regular part of the parish life.

Wednesday, June 9

COLUMBA, 597; AIDAN, 651; BEDE, 735; CONFESSORS

Today we commemorate three monks from the British Isles who kept alive the light of learning and devotion during the Middle Ages. Columba founded three monasteries, including one on the island of Iona, off the coast of Scotland. That monastery was left in ruins after the Reformation but today is home to an ecumenical religious community. Aidan was known for his pastoral style and ability to stir people to charity and good works. Bede was a Bible translator and scripture scholar. He wrote a history of the English church and was the first historian to date events *anno Domini* (A.D.). Bede is also known for his hymns, including "A hymn of glory let us sing!" (LBW 157).

Friday, June 11

ST. BARNABAS, APOSTLE

The Eastern church commemorates Barnabas as one of the seventy commissioned by Jesus. Though he was not among the twelve mentioned in the gospels, the book of Acts gives him the title of apostle. His name means "son of encouragement." When Paul came to Jerusalem after his conversion, Barnabas took him in over the fears of the other apostles, who doubted Paul's discipleship. Later, Paul and Barnabas traveled together on missions.

At the Council of Jerusalem, Barnabas defended the claims of Gentile Christians regarding the Mosaic law. How can his work on behalf of others and his support of other Christians serve as a model for contemporary Christians and churches?

June 13, 2004

Second Sunday after Pentecost
Proper 6

239

INTRODUCTION

Confession and forgiveness frequently serve as a doorway to worship. We come into God's presence not because we earn it, but purely as an act of grace. Today's readings introduce us to some of the world's great sinners, and we take our place among them, hungry to taste the wonderful love of God.

PRAYER OF THE DAY

God, our maker and redeemer, you have made us a new company of priests to bear witness to the Gospel. Enable us to be faithful to our calling to make known your promises to all the world; through your Son, Jesus Christ our Lord.

VERSE

Alleluia. Let your priests be clothed with righteousness; let your faithful people sing for joy. Alleluia. (Ps. 132:9)

READINGS

2 Samuel 11:26—12:10, 13-15

King David has misused his royal power by taking advantage of his neighbor Bathsheba and is responsible for killing her husband, Uriah, by sending him into battle without proper support to defend him. God sends the prophet Nathan to confront the king with his guilt.

Psalm 32

Then you forgave me the guilt of my sin. (Ps. 32:6)

Galatians 2:15-21

Paul explores the dynamics of grace. We are made right with God through Jesus and are crucified with Christ. We trade the old life of sin for a new life with God.

Luke 7:36—8:3

A forgiven sinner expresses great love for Jesus. This humble act reveals what is lacking in the self-righteous who feel no need to be forgiven.

Alternate First Reading/Psalm

1 Kings 21:1-10 [11-14] 15-21a

Ahab and Jezebel ruled Israel in the days of Elijah. After they cheated Naboth out of the vineyard that was his family inheritance, God sent the prophet to confront them with their sin.

Psalm 5:1-8

Lead me, O LORD, in your righteousness; make your way straight before me. (Ps. 5:8)

COLOR   Green

THE PRAYERS

Confident in God's steadfast love through Jesus Christ and guided by the Holy Spirit, let us pray for the church, the world, and all people according to their needs.

A BRIEF SILENCE.

Let us pray for the church, that God will empower all the church's members to be bold witnesses of the Christ who lives in them. God of grace,
let our prayer come before you.

Let us pray for the leaders of the world, that they will heed the prophetic voices in their midst speaking God's truth and justice. God of grace,
let our prayer come before you.

Let us pray for all those burdened with the weight of sin, that God will surround them with the assurance of forgiveness and give them upright hearts. God of grace,
let our prayer come before you.

Let us pray for the sick and dying *(especially)*, that God will strengthen, heal, and comfort them in every need. God of grace,
let our prayer come before you.

Let us pray for this congregation, that God will enliven in us joy in the confidence of forgiveness and strengthen our faith in Jesus Christ. God of grace,
let our prayer come before you.

HERE OTHER INTERCESSIONS MAY BE OFFERED.

Let us give thanks for *(names* and*)* all the faithful departed who have died and yet who through faith in Jesus Christ live in you. God of grace,
let our prayer come before you.

Teach us to pray, O God, and grant to all for whom we pray the good gifts that you have promised, through Jesus Christ our Lord.
Amen

IMAGES FOR PREACHING

Watch out what you do, for one thing leads to another. Parents frequently issue that admonition to headstrong children. The active conscience raises that warning when one is in the process of overeating. Teachers and pastors frequently stress the theme of courtesy and hospitality in human relations. Habits can spell the difference between whole and broken relationships. Watch what you are doing, therefore, for one thing leads to another.

When Jesus accepted the invitation to eat with Simon the Pharisee, he initiated a series of events in which one thing led to another. Entering the Pharisee's house, Jesus reclined for the meal. A woman, simply described as a sinner, approached Jesus and washed his feet with her copious tears. This kissing and anointing provoked disapproving thoughts in the mind of the Pharisee host. Somehow Jesus discerned the thought, leading him to tell a brief parable with a question about debt cancellation and love. Simon answered rightly, and Jesus then proceeded to speak about hospitality, love, sin, and forgiveness. Not everyone present liked the story. (*Who is this who even forgives sins?*) Yet it concluded with a surprising grace note. (*Your faith has saved you; go in peace.*) In other words, what began as an dinner invitation ended with a redemptive word.

It is a compelling word for all who have ears to hear. We are invited to a meal where we encounter the risen Christ. We sinners are free to approach the living Lord and receive forgiveness. We can read the story about a tearful woman and learn about hospitality and respect for the guest in our midst. If we listen, we hear the teacher observe that we should watch what we are doing, for one thing leads to another. An encounter with Jesus could take us anywhere.

WORSHIP MATTERS

The gospel reading for this Sunday is filled with an abundance of tactile, sensual actions: bathing feet with tears and then wiping them with hair, anointing feet with precious moisturizers, kissing. These are the gestures that parents offer their young children: they bathe, dry, moisten, and kiss. All these actions done with love are signs of a parent's care for the life of this child.

So it is in the liturgy. God comes to us and reveals a father's or a mother's love through simple actions: bathing, anointing, kissing. What is the fear that prevents so many of our churches from engaging in this "evangelization" of all the senses? Why do so many people accept a worship service filled with only words spoken and sung when the scriptures speak so clearly of the many bodily actions through which Christ embodied the reign of God's mercy and peace?

LET THE CHILDREN COME

This Sunday marks the beginning of "ordinary time" in the church year. We dress our sanctuary in green. The greens in God's creation are rich and varied, from dark green fir needles to bright green willow leaves. In advance of this Sunday invite the congregation to dress in green. Point out that all of us are part of God's amazing cre-

240

ation. Consider introducing the first two stanzas of "All creatures of our God and King" (LBW 527). In the upcoming five Sundays add a stanza until you have introduced all seven stanzas. Young children will quickly learn the refrain and will feel at ease as they sing a familiar hymn with their church family.

HYMNS FOR WORSHIP

GATHERING

Open now thy gates of beauty   LBW 250
God is here!   WOV 719

HYMN OF THE DAY

Healer of our every ill   WOV 738

ALTERNATE HYMN OF THE DAY

O Jesus, joy of loving hearts   LBW 356
You are my hiding place   W&P 160

COMMUNION

I lay my sins on Jesus   LBW 305
O Lord, we praise you   LBW 215

SENDING

My God, how wonderful thou art   LBW 524
Great is thy faithfulness   WOV 771

ADDITIONAL HYMNS AND SONGS

Give me a clean heart   RWSB, TFF 216
Heal this old heart   ASG 16
Wonderful grace of Jesus   TFF 184
Holy woman, graceful giver   OBS 100, RWSB

MUSIC FOR THE DAY

PSALMODY

Cooney, Rory. "Forgive the Wrong I Have Done" in PCY, vol. 4.
Haas, David. "God, I Confess My Wrong" in PCY, vol. 9.
Howard, Julie. *Sing for Joy: Psalm Settings for God's Children.*
   LP 0814620787.
Isele, David Clark and Hal H. Hopson. "Psalm 32" in TP.
Shields, Valerie. PW, Cycle C.
Stewart, Roy James. "I Turn to You, Lord" in PCY, vol. 5.
See Fourth Sunday in Lent and Proper 26.

CHORAL

Bach, J. S. "Salvation unto Us Has Come" in *Bach for All Seasons*. SATB.
   AFP 080065854X.

Handel, G.F. "How Beautiful Are the Feet of Them" in *Messiah*. S solo, kybd. Various ed.
Hilton, John, ed. K. Lee Scott. "Wilt Thou Forgive?" in *Sing Forth God's Praise*. AFP 0800675266 (MH voice); AFP 080067538X (ML voice).
Kallman, Daniel. "Walk as Children of Light." SATB, org.
   MSM 50-9047.
Livingston, Hugh. "O God Unseen Yet Ever Near." SATB, kybd.
   AFP 0800675436.
Walton, William. "A Litany" (Drop Slow Tears) in *Anthems for Choirs IV*. SATB. OXF 353018X.

CHILDREN'S CHOIR

Hanson, Handt. "Go in Peace and Serve the Lord" in LS. U, kybd.
Hopson, Hal H. "Come, Sing a Song to the Lord." U, kybd, opt perc.
   AFP 0800675460.
Ziegenhals, Harriet Ilse. "Sing, Dance, Clap Your Hands." (Ps. 32:11)
   U, opt desc, kybd. CG CGA625.

KEYBOARD/INSTRUMENTAL

Cherwien, David. "I Come With Joy" in *Evening and Morning: Hymn Settings for Organ*. Org. AFP 080067572X.
Honoré, Jeffrey. "Healer of Our Every Ill" in *Contemporary Hymn Settings for Organ*. Org. AFP 0800674782.
Lindberg, Oskar. "Gammal fäbodpsalm" in *Augsburg Organ Library: Epiphany*. Org. AFP 0800659341.

HANDBELL

Dobrinski, Cynthia. "Great Is Thy Faithfulness." AG 1279 (2 oct);
   AG 1280 (3-5 oct.).
McChesney, Kevin. "My Faith Looks Up to Thee." 3 oct. AG 1637.

PRAISE ENSEMBLE

Dyer, Scott and Joe Horness. "Everything I Am" in *Praise Hymns and Choruses*, 4th ed. MAR 3010130368.
Redman, Matt. "Friend of Sinners" in *Best of the Best*. FEL 1891062018.
Zschech, Darlene. "Shout to the Lord" in W&P.

Monday, June 14

BASIL THE GREAT, BISHOP OF CAESAREA, 379;
GREGORY OF NAZIANZUS, BISHOP OF CONSTANTINOPLE,
C. 389; GREGORY, BISHOP OF NYSSA, C. 385

These three are known as the Cappadocian fathers, and all three of them explored the mystery of the Holy Trinity.

241

Basil was influenced by his sister Macrina to live a monastic life, and he settled near his home. Basil's Longer Rule and Shorter Rule for monastic life are the basis for Eastern monasticism to this day. In his rule, he establishes a preference for communal, rather than eremetical monastic life by making the case that Christian love and service are by nature communal. Gregory of Nazianzus was sent to preach on behalf of the orthodox faith against the Arians in Constantinople, though the orthodox did not have a church there at the time. He defended orthodox trinitarian and christological doctrine, and his preaching won over the city. Gregory of Nyssa was the younger brother of Basil the Great. He is remembered as a writer on spiritual life and the contemplation of God in worship and sacraments.

June 20, 2004

Third Sunday after Pentecost
Proper 7

INTRODUCTION

Before God saves us in baptism, we are held prisoner to hostile spiritual forces. Some of them are known to us, and some are of our own making. Often we do not see or recognize the spirits that trouble us. As we come into God's presence today, a word of liberation is announced to us.

PRAYER OF THE DAY

O God our defender, storms rage about us and cause us to be afraid. Rescue your people from despair, deliver your sons and daughters from fear, and preserve us all from unbelief; through your Son, Jesus Christ our Lord.

VERSE

Alleluia. Because you are children, God has sent the Spirit of his Son into your hearts, crying, "Abba! Father!" Alleluia. (Gal. 4:6)

READINGS

Isaiah 65:1-9

The prophet announces God's impatience. The people's self-absorption is idolatry, and images from pagan worship fill this reading. Like a vintner who crushes the grape to release the wine, God will use Israel's exile to establish a new community of the faithful.

Psalm 22:18-27 (Psalm 22:19-28 NRSV)

In the midst of the congregation I will praise you. (Ps. 22:21)

Galatians 3:23-29

For Paul, baptism is a powerful bond that unites people in faith. Those who are baptized experience a radical equality that removes distinctions based on race, social class, or gender.

Luke 8:26-39

In response to being healed, the Gerasene indicated his willingness to be Jesus' disciple by sitting at Jesus' feet. Unlike the rest of the Gerasenes who, in their fear, ask Jesus to leave, the man who has been healed testifies to what Jesus has done for him.

Alternate First Reading/Psalm

1 Kings 19:1-4 [5-7] 8-15a

In the previous chapter, Elijah had triumphed over the prophets of Baal through the power of the Lord. Now, terrified by Queen Jezebel's threats, Elijah flees into the wilderness, where he seeks refuge at Horeb (Sinai), the mountain of God. God addresses Elijah's dejection by sending him on to Damascus to anoint Elisha as his successor.

Psalms 42 and 43

Send out your light and truth that they may lead me. (Ps. 43:3)

COLOR   Green

THE PRAYERS

Confident in God's steadfast love through Jesus Christ

and guided by the Holy Spirit, let us pray for the church, the world, and all people according to their needs.

A BRIEF SILENCE.

God of faithfulness, enliven all those baptized into Christ to be witnesses of the church's oneness in Christ Jesus, that all the world may be drawn to you. God of grace,

let our prayer come before you.

God of faithfulness, turn the hearts of the leaders of all nations to compassion for the poor and hungry everywhere and move them to action on behalf of all in need. God of grace,

let our prayer come before you.

God of faithfulness, protect and heal all those afflicted with the demons of despair, addiction, and abuse, that they may one day live to declare how much you have done for them. God of grace,

let our prayer come before you.

God of faithfulness, comfort the sick and the dying (*especially*) and let them experience your love through their families and those who care for them. God of grace,

let our prayer come before you.

God of faithfulness, bless the fathers in our congregation and fathers everywhere with wisdom, patience, and understanding, that they may nurture with love and discipline the children you have entrusted to them. God of grace,

let our prayer come before you.

HERE OTHER INTERCESSIONS MAY BE OFFERED.

God of faithfulness, we give you thanks for all the faithful departed who are heirs according to your promise. Let their lives be for us models of faithfulness until we too join with them in praising you forever. God of grace,

let our prayer come before you.

Teach us to pray, O God, and grant to all for whom we pray the good gifts that you have promised, through Jesus Christ our Lord.

Amen

IMAGES FOR PREACHING

Chains, shackles, ranting demons, the destruction of a large herd of swine, the manifest fear of the onlookers, their desire to be rid of this disturbing healer-exorcist: this is a strange healing story. It is a noisy narrative full of sound and fury, violence and anxiety. Its elements seem to come from a film in the tradition of *The Exorcist*.

Yet there is still more going on in this scenario. When the story began, Jesus and his disciples entered a seemingly bucolic scene; but at story's end, Jesus left amid great agitation. The possessed man, however, at the outset shouted and raved, subject to demonic seizures. In the end, he calmly sat at Jesus' feet, clothed and in his right mind. He begged to accompany his liberator, but Jesus sent him home not to be a disciple but an evangelist.

The gyrations in this story are like one of those turbulent rides at the state fair. We know that things will turn out all right; but the ride, while it lasts, is choppy and unsettling. Likewise, this is a jarring healing story. The disturbing healer rousted the demons and sacrificed a herd of unclean animals in the process. He instilled so much fear in the populace that they begged him to leave the district. He made a convert, but he did not allow him to follow, though he did send him home to declare how much God had done for him. It is a story that zigs and zags like a bolt of lightning.

Most of all, it is a story about the one who still reaches out and breaks the chains that bind lives. He is the one who faces down demons and restores wholeness to broken lives. Having undergone the happy exchange, he takes our demons upon himself and gives health in return. In his unpredictably redemptive way Jesus sends his followers into the world to declare God's healing power. Jesus is both demon chaser and disturbing healer who offers—and gives—fullness of life to all in bondage.

WORSHIP MATTERS

Whether the context is a congregational meeting or a churchwide assembly, we often mistakenly think that in order for the church to be united we must all agree. Because there is no longer Jew or Greek, slave or free, male or female (Gal. 3:28), we think that we must agree in all things. In so thinking we mistake differences for divisions. Christ has not done away with our differences. Christ has overcome the power of our differences to divide us. The church is united not by our agreement, not by the fact that we are all the same, but because Christ Jesus has made us all children of God through faith (Gal. 3:26). Clothed in Christ through baptism, our differences become opportunities to creatively live out our calling as heirs according to God's promise (Gal. 3:29) within the one, catholic church.

243

LET THE CHILDREN COME

Even the youngest children understand the concept of family. When we are baptized we become part of a much larger family—God's family. Invite parents with younger children to be greeters today. Encourage the congregation to welcome visitors and help them to get settled into your church home. As you pass the peace, join hands with the people seated nearby to show that we are joined together in Christ's love. Add the third stanza to "All creatures of our God and King" (LBW 527), introduced in Proper 6.

HYMNS FOR WORSHIP

GATHERING

O Savior, precious Savior   LBW 514
He comes to us as one unknown   WOV 768
Here in this place   WOV 718

HYMN OF THE DAY

Oh, praise the gracious power   WOV 750

ALTERNATE HYMN OF THE DAY

Rise, shine, you people!   LBW 393
Let us put on the clothes of Christ   HFW

COMMUNION

Oh, that I had a thousand voices   LBW 560
One bread, one body   WOV 710

SENDING

My God, how wonderful thou art   LBW 524
Go, my children, with my blessing   WOV 721

ADDITIONAL HYMNS AND SONGS

We come to you for healing, Lord   RWSB
Shout to the Lord   W&P 127, RWSB
Satan, we're going to tear your kingdom down   TFF 207
Amid the thronging worshipers (Ps. 22)   TWC 340

MUSIC FOR THE DAY

PSALMODY

Guimont, Michel. "Psalm 22: I Will Praise You, Lord" in RS.
Hopson, Hal H. Psalm Refrains and Tones. HOP 425.
Hughes, Howard. *Psalms for all Seasons: An ICEL Collection.* OCP 6111.
Shields, Valerie. PW, Cycle C.
See Good Friday.

CHORAL

Bach, J. S. "Salvation unto Us Has Come" in *Bach for All Seasons.* SATB. AFP080065854X.
Berger, Jean. "The Eyes of All Wait upon Thee." SATB. AFP 0800645596.
Copland, Aaron. "Help Us, Lord." SATB. B&H 6018.
Ferguson, John. "By Gracious Powers." SATB, fl, org, opt cong. AFP 0800675495.
Zingarelli, Niccolò Antonio. "Go Not Far from Me, O God." SATB. Gsch 4889.

CHILDREN'S CHOIR

Mitchell, Tom. "Celebrate the Good News." (Gal. 3:28) 2 pt, kybd, opt hb, opt DB. CG CGA381.
Riehle, Kevin. "Song for Beginnings." (Ps. 22) U/2 pt, kybd, opt C inst, opt cong. CG CGA493.

KEYBOARD/INSTRUMENTAL

Fields, Tim. "All Hail the Power of Jesus' Name." Org. AFP 0800658736.
Hassell, Michael. "Jesus Loves Me" in *Jazz Americana.* Pno. AFP 0800675789.
Linker, Janet. "Blessed Assurance" in *John Ness Beck Favorites for Organ.* Org. BEC OC9.

HANDBELL

Linker, Janet and Jane McFadden. "Rise, Shine, You People." 3-5 oct, org, opt tpt. AFP 0800655044 (full score). OP. AFP 0800655052 (hb pt). OP.
Thompson, Martha Lynn. "God of Grace." 4-5 oct. MSM 30-810.

PRAISE ENSEMBLE

Founds, Rick. "Lord, I Lift Your Name on High!" in W&P.
Morgan, Reuben. "What the Lord Has Done in Me" in *Worship Leader's Song Discovery,* vol. 29. Worship Leader 2001-11-LS.
Sims, Randy, arr. Dan Goeller. "You Are the Lord of Me." SAB, pno, opt C inst, cong. AFP 0800674421.

Monday, June 21

ONESIMOS NESIB, TRANSLATOR, EVANGELIST, 1931

Onesimos was born in Ethiopia. He was captured by slave traders and taken from his Galla homeland to Eritrea, where he was bought, freed, and educated by Swedish missionaries. He translated the Bible into Galla and returned to his homeland to preach the gospel there. His tombstone includes a verse from Jeremiah 22:29, "O land, land, land, hear the word of the Lord!"

Does your congregation support mission work through synod or churchwide offerings, or do you support a specific missionary? Let the commemoration of Onesimos Nesib be a way for your congregations to focus on missions during the summer months.

Thursday, June 24

THE NATIVITY OF ST. JOHN THE BAPTIST

The Nativity of St. John the Baptist is celebrated exactly six months before Christmas Eve. For Christians in the Northern Hemisphere, these two dates are deeply symbolic. John said that he must decrease as Jesus increased. John was born as the days are longest and then steadily decrease. Jesus was born as the days are shortest and then steadily increase. In many countries this day is celebrated with customs associated with the summer solstice. Midsummer is especially popular in northern European countries that experience few hours of darkness at this time of year.

At this time of year, parishes could consider having a summer festival shaped by the pattern of the liturgical year. Consider a church picnic on or near this date, and use John's traditional symbols of fire and water in decorations and games.

Friday, June 25

PRESENTATION OF THE AUGSBURG CONFESSION, 1530; PHILIPP MELANCHTHON, RENEWER OF THE CHURCH, 1560

The University of Wittenberg hired Melanchthon as its first professor of Greek, and there he became a friend of Martin Luther. Melanchthon was a popular professor—even his classes at six in the morning had as many as six hundred students. As a reformer he was known for his conciliatory spirit and for finding areas of agreement with fellow Christians. He was never ordained. On this day in 1530 the German and Latin editions of the Augsburg Confession were presented to Emperor Charles of the Holy Roman Empire. The Augsburg Confession was written by Melanchthon and endorsed by Luther. In 1580 when the Book of Concord was drawn up, the unaltered Augsburg Confession was included as the principal Lutheran confession.

In the spirit of Melanchthon's work, consider a summer ecumenical study group with a nearby Roman Catholic parish. Use the Augsburg Confession and the Joint Declaration on the Doctrine of Justification as study documents.

245

June 27, 2004

Fourth Sunday after Pentecost
Proper 8

INTRODUCTION

As we are called by Jesus, we leave one life behind and take up another. The readings for this day invite us to take the bold step that brings us into a new world—one that asks of us a radical commitment to the freedom and risk of the gospel.

PRAYER OF THE DAY

O God, you have prepared for those who love you joys beyond understanding. Pour into our hearts such love for you that, loving you above all things, we may obtain your promises, which exceed all that we can desire; through your Son, Jesus Christ our Lord.

VERSE

Alleluia. May the God of our Lord Jesus Christ enlighten the eyes of our hearts that we may know the hope to which he has called us. Alleluia. (Eph. 1:17-18)

READINGS

1 Kings 19:15-16, 19-21

In the story preceding today's reading, the prophet Elijah flees for his life to the security of God's mountain. There the Lord reveals to Elijah the work that is to be done and promises to be present wherever God's people are faithful in their work.

Psalm 16

I have set the LORD always before me. (Ps. 16:8)

Galatians 5:1, 13-25

For Paul, the freedom Christ gives is not permission to do whatever we want. It is the ability to be what we could not be otherwise. The power and guidance of the Spirit produce a different kind of life, one marked by the qualities Paul lists in this reading.

Luke 9:51-62

Luke's gospel describes a long journey to Jerusalem during which Jesus teaches his followers about the costs of discipleship. Today's reading describes the outset of this journey and the resolute action needed for travel.

246

Alternate First Reading/Psalm

2 Kings 2:1-2, 6-14

Elijah's ministry comes to a successful conclusion, and a new chapter of the story begins as Elisha accepts the spirit of his teacher to carry on God's ministry.

Psalm 77:1-2, 11-20

By your strength you have redeemed your people. (Ps. 77:15)

COLOR   Green

THE PRAYERS

Confident in God's steadfast love through Jesus Christ and guided by the Holy Spirit, let us pray for the church, the world, and all people according to their needs.

A BRIEF SILENCE.

That your whole church, bishops, pastors, diaconal ministers, associates in ministry, and all the baptized may be led by your Spirit to answer Christ's call and proclaim the reign of God, we cry out: God of grace,

let our prayer come before you.

That all who till the land may be blessed with favorable weather, abundant yields, and fair prices so that there may be peace and prosperity throughout the world, we cry out: God of grace,

let our prayer come before you.

That all people in need, those enslaved by others, those persecuted for following Christ, those who are sick, dying, or in despair *(especially)* may live and die in the confidence that you are their saving help, we cry out: God of grace,

let our prayer come before you.

That those from our congregation who are vacationing may experience rest and renewal and may return home safely, we cry out: God of grace,

let our prayer come before you.

HERE OTHER INTERCESSIONS MAY BE OFFERED.

We remember with thanksgiving the lives of those who answered Christ's call to follow him. That we, like those who have gone before us, may boldly proclaim you as our

chosen portion and lot, we cry: God of grace,
let our prayer come before you.
Teach us to pray, O God, and grant to all for whom we
pray the good gifts that you have promised, through
Jesus Christ our Lord.
Amen

IMAGES FOR PREACHING

It is appropriate that the disciples who suggested a fiery
fate for the Samaritan village were James and John. In
Mark 3:17 Jesus calls these sons of Zebedee "Boanerges,"
which means "Sons of Thunder." That designation suggests impetuous spirits and flashing tempers. Therefore it
is not surprising nor does it seem out of character for
James and John to want to command fire to come down
and consume the inhospitable Samaritan village.

Prejudice against Samaritans in general provoked
hostility among the wider population—which may help
explain why James and John were so willing to bring
down fire on the Samaritan village. Jesus, however, did
not share James and John's blistering approach and
looked more benignly on the people of this district. He
often favored the outcast—remember the good Samaritan and the woman at the well. Instead of firebombing
the village as the Zebedee brothers were eager to do,
Jesus rebuked the disciples.

This inversion of expectations suggests something
important about caring for those whom others despise
or reject. Jesus' unwillingness to approve harsh action
against outsiders (like the inhospitable village) strongly
hints that the disciples were under some obligation to
cultivate a more open and accepting attitude. It is worth
noting that, as the story unfolds, Jesus demonstrated a
more forgiving stance toward inhospitable Samaritans
than he did to those he met along the way, those who
balked when he issued the invitation to follow.

In this story Jesus is a man on a mission. He has set
his face to go to Jerusalem where he will be handed over
to die. Yet along the way, quite unexpectedly, he demonstrates an openness of mind to outsiders who were not
on the approved list and an impatience with those who
were. Disciples like James and John—and all who have
strong, firmly cemented opinions—are bound to be
caught off guard by the call and mission of Jesus.

WORSHIP MATTERS

What is the essence of presiding at Holy Communion?
Many would suggest that it is hospitality. A truly hospitable presider always will know what is coming next
and lead the people in prayer so they do not become ner-
vous or feel insecure. A thoughtful presider will take the
time during worship planning to imagine how people
will respond to hymns, anthems, and other optional portions of the service. The gracious presider will welcome
worshipers with gestures that are full without being the-
atrical, and so well-rehearsed that they are natural, a genuine part of each celebration. Through appropriate eye
contact, a pleasant facial expression, and unhurried
movements, the good presider will communicate that
each worshiper is a beloved child of God.

LET THE CHILDREN COME

In many places of the world summer is beginning. With
summer comes God's bountiful array of flowers, fruits,
and vegetables. Today place a large basket filled with nine
different fruits on the altar. After the worship service invite the congregation to eat fruit together to celebrate
the nine fruits of the Spirit. Pray to give thanks for these
sweet and juicy gifts. As you share this fellowship help
the children begin to sense that God fills us up with lots
of good things: love, joy, peace, patience, kindness, generosity, faithfulness, gentleness, and self-control. Add the
fourth stanza of "All creatures of our God and King"
(LBW 527), introduced in Proper 6.

HYMNS FOR WORSHIP
GATHERING
O Christ, our hope   LBW 300
Oh, sing to God above   WOV 726
Stand in the congregation   W&P 131, RWSB

HYMN OF THE DAY
Lord, thee I love with all my heart   LBW 325

ALTERNATE HYMN OF THE DAY
In the morning when I rise   WOV 777
O Jesus, I have promised   LBW 503

COMMUNION
You satisfy the hungry heart   WOV 711

247

I heard the voice of Jesus say   LBW 497, RWSB

SENDING

He leadeth me: oh, blessed thought!   LBW 501
Praise to you, O God of mercy   WOV 790

ADDITIONAL HYMNS AND SONGS

Lead me, guide me   TFF 70, RWSB
I can hear my Savior calling   TFF 146
O Christ, who called the Twelve   HFG 55
The summons   W&P 137, RWSB

MUSIC FOR THE DAY
PSALMODY

Haas, David. "Show Me the Path" in PCY, vol. 8.

Inwood, Paul. "Psalm 16: Center of My Life" in STP, vol. 1.

Makeever, Ray. "You Show Us the Path of Life" in *Joyous Light Evening Prayer.* AFP 0800659317.

Shields, Valerie. PW , Cycle C.

Soper, Scott. "Psalm 16: The Path of Life" in STP, vol. 3.

O God, protect me   SP 6

CHORAL

Wood, Charles. "King Jesus Had a Garden" in *Carols for Choirs I.* SATB. OXF 3532220.

Duruflé, Maurice. "Ubi caritas." SATB. DUR 312-41253.

Friedell, Harold W. "Draw Us in the Spirit's Tether." SATB, org. WAR CMR 2472.

Grieg, Edvard, arr. Oscar R. Overby. "God's Son Has Set Me Free." SATB. AFP 0800645561.

Hobby, Robert A. "Beloved, God's Chosen" in *To God Will I Sing.* AFP 0800674332 (MH voice); AFP 0800674340 (ML voice).

CHILDREN'S CHOIR

Christopherson, Dorothy. "God Our Maker, Give Us Peace." (Gal. 5:22) U/2 pt, kybd, opt cong, 8 hb/C inst. CG CGA632.

Dietterich, Philip. "Come One, Come All, Come Follow." (Luke 9:59-61) U, antiphonal vcs, kybd. CG CGA553.

KEYBOARD/INSTRUMENTAL

Behnke, John A. "Siyahamba" in *Three Global Songs.* Org. HOP 8057.

Hayes, Mark. "Just a Closer Walk with Thee" in *Well-Tempered Jazz.* Pno. SHW HE5044.

Johnson, David N. "Trumpet Tune in D" in *Trumpet Tunes for Organ.* Org. AFP 0800674820.

HANDBELL

Kinyon, Barbara Baltzer. "O Jesus, I Have Promised." 3-5 oct. BEC HB91.

Nelson, Susan T. "Give Me Jesus." 3-4 oct. AFP 0800658132.

PRAISE ENSEMBLE

Adler, Dan, arr. Dan Goeller. "Your Ways Are Right." SAB, kybd, opt cong. AFP 080067443X.

Cloninger, Claire and Martin J. Nystrom. "Come to the Table" in RW5.

Zschech, Darlene. "The Potter's Hands" in *Best of the Best.* FEL 1891062018.

Monday, June 28

IRENAEUS, BISHOP OF LYONS, C. 202

Irenaeus believed that the way to remain steadfast to the truth was to hold fast to the faith handed down from the apostles. He believed that only Matthew, Mark, Luke, and John were trustworthy gospels. Irenaeus was an opponent of gnosticism and its emphasis on dualism. As a result of his battles with the gnostics he was one of the first to speak of the church as "catholic." By "catholic" he meant that congregations did not exist by themselves, but were linked to one another throughout the whole church. He also maintained that this church was not contained within any national boundaries. He argued that the church's message was for all people, in contrast to the gnostics who emphasized "secret knowledge."

What do we mean when we say that the church is catholic and apostolic? How is the apostolic faith passed down through the generations?

Tuesday, June 29

ST. PETER AND ST. PAUL, APOSTLES

These two are an odd couple of biblical witnesses to be brought together in one commemoration. It appears that Peter would have gladly served as the editor of Paul's letters: in a letter attributed to Peter, he says that some things in Paul's letters are hard to understand. Paul's criticism of Peter is more blunt. In Galatians he points out ways that Peter was wrong. One of the things that unites Peter and Paul is the tradition that says they were martyred together

248

on this date in A.D. 67 or 68. What unites them more closely is their common confession of Jesus Christ. In the gospel reading Peter declares that Jesus is the Christ through whom the foundation of the church is established. In the second reading Paul tells the Corinthians that they are the temple of Christ. Together Peter and Paul lay a foundation and build the framework for our lives of faith through their proclamation of Jesus Christ.

Wednesday, June 30

JOHAN OLOF WALLIN, ARCHBISHOP OF UPPSALA, HYMNWRITER, 1839

Wallin was consecrated archbishop of Uppsala and primate of the Church of Sweden two years before his death. He was considered the leading churchman of his day in Sweden, yet his lasting fame rests upon his poetry and his hymns. Of the five hundred hymns in the Swedish hymnbook of 1819, 130 were written by Wallin, and approximately two hundred were revised or translated by him. For more than a century the Church of Sweden made no change in the 1819 hymnbook.

Three Wallin hymns are included in *Lutheran Book of Worship:* "All hail to you, O blessed morn!" (73), "We worship you, O God of might" (432), and "Christians, while on earth abiding" (440).

Thursday, July 1

CATHERINE WINKWORTH, 1878;
JOHN MASON NEALE, 1866; HYMNWRITERS

Neale was an English priest associated with the movement for church renewal at Cambridge. Winkworth lived most of her life in Manchester, where she was involved in promoting women's rights. These two hymnwriters translated many hymn texts into English. Catherine Winkworth devoted herself to the translation of German hymns, and John Mason Neale specialized in ancient Latin and Greek hymns. Winkworth has thirty hymns in *LBW*, and Neale has twenty-one. In addition, two texts by Neale are in *WOV*. Use the indexes at the back of both books to discover some of their most familiar translations.

249

July 4, 2004

Fifth Sunday after Pentecost
Proper 9

INTRODUCTION

We are nurtured; we are nurturing. Today's readings remind us how God cares for us. We are called to adopt God's sustaining ways. We are fed at the table, and we are sent into the world to care for others.

PRAYER OF THE DAY

God of glory and love, peace comes from you alone. Send us as peacemakers and witnesses to your kingdom, and fill our hearts with joy in your promises of salvation; through your Son, Jesus Christ our Lord.

VERSE

Alleluia. Happy are they who hear the word, hold it fast in an honest and good heart, and bear fruit with patient endurance. Alleluia. (Luke 8:15)

READINGS

Isaiah 66:10-14

Those who returned from the exile found that the hopes and expectations for the glorious restoration of Judah were not fulfilled. For these disappointed people, the prophet envisions salvation in the image of a nursing woman. Mother Jerusalem and a mothering God remind the community how they are sustained and supported.

Psalm 66:1-8 (Psalm 66:1-9 NRSV)

God holds our souls in life. (Ps. 66:8)

Galatians 6:[1-6] 7-16

In this letter, Paul insists that all people are made right with God through faith in Jesus Christ. Here Paul offers practical advice about how people who believe this truth will live, exercising common concern for one other in "the family of faith."

Luke 10:1-11, 16-20

Jesus commissions his followers to go where he would go and do what he would do. Risking hardship and danger, they offer peace and healing as signs that the reign of God is near.

Alternate First Reading/Psalm

2 Kings 5:1-14

Naaman, a Syrian general, suffers from leprosy. In this passage Elisha miraculously cures his illness, but only after Naaman realizes, with the help of his servants, that his real problem lies in his pride.

Psalm 30

My God, I cried out to you, and you restored me to health. (Ps. 30:2)

COLOR   Green

THE PRAYERS

Confident in God's steadfast love through Jesus Christ and guided by the Holy Spirit, let us pray for the church, the world, and all people according to their needs.

A BRIEF SILENCE.

Mothering God, watch over your church; bring forth from the church laborers to work in the plentiful harvest, so that your comfort and consolation may be known throughout the world. God of grace,

let our prayer come before you.

Mothering God, watch over our nation; let it be a place where individual freedom is guarded, where justice is upheld, where democracy flourishes, and where religious liberty is protected. God of grace,

let our prayer come before you.

Mothering God, comfort and nurse all your children in need; provide meaningful work and fair wages to the unemployed and underemployed; grant health and wholeness to the sick *(especially)*; give peace and companionship to the lonely. God of grace,

let our prayer come before you.

Mothering God, watch over our congregation; let us not grow weary in working for the good of all; use us to show forth your new creation. God of grace,

let our prayer come before you.

HERE OTHER INTERCESSIONS MAY BE OFFERED.

Mothering God, we give you thanks for the saints and martyrs. Nurture our faith in Christ so that throughout our lives we may rejoice that our names are written in heaven and look forward to sharing the joy of full communion with you and all whom you hold in life. God of grace,

let our prayer come before you.

Teach us to pray, O God, and grant to all for whom we pray the good gifts that you have promised, through Jesus Christ our Lord.

Amen

IMAGES FOR PREACHING

Much of the time the disciples tended to get things wrong, as when James and John wanted to bring down fire on a Samaritan village. But there were occasions when they seemed to get it right. When seventy selected followers went out in pairs against all odds, they returned astonished. They discovered that even the demons submitted to them. Jesus had told them how tough their mission could be. Yet when they returned, they came back with a glowing report.

Even when they managed to get it right, though, they still didn't get it *entirely* right. In this case Jesus affirmed what they had seen and done, and then he raised the ante. He indicated they would have the kind of authority that would allow them to tread on snakes and scorpions. Yet, he cautioned, they were not to be taken in by the special effects. Rather than being impressed with having power over the enemy on earth, they were to rejoice in their abiding relationship with their Father in heaven.

All who have been baptized in the name of the triune God are called and sent on some form of mission. Wherever they serve, many may feel unwelcome like sheep among wolves. On the other hand, some may experience the rare sight of watching Satan fall from heaven like a flash of lightning. Jesus seems to indicate that neither the struggle nor the achievement is the point of discipleship. The Lord of the harvest calls followers not to success but to faithfulness. What counts is not the spectacle nor our feelings. The abiding significance in serving Christ resides in the relationship with God. In the end, Jesus will call us to remember that we rejoice not over the spirits who submit but over the fact that our names are written in heaven.

WORSHIP MATTERS

In today's gospel, Jesus sends out workers into every town and every place. That mission has continued through the ages and to every corner of the world. The invitation to go out into the harvest has also been carried out by persons with many and diverse gifts. How do we celebrate all the diverse vocations and ministries in our communities in the midst of the liturgy? We could do it in the Easter season when the message of the resurrection is being spread. We could do it around Pentecost as the Holy Spirit's work among the nations is celebrated. We could do it in November, beginning with All Saints Day, when our thoughts are drawn to the harvest, to stewardship, and the fulfillment of all God's promises. Review and consider using these resources available in *Occasional Services*: Affirmation of the Vocation of Christians in the World (p. 147), Recognition of Ministries in the Congregation (p. 143), or General Order of Blessing (p. 183), adaptable for a variety of circumstances.

LET THE CHILDREN COME

In advance, encourage children to bring friends to worship today. (In the United States friends or relatives may be in town to celebrate this nation's independence.) What a wonderful way for young ones to discover that anyone can bring the good news to others. Provide a green ribbon for the guests to wear to match the paraments. Extend hospitality by recognizing them and greeting them after the service. Add the fifth stanza of "All creatures of our God and King" (LBW 527), introduced in Proper 6.

HYMNS FOR WORSHIP

GATHERING

Love divine, all loves excelling   LBW 315

Lord, you give the great commission   WOV 756

HYMN OF THE DAY

Hark, the voice of Jesus calling   LBW 381

ALTERNATE HYMN OF THE DAY

The summons   W&P 137, RWSB

We all are one in mission   WOV 755

251

COMMUNION

Spread, oh, spread almighty Word   LBW 379

Mothering God, you gave me birth   WOV 769

SENDING

Guide me ever, great Redeemer   LBW 343

Let us talents and tongues employ   WOV 754

ADDITIONAL HYMNS AND SONGS

Dancing at the harvest   DH 40

Lord Jesus, you shall be my song   RWSB

Glory and praise to our God   W&P 43, RWSB

Come, labor on   PH 415, HFW

MUSIC FOR THE DAY

PSALMODY

Cooney, Rory. "Let All the Earth Cry Out" in STP, vol. 4.

Haugen, Marty and David Haas. "Let All the Earth" in PCY, vol. 10.

Shields, Valerie. PW , Cycle C.

Warner, Steven C. "Psalm 66: Cry Out to the Lord" in STP, vol. 2.

CHORAL

Copland, Aaron. "Sing Ye Praises." SATB. B&H OCTB6021.

Handel, G.F. "Rejoice Greatly" in *Messiah.* S solo, kybd. Various ed.

Hopson, Hal H. "Sing Forth God's Glory." SAB, kybd. AFP 0800675444.

Mendelssohn, Felix. "For the Lord Will Lead" in *To God Will I Sing.* AFP 0800674332 (MH voice); AFP 0800674340 (ML voice).

Rutter, John. "Praise Ye the Lord." SATB, org. OXF E120.

CHILDREN'S CHOIR

Angerman, David. "The Lord Never Closes His Eyes." (Luke 10:3) U/2 pt, kybd, opt C inst. Triune Music 10/2175K.

Marshall, Jane. "Psalm 66:1-2" in *Psalms Together.* U, kybd. CG CGC18.

KEYBOARD/INSTRUMENTAL

Hassell, Michael. *Jazz Americana.* Pno. AFP 0800675789.

Hobby, Robert A. "This Is My Father's World" in *Three Hymns of Praise, Set 4.* Org. MSM 10-759.

Wagner, Douglas E. "Seek Ye First" in *Praise and Worship for Organ.* Org. HOP 8086.

Wold, Wayne L. *Harmonies of Liberty.* Org. AFP 0800675754.

HANDBELL

McFadden, Jane. "How Can I Keep from Singing?" 3-5 oct. AFP 0800658124.

Sherman, Arnold B. "America the Beautiful." 3-6 oct. RR HB0002.

Wagner, Douglas E. "Eternal God of Our Fathers." 4-5 oct. BEC HB51.

PRAISE ENSEMBLE

Hanson, Handt. "Go, Make Disciples" in *Spirit Calls . . . Rejoice.* SATB. CCF 0933173393 (pew ed); CCF 0933173385 (acc ed).

Schutte, Daniel. "Here I Am, Lord" in WOV.

Tuesday, July 6

JAN HUS, MARTYR, 1415

Jan Hus was a Bohemian priest who spoke against abuses in the church of his day in many of the same ways Luther would a century later. He spoke against the withholding of the cup at Holy Communion and because of this stance was excommunicated, not for heresy but for insubordination toward his archbishop. He preached against the selling of indulgences and was particularly mortified by the indulgence trade of two rival claimants to the papacy who were raising money for war against each other. He was found guilty of heresy by the Council of Constance and burned at the stake.

The followers of Jan Hus became known as the Czech Brethren and later became the Moravian Church. The Evangelical Lutheran Church in America and the Moravian Church in America are in full communion with each other.

July 11, 2004

Sixth Sunday after Pentecost
Proper 10

INTRODUCTION

God can be as near as a neighbor, and our opportunities
to share God's love are as close as the words that leave
our lips. The peace of Christ we exchange in this community we also take with us into the world to share with
others.

Today the church recalls the ground-breaking work
of Benedict of Nursia, a sixth-century Italian Christian
who was disturbed by the immorality of his time and responded by founding the Western monastic movement,
guided by the *Rule* he developed.

PRAYER OF THE DAY

Almighty God, we thank you for planting in us the seed
of your word. By your Holy Spirit help us to receive it
with joy, live according to it, and grow in faith and hope
and love; through your Son, Jesus Christ our Lord.
or
Lord God, use our lives to touch the world with your
love. Stir us, by your Spirit, to be neighbor to those in
need, serving them with willing hearts; through your
Son, Jesus Christ our Lord.

VERSE

Alleluia. The word is very near to you; it is in your
mouth and in your heart for you to observe. Alleluia.
(Deut. 30:14)

READINGS

Deuteronomy 30:9-14

Moses calls the people to renew the covenant God made
with their ancestors. Through this covenant God gives
life and asks obedience. God's word is brought near to
the people, so that they may remain true to the covenant.

Psalm 25:1-9 (Psalm 25:1-10 NRSV)

Show me your ways, O LORD, and teach me your paths.
(Ps. 25:3)

Colossians 1:1-14

The letter to the Colossians was written to warn its
readers of various false teachings. The first part of the
letter is an expression of thanks for the faith, hope, and
love that mark this community. It concludes with a
prayer for continued growth in understanding.

Luke 10:25-37

In this well-known parable, Jesus shifts the focus of concern from speculation concerning who is one's neighbor
to the treatment of one's neighbor with mercy.

Alternate First Reading/Psalm

Amos 7:7-17

Amos, a shepherd from the southern village of Tekoa, is
called by God to preach against Israel, the Northern
Kingdom, in a time of economic prosperity. Today's
reading illustrates how Amos's stinging criticism of
those in authority alienated him from both king and
priest.

Psalm 82

Arise, O God, and rule the earth. (Ps. 82:8)

COLOR   Green

THE PRAYERS

Confident in God's steadfast love through Jesus Christ
and guided by the Holy Spirit, let us pray for the church,
the world, and all people according to their needs.
A BRIEF SILENCE.

Let us pray for the whole church, that filled with your
Spirit, the church will, in action and word, proclaim
boldly the word of truth that is near, we pray: God of
grace,
let our prayer come before you.

Let us pray for all creation, that God will move nations
and peoples to be good stewards of the gifts of the earth
and work toward a sustainable world in which all might
share its blessings, we pray: God of grace,
let our prayer come before you.

Let us pray for all those abandoned and forgotten in our
world: those who are mentally ill or disabled, children
missing and living in neglect, those in nursing homes
without caring families. Increase our love for you, God,
so that we might show that love more fully to these
neighbors in need, we pray: God of grace,

253

let our prayer come before you.

Let us pray for all the sick and those close to death (*especially*), that God will prepare them to endure everything with patience and bring them to wholeness, we pray: God of grace,

let our prayer come before you.

Let us pray for this congregation, that through the word proclaimed and sacrament shared here, we might bear fruit and truly comprehend the grace of God, we pray: God of grace,

let our prayer come before you.

HERE OTHER INTERCESSIONS MAY BE OFFERED.

Let us thank God for the inheritance given to the saints in light, especially Benedict of Nursia, abbot and renewer of the church. May we follow his example of hospitality to strangers as a witness of our faith in Christ, we pray: God of grace,

let our prayer come before you.

Teach us to pray, O God, and grant to all for whom we pray the good gifts that you have promised, through Jesus Christ our Lord.

Amen

IMAGES FOR PREACHING

In 1633 Rembrandt van Rijn produced an etching of the Good Samaritan. One may find this work reproduced on page 413 in Simon Schama's book *Rembrandt's Eyes* (Alfred A. Knopf, 1999), or on the Web. Unlike other artists, Rembrandt chose to portray the story at the point where the Samaritan delivers the wounded man at an inn. He is being hauled like a sack of potatoes on the shoulder of a burly attendant. In the foreground a boy holds the reins of the sturdy horse, and off to the side a woman reaches into a well for water. This scene of bright light and deep shadow comes at the ending of Jesus' parable. In its muscular stillness the etching shows the practical result of the traveler's charity.

If viewers look closely, they will see a dog in the right foreground and become aware of an extraordinarily profane intrusion into this otherwise sacred scene. The dog unceremoniously squats, very clearly answering a call of nature. The pile of evidence is quite obvious, though the reason Rembrandt included this incongruous detail is not. It might make some blush and wish to turn the page. Yet the unexpected detail does say something about the juxtaposition of the profane with the sacred and the intrusion of the ordinary into an otherwise elevated narrative.

Perhaps Rembrandt was playing a visual joke. Or maybe he was performing a unique bit of exegesis. Jesus always emphasized the commonplace, using things like water, bread, and wine—even offal (Luke 13:8)—to make some uncommon statement about salvation. Today's story began with a lofty question about eternal life. At its conclusion Jesus commended an everyday act of mercy. He also instructed the listener to go and do likewise. For humans, eternal life is grounded in the ordinary, even gross, aspects of our world. There are almost always surprising messages hidden in the landscape well worth sniffing out. Even a squatting dog can support a larger truth.

WORSHIP MATTERS

How do we pray without ceasing (Col. 1:9)? Many of us find it difficult to slow the pace of our lives in order to find time to pray. The truth is that prayer is like exercise. We stay in shape by incorporating physical activity into our way of living. So Paul hints at some of the exercises we can do that will make for prayer-filled living. Always thank God, especially for faith. Seek God's will in all things. Lead lives worthy of the Lord. Be prepared to endure everything with patience. Even a few minutes of this kind of serious exercise every day will drive us to our knees, turn us to our God, and fill our lives with prayer.

LET THE CHILDREN COME

Teach the children the prayer response you will use for the intercessory prayers today. Consider singing a prayer response with instrumental accompaniment. Children easily learn musical phrases and will discover that we can pray by singing. You may also sing "Lord, listen to your children praying"(WOV 775). To carry daily prayers into the home, provide a children's bulletin that can easily transform into a prayer tent to place on the kitchen table. Add the sixth stanza of "All creatures of our God and King" (LBW 527), introduced in Proper 6.

HYMNS FOR WORSHIP
GATHERING

Open now thy gates of beauty   LBW 250
Be thou my vision   WOV 776

HYMN OF THE DAY

Forth in thy name, O Lord, I go   LBW 505

ALTERNATE HYMN OF THE DAY

Jesu, Jesu, fill us with your love   WOV 765, TFF 83

O God of mercy, God of light   LBW 425

COMMUNION

Joyful, joyful we adore thee   LBW 551

Where true charity and love abide / *Ubi caritas et amor*
WOV 665, RWI 92

SENDING

Lead on, O King eternal!   LBW 495

The Spirit sends us forth to serve   WOV 723

God forgave my sin in Jesus' name   TFF 187

ADDITIONAL HYMNS AND SONGS

Goodness is stronger than evil   RWSB

Make me a channel of your peace   W&P 95, RWSB

They asked, "Who's my neighbor?"   NCH 541

Help me, Jesus   TFF 224

MUSIC FOR THE DAY

PSALMODY

Artman, Ruth. "Teach Me Your Ways, O Lord" in *Sing Out! A Children's Psalter.* WLP 7191.

Haugen, Marty. "To You, O Lord" in PCY, vol. 10.

Kreutz, Robert. "Come, O Lord" in *Psalms and Selected Canticles.* OCP TM-8311.

Shields, Valerie. PW, Cycle C.

Soper, Scott. "Psalm 25: To You, O Lord" in STP, vol. 1.

See First Sunday in Advent.

CHORAL

Attwood, Thomas. "Teach Me, O Lord, the Way of Thy Statutes." SATB. GIA G-3045.

Bouman, Paul. "O God of Mercy" in *To God Will I Sing.* AFP 0800674332 (MH voice);   AFP 0800674340 (ML voice).

Jennings, Kenneth. "Thee Will I Love." SATB. KJO 8724.

Purcell, Henry. "Thou Knowest, Lord, the Secrets of Our Hearts." SATB, org. ECS No. 170 (376 Archive Reprints).

Roberts, J. Varley. "Seek Ye the Lord." SATB, T solo, kybd. Gsch 3731.

Wilby, Philip. "If Ye Love Me." SSATB, org.   PVN 8300561.

CHILDREN'S CHOIR

Horman, John. "The Good Samaritan." (Luke 10:25-37) 2 pt, kybd. CG CGA281.

Marshall, Jane. "Dear Lord, Lead Me Day by Day." (Ps. 25:5) U, kybd, opt fl. CG CGA637.

KEYBOARD/INSTRUMENTAL

Cherwien, David. "Guide Me, O Thou Great Jehovah" in *Interpretations, Book VI.* Org.   AMSI SP-103.

Linker, Janet. *Meditation and Variations on How Great Thou Art.* Org. BEC OC10.

Wold, Wayne L. *Eternal Father, Strong to Save.* Org. AFP 080067569X.

HANDBELL

Helman, Michael. "Jesu, Jesu, Fill Us with Your Love." 3-5 oct, opt hc. AFP 0800658876.

McChesney, Kevin. "Beach Spring." 2-3 oct. AFP 080065885X.

McChesney, Kevin. "Jesu, Jesu, Fill Us with Your Love." 2-3 oct. AFP 0800658116.

PRAISE ENSEMBLE

Adler, Dan, arr. Dan Goeller. "Make Me an Answer to Prayer." SAB, pno, 1/2 C inst, opt cong. AFP 0800674405.

Hanson, Handt. "Good Soil." in *Spirit Calls . . . Rejoice.* SATB. CCF 0933173393 (pew ed); CCF 0933173385 (acc ed).

Zehnder, Michael. "Someone Else Living in You" in *Best of the Best.* FEL 1891062018.

255

Sunday, July 11

BENEDICT OF NURSIA, ABBOT OF MONTE CASSINO, C. 540

Benedict is known as the father of Western monasticism. He was educated in Rome but was appalled by the decline of life around him. He went to live as a hermit, and a community of monks came to gather around him. In the prologue of his rule for monasteries he wrote that his intent in drawing up his regulations was "to set down nothing harsh, nothing burdensome." It is that moderate spirit that characterizes his rule and the monastic communities that are formed by it. Benedict encourages a generous spirit of hospitality in that visitors to Benedictine communities are to be welcomed as Christ himself.

Benedictine monasticism continues to serve a vital role in the contemporary church. A summer reading group might choose *A Share in the Kingdom* by Benet Tvedten, OSB (Liturgical Press, 1989) to learn about Benedict's Rule and hear this ancient voice speak to the church today.

Monday, July 12

NATHAN SÖDERBLOM, ARCHBISHOP OF UPPSALA, 1931

In 1930, this Swedish theologian, ecumenist, and social activist received the Nobel Prize for peace. He saw the value of the ancient worship of the catholic church and encouraged the liturgical movement. He also valued the work of liberal Protestant scholars and believed social action was a first step on the path toward a united Christianity. He organized the Universal Christian Council on Life and Work, which was one of the organizations that in 1948 came together to form the World Council of Churches.

As you commemorate Söderblom, discuss the ecumenical situation in the church now in this new millennium. What are some of the achievements of the past century? What hopes of Söderblom's might still wait to be achieved?

Thursday, July 15

VLADIMIR, FIRST CHRISTIAN RULER OF RUSSIA, 1015;
OLGA, CONFESSOR, 969

Princess Olga became a Christian about the time she made a visit to Constantinople, center of the Byzantine church. She had no success persuading her son or her fellow citizens to receive the gospel. Vladimir was Olga's grandson, and he took the throne at a ruthless time and in a bloodthirsty manner: he killed his brother for the right to rule. After Vladimir became a Christian he set aside the reminders of his earlier life, including pagan idols and temples. He built churches, monasteries, and schools, brought in Greek missionaries to educate the people, and was generous to the poor. Together Vladimir and Olga are honored as the first Christian rulers of Russia.

Saturday, July 17

BARTOLOMÉ DE LAS CASAS,
MISSIONARY TO THE INDIES, 1566

Bartolomé de las Casas was a Spanish priest and a missionary in the Western Hemisphere. He first came to the West while serving in the military, and he was granted a large estate that included a number of indigenous slaves. When he was ordained in 1513, he granted freedom to his servants. This act characterized much of the rest of de las Casas's ministry. Throughout the Caribbean and Central America he worked to stop the enslavement of native people, to halt the brutal treatment of women by military forces, and to promote laws that humanized the process of colonization.

In a time when churches continue to work for the rights of all people we can recall the words of de las Casas: "The Indians are our brothers, and Christ has given his life for them. Why, then, do we persecute them with such inhuman savagery when they do not deserve such treatment?"

July 18, 2004

Seventh Sunday after Pentecost
Proper 11

INTRODUCTION

Stay alert! You might be entertaining God! Today we are introduced to people who hosted God in their homes, although they were not always aware of God's presence. God comes close to us—even within us, as Paul exclaims.

PRAYER OF THE DAY

O Lord, pour out upon us the spirit to think and do what is right, that we, who cannot even exist without you, may have the strength to live according to your will; through your Son, Jesus Christ our Lord.

or

O God, you see how busy we are with many things. Turn us to listen to your teachings and lead us to choose the one thing which will not be taken from us, Jesus Christ our Lord.

VERSE

Alleluia. My word shall accomplish that which I purpose, and succeed in the thing for which I sent it. Alleluia. (Isa. 55:11)

READINGS

Genesis 18:1-10a

The Lord visits Abraham and Sarah and promises the birth of a child even though they are too old to start a family.

Psalm 15

Who may abide upon your holy hill? Whoever leads a blameless life and does what is right. (Ps. 15:1-2)

Colossians 1:15-28

The great mystery of God is "Christ in you." Because Christ is present in his body, the church, Christians share in his life, suffering, and glory.

Luke 10:38-42

Jesus speaks with two disciples. One is very busy, but the other sits quietly and listens.

Alternate First Reading/Psalm

Amos 8:1-12

Amos announces the coming of God's judgment upon the people of Israel, who have continued to oppress the poor, engage in unethical business practices, and break God's commands. Amos's vision is based on a Hebrew wordplay: he sees a basket of summer fruit *(qayits)* that will ripen at the end *(qets)* of the summer. The end of Israel will come through a famine of hearing the word of the Lord.

Psalm 52

I am like a green olive tree in the house of God. (Ps. 52:8)

COLOR   Green

THE PRAYERS

Confident in God's steadfast love through Jesus Christ and guided by the Holy Spirit, let us pray for the church, the world, and all people according to their needs.

A BRIEF SILENCE.

Give to your church, O God, faithful stewards of the mystery revealed in Christ Jesus that through Christ's body, the church, all people might be reconciled to you and brought to peace through the blood of the cross. God of grace,

let our prayer come before you.

We are easily distracted, O God. Guard us from the affliction of mere busyness, and even as we serve, keep our attention focused on your liberating gospel. God of grace,

let our prayer come before you.

Direct, O God, the leaders of all nations to work for the end of war, violence, and injustice in their lands that all people might live and prosper in peace and safety. God of grace,

let our prayer come before you.

Make your presence known, O God, to all who are sick or living without hope *(especially)*, that they might find strength and healing, and may trust in your lovingkindness. God of grace,

let our prayer come before you.

Move us, O God, to show hospitality to the stranger among us in our neighborhoods, our workplaces, and here in our worshiping assembly, that through our actions all might know that Christ holds first place in our lives.

257

God of grace,

let our prayer come before you.

HERE OTHER INTERCESSIONS MAY BE OFFERED.

We give you thanks, O God, for those whom you declared blameless through faith in your Son and who now dwell with you. Keep us also faithful to Christ, who is the beginning, the firstborn from the dead, and our end. God of grace,

let our prayer come before you.

Teach us to pray, O God, and grant to all for whom we pray the good gifts that you have promised, through Jesus Christ our Lord.

Amen

IMAGES FOR PREACHING

One of the awesome acts in the circus involves a troupe of performers who climb up or leap onto the shoulders of one another. By climbing and leaping, they fashion a shaky vertical column. When the feat is at its height, as many as six performers may be balanced one on top of another. If the timing were off, if someone leaped or leaned too far, the human tower would collapse and the balancing act would fall apart.

In discussions of ministry and vocation, matters of balance often arise. In order to keep from falling apart or burning out, it seems that an intentional balance needs to be struck between activity and leisure, between involvement and withdrawal, between work and family. If balances are not maintained, the structure of ministry (lay and ordained) eventually teeters and the joy of doing often becomes drudgery.

At the core of Jesus' encounter with Mary and Martha is this concern over balance. In commending Mary, Jesus did not deride Martha's work of hospitality. Rather, he expressed disquiet at her distraction. Jesus observed that she was so busy with work that she had lost her sense of balance and proportion, leaving insufficient room for the better part. It is as if one of the members of the troupe had overshot a leap, lost the balance, and landed topsy-turvy.

In a different story (John 11) Martha eventually got things right, her balance clearly in place. She was upset about her brother's death. Even so, she responded to Jesus in a way that showed she had regained her equilibrium. Questioned about resurrection and belief, Martha gave a commendably balanced response: "Yes, Lord, I believe that you are the Messiah, the Son of God, the one coming into the world"(John 11:27). When seeking to serve, busy is not bad; but balance is better.

WORSHIP MATTERS

Where would our worship be without the Marthas in our congregation? We need to thank those who prepare the altar, provide bread and wine, mark the Bible, light the candles, fill the font, pass out bulletins, greet visitors, sing, and chant, we sometimes we forget that these tasks are not ends in themselves, but are meant to help us receive God's gifts to us in word and sacrament. Sometimes we allow these tasks to become a burden that colors our whole experience of worship. Then we need to take a cue from Mary and sit at the Lord's feet, for the focus of our worship is God's gift of word and sacrament, and we cannot allow our works in ministry to take this gift from us.

LET THE CHILDREN COME

We celebrate Christ's presence in the eucharist, at one level a simple meal of bread and wine. Beginning this Sunday, serve bread that children and their families have baked. Invite others to help distribute the elements. Set up a schedule to follow throughout the summer months and into the fall. Children who bake bread and help serve eucharist will begin to sense that Christ's love comes to us in very real, ordinary ways. In some congregations, young children receive a blessing instead of a meal during Holy Communion. As they come forward for the blessing, take care so that each child may sense Christ's presence in a gentle touch and words of Jesus' love. Add the last stanza of "All creatures of our God and King" (LBW 527).

HYMNS FOR WORSHIP
GATHERING

When morning gilds the skies   LBW 545, 546

All things bright and beautiful   WOV 767

HYMN OF THE DAY

Be thou my vision   WOV 776

ALTERNATE HYMN OF THE DAY

Dearest Jesus, at your word   LBW 248

O Christ the same   WOV 778

COMMUNION

Jesus, the very thought of you   LBW 316

In the morning when I rise   WOV 777

SENDING

I love to tell the story   LBW 390, RWI 40

Oh, that the Lord would guide my ways   LBW 480

ADDITIONAL HYMNS AND SONGS

Come to me   RWSB

As the deer   W&P 9, RWSB

Jesus, we are gathered   TFF 140

MUSIC FOR THE DAY

PSALMODY

Gelineau, Joseph. "Psalm 15" in RS.

Haas, David. "They Who Do Justice" in PCY, vol. 3.

Hopson, Hal H. *Psalm Refrains and Tones.* HOP 425.

Paradowski, John. PW , Cycle C.

CHORAL

Bisbee, B. Wayne. "God of Peace." 2 pt mxd/equal vcs, kybd.
AFP 0800675126.

Dawson, William. "There Is A Balm in Gilead." SATB, S solo.
KJO T105.

Dvořák, Antonín. "Search Me, O God" in *Lift Up Your Voice.* M voice
solo, kybd.   PRE.

Lassus, Orlando. "Adoramus Te." SATB. PRE MC76.

Scott, K. Lee. "Redeeming Grace" in *Sing a Song of Joy: Vocal Solos for
Worship.* AFP 0800647882 (MH voice); AFP 0800652827
(ML voice).

CHILDREN'S CHOIR

Bach, J.S., arr. Stephen Roddy. "Rejoice, Ye Children of God." (Luke
10:38-42) U, kybd, opt fl. Gentry JG2246.

Wagner, Douglas E. "Sing, Sing." U, kybd. Triune Music 10/2460K.

KEYBOARD/INSTRUMENTAL

Harbach, Barbara. "On Our Way Rejoicing" in *On Our Way Rejoicing.*
Org. AFP 0800675657.

Rodriguez, Penny. "Be Thou My Vision" in *Images II.* Pno. BEC PC8.

Walther, Johann. "Praise to the Lord, the Almighty." Various ed. Also
in *The Complete Wedding Collection.* BEC OC21.

HANDBELL

McFadden, Jane. "Londonderry Air." (O Christ the Same) 2-3 oct,
opt hc. AFP 0800656296.

McKlveen, Paul. "Be Thou My Vision." 3-5 oct. ALF 16465.

PRAISE ENSEMBLE

Beaker. "Step by Step" in *More Songs for Praise and Worship.* SATB. WRD
3010387016 (vocal ed); WRD 3010186363 (pno, vcs, perc).

Jerrigan, Dennis. "You Are My All in All" in *Best of the Best.*
FEL 1891062018.

Thursday, July 22

ST. MARY MAGDALENE

The gospels report Mary Magdalene was one of the
women of Galilee who followed Jesus. She was present at
Jesus' crucifixion and his burial. When she went to the
tomb on the first day of the week to anoint Jesus' body,
she was the first person to whom the risen Lord appeared. She returned to the disciples with the news and
has been called "the apostle to the apostles" for her
proclamation of the resurrection. Because John's gospel
describes Mary as weeping at the tomb, she is often portrayed in art with red eyes. Icons depict her standing by
the tomb and holding a bright red egg.

This glimpse of Easter in the middle of summer invites us to keep our eyes open for the signs of Christ's
resurrection and new life that are always around us.

Friday, July 23

BIRGITTA OF SWEDEN, 1373

Birgitta was married at age thirteen and had four daughters with her husband. She was a woman of some standing
who, in her early thirties, served as the chief lady-in-
waiting to the Queen of Sweden. She was widowed at the
age of thirty-eight, shortly after she and her husband had
made a religious pilgrimage. Following the death of her
husband the religious dreams and visions that had begun
in her youth occurred more regularly. Her devotional
commitments led her to give to the poor and needy all
that she owned while she began to live a more ascetic life.
She founded an order of monks and nuns, the Order of
the Holy Savior (Birgittines), whose superior was a
woman. Today the Society of St. Birgitta is a laypersons'
society that continues her work of prayer and charity.

259

July 25, 2004

St. James the Elder, Apostle

INTRODUCTION

James, brother of John and son of Zebedee, had a remarkable journey with Jesus and beyond. Called from their father's fishing boat, James and John became committed, if sometimes contentious, disciples—to the extent that they earned the nickname "sons of thunder." But James was indeed faithful unto death, becoming the first apostle to be martyred for his faith, the only death of an apostle recorded in the Bible.

PRAYER OF THE DAY

O gracious God, we remember before you today your servant and apostle James, first among the Twelve to suffer martyrdom for the name of Jesus Christ. Pour out upon the leaders of your Church that spirit of self-denying service which is the true mark of authority among your people; through Jesus Christ our Lord, who lives and reigns with you and the Holy Spirit, one God, now and forever.

VERSE

Alleluia. Blessed are those who are persecuted for righteousness' sake, for theirs is the kingdom of heaven. Alleluia. (Matt. 5:10)

READINGS

1 Kings 19:9-18

After great cataclysmic events, Elijah hears God in the silence.

Psalm 7:1-11 (Psalm 7:1-10 NRSV)

God is my shield and defense. (Ps. 7:11)

Acts 11:27—12:3a

King Herod orders the death of the apostle James.

Mark 10:35-45

James and John seek the seats of honor in Christ's kingdom. Jesus teaches the disciples that greatness is not measured in terms of honor, but rather in their willingness to be servants of all people.

COLOR   Red

THE PRAYERS

Confident in God's steadfast love through Jesus Christ and guided by the Holy Spirit, let us pray for the church, the world, and all people according to their needs.

A BRIEF SILENCE.

Raise up for your church leaders like the prophet Elijah and the apostle James, zealous for you and willing to suffer death in the name of Christ. God of grace,

let our prayer come before you.

Give to the nations of the world enlightened leaders so that there might be an end to all religious discrimination and persecution. God of grace,

let our prayer come before you.

Grant relief to those who suffer from hunger throughout the world, and inspire us to greater generosity in sharing of our resources. God of grace,

let our prayer come before you.

Sustain and strengthen all people who are sick *(especially)* and all people in any kind of need, especially those who are suffering because of their faith in Christ. God of grace,

let our prayer come before you.

Stir up among your servants in this congregation greater zeal for you, and teach us to listen and watch for your presence in quiet and unremarkable ways. God of grace,

let our prayer come before you.

HERE OTHER INTERCESSIONS MAY BE OFFERED.

Our thanks we offer to you, O God, for the lives of your servant James the Elder *(and other names)* and all your saints. May they inspire us to lives of greater faith and service in Christ's name, until with them we offer you the full and perfect praise in heaven. God of grace,

let our prayer come before you.

Teach us to pray, O God, and grant to all for whom we pray the good gifts that you have promised, through Jesus Christ our Lord.

Amen

MAGES FOR PREACHING

About a month ago in the lectionary, Zebedee's sons demonstrated their fiery temper by counseling Jesus to destroy an inhospitable Samaritan village. Today James and John appear in two separate scriptural accounts. In Mark's lesson the brothers brashly put themselves forward, asking Jesus for special privilege. They want the best seats in the house.

This conspicuous display of ambition was a misunderstanding of kingdom dynamics and it earned James and John the heated indignation of their fellow disciples. Jesus, however, responded with understanding and patience. First he pointed out that he was unable to control the seating arrangements in the coming kingdom. Then he explained that, while he could not assure any particular form of glory, he *could* envisage suffering for them.

The references to drinking from the cup and sharing the baptism are interpreted by some as having sacramental overtones. When the disciples gathered at the last supper they all did drink from the cup Jesus offered. When Paul later gave his interpretation of baptism (Rom. 6), he noted that by being baptized into Christ Jesus we are baptized into his death.

On the other hand, Jesus may have been speaking wistfully rather than sacramentally in this passage. It doesn't really matter, for the story has peculiar poignancy for James and John. In Acts 12:1-2 we learn that King Herod—apparently pandering for some political purpose—had James killed. That tragic act finally brought home the truth of Jesus' words about drinking the cup that he drank and being baptized with the baptism that he was baptized with. The cost of discipleship has nothing to do with the seating arrangement in the kingdom, as the sons of Zebedee finally discovered. It is about serving the Lord wherever he sends us. It's not the seating, it's the sending.

WORSHIP MATTERS

Who invites the assembly to worship? Who calls the assembly to worship? The church has one simple answer to these questions: It is God—Father, Son, and Holy Spirit—who calls and enlightens the people of God in the journey of faith. This is why the church intends that the first greeting to the assembly should speak this truth. It is God who invites and calls. Thus the Brief Order for Confession begins with the invocation of God's name, not "Good morning, everyone." Thus, the Holy Communion begins with the apostolic greeting and welcome in God's threefold name, not "We're so happy to welcome you."

LET THE CHILDREN COME

Fishing is a favorite summer pastime for many. For others, like St. James the Elder, it is a livelihood. St. James was a fisherman and one of Jesus' disciples. Jesus' call changed the focus of St. James' fishing—Jesus called him to catch people, not fish. How do we, as Christians, catch people? To fish for people, we must serve them. Give children the opportunity to serve by having them help with the worship service. Invite young adults to mentor children as they work as ushers and greeters. Wear fish tags as a reminder that we have all been caught in Christ's net of love.

HYMNS FOR WORSHIP

GATHERING
Faith of our fathers   LBW 500, RWI 26
Rejoice in God's saints   WOV 689

HYMN OF THE DAY
For all your saints, O Lord   LBW 176

ALTERNATE HYMN OF THE DAY
By all your saints in warfare   LBW 178 (I, 16, 3)
By gracious powers   WOV 736

COMMUNION
I received the living God   WOV 700
Strengthen for service, Lord   LBW 218, RWI 69

SENDING
Oh, what their joy   LBW 337
Sing with all the saints in glory   WOV 691

ADDITIONAL HYMNS AND SONGS
Give thanks for saints   RWSB
Make me a servant   W&P 96
For thy blest saints   H82 276
Lord, help us walk your servant way   HFG 150

MUSIC FOR THE DAY

PSALMODY
Turner, Ronald. PW, Cycle C.
O Lord my God, from you alone comes aid   PsH 7

261

CHORAL

Bach, J. S. "We All Believe In One True God" in *Bach for All Seasons.* SATB. AFP 080065854X.

Carter, John. "We Are Called to Be His Servants." U, opt div, pno. AFP 0800675452.

Scott, K. Lee. "So Art Thou to Me" in *Rejoice Now My Spirit: Vocal Solos for the Church Year.* AFP 0800651081 (MH voice); AFP 080065109X (ML voice).

Stainer, John. "God So Loved the World." SATB. CFI 25792-4.

CHILDREN'S CHOIR

Hruby, Dolores. "Go Now to Love and Serve the Lord." U, kybd, opt fl. CG CGA354.

Willard, Kelly. "Make Me a Servant" in LS. (Mark 10:35-45)

KEYBOARD/INSTRUMENTAL

Frahm. Frederick. "Von Gott will ich nicht lassen" in *Faith Alive.* Org. AFP 0800675738.

Shearing, George. "Amazing Grace" in *Sacred Sounds from George Shearing for Organ.* Org. SMP - KK 229.

Sowash, Bradley. "Wade in the Water" and "You Gotta Sing" in *We Gather Together,* vol. I. Pno. AFP 0800675622.

HANDBELL

Afdahl, Lee J. "Rejoice in God's Saints." 3-5 oct, opt perc. AFP 0800656695.

Dicke, Martin. "Rondo for Bells." 2 oct. AFP 0800659945.

PRAISE ENSEMBLE

Brown, Clint. "I Want to Be More Like You" in *Best of the Best.* FEL 1891062018.

Cook, Steve and Vikki Cook. "Jesus, You Reign over All" in *Praise Hymns and Choruses, 4th ed.* MAR 3010130368.

Willard, Kelly. "Make Me a Servant" in W&P.

July 25, 2004

Eighth Sunday after Pentecost
Proper 12

INTRODUCTION

We want to learn how to pray, and our prayers have many shapes. Jesus' model prayer shapes our own and leads us to a fuller realization of God's presence in our lives and in the world—a vision shared by Paul as he proclaims Christ's new day. Today the church remembers St. James the Elder, son of Zebedee and brother of John. James is the only apostle whose death is recorded in the Bible.

PRAYER OF THE DAY

O God, your ears are open always to the prayers of your servants. Open our hearts and minds to you, that we may live in harmony with your will and receive the gifts of your Spirit; through your Son, Jesus Christ our Lord.

VERSE

Alleluia. Lord, to whom shall we go? You have the words of eternal life. Alleluia. (John 6:68)

READINGS

Genesis 18:20-32

In today's first reading, Abraham fulfills the commission given him by God, that all the nations of the earth should bless themselves through him. Abraham's call is to teach God's way of justice and righteousness.

Psalm 138

Your love endures forever; do not abandon the works of your hands. (Ps. 138:9)

Colossians 2:6-15 [16-19]

The letter to the Colossians warns about "the empty lure" of ideas that compromise the faith into which people are baptized. Through baptism, the church is rooted in Christ.

Luke 11:1-13

In Luke's gospel Jesus prays often and urges his disciples to do the same. Here, he teaches them to pray and encourages them to trust in God at all times.

Alternate First Reading/Psalm

Hosea 1:2-10

Hosea's marriage to a faithless wife symbolizes Israel's faithless disregard of the covenant. Even the names of Hosea's children—Jezreel (where Israel's idolatrous kings had been killed), Lo-ruhamah ("she is not pitied"), and Lo-ammi ("not my people")—announce the nation's coming doom, countered by the proclamation that sinful Israel remains a child of the living God.

Psalm 85

Righteousness and peace shall go before the LORD. (Ps. 85:13)

COLOR   Green

THE PRAYERS

Confident in God's steadfast love through Jesus Christ and guided by the Holy Spirit, let us pray for the church, the world, and all people according to their needs.

A BRIEF SILENCE.

God of enduring love, give to your church the boldness and persistence of Abraham to intercede on behalf of those whose hearts are turned away from you. God of grace,

let our prayer come before you.

God of enduring love, raise up among the nations of the world leaders who desire justice and seek peace for all people. God of grace,

let our prayer come before you.

God of enduring love, make known your presence among the lowly: the poor, the immigrant, those suffering from depression, those without hope, and the sick (*especially*), that they might be uplifted and strengthened by your hand. God of grace,

let our prayer come before you.

God of enduring love, empower your servants in this congregation to pray with persistence on behalf of our members and for the needs of the world. God of grace,

let our prayer come before you.

HERE OTHER INTERCESSIONS MAY BE OFFERED.

God of enduring love, we thank you for James the Elder, apostle, and all the saints and martyrs who were buried with Christ in baptism and have come to fullness in Christ. Give to us perseverance in faith that we too may share in that fullness with Christ and all the faithful. God of grace,

let our prayer come before you.

Teach us to pray, O God, and grant to all for whom we pray the good gifts that you have promised, through Jesus Christ our Lord.

Amen

IIMAGES FOR PREACHING

If we are curious about the act of praying, we would do well to look at Luke's narrative. In this gospel, more than anywhere else, Jesus withdrew to pray; he urged others to pray, he encouraged corporate prayer, he warned against the misuse of prayer, and he *taught* prayer. In today's gospel he teaches *the* prayer, the one we now call the Lord's Prayer.

Jesus taught the prayer in direct response to his disciples' specific request, "Lord, teach us to pray." In this prayer Jesus virtually taught his disciples to breathe, for the prayer has become like respiration. It is the great community prayer in which we ask God to hear and answer us. As a corporate expression, it is the prayer of the body of Christ and not only of isolated individuals.

This address to God, Luther said, is an enticement to believe that God is our Father and we are his children. In this prayer Jesus invited all disciples into a living relationship with God, in which we gather all our earthly hopes and desires and bring them to our heavenly Father. We know that God knows what we know and want, but we pray anyway. We pray for God's holy name; for God's dominion; for daily bread; for forgiveness of sins; for deliverance. Without this prayer we would be left breathless and speechless. We would be petitioners without the right of petition.

Jesus also taught the disciples the implications of prayer. Neighborliness and persistence, asking and searching, proper response and giving good gifts: these all derive from the prayer. We pray in the world where God encounters us and we engage one another. Praying, Jesus taught, involves the Holy Spirit who calls, gathers, and inspires. When the disciples asked Jesus how to pray, they got much more than they bargained for. So do we.

WORSHIP MATTERS

Why do the prayers of the church usually begin with the first person plural? We pray "Our Father," "In peace, let us pray to the Lord," "This is the feast of victory for our God," "Lord, to whom shall we go?" "Hear our prayer,"

263

"Fill to the brim our cup of blessing," "Come, Lord Jesus, be our guest."

The clue is in the words of the Lord's Prayer: Our Father. Despite the fact that we live in a culture that would have us pray, "My father," or "In peace, I want to pray to the Lord," or "Fill to the brim my cup of blessing," the church's liturgy would have us see the truth of what we do: the liturgy—the work of the people—is a communal action of the Holy Trinity and the worshiping assembly. In baptism we have been bound to the community of Father, Son, and Holy Spirit in the community of baptized brothers and sisters.

The Spirit is given to all for the strengthening of the body of Christ, a reality that can be difficult to discern in a culture of lonely individuals.

LET THE CHILDREN COME

Jesus teaches us: "Give us each day our daily bread" (Luke 11:3). In other words, Jesus is teaching us to ask God for what we need through prayer. Today invite someone who knows American Sign Language to lead the congregation in signing the Lord's Prayer, petition by petition. Sing all seven stanzas of "All creatures of our God and King" (LBW 527). Children will discover that we can pray to God with words, actions, silently, in song, and in all languages.

HYMNS FOR WORSHIP
GATHERING

Oh, for a thousand tongues to sing   LBW 559
When long before time   WOV 799
We have come into his house   TFF 136

HYMN OF THE DAY

Day by day   WOV 746

ALTERNATE HYMN OF THE DAY

Lord, teach us how to pray aright   LBW 438
O thou, who hast of thy pure grace   LBW 442

COMMUNION

What a friend we have in Jesus   LBW 439
Lord, listen to your children praying   WOV 775

SENDING

Christians, while on earth abiding   LBW 440
Seek ye first   WOV 783, TFF 149, W&P 122

ADDITIONAL HYMNS AND SONGS

Your will be done / *Mayenziwe*   TFF 243, RWSB
Lord, listen to your children   W&P 91, RWSB
Lord, teach us how to pray   HFG 22
Let all who pray the prayer Christ taught   PH 349

MUSIC FOR THE DAY
PSALMODY

Cooney, Rory. "On the Day I Called" in STP, vol. 4.
Haas, David. "In the Presence of the Angels" in PCY, vol. 3.
Paradowski, John. PW , Cycle C.
Stewart, Roy James. "Lord, Your Love Is Eternal" in PCY, vol. 5.
See Fifth Sunday after the Epiphany.

CHORAL

Duruflé, Maurice. "Notre Pere." SATB. DUR 362-03307.
Ellingboe, Bradley. "The Lord's Prayer." SATB, pno. KJO 8952.
Organ, Anne Krentz. "Come and Find the Quiet Center." SAB, kybd. AFP 0800675096.
Peeters, Flor. "The Lord's Prayer." SATB, kybd. PET 6200.
Poole, David. "Somebody's Knockin' At Your Door." SATB, pno. KJO 8949.
Schubert, Franz. "Lord, to Whom Our Prayers Ascend" in *Rejoice Now My Spirit: Vocal Solos for the Church Year.* AFP 0800651081 (MH voice); AFP 080065109X (ML voice).

CHILDREN'S CHOIR

Barta, Dan. "Ask and Seek and Knock." (Luke 11:9) 2 pt, kybd, opt C inst. CG CGA683.
Horman, John. "The Unexpected Guest." (Luke 11:1-8) U, pno, narr, hc, wood block. ABI 07255-7.

KEYBOARD/INSTRUMENTAL

Biery, James. "Rendez á Dieu." Org. AFP 0800658744.
Boellmann, Léon. "Prayer." (Prière à Notre-Dame) Org. Various ed. Also in *The Complete Wedding Collection.* BEC OC21.
Hayes, Mark. "His Eye Is on the Sparrow" in *Well-Tempered Jazz.* Pno. SHW HE 5044.
Sedio, Mark. "Foundation" in *Two on a Bench.* Pno duet. AFP 0800659090.

264

HANDBELL

McChesney, Kevin. "Day by Day." 3 oct. JEF JHS9182.

Wagner, Douglas E. "What a Friend We Have in Jesus." 3-5 oct.
AG 1681.

PRAISE ENSEMBLE

Hanson, Handt. "Hear Our Prayer" in *Spirit Calls . . . Rejoice*. SATB.
CCF 0933173393 (pew ed); CCF 0933173385 (acc ed).

Whittemore, Dan. "Just a Prayer Away" in *The Ultimate Praise Songbook
for Kids*. LIL MB-681.

Sunday, July 25

ST. JAMES THE ELDER, APOSTLE

See pages 260–62.

Wednesday, July 28

JOHANN SEBASTIAN BACH, 1750; HEINRICH SCHÜTZ,
1672; GEORGE FREDERICK HANDEL, 1759; MUSICIANS

These three composers have done much to enrich the
worship life of the church. Johann Sebastian Bach drew
on the Lutheran tradition of hymnody and wrote about
two hundred cantatas, including at least two for each
Sunday and festival day in the Lutheran calendar of his
day. He has been called "the fifth evangelist" for the
ways that he proclaimed the gospel through his music.
George Frederick Handel was not primarily a church
musician, but his great work, *Messiah*, is a musical proclamation of the scriptures. Heinrich Schütz wrote choral
settings of biblical texts and paid special attention to
ways his composition would underscore the meaning of
the words.

A musical gathering might be planned to commemorate these and other great church composers. Remember to include a prayer of thanksgiving for organists,
choir directors, composers, and all who make music in
worship.

Thursday, July 29

MARY, MARTHA, AND LAZARUS OF BETHANY

Mary and Martha are remembered for the hospitality
and refreshment they offered Jesus in their home. Following the characterization drawn by Luke, Martha
represents the active life, and Mary, the contemplative.
Mary is identified in the fourth gospel as the one who
anointed Jesus before his passion and who was criticized for her act of devotion. Lazarus, Mary's and
Martha's brother, was raised from the dead by Jesus as
a sign of the eternal life offered to all believers. It was
over Lazarus's tomb that Jesus wept for love of his
friend. Congregations might commemorate these three
early witnesses to Christ by reflecting on the role of
hospitality in both home and church and the blessing
of friendship.

Thursday, July 29

OLAF, KING OF NORWAY, MARTYR, 1030

Olaf is considered the patron saint of Norway. In his
early career he engaged in war and piracy in the Baltic
and in Normandy. It was there he became a Christian.
He returned to Norway, declared himself king, and from
then on Christianity was the dominant religion of the
realm. He revised the laws of the nation and enforced
them with strict impartiality, eliminating the possibility
of bribes. He thereby alienated much of the aristocracy.
The harshness that he sometimes resorted to in order to
establish Christianity and his own law led to a rebellion.
After being driven from the country and into exile, he
enlisted support from Sweden to try to regain his kingdom, but he died in battle.

Olaf reminds the church of the temptation to
establish Christianity by waging war, whether military or
social. How might the church bear witness to the one
who calls us to pray for enemies and persecutors?

August 1, 2004

Ninth Sunday after Pentecost
Proper 13

INTRODUCTION

The church prays, "We offer with joy and thanksgiving what you have first given us—our selves, our time, and our possessions." We do much more than support the work of our congregation as we make our contributions. We actually reorient ourselves toward what we possess and what we value the most. God's word speaks to us about this fundamental realignment of our lives.

PRAYER OF THE DAY

Gracious Father, your blessed Son came down from heaven to be the true bread which gives life to the world. Give us this bread, that he may live in us and we in him, Jesus Christ our Lord.

or

Almighty God, judge of us all, you have placed in our hands the wealth we call our own. Give us such wisdom by your Spirit that our possessions may not be a curse in our lives, but an instrument for blessing; through your Son, Jesus Christ our Lord.

VERSE

Alleluia. Jesus said, Those who love me will keep my word, and my Father will love them, and we will come to them and make our home with them. Alleluia.
(John 14:23)

READINGS

Ecclesiastes 1:2, 12-14; 2:18-23

The teacher of wisdom who wrote Ecclesiastes sees that working for mere accumulation of wealth turns life into an empty game.

Psalm 49:1-11 (Psalm 49:1-12 NRSV)

We can never ransom ourselves or deliver to God the price of our life. (Ps. 49:6)

Colossians 3:1-11

Life in Christ includes a radical reorientation of our values. Just as the newly baptized shed their old clothes in order to put on new garments, so Christians are called to let go of greed and take hold of a life shaped by God's love in Christ.

Luke 12:13-21

The gospel of Luke tells not only how Jesus brought good news to the poor, but also how he sought to save those who were rich. Here he warns against identifying the worth of one's life with the value of one's possessions.

Alternate First Reading/Psalm

Hosea 11:1-11

The prophet compares God's love of Israel to the love parents have for their children. Whether teaching toddlers to walk or supporting them in the midst of rebellion, good parents continue to love their children as they try to lead them to life. In the same way, God's love will not let Israel go.

Psalm 107:1-9, 43

Give thanks to the LORD, all those whom the LORD has redeemed. (Ps. 107:1-2)

COLOR Green

THE PRAYERS

Confident in God's steadfast love through Jesus Christ and guided by the Holy Spirit, let us pray for the church, the world, and all people according to their needs.

A BRIEF SILENCE.

For all people, leaders, and ministers of the church, that our minds may be set on things above, we implore you: God of grace,

let our prayer come before you.

For wealthy nations and peoples in the world, that they might recognize the futility of storing up possessions and be moved to share their material blessings with others, we implore you: God of grace,

let our prayer come before you.

For all those living vain and empty lives, that they might seek and find the fullness of life in Christ, we implore you: God of grace,

let our prayer come before you.

For those who are victims of violence and oppression, that they might live in safety and freedom, we implore you: God of grace, let our prayer come before you.

For the sick *(especially)*, that they might be brought to health and wholeness, and for the dying *(especially)*, that the peace of Christ might rule in their hearts, we implore you: God of grace,

let our prayer come before you.

For our congregation, that we might be renewed in knowledge according to the image of you, our creator, and welcome in our midst those who differ from us, we implore you: God of grace,

let our prayer come before you.

HERE OTHER INTERCESSIONS MAY BE OFFERED.

For all the faithful who have gone before us *(especially)*, we give thanks. Keep us, who have died to all things earthly through our baptism, safely hidden with Christ until we will be revealed with him in glory; we implore you: God of grace,

let our prayer come before you.

Teach us to pray, O God, and grant to all for whom we pray the good gifts that you have promised, through Jesus Christ our Lord.

Amen

IMAGES FOR PREACHING

Dorothy Sayers once wrote an essay called "The Other Six Deadly Sins." In that piece she noted there are sins other than sex. Among them was greed, today's featured sin. In the gospel narratives Jesus seems to have varying views of money and the marketplace. One time he commended sharp practices (Luke 16:1-13). Another time he was critical of wealth (Luke 18:18-25). Or Jesus could play it coyly, as he did in the question regarding taxes (Luke 20:20-26).

About the deadly sin of greed, though, Jesus was quite eloquent. He told the inheritance seeker that one's life does not consist simply in the abundance of possessions. Jesus then told a parable about someone who had a life of wealth but lost his length of life. The question of abundance and inheritance, on the night of the man's unexpected death, became moot.

The man had felt he had ample goods and many years to enjoy them. He smugly paraphrased Ecclesiastes 9:7 by way of self-justification: *Relax, eat, drink, be merry,* he crooned, little realizing that his life was forfeit. The irony is that Isaiah 22:13 was more apposite: *Let us eat and drink, for tomorrow we die.*

The greedy, self-satisfied man little realized that it was *not* "well with his soul," as we sing in "When peace, like a river" (TFF 194). Soul satisfaction will not come from the vastness of one's holdings or the spread of one's estate. Instead, consider the satisfaction the writer sings of particularly in stanza two:

> Though Satan should buffet, though trials should come,
> Let this blest assurance control,
> That Christ hath regarded my helpless estate
> And hath shed his own blood for my soul.

WORSHIP MATTERS

The gospels present Jesus as one who lived among the poor, a wandering teacher who owned no property and carried little, if any, cash. Reflecting on the growing numbers of poor people in the world today and the terrible sufferings they endure, some Christian communions have begun to speak strongly about following Jesus who wanted to be among the poor, the homeless, and the powerless people of his culture. Making a fundamental choice to serve the poor takes precedence over building large congregations and larger buildings to house them.

How do the poor and the powerless enter into the worship of largely middle-class North American congregations? How do we insulate ourselves from the fear of being "without" and how does that fear shape our perceptions of God?

LET THE CHILDREN COME

Before children can understand what it means to have treasures or riches, they must be treasured at home and in your church family. Every Sunday have ushers welcome families with young children and seat them near the front of the sanctuary. Children will be able to see and experience worship firsthand. Teach greeters to welcome young ones by meeting their eyes and expressing their pleasure at seeing them. If our greatest treasure is God's love for us, then children will discover that this gift is for them as they are wrapped up in the loving arms of their church family.

HYMNS FOR WORSHIP
GATHERING

Sing praise to God, the highest good   LBW 542
Shout for joy loud and long   WOV 793

HYMN OF THE DAY

O Jesus, king most wonderful!   LBW 537

ALTERNATE HYMN OF THE DAY

All my hope on God is founded   WOV 782
Fear not for tomorrow   LS 161, HFW

COMMUNION

O living Bread from heaven   LBW 197
One bread, one body   WOV 710

SENDING

God, whose giving knows no ending   LBW 408
My life flows on in endless song   WOV 781

ADDITIONAL HYMNS AND SONGS

I'd rather have Jesus   TFF 233
We raise our hands to you   RWSB
Lead me, guide me   TFF 70, W&P 84, RWSB
We cannot own the sunlit sky   NCH 563

268

MUSIC FOR THE DAY
PSALMODY

Hopson, Hal H. "Psalm 49" in TP.
Howard, Julie. *Sing for Joy: Psalm Settings for God's Children.* LP 0814620787.
Paradowski, John. PW , Cycle C.
Psalms for Praise and Worship: A Complete Liturgical Psalter. ABI 0687093260.

CHORAL

Bach, J.S. "O, Mortal World" in *Lift Up Your Voice.* M voice solo, kybd. PRE.
Benson, Robert A. "Prayer of St. Benedict." SATB, org, opt hb. AFP 0800675541.

Brahms, Johannes. "Ah Thou Poor World" in *Anthems for Choirs 1.* SATB. OXF 353214X.
Ellingboe, Bradley. "The Food of Life." SATB, pno. KJO 8966.
Rutter, John. "God Be in My Head." SATB. OXF 94.326.
Young, Carlton R. "Bread of the World, in Mercy Broken." 2 pt mxd, kybd. AFP 0800675592.

CHILDREN'S CHOIR

Collins, Dori Erwin. "God Will Always Be with Me." U, pno, opt fl. AFP 0800675193.
Sleeth, Natalie. "Fear Not for Tomorrow" in LS. U, kybd.

KEYBOARD/INSTRUMENTAL

Linker, Janet. "Devotion" ("I Am Thine, O Lord" and "Lord, I Want to be a Christian") in *John Ness Beck Favorites for Organ.* Org. BEC OC9.
Mann, Adrian. "I Want Jesus to Walk with Me" in *Arise and Rejoice: Preludes for Treble Instrument and Keyboard.* Kybd, inst. AFP 0800674960.
Rodriguez, Penny. "Praise to the Lord, the Almighty" in *Portraits of Praise.* Pno. BEC PC2.

HANDBELL

McChesney, Kevin. "God of Grace and God of Glory." 3-5 oct. CPH 97-6584.
Morris, Hart. "First in My Heart." 3-5 oct. RR HB0029.

PRAISE ENSEMBLE

Bancroft, Charite Lees and Vikki Cook. "Before the Throne of God" in *Worship Leader's Song Discovery,* vol. 28. Worship Leader 2001-09-LS.
Mann, Robin. "Father Welcomes" in *Best of the Best.* FEL 1891062018.

August 8, 2004

Tenth Sunday after Pentecost
Proper 14

INTRODUCTION

"Faith is the conviction of things not seen," the second reading announces. "We've come this far by faith, leaning on the Lord," the hymn by Albert Goodson proclaims. This day we gather as a community of faith and seek renewed vision, so that we might make our way more boldly into the world as bearers of God's saving love.

Dominic, commemorated today, was a Spanish priest who battled heretics and founded the Order of Preachers (Dominicans). He died in 1221.

PRAYER OF THE DAY

Almighty and everlasting God, you are always more ready to hear than we are to pray, and to give more than we either desire or deserve. Pour upon us the abundance of your mercy, forgiving us those things of which our conscience is afraid, and giving us those good things for which we are not worthy to ask, except through the merit of your Son, Jesus Christ our Lord.

VERSE

Alleluia. Faith is the assurance of things hoped for, the conviction of things not seen. Alleluia. (Heb. 11:1)

READINGS

Genesis 15:1-6

God promises childless Abram that a child of his own will be his heir and that his descendants will number as many as the stars. Abram trusts God's promise and through this faith, he is considered righteous.

Psalm 33:12-22

Let your lovingkindness be upon us, as we have put our trust in you. (Ps. 33:22)

Hebrews 11:1-3, 8-16

Abraham and Sarah exemplify the vision of faith that people of God need in every age. Their hope and trust in God's promise allowed them to face an unknown future.

Luke 12:32-40

Jesus encourages his followers to recognize the true value of God's kingdom, so that their hearts may be where their real treasure lies. Instead of facing life with fear,

those who know God's generosity are always ready to receive from God and to give to others.

Alternate First Reading/Psalm

Isaiah 1:1, 10-20

Isaiah announces God's displeasure with the offerings and sacrifices of a people who are without compassion and pleads with Judah, the Southern Kingdom, to return to the Lord that they might be cleansed.

Psalm 50:1-8, 22-23

To those who keep in my way will I show the salvation of God. (Ps. 50:24)

COLOR   Green

269

THE PRAYERS

Confident in God's steadfast love through Jesus Christ and guided by the Holy Spirit, let us pray for the church, the world, and all people according to their needs.
A BRIEF SILENCE.

Let us pray for the church, that as we wait in hope for the return of our master, we will be found to be faithful servants of Christ in the world. God of grace,
let our prayer come before you.

Let us pray for all those who promote the health and safety of others in our country and our community, that they would experience joy in their service to others. God of grace,
let our prayer come before you.

Let us pray for all those who are living without hope: the homeless, the mentally ill, those with chronic illness, the childless, and for the sick *(especially)*, that they may not be afraid but may come to know that it is the Father's good pleasure to give them the kingdom. God of grace,
let our prayer come before you.

Let us pray for those from our congregation vacationing, that they may obtain rest from their labors and renewal of their spirits. God of grace,
let our prayer come before you.

HERE OTHER INTERCESSIONS MAY BE OFFERED.

Let us give thanks for all those whose faith sustained

them even as they longed for their heavenly home, especially Dominic, renewer of the church (and *names*). Sustain our faith and grant us your unfailing treasure in heaven. God of grace,

let our prayer come before you.

Teach us to pray, O God, and grant to all for whom we pray the good gifts that you have promised, through Jesus Christ our Lord.

Amen

IMAGES FOR PREACHING

Some of Jesus' words are easier to take than others. When counseling hearers not to fear because God is in charge, he speaks a smoother sounding word than when he urges the sale of one's possessions. That difference is like singing the soothing hymn "Have no fear, little flock" (LBW 476) in contrast to the more demanding aspects of "Take my life, that I may be," stanza 3: "Take my silver and my gold, not a mite would I withhold" (LBW 406).

The riptide in today's text both disturbs and uplifts. Rough currents provoke both caution and comfort. The observation about treasure being where the heart is provides a sobering echo of last week's gospel story about the greedy inheritance seeker. The matter of keeping lamps lit and being alert for the unexpected return of the master is a précis of Jesus' parable of the ten bridesmaids in Matthew 25. Keeping a lookout for the thief in the night is disturbing for any householder, while the pointed advice to watch and be ready sounds like the distant early warning signs of Advent—and it is still midsummer!

We customarily regard Jesus as a storyteller or a miracle doer, one who gives parables and offers advice and inspiration to disciples. Today, though, Jesus is a maker of aphorisms. That is, he frames tersely phrased statements of truth like the sage in the book of Proverbs.

In Luke 9 we learned that Jesus "set his face to go to Jerusalem." Today, still on the road, he is in the midst of a gutsy discourse on discipleship. It is turning out to be a long and challenging journey. Perhaps fatigued, he has becomes tersely aphoristic. What he says in brief form is punchy and worthwhile. "Do not be afraid." "Don't set your heart on transient things." "Be dressed for action and have your lamps lit." But mostly, "Be

prepared to meet the Son of Man, the one who comes in unexpected ways at an unexpected hour."

WORSHIP MATTERS

There is a difference between reading and proclaiming scripture. "Reading" scripture is reading the words of a text so that other people can hear them. You know when someone is reading at you: it is clear that the reader's primary goal is to get through the text with the least number of slips or mistakes.

"Proclaiming" the text is something quite different. The one who proclaims the text knows the text so well that the words have become a part of the person. The reader is clearly conveying the meaning rather than the emotional tone of the text. The reader is deliberate in his or her proclamation, using appropriate pauses so the listeners can let the meaning of the words roam around inside them.

Someone who knows the text thoroughly and proclaims to the worshiping assembly a story that he or she wants to communicate is no longer reading words off a page. The reader is now proclaiming a living word. The difference between the two only becomes apparent with practice, reflection, and prayer.

LET THE CHILDREN COME

These words precede the Great Prayer of Thanksgiving: "Let us give thanks to the Lord our God. It is right to give our thanks and praise."

In the post-communion canticle we may sing "Thank the Lord and sing his praise" and later "with shouts of thanksgiving." Part of the work of the congregation is to give thanks to God for the richness of God's blessings. Today invite families to focus on the words "thanks" and "thanksgiving" in your worship service. Young children will grow in their familiarity with the liturgy as well as see that one way we can worship God is by giving thanks for our blessings.

HYMNS FOR WORSHIP
GATHERING

O Holy Spirit, enter in   LBW 459
Oh, sing to God above   WOV 726
Oh, come, let us sing   W&P 107

HYMN OF THE DAY

Have no fear, little flock   LBW 476

ALTERNATE HYMN OF THE DAY

Many and great, O God, are your works   WOV 794
How great thou art   LBW 532

COMMUNION

Soul, adorn yourself with gladness   LBW 224
God, who stretched the spangled heavens   LBW 463

SENDING

If you but trust in God to guide you   LBW 453
Great is thy faithfulness   WOV 771
We've come this far by faith   TFF 197, RWSB

ADDITIONAL HYMNS AND SONGS

Lord Jesus, you shall be my song   RWSB
Holy is our God / *Santo, santo, santo*   TFF 203, RWSB
That Christ be known   W&P 133
Faith is a living power from heaven   CW 404

MUSIC FOR THE DAY

PSALMODY

Cooney, Rory. "Happy the People You Have Chosen" in STP, vol. 4.
Dufford, Bob. "Lord, Let Your Mercy" in STP, vol. 4.
Foley, John. "Psalm 33: God, Let Your Mercy" in PCY, vol. 7.
Haugen, Marty. "Let Your Mercy Be on Us" in PCY, vol. 2.
Inwood, Paul. "Psalm 33: The Lord Fills the Earth with His Love" in STP, vol. 3.
Paradowski, John. PW, Cycle C.

CHORAL

Bach, J. S. "Jesu meine Freude" in *Bach for All Seasons*. SATB. AFP 080065854X.
Bach, J. S. "Zion Hears the Watchmen Singing" in *Bach for All Seasons*. U. AFP 080065854X.
Brahms, Johannes. "Ah Thou Poor World" in *Anthems for Choirs 1*. SATB. OXF 353214X.
Johnson, Carolyn. "Have No Fear, Little Flock." SATB, kybd. AFP 0800674545.
Mendelssohn, Felix. "O Rest in the Lord" in *Elijah*. A solo, kybd. Various ed.
Scott, K. Lee. "Keep Your Lamps Trimmed and Burning" in *Sing Forth God's Praise*. AFP 0800675266 (MH voice); AFP 080067538X (ML voice).

Walter, Johann. "Rise Up! Rise Up!" in *Chantry Choirbook*. SATB. AFP 0800657772.

CHILDREN'S CHOIR

Kemp, Helen. "Psalm 33:20-22" in *Speak and Sing of God's Glory*. U/2 pt, kybd. CG CGA563.
Schlosser, Don. "I Will Trust in God." U/2 pt, pno. CG CGA895.

KEYBOARD/INSTRUMENTAL

Cherwien, David. "Have No Fear, Little Flock" in *Interpretations, Book XI*. Org. AMSI SP-108.
Kolander, Keith. *Voluntaries for Trumpet and Organ*. Org, tpt. AFP 0800659406.
Rodriguez, Penny. " 'Tis a Gift to Be Simple" in *Images*. Pno. BEC PC7.
Sowash, Bradley. "Bringing In the Sheaves" in *We Gather Together*, vol. 1. Pno. AFP 0800675622.

HANDBELL

Rogers, Sharon Elery. "God, Who Stretched the Spangled Heavens." 3-5 oct. AFP 0800657373.
Rogers, Sharon Elery. "How Great Thou Art." 3-5 oct, opt hc. AFP 0800659910.

PRAISE ENSEMBLE

Baloche, Paul. "Open the Eyes of My Heart" in RW5.
Cortez, Jaime. "Rain Down" in *Glory & Praise*. OCP 5910GC.

Sunday, August 8

DOMINIC, PRIEST, FOUNDER OF THE ORDER OF THE DOMINICANS, 1221

Dominic was a Spanish priest who preached against the Albigensians, a heretical sect that held gnostic and dualistic beliefs. Dominic believed that a stumbling block to restoring heretics to the church was the wealth of clergy, so he formed an itinerant religious order, the Order of Preachers (Dominicans) who lived in poverty, studied philosophy and theology, and preached against heresy. The method of this order was to use kindness and gentle argument, rather than harsh judgment, when bringing unorthodox Christians back to the fold. Dominic was opposed to burning Christians at the stake. Three times Dominic was offered the office of bishop, which he refused so that he could continue his work of preaching.

Tuesday, August 10

LAWRENCE, DEACON, MARTYR, 258

Lawrence was one of seven deacons of the congregation at Rome and, like the deacons appointed in Acts, was responsible for financial matters in the church and for the care of the poor. Lawrence lived during a time of persecution under the emperor Valerian. The emperor demanded that Lawrence surrender the treasures of the church. Lawrence gathered lepers, orphans, the blind and lame. He brought them to the emperor and said, "Here is the treasure of the church." This act enraged the emperor, and Lawrence was sentenced to death. Lawrence's martyrdom was one of the first to be observed by the church.

Amid the concerns for the institutional church, reflect on what we consider the treasures of the church today. If the people on the margins of life are treasured in God's eyes, consider ways a congregation can sharpen its vision for social ministry.

272

Friday, August 13

FLORENCE NIGHTINGALE, 1910; CLARA MAASS, 1901;
RENEWERS OF SOCIETY

When Florence Nightingale decided she would be a nurse, her family was horrified. In the early 1800s nursing was done by people with no training and no other way to earn a living. Florence trained at Kaiserswerth, Germany, with a Lutheran order of deaconesses. She returned home and worked to reform hospitals in England. Nightingale led a group of thirty-eight nurses to serve in the Crimean War, where they worked in appalling conditions. She returned to London as a hero and there resumed her work for hospital reform. Clara Maass was born in New Jersey and served as a nurse in the Spanish-American War, where she encountered the horrors of yellow fever. She later responded to a call for subjects in research on yellow fever. During the experiments, which included receiving bites from mosquitoes, she contracted the disease and died. The commemoration of these women invites the church to give thanks for all who practice the arts of healing.

August 15, 2004

Mary, Mother of Our Lord

INTRODUCTION

Mary, the mother of Jesus, is traditionally believed to have died on this date. Faithful to the last, Mary has been important to Christian devotion throughout history because in her, the God-bearer, is seen a representation of the church itself. Mary's song (the Magnificat) is our gospel for the day. It is a powerful statement of justice, still apt for us today as we come with our own neediness to experience God's justice and mercy in word and sacrament.

PRAYER OF THE DAY

Almighty God, you chose the virgin Mary to be the mother of your only Son. Grant that we, who have been redeemed by his blood, may share with her in the glory of your eternal kingdom; through your Son, Jesus Christ our Lord, who lives and reigns with you and the Holy Spirit, one God, now and forever.

VERSE

Alleluia. Greetings, O favored one! The Lord is with you. The Holy Spirit will come upon you. Alleluia. (Luke 1:28, 35)

or

Alleluia. From this day all generations will call me blessed: the Almighty has done great things for me, and holy is his name. Alleluia. (Luke 1:48–49)

READINGS

Isaiah 61:7-11

God's beleaguered people will enjoy a reversal of fortune when God shows faithfulness, causing the saved to rejoice in the Lord.

Psalm 45:11-16 (Psalm 45:10-15 NRSV)

I will make your name to be remembered from one generation to another. (Ps. 45:18)

Galatians 4:4-7

Through Christ's birth from a woman, we are no longer slaves governed by the law, but children and heirs of God.

Luke 1:46-55

Upon hearing that she was to become the mother of Jesus, Mary sings a song rejoicing in the Lord. In it she reflects the world-shaking priorities of God who favors the lowly and hungry.

COLOR White

THE PRAYERS

Confident in God's steadfast love through Jesus Christ and guided by the Holy Spirit, let us pray for the church, the world, and all people according to their needs.

A BRIEF SILENCE.

Mighty God, stir up your church to magnify your name, to rejoice in your salvation, and to bring forth your saving word for the sake of the world. God of grace,

let our prayer come before you.

Righteous God, make your justice known among the nations and leaders of the world, bring down the powerful, and lift up the lowly and oppressed. God of grace,

let our prayer come before you.

Faithful God, remember all those in need, especially those who are poor, hungry, orphaned, and those deprived of their land; show them the strength of your arm through those who work for justice. God of grace,

let our prayer come before you.

Compassionate God, look with favor upon the sick and dying everywhere *(especially)* and grant them healing, comfort, and peace. God of grace,

let our prayer come before you.

Merciful God, bless the members of this congregation through the proclamation of your word and participation in the sacrament, and fill us with your Holy Spirit. God of grace,

let our prayer come before you.

HERE OTHER INTERCESSIONS MAY BE OFFERED.

Redeeming God, we give you thanks for Mary, the mother of our Lord *(for names)*, and for all the saints who have received adoption as your children through baptism and now rest in your arms. Keep us in our baptismal

273

faith so that we too may be heirs of your heavenly king-dom. God of grace,

let our prayer come before you.

Teach us to pray, O God, and grant to all for whom we pray the good gifts that you have promised, through Jesus Christ our Lord.

Amen

IMAGES FOR PREACHING

If we didn't know that this was Mary's song, we might mistake it for a psalm of David, who was Mary's grand-father twenty-eight generations earlier (according to Matthew 1:17). If we didn't know about divine inver-sion, we might fail to realize how dramatically God turns things upside down. Mary's song is for all seasons. It is healing balm for those singed by the fires of the world; and it is ballast for those off balance. Long associated with evening prayer, this is the true soul music, for it is full of promise and affirmation for the soul.

Mary's song is surprisingly nuanced, with beat and rhythm. God, Mary croons, has looked with favor by lifting up a lowly servant. While there is no direct men-tion that she who sings is carrying God's son, that preg-nant reality is implied in every syllable. We know who is in Mary's womb. She and anyone can rejoice that God provides a Savior.

We must not overlook the great inversions. In Mary's song everything is condition-contrary-to-fact: the proud are scattered, the powerful are brought low, the lowly are raised up, the hungry are filled, the rich are sent away empty. That's not the way things are, of course, but that's the way the song goes.

Many literal-minded people find little sense in this exultant expression. How sad, for countless generations have called Mary blessed. They have been lifted by her sacred song which is, after all, the poetry of faith in which things do not have to be *literally* true to be *really* true. Mary sang her psalm, like her venerable grandfather from twenty-eight generations back. More than a hun-dred generations since, believers are still joining the song. With the voice of faith we sing not of the way things are, but of the way things *really* are. We sing of God's grace, God's giving, God's inversions. God chose Mary to bear a son who was and is the savior of the world. That is such a good story, it deserves the best song.

WORSHIP MATTERS

For centuries the church has sung Mary's song (Luke 1:46-55) as a canticle at evening prayer. Mary personifies the faith of the whole Christian church that is always ready to answer God's call to service. Far from being words of mere submission, though, Mary's song gives witness to a God of justice who brings down the power-ful and fills hungry people with good things. Consider using various forms of Mary's song throughout the year to give expression to the full range of emotions present in this great canticle. Among many hymn paraphases of this canticle are "My soul now magnifies the Lord" (LBW 180), "My soul proclaims your greatness" (WOV 730), "My soul does magnify the Lord" (TFF 168), "Canticle of the turning" (W&P 26), and "My heart sings out with joyful praise" (RWSB). How do each of these settings express one or more aspects of the canticle?

LET THE CHILDREN COME

In advance, invite each member of the congregation to bring one cut flower to worship today. Wildflowers and flowers from the garden are both appropriate. In the narthex have cut flowers ready for those who arrive empty-handed. Before the worship service begins, greeters and ushers may direct people to place their flow-ers in a large vase that sits on or near the altar. Encour-age parents to lift up the little ones, so each child can place a flower in the vase. The beautiful bouquet re-minds us of a beautiful person, one God chose to be Jesus' mother. Many of the youngest children will know that Mary was Jesus' mother and that today we can cele-brate the wonderful way she served God.

HYMNS FOR WORSHIP
GATHERING

Love divine, all loves excelling   LBW 315
Our Father, by whose name   LBW 357

HYMN OF THE DAY

Sing of Mary, pure and lowly   WOV 634

ALTERNATE HYMN OF THE DAY

Ye watchers and ye holy ones   LBW 175
My soul now magnifies the Lord   LBW 180

COMMUNION

Of the Father's love begotten   LBW 42

O Lord, we praise you   LBW 215

My soul proclaims your greatness   WOV 730

SENDING

Now thank we all our God   LBW 533, 534

For all the faithful women   WOV 692

ADDITIONAL HYMNS AND SONGS

Magnificat   RWSB

All who hunger, gather gladly   RWSB

I sing a maid   RS 899

When to Mary, the Word   HFG 144

MUSIC FOR THE DAY

PSALMODY

Jennings, Carolyn. PW , Cycle C.

"Psalm 45" in TP.

CHORAL

Carter, Andrew. "Mary's Magnificat." SATB, org. OXF X299.

Duruflé, Maurice. "Tota pulchra es." SSA. PRE 312-416721.

Holst, Gustav. "Jesu, Thou the Virgin-Born" in *Church Choir Book II.*
SATB, org. CPH 97-5610.

Jennings, Carolyn. "A New Magnificat." SATB, org, SA soli, opt cong.
AFP 080065255X. Also in *The Augsburg Choirbook.*
AFP 0800656784.

Laster, James. "Sing of Mary, Pure and Lowly." SATB, org.
AFP 0800674235.

Schulz-Widmar, Russell. "Mary Said Yes." SATB, kybd. SEL 405-201.

CHILDREN'S CHOIR

Rotermund, Donald. "A Responsorial Magnificat." (Luke 1:46-55) U,
org, 2 oct hb, cong. CPH 98-3576.

Telemann, G.P., arr. Schoenfeld. "I Will Rejoice in the Lord." (Isaiah
61:10) 2 pt, kybd. CG CGA817.

KEYBOARD/INSTRUMENTAL

Manz, Paul. "Tell Out, My Soul" (Woodlands) in *Six Advent Improvisations.* Org. MSM 10-002.

Porter, Emily Maxson. "For all the Faithful Women" in *For All the
Faithful: Hymn Settings for Organ.* Org. AFP 0800659422.

Uehlein, Christopher. "Postlude on an Original Antiphon" in *Blue
Cloud Abbey Organ Book.* Org. AFP 0800653343.

Young, Jeremy. "Ave Maria" in *Pianoforte Christmas.* Pno.
AFP 0800655702.

HANDBELL

Keller, Michael. "The Angel Gabriel from Heaven Came." 3-5 oct.
ALF 16475.

McChesney, Kevin. "Of the Father's Love Begotten." 3-5 oct.
BEC HB206.

PRAISE ENSEMBLE

Baloche, Rita. "But for Your Grace" in *God of Wonders Songbook.* 2 pt
trbl. HOS 20567.

Walker, Tommy. "He Knows My Name" in *Never Gonna Stop Songbook.*
3 pt trbl. HOS 18467.

275

August 15, 2004

Eleventh Sunday after Pentecost
Proper 15

INTRODUCTION

The candles that grace our worship seem like gentle lights, but fire is a powerful and purging force. Fire is used to purify molten ore and burn away the dross. In this day's worship, God's word comes among us like raging fire, consuming what is false and leaving behind pure gold.

Today the church honors Mary, the mother of our Lord. Her example of faithfulness serves as a model for the whole church.

PRAYER OF THE DAY

Almighty and ever-living God, you have given great and precious promises to those who believe. Grant us the perfect faith which overcomes all doubts, through your Son, Jesus Christ our Lord.

VERSE

Alleluia. The word of God is living and active, sharper than any two-edged sword, able to judge the thoughts and intentions of the heart. Alleluia. (Heb. 4:12)

READINGS

Jeremiah 23:23-29

Because Jeremiah preaches the unpopular message of God's judgment, he suffers rejection. Today's reading speaks of the mistaken notion that God sees only what is happening in the temple. Rather, Jeremiah points out, God's distance allows for a panoramic view of all the universe, including the lies and deceptions of false prophets.

Psalm 82

Arise, O God, and rule the earth. (Ps. 82:8)

Hebrews 11:29—12:2

The author of Hebrews presents us with a long list of biblical heroes whose exemplary faith enabled them to face the trials of life. In addition to this "cloud of witnesses," we have Jesus, the perfect model of faithful endurance.

Luke 12:49-56

Today's gospel contains harsh words concerning the purifying and potentially divisive effects of God's call.

People who follow the way of Christ often encounter hostility and rejection, even from those they love.

Alternate First Reading/Psalm

Isaiah 5:1-7

The prophet begins to sing about a beautiful vineyard, but the beautiful song becomes chilling as Isaiah describes the vineyard's destruction and suggests it is a picture of Israel.

Psalm 80:1-2, 8-19

Look down from heaven, O God; behold and tend this vine. (Ps. 80:14)

COLOR   Green

THE PRAYERS

Confident in God's steadfast love through Jesus Christ and guided by the Holy Spirit, let us pray for the church, the world, and all people according to their needs.
A BRIEF SILENCE.

God of fire, ignite those who preach and teach in your church to proclaim your word faithfully to those committed to their care. God of grace,

let our prayer come before you.

God of all nations, cause your justice to rule among all people so that the weak and orphaned, the lowly and the destitute are upheld and protected throughout the world. God of grace,

let our prayer come before you.

God of deliverance, heal the sick *(especially)*, feed the hungry, give hope to those in despair, and shower abundant blessings on the poor. God of grace,

let our prayer come before you.

God of power, strengthen the faith of your people in this congregation as we listen to your word and share in the holy meal prepared for us. God of grace,

let our prayer come before you.

HERE OTHER INTERCESSIONS MAY BE OFFERED.

God of the faithful, we give you thanks for the cloud of witnesses, especially Mary, mother of our Lord *(and)*, who surround us. May their lives draw us to Jesus, pioneer and perfecter of our faith, as we run the race set before us. God of grace,

let our prayer come before you.

Teach us to pray, O God, and grant to all for whom we pray the good gifts that you have promised, through Jesus Christ our Lord.

Amen

IMAGES FOR PREACHING

Untold numbers of viewers regularly turn to cable TV's Weather Channel for updates, feeding their insatiable interest in weather. With radar and satellites, frontal systems and weather maps, we have added scientific knowledge to the ability to interpret the appearance of earth and sky. Jesus doubtless had something different in mind when he addressed his remarks to the hypocrites in the crowd in today's gospel. Nonetheless, he wanted his hearers to know that a storm was brewing.

The stewing images of judgment and destruction—of nature and community out of joint—are still very disquieting and not easily interpreted. They are like an abstract painting whose power is apparent but whose meaning is elusive. Minnesota artist Luc Le Bon painted a picture suggestively called "Boundary Waters." The bottom four-fifths of this striking piece consists of alternating zones of streaked black and smoky white with small patches of green throughout. The uppermost zone is a contrasting strip of blood red punctuated with a mottled, hazy yellow disk, suggestive of a squashed sun on the horizon.

The painting, in spite of its title, eludes precise interpretation, very much like Jesus' jeremiad in today's passage. In Le Bon's painting it is not certain whether the sun is rising or setting. In Jesus' oracle one is not sure whether to cower in fear or seek space for hope in the midst of the storm. If in faith—not fear—one chooses the latter, it is essential to remember that no matter how great the disruption, the victory is ultimately God's. Whatever the shape and scope of judgment, we are obliged to remember that Jesus has destroyed death by his death. While we his people live in the midst of death, we also live in anticipation of new life. Those who have a weather eye would do well to keep it wide open for signs of God's judgment *and promise* during the present and the time to come.

WORSHIP MATTERS

How does the liturgy speak its own words of fire? If you look carefully, the church's worship is filled with fire and flames. During Advent, we light candles on the evergreen wreath. On Christmas Eve, we may hold burning candles in our hands as a sign of our baptismal call to be people of the light of Christ. At the Easter Vigil, the assembly gathers around the new fire—a bonfire!—and the paschal candle and then processes into the worship space holding brightly burning tapers. On Pentecost Sunday, many congregations fill their worship space with brightly burning candles. These actions allow the worshiping assembly to come into contact with living fire.

Of course, if we only see candles at a distance set next to an altar or pulpit and never hold them or come close to a bonfire, the powerful fire images of the gospels are diminished. The wise worship planner will ensure that the assembly comes in contact with (albeit safe) fires and flames. The wise preacher will draw the connection between the fire and flames we hold in our hands throughout the year and the fire of the gospel we are to be in daily life.

LET THE CHILDREN COME

Today help children make the connection between our actions in worship and our actions in our everyday lives. Followers of Christ carry their Sunday lives into their weekday ones. Here are some examples:

We pray before the meal of the Lord's Supper / We can pray before we eat meals.

In worship we confess our sins, we tell God we are sorry. / We can tell others we are sorry.

In worship we sing praises to God. / We can sing our church songs every day.

In worship we listen to God's word. / We can read the Bible daily in family devotions.

In worship we give our offering, our gifts of money. / Every day we can share our gifts of talents and abilities with others.

HYMNS FOR WORSHIP
GATHERING

Immortal, invisible, God only wise   LBW 526

He comes to us as one unknown   WOV 768

HYMN OF THE DAY

Lead on, O King eternal! LBW 495

ALTERNATE HYMN OF THE DAY

If God himself be for me LBW 454

We've come this far by faith TFF 197, RWSB

COMMUNION

I come, O Savior, to your table LBW 213

I want to walk as a child of the light WOV 649

SENDING

How firm a foundation LBW 507

Have thine own way, Lord TFF 152

ADDITIONAL HYMNS AND SONGS

Guide my feet TFF 153

Take, O take me as I am RWSB

We have seen the Lord/*Ni me mwana bwana* RWSB

Be bold, be strong W&P 15

MUSIC FOR THE DAY

PSALMODY

Paradowski, John. PW , Cycle C.

Psalms for Praise and Worship: A Complete Liturgical Psalter. ABI 0687093260.

Williams, Kenneth E. "Psalm 82" in TP.

CHORAL

Attwood, Thomas, arr. K. Lee Scott. "Come, Holy Ghost" in *Sing Forth God's Praise.* AFP 0800675266 (MH voice); AFP 080067538X (ML voice).

Berger, Jean. "O Give Thanks unto the Lord." SATB. AFP 11-1982. OP.

Buxtehude, Dietrich. "Lord, Keep Us Steadfast in Thy Word." SATB, str trio, kybd. CPH 97-6331.

Ellingboe, Bradley. "Let Us Run to Jesus." SATB, org, cong., brass. KJO 8901.

Handel, G. F. "Why Do the Nations So Furiously Rage?" in *Messiah.* B solo, kybd. Various ed.

CHILDREN'S CHOIR

Callahan, Charles. "A Children's Carol." U, kybd. MSM 50-3751.

Shepherd, John. "A Living Faith." U/2 pt, kybd. CG CGA580.

KEYBOARD/INSTRUMENTAL

Callahan, Charles. "Awake, Awake to Love and Work" in *American Folk Hymn Suite.* Pno. CPH 97-6972.

Cherwien, David. "Triptych on 'The Ash Grove.'" Org. AFP 0800658256.

Helman, Michael. "Lancashire" in *Three for Easter.* Org. AFP 0800674790.

Linker, Janet. "Variations on 'Foundation.'" Org. CPH 97-6586.

Wasson, Laura. "You Are Near" in *A Piano Tapestry,* vol. 2. Pno. AFP 0800658183.

HANDBELL

Bisbee, B. Wayne. "Faith of Our Fathers." 3-4 oct. National HB209.

McChesney, Kevin. "Praise God, Praise Him." 2-3 oct. AFP 0800655060.

PRAISE ENSEMBLE

Adler, Dan, arr. Dan Goeller. "Your Ways Are Right." SAB, kybd, opt cong. AFP 080067443X.

Beaker. "Step by Step" in *More Songs for Praise and Worship.* SATB. WRD 3010387016 (vocal ed); WRD 3010186363 (pno, vcs, perc).

DeShazo, Lynn. "Worthy of Praises" in *Sing for Joy Songbook Hosanna!* 3 pt trbl. HOS 21377.

Sunday, August 15

MARY, MOTHER OF OUR LORD

See pages 273–75.

Friday, August 20

BERNARD, ABBOT OF CLAIRVAUX, 1153

Bernard was a Cistercian monk who became an abbot of great spiritual depth. He was a mystical writer deeply devoted to the humanity of Christ and consequently to the affective dimension of spirituality. He was critical of one of the foremost theologians of the day, Peter Abelard, because he believed Abelard's approach to faith was too rational and did not provide sufficient room for mystery. Bernard's devotional writings are still read today. His sermon on the Song of Solomon treats that book as an allegory of Christ's love for humanity. Bernard wrote several hymns, five of which are in *LBW*. Singing his hymn "Jesus the very thought of you" (316) could be a way to commemorate this monk at gatherings within the congregation today.

August 22, 2004

Twelfth Sunday after Pentecost
Proper 16

INTRODUCTION

Early Christians referred to Sunday as the Lord's Day, the eighth day of the week, the day beyond time in which a new creation is born. We gather this day for new beginnings, eager to be recreated by the Word who raises us to new life. Jesus insists that the older sabbath, too, is intended to be a blessing, not a strict rule.

PRAYER OF THE DAY

God of all creation, you reach out to call people of all nations to your kingdom. As you gather disciples from near and far, count us also among those who boldly confess your Son Jesus Christ as Lord.

VERSE

Alleluia. Our Savior Jesus Christ abolished death and brought life and immortality to light through the gospel. Alleluia. (2 Tim. 1:10)

READINGS

Isaiah 58:9b-14

The Lord promises those who have returned from exile that where justice and mercy prevail, the ruins will be rebuilt and light will rise in the darkness. It is a day for new beginnings.

Psalm 103:1-8

The LORD crowns you with mercy and lovingkindness. (Ps. 103:4)

Hebrews 12:18-29

The writer to the Hebrews presents a striking vision of the eternal dwelling place and the one who welcomes the righteous. It holds no fear, only forgiveness through Christ's blood.

Luke 13:10-17

Jesus heals a woman on the sabbath, offering her a new beginning for her life. When religious leaders are angered because Jesus did work on the sabbath, Jesus insists that new creation is not constrained by a legalistic reading of an ancient calendar.

Alternate First Reading/Psalm

Jeremiah 1:4-10

The call of the prophet Jeremiah is a reminder that age is not an obstacle to being a witness for God. Jeremiah's difficult ministry in the years before the Babylonian exile is part of a plan God made before Jeremiah was born. God will give the prophet the words he needs to say.

Psalm 71:1-6

From my mother's womb you have been my strength. (Ps. 71:6)

COLOR   Green

THE PRAYERS

Confident in God's steadfast love through Jesus Christ and guided by the Holy Spirit, let us pray for the church, the world, and all people according to their needs.

A BRIEF SILENCE.

For all the baptized, that we would take delight in the sabbath, gladly hear your word, receive with joy your forgiveness, and savor the feast you have prepared for us. God of grace,

let our prayer come before you.

For all nations and peoples, that you would raise up leaders in the world who will feed the hungry, bring justice to the oppressed, and work for peace. God of grace,

let our prayer come before you.

For all those afflicted with chronic diseases, for those cut off from family and loved ones through wars and conflicts, for the sick and dying *(especially)*, that you would provide wholeness, reconciliation, and healing in their lives. God of grace,

let our prayer come before you.

For our congregation, that we would be the body of Christ in the world and bring justice and healing to the oppressed in our community. God of grace,

let our prayer come before you.

HERE OTHER INTERCESSIONS MAY BE OFFERED.

In thanksgiving for *(names,* and) all the saints who dwell with you in the heavenly Jerusalem, that we, following the example of their faith in Christ, might one day also

279

enjoy your reign that cannot be shaken. God of grace,
let our prayer come before you.
Teach us to pray, O God, and grant to all for whom we
pray the good gifts that you have promised, through
Jesus Christ our Lord.
Amen

IMAGES FOR PREACHING

Technically, the leader of the synagogue in today's gospel
was correct, for in Israel the command to observe the sabbath was foundational (Exod. 20:8-11). Jesus' healing
could indeed be regarded as a violation of the rules. We recall that this was neither the first nor the last time Jesus
tested the limits of this commandment. He was twice cited
for sabbath violations in Luke 6 and again in Luke 14.

In each case, by stressing the humane over the legal,
Jesus tested the limits of both the law and common
sense. Even the strictest law keeper had to recognize that
there were exceptions. If one was allowed to untie an ani-
mal on the sabbath, he argued, it was also legitimate to
set someone free from bondage, hunger, or illness on
that day. Jesus, like any gifted rabbi, could have made a
case in religious law on this point.

However, he called those who disagreed with him
hypocrites, and he put to shame those with whom he argued, thus landing in deep trouble. Arguing fine points
of law is one thing; humiliating your opponents—
especially when they have clout—is quite another.
Standoffs like this had a cumulative effect. They enraged
his opponents and encouraged the adverse opinion,
which eventually led to Jesus' arrest, trial, and death.

Clearly Jesus regarded issues of health and holiness
as significant enough to stake his life on. His overriding
concern was with releasing the captives, the recovery of
sight, letting the oppressed go free—even on the sabbath. Jesus adopted this prophetic mandate at the beginning of his public ministry (Luke 4); and he remained
unwavering, as we see in this controversy. For him it was
right that the woman bound for eighteen long years be
set free from her bondage even on the sabbath. The God
of law and love still calls for proclamation and liberation
every day of the week.

WORSHIP MATTERS

A pastor may often communicate the healing power of
Christ with a knowing look or a genuine smile, or

through a firm handshake, a gentle hug, or a reassuring
grasp on the shoulder. A pastor will also communicate
the healing power of Christ through the laying on of
hands with prayer and anointing with oil (James 5:14).
In his proclamation of the coming reign of God, Jesus
promised not only *shalom* (peace) but wholeness for all
those who are broken by sin, illness, or despair. In all
these ways, the pastor and the healing community of the
church become vehicles through which the reign of God
breaks into our world and brings us Christ's healing and
new life.

When does your congregation gather to celebrate a
service of the word for healing? See *Renewing Worship 4:
Life Passages* for newer provisional healing rites.

LET THE CHILDREN COME

Today draw attention to the beauty of your worship
space. This space is holy—set aside—to celebrate God's
love. Even if your worship space is a multipurpose place,
whenever you worship it is transformed into a sacred
space. Let the children decorate the space today. Consider large baskets of late summer flowers. Make paper
chains from a variety of colors of green paper, perhaps
adding a few golds and oranges of the autumn season,
which is approaching for many in North America. Children may create designs for bulletin covers. Find simple
ways for the children to process into the sanctuary at the
beginning of the worship service, adding the decorations
as they go.

HYMNS FOR WORSHIP
GATHERING

O day of rest and gladness   LBW 251
Many and great, O God, are your works   WOV 794

HYMN OF THE DAY

Glories of your name are spoken   LBW 358

ALTERNATE HYMN OF THE DAY

How firm a foundation   LBW 507
Come, we that love the Lord   WOV 742, TFF 135

COMMUNION

Let us break bread together   LBW 212
Grains of wheat   WOV 708

SENDING

Rejoice, O pilgrim throng!   LBW 553

Praise to you, O Christ, our Savior   WOV 614, W&P 118

ADDITIONAL HYMNS AND SONGS

Canticle of the turning   W&P 26, RWSB

Praise the one who breaks the darkness   ASG 34, RWSB

Heal me, O Lord   TFF 189

Standing at the future's threshold   NCH 538

MUSIC FOR THE DAY

PSALMODY

Norbert, Gregory. "Psalm 103: O Bless the Lord" in *Morning Prayer–Evening Prayer.* OCP 10372.

Paradowski, John. PW , Cycle C.

Ziegenhals, Harriet Ilse. "The Lord Is Kind and Merciful" in *Sing Out! A Children's Psalter.* WLP 7191.

My soul, now praise your maker!   LBW 519

Praise to the Lord, the Almighty   LBW 543

Praise, my soul, the King of heaven   LBW 549

Bless the Lord, O my soul   WOV 798

CHORAL

Beethoven, Ludwig van. "The Heavens Sing Praises" in *Sing Forth God's Praise.* AFP 0800675266 (MH voice); AFP 080067538X (ML voice).

Handel, G. F. "But Who May Abide" in *Messiah.* B solo, kybd. Various ed.

Handel, G. F. "Thus Saith the Lord" in *Messiah.* B solo, kybd. Various ed.

Shute, Linda Cable. "You Satisfy the Hungry Heart." SATB, org, opt cong. AFP 0800674693.

Thompson, Randall. "Alleluia." SATB. ECS 1786.

CHILDREN'S CHOIR

Kosche, Kenneth. "Bless God's Holy Name." (Ps. 103:1, 4-5) 2 pt, kybd, opt 6 hb, 2 oct range. CG CGA766.

Page, Sue Ellen. "Jesus' Hands Were Kind Hands." U, kybd, fl. CG CGA485.

KEYBOARD/INSTRUMENTAL

Hustad, Don. "Glorious Things of Thee Are Spoken" in *Collected Works of Don Hustad.* Org. HOP 353.

Meyer, Lawrence. "Processional of Joy." Pno/org. AFP 080065658X. OP.

Porter, Rachel Trelstad. "It Is Well" in *Day by Day.* Pno. AFP 0800656326.

HANDBELL

Honoré, Jeffrey. "Marching to Zion." 3-5 oct. AFP 080067488X.

Hopson, Hal H. "How Firm a Foundation." 3-5 oct. ALF 12408.

Keller, Michael. "Marching to Zion." 3-5 oct. ALF 12409.

Page, Anna Laura. "How Firm a Foundation." 2-3 oct. MSM 30-806.

PRAISE ENSEMBLE

Sadler, Gary and Jamie Harvill. "Ancient of Days" in *Best of the Best.* FEL 1891062018.

Willard, Kelly. "Make Me a Servant" in W&P.

Tuesday, August 24

ST. BARTHOLOMEW, APOSTLE

Bartholomew is mentioned as one of Jesus' disciples in Matthew, Mark, and Luke. The list in John does not include him but rather Nathanael, and these two are often assumed to be the same person. Except for his name on these lists of the twelve, little is known. Some traditions say Bartholomew preached in India or Armenia following the resurrection. In art, Bartholomew is pictured holding a flaying knife to indicate the manner in which he was killed.

In Bartholomew we have a model for the way many Christians live out their faith: anonymously. Like Bartholomew we are called by name to follow, though much of what we do in faith is quiet and unrecognized. Today we can look to the example of Bartholomew and pray for strength and guidance as we continue to live as disciples of Christ.

Saturday, August 28

AUGUSTINE, BISHOP OF HIPPO, 430

Augustine was one of the greatest theologians of the Western church. Born in North Africa, he was a philosophy student in Carthage, where he later became a teacher of rhetoric. Much of his young life was a debauched one. As an adult he came under the influence of Ambrose, the bishop of Milan, and through him came to see Christianity as a religion appropriate for a philosopher. Augustine was baptized by Ambrose at the Easter Vigil in 387. He was ordained four years later and made

281

bishop of Hippo in 396. Augustine was a defender of the Christian faith and argued, against the Donatists, that the holiness of the church did not depend on the holiness of its members, particularly the clergy, but that holiness comes from Christ, the head of the church. Augustine's autobiography, *Confessions*, tells of his slow move toward faith and includes the line, "Late have I loved thee."

August 29, 2004

Thirteenth Sunday after Pentecost
Proper 17

INTRODUCTION

Who is welcome in your community of faith? And how would they know that they are? Today's readings ask us to think about hospitality, especially as it is practiced at the table. The feast of God's radical grace calls us into this place and connects friends and strangers with each other.

PRAYER OF THE DAY

O God, we thank you for your Son who chose the path of suffering for the sake of the world. Humble us by his example, point us to the path of obedience, and give us strength to follow his commands; through your Son, Jesus Christ our Lord.

VERSE

Alleluia. Your words became to me a joy and the delight of my heart. Alleluia. (Jer. 15:16)

READINGS

Proverbs 25:6-7

The book of Proverbs is known as wisdom literature. It gave directions to Israel's leaders and people for the conduct of daily life. Today's reading is about humility.

or Sirach 10:12-18

Judgment rests upon the proud.

Saturday, August 28

MOSES THE BLACK, MONK, C. 400

A man of great strength and rough character, Moses the Black was converted to Christian faith toward the close of the fourth century. Prior to his conversion he had been a thief and a leader of a gang of robbers. The story of his conversion is unknown, but eventually, he became a desert monk at Skete. The habit of his monastic community was white, though Moses is reported to have said, "God knows I am black within." The change in his heart and life had a profound impact on his native Ethiopia. He was murdered when Berbers attacked his monastery.

Psalm 112

The righteous are merciful and full of compassion. (Ps. 112:4)

Hebrews 13:1-8, 15-16

The conclusion of the letter to the Hebrews contains many suggestions for the conduct of life, all of which are shaped by God's love toward us in Jesus Christ.

Luke 14:1, 7-14

In Luke's gospel, Jesus often tells parables about meals in order to illustrate God's unexpected grace and to lead people to a faithful response. Here, we have two examples of these stories: one encourages humility, and in the other Jesus invites his listeners to review their guest list.

Alternate First Reading/Psalm

Jeremiah 2:4-13

God, who has remained faithful despite Israel's rebellion, calls upon the heavenly council to witness the incredible foolishness of a people who, under the flawed leadership of priests, rulers, and prophets, willingly abandon God's life-giving water for leaky cisterns in the wilderness.

Psalm 81:1, 10-16

I feed you with the finest wheat and satisfy you with honey from the rock. (Ps. 81:16)

THE PRAYERS

Confident in God's steadfast love through Jesus Christ and guided by the Holy Spirit, let us pray for the church, the world, and all people according to their needs.

A BRIEF SILENCE.

That the leaders of the church may serve you and your people with humility and integrity. God of grace,

let our prayer come before you.

That all people would honor your gift of creation and strive to preserve its resources for future generations. God of grace,

let our prayer come before you.

That all those in prison would be remembered by family and loved ones, and that all the sick *(especially)* would feel your healing touch. God of grace,

let our prayer come before you.

That our congregation would be a place of hospitality, where the stranger is welcomed and the lowly are given a place of honor. God of grace,

let our prayer come before you.

HERE OTHER INTERCESSIONS MAY BE OFFERED.

In thanksgiving for those saints who have modeled humility and hospitality *(especially)*; may their lives inspire us to greater faith in Christ and service to the world. God of grace,

let our prayer come before you.

Teach us to pray, O God, and grant to all for whom we pray the good gifts that you have promised, through Jesus Christ our Lord.

Amen

IMAGES FOR PREACHING

Manners at meals can be troublesome, especially if someone is critically watching. Which fork to use, a stain that blooms where the napkin is not—these are just a couple of potentially embarrassing moments for the self-conscious diner. Where one sits and with whom can also be matters of concern, as it was in today's meal story. The matter of manners is sticky at this sabbath dinner party, for we learn at the outset that Jesus was under scrutiny. Considering the kind of unsettling behavior he had demonstrated on other sabbath days, that should not have been surprising.

When things begin to go wrong, one can try telling a story, hoping it might take the edge off awkwardness. Jesus did that by telling a parable about hospitality.

People had been watching him critically throughout the meal while hypocritically seeking pride of place for themselves. Jesus acknowledged that move in his story; and he actually turned the tables on his critics when his parable moved from hospitality to humbleness. In the story Jesus skillfully illustrated the danger inherent in self-advancement. Watch out how you position yourself, he cautioned, for someone is always waiting and willing to leap over or outflank you.

Perhaps it was during a later course that Jesus broadened his observation about self-promotion and humbleness. Diners listened to Jesus as he shifted focus from table place to guest list. The banquet in the expanded story was no longer for cronies; it was for the outsider and those who would normally not even have a place at the table. The meal clearly pointed to something far different. The phrase "resurrection of the righteous" rang a bell and moved the story to a different plane. In the end Jesus was no longer talking about manners and etiquette. He was giving his listeners much more, a glimpse of something else, a foretaste of the feast to come. His story—like the meal itself—is something to savor.

WORSHIP MATTERS

In the communion, Christ feeds us with his body and blood. He gives himself to us as food for the journey of life. He draws us into an intimate union with himself and the communion of saints. He forgives, restores, and enlivens faith.

Have you ever noticed the "economy" of communion? Christ gives himself to each person regardless of gender, age, race or ethnic group, education, income, strength, or mental ability. He gives himself equally to each person: one group or type of person does not receive more than another group or type. There seems to be a prodigality in the way Christ offers himself to his brothers and sisters. This food—ordinary and extraordinary—is given without discrimination.

Is there a model here for the manner in which we are to share food with each other? It would seem that Paul thought so. He was quick to point out to the well-fed and well-off Corinthian Christians that they mocked Christ's prodigal gift of himself in the eucharist by refusing to see its implication for sharing food with the poor.

How might the "economy" of Holy Communion

lead to a just and equitable sharing of food in our society where thousands of children go to bed hungry every night?

LET THE CHILDREN COME

How does your congregation care for visitors? In advance, meet with families with a variety of ages of children who would be willing to meet with and sit with visitors. As they worship with visitors, the children in your congregation can mentor the children who are visiting, helping them to follow the order of worship, locate hymns, and bringing them up for the eucharist. Visitors will feel welcome and at ease knowing someone is caring for them, leading them through the maze of a Sunday worship service. Children, who are members, will experience the joy of hospitality.

HYMNS FOR WORSHIP

GATHERING

Joyful, joyful we adore thee   LBW 551
O God beyond all praising   WOV 797

HYMN OF THE DAY

Jesus, the very thought of you   LBW 316

ALTERNATE HYMN OF THE DAY

Here in this place   WOV 718
O God of earth and altar   LBW 428

COMMUNION

Now we join in celebration   LBW 203
We come to the hungry feast   WOV 766

SENDING

Forth in thy name, O Lord, I go   LBW 505
O Christ the same   WOV 778
Jesus in the morning   TFF 167

ADDITIONAL HYMNS AND SONGS

Welcome table   TFF 263, RWSB
Let us go now to the banquet / *Vamos todos al banquete*
LLC 410, RWSB
Break with the hungry ones your bread   RWSB
Praise the Savior, ye who know him   TWC 125

MUSIC FOR THE DAY
PSALMODY

Guimont, Michel. "Psalm 112: A Light Rises in the Darkness" in RS.
Hopson, Hal H. *Psalm Refrains and Tones.* HOP 425.
Paradowski, John. PW , Cycle C.

CHORAL

Christiansen, F. Melius. "Psalm 50, Movement II: Offer Unto God." SATB. AFP 0800657578.
Dowland, John. "He That Is Down Need Fear No Fall" in *Oxford Book of Easy Anthems.* SATB. OXF 3533219.
Handel, G.F. "Every Valley" in *Messiah.* T solo, kybd. Various ed.
Hayes, Mark. "Welcome Table." SATB, pno. AFP 0800676033.
Mendelssohn, Felix. "For the Lord Will Lead" in *To God Will I Sing.* AFP 0800674332 (MH voice); AFP 0800674340 (ML voice).
Moore, Philip. "He That Is Down Need Fear No Fall." SATB, org. RME.
Vaughan Williams, Ralph. "O Taste and See." SATB, org. OXF 43.909.

CHILDREN'S CHOIR

Page, Sue Ellen. "Every Morning's Sun." U, kybd, opt 2 glock. CG CGA193.
Wold, Wayne L. "To the Banquet, Come" in LS. U, kybd.

KEYBOARD/INSTRUMENTAL

Guilmant, Alexandre. "Adagio Molto" from *Third Sonata for Organ.* Org. Various ed. Also in *The Complete Wedding Collection, Book. II.* BEC OC23.
Miller, Aaron David. "Great Is Thy Faithfulness" in *Three Gospel Favorites for Organ.* Org. MSM 10-871.

HANDBELL

Helman, Michael. "Variations on 'Gather Us In.'" 3-5 oct, opt hc. AFP 0800674928.
Honoré, Jeffrey. "Gather Us In." 3-5 oct. CPH 97-6556.
Mathis, William. "We Come to the Hungry Feast" in *Let Us Talents and Tongues Employ and We Come to the Hungry Feast.* 3-5 oct, opt hc. AFP 0800658884.

PRAISE ENSEMBLE

Morgan, Reuben. "Hear Our Praises" in *Worship Leader's Song Discovery,* vol. 13. Worship Leader 1999-03-LS.
Nystrom, Martin. "As the Deer" in W&P

284

Tuesday, August 31

JOHN BUNYAN, TEACHER, 1688

John Bunyan had little schooling but became one of the most remarkable figures of seventeenth-century literature. He was a lay preacher who made his living as a tinker. After the restoration in England he was ordered to stop preaching, but he refused and was jailed several times. His spiritual pilgrimage is revealed in his works, particularly *The Pilgrim's Progress*. It is an allegory of a person's experience from his first awareness of sin, through a personal conversion to Christ, then on to the life of faith and then finally to the "Celestial City," the true and eternal home. His commemoration and his own journey offer strength for people to continue their own quest for spiritual truth.

Thursday, September 2

NIKOLAI FREDERIK SEVERIN GRUNDTVIG, BISHOP, RENEWER OF THE CHURCH, 1872

Grundtvig was one of two principal Danish theologians of the nineteenth century; the other was Søren Kierkegaard. Grundtvig's ministry as a parish pastor had a difficult start. He was officially censured after his first sermon, though he did receive approval a year later to be ordained. He served with his father for two years but was unable to receive a call for seven years after that. In 1826 he was forced to resign after he attacked the notion that Christianity was merely a philosophical idea rather than God's revelation made known to us in Christ and through word and sacrament. This belief would be a hallmark of Grundtvig's writing. He spent the last thirty-three years as a chaplain at a home for elderly women. From his university days he was convinced that poetry spoke to the human spirit better than prose, and he wrote more than a thousand hymns. Eight of his hymns are in *LBW*.

Saturday, September 4

ALBERT SCHWEITZER, MISSIONARY TO AFRICA, 1965

Schweitzer was a philosopher, theologian, and an ordained Lutheran minister. He wrote *The Quest for the Historical Jesus*. He was also an organist who published a study of Johann Sebastian Bach. But he set aside careers as a university lecturer and musician, went to medical school, and became a missionary in the Gabon province of French Equatorial Africa. He believed that the solution to the world's problems was simple: have reverence for life. His style of practicing medicine shocked some, but he was a humanitarian who served Christ by serving his neighbors in need.

Now that school is resuming in many places, parishes can hold up Schweitzer as an example of someone who used vast knowledge for service and ministry to others.

285

AUTUMN

Coming home to Christ in the liturgy

Images *of the* Season

A visit to an antique shop or second-hand store

reveals the "in between" way in which objects

are categorized. An old tattered quilt, an incomplete

set of dishes, a refinished chest of drawers, faded paintings and pictures that are too good to throw away—all of these items remind us that times passes, yet has not concluded. Likewise, an item's worth can change: its value increases for some and it decreases for others. An in-between time, betwixt the beginnings and endings, the feasts and the fasts—this is autumn liturgy.

In a way, autumn is an arbitrary and ambiguous time of the year. With the post-Pentecost season's length extending from early summer to early winter, the church often struggles with a focus at this midpoint. Of course, it is a time for continuing growth in faith, a time for building on the foundations that have been witnessed through the resurrection appearances. Yet the challenge of this time of year often overwhelms. Where is the church headed? It is like waiting for a train that can be heard in the distance, yet seems to take forever to arrive.

The biblical stories are familiar and well-worn. They have tinges of memories associated with them. They have been heard before. Once in a while, there is something new and fresh, vital and surprising about the stories; more usually, though, they are retold with a rehearsed expectation and familiarity. They are, after all, part of the celebrated canon. They are a given.

Yet, at the very same time, it is the richness found in the retelling that offers a breath for new life. That which is well-worn is revitalized through an intimacy in a deep and abiding recollection of what is true and good, honorable and pure. Autumn liturgy is a time for homecoming, a coming home to Christ.

Autumn itself always brings about a number of changes. The seasons are marked by cycles of reversals: the stars shift in the sky; the natural world finds new ways of living. Likewise, school's days begin or end, new calendar years are established, old patterns of living are undertaken. A cabin might be closed for the winter, new windows put up on the house, clothing styles changed— these are marks of a shifting and transitional time.

Even though this change is apparent, it takes different ears and eyes to notice that the changes are not always dramatic or even recognizable. Conversion is much the same, seldom happening in an earth-shaking way. More often, transformation takes place in the ways that are hidden in the heart.

Perhaps it is the time of year to look for the subtle and simple nuances that contribute to a common faith. Perhaps it is the time of the year to revisit those aspects of faith that are considered understood and agreed upon. That would give an opportunity to interrogate and discover anew the richness of a life lived within the liturgy of the church.

To investigate the pattern of the liturgy might be a good place to start. To see the possibilities within the pattern of gathering, receiving, experiencing, and sending through the word and sacraments affords the chance of liturgical formation. This is not to say that everything ought to be explained in great detail. That kind of didactic teaching can rob the liturgy of its multiple meanings. Rather, to reflect briefly in a homily or in a Sunday bulletin about the pattern that shapes community life—that might be the way to look anew at what is given, to see afresh what is gift. Liturgical formation is reflecting on how an understanding of the liturgy can help to shape the Christian life.

Patterns of formation are abundantly present in the texts for this time of year: teachings and healings, parables and ponderings. This was the reason Jesus gathered people together, to shape both their understanding and their living—to form them as children of God. This is the task of any catechesis: to shape individuals as individuals and to shape them all into one community.

Likewise, to revisit the historic creeds and confessions provides another opportunity to eke out new and profound commitments to the oldest expressions of faith to which the church attests. It might be the right time to look at the Small Catechism. Or work more intentionally

288

with the church year's lesser festivals and commemorations. Working in consultation with ecumenical partners, the lengthy Pentecost season provides ample chances to explore common convictions and unique gifts.

It could also be the time of year to consider exploring hymnody at a greater depth.

Telling the stories of composers or poets or bringing a practicing composer or poet to the congregation would add layers of meaning to all of the hymns. Calling upon musicians and artists in the community to share their talents and understandings could be a way to enhance appreciation for the old but new story.

In Christ, that is is old can become new. That is why the liturgical year has a lengthy time of reflecting on the saving and redemptive work of the Christ who lives in the daily-ness of existence. Using the ordinary to usher in the extraordinary, drawing attention to the commonplace to bring to light the uncommon truth, pointing beyond the seen to the unseen, these are the tasks during autumn liturgy. When, for instance, the community gathers around a paten with some bread on it and a chalice with some wine in it, mystery across time speaks. The servers hold the real presence of Christ's body and blood which time itself cannot hold.

Antiques have value not only for how they function, but for how they form a frame of reference for our experience. They have stood the test of time with generations of hands cleaning them faithfully, wiping dust from them. Old beds have been wrapped in blankets of prayers providing rest and refreshment to generations. An antique clock speaks about the confirmation or the wedding that was the occasion of its giving. The sideboard recounts the sustenance that has been prepared by generations. Through the subtle changes that are seen in the common and ordinary, a deepening and abiding faith is nurtured and sustained.

Environment *and* Art *for the* Season

It seems like the Sundays after Pentecost go on

and on. In the midst of this long, green season

of the church year, there are a couple of natural

turning points in our routine, day-to-day existence. We need the breaks that a change of meteorological seasons brings us. They keep us from the feeling that one week is just like the last. As summer comes to a close and we shift into our autumn schedules, church education programs as well as other committees and ministry groups begin again if they took a summer break. Time seems to speed up, and more and more people, excited and refreshed from traveling and vacations, are around to take advantage of opportunities to learn and grow. New learning opportunities present us with a time of renewed discipleship. The more we learn and grow, the more we appreciate the work of the Holy Spirit in our lives.

ANALYZING YOUR SPACE

This would be a good time for those interested in the environment and art of the church to convene in order to discuss and reflect on issues related to the worship space. Set aside a time to get together with any interested parties, especially those who visited other churches with a questionnaire in hand. (See Environment and Art for summer to review the questionnaire.) The experiential learning gained from seeing and reflecting on other worship spaces is important. However, we also need to allow the thoughts and insights of others into our conversation. Two ways in which you might bring another perspective to your learning are: 1) Hold a series of classes for anyone interested to study the foundational document of the Renewing Worship project, *Renewing Worship 2: Principles for Worship* (available from Augsburg Fortress). It includes a section dealing specifically with liturgical space, a wonderful resource for anyone working in this area of the church's worship. 2) Bring in someone with experience and education in liturgical consulting. Liturgical consulting, sometimes called "liturgical design consulting" is a growing field in the church. Liturgical consultants work with communities who are interested in building or renovating their worship space and related spaces or who are interested in making better liturgical use of the space they have. If you are interested in bringing someone in, contact your denominational office for suggestions. (The design studio of the ELCA is located at Augsburg Fortress in Philadelphia, 800/348-5887.)

ART FOR THE SEASON

With classes back in session, now would be a good time to involve different groups in creating art for your worshiping community. You can have the students (or anyone interested) in your church draw something related to an image or a scene from the appointed texts for each Sunday. Of course, they will need to be working in advance. Challenge the artists to get us thinking about the reading in a new way—perhaps focus on an overlooked detail, move the action to the present day, or depict not the reading itself but the consequences or implications for us. Some of the best art sneaks up on you and touches you at an unexpected time from an unexpected place.

These pictures can be displayed in a number of ways. You could mount them as individual works along the walls and doors of your entrance and gathering spaces. You could display them along the walls of your worship space. You could arrange them artfully on larger pieces of green backing and make weekly, textural paraments and cover the front of the altar and places where the word is read. From far away, it will look like green with other colors mixed in. From close up, it will be your community's rendering of the texts for people to reflect

on as they come forward for communion or before and after church. This also has the benefit of providing a change in paraments even though the liturgical color remains green. Another way to display these works of art is to use projection technology. Find a suitable spot to project the images, then do so using one of the following methods. Use a plain paper overhead projector (or "opaque projector"). Have the drawings turned into overheads at a local copy shop and use a standard overhead projector. Scan them into a computer and connect it to a computer projector. Take slide photographs of drawings and then show them from a slide projector. Find the technology that you are most comfortable with and can afford. Most likely, you don't have to invest in anything other than slide film and developing costs or the cost of having pictures turned into overheads.

Another fun multiple-session project that would get everyone in the church thinking about your worship space in different ways is to invite people to make foam board models of the worship space. These can be made in various sizes. You can focus on both the inside and the outside of the space. While working on this, see if you can find the architectural plans of the church to use as inspiration. This type of model is what many architects use to help a client see in three dimensions what is going on in a particular space. You could even group people into teams of different ages and use this as an intergenerational project for the congregation. Make sure when you create your models that you try to get the proportions right. You will have to take some basic measurements in order to do this, which should be easy enough to do. Once the model of the existing building is created, it's easier to visualize changes that might enhance the worship, and to demonstrate your perspective to others.

Preaching *with the* Season

For better or worse, we get several fresh, new starts

at life per year. As Christian communities, we begin

anew with the coming of Advent. In the darkness of

December, we take stock, repent, and prepare to enter the light of Christ's coming. Soon thereafter, along with the rest of the world we hang a new calendar on January I and firmly resolve that this time around we'll break old habits and establish new patterns. On top of that, we each get our annual birthday and with it a new year of life.

Autumn also offers many of us a chance to start over. Students and teachers begin again with clean slates and high hopes. The rest of us have spent enough years in school so that we, too, still experience the coming of fall as a time of confident expectation and new beginnings. The return of those familiar yellow buses triggers an old instinct to sharpen a few pencils and buy a new box of crayons. Any hallway with freshly waxed tiles smells like hope.

Ironically, the odor of death comes to linger in autumn's crisp air as well. Frost kills, leaves fall, and moisture begins the work of recycling summer's verdant bounty into next year's humus. Cooler, shortening days remind us that we, too, live in the rhythm of things that return to dust.

Add to this the fact that most of us will never again in our lifetime enter autumn without graphic reminders of what happened on September II, 2001, a day when death came visiting in a particularly awful way. We'll breathe dust and ashes for years to come, even as our parents and grandparents have tasted blood on December 7.

Grace allows another angle of vision on some of this dying. The leaves grow tired of being green, say the poets of what happens in late summer. To escape their boredom, boughs of leaves break ranks with the grass and evergreens. They don parade hues and show off for a spell. They wish to show us, perhaps, that they've watched the sunsets and learned the heavens' tricks, and how the sun struts its stuff in those last moments before it sinks beneath our world.

Soon enough, it's true, we'll rake up their lifeless remains to burn or bury. Of this year's billions, only two or three will find their way into some child's scrapbook. Someone, someday, may look at them and remember the leaves of 2004. Or perhaps not.

The full tale of autumn's painted epiphany reveals a precious secret. The tree births its leaves in spring, nurtures them with sweet sap, and all through summer the leaves soak up the sun's glory. Now comes the season of giving back, of returning the gift of life to the community of twigs and branches and trunk. Leaves make a gift of their lives and go out in a blaze of splendor.

Those who watch closely the human family see the same drama played out there. So often the richest blessings people bestow on one another come not amidst life's green season, but in the autumn of our lives. Our elders' bequests flow from deep resources of love, wisdom, and goodness stored up over the years—gifts that came from those who went before, leaves of a still earlier season in the long story of our family tree. Though we marvel over the glory of maples, oaks, and beeches, we can easily miss an elder's autumnal outpouring, or devalue our own in the homestretch of our journeys. Our strength *is* made perfect in weakness, though we don't wait longingly for such a time.

The lectionary of this season brings us along on Jesus' autumnal journey. Jerusalem beckoned, and there Jesus would die. Though young and still in his green season, he prepares for the end. Gifting characterizes the days before Jesus gets nailed to a dead tree and sealed in a tomb. Luke's gospel bids us come along on this journey of daily cross-bearing, the way of giving and letting go. On our itinerary we find the steps where poor Lazarus waits. It winds as well through the desolate place where lepers sit in exile, and includes a stop in the home of Zacchaeus, a little man in every way until called by Jesus.

In all those places, and everywhere in between, the man bound for Jerusalem gives away all he has. We come along. Slowly but surely, and only by God's grace, we learn to do the same. We find our lives in losing them.

291

Shape *of* Worship *for the* Season

BASIC SHAPE OF THE EUCHARISTIC RITE

- Confession and Forgiveness: see alternate worship text for autumn in *Sundays and Seasons* as an option to the text in the liturgy setting

GATHERING

- Greeting: see alternate worship text for autumn, page 303
- Omit the Kyrie during autumn (except, perhaps, for festivals)
- Omit or use the hymn of praise during autumn (use "Glory to God" or hymn equivalent for Reformation Day)

WORD

- Use the Nicene Creed for Reformation celebration; use the Apostles' Creed for remaining Sundays in this season
- The prayers: see the prayers for each Sunday in the autumn section

MEAL

- Offertory prayer: see alternate worship text for autumn
- Use the proper preface for Sundays after Pentecost
- Eucharistic prayer: in addition to four main options in *LBW*, see "Eucharistic Prayer H: Autumn" in *WOV* Leaders Edition, p. 72
- Invitation to communion: see alternate worship text for autumn
- Post-communion prayer: see alternate worship text for autumn

SENDING

- Benediction: see alternate worship text for autumn
- Dismissal: see alternate worship text for autumn

OTHER SEASONAL POSSIBILITIES

- Blessing of Teachers and Students (see seasonal rites section)
- See Recognition of Ministries in the Congregation in *Occasional Services*, pp. 143–46

DISTRIBUTION OF BIBLES

- If Bibles are publicly distributed to young readers, consider having their parents or sponsors involved in physically handing over the Bibles (as a follow-up to promises made at baptism)

BLESSING OF ANIMALS

- Traditionally celebrated on or near October 4 (Francis of Assisi, renewer of the church, 1226); see a possible order for this celebration in the seasonal rites section

HARVEST FESTIVAL OR HARVEST HOME

- Many congregations celebrate the harvest sometime each fall. Readings are appointed on page 39 of *LBW* for the occasion of harvest.

REFORMATION DAY

- Since this falls on a Sunday this year, there may be added impetus to observe the festival. It is less of a universal church festival than most others, though, so some congregations choose to celebrate it by using lectionary readings for Proper 26, but using the prayers of the day for both Proper 26 and Reformation Day. Preaching might be based on the Zacchaeus gospel while incorporating reference to the principles of the Reformation. Prayers, hymns, and other music could also reflect both the lectionary day and the festival. The color for the day could be red.

SERVICE OF THE WORD FOR HEALING

- See the seasonal rites section for this order, which may be used on or near the festival of St. Luke, Evangelist (October 18)

Assembly Song *for the* Season

Most church activities, including choirs and other

musical leadership ensembles, restart in September,

beginning a headlong drive toward Christmas.

As students of all ages resume this time of learning, their curiosity and skills are sharpened. Harness this renewed energy, pouring it into new liturgical music, songs, and hymns.

GATHERING

Survey renewed settings of American hymns, such as "In Christ there is no east or west" (RWI 41), and "There's a wideness in God's mercy" (RWI 77). Or, enliven the entrance procession by singing the enjoyable psalm settings from *This Far by Faith*, such as Psalm 24 "Lift up your heads" (TFF 4), or Psalm 122 "Let us go rejoicing" (TFF 17). Have the assembly sing the refrain and skilled soloists improvise the verses or sing them to the reharmonized psalm tones.

In addition to Kyrie settings found in *LBW*, *WOV*, and *TFF* communion settings, two good alternatives include a Ukrainian setting of the Kyrie (WOV 602), and a setting of "Holy God" (*Trisagion*) by David Hurd (WOV 603).

Encourage the assembly to memorize parts of the liturgy by singing short refrains, such as the Taizé "Gloria" (WOV 640), sung as a four-part canon, accompanied by flutes, violins, and recorders. A strong alternative is "Bless his holy name" (W&P 19) by Andraé Crouch, a gospel setting for strong congregational singing and piano.

WORD

The ordinary time of Autumn provides ample time to sing a variety of gospel verses, or hymns in place of the verse. Introduce the chant "Alleluia" (WOV 611a), sung first by a cantor or children's choir, then by all, using simple keyboard accompaniment, handbells on cue notes, or sung a cappella. Alternatively, sing "Lord, let my heart be good soil" (W&P 52, WOV 713), or "Alleluia! Lord and Savior" (RWI 10).

On October 3, the day before the commemoration of Francis of Assisi, consider singing the retranslated version of his hymn, "All creatures, worship God most high!" (RWI 8), or a piece based on his prayer, "Make me a channel of your peace" (W&P 95). For Reformation, sing a renewed setting of "A mighty fortress" (RWI 2-3).

MEAL

Anchor the assembly in familiar *LBW* settings, such as Setting 1, for the offertory, Sanctus, and Lamb of God. Two alternate and renewed offertory hymns are "As saints of old" (RWI 12) and "Oh, what shall I render" (RWI 56).

Encourage singing at the communion using short hymns or hymns with refrains. Two good choices are "Come and taste" (W&P 30) led by a vocal team, and "Taste and see" (TFF 126) for assembly, piano, and improvisational vocal solos.

SENDING

Learn a new post-communion or closing hymn, such as "I'm so glad Jesus lifted me" (WOV 673, TFF 191), "Go in peace and serve the Lord" (W&P 46), "Go, make disciples" (W&P 47), or "Thank the Lord, your voices raise" (RWI 70).

293

Music *for the* Season

VERSE AND OFFERTORY

Busarow, Donald. *Verses and Offertories (Pentecost 21–Christ the King).*
AFP 0800648986.

Cherwien, David. *Verses for the Season of Pentecost, Set 3.* Mxd vcs, kybd.
MSM 80-543.

Cherwien, David. *Verses for the Fall Festivals.* U/SATB, opt brass qrt, org.
MSM 80-880.

Schiavone, J. *Gospel Acclamation Verses for Sundays of the Year, I, II, III.*
GIA G-2495, 2496, 2497.

Verses and Offertory Sentences, Part VII (Pentecost 19–Christ the King).
CPH 97-5507.

CHORAL

Hassler, Hans L. "We Give Thanks Unto Thee." SATB.
CPH 98-3378.

Hayes, Mark. "Welcome Table." SATB, pno. AFP 0800676033.

Pachelbel, Johann. "On God, and Not on Human Trust." SATB.
CPH 98-1006.

Schütz, Heinrich. "Lift Up Your Voice" in *Chantry Choirbook.* SATB.
AFP 0800657772.

Shepperd, Mark. "In Whom I Trust." SATB, pno.
AFP 0800675991.

Sjolund, Paul. "Children of the Heavenly Father" in *The Augsburg
Choirbook.* SATB, org. AFP 0800656784.

Tyler, Edward. "St. Theresa's Bookmark." SSATBB.
AFP 0800658329.

Vaughan Williams, Ralph. "At the Name of Jesus." SATB.
OXF 40-100.

Ylvisaker, John, arr. John Helgen. "I Was There to Hear Your Borning
Cry." SATB, pno, rec. KJO 8826.

CHILDREN'S CHOIR

Bedford, Michael. "Come Worship God This Holy Day." U, kybd,
opt fl, opt tamb. CG CGA806.

Edwards, Rusty. "Simple Song/O Lord, I Worship You." U, kybd, opt
fl. AFP 0800674219.

Leaf, Robert. "Come Feel the Joy." U, kybd. CG CGA742.

Page, Anna Laura. "Come, Sing a Song of Praise." U/2 pt, kybd.
AFP 0800675924.

Taylor, Jim. "A Call to Praise." U/2 pt, kybd, opt fl. CG CGA793.

Walker, Naomi King. "Purer in Heart." U, pno, fl. MSM 50-9458.

Wold, Wayne L. "Build New Bridges." U/2 pt, kybd.
AFP 0800657438.

KEYBOARD/INSTRUMENTAL

Augsburg Organ Library: Autumn. Org. AFP 0800675797.

Augsburg Organ Library: November. Org. AFP 0800658965.

Held, Wilbur. *Hymn Preludes for Autumn Festivals.* Org. CPH 97-5360.

Helvey, Howard. "All Creatures of Our God and King" in *Meditation
and Majesty.* Pno. BEC PC4.

Hustad, Don. *The Collected Works of Don Hustad.* Org. HOP 353.

Rutter, John. "Toccata in Seven" in *A Second Easy Album for Organ.* Org.
OXF 193751291.

HANDBELL

Afdahl, Lee J. "You Have Come Down to the Lakeshore" in *Two
Spanish Tunes for Handbells.* 3-5 oct, opt perc. AFP 0800657381.

Dobrinski, Cynthia. "Come, Thou Fount of Every Blessing." 3-5 oct.
AG 1832.

Helman, Michael. "Let Us Talents and Tongues Employ." 2-3 oct.
AFP 0800659937.

Rogers, Sharon Elery. "God, Who Stretched the Spangled Heavens."
3-5 oct, opt hc. AFP 0800657373.

PRAISE ENSEMBLE

Batstone, Bill. "Your Everlasting Love" in *Best of the Best.*
FEL 1891062018.

Brown, Brenton. "Lord, Reign in Me" in *Come, Now is the Time to Worship
Songbook.* Vineyard Music VMB9347.

Mullins, Rich. "Awesome God" in W&P.

Alternate Worship Texts

CONFESSION AND FORGIVENESS

In the name of the Father, and of the ✛ Son,
and of the Holy Spirit.
Amen

Recognizing our need for God's mercy,
let us confess our sin,
and seek reconciliation with God and each other.

Silence for reflection and self-examination.

God of justice and compassion,
we confess that we have sinned against you
in thought, word, and deed.
We have not loved our neighbors as ourselves,
We have not been faithful stewards of your creation.
We have failed to share the bounty of your harvest
with the poor and needy.
Forgive our sin, increase our faith,
strengthen us in service,
and bring us to everlasting life. Amen

Heaven rejoices when a sinner repents
and a lost sheep is found.
In the mercy of God,
Jesus Christ was given to die for you,
and for his sake, God forgives you all your sins.
Amen

GREETING

The rich presence of God,
the beginning and end of all that is good,
be with you now and always.
And also with you.

PRAYERS

Remembering God's marvelous work and living in hope,
let us pray for the church, the world,
and all people according to their needs.

A brief silence.

Each petition ends:

Lord, in your mercy,
hear our prayer.

Concluding petition:

God of faithfulness, encircled in your lovingkindness,
we lift up to you all in need.
Hear our prayers on behalf of others
and sustain us as we await the coming of your Son,
Jesus Christ our Lord, in whose name we pray.
Amen

OFFERTORY PRAYER

God our provider,
all that we have is a sign of your love;
all that we are is a gift from your hand.
Receive these offerings
along with our thanksgiving,
that our lives may proclaim your care for creation
redeemed by Jesus Christ our Lord.
Amen

INVITATION TO COMMUNION

Set your hope on God,
who richly provides us with every good thing.

POST-COMMUNION PRAYER

We give you thanks, faithful God,
for feeding us with this one heavenly food.
Transform us through this meal
into the likeness of your Son,
and unite us in love for one another,
that we may be your body in the world;
in Jesus' name we pray.
Amen

BLESSING

Almighty God, Father, ✛ Son, and Holy Spirit,
watch over your going out and your coming in,
from this time forth and forevermore.
Amen

DISMISSAL

Go in peace, equipped by God for every good work.
Thanks be to God.

295

Seasonal Rites

Blessing of Teachers and Students

HYMN
Earth and all stars! LBW 558

If used on a Sunday morning the following prayer may be used during or following the prayers.

Let us pray for all who are beginning a new school year, that both students and teachers will be blessed in their academic endeavors.

Almighty God, you give wisdom and knowledge. Grant teachers the gift of joy and insight, and students the gift of diligence and openness, that all may grow in what is good and honest and true. Support all who teach and all who learn, that together we may know and follow your ways; through Jesus Christ our Lord.
Amen

Service of the Word for Healing

This service may be celebrated at any time. It may be especially appropriate on or near the festival of St. Luke, Evangelist (October 18), who was a physician. See also the liturgy in Renewing Worship 4: Life Passages, pp. 27–39.

HYMN
O Christ, the healer, we have come LBW 360
Word of God, come down on earth WOV 716
Heal me, O Lord TFF 189

GREETING AND WELCOME
The grace of our Lord Jesus Christ, the love of God, and the communion of the Holy Spirit be with you all.
And also with you.

We gather to hear the word of God, pray for those in need, and ask God's blessing on those who seek healing and wholeness through Christ our Lord.

PRAYER OF THE DAY
The proper prayer of the day may be used, or the prayer for St. Luke (October 18), LBW p. 35, or the following:

Great God, our healer, by your power the Lord Jesus healed the sick and gave hope to the hopeless. As we gather in his name,

look upon us with mercy, and bless us with your healing Spirit. Bring us comfort in the midst of pain, strength to transform our weakness, and light to illuminate our darkness. We ask this in the name of Jesus Christ, our crucified and risen Lord, who lives and reigns with you and the Holy Spirit, one God, now and forever.
Amen

READINGS
These readings, the readings listed for St. Luke, Evangelist (LBW, p. 35), or the readings listed on pp. 96–97 of Occasional Services may be used.

Isaiah 61:1-3a
Psalm 23
The LORD is my shepherd; I shall not be in want. (Ps. 23:1)
Luke 17:11-19

SERMON

HYMN
Lord, whose love in humble service LBW 423
Healer of our every ill WOV 738
We come to you for healing, Lord RWSB
Come, ye disconsolate TFF 186

THE PRAYERS
This litany or the prayers in Occasional Services (pp. 91–93) may be used.

God the Father, you desire the health and salvation of all people.
We praise you and thank you, O Lord.
God the Son, you came that we might have life
and might have it more abundantly.
We praise you and thank you, O Lord.
God the Holy Spirit,
you make our bodies the temples of your presence.
We praise you and thank you, O Lord.
Holy Trinity, one God,
in you we live and move and have our being.
We praise you and thank you, O Lord.
Lord, grant your healing grace to all who are sick, injured, or disabled, that they may be made whole;
hear us, O Lord of life.
Grant to all who are lonely, anxious, or despondent
the awareness of your presence;
hear us, O Lord of life.

296

Mend broken relationships, and restore those in emotional distress
to soundness of mind and serenity of spirit;
hear us, O Lord of life.
Bless physicians, nurses, and all others who minister
to the suffering; grant them wisdom and skill,
sympathy and patience;
hear us, O Lord of life.
Grant to the dying a peaceful, holy death,
and with your grace strengthen those who mourn;
hear us, O Lord of life.
Restore to wholeness whatever is broken in our lives,
in this nation, and in the world;
hear us, O Lord of life.
Turn your ear to us, O God:
heal us, and make us whole.

Gracious God, in baptism you anointed us with the oil of salvation, and joined us to the death and resurrection of your Son.
Bless all who seek your healing presence in their lives. In their
suffering draw them more deeply into the mystery of your love,
that following Christ in the way of the cross, they may know the
power of his resurrection; who lives and reigns forever and ever.
Amen

LAYING ON OF HANDS AND ANOINTING

*Those who wish to receive the laying on of hands (and anoint-
ing) come to the altar and, if possible, kneel. The minister lays
both hands on each person's head in silence, after which he or
she may dip a thumb in the oil and make the sign of the cross
on the person's forehead, saying:*

(Through this holy anointing) may God's love and mercy uphold
you by the grace and power of the Holy Spirit.
Amen

*During the anointing, the assembly may sing various hymns and
songs, instrumental music may be played, or a simple interval of
silence may be observed.*

PRAYER

After all have returned to their places, the minister may say:

As you are anointed with this oil, may God bless you with the
healing power of the Holy Spirit. May God forgive you your sins,
release you from suffering, and restore you to wholeness and
strength. May God deliver you from all evil, preserve you in all
goodness, and bring you to everlasting life, through Jesus Christ
our Lord. Amen

THE LORD'S PRAYER

BLESSING AND DISMISSAL

HYMN
Abide with us, our Savior   LBW 263
Go, my children, with my blessing   WOV 721, TFF 161
There is a balm in Gilead   WOV 737, TFF 185

297

September 5, 2004

Fourteenth Sunday after Pentecost
Proper 18

INTRODUCTION

In remembrance of baptism, many Christians make the sign of the cross. We are the people marked with Jesus' cross. But that cross is costly, and those who bear it must be prepared to let go of everything in order to take up the new life of the crucified and risen Christ.

PRAYER OF THE DAY

Almighty and eternal God, you know our problems and our weaknesses better than we ourselves. In your love and by your power help us in our confusion and, in spite of our weakness, make us firm in faith; through your Son, Jesus Christ our Lord.

VERSE

Alleluia. Rejoice in the Lord always; again I will say, Rejoice. Alleluia. (Phil. 4:4)

READINGS

Deuteronomy 30:15-20

Life and blessing are the benefits of keeping the law God has given through Moses. In this passage, Moses presents the consequences of choosing between life and death.

Psalm 1

Their delight is in the law of the LORD. (Ps. 1:2)

Philemon 1-21

While Paul was in prison, he was aided by a runaway slave named Onesimus. The slave's master, Philemon, was a Christian friend of Paul. Paul told Onesimus to return to his master but encouraged Philemon to receive Onesimus back as a brother.

Luke 14:25-33

Jesus speaks frankly about the costs of discipleship. Those who follow him should know from the outset that they will have to renounce allegiance to all competing concerns.

Alternate First Reading/Psalm

Jeremiah 18:1-11

God teaches Jeremiah a lesson at a potter's shop. Just as a potter is able to destroy an unacceptable vessel, starting over to refashion it into one of value, so God molds and fashions the nations, including Israel.

Psalm 139:1-5, 12-17 (Psalm 139:1-6, 13-18 NRSV)

You have searched me out and known me. (Ps. 139:1)

COLOR   Green

THE PRAYERS

Remembering God's marvelous work and living in hope, let us pray for the church, the world, and all people according to their needs.

A BRIEF SILENCE.

God of life, let your church be like a tree planted by baptismal streams of water, bearing the fruit of the gospel for the sake of the world. Lord, in your mercy, **hear our prayer.**

God of life, bring to an end wars and conflicts among nations and peoples, so that all may live in peace and safety. Lord, in your mercy, **hear our prayer.**

God of life, free those who are enslaved by others, turn the hearts of those whose choices are leading them to death, and empower and rescue victims of violence. Lord, in your mercy, **hear our prayer.**

God of life, make your living presence known to all who are sick *(especially)* and strengthen them in every need. Lord, in your mercy, **hear our prayer.**

God of life, look upon all who work to improve their lives and those of others, as well as all who cannot find adequate employment. Grant them fulfillment in their labor and a just reward for their work. Lord, in your mercy, **hear our prayer.**

God of life, give to our congregation the courage to carry our cross and stir us up to follow Christ's radical call to discipleship. Lord, in your mercy, **hear our prayer.**

HERE OTHER INTERCESSIONS MAY BE OFFERED.

God of life, we give you thanks for the saints who gave

up all to follow Jesus Christ. Let their lives of faith and obedience inspire and encourage us to follow Christ and so enjoy fullness of life at the coming of your kingdom. Lord, in your mercy,

hear our prayer.

God of faithfulness, encircled in your lovingkindness, we lift up to you all in need. Hear our prayers on behalf of others and sustain us as we await the coming of your Son, Jesus Christ our Lord, in whose name we pray. **Amen**

IMAGES FOR PREACHING

Brochures that beckon visitors to Alaska depict breathtaking mountains, pristine seascapes, and plentiful opportunity. Few explain how difficult life can become there. Hence, newcomers experience some surprise at the array of abandoned homes, vehicles, and places of business that dot the Alaskan landscape. Unfinished and barely used structures stand in silent testimony to the harsh, unforgiving winters and to dreams that failed under their assault.

Similar ghosts haunt the landscapes of our lives. As unfinished projects clutter our attics, so do abandoned marriages and friendships lie strewn in our wake. Perhaps we didn't count the cost or couldn't imagine what genuine commitment might ultimately require. The same goes for our responses to vocation and discipleship. Most of us know too well the builder Jesus describes, the one with a half-built tower that's become the town joke, or the general who entered battle short-handed. Perhaps we'll do better one day, but we'll never be rid of all our failures.

In the end, it doesn't matter how much debris we leave behind. Christ, who calls us to discipleship, finished his project. He faced an army alone. His curious tower, the cross outside Jerusalem, stands complete. That's enough, both for him and for us who are baptized into his cruciform project.

When visitors ask Alaskans why nobody cleans up those abandoned vehicles and buildings, they respond with their own surprise. "Are you kidding?" they reply. "That's our parts department. If we need wood, wire, or a whole wall, we go to one of those and get it! The same if someone lacks a starter motor or a headlight." In a way, the body of Christ works like that. To God, even our unfinished projects have some use. By God's grace, a bit of mine and a piece of yours eventually amount to a whole tower.

God hasn't finished with any of us just yet.

WORSHIP MATTERS

Some scholars would suggest that in the background of Jesus' admonition to "carry the cross," was the first-century Jewish practice of making a T or "tau" (+ or ✕) on the forehead (see Ezek. 9:4-6). The one who received this "cross" was branded as one whose heart was open to God, ready to receive the word and act on it. Perhaps it is this Jewish practice that enters early Christian baptismal practice and was reinterpreted in light of the death and resurrection of Christ: the cross of Christ is traced on the forehead signifying that this person has been claimed, anointed by Christ, for a mission (see Luke 4:18). This gesture, tracing the cross on the forehead, is one of the identifiable marks of the Christian "family."

299

LET THE CHILDREN COME

Today have the children process, with one carrying the cross, followed by others carrying streamers of red, orange, green, bronze, and gold to mark the time of transition to the natural season of autumn. This is a strong visual reminder to children and adults alike that as Christians, we follow the way of Jesus. It will also serve to highlight the text from the gospel of Luke: "Whoever does not carry the cross and follow me cannot be my disciple" (Luke 14:27). As the children leave worship, consider sending home Bible bookmarks with crosses on them as a reminder that Sunday programming has resumed or will be resuming soon.

HYMNS FOR WORSHIP
GATHERING

When in our music God is glorified   LBW 555, WOV 802
We have come into his house   TFF 136

HYMN OF THE DAY

All my hope on God is founded   WOV 782

ALTERNATE HYMN OF THE DAY

Take my life, that I may be   LBW 406
Must Jesus bear the cross alone   TFF 237

COMMUNION

Day by day   WOV 746

Spirit of God, descend upon my heart   LBW 486

SENDING

O Jesus, I have promised   LBW 503

For the fruit of all creation   WOV 760

ADDITIONAL HYMNS AND SONGS

Jesus, keep me near the cross   RWSB, TFF 73

Just a closer walk with thee   RWSB, TFF 253

I will delight   W&P 72

Now in the days of youth   NCH 350

MUSIC FOR THE DAY

PSALMODY

Bell, John L. "Happy Is the One" in *Psalms of Patience, Protest and Praise.* GIA G-4047.

Christopherson, Dorothy. PW , Cycle C.

Cooney, Rory. "Psalm 1: Roots in the Earth." U, cong, gtr, kybd. GIA G-3969.

Howard, Julie. *Sing for Joy: Psalm Settings for God's Children.* LP 0814620787.

Schoenbachler, Tim and Sheryl Soderberg. "Psalm 1: Happy Are They" in STP, vol. 2.

Happy are they   TFF 1

See Sixth Sunday after the Epiphany.

CHORAL

Bisbee, B. Wayne. "God of Peace." 2 pt mxd/equal vcs, kybd. AFP 0800675126.

Grundahl, Nancy. "The Best of Rooms." SATB, org. KJO 8899.

Hayes, Mark. "Day by Day." SATB, pno. AFP 0800658345.

Kallman, Dan. "In Thee Is Gladness." SATB, org. MSM 50-9058.

Patterson, Mark. "Come, Worship the Lord." SATB, kybd. AFP 0800675479.

Stanford, Charles Villiers. "O for a Closer Walk with God" in *Anthems for Choirs 1.* SATB, org. OXF 353214X.

Wesley, Samuel. "Lead Me Lord." SATB, kybd. NOV 29 0305.

CHILDREN'S CHOIR

Cool, Jayne Southwick. "I'm a Disciple, Too!" U/2 pt, kybd. AFP 080067457X.

Howard, Julie. "Like a Tree" in LS (Ps. 1). U, kybd, opt hb/fl.

Sleeth, Natalie. "If You Love Me" in LS. U, kybd.

KEYBOARD/INSTRUMENTAL

Hustad, Don. "I Will Arise and Go to Jesus" in *Early American Folk Hymns for Organ.* Org. HOP 349.

Kerr, J. Wayne. "Simple Gifts" in *Augsburg Organ Library: Easter.* Org. AFP 0800659368.

Linker, Janet. "Festive Procession." ("Lift High the Cross" and "Rejoice, the Lord is King") Org, opt tpt solo. BEC OC6. Also in *The Complete Wedding Collection, Book II.* BEC OC23.

HANDBELL

Afdahl, Lee J. "Thaxted: O God beyond All Praising." 3-5 oct. AFP 0800658140.

Dobrinski, Cynthia. "Lift High the Cross." 3-5 oct. AG 1491.

PRAISE ENSEMBLE

Beaker. "Step by Step" in W&P.

Butler, Terry. "Cry of My Heart" in *Best of the Best.* FEL 1891062018.

Thursday, September 9

PETER CLAVER, PRIEST, MISSIONARY TO COLOMBIA, 1654

Peter Claver was born into Spanish nobility and was persuaded to become a Jesuit missionary. He served in Cartagena (in what is now Colombia) by teaching and caring for the slaves. The slaves arrived in ships, where they had been confined in dehumanizing conditions. Claver met and supplied them with medicine, food, clothing, and brandy. He learned their dialects and taught them Christianity. He called himself "the slave of the slaves forever." Claver also ministered to the locals of Cartagena who were in prison and facing death.

Claver's advocacy on behalf of the rights of slaves is a witness to a gospel that is for all people. Pray for contemporary ministries and for persons who offer care and compassion to people living in substandard living conditions.

September 12, 2004

Fifteenth Sunday after Pentecost
Proper 19

INTRODUCTION

Only the lost can be found. The confession of sins is our admission that we do not know the way to God. But God has been looking for us. This day we are surrounded by images of people who "once were lost." Those who are found enter the joy of the Lord.

PRAYER OF THE DAY

O God, you declare your almighty power chiefly in showing mercy and pity. Grant us the fullness of your grace, that, pursuing what you have promised, we may share your heavenly glory; through your Son, Jesus Christ our Lord.

VERSE

Alleluia. Whatever was written in former days was written for our instruction, so that by steadfastness and by the encouragement of the scriptures we might have hope. Alleluia. (Rom. 15:4)

READINGS

Exodus 32:7-14

Prior to this chapter, Moses receives instructions from God on Mount Sinai. Meanwhile, the people grow rebellious and decide to make a golden calf. Today's reading suggests a court setting in which God acts as prosecuting attorney and Moses serves as defense attorney in a lawsuit against the people.

Psalm 51:1-11 (Psalm 51:1-10 NRSV)

Have mercy on me, O God, according to your lovingkindness. (Ps. 51:1)

1 Timothy 1:12-17

The letters to Timothy are called the pastoral epistles because they contain advice especially intended for leaders in the church. Here the mercy shown to Paul, who once persecuted the church, is cited as evidence that even the most unworthy may become witnesses to the grace of God.

Luke 15:1-10

Jesus tells two stories about repentance to indicate that God takes the initiative in finding us. We are precious to God, and our recovery brings joy in heaven.

Alternate First Reading/Psalm

Jeremiah 4:11-12, 22-28

The sinfulness of the people will surely bring their destruction. God's searing wind of judgment, in the form of a massive army from the north, will reduce the land to its primeval state of waste and void.

Psalm 14

The LORD looks down from heaven upon us all. (Ps. 14:2)

COLOR   Green

THE PRAYERS

Remembering God's marvelous work and living in hope, let us pray for the church, the world, and all people according to their needs.

A BRIEF SILENCE.

God of mercy, your church has often turned within itself, and away from your passion for those who are lost. Draw us out of our self-righteousness and closer to you, that we might be a saving witness to the world. Lord, in your mercy,

hear our prayer.

God of mercy, we continue to neglect and exploit your good creation. Give us the courage and wisdom to become prudent caretakers of the natural resources entrusted to us. Lord, in your mercy,

hear our prayer.

God of mercy, heaven rejoices over one sinner who repents. Show your mercy to those who are crushed and in despair over their sins and open their ears to hear with joy and gladness the good news of forgiveness offered through Jesus Christ. Lord, in your mercy,

hear our prayer.

God of mercy, you know the needs of all. Bring healing and wholeness to all who are sick *(especially)*, bear in your arms those who have lost loved ones to terrorism, and comfort all those who mourn. Lord, in your mercy,

hear our prayer.

God of mercy, you pour out your gifts on all people. Enlighten and inspire those in our congregation who teach the faith to our children, those whose voices enhance

301

our worship with their song, and those who practice hospitality for others. Lord, in your mercy,

hear our prayer.

HERE OTHER INTERCESSIONS MAY BE OFFERED.

God of mercy, give us courage to daily die to ourselves and live to you so that one day we *(with names)* will enjoy the eternal life prepared for all whom you love. Lord, in your mercy,

hear our prayer.

God of faithfulness, encircled in your lovingkindness, we lift up to you all in need. Hear our prayers on behalf of others and sustain us as we await the coming of your Son, Jesus Christ our Lord, in whose name we pray.

Amen

IMAGES FOR PREACHING

Had Jesus lived in Texas, his parable of the restless God who will not abide the loss of anyone, whether a murmuring multitude or a lone sheep, might have gone somewhat differently. Out on vast rangelands, where individual cattle and horses inevitably stray from their herds, ranchers have always had ways to retrieve lost animals. Today they use aircraft and trucks. Not long ago they employed donkeys for such work.

A healthy, well-fed donkey is smart, stubborn, and strong, and it loves nothing more than being at home. If left some distance away, a donkey will return home no matter the obstacles it faces. To get a wandering critter back, ranchers simply tied one end of a rope to a stray and the other to one of their donkeys, then left the pair to work things out. Sooner or later both animals would show up at the ranch. Upon arrival, they might both look worse for wear, but they'd be home. If retraced, their tracks would likely appear as a sequence of donkey hoofprints and whole lot of skid marks.

So it is that God gets us back from our meandering, strays that we so often make of ourselves. God's Son takes the pounding, for we never make his journey easy or simple. Indeed, it costs him his life, for the rangeland he must traverse includes the Abyss. But he will not be stopped until each of us rests at home.

God puts the same, persistent Spirit in each of us and into our communities of baptized, gathered ones, and ties around our necks the same sort of harness—the yoke of discipleship that draws us along, always in the footsteps of the eternally restless searcher.

302

And what a joyous celebration breaks out as we come over the horizon and find ourselves here, and home at last.

WORSHIP MATTERS

Two proclamations are central in the Holy Communion: the gospel reading and the great thanksgiving/eucharistic prayer. The gospel reading leads to preaching, the feeding of the community on the word proclaimed in the readings. The creed and the prayers respond to this proclamation of the word. The great thanksgiving/eucharistic prayer leads to communion, receiving the body and blood of Christ. The post-communion song and prayer respond to the communion of the assembly. There is a certain order of primary and secondary elements in the worship service.

The proportions of the liturgy should reflect this order. If one is concerned about time, shorten the announcements, shorten the sermon or a children's sermon, place instrumental or choral works before worship begins, during the offertory or at the communion of the people, resist the temptation to use every liturgical option (both Kyrie and hymn of praise). Keep what is primary, primary. Let all other elements be shaped according to what is primary.

LET THE CHILDREN COME

For many congregations this is "Rally Sunday," a day when Sunday programming begins. This may be an overwhelming time for many children, with school and Sunday school classes beginning. As a welcome back greeting, invite youth in your congregation to use face paint to mark each child's hand or cheek with a colorful cross. The cross will remind them that they belong to Jesus. As the youth are painting, have them talk to the children about events in their lives and offer the assurance that we all are part of God's big and loving family. Like the lost sheep and the lost coin from today's gospel message, each one of us is precious to God.

HYMNS FOR WORSHIP

GATHERING

Come, thou Fount of every blessing   LBW 499
Christ is made the sure foundation   WOV 747
Lord, I lift your name on high   W&P 90, RWSB

HYMN OF THE DAY

Jesus sinners will receive   LBW 291

ALTERNATE HYMN OF THE DAY

Amazing grace, how sweet the sound   LBW 448
Softly and tenderly Jesus is calling   WOV 734

COMMUNION

One there is, above all others   LBW 298
Lord, listen to your children praying   WOV 775

SENDING

There's a wideness in God's mercy   LBW 290, RWI 76, 77
Praise to you, O God of mercy   WOV 790

ADDITIONAL HYMNS AND SONGS

Beloved, God's chosen   RWSB
Build us up, Lord   RWSB
Create in me a clean heart   W&P 34, 35
A woman and a coin—the coin is lost   VU 360

MUSIC FOR THE DAY

PSALMODY

Bedford, Michael. "Be Merciful, O Lord" in *Sing Out! A Children's Psalter.* WLP 7191.

Christopherson, Dorothy. PW, Cycle C.

Haugen, Marty. "Be Merciful, O Lord" in PCY, vol. 1.

Jenkins, Steve. "Create in Me." 2 pt, cong, kybd. MSM 80-302.

Marshall, Jane. *Psalms Together II.* CG CGC21.

Walker, Christopher. "Give Me a New Heart, O God" in STP, vol. 3.

Create in me a clean heart   WOV 732

See Ash Wednesday.

CHORAL

Bouman, Paul. "Create in Me a Clean Heart." SA, kybd. CPH 98-1143.

Brahms, Johannes. "Create in Me a Clean Heart." SATBB. Gsch 7504.

Christiansen, Paul J. "Create in Me a Clean Heart." SATB. AFP 0800645847.

Farlee, Robert Buckley. "Holy God." SATB, org. AFP 0800675207.

Hayes, Mark. "Go Down Moses." SATB, pno. HIN HMC-704.

Johnson, Carolyn. "Have No Fear, Little Flock." SATB, kybd. AFP 0800674545.

Shute, Linda Cable. "A Shepherd Knows." SATB, org. AFP 0800675118.

CHILDREN'S CHOIR

Folkening, John. "One in a Hundred" in LS. (Luke 15:3-7) U, kybd.

Hopson, Hal H. "Gentle Shepherd, Kind and True." U, kybd, opt 2 hb. CG CGA687.

Nygard, Jr., Carl. "Grateful Praise." 2 pt, kybd. AFP 0800675185.

KEYBOARD/INSTRUMENTAL

Campra, André. "Rigaudon" in *The Complete Wedding Collection, Book I.* Org. BEC OC23.

Gehring, Philip. "New Britain" in *Augsburg Organ Library: Lent.* Org. AFP 0800658973.

Harbach, Barbara. "Festive Proclamation" in *Organ Music for the Seasons,* vol. 3. Org. AFP 0800675649.

Rodriguez, Penny. "When Morning Gilds the Skies" in *Portraits of Praise.* Pno. BEC PC2.

HANDBELL

Dobrinski, Cynthia. "Amazing Grace." 2-3 oct. LAK HB00067.

Dobrinski, Cynthia. "Come, Thou Fount of Every Blessing." 3-5 oct. AG 1832.

Honoré, Jeffrey. "Softly and Tenderly." 3-4 oct. CG CGB162.

PRAISE ENSEMBLE

Doerksen, Brian. "Refiner's Fire" in *More Songs for Praise and Worship.* SATB. WRD 3010387016 (vocal ed); WRD 3010186363 (pno, vcs, perc).

Espinosa, Eddie. "Change My Heart, O God" in W&P.

Nelson, Jeff. "Purify My Heart" in *Best of the Best.* FEL 1891062018.

Monday, September 13

JOHN CHRYSOSTOM, BISHOP OF CONSTANTINOPLE, 407

John was a priest in Antioch and an outstanding preacher. His eloquence earned him the nickname "Chrysostom" ("golden mouth"), but it also got him into trouble. As bishop of Constantinople he preached against corruption among the royal court. The empress, who had been his supporter, sent him into exile. His preaching style emphasized the literal meaning of scripture and its practical application. This interpretation stood in contrast to the common style at the time, which emphasized the allegorical meaning of the text. Chrysostom's skill in the pulpit has led many to describe him as the patron of preachers. This week at gatherings of parish groups, include prayers for pastors and all who proclaim the gospel through preaching.

303

Thursday, September 16

CYPRIAN, BISHOP OF CARTHAGE, MARTYR, C. 258

Cyprian worked for the unity of the church and cared for his flock in North Africa during a time of great persecution. During Cyprian's time as bishop many people had denied the faith under duress. In contrast to some who held the belief that the church should not receive these people back, Cyprian believed they ought to be welcomed into full communion after a period of penance. Cyprian insisted on the need for compassion in order to preserve the unity of the church. His essay "On the Unity of the Catholic Church" stressed the role of bishops in guaranteeing the visible, concrete unity of the church. Cyprian was also concerned for the physical well-being of the people under his care. He organized a program of medical care during a severe epidemic in Carthage.

Saturday, September 18

DAG HAMMARSKJÖLD, PEACEMAKER, 1961

Dag Hammarskjöld was a Swedish diplomat and humanitarian who served as Secretary General of the United Nations. He was killed in a plane crash on this day in 1961 in what is now Zambia while he was on his way to negotiate a cease-fire between the United Nations and the Katanga forces. For years Hammarskjöld had kept a private journal, and it was not until that journal was published as *Markings* that the depth of his Christian faith was known. The book revealed that his life was a combination of diplomatic service and personal spirituality, a combination of contemplation on the meaning of Christ in his life and action in the world.

To commemorate Hammarskjöld, pray for the work of the United Nations and for all peacemakers. Here is an example of a person whose quiet contemplation led to visible action in the world.

September 19, 2004

Sixteenth Sunday after Pentecost
Proper 20

INTRODUCTION

Early in the academic year may seem a strange time to think about the final exam, but on this day Jesus reminds us that each of us needs to give an accounting of all that is entrusted to us. In the new logic of God's reign, knowing the riches of grace we possess demands resolute action from us; we risk it all for possessing the lavish love of God offered to us.

PRAYER OF THE DAY

Lord God, you call us to work in your vineyard and leave no one standing idle. Set us to our tasks in the work of your kingdom, and help us to order our lives by your wisdom; through your Son, Jesus Christ our Lord.

VERSE

Alleluia. Live your life in a manner worthy of the gospel of Christ; strive side by side for the faith of the Gospel. Alleluia. (Phil. 1:27)

READINGS

Amos 8:4-7

Amos was called by God to prophesy in the Northern Kingdom for a brief period of time. Peace and prosperity in Israel led to corruption and an increased gap between rich and poor. The prophet declares that God will not tolerate such a situation.

Psalm 113

The LORD lifts up the poor from the ashes. (Ps. 113:6)

1 Timothy 2:1-7

The pastoral epistles offer insight into how early Christians understood many practical matters, such as church administration and worship. The church's focused prayer for others is an expression of the single-minded passion God has toward us in Jesus.

Luke 16:1-13

Jesus tells the story of a dishonest man who cheats his employer and then is commended by him for having

Order next year's resources now!

Sundays and Seasons 2005
YEAR A

Make worship planning easy with this new comprehensive resource! Based on the ecumenical lectionary and church year, this guide will provide you with the materials needed to prepare worship for Sundays and seasons of the church year. This annual guide is organized around the three major cycles: Advent, Christmas, and Epiphany; Lent, Holy Week, and Easter; and Time of the Church: Summer, Autumn, and November. Call about our new standing order program!

ISBN 0-8066-4674-8 $35.00
Three or more $29.00 each

Worship Planning Calendar 2005
YEAR A

Order next year's copy today! It's the perfect complement to *Sundays and Seasons*. Use this worship planning guide, daily devotional, and appointment calendar as your workbook.

ISBN 0-8066-4673-X $20.00

Words for Worship 2005
CD-ROM YEAR A

This CD-ROM contains resources for use with the Revised Common Lectionary, Cycle A. These easy-to-use text and graphic files are organized by calendar date. Includes readings, prayers, introductions to the day, psalm refrains and tones, seasonal rites and texts, and the *LBW* Symbol font.

CD-ROM AND COPYRIGHT LICENSE

ISBN 0-8066-4668-3 $139.00

Sundays and Seasons Leader Edition
NEW THIS YEAR!

This elegant, practical volume contains the intercessory prayers and other proper material from *Sundays and Seasons*, for every Sunday and principal festival of the church year. Designed and bound for use in worship, the larger type and convenient layout will help worship leaders lead with confidence. Plus, blank space is provided for local prayer requests and intercessions to be added. A welcome addition to the Sundays and Seasons family of worship products.

Call to order.

Sundays and Seasons/Worship Planning Calendar Combo Pack

Sundays and Seasons and the *Worship Planning Calendar* are designed to work together to provide you with all the planning tools for meaningful worship and helpful time management. Order this Combo Pack and you'll get both must-have resources at a savings of over 10%!

ISBN 6-0001-6904-3 $49.00
($55.00 if purchased separately)

Shipping and Handling

Note: Prices and availability are subject to change without notice.

Shipping Charges: Shipping charges are additional on all orders. For orders up through $10.00 add $2.50; $10.01–$20.00 add $4.00; $20.01–$35.00 add $5.50; $35.01 and above add 6.50%. Actual shipping charges will be assessed for all orders over 35 lbs. in weight (bulk), and for expedited shipping service. Promotion orders are shipped separately from other orders. Additional shipping charges for international shipments. For Canadian orders, actual shipping costs will be charged. This policy is subject to change without notice. **Sales Tax:** Add appropriate state/province and local taxes where applicable. Tax exempt organizations must provide tax exempt numbers on all orders. **Return Policy:** All U. S. mail, fax and telephone order returns must be shipped postage prepaid to the Augsburg Fortress Distribution Center, 4001 Gantz Road, Suite , Grove City, Ohio 43123-1891. Permission is not required for returns. Non-damaged, in-print product in saleable condition may be returned for up to 60 days after the invoice date. Defective products, products damaged in shipment, or products shipped in error may be returned at any time and postage will be reimbursed. Special order or clearance items may not be returned. Canadian orders must be returned to the location from which the order was shipped.

Augsburg Fortress **Order Form**
Worship Planning Resources 2005, Year A

Just complete this order card, affix postage, and drop it in the mail.
To order by phone: 1-800-328-4648 By fax: 1-800-722-7766

Send to: _____
Address: _____
City: _____ State: _____ Zip: _____
Phone: _____

Bill to: _____
Address: _____
City: _____ State: _____ Zip: _____

Method of Payment *(check one)*
❑ Augsburg Fortress Acct #_____
❑ Credit Card #_____
Exp. Date:_____
(Must be valid for Sept. 2004. Products ship August 2004.)

Signature:_____
(Required on all credit card orders.)

❑ Check *(Place check and order card in envelope and mail to address on reverse. Include proper shipping charges and sales tax.)*

Qty.	Title / ISBN	Price
____	Sundays and Seasons 2005 0-8066-4674-8	$35.00
____	Worship Planning Calendar 2005 0-8066-4673-x	$20.00
____	Word for Worship CD-ROM 2005 0-8066-4668-3	$139.00
____	Hymns for Worship 2005 0-8066-4074-X	$329.00
____	Kids Celebrate Bulletins Year A 0-8066-4671-3	$44.99
____	Calendar of Word and Season 2005 w/o imprint 0-8066-4670-5	$9.95
____	Church Year Calendar 2005 Year A 0-8066-4672-1	$1.95
____	Sundays and Seasons/Worship Planning Calendar Combo Pack 6-0001-6904-3	$49.00

Thank you for your order.
Prices valid through April 15, 2004.

Calendar of Word and Season 2005

YEAR A

This beautiful full-color wall calendar will keep you on track at a glance. Identifies church festivals, and U.S. and Canadian holidays. Large date blocks note Bible readings from the Revised Common Lectionary for Sundays and church festivals and identify the seasonal or festival color. Makes a great gift with custom imprinting available. Create a reference tool for each household, or staff and committee members! 10⅞ x 8⅜". Spiral bound, punched for hanging, 28 pages. Call for details regarding custom imprinting.

ISBN 0-8066-4670-5 $9.95 EACH
12-49 $4.25 EACH   50-99 $3.25 EACH
100-499 $3.00 EACH   500+ $2.00 EACH

Church Year Calendar 2005

YEAR A

This simple sheet is a useful tool for anyone in your church: committee members, choir members, worship planners, the altar guild, teachers, and pastors. The full-color calendar gives dates, Bible readings, hymn of the day, and liturgical color for each Sunday and festival of the church year. Two sides 11 x 8½

ISBN 0-8066-4672-1 $1.95 EACH $0.83 each 12 or more

Hymns for Worship

Hymn graphics on CD-ROM! More than 1,300 hymns and so from *LBW, With One Voice, Thi Far by Faith, Worship and Prais* and other sources make this a must have addition. A Playback feature allows you to hear the melodies you've selected and ar easy to use search engine will quickly locate the hym and songs you have in mind. Printing or downloadir any hymn requiring copyright permission automatically generates the necessary information ar paperwork for submission to the publisher.

ISBN 0-8066-4074-X $329.00

Kids Celebrate

Bulletins Year A

An entire year of **reproducible** worship bulletins for lower elementary age users. Activities, prayers, and suggestions for intergenerational interaction followir the texts of the revised common lectionary. The bulletins are undated so you can reuse this volume every Year A starting in December.

Book and CD-ROM
ISBN 0-8066-4671-3 $44.99

Place
Stamp
Here

AUGSBURG FORTRESS PUBLISHERS
ATTN MAILING CENTER
PO BOX 59303
MINNEAPOLIS, MN 55459-0303

acted so shrewdly. Jesus reminds his listeners that God will not stand to be merely one of many commitments.

Alternate First Reading/Psalm

Jeremiah 8:18—9:1

Jeremiah's primary task as God's prophet was to announce the terrible destruction that awaited the people of Israel because of their sin. In this passage, a grief-stricken Jeremiah anguishes over the sadness of that message and weeps day and night for his people.

Psalm 79:1-9

Deliver us and forgive us our sins, for your name's sake. (Ps. 79:9)

COLOR   Green

THE PRAYERS

Remembering God's marvelous work and living in hope, let us pray for the church, the world, and all people according to their needs.

A BRIEF SILENCE.

Let us pray for the church, that its leaders and ministers will be faithful heralds of the one mediator, Jesus Christ, and draw others to the knowledge of the truth. Lord, in your mercy,

hear our prayer.

Let us pray for the leaders of the world, that they will govern wisely and protect those under their care, so that all people may live a quiet and peaceable life. Lord, in your mercy,

hear our prayer.

Let us pray for the poor and for all people oppressed and exploited by dishonest business practices, that they might receive justice. Lord, in your mercy,

hear our prayer.

Let us pray for those who mourn because they are childless, that God will give them comfort, hope, and fulfillment. Lord, in your mercy,

hear our prayer.

Let us pray for all who are sick and dying (*especially*), that they would be lifted from their pain and despair to healing and hope. Lord, in your mercy,

hear our prayer.

Let us pray for our congregation, that we would be called away from the lure of wealth and everything that might impede our service to God and others. Lord, in your mercy,

hear our prayer.

HERE OTHER INTERCESSIONS MAY BE OFFERED.

Let us give thanks for (*names,* and all) the saints who lived in the knowledge of the truth of Jesus Christ and now rest securely with him. Bring us also to that rest. Lord, in your mercy,

hear our prayer.

God of faithfulness, encircled in your lovingkindness, we lift up to you all in need. Hear our prayers on behalf of others and sustain us as we await the coming of your Son, Jesus Christ our Lord, in whose name we pray. **Amen**

IMAGES FOR PREACHING

The manager in Jesus' parable resembles certain characters in this decade's business scandals. He's cooked the books, and when caught he doctors them again.

Curiously, Jesus' own behavior isn't much different. He's wasted God's mercy on tax collectors and sinners, and soon his critics will not only fire Jesus, they'll have him killed. How dare he spend God's time and wealth on scum!

If that's not bad enough, Jesus continues to cook the books—God's books. Like the manager in the parable, he invests, while he can, in people, not in stocks and commodities. Perhaps that's simple prudence, making friends as a hedge against market crashes. Such are the riches of heaven.

"You know that 500 gallons you owe? Repay 250. Does that work for you?"

Soon the boss catches on, but what can he do? The manager didn't tell customers whose idea this was, so for all they know the owner cut everyone's bills in a fit of generosity. The boss can hardly tell everyone, "Wait! I'm not the generous guy my crazy manager makes me seem! You must all pay every last penny!"

Manager Jesus squandered his Master's goods, and now he's changed everyone's bill. He's forgiven the tax collectors, prostitutes, and many others including us, and trusted that God will make good on his outrageous promise.

By virtue of our baptism, we're in the same business—wasting God's goods on those who don't deserve forgiveness or inclusion. As the Body of Christ, we're

305

today's version of the crooked manager who doctors God's books. God makes good on our promises of forgiveness in a world that wants nothing more than for everybody to pay for their sins.

That manager in the parable sought a home, a table to sit at when he could no longer do what he'd learned as a job. We've found that table here. In this company we enjoy the eternal habitations.

WORSHIP MATTERS

The prayers of the people are an integral part of the assembly's worship. It is here that God's children offer their joys and concerns to the creator. For whom and for what does the assembly pray? Within any congregation, a myriad of prayer concerns is possible, which reflects the diversity among the people. Worship leaders must be aware of the community's needs, and the community must be encouraged to share prayer requests with the pastor and other leaders.

The Christian church, local congregations of like and different denominations, those who are sick or grieving, new and expectant parents—all must have a place within the assembly's prayers. In the second reading Paul encourages us to remember our political leaders in prayer. No matter what our political convictions may be, we recognize that our leaders need our spiritual support and God's wisdom as they do the work to which they have been called.

LET THE CHILDREN COME

One way we can follow Jesus is by giving gifts of money. Today pair children with ushers. If the ushers wear special badges, provide similar ones for the children. This Sunday designate a portion of the offering to help a needy family or to give to a charitable organization that helps needy families. In a bulletin announcement, provide information about who will receive this money and how it will be used. If possible, have the recipient follow up with a letter that may be posted on a bulletin board near the Sunday school classrooms and copied to be read aloud in each class.

HYMNS FOR WORSHIP
GATHERING

O God, my faithful God   LBW 504

Be thou my vision   WOV 776

HYMN OF THE DAY

All depends on our possessing   LBW 447

ALTERNATE HYMN OF THE DAY

Let justice flow like streams   WOV 763

Let justice roll like a river   W&P 85, RWSB

COMMUNION

Son of God, eternal Savior   LBW 364

One bread, one body   WOV 710

SENDING

Take my life, that I may be   LBW 406

Bind us together   WOV 748

May you run and not be weary   W&P 97

ADDITIONAL HYMNS AND SONGS

When the poor ones / *Cuando el pobre*   RWSB, LLC 508

Goodness is stronger than evil   RWSB

I've got a robe   TFF 210

We offer Christ   NCH 527

MUSIC FOR THE DAY
PSALMODY

Christopherson, Dorothy. PW , Cycle C.

Joncas, Michael. "Psalm 113: Praise God's Name" in RS.

Marchionda, James V. "Psalm 113" in *Psalms for the Cantor*, vol. IV. WLP 2506.

"Psalm 113" in TP.

Praise to the Lord   RWSB

CHORAL

Bach, J.S. "Jesu, meine Freude" in *Bach for All Seasons*. SATB. AFP 080065854X.

Ellen, Jane. "Love One Another." SA, pno, opt fl. KJO 6271.

Ferguson, John. "Be Thou My Vision." SATB, org. AFP 0800657934.

Hopson, Hal H. "Psalm 113:1" in *Praise the Lord: Service Music*. U/2 pt, kybd, opt inst. CG CGA530.

Mozart, W.A. "Laudate pueri." SATB, kybd. AMC AE 455.

Willcock, Christopher. "Give Us a Pure Heart." SATB, org. Trinitas 4529.

CHILDREN'S CHOIR

McRae, Shirley. "Let Us Praise God." U/2 pt, Orff, opt kybd. AFP 0800647785.

306

Page, Anna Laura. "Come, Sing a Song of Praise." U/2 pt, kybd. AFP 0800675924.

KEYBOARD/INSTRUMENTAL

Karg-Elert, Siegfried. "Abide, O Dearest Jesus" in *Wedding Music, Part II.* Org. CPH 97-1370.

Langlais, Jean. "Chant de Paix" in *Augsburg Organ Library: November.* Org. AFP 0800658965.

Willan, Healey. "Finale Jubilante" in *The Complete Wedding Collection, Book. II.* Org. BEC OC23.

Wood, Dale. "Alles ist an Gottes segen" in *Preludes and Postludes,* vol. 3. Org. AFP 0800648560.

HANDBELL

McKlveen, Paul. "Be Thou My Vision." 3-5 oct. ALF 16465.
Morris, Hart. "First in My Heart." 3-5 oct. Red River HB0029.

PRAISE ENSEMBLE

Mohr, Jon. "Find Us Faithful" in *Best of the Best.* FEL 1891062018.
Smith, Harry. "Give Thanks" in W&P.

Monday, September 20

NELSON WESLEY TROUT, BISHOP, 1996

Trout was born in Columbus, Ohio, and attended the Evangelical Lutheran Theological Seminary in Columbus. Ordained in 1952, he served parishes in Montgomery, Alabama; Los Angeles, California; and Eau Claire, Wisconsin. Trout also served in staff positions with the American Lutheran Church, Lutheran Social Services of Dayton, and the Columbus seminary. In 1983 Trout was elected bishop of the South Pacific District of the American Lutheran Church, the first African American to serve in such a capacity.

Tuesday, September 21

ST. MATTHEW, APOSTLE AND EVANGELIST

Matthew was a tax collector for the Roman government in Capernaum. Tax collectors were distrusted because they were dishonest and worked as agents for a foreign ruler, the occupying Romans. In the gospels, tax collectors are mentioned as sinful and despised outcasts, but it was these outcasts to whom Jesus showed his love. Matthew's name means "gift of the Lord."

In the gospels Jesus tells his disciples to treat notorious sinners as Gentiles and tax collectors. That has often been taken as a mandate for the church to avoid such people. But Jesus brought his ministry to these very people. In what ways might the church not shun "tax collectors" and sinners but extend its ministry to them and see them as gifts of the Lord?

Saturday, September 25

SERGIUS OF RADONEZH,
ABBOT OF HOLY TRINITY, MOSCOW, 1392

The people of Russia honor Sergius as the most beloved of all their saints and a model of Russian spiritual life at its best. At the age of twenty he began to live as a hermit, and others joined him. From their monastery in the forest, Sergius led the renewal of Russian monastic life. His monastery, the Monastery of the Holy Trinity, was a center for pilgrimage where people came to worship and receive spiritual support. Sergius was also a peacemaker whose influence stopped four civil wars between Russian princes. Sergius left no writings, but his disciples founded seventy-five monasteries and spread his teachings.

The commemoration of Sergius is an opportunity to consider the Russian church and the traditions of Russian Orthodoxy. For example, a discussion could begin about the place of icons in Orthodox spirituality and ways icons can find a home among other Christians.

September 26, 2004

Seventeenth Sunday after Pentecost
Proper 21

INTRODUCTION

The readings for this day continue the theme of the past several weeks asking God's people to consider their relationship to wealth. Our money can be a powerful tool for alleviating suffering in the world, but it can just as easily become a strong force that alienates us from the riches of God's love. We need to know where we place our deepest values.

PRAYER OF THE DAY

God of love, you know our frailties and failings. Give us your grace to overcome them; keep us from those things that harm us; and guide us in the way of salvation; through your Son, Jesus Christ our Lord.

VERSE

Alleluia. At the name of Jesus every knee should bend, and every tongue should confess that Jesus Christ is Lord, to the glory of God the Father. Alleluia. (Phil. 2:10–11)

READINGS

Amos 6:1a, 4-7

The prophet Amos announces that Israel's great wealth is not a cause for rejoicing but rather for sorrow, because God's people have forgotten how to share their wealth with the poor.

Psalm 146

The LORD gives justice to those who are oppressed. (Ps. 146:6)

1 Timothy 6:6-19

Timothy is reminded of the confession he made at his baptism and of its implications for daily life. His priorities will be different from those of people who merely want to be rich.

Luke 16:19-31

When Jesus taught that no one can serve both God and wealth, some of his hearers mocked him. He responded with the story of the rich man and Lazarus.

Alternate First Reading/Psalm

Jeremiah 32:1-3a, 6-15

In the year before Israel fell to the Babylonians, while the attack had already begun, Jeremiah was prisoner in the palace of the king. He arranged to purchase a tract of land to express hope in God's ultimate restoration of Israel after the tragedy of the exile.

Psalm 91:1-6, 14-16

You are my refuge and my stronghold, my God in whom I put my trust. (Ps. 91:2)

COLOR Green

THE PRAYERS

Remembering God's marvelous work and living in hope, let us pray for the church, the world, and all people according to their needs.

A BRIEF SILENCE.

God of justice and hope of the poor, stir up your church to be a prophetic voice for who today are like Lazarus, and for those oppressed everywhere. Lord, in your mercy, **hear our prayer.**

God of justice and hope of the poor, open the eyes of wealthy nations and people to see injustice in the world and move them to become advocates for those exploited by others. Lord, in your mercy, **hear our prayer.**

God of justice and hope of the poor, feed the hungry, set free those wrongly imprisoned, protect the stranger, heal the sick *(especially)*, and sustain all families broken by death, separation, and divorce. Lord, in your mercy, **hear our prayer.**

God of justice and hope of the poor, make our congregation rich in good works and ready to share our bounty with others. Lord, in your mercy, **hear our prayer.**

HERE OTHER INTERCESSIONS MAY BE OFFERED.

God of justice and hope of the poor, we thank you for *(names, and)* all your saints who have fought the good fight of faith and taken hold of eternal life. Bring us with them to dwell with you in the light of glory. Lord, in your mercy,

hear our prayer.

God of faithfulness, encircled in your lovingkindness, we lift up to you all in need. Hear our prayers on behalf of others and sustain us as we await the coming of your Son, Jesus Christ our Lord, in whose name we pray.

Amen

IMAGES FOR PREACHING

Poor Lazarus lost his job. Too weak to dig, now he begged. This rich man's doorstep was the best he'd found. At others he'd received nothing. The rich man benefited, too. Why feed perfectly good leftovers *straight* to the dogs? Let the beggar have them. That's the humane thing to do. He never thought, however, to invite Lazarus inside.

Does the chasm between Lazarus and the rich man exist only in parables? Bread for the World estimates that an American city discards as garbage sufficient food to supply a comparable European city, and a European city throws away enough to feed an Asian or African city. Warnings about such disparities rarely prompt change. Every generation hears prophetic tirades, and the letter to Timothy repeats an old saw with its reminder that hearses don't pull U-Haul trailers.

Sadly, the rich man in Jesus' story was poor even before he died. He'd given his heart to a fickle lover, namely, the 401(k), health insurance, and security system he trusted to keep him from becoming like Lazarus.

Our only hope of avoiding the rich man's fate is to lie outside the gates with only crumbs for supper and dogs to lick our wounds clean. We, too, must die. Hard as it sounds, we've already done this—in baptism. Now, in Abraham's bosom, with our wealth and virtues washed away with our sins, we join the one who crosses the chasm. The storyteller has set his face toward Jerusalem, heading not for the palace table, but a place outside the gates. On the cross, as dogs awaited his blood, he knew the torment of all who suffer with none to comfort them.

"He descended to hell," we confess. There he joins us kinfolk of that sorry rich man. With those ruined hands and feet he seems a beggar. "Come," he says, "here is bread for your hunger, wine for your soul. Take. Eat."

As always, there are leftovers. We may take some if

w

e wish, to feed others outside. But really, there's room inside for everybody.

WORSHIP MATTERS

"Go in peace. Serve the Lord." "Thanks be to God!" Thanks be to God for the transforming and revitalizing power of the word, the word that calls us to look beyond ourselves and our own needs. Thanks be to God that the liturgy calls us to justice and service. Thanks be to God that in our worship we are forgiven, taught, fed, and strengthened, so that we might go forth as ambassadors of God's love—God's love of people, as well as God's love of justice for the world God created. Thanks be to God that the Spirit will lead us to places of need and empower us to ensure that those needs might be met. Thanks be to God for the opportunity to serve the Lord in so many diverse ways.

LET THE CHILDREN COME

In advance, invite members of the congregation to bring gifts of nonperishable food items, good used clothing, and clean unused toys for the same organization or family you selected last week or another charitable organization. This highlights another way we can follow Jesus: by sharing our possessions. All that we have belongs to God. If you celebrate Reformation Sunday on October 31, have the children begin to practice a hymn or portion of a hymn by Martin Luther to sing during worship. Consider "A mighty fortress is our God" (LBW 228, 229) or "Lord, keep us steadfast in your word" (LBW 230). Practice it over the next several weeks.

HYMNS FOR WORSHIP

GATHERING

Rise up, O saints of God!   LBW 383

My soul proclaims your greatness   WOV 730

HYMN OF THE DAY

Lord, whose love in humble service   LBW 423

ALTERNATE HYMN OF THE DAY

Oh, praise the Lord, my soul!   LBW 538

Let me be your servant, Jesus   HFW

COMMUNION

We come to the hungry feast   WOV 766

Lord of all nations, grant me grace   LBW 419

309

SENDING

God of grace and God of glory   LBW 415

Hallelujah! We sing your praises   WOV 722, TFF 158

ADDITIONAL HYMNS AND SONGS

Come to the table   RWSB, W&P 33

Will you let me be your servant   RWSB

Christ, be our host   VU 465

Let your heart be broken for a world in need   TWC 429

MUSIC FOR THE DAY

PSALMODY

Christopherson, Dorothy. *PW* , Cycle C.

Joncas, Michael. "Psalm 146: Lord, Come and Save Us" in STP, vol. 2.

Smith, H. Hamilton. "Psalm 146" in *Psalms for the Cantor*, vol. III. WLP 2504.

Stewart, Roy James. "Praise the Lord" in PCY, vol. 5.

Oh, praise the Lord, my soul!   LBW 538

Praise the Almighty   LBW 539

CHORAL

Bach, J. S. "Jesu, meine Freude" in *Bach for All Seasons.* SATB. AFP 080065854X.

Bach, J. S. "Lord, Thee I Love With All My Heart" in *Bach for All Seasons.* SATB. AFP 080065854X.

Cool, Jayne Southwick. "As Trees by the Waters." SAB, kybd, opt 4 hb, cong. AFP 080067507X.

Fauré, Gabriel. "In Paradisum" in *Requiem.* SATB div, opt orch, org. HIN HMB 147A.

Gardner, John. "Fight the Good Fight." SATB, kybd. OXF 42.874.

Gunderson, Jerry. "We Come to the Hungry Feast." SAB, pno, 1/2/3 C inst, opt cong. AFP 080065871X.

Hairston, Jester. "Poor Man Laz'rus." SATB. BRN 187567.

Helgen, John. "That Priceless Grace" in *The Augsburg Easy Choirbook.* 2 pt mxd, kybd. AFP 0800676025.

CHILDREN'S CHOIR

Mitchell, Tom. "Song of Hope." U, kybd, opt desc, opt instr. (Ps. 146:5) CG CGA638.

Powell, Robert J. "Remember Your Lord God." U, kybd. AFP 0800656377. OP.

KEYBOARD/INSTRUMENTAL

Carter, John. "Beach Spring" in *Contemplative Folk Tunes for Piano.* Pno. AFP 0800659775.

Gawthrop, Daniel. "Toccata Brevis." Org. AMSI OR-7.

Linker, Janet. "Prelude on Beach Spring" in *Sunday Morning Suite: Three Preludes on Early American Hymns.* Org. AFP 0800675606.

Wold, Wayne L. "Beach Spring" in *Augsburg Organ Library: Lent.* Org. AFP 0800658973.

HANDBELL

Manz, Paul, arr. Martha Lynn Thompson. "God of Grace." 4-5 oct. MSM 30-810.

Wagner, H. Dean. "Fantasy on 'Kingsfold.'" 3-5 oct, opt hc. AG 2134.

PRAISE ENSEMBLE

Butler, Terry. "Cry of My Heart" in *Best of the Best.* FEL 1891062018.

Haugen, Marty. "Gather Us In." U/SATB, kybd, opt solo, cong, gtr, 2 fl. GIA G-2651.

Tuesday, September 28

JEHU JONES, MISSIONARY, 1852

A native of Charleston, South Carolina, Jones was ordained by the New York Ministerium in 1832, and was the Lutheran church's first African American pastor. Upon returning to South Carolina he was arrested under a law prohibiting free blacks from reentering the state, so was unable to join the group of Charlestonians he had been commissioned to accompany to Liberia. For nearly twenty years Jones carried out missionary work in Philadelphia in the face of many difficulties. There he led the formation of the first African American Lutheran congregation, St. Paul's, and the construction of its church building.

Wednesday, September 29

ST. MICHAEL AND ALL ANGELS

On this festival day we ponder the richness and variety of God's created order and the limits of our knowledge of it. The scriptures speak of angels who worship God in heaven, and in both testaments angels are God's messengers on earth. They are remembered most vividly as they appear to the shepherds and announce the birth of the savior. Michael is an angel whose name appears in Daniel as the heavenly being who leads the faithful dead to God's throne on the day of resurrection. In Revelation,

Michael fights in a cosmic battle against Satan.

Sing "Ye watchers and ye holy ones" (LBW 175) today. The hymn delights in the presence of the whole heavenly host of seraphs, cherubim, thrones, archangels, virtues, and angel choirs all led in praise of God by Mary, the "bearer of the eternal Word."

Thursday, September 30

JEROME, TRANSLATOR, TEACHER, 420

Jerome is remembered as a biblical scholar and translator.

Rather than choosing classical Latin as the basis of his work, he translated the scriptures into the Latin that was spoken and written by the majority of people in his day. His translation is known as the Vulgate, which comes from the Latin word for "common." While Jerome is remembered as a saint, he could be anything but saintly. He was well known for his short temper and his arrogance, although he was also quick to admit to his personal faults.

Thanks to the work of Jerome, many people received the word in their own language and lived a life of faith and service to those in need.

October 3, 2004

Eighteenth Sunday after Pentecost
Proper 22

311

INTRODUCTION

Faith is the foundation of our worship, not hope for any reward based on our deeds. We adore the God who has brought us into loving relationship, and we receive God's grace that continues to build up our faith.

PRAYER OF THE DAY

Our Lord Jesus, you have endured the doubts and foolish questions of every generation. Forgive us for trying to be judge over you, and grant us the confident faith to acknowledge you as Lord.

VERSE

Alleluia. I will proclaim your name to my brothers and sisters; in the midst of the congregation I will praise you. Alleluia. (Heb. 2:12)

READINGS

Habakkuk 1:1-4; 2:1-4

The injustices of the Judean king and the violence of the Chaldeans (Babylonians) move this prophet to write during the years leading up to the Babylonian exile of Judah. The central issue for the prophet is: How can a good and all-powerful God see evil in the world and seemingly remain indifferent?

Psalm 37:1-10 (Psalm 37:1-9 NRSV)

Commit your way to the LORD; put your trust in the LORD. (Ps. 37:5)

2 Timothy 1:1-14

These words preserve a personal message to a prominent leader in the early Christian church. In the face of hardship and persecution, Timothy is reminded that his faith is a gift of God. He is encouraged to exercise that faith with the help of the Holy Spirit.

Luke 17:5-10

On the way to Jerusalem, Jesus instructs his followers concerning the duties of discipleship. He wants his disciples to exhibit mutual support and forgiveness, to realize the power of faith, and to adopt the attitude of servants who do what is right without thought of reward.

Alternate First Reading/Psalm

Lamentations 1:1-6

Jeremiah's announcement of destruction had become a reality. Now Israel is in exile. The book of Lamentations contains five poems mourning the exile. In this passage, Jerusalem is portrayed as a widow with no one to comfort her.

Lamentations 3:19-26

Great is your faithfulness, O LORD. (Lam. 3:23b)

or Psalm 137

Remember the day of Jerusalem, O LORD. (Ps. 137:7)

COLOR Green

THE PRAYERS

Remembering God's marvelous work and living in hope, let us pray for the church, the world, and all people according to their needs.

A BRIEF SILENCE.

That God will pour out the Spirit of power, love, and self-discipline upon the church, so that confident of our salvation, we might live according to God's holy calling in the world, we pray: Lord, in your mercy,

hear our prayer.

That God will bring an end to destruction and violence in the world and make justice to shine like the noonday, we pray: Lord, in your mercy,

hear our prayer.

That God will strengthen the faith of all who suffer for the sake of the gospel and deliver them, that they might not be ashamed of their suffering but be powerful witnesses to God's grace, we pray: Lord, in your mercy,

hear our prayer.

That God will heal the sick *(especially)*, uphold the dying, and that those who care for the sick and dying will gain strength from their faith, we pray: Lord, in your mercy,

hear our prayer.

That God will increase the faith of all in our congregation and so increase our love for and service to others, we pray: Lord, in your mercy,

hear our prayer.

HERE OTHER INTERCESSIONS MAY BE OFFERED.

We remember with thanksgiving your saints Lois and Eunice, who nurtured in Timothy a living faith, and all parents and grandparents who nurtured in children and grandchildren that same faith in Jesus Christ. Give us a living faith to do the same until we are finally united with Christ and all the saints in light. Lord, in your mercy,

hear our prayer.

God of faithfulness, encircled in your lovingkindness, we lift up to you all in need. Hear our prayers on behalf of others and sustain us as we await the coming of your Son, Jesus Christ our Lord, in whose name we pray.

Amen

IMAGES FOR PREACHING

Jesus sounds annoyed at his disciples' request for additional megabytes of faith. He started the numbers game himself, however. "Even if somebody wrongs you seven times a day, and each time returns to apologize, you must keep on forgiving," Jesus said (Luke 17:4). Three times they might have handled, or even five. But seven? Sorry, Jesus. That's beyond capacity. How about an upgrade?

Jesus uses the mustard seed analogy to teach that faith and faithfulness aren't matters of quantity and size but of relationship and identity. We glimpse this truth about faith in our English words *believe* and *creed*. "To believe" comes from an old, Anglo-Saxon word for being in love. "Creed" derives from *credo*, Latin for "I give my heart."

Faith, therefore, resembles marriage. You entrust your whole self to another. You stake your life, your lone chance at being human on this earth, on that one's faithfulness. In riches or poverty, sickness or health, we belong to each other. I am yours. You are mine. So we also say to God, and God says to us.

Married people don't receive bonus points for remaining faithful any more than students get extra credit for attending class. Spouses simply love, honor, and cherish each other so long as they both live, or the marriage breaks. For one whose heart belongs to Christ, failing or refusing to forgive falls in the category of cheating on one's spouse. Forgiveness is simply what we do, a part of who we are. "A slave is a slave is a slave," Jesus explained, "and slaves don't sit down until their work is complete." Likewise, faith is faith is faith, and a forgiver is a forgiver is a forgiver, and the faithful don't quit forgiving until that work is finished.

Jesus didn't say it would be easy. In fact, he says it will kill us, as it did him. But as strength and comfort for this work, we don't merely have faith. Christ gives us his own heart.

WORSHIP MATTERS

Leading prayer is not reading prayers. Some people pray well. Whether gift or skill, we have all experienced worship where presider or assistant prayed well and through their leadership invited the whole assembly into active participation. Active participation includes not only the hymns and congregational responses, but also drawing the assembly into the prayer of that hour. Such prayers as the eucharistic prayer are not the prayer of the presider or assistant. They are the prayers of the assembly, shaped by the continued use of the church. This week, think about how you invite the congregation into these prayers. Have you practiced the prayers that you will speak publicly this week? Do you know them so well that they have become one with you and you with them? Have you practiced leading them so that you can look at the people as you invite them to pray? Do you wait for congregational responses? What gestures, inflection, posture will you use? What have you done recently to hone your skills at leading prayer, rather than reading prayers?

LET THE CHILDREN COME

Today invite older elementary children to teach this congregational response to the prayers in three graceful motions: *Hear*—lightly touch ears with hands; *our*—tuck elbows in at sides and raise palms upward to chest height, beginning with hands touching, then spreading them apart; and *prayer*—lift high open palms. Print these actions in your worship bulletin, too. Have youth read the prayer petitions. Set aside time before the worship service for youth to practice reading aloud. Encourage families to use this action response to their prayers at home.

HYMNS FOR WORSHIP
GATHERING
Lord Jesus Christ, be present now   LBW 253
God is here!   WOV 719

HYMN OF THE DAY
O Spirit of life   WOV 680

ALTERNATE HYMN OF THE DAY
My God, how wonderful thou art   LBW 524
Don't be worried   TFF 212

COMMUNION
Dear Lord and Father of mankind   LBW 506
As the grains of wheat   WOV 705

SENDING
You are the way   LBW 464
For the fruit of all creation   WOV 760, LBW 563
When peace, like a river   TFF 194, RWI 89

ADDITIONAL HYMNS AND SONGS
As the deer   RWSB, W&P 9
Keep the faith   DH 98
I know my faith is founded   LW 354

MUSIC FOR THE DAY
PSALMODY
Christopherson, Dorothy. PW , Cycle C.
Hopson, Hal H. "Psalm 37" in TP.
Marshall, Jane. "Psalm 37" in *Psalms Together.* CG CGC18.
See Seventh Sunday after the Epiphany.

CHORAL
Candlyn, T. Frederick H. "Thee We Adore." SATB, org.
    CFI CM 492.
Loosemore, Henry. "O Lord, Increase My Faith." SATB.
    BBL CR 11.
Patterson, Mark. "The Banquet Awaits." SATB, kybd, opt ob.
    AFP 0800675843.
Thliverus, Beth. "Give Us Your Blessing." SATB. KJO 8844.
Vaughan Williams, Ralph. "O Taste and See." SATB, org.
    OXF 43.909.
Wold, Wayne L. "As This Broken Bread" in *The Augsburg Easy Choirbook.*
    2 pt mxd, kybd. AFP 0800676025.

CHILDREN'S CHOIR
Marshall, Jane. "Psalm 37:3-4" in *Psalms Together.* U, kybd, cong.
    CG CGC18.
Page, Sue Ellen. "Sing Alleluia" in LS. U, kybd, opt Orff.

KEYBOARD/INSTRUMENTAL
Frahm, Frederick. "Schmücke dich" in *Faith Alive.* Org.
    AFP 0800675738.
Hassell, Michael. "McKee" in *Jazz Plain and Simple.* Pno.
    AFP 0800657268.
Hobby, Robert A. "What a Friend We Have in Jesus" in *For All the Saints.* Org. AFP 0800675371.
Peeters, Flor. "Aria." Org. PRE 513-00436.
Wood, Dale. "In Christ There Is No East or West" in *Wood Works,* vol.
    2. Org. SMP KK400.

HANDBELL
Afdahl, Lee J. "Abbot's Leigh." 3-5 oct. AG 2103.
McChesney, Kevin. "O Master, Let Me Walk with Thee." 2-3 oct.
    Ringing Word 8101.

313

PRAISE ENSEMBLE

Dengler, Lee. "Look at the Birds of the Air." SATB, kybd, opt fl. CPH 98-3125.

Sadler, Gary and Jamie Harvill. "Ancient of Days" in *Best of the Best*. FEL 1891062018.

Monday, October 4

FRANCIS OF ASSISI, RENEWER OF THE CHURCH, 1226

Francis was the son of a wealthy cloth merchant. In a public confrontation with his father he renounced his wealth and future inheritance and devoted himself to serving the poor. Francis described this act as being "wedded to Lady Poverty." Under his leadership the Order of Friars Minor (Franciscans) was formed, and they understood literally Jesus' words to his disciples that they should take nothing on their journey and receive no payment for their work. Their task in preaching was to "use words if necessary." Francis had a spirit of gladness and gratitude for all of God's creation. This commemoration has been a traditional time to bless pets and animals, creatures Francis called his brothers and sisters. A prayer attributed to St. Francis is included in *LBW* (p. 48) and could be used at gatherings in the congregation today.

Monday, October 4

THEODORE FLIEDNER, RENEWER OF SOCIETY, 1864

Fliedner's work was instrumental in the revival of the ministry of deaconesses among Lutherans. While a pastor in Kaiserswerth, Germany, he also ministered to prisoners in Düsseldorf. Through his ministry to prisoners he came in contact with Moravian deaconesses, and it was through this Moravian influence that he was convinced that the ministry of deaconesses had a place among Lutherans. His work and writing encouraged women to care for those who were sick, poor, or imprisoned. Fliedner's deaconess motherhouse in Kaiserswerth inspired Lutherans all over the world to commission deaconesses to serve in parishes, schools, prisons, and hospitals. At this motherhouse in Kaiserswerth, Florence Nightingale received her training as a nurse (see August 13).

Wednesday, October 6

WILLIAM TYNDALE, TRANSLATOR, MARTYR, 1536

William Tyndale was ordained in 1521, and his life's desire was to translate the scriptures into English. When his plan met opposition from Henry VIII, Tyndale fled to Germany, where he traveled from city to city and lived in poverty and constant danger. He was able to produce a New Testament in 1525. Nine years later he revised it and began work on the Old Testament, which he was unable to complete. He was tried for heresy and burned at the stake. Miles Coverdale completed Tyndale's work, and the Tyndale-Coverdale version was published as the "Matthew Bible" in 1537. The style of this translation has influenced English versions of the Bible such as the King James (Authorized Version) and the New Revised Standard Version for four centuries.

Thursday, October 7

HENRY MELCHIOR MUHLENBERG, MISSIONARY TO NORTH AMERICA, 1787

Muhlenberg was prominent in setting the course for Lutheranism in this country. He helped Lutheran churches make the transition from the state churches of Europe to independent churches of America. Among other things, he established the first Lutheran synod in America and developed an American Lutheran liturgy. His liturgical principles became the basis for the Common Service of 1888, used in many North American service books for a majority of the past century.

The commemoration of Muhlenberg invites congregations to look back on what has shaped their identity, worship, and mission in the past and to look ahead to what might shape it in the future.

October 10, 2004

Nineteenth Sunday after Pentecost
Proper 23

INTRODUCTION

"Kyrie, eleison," the church cries: "Lord, have mercy." In Jesus, God *does* have mercy—mercy upon lepers who are outcasts, mercy on apostles who are in chains. God has mercy upon foreigners, breaking through boundaries of nationality and political alienation.

Today the church remembers Massie L. Kennard, an African American pastor who worked effectively toward increasing racial and ethnic inclusiveness in the Lutheran church of the twentieth century.

PRAYER OF THE DAY

Almighty God, source of every blessing, your generous goodness comes to us anew every day. By the work of your Spirit lead us to acknowledge your goodness, give thanks for your benefits, and serve you in willing obedience; through your Son, Jesus Christ our Lord.

VERSE

Alleluia. This is the LORD for whom we have waited; let us be glad and rejoice in his salvation. Alleluia. (Isa. 25:9)

READINGS

2 Kings 5:1-3, 7-15c

Naaman, a Syrian general, suffers from leprosy. In this passage Elisha miraculously cures his illness but only after Naaman realizes, with the help of his servants, that he also needs healing for his pride.

Psalm 111

I will give thanks to the LORD with my whole heart. (Ps. 111:1)

2 Timothy 2:8-15

Though Paul is chained as a prisoner, he reminds Timothy that the word of God is never shackled. He encourages his young friend to proclaim that word of freedom in an honest and upright life as well as in his teaching and preaching.

Luke 17:11-19

A Samaritan leper becomes a model for thanksgiving. This one who was healed does not take for granted the kindness shown to him but offers thanks to Jesus and glorifies God.

Alternate First Reading/Psalm

Jeremiah 29:1, 4-7

From Jerusalem during the years of exile, Jeremiah sends a letter to those in Babylon encouraging them, while they live in this strange and alien place, to be in ministry for the sake of their Babylonian neighbors.

Psalm 66:1-11 (Psalm 66:1-12 NRSV)

God holds our souls in life. (Ps. 66:8)

COLOR   Green

315

THE PRAYERS

Remembering God's marvelous work and living in hope, let us pray for the church, the world, and all people according to their needs.

A BRIEF SILENCE.

Let us pray for the church, that those who preach the word of God will proclaim God's faithfulness and mercy to your people and the world. Lord, in your mercy,
hear our prayer.

Let us pray for favorable weather during harvest time and for fair prices in the marketplace for those who work the land. Lord, in your mercy,
hear our prayer.

Remember those who are struggling with addictions, those struggling with despair and loneliness, those who are sick *(especially)*, and those struggling to keep their faith. Bless them with the grace of your presence. Lord, in your mercy,
hear our prayer.

Let us pray for the strangers and foreigners in our midst, that the people of God will welcome them, offer them hospitality, and so be a sign of God's love for all. Lord, in your mercy,
hear our prayer.

Let us pray for our congregation, that we will give thanks with our whole hearts for the forgiveness that makes us clean, and for all God's blessings. Lord, in your mercy,

hear our prayer.

HERE OTHER INTERCESSIONS MAY BE OFFERED.

Let us give thanks for Massie Kennard, *(names)*, and all the saints whose lives of faith point us to the One who remains faithful to us, Christ Jesus. Lord, in your mercy, **hear our prayer.**

God of faithfulness, encircled in your lovingkindness, we lift up to you all in need. Hear our prayers on behalf of others and sustain us as we await the coming of your Son, Jesus Christ our Lord, in whose name we pray. Amen

IMAGES FOR PREACHING

Conventional wisdom says there aren't many atheists in foxholes. The same goes, no doubt, for hospital emergency rooms and any place a newly diagnosed cancer patient collects his or her thoughts. In times of danger our instincts override whatever theology we may or may not affirm, and we hurl toward heaven a plea for mercy.

When disease threatens, we pray for healing, but we really want cure. Sometimes we get cure, sometimes not, no matter how fervent our prayers. The patient petitioner always receives healing, however. Even if disease wins and death comes earlier than we'd like, turning one's case over to God means we do not die alone, our humanity crushed. Whether we live in God's care, or die in God's embrace, we have healing and wholeness.

Ten desperate lepers once begged Jesus for mercy. All ten received cure. As far as we know, only one found healing. Not only his disintegrating skin changed, his heart filled with thanks, and he couldn't help but return to express his praise and gratitude as directly as he'd once launched cries for help.

A heart full of thanks is a sign of wholeness. It appears often on a deathbed where cure has never arrived. The teacher says also to that one, "Go on your way; your faith has made you whole."

For Christians, the secret of this healing story, and all others as well, lies in the paths that crossed out there in the desolate region where lepers lived out their days. Jesus had set his face toward Jerusalem. There he would show himself to the priests, who would judge him unclean, far from whole. He would pray for God's aid, but he would die broken. Yet, "by his bruises we are healed" (Isa. 53:5).

First, though, Jesus sends these ten to Jerusalem and the priests. If the nine found healing, they got it as Jesus and the Samaritan did—with arms outstretched in the ancient posture that fits both crucifixion and thanksgiving.

WORSHIP MATTERS

"Kyrie eleison!" "Lord have mercy!" It is the cry of the faithful as we bring the cares and concerns both of the past week and of our lives before God. These words are found in the gathering rite and are frequently included in the prayers of the church. Kyrie eleison . . . as we pray for the church, our world and ourselves. Kyrie eleison . . . as we confess to our brokenness and seek God's forgiveness. Kyrie eleison . . . as we ask for strength to face what may lie ahead.

The Bread of Life setting (setting five in *With One Voice*) provides a wonderful opportunity to use this simple yet powerful request for God's mercy. The Kyrie offers the chance to hear and sing both the Greek words and the English equivalent. Worship planners would do well to use the Greek—even if it means taking extra time to teach pronunciation. Those two "foreign" words link us in an additional way with countless Christians of many times and tongues.

LET THE CHILDREN COME

In advance, have each Sunday school class work together to prepare one of the petitions for the congregational prayers. Assign a theme to each class. Choose themes that reflect the concerns and joys of your congregation. You may also include the world, your congregation, people with special needs, people who are hospitalized, the harvest, and government and community leaders. Conclude each petition with: "Lord in your mercy . . ." Be sure to have teachers explain that when we ask for God's mercy, we are humbly asking for God's love. If time permits, print the children's petitions in the bulletin. Consider reviewing and using the prayer response from Proper 22.

HYMNS FOR WORSHIP
GATHERING

Praise to the Lord, the almighty   LBW 543, RWI 58
Each morning brings us   WOV 800
We bow down   W&P 149

HYMN OF THE DAY

Your hand, O Lord, in days of old   LBW 431

ALTERNATE HYMN OF THE DAY

I've just come from the fountain   WOV 696, TFF 111

Baptized in water   WOV 693

COMMUNION

Here, O my Lord, I see thee   LBW 211

Healer of our every ill   WOV 738

SENDING

Praise to you, O God of mercy   WOV 790

To God be the glory   TFF 264

ADDITIONAL HYMNS AND SONGS

Healing river   RWSB

Lord, I lift your name on high   RWSB, W&P 90

Thank you, Lord   TFF 293

An outcast among outcasts   NCH 201

MUSIC FOR THE DAY

PSALMODY

Cherwien, David. "I Will Give Thanks to the Lord." U, hb.
CPH 98-2930.

Christopherson, Dorothy. PW , Cycle C.

Hopson, Hal H. TP.

Proulx, Richard. "My Heart Is Full Today." 2 pt, kybd, hb, perc.
AFP 11-0645. OP.

Psalms for Praise and Worship: A Complete Liturgical Psalter.
ABI 0687093260.

CHORAL

Cherwien, David. "I've Just Come from the Fountain." 2 pt, kybd.
AMSI 832.

Farlee, Robert Buckley. "O Blessed Spring" in *The Augsburg Choirbook.*
SATB, org.   AFP 0800656784.

Handel, G.F. "Since by Man Came Death" in *Messiah.* SATB, kybd.
Various ed.

Helgen, John. "Praise the Living God Who Sings." SATB, org.
AFP 0800674618.

Hopson, Hal H. "Sing Praise to the Lord." SATB, org, opt children's
choir, brass qnt, hb.   AFP 0800676009.

Mendelssohn, Felix. "Above All Praise and All Majesty" in *The Oxford Book of Easy Anthems.* SATB, kybd.   OXF 3533219.

CHILDREN'S CHOIR

Carter, John. "How Excellent Is Your Name." 2 pt, kybd.
AFP 0800674553.

Hassell, Michael. "Is There Anybody Here Who Loves My Jesus?"
2 pt, kybd.   AFP 0800674596.

Horman, John. "Tell All the World." 2 pt, kybd, opt 2 oct hb, opt
Orff.   CG CGA681.

Telemann, G. P., arr. Susan Palo Cherwien. "I Want to Praise the Lord
All of My Life." 2/3 pt, kybd, opt solo inst.   CPH 98-3350.

KEYBOARD/INSTRUMENTAL

Billingham, Richard. "His Name So Sweet" in *Seven Reflections on African
American Spirituals for Organ.* Org.   AFP 0800656229.

Larson, Lloyd. "Where Cross the Crowded Ways of Life" in *Powerful
Preludes.* Pno.   LOR 70/1288L.

Westenkuehler, Jerry. "O the Deep, Deep Love of Jesus" (Ebenezer)
in *I Sing the Mighty Power of God.* Org.   HWG GB9903.

HANDBELL

Baker, Cheryl. "A Stroll on Duke Street." 3-6 oct.   Bronze FX 006.

Kerr, J. Wayne. "Jesus Shall Reign Where'er the Sun." 2-3 oct.
CG CGB113.

Page, Anna Laura. "Morning Has Broken." 3-5 oct.   JEF JHS9190.

PRAISE ENSEMBLE

DeShazo, Lynn. "Worthy of Praises" in *Sing for Joy Songbook Hosanna!*
HOS 21377.

Ruis, David. "You Are Worthy of My Praise" in *More Songs for Praise
and Worship.* SATB.   WRD 3010387016 (vocal ed);
WRD 3010186363 (pno, vcs, perc).

Sunday, October 10

MASSIE L. KENNARD, RENEWER OF THE CHURCH, 1996

Massie L. Kennard was a native of Chicago, Illinois. He
was a major figure in supporting and working toward
ethnic and racial inclusiveness in the former Lutheran
Church in America. Ordained in 1958, he served the
church in various staff positions, including work as the
director for Minority Concerns of the Division for Mission in North America.

Monday, October 11

DAY OF THANKSGIVING (CANADA)

See Day of Thanksgiving (U.S.A.), pages 358–60.

Friday, October 15

TERESA DE JESÚS, TEACHER,
RENEWER OF THE CHURCH, 1582

Teresa de Jesús is also known as Teresa of Avila. She may also be commemorated with John of the Cross on December 14. Teresa chose the life of a Carmelite nun after reading the letters of Jerome. She was frequently sick during her early years as a nun and found that when she was sick her prayer life flowered, but when she was well it withered. Steadily her life of faith and prayer deepened, and she grew to have a lively sense of God's presence with her. She worked to reform her monastic community in Avila, which she believed had strayed from its original purpose. Her reforms asked nuns to maintain life in the monastic enclosure without leaving it and also to identify with those who are poor by not wearing shoes. Teresa's writings on devotional life are widely read by members of various denominations.

October 17, 2004

Twentieth Sunday after Pentecost
Proper 24

INTRODUCTION

The life of faith means that we might wrestle with God. Jesus commends to us the story of a widow who would not take no for an answer. Paul commends to Timothy a life of persistence in proclaiming good news, even when the world may not be eager to hear it. We contend with God, and we find our peace when God assures us of our identity and blesses us.

Ignatius, a second-century bishop of Antioch, is remembered today on the anniversary of his martyrdom. Known to us through his letters, he is an important link between the apostolic times and the early church.

PRAYER OF THE DAY

Almighty and everlasting God, in Christ you have revealed your glory among the nations. Preserve the works of your mercy, that your Church throughout the world may persevere with steadfast faith in the confession of your name; through your Son, Jesus Christ our Lord.

VERSE

Alleluia. In fulfillment of his own purpose God gave us birth by the word of truth, so that we would become a kind of first fruits of his creatures. Alleluia.
(James 1:18)

READINGS

Genesis 32:22-31

Returning to the home he had fled after stealing his brother's birthright and his father's blessing, Jacob wrestles all night long with an adversary who ultimately blesses him and changes his name to "Israel," a name that means "he wrestles with God."

Psalm 121

My help comes from the LORD, the maker of heaven and earth. (Ps. 121:2)

2 Timothy 3:14—4:5

Paul continues his instruction of Timothy, his younger colleague in ministry, by emphasizing the importance of faithful teaching despite opposition.

Luke 18:1-8

Jesus tells a story reminding his listeners they are to be persistent in prayer, unceasing in their appeals. If an unethical judge will ultimately grant the plea of a persistent widow, how much more will our loving God hear those who call upon him!

Alternate First Reading/Psalm

Jeremiah 31:27-34

Jeremiah announces a day when Israel and Judah will be bound to God in a new covenant written upon their hearts and sealed with God's forgiveness.

Psalm 119:97-104

Your words are sweeter than honey to my mouth.
(Ps. 119:103)

COLOR   Green

THE PRAYERS

Remembering God's marvelous work and living in
hope, let us pray for the church, the world, and all
people according to their needs.
A BRIEF SILENCE.

Stir up your church to do the work of evangelism and
proclaim the message of the salvation through faith in
Christ Jesus to the world. Lord, in your mercy,
hear our prayer.

Enlighten world leaders with new and creative ways to
become good stewards of the earth's resources for the
sake of future generations. Lord, in your mercy,
hear our prayer.

Watch over all who suffer from injustice, hear and answer their cry, and preserve them from all evil. Lord, in
your mercy,
hear our prayer.

Let us pray for all the sick *(including)* and especially for
those with AIDS and those who are HIV positive, that
God will give health and strengthen their faith. Lord, in
your mercy,
hear our prayer.

Inspire our congregation to persistent prayer and steadfast study of the scriptures, so that we will be equipped
for every good work. Lord, in your mercy,
hear our prayer.

HERE OTHER INTERCESSIONS MAY BE OFFERED.

We give you thanks for the witness of Ignatius, bishop
and martyr *(and names)*. Give us persistence of faith until
we, with all the saints, may see you face to face. Lord, in
your mercy,
hear our prayer.

God of faithfulness, encircled in your lovingkindness, we
lift up to you all in need. Hear our prayers on behalf of
others and sustain us as we await the coming of your
Son, Jesus Christ our Lord, in whose name we pray.
Amen

IMAGES FOR PREACHING

Jacob worked hard, constantly finagling for some advantage

and often making enemies. Eventually came the inevitable confrontation with the man he'd cheated worst,
his brother Esau. First, however, Jacob got into one more
fight. A mysterious night stranger wrestled him to a
draw. At daybreak, when the opponent sought release,
Jacob demanded a blessing. He received one, along with
a new name and dislocated hip. Jacob became *Israel,*
"One who fights with God." Next morning, the dreaded
meeting proved a joyous reunion. Esau didn't see in Jacob
the enemy; rather, he saw the face of God (Gen. 33:10).
Jacob, too, viewed things differently. His real struggles
weren't with rivals, but with God.

Ever since, Israel's poets and prophets have got in
God's face and helped others do likewise. (If only Cain
had learned this before he wrung his brother's neck,
when the real culprit seemed untouchable!)

Though she's only a character in a parable, the
widow who wears down the crooked judge in Jesus' story
grasps this truth. She won't let the judge go until he
blesses her. Eventually she wins him over.

When we ponder this parable long enough, we see
the face of God in the wrestling widow, not the fickle
judge. All through our nights of anxiety, rage, and confusion, God grapples faithfully with us. Our best punches
land on God, not on each other. God, however, can bear
the lethal load of vengeance we'd love to dump on some
family member or rival, and still come back for more.

Jesus knew the widow's plight better than anyone. He
prayed those vindication psalms through his own night of
torture. Many, including friends, deserved a black eye or
worse for what happened. Instead of retaliating, Jesus
prayed Psalm 31, which says, "Into your hands I commit
my spirit." It also says, "Let the wicked be put to shame;
let them go dumbfounded to Sheol" (v. 17).

God heard every word. But God let us out of Sheol
anyway.

WORSHIP MATTERS

Parents, Luther reminds us, are the bishops, priests, and
deacons in the home. He says this in order to help the
church understand that faith is first nurtured in the
home. It is "learned" by watching, acting, and listening.
While many parents want their children "raised in the
faith," rarely does the church help parents fulfill their
baptismal ministry in the home.

Who is responsible in your parish for gathering

319

parents together and leading them in a discussion of the basics of faith formation in the home? The assumption that parents know how to pray in the home because they come to church regularly needs to be tested by listening to parents' questions and concerns. Of course, there will be a few parents who expect church professionals to carry out such work for them. At times, this is because they may feel a lack of confidence in their own abilities. For those who view the church as a dispenser of "goods and services" that are "purchased" through offerings, it may be helpful to reflect on the promises that parents and godparents make at baptism.

LET THE CHILDREN COME

Today teach that we can pray in all places. Before the worship service begins, have a pastor lead the children in a prayer in the narthex. Read the prayers of the day from various locations in your sanctuary: at the back of the church, near the font, at the lectern, from a balcony, from the center of the sanctuary, and so on. Another possibility is to sprinkle readers throughout the congregation. After the service, have the pastor lead the children on a prayer journey. Pray in the church nursery, in a classroom, outdoors, and in fellowship hall. At the end of the journey, give each child a little sticker that says *pray* to place on a light switch plate at home. Each time family members turn on or off the light they can be reminded to pray.

HYMNS FOR WORSHIP
GATHERING

Give to our God immortal praise   LBW 520
By gracious powers   WOV 736
We have come into his house   TFF 136

HYMN OF THE DAY

Christians, while on earth abiding   LBW 440

ALTERNATE HYMN OF THE DAY

Day by day   WOV 746
Unto the hills   LBW 445

COMMUNION

O Lord, hear my prayer   WOV 772
Eternal Spirit of the living Christ   LBW 441

SENDING

My hope is built on nothing less   LBW 293, 294
I will sing of the mercies of the Lord   W&P 74

ADDITIONAL HYMNS AND SONGS

Lord, listen to your children   RWSB, W&P 91
O God in heaven   RWSB
When the storms of life are raging   TFF 198
Come, O thou Traveler unknown   H82 638

MUSIC FOR THE DAY
PSALMODY

Bobb, Barry L. "Psalm 121." U, opt cong, kybd. AFP 11-4656. OP.
Christopherson, Dorothy. PW, Cycle C.
Cotter, Jeanne. "Our Help Is from the Lord" in PCY, vol. 3.
Cox, Joe. "I Lift Up My Eyes to the Hills" in *Psalms for the People of God.* SMP 45/1037S.
Edwards, Rusty and LaJuana Fiester. "We Lift Our Eyes" in ASG.
Lovelace, Austin. "Psalm 121." U, fl. CG CGC361.

CHORAL

Ferguson, John. "By Gracious Powers." SATB, org, fl, opt cong. AFP 0800675495.
Handel, G. F. "Let Justice and Judgement" in *Four Coronation Anthems.* SAATB, kybd. OXF 3352591.
Helgen, John. "O Jesus, Blessed Lord." SATB, pno. KJO 8968.
Mendelssohn, Felix. "Lift Thine Eyes" in *Elijah.* SSA. CFI CM618.
Petker, Allan. "I Will Follow Your Call." SATB, hrp/pno. PVN P1203.
Schute, Linda Cable. "Jesus Is Mine." SATB, kybd. AFP 0800675487.

CHILDREN'S CHOIR

Jothen, Michael. "Over All (Sabre todos)." (Ps. 121) U, kybd, opt gtr, opt C inst. CG CGA835.
Pethel, Stan. "Three Psalms." (Ps. 121) U/2 pt, pno. CG CGA931.

KEYBOARD/INSTRUMENTAL

Carlson, J. Bert. "Precious Lord" in *This Little Light of Mine.* Pno. AFP 0800659503.
Ferguson, John. "Children of the Heavenly Father" in *Thy Holy Wings.* Org. AFP 0800647955.
Kohrs, Jonathan. "Linstead" in *Four Tunes for Piano and Two Instruments.* Kybd, inst. AFP 0800658787.

Schroeder, Hermann. "Piece 6" in *Kleine Preludien und Intermezzi.* Org. Schott 2221.

HANDBELL

Lamb, Linda R. "What a Friend We Have in Jesus." 2-3 oct. CPH 97-6927.

McFadden, Jane. "Day by Day" in *Two More Swedish Melodies for Handbells.* 3-4 oct, opt hc. AFP 0800657357.

Sherman, Arnold B. "What a Friend We Have in Jesus." 3-6 oct. RR HB0032.

Young, Philip M. "Day by Day." 3-5 oct. LOR 20/1100L.

PRAISE ENSEMBLE

Hanson, Handt. "Listen to My Prayer" in *Spirit Calls . . . Rejoice.* SATB. CCF 0933173393 (pew ed); CCF 0933173385 (acc ed).

Whittemore, Dan. "Just a Prayer Away" in *The Ultimate Praise Songbook for Kids.* LIL MB-681.

Sunday, October 17

IGNATIUS, BISHOP OF ANTIOCH, MARTYR, C. 115

Ignatius was the second bishop of Antioch in Syria. It was there that the name "Christian" was first used to describe the followers of Jesus. Ignatius is known to us through his letters. In them he encouraged Christians to live in unity sustained with love while standing firm on sound doctrine. Ignatius believed Christian martyrdom was a privilege. When his own martyrdom approached, he wrote in one of his letters, "I prefer death in Christ Jesus to power over the farthest limits of the earth. . . . Do not stand in the way of my birth to real life."

Ignatius and all martyrs are a reminder that even today Christians face death because of their faith in Jesus. Still, 2 Timothy reminds us, "If we died with him, we shall also live with him" (2:11).

Monday, October 18

ST. LUKE, EVANGELIST

Luke is identified as the author of both Luke and Acts. Luke is careful to place the events of Jesus' life in both their social and religious contexts. Some of the most loved parables, including the good Samaritan and the prodigal son, are found only in this gospel. Luke's gospel has also given the church some of its most beautiful songs: the Benedictus sung at morning prayer, the Magnificat sung at evening prayer, and the Nunc dimittis sung at the close of the day. These songs are powerful witnesses to the message of Jesus Christ.

Paul calls Luke the "beloved physician," and some congregations use the day of St. Luke to remember and pray for those in healing professions. The Service of the Word for Healing in the seasonal rites section may be used, or the one in *Life Passages: Marriage, Healing, Funeral, Renewing Worship,* vol. 4.

321

Saturday, October 23

JAMES OF JERUSALEM, MARTYR

James became an early leader of the church in Jerusalem. He is described in the New Testament as the brother of Jesus, and secular historian Josephus calls James the brother of Jesus, "the so-called Christ." Little is known about him, but Josephus reported that the Pharisees respected James for his piety and observance of the law. His enemies had him put to death.

Was James a blood brother of the Lord? It is difficult to answer that question because the Aramaic word for brother can also mean cousin. Jesus also said, "Whoever does the will of God is my brother and sister and mother." The commemoration of James and his connection to Jesus as "brother" can spark further discussion about how we all share Christ as our brother through baptism into his death and resurrection.

October 24, 2004

Twenty-first Sunday after Pentecost
Proper 25

INTRODUCTION

Those who seem the farthest from God may be the closest to mercy. That is the theme of today's gospel, and it is echoed in the other readings. It is the dynamic that supports the dialogue in the first reading. We get close to God as we confess that we are in need of grace.

PRAYER OF THE DAY

Almighty and everlasting God, increase in us the gifts of faith, hope, and charity; and, that we may obtain what you promise, make us love what you command; through your Son, Jesus Christ our Lord.

VERSE

Alleluia. The Lord will rescue me from every evil attack and save me for his heavenly kingdom. Alleluia. (2 Tim. 4:18)

READINGS

Jeremiah 14:7-10, 19-22

The prophet identifies with his people in this anguished prayer following the onslaught of the Babylonians and the destruction of Jerusalem.

or Sirach 35:12-17

God is impartial in justice and hears the powerless.

Psalm 84:1-6 (Psalm 84:1-7 NRSV)

Happy are the people whose strength is in you. (Ps. 84:4)

2 Timothy 4:6-8, 16-18

The conclusion of this letter to a young minister offers a final perspective on life from one who is now facing death. Though others have let him down, Paul is sure of his faith in the Lord, who has stood by him and lent him strength.

Luke 18:9-14

At the time of Jesus, Pharisees were regarded as exceptionally religious persons, and tax collectors were treated as outcasts. In this parable Jesus contrasts the two in a surprising way to make a point about approaching God in humbleness.

Alternate First Reading/Psalm

Joel 2:23-32

The prophet Joel uses the image of a plague of locusts as a reminder of Judah's destruction at the hands of hostile armies. Today's reading points beyond the judgment of the Day of the Lord, when the Lord will repay "the years that the swarming locust has eaten" and everyone who calls on the Lord's name will be saved.

Psalm 65

Your paths overflow with plenty. (Ps. 65:12)

COLOR Green

THE PRAYERS

Remembering God's marvelous work and living in hope, let us pray for the church, the world, and all people according to their needs.

A BRIEF SILENCE.

Let us pray that God will stand by the church and give it strength, so that the message of the gospel will be proclaimed fully in an age of discord and unbelief. Lord, in your mercy,

hear our prayer.

Let us pray that God will bring peace to nations and peoples in warfare and healing where there is terror and strife. Lord, in your mercy,

hear our prayer.

Let us pray that God will be merciful to penitent sinners, will lead those in the desolate valley of hopelessness to a place of springs, and will exalt those who humble themselves before God. Lord, in your mercy,

hear our prayer.

Let us pray that God will be the source of healing on whom all who are sick and dying *(especially)* will set their hope, and will find that hope rewarded. Lord, in your mercy,

hear our prayer.

Let us pray that God will place in the soul of this congregation a desire to hear the word of God preached and a longing to share the feast of love prepared for us. Lord, in your mercy,

hear our prayer.

HERE OTHER INTERCESSIONS MAY BE OFFERED.

Let us give thanks for *(names, and all)* those who have fought the good fight, finished the race, and kept the faith. Preserve us, gracious God, in that same faith so that we, with them, may enjoy the crown of righteousness reserved for us. Lord, in your mercy,

hear our prayer.

God of faithfulness, encircled in your lovingkindness, we lift up to you all in need. Hear our prayers on behalf of others and sustain us as we await the coming of your Son, Jesus Christ our Lord, in whose name we pray.

Amen

IMAGES FOR PREACHING

The Pharisee in Jesus' parable presents himself as one who offers thanks to God. In truth, he's come to the temple to do some banking. He means to make a deposit. To his already substantial account, today he adds two fast days, not merely one, and a full tithe, plus motives far superior to "other people," like those inclined toward greed, impiety, and lust.

The Pharisee suspects he'll need his savings account one day. He banks on God's justice. In a day of trouble, or threatened persecution, the Pharisee can make a withdrawal like the one the psalmist attempts in the prayer we know as Psalm 17. There, David, according to the superscription, calls on God to save him from enemies as a reward for perfect righteousness. "Just test me," this psalm dares God, "and you'll find no trace of anything wrong in me. Therefore, destroy my enemies, Lord, and their children and grandchildren, too, while you're at it."

We don't know this particular Pharisee, but we do know David, and he's not fooling us when he writes out his withdrawal slip that way. We expect he's not fooling God, either. How arrogant, this Pharisee! Thankfully, we're not like that. Our theology is much better. We're banking on it, in fact.

In the shadows, far from the teller's window, stands the tax collector. He offers no deposit. Instead, he banks on God's mercy.

By that same mercy, we stand with the tax collector. We go home with him, too, and there, in our prayer closet, we dare to sing Psalm 17. "Visit me in the dead of night, O God. Test me."

We don't bank on our own righteousness, however. Instead, we trust God will examine us, scrutinize our accounts, and see not our debts, with all our righteousnesses piled like filthy rags, but the startling record reflected in the baptismal garment we wear.

WORSHIP MATTERS

From where does the pastor lead the order for confession and forgiveness? If the arrangement of your church building permits, the font is an ideal place from which to lead the congregation in the confession of sin and to announce God's forgiveness.

Baptism, confession, and forgiveness are intrinsically linked. It is in the cleansing waters that we are reborn and raised to a new existence as God's forgiven children. A visual reminder of this connection will illustrate the tie between the waters and our need for continual cleansing. Ideally, then, the font should be in a visible location in the worship space. Perhaps it might be placed near the entrance, so that all could not help but notice it as they came to worship. The order for confession and forgiveness could then be led from this place, illustrating the rite as preparatory to the service, as an entrance to our corporate worship of God.

Another option would be to place the font front and center, so that all would pass by on their way to the Lord's table. Either way, the visible font filled with water, together with the powerful words of confession and absolution, will remind the assembly of our baptism into God's family and our rebirth in the Spirit.

LET THE CHILDREN COME

Today focus on confession and forgiveness. All of us need to say we're sorry to God and to each other. Before the worship service starts, perhaps during announcements, teach the congregation about the moment of silence during the confession. Invite the children, and the whole congregation, to think of one thing for which they would like to ask God's forgiveness. Assure young children that God always hears our prayers. Parents may write down young children's responses. Pause during the moment of silence to give everyone time to pray. Young children may even whisper their responses. If you celebrate Reformation, wear red next Sunday.

HYMNS FOR WORSHIP

GATHERING

Praise, my soul, the King of heaven   LBW 549
Praise, my soul, the God of heaven   RWI 59
My soul proclaims your greatness   WOV 730

HYMN OF THE DAY

To you, omniscient Lord of all   LBW 310

ALTERNATE HYMN OF THE DAY

In all our grief   WOV 739
The walls will echo praises   HFW

COMMUNION

Just as I am, without one plea   LBW 296
You satisfy the hungry heart   WOV 711

SENDING

How firm a foundation   LBW 507
All my hope on God is founded   WOV 782

ADDITIONAL HYMNS AND SONGS

Come and fill   RWSB
Holy God, holy and glorious   RWSB
Guide my feet   TFF 153
Change my heart, O God   W&P 28

MUSIC FOR THE DAY

PSALMODY

Cherwien, David. PW , Cycle C.
Haas, David. "How Lovely" (Psalm 84) in PCY, vol. 9.
Joncas, Michael. "Psalm 84: How Lovely Is Your Dwelling Place" in STP, vol. I.
Mackie, Ruth E. "Psalm 84." SATB, cong, inst, org.   CPH 98-3305.
Porter, Tom. "Happy Are They Who Dwell in Your House." Cong, choir, kybd, gtr, inst.   GIA G-3026.

CHORAL

Dowland, John. "He That Is Down Need Fear No Fall" in *Oxford Book of Easy Anthems.* SATB.   OXF 3533219.
Fauré, Gabriel, arr. Hal H. Hopson. "Psalm 84: Cantique de Jean Racine." SATB, kybd.   CFI CM 8042.
Gardner, John. "Fight the Good Fight." SATB, kybd.   OXF 42.874.
Handel, G.F. "Every Valley" in *Messiah.* T solo, kybd. Various ed.
Hassell, Michael. "Jesus Loves Me." SATB, kybd, sax.

AFP 0800656512.
Moore, Philip. "He That Is Down Need Fear No Fall." SATB, org.   RME.
Shepperd, Mark. "In Whom I Trust." SATB, kybd.   AFP 0800675991.

CHILDREN'S CHOIR

Christopherson, Dorothy. "Come and Pray with Me." U, pno.   ABI 029627.
McClune, Ellen and A. Steven Taranto. "Let Us Go to the House of the Lord." (Ps. 84) U, kybd. CG CGA872.

KEYBOARD/INSTRUMENTAL

Burkhardt, Michael. *All My Hope on God Is Founded.* Org.   MSM 10-734.
Callahan, Charles. *Aria.* Org. MSM 10-902.
Hamilton, Gregory. "Prelude" (New Britain) in *The Marilyn Mason Music Library,* vol. I. Org. MSM 10-990.
Hassell, Michael. "De colores" in *Folkways.* Kybd, inst.   AFP 0800656903.

HANDBELL

Helman, Michael. "There Is a Balm in Gilead." 3-5 oct. ALF 18572.
Larson, Katherine Jordahl. "I Lay My Sins on Jesus." 3-5 oct.   AMSI HB-29.
Young, Philip M. "There Is a Balm in Gilead." 3-4 oct.   AFP 0800653572. OP.

PRAISE ENSEMBLE

Brown, Brenton. "Lord, Reign in Me" in *Come, Now Is the Time to Worship Songbook.* Vineyard Music VMB9347.
Espinosa, Eddie. "Change My Heart, O God" in W&P.
McLean, Terry Bocklund, arr. Dan Goeller. "Lord of Life." SAB, kybd. AFP 0800675827.

Tuesday, October 26

PHILIPP NICOLAI, 1608; JOHANN HEERMANN, 1647;
PAUL GERHARDT, 1676; HYMNWRITERS

These three outstanding hymnwriters all worked in Germany in the seventeenth century during times of war and plague. When Philipp Nicolai was a pastor in Westphalia, the plague killed thirteen hundred of his parishioners. One hundred seventy people died in one week. His hymns "Wake, awake, for night is flying" (LBW 31)

324

and "O Morning Star, how fair and bright!" (LBW 76) were included in a series of meditations he wrote to comfort his parishioners during the plague. The style of Johann Heermann's hymns moved away from the more objective style of Reformation hymnody toward expressing the emotions of faith. Three of his hymns are in *LBW*, including his plaintive text, "Ah, holy Jesus" (123). Paul Gerhardt lost a preaching position at St. Nicholas's Church in Berlin because he refused to sign a document stating he would not make theological arguments in his sermons. Some have called him the greatest of Lutheran hymnwriters.

October 31, 2004

Reformation Day

INTRODUCTION

This day the Lutheran church remembers with thanksgiving the events of the sixteenth-century Reformation. We rightly celebrate the Reformation not when we glory in the events of the past, but rather when we pray, "Come, Holy Spirit!" The church is always in need of reform, always in need of dying again in Christ and being raised from the dead, so that it might be truly free.

PRAYER OF THE DAY

Almighty God, gracious Lord, pour out your Holy Spirit upon your faithful people. Keep them steadfast in your Word, protect and comfort them in all temptations, defend them against all their enemies, and bestow on the Church your saving peace; through your Son, Jesus Christ our Lord, who lives and reigns with you and the Holy Spirit, one God, now and forever.

VERSE

Alleluia. If you continue in my word, you are truly my disciples, and you will know the truth, and the truth will make you free. Alleluia. (John 8:31–32)

Thursday, October 28

ST. SIMON AND ST. JUDE, APOSTLES

We know little about Simon and Jude. In New Testament lists of the apostles, Simon the "zealot" or Cananean is mentioned, but he is never mentioned apart from these lists. Jude, sometimes called Thaddeus, is also mentioned in lists of the twelve. At the last supper Jude asked Jesus why he had chosen to reveal himself to the disciples but not to the world. A traditional story about Simon and Jude says that they traveled together on a missionary journey to Persia and were both martyred there.

The Prayer of the Day for this lesser festival asks that as Simon and Jude "were faithful and zealous in their mission, so we may with ardent devotion make known the love and mercy of our Lord and Savior Jesus Christ."

READINGS

Jeremiah 31:31-34

The exiles in Babylon blamed their captivity on their ancestors who had broken the covenant established at Mount Sinai. But the prophet envisions a future day when the people can no longer make such a complaint, for there will be no need to teach the law. Knowledge of God and of God's laws will be a gift from God, written on the heart.

Psalm 46

The LORD of hosts is with us; the God of Jacob is our stronghold. (Ps. 46:4)

Romans 3:19-28

Martin Luther and other leaders of the Reformation believed the heart of the gospel was found in these words of Paul written to the Romans. All people have sinned, but God offers forgiveness of sins through Christ Jesus. We are justified—put right with God—by the gift of God's grace, through faith in Jesus.

John 8:31-36

The Reformation sought to emphasize that true freedom is not related to ethnic distinctions or social class. Only

Jesus can free us from slavery to sin, which he does through the truth of the gospel.

COLOR Red

THE PRAYERS

Remembering God's marvelous work and living in hope, let us pray for the church, the world, and all people according to their needs.

A BRIEF SILENCE.

Renew your church and strengthen it to continue in your word, so that the church will proclaim with boldness the message of freedom that Jesus Christ brings. Lord, in your mercy,

hear our prayer.

Break the bow, shatter the spear, burn the shield, and make wars to cease in all the world, that everyone may live in peace, safety, and freedom. Lord, in your mercy,

hear our prayer.

Give wisdom to the citizens of the United States as they approach this week's elections, that they may be encouraged to participate, and may vote with an eye to the welfare of all the earth and its people. Lord, in your mercy,

hear our prayer.

Be a stronghold for those who are victims of abuse, for those who feel imprisoned by life's circumstances, and for all who are sick (*especially*), so that they may live without fear. Lord, in your mercy,

hear our prayer.

Stir up in this congregation thankful hearts for the righteousness of God disclosed through faith in Jesus Christ, given through baptism. Lord, in your mercy,

hear our prayer.

HERE OTHER INTERCESSIONS MAY BE OFFERED.

We give you thanks for Martin Luther, renewer of the church, and for all the saints throughout the ages who have called the church to faithful witness of Jesus Christ. Renew your covenant with us, so that we may live in the confidence that we are your people and you are our God until we are united with you and all the saints in heaven. Lord, in your mercy,

hear our prayer.

God of faithfulness, encircled in your lovingkindness, we lift up to you all in need. Hear our prayers on behalf of others and sustain us as we await the coming of your Son, Jesus Christ our Lord, in whose name we pray.

Amen

326

IMAGES FOR PREACHING

Not every truth grants freedom. Indeed, many enslave us. The truth of our private hatreds, sometimes of those closest and most dear, imprisons us. Our strength and wit goes wasted in hiding the truth of our addictions, shame, or gnawing despair from both ourselves and the one from whom, ultimately, no secrets are hid.

In countless triangles, a furtive truth that two know, but a third does not, makes captives of all three. Words like cancer, layoff, or divorce take us hostage when they appear in the same sentence as our names. Rumor and gossip, even when truthful, pin us helplessly to a wall of public scrutiny. We arm for volleys of dueling truths whose purpose is to maim and demean, whether in marriage, church squabbles, or political campaigns.

"Tell all the Truth but tell it slant," advised Emily Dickinson. An old Yugoslavian proverb says, "Tell the truth and run." Many a prophet has paid dearly for ignoring such advice.

We seem condemned to live in solitary prisons. Except for one thing. *The* truth. "Abide in my word," Jesus says, "there you know truth and have genuine freedom." What is that word? "As the Father has loved me, so I have loved you; abide in my love" (John 15:9). God's incarnate Word is God's love, and also our dwelling place of freedom. We entered through baptism and abide thanks to the Spirit's persistent calling, urging, and faithfulness.

In the embrace of Christ's body, we see that truth written in flesh and blood. Here, words of absolution trump the truth of accusations. Words of comfort lift us from the prison of disintegrating bodies.

Christ lived the truth and didn't run. Each of us, and all of us together, are worth everything, including life itself, to the God revealed in Christ. Of all that's true about any of us, this truth ultimately counts.

The same truth gives the church life, freedom, and the strength to repent and seek reform. Christ's gospel, spoken truthfully, never isolates, alienates, or excludes. Rather, it reforms our lives, families, church, and world.

WORSHIP MATTERS

In the western church, the color red is associated with blood, fire, and the Holy Spirit. These associations are partly natural, partly cultural, and partly arbitrary. The system of colors now in use generally among western

Christians has not always been so uniform. Individual dioceses or territorial churches developed their own use of colors over the centuries. Some colors have all but disappeared from use, like yellow for example, or blue, which was only reintroduced twenty years ago among most Lutherans in North America. The use of colors to mark the passage of the festivals and seasons of the church year is popular among Christians today.

The use of red for Reformation Day (October 31) is based not so much on the associations of blood and fire—though the Reformation had its share of martyrs and destruction in Northern Europe and England—as on the conviction that it is a time to celebrate the work of the Holy Spirit in renewing the church. Like Pentecost it is a time to celebrate the power of God's Spirit to move, shape, and reshape (reform) the church. Reformation churches and especially Lutherans observe this festival not out of chauvinistic pride in our rightness and everyone else's wrongness. Rather, it is offered as an opportunity to celebrate the power of Pentecost moving through the church in our present day.

LET THE CHILDREN COME

We dress the church in red today. Red paraments, red banners, and red clothing can all remind us of fire, and, in turn, of the work of the Holy Spirit in Martin Luther's life. Have a children's choir lead the congregation in singing one of Martin Luther's hymns. Print a brief child-friendly biography about Luther in your church bulletin. Invite an adult to dress like Martin Luther and tell highlights of Luther's life before and after the worship service, perhaps roaming around fellowship hall. Display a poster of Luther's seal with the meaning of the six symbols. Offer gold chocolate coins to children as reminders that the gold circle in Luther's symbol reminds us of God's never-ending love for us.

HYMNS FOR WORSHIP

GATHERING

The Church's one foundation   LBW 369
Oh, praise the gracious power   WOV 750

HYMN OF THE DAY

Lord, keep us steadfast in your Word   LBW 230

ALTERNATE HYMN OF THE DAY

Listen, God is calling   WOV 712, TFF 130
God, my Lord, my strength   LBW 484

COMMUNION

For the bread which you have broken   LBW 200
What feast of love   WOV 701

SENDING

A mighty fortress is our God   LBW 228, 229; RWI 2, 3
What a mighty word God gives   W&P 155

ADDITIONAL HYMNS AND SONGS

For by grace you have been saved   RWSB
Glory, glory, hallelujah   RWSB, TFF 148
God, our help and constant refuge   PH 192
By grace I'm saved   LW 351

MUSIC FOR THE DAY

PSALMODY

327

Burkhardt, Michael. *Three Psalm Settings.* U, cong, perc, org. MSM 80-705.

Cherwien, David. PW, Cycle C.

Cherwien, David. "Psalm 46: God Is Our Refuge." U, cong, org. MSM 80-800.

Folkening, John. *Six Psalm Settings with Antiphons.* SATB, U, cong, kybd. MSM 80-700.

Wood, Dale. PW, Cycle C.

Ziegenhals, Harriet Ilse. "God Is Our Help in Time of Trouble" in *Sing Out! A Children's Psalter.* WLP 7191.

CHORAL

Bach, J. S. "A Mighty Fortress" in *Bach for All Seasons.* SATB. AFP 080065854X.

Buxtehude, Dietrich. "Lord, Keep Us Steadfast in Thy Word." SATB, str trio, org. CPH 97-6331.

Distler, Hugo. "Salvation unto Us Has Come" in *Chantry Choirbook.* SATB. AFP 0800657772.

Ferguson, John. "Psalm 46." SATB, org. AFP 0800656067.

Hassler, Hans L. "A Mighty Fortress Is Our God" in *Chantry Choirbook.* SATB. AFP 0800657772.

Walter, Johann. "I Build on God's Strong Word" in *Chantry Choirbook.* SATB. AFP 0800657772.

Ylvisaker, John. "Lord, Keep Us Steadfast in Your Word." SATB, kybd, opt perc, db. KJO 8864.

CHILDREN'S CHOIR

Comer, Marilyn. "God Is Our Refuge and Strength" in LS. (Ps. 46) U, kybd, opt Orff.

Gay, Sandra. "Sing Thankful Songs." (John 8:31-32) U/2 pt, pno, 3 oct hb/hc. CG CGA828.

KEYBOARD/INSTRUMENTAL

Cherwien, David. "A Mighty Fortress" in *Interpretations, Book I.* Org. AMSI OR-3.

Cherwien, David. "Christ Is Made the Sure Foundation" in *Interpretations, Book XII.* Org. AMSI SP-109.

Hobby, Robert A. "A Mighty Fortress Is Our God" in *For All the Saints.* Org. AFP 0800675371.

Wold, Wayne L. "A Mighty Fortress" in *Songs of Thankfulness and Praise, Set I.* Org. MSM 10-711.

HANDBELL

Helman, Michael. "Built on a Rock." 3-5 oct, opt hc, opt cong. ALF 19006.

Linker, Janet and Jane McFadden. "Built on a Rock: Hymn Concertato." 3 oct hb, org, opt choir, opt tpt. AFP 0800655680 (full score). OP.

Page, Anna Laura. "A Mighty Fortress Is Our God." 3-5 oct, opt hc. AFP 0800658841.

Tucker, Sondra. "The Church's One Foundation." 2-3 oct. CPH 97-6903.

PRAISE ENSEMBLE

Gordon, Nancy and Jamie Harvill. "Because We Believe" in *More Songs for Praise and Worship.* SATB. WRD 3010387016 (vocal ed); WRD 3010186363 (pno, vcs, perc).

Zschech, Darlene. "Shout to the Lord" in W&P.

October 31, 2004

Twenty-second Sunday after Pentecost
Proper 26

INTRODUCTION

In today's gospel, Jesus invites himself to the home of a known sinner. This day God invites us into grace, even though we do not deserve it. "Today salvation has come to this house." Therefore, we always "enter God's courts with praise."

Today the Lutheran church recalls its roots, the principles and actions that grew out of the sixteenth-century Reformation.

PRAYER OF THE DAY

Stir up, O Lord, the wills of your faithful people to seek more eagerly the help you offer, that, at the last, they may enjoy the fruit of salvation; through our Lord Jesus Christ.

VERSE

Alleluia. Let the word of the Lord spread rapidly and be glorified everywhere, for the Lord is faithful and will strengthen you. Alleluia. (2 Thess. 3:1, 3)

READINGS

Isaiah 1:10-18

Isaiah announces God's displeasure with the offerings and sacrifices of a people who are sinful and without compassion. He pleads with Judah, the Southern Kingdom, to return to the Lord that they might be cleansed.

Psalm 32:1-8 (Psalm 32:1-7 NRSV)

All the faithful will make their prayers to you in time of trouble. (Ps. 32:7)

2 Thessalonians 1:1-4, 11-12

The letters of Paul typically begin with a salutation, a blessing, and a few words of praise for what God is accomplishing among the recipients. By remaining faithful and growing spiritually during hardship, the Thessalonian Christians have become witnesses to the glory of God.

Luke 19:1-10

The story of Jesus and Zacchaeus illustrates well the central theme of Luke's gospel: Jesus is the Savior of all, especially those whom others reject.

Alternate First Reading/Psalm
Habakkuk 1:1-4; 2:1-4

The injustices of the Judean king and the violence of the Chaldeans (Babylonians) move this prophet to write during the years leading up to the Babylonian exile of Judah. The central issue for the prophet is: How can a good and all-powerful God see evil in the world and seemingly remain indifferent?

Psalm 119:137-144

Grant me understanding, that I may live. (Ps. 119:144)

COLOR   Green

THE PRAYERS

Remembering God's marvelous work and living in hope, let us pray for the church, the world, and all people according to their needs.
A BRIEF SILENCE.

Ignite your church to proclaim your message of repentance and forgiveness to everyone, and stir up its zeal to seek out and save the lost. Lord, in your mercy,
hear our prayer.

Turn the hearts of all nations to seek justice, to rescue the oppressed, to defend those who are orphaned or widowed. Lord, in your mercy,
hear our prayer.

Give wisdom to the citizens of the United States as they approach this week's elections, that they may be encouraged to participate, and may vote with an eye to the welfare of all the earth and its people. Lord, in your mercy,
hear our prayer.

Strengthen the faith of all those who suffer persecution for confessing the name of Jesus Christ and bring an end to their suffering. Lord, in your mercy,
hear our prayer.

Deliver from despair those burdened by their sins and assure them of your salvation. Lord, in your mercy,
hear our prayer.

Comfort and heal those who are dying or sick *(especially)*, and make your presence known to them in times of trouble. Lord, in your mercy,

hear our prayer.

Awaken in this congregation the desire to welcome as your guest the outsider whom we fear or hate, and increase our love for one another. Lord, in your mercy,
hear our prayer.

HERE OTHER INTERCESSIONS MAY BE OFFERED.

We give thanks to you, O God, for those whom you made worthy of your calling, especially *(names,* and) Martin Luther, renewer of the church. Make our faith grow in abundance so that the name of the Lord Jesus may be glorified in us until we offer the full and perfect praise with all your saints in heaven. Lord, in your mercy,
hear our prayer.

God of faithfulness, encircled in your lovingkindness, we lift up to you all in need. Hear our prayers on behalf of others and sustain us as we await the coming of your Son, Jesus Christ our Lord, in whose name we pray.
Amen

IMAGES FOR PREACHING   329

When Jesus invited himself into Zacchaeus's home, the surprised host rejoiced at his good fortune. Everyone else murmured. The way Luke tells the story of Jesus, however, a sojourn in Zacchaeus's home was anything but optional.

The statement, "I must stay at your house today," bears several of Luke's code words for Jesus' mission. It was *necessary*, and indeed *high time*, that Jesus *abide* with Zacchaeus. This visit was part of the Father's business Jesus had to be about (Luke 2:49), the purpose for which he was sent (4:43), a piece of the fateful journey to Jerusalem (13:33) that would end in the messiah's necessary suffering and death (9:22; 17:25; 19:5; 22:37; 24:7, 44). In short, when Jesus got Zacchaeus down out of a tree he was mostly fixing to switch places with the startled tax collector.

Zacchaeus hadn't invited Jesus into his heart. He only wanted a look at the famous man. But the Son of Man doesn't always wait for an invitation. He restlessly seeks out lost ones, invites himself in, and makes himself at home.

In yet another turnabout, a man whose profession consisted of collecting wealth began to give money away—with abandon. His motive remains hidden in Luke's narrative. We're left to assume that joy gave birth to generosity.

Whatever caused it, the new way of living at Zacchaeus's house was a sign that this was also Jesus' home. Salvation—and Jesus' name means "salvation"— had come to stay in that home, and the joyful generosity that flowed there showed it hadn't been a one-night stand. The crucified and risen one lived there as surely as he did in Emmaus and every other abiding spot along the way that leads to and from Calvary.

WORSHIP MATTERS

There is a simple pattern in the table liturgy. We bring the gifts of bread and wine to the altar. We offer thanks to God over these gifts and ask God to send the Holy Spirit upon them and us. The ministers then break the bread and pour the wine. We eat and drink these gifts in thanksgiving. We conclude this communion with a simple prayer.

The institution narrative offers us this pattern we now use in the table liturgy: he took the bread and cup (presentation of the gifts), he offered thanks (thanksgiving prayer), he broke the bread and poured the wine, then gave this bread and the cup to his disciples (communion). The church follows this pattern of offering, thanksgiving, breaking/pouring, and sharing.

LET THE CHILDREN COME

Today's gospel story of Jesus dining with Zacchaeus is a favorite of many children. They know what it's like to be short and unable to see above the heads of others. They know how fun it is to have a friend come over for dinner. Have the children bring a friend to worship. After the worship service, they can enjoy table fellowship with their friends as they eat snacks together in the fellowship hall. Have children's bookmarks available to give to visitors. These might include the name of your church and the schedule of worship services and educational programming on Sundays and throughout the week.

HYMNS FOR WORSHIP
GATHERING

God himself is present   LBW 249

God is truly present   RWI 32

O Christ the same   WOV 778

HYMN OF THE DAY

Salvation unto us has come   LBW 297

ALTERNATE HYMN OF THE DAY

Shout for joy loud and long   WOV 793

Once he came in blessing   LBW 312

COMMUNION

Soul, adorn yourself with gladness   LBW 224

Today your mercy calls us   LBW 304

SENDING

Blest be the tie that binds   LBW 370

What a fellowship, what a joy divine   WOV 780

ADDITIONAL HYMNS AND SONGS

I come with joy   RWSB

Bread of life from heaven   RWSB

Pass me not, O gentle Savior   TFF 150

You are my hiding place   W&P 160

MUSIC FOR THE DAY
PSALMODY

Cherwien, David. PW , Cycle C.

Haas, David. "God, I Confess My Wrong" in PCY, vol. 9.

Howard, Julie. *Sing for Joy: Psalm Settings for God's Children.* The Liturgical Press 0814620787.

Stewart, Roy James. "I Turn to You, Lord" in PCY, vol. 5.

See Fourth Sunday in Lent and Proper 6.

CHORAL

Carter, John. "Shout for Joy to the Lord." SATB, org, brass. AFP 0800675223.

Clausen, René. "Thank the Lord." SATB. SHW 1207596.

Nelson, Eric. "How Can I Keep from Singing." SATB. AFP 0800675177.

Petker, Allan. "I Will Sing Praises." PVN P1116.

CHILDREN'S CHOIR

African American Spiritual. "I Want Jesus to Walk with Me" in LS. U, kybd.

Hassell, Michael. "Is There Anybody Here Who Loves My Jesus?" 2 pt, kybd. AFP 0800674596.

KEYBOARD/INSTRUMENTAL

Albrecht, Timothy. "A Mighty Fortress" in *Grace Notes VI.* Org. AFP 0800656865.

Behnke, John A. "Es ist das Heil" in *Variations for Seven Familiar Hymns.* Org. AFP 0800655605.

Linker, Janet. "Jubilant Processional" (Hymn to Joy and Ein feste Burg). Org, opt tpt. BEC O8.

HANDBELL

Mallory, Ron. "Rock of Ages, Cleft for Me." 3-5 oct. Ringing Word 8143.

McChesney, Kevin. "Come, Thou Fount of Every Blessing." 3-5 oct. JEF JHS9186.

Patterson, Mark. "Let Praise Be the First Word." U/2 pt, kybd. AFP 0800675347.

PRAISE ENSEMBLE

Park, Andy. "In the Secret" in *Best of the Best*. FEL 1891062018.

Ragsdale, Steve. "Hide Me in Your Holiness" in *Praise Hymns and Choruses, 4th ed.* MAR 3010130368.

Monday, November 1

ALL SAINTS DAY

The custom of commemorating all of the saints of the church on a single day goes back at least to the third century. Our All Saints Day celebrates the baptized people of God, living and dead, who make up the body of Christ. Today, or on this upcoming All Saints Sunday, many congregations will remember the faithful who have died during the past year.

Our liturgy abounds with references to the saints and to our continual relationship with them. The preface for All Saints describes the relationship this way: "that moved by their witness and supported by their fellowship, we may run with perseverance the race that is set before us and with them receive the unfading crown of glory." Today and this week invite people to reflect on others—living and dead—who have moved and supported us in our lives of faith.

Wednesday, November 3

MARTÍN DE PORRES, RENEWER OF SOCIETY, 1639

Martín was the son of a Spanish knight and Ana Velázquez, a freed black slave from Panama. Martín apprenticed himself to a barber-surgeon in Lima, Peru, and was known for his work as a healer. Martín was a lay brother in the Order of Preachers (Dominicans) and engaged in many charitable works. He was a gardener as well as a counselor to those who sought him out. He was noted for his care of all the poor, regardless of race. His own religious community described him as the "father of charity." His work included the founding of an orphanage, a hospital, and a clinic for dogs and cats. He is recognized as an advocate for Christian charity and interracial justice.

331

NOVEMBER

The church moves toward the fulfillment of all time

Images *of the* Season

The old cathedrals and churches in Europe share

in common thick stone walls supported by buttresses.

They stand as sentinels on the landscape of faith.

The witness cultivated in these communities of faith sent their children across the globe carrying the message of the gospel for planting in new places. Every so often, these walls are cleaned or repainted, repaired or replaced, and in doing this work, stories are uncovered. Layer after layer of dirt and dust have covered beautiful etchings and frescos from other ages. At the same time, these walls have also withstood plagues and strife, the ravages of war and famine, and they have lived through centuries of human error and deceit. A haunting phrase in Swedish, "Om bara dessa väggar kunde tala" translates "if only these walls could speak," but in any language, the inference is the same: these stone walls have witnessed the church in the worst of times.

In important and paradoxical ways, these stone walls have also held the church together throughout the ages. In much the same pattern, the gathered assembly in this time and place has faced trial and tribulation, yet has been sustained by a rock that will never falter. The Lord of hosts is with us, the God of Jacob is our stronghold.

As the church moves into November time, the procession of the faithful returning to gravestones is a lasting reminder of those who have gone before and by their witness have helped to sustain the church. Etched into memory and written into tablets of human hearts, our loved ones give us a living faith even in their dying. A cemetery walk at this time of year helps the members of its community ground itself in a story that extends far beyond what normally seems visible. At the graves, the faithful stand at the gate to eternal life. In this way, the church begins its move toward the end of the year, toward the fulfillment of all time, toward the culmination of twelve months of God's grace.

We remember that in every place, but certainly at the grave and in the church, the common prayers of the people have been shared. Our Kyries are a cry for peace. At times of grief and loss, we realize poignantly how prayer unites a people, even if the prayer consists of only a few words or even simple silence. This is counterintuitive to a culture that depends on convincing its members of the value of things through blizzards of word and image. The November church would do well to hold to silence in remembering the past.

The task of laying to rest the past becomes an important metaphor in this time before Advent. Almost liminal in character, the church is drawn to the edge of time to witness the culmination of the Christ story by remembering the humility of its servant.

Christ the King, Christ the Servant is the cornerstone, the rock on which the church is not only built but continues to rest. Judgment cannot be denied, nor ought it be feared. The judging time of the church ushers in the righteous One of Israel whose clearest commitment is to lead to forgiveness and justice.

The church is God's house of living stones. Here we discover an interesting paradox. The stones of the church upon which the faithful promise their lives are enduring and unmovable, and yet, at the same time, the church needs to fight against being unmoving and inflexible. The liturgy of the church provides an important model for this dichotomy of needs. Stable and predictable while being adaptable and changeable, the liturgy embodies the paradox and holds it in tension. Sunday after Sunday, the church gathers around the word and table, the font and the prayers to be sent in mission to a dying world. Within this stability, hymns and texts, homilies and prayers provide a variety and surprise that make the church grounded and able to reach out at the same time.

Perhaps the holding together of last things as first things, of endings as beginnings, and of death as a rebirth gives us Glorias as well. In the strains of a hymn of praise, we move toward being able to celebrate a victory that comes not only through death but also over death itself.

Even the stones will cry out with the promise of responding to injustice and challenging inequity. A stone might seem an unlikely symbol of risk, yet this important biblical image assists in crossing over to a promised land. The journey is made over uneven ground, strewn with everything from pebbles to boulders, yet in just a few weeks the church will be reminded that the valleys shall be lifted up and the rough places made plain. November liturgy helps a community to see intimately the landscape of faith.

This time of closure for the church has the shape of the valley of the shadow of death. The promise that God's rod and staff will be present allows those who mourn to be comforted. Healing services at this time of year can help prepare for the upcoming Advent fast. The more opportunities to confront loss, the greater the

chance to grow and mature into a fuller life in Christ.

A stone rests on the edge of a grave marker, the church is built upon the rock of faith, and all who come to know Jesus Christ remember that when Moses touched the rock, living water burst forth. Running water murmuring over the layered bedrock reminds the believing community of the dynamic and provocative promise of God. Bread and wine with the promise of God become resurrection feast, recalling that the stone was rolled away and we are no longer enclosed and trapped in our self-imposed prisons.

If these walls could speak, the saving gospel sound would be mingled with the prayers of countless pilgrims trusting in the promises of God.

Environment *and* Art *for the* Season

We say that the church is the manifestation of the reign of God in the world. Some would dare to call our churches mission centers where missionaries

335

are trained to work in the fields, bringing the good news of Jesus Christ to all who need it. (That would be, of course, to everyone.) Most of us in the church would agree that our worship space is the house of God—in it God is present, though not in an exclusive sense. We would argue that the space itself is holy as are the things inside. We are awed by and attracted to what we think is holy in the world—those moments and places in our lives where we have a heightened awareness of the presence of God. The gospel preacher for this month, Luke, has a vision of the kingdom of God that includes the poor. In fact, this realm belongs to the poor. If we are charged with maintaining the physical buildings of the church, and they are the places where we say the reign of God is profoundly felt, then doesn't it follow that we should see the poor and the needy in our worship space itself?

ANALYZING YOUR SPACE

Over this past church year we have reflected and maybe even struggled over issues involving liturgical furnishings and their locations, art in worship, lighting, acoustics,

and so forth. We who care for God's house and the worship that takes place within often develop a strong sense of ownership of the holy in our particular space. We value the symbols and the art. We have encouraged others in our worshiping community to value those things, too. We have given of our time and our talents to make this place a place where people want to come to experience the presence of God, not only during worship but also in times of silent prayer and reflection. We have also given of our resources—liturgical furnishings and appointments are often expensive—because we believe that the cost is not too high as long as we are also ministering to the practical needs of those in our neighborhood and around the world.

Is your church open to the public at all times? Any times other than Sunday morning? If not, what is preventing that?

Many communities have concerns about who is going to be in the church. We don't want anyone breaking or stealing anything. We have lists of rules for weddings and other events that happen outside of worship. Most church communities prohibit food or drink in their worship spaces (except, of course, for the eucharist). Many of our churches are not open to the public unless there is something already going on.

Some churches have already taken a step toward an open-door environment by reflecting on how their exterior space communicates an atmosphere of hospitality. They have assessed the needs of the community around their church building and have thought of ways to meet some of those needs through creative use of their space and resources. For example, a church that has a bus stop right in front invests in a nice bench or protective niche for people who are waiting for the bus there. Another church creates a prayer garden or other form of respite outside for people in their neighborhood. Some congregations never lock their doors, allowing homeless people to sleep within and in turn, watch over the physical plant. These communities have begun to see how their space extends into the community, which speaks volumes to those who may otherwise not think about coming into the church.

How do we communicate the kingdom of God for those who aren't sure it exists when we close our churches to the public?

We should never be without care when it comes to our places of worship. For many communities of faith, there is still room to grow in our understanding of what it means to be a witness to the openness of God through the use of our buildings and our spaces. Keeping our spaces closed and secure does two things. On the one hand, it prevents "undesirable" people (and think about that description from the viewpoint of Jesus!) from entering and messing up that which we have worked so hard to maintain. On the other hand, it hinders an encounter between the world and its needs, and the church that sees itself as the repository of God's love for all. We hope that our worship spaces communicate what we believe to be true about God and God's people. We certainly want the whole world to know the God in whom we believe and hope and trust.

If your congregation does not already have an open door policy for your building, here are some questions to help begin the process of reflection in order to help address concerns.

- *Is it possible to secure parts of the building while leaving the main worship space open?*
- *Is there a way to have timer locks on your doors set in the evening for overnight?*

- *Are there volunteers who would be interested in helping keep the church open during the day?*
- *Does your church have a separate chapel that could be used for the public?*
- *Does your church have another space that could be converted into a day chapel for regular public use?*

The process of reflecting on the use of our space in this way can be challenging for many of us. People in your congregation may have strong feelings about this. Be sensitive to everyone's position. Allow for conversation to take place where everyone can share their dreams and their concerns. If your worship space can be more open to the surrounding community, that can in itself be a strong witness.

ART FOR THE SEASON

Staying with the theme of reaching out to communities in need, here are a few suggestions on how to raise awareness through art. Many of us are familiar with various forms of "naïve art," art that is created by people who are self-taught, or art from various indigenous communities around the world. The wooden crosses and plaques from Central America are prolific examples in our current church culture. Many of the people who create this very appealing and fashionable art are exploited and paid extremely small sums of money for their work. There are organizations that work to ensure that the individuals from developing nations who produce anything from art to coffee are justly compensated for their labors. These organizations use the term "fair trade" to signify this concept of just compensation for one's work. You can contact your national and regional church offices and ask to speak with whomever deals with issues of fair trade. They can certainly put you in touch with approved organizations. From there, you can purchase small pieces of art like crosses and make them available for the congregation to purchase for use in their homes and, in the process, educate everyone about fair trade.

Another project would be to go around your community and collect, purchase, or borrow objects that symbolize life in your community. Creating a mass sculpture of these things for use inside the church might be a powerful way to bring the "community" into your worship space as an encouragement toward even more integration between the church and the community. Creating a cross or some other symbol out of signs, shopping carts, trash cans, and other common materials is the kind of juxtaposition that makes for thought-provoking art.

Whatever you decide to do to raise awareness, the goal is not to trivialize the community and especially not the poor. The goal is to help us begin to see the holy beyond our own worship spaces.

Preaching *with the* Season

At first glance, the disjunction between our daily

preoccupations and the liturgical season's prompts

could hardly be greater than what we experience

in November. We begin with a celebration of saints, a host of them to be exact, but one of their number, Saint Nick, now co-opts that very day as the kickoff for his annual capital campaign. A certain Rudolph serves as his acolyte and his anthem is "Jingle Bells." In the blink of an eye the marts and malls shift from Halloween to Christmas, and television commercials begin a clever, concerted effort to build within us, and especially in our children, a burning need for the latest, indispensable array of *things*.

At the same time, well before Advent, the darkness that gathers about us begins to make us uneasy. The liturgy helps us to see the sources of our questions and the depth of our needs and dreads. When the Sadducees among us ask trick questions about the marriage laws that may apply in heaven (Luke 20:27-38, Proper 27), we really confess in a backhanded way our despairing suspicion that life will prove in the end no more than a series of failed ventures. We also join Luke's first readers in eavesdropping on the disciples as they admire the great temple and its massive stones (Luke 21:5-19, Proper 28). Most of those disciples didn't live to see what we have witnessed. Glorious temples and towers do inevitably fall, and when they do, everything trembles—especially our faith and confidence.

We sense a critique in the offing, too, an accounting of the harvest as we put this year's crop in the barns, silos, and ledgers. This season's collects articulate our fears quite aptly when they confess, for example (Proper 27), "Lord, when the day of wrath comes we have no hope except in your grace." The prospects of an end to all things and a day of judgment leave us calling for our

attorney, the Counselor. Thus we pray on Proper 28, "So rule and govern our hearts and minds by your Holy Spirit that . . . we may be stirred up to holiness."

The Counselor's agents show up in this season to accompany us in the dim light and to stand by us in the day of reckoning. Saints, the whole great cloud of witnesses, surround us. We're never so alone as we think. Besides the local saints that appear in our homes and workplaces, we travel with Søren Kierkegaard, who in his short life knew gloom of every kind, but none that the shadow of the cross failed to touch. We find among us John Christian Frederick Heyer, who as a child fled the Napoleonic wars and never again knew a homeland, really, but found his place in the body of Christ. With Martin of Tours, we wrestle the tough questions of vocation in a world that draws us into combat and would teach us to love war.

Along with the blessed hungry and poor, we give thanks with and for Elizabeth of Thuringia, a princess bride at age 14, three times a mother by 19, a widow at 20, and buried herself at 24, and through it all the soul of hospitality. Lest we find our tongues tied and our hearts without a song, we travel in the company of Isaac Watts, who leads our singing throughout the year and now poignantly gives words to our plea that God would be our guard while troubles last and our eternal home (LBW 320).

In this company we process with thankful hearts. The candles of those the Spirit sends to join us help us to see and acknowledge the generous goodness that comes to us new every day. Into the gathering dusk we move along until we reach the place where the end does come, and we find our arms stretched out in the posture of crucifixion, only to discover that there, too, we have company. In the fellowship of the crucified, we find a place saved for each of us—and for all of us together.

Shape *of* Worship *for the* Season

BASIC SHAPE OF THE EUCHARISTIC RITE

- Confession and Forgiveness: see alternate worship text for November on page 349 as an option to the text in the liturgy setting

GATHERING

- Greeting: see alternate worship text for November
- Omit the Kyrie during November (except on the festivals of All Saints and Christ the King)
- Use the hymn of praise throughout November (or use "This is the feast of victory" just for the festivals of All Saints and Christ the King)

WORD

- Use the Nicene Creed for the festivals of All Saints and Christ the King; use the Apostles' Creed for the remainder of the month
- The prayers: see the prayers for each Sunday in the November section
- Incorporate the names of those who have died into one of the prayer petitions on All Saints Sunday

BAPTISM

- Consider observing All Saints Sunday (November 7) as a baptismal festival. If there are no baptisms, use the Remembrance of Baptism from *Holy Baptism and Related Rites* with the thanksgiving prayer for All Saints, p. 110.

MEAL

- Offertory prayer: see alternate worship text for November
- Use the proper preface for Sundays after Pentecost; for the festival of All Saints, use the proper preface for All Saints; *WOV* Leaders Edition provides a proper preface for Christ the King
- Eucharistic prayer: in addition to four main options in *LBW*, see "Eucharistic Prayer I: November" in *WOV* Leaders Edition, p. 73
- Invitation to communion: see alternate worship text for November
- Post-communion prayer: see alternate worship text for November

SENDING

- Benediction: see alternate worship text for November
- Dismissal: see alternate worship text for November

338

Assembly Song *for the* Season

November begins with All Saints Day and invites

contemplation of our own mortality and our

position among God's saints of all times and places.

It is a time to recall, in the words of the hymn, that in the church "there is welcome for the sinner, and a promised grace made good; / there is mercy with the Savior; there is healing in his blood. / There is grace enough for thousands of new worlds as great as this; / there is room for fresh creations in that upper home of bliss" (LBW 290, RWI 76, 77). Explore music that helps, heals, and makes room enough for thousands.

GATHERING

Focus the community on prayer with "Lord, listen to your children praying" (WOV 775, TFF 247, W&P 92). Sing a setting of "Glory to God" such as the one in *LBW* Setting I, in anticipation of the festival of Christ the King, November 21. True, we might tend to think of "This is the feast" as the better canticle for that feast, but the "Glory to God," with its eschatological overtones, also works well. Its use in November can also help to close the church year circle and connect November with the coming Christmas cycle.

WORD

Sing psalms from Peter Hallock's *Ionian Psalter* (Ionian Arts), with beautifully written choral verses and accessible congregational refrains.

Try the South African choral "Alleluia" found at WOV 610 or TFF 26, sung first by the choir, then the assembly. Reinforce the celebration of All Saints Day

with "Blest are they" (WOV 764) and "Taste and see" (TFF 126).

On All Saints Sunday, if your congregation remembers by name the local saints who have died in the past year (either as part of the gathering or the prayers), consider adding also the names of the saints who have been baptized in that time. Close the reading with a hymn such as "For all the saints" (LBW 174) or "Sing with all the saints in glory" (RWI 68 or WOV 691).

MEAL

Continue using a familiar setting of the Holy Holy Holy and Lamb of God, such as in *LBW* Setting I or *WOV* Setting 5. Or on a special occasion, have the choir lead an a cappella setting of "Holy, holy, holy Lord" (TFF 32) or "O Lamb of God" (TFF 36).

SENDING

Go into the world giving thanks, singing one of the "Thank the Lord" canticles, such as *LBW* setting I or *WOV* Setting 5. Or, sing the ancient and imaginative text "Father, we thank you" (WOV 704), a great hymn for harmony singing. "Bread of the world" (RWI 14) is another text set to the same tune. If it were sung during the communion and "Father, we thank you" as a sending hymn, the tune could be reinforced and the ending of the liturgy unified.

Music *for the* Season

VERSE AND OFFERTORY

Hobby, Robert A. "Offertory for All Saints Day." 2 pt mxd.
MSM 80-811.

Hobby, Robert A. "Verse for All Saints Day." 2 pt mxd.
MSM 80-810.

See also Music for the Season of Autumn.

CHORAL

Berger, Jean. "The Eyes of All Wait upon Thee." SATB.
AFP 0800645596.

Carter, John. "Shout for Joy to the Lord." SATB, org, brass.
AFP 0800675223.

Forsberg, Charles. "Fairest Lord Jesus." SATB, pno.
AFP 0800656962.

Handel, G. F. "But Who May Abide the Day of His Coming?" in
Messiah. A/B solo, kybd. Various ed.

Handel, G. F. "The Trumpet Shall Sound" in *Messiah.* B solo, kybd,
opt. tpt. Various ed.

Johnson, David N., adapt. Susan Palo Cherwien. "Souls of the Righteous" in *To God Will I Sing.* AFP 0800674332 (MH voice);
AFP 0800674340 (ML voice).

Manz, Paul. "E'en So, Lord Jesus, Quickly Come." SATB.
MSM 50-0001.

Schultz, Donna Gartman. "Shall We Gather at the River." SATB,
kybd. AFP 0800659376.

CHILDREN'S CHOIR

Bedford, Michael. "I Sing the Mighty Power of God." U/2 pt, cong,
fl, ob, org, opt 3 oct hb. CG CGA884.

Franck, César, arr. Dale Grotenhuis. "O Lord Most Holy." 2 pt,
kybd. MSM 50-9419.

Hassell, Michael. "I Sing a Song of the Saints of God." 2 pt, pno, fl.
AFP 0800658515.

Matthews, Peter. "Praise the Lord, His Glories Show." U, pno.
CG CGA864.

Nygard, Carl J. "Grateful Praise." 2 pt, kybd. AFP 0800675185.

KEYBOARD/INSTRUMENTAL

Augsburg *Organ Library: November.* Org. AFP 0800658965.

Burkhardt, Michael. *Praise and Thanksgiving, Set 6.* Org. MSM 10-703.

Callahan, Charles. *A Thanksgiving Prelude for Flute and Organ.* Org, fl.
MSM 20-660.

Helvey, Howard. "We Gather Together" in *Hymns From Around the
World.* Pno. BEC PC6-3.

Hobby, Robert A. *For All the Saints.* Org. AFP 0800675371.

Langlais, Jean. "Pasticcio" in *Organ Book.* Org. Elkan-Vogel 463-
00006.

Rembt, Johann. "Now Thank We All Our God" in *The Complete Wedding Collection, Book II.* Org. BEC OC23.

West, John. *Now Thank We All Our God.* Org, MIDI. AFP 0800675673.

HANDBELL

Bartsch, Jr., John. "This Is My Father's World." 3-5 oct.
NMP HB259.

Helman, Michael. "This Is My Father's World." 2-3 oct.
LOR 20/1099L.

Honoré, Jeffrey. "Now We Offer / *Te Ofrecemos.*" 2-3 oct, opt perc.
AFP 0800674898.

McFadden, Jane. "How Can I Keep from Singing?" 3-5 oct.
AFP 0800658124.

PRAISE ENSEMBLE

Hayford, Jack. "Majesty" in W&P.

Ruis, David. "You Are Worthy of My Praise" in *More Songs for Praise
and Worship.* SATB. WRD 3010387016 (vocal ed); WRD
3010186363 (pno, vcs, perc).

Zschech, Darlene. "Shout to the Lord" in W&P.

Alternate Worship Texts

CONFESSION AND FORGIVENESS

In the name of the Father, and of the ✛ Son,
and of the Holy Spirit.

Amen

Let us confess our sin in the presence of God,
the whole company of heaven,
and our sisters and brothers in this community.

Silence for reflection and self-examination.

Holy and gracious God,
we confess that we have sinned against you
in thought, word, and deed.
We have not protected and cared for
the gifts of sisters and brothers past,
the well-being of your people in our time,
the hopes of those to come.
Have mercy on us, forgive our sins,
and bring us to everlasting life;
through Jesus Christ our Lord. Amen

How blessed are those whose sins are forgiven!
In the mercy of almighty God,
I announce to you the entire forgiveness of your sins,
in the name of the Father, and of the ✛ Son,
and of the Holy Spirit.

Amen

GREETING

May the God of hope give you fullness of peace,
and may the Lord of life be with you all.

And also with you.

PRAYERS

Encouraged by the company
of the saints of every time and place,
let us pray for the church, the world,
and all people according to their needs.

A brief silence.

Each petition ends:

Let us pray to the Lord.
Lord, have mercy.

Concluding petition:

Holy God, enthroned in glory and surrounded by saints and angels,
we bring before you these petitions
and all else that you know we need.
Hear our prayers for the sake of our Savior and King,
Jesus Christ our Lord.

Amen

OFFERTORY PRAYER

God of our salvation,
your faithfulness extends from generation to generation.
Receive these gifts, signs of your gracious love,
give us a foretaste of the feast to come,
and lead us to the eternal communion
of Jesus Christ our Lord.
Amen

INVITATION TO COMMUNION

341

Blessed are all who hunger now,
for they shall be filled.

POST-COMMUNION PRAYER

God of the living,
you gather and shepherd your flock,
satisfying us with bread from heaven.
Sustain us through this meal
until the day of resurrection,
when we shall see you face to face;
in the name of our living redeemer, Jesus Christ.

Amen

BLESSING

May God who loves you,
and through the grace of Jesus Christ gives you good hope,
✛ bless you and comfort your hearts
by the power of the Holy Spirit.

Amen

DISMISSAL

Surrounded by so great a cloud of witnesses,
let us go forth in peace to serve the Lord.

Thanks be to God.

Seasonal Rites

Vigil of All Saints

This order of worship may be used on All Hallows Eve, October 31, or on November 6, the evening before All Saints Sunday.

SERVICE OF LIGHT
PROCESSION

All stand as the lighted paschal candle is carried in procession to its stand in front of the assembly. The people may light hand-held candles from its flame.

In the new Jerusalem there will be no need of | sun or moon,
for the glory of God will be its | light.
Before the Lamb is a multitude from | every nation,
and they worship God night and | day.
Surely he is | coming soon.
Amen. Come, Lord | Jesus.

HYMN OF LIGHT

As this hymn is sung, the candles on and near the altar are lighted from the flame of the paschal candle.

Joyous light of glory:
of the immortal Father;
heavenly, holy, blessed Jesus Christ.
We have come to the setting of the sun,
and we look to the evening light.
We sing to God, the Father, Son, and Holy Spirit:
You are worthy of being praised
with pure voices forever.
O Son of God, O Giver of light:
The universe proclaims your glory.

THANKSGIVING FOR LIGHT
The Lord be with you.
And also with you.
Let us give thanks to the Lord our God.
It is right to give our thanks and praise.
Blessed are you, O Lord our God, king of the universe,
who led your people Israel by a pillar of cloud by day
and a pillar of fire by night:
Enlighten our darkness by the light of your Christ;
may his Word be a lamp to our feet and a light to our path;
for you are merciful, and you love your whole creation,
and we, your creatures, glorify you, Father, Son, and Holy Spirit.
Amen

LITURGY OF THE WORD
FIRST READING
Genesis 12:1-8
Psalm 113

SECOND READING
Daniel 6:[1-15] 16-23
Psalm 116

THIRD READING
Hebrews 11:32—12:2
Psalm 149

FOURTH READING
Revelation 7:2-4, 9-17

CANTICLE
This is the feast of victory

GOSPEL
Matthew 5:1-12

SERMON

HYMN OF THE DAY

THANKSGIVING FOR BAPTISM

If possible, the people may gather around the font. After the prayer each person may dip a hand in the water and make the sign of the cross in remembrance of baptism.

The Lord be with you.
And also with you.
Let us give thanks to the Lord our God.
It is right to give our thanks and praise.
Holy God and mighty Lord, we give you thanks,
for you nourish and sustain us and all living things
with the gift of water.
In the beginning your Spirit moved over the waters,
and you created heaven and earth.
By the waters of the flood you saved Noah and his family.
You led Israel through the sea out of slavery
into the promised land.
In the waters of the Jordan
your Son was baptized by John and anointed with the Spirit.
By the baptism of his death and resurrection
your Son set us free from sin and death

and opened the way to everlasting life.
We give you thanks, O God,
that you have given us new life in the water of baptism.
Buried with Christ in his death,
you raise us to share in his resurrection
by the power of the Holy Spirit.
Through it we are united to your saints
of every time and place
who proclaim your reign
and surround our steps as we journey
toward the new and eternal Jerusalem.
May all who have passed through the waters of baptism
continue in the risen life of our Savior.
To you be all honor and glory, now and forever.
Amen

LITURGY OF THE EUCHARIST

After all have returned to their places, the liturgy continues with the preparation of the altar and the presentation of the gifts.

NOTES ON THE SERVICE:

- *The opening verses in the procession of the paschal candle may be sung using the musical setting found in LBW, p. 142.*
- *The hymn of light is found in LBW, p. 143. An alternate hymn is "O Light whose splendor thrills" (WOV 728).*
- *The thanksgiving for light (LBW, p. 144) may be sung or spoken by the leader.*
- *The psalm responses to the readings may be sung or spoken by the assembly.*
- *The canticle is sung using one of the available musical settings of this text.*
- *For the hymn of the day, one of the following hymns is suggested: "Sing with all the saints in glory" (WOV 691) or "Who is this host arrayed in white" (LBW 314).*
- *If the people cannot gather at the font, the worship leaders may process there during the singing of the hymn of the day.*

343

November 7, 2004

All Saints Sunday

INTRODUCTION

"With the Church on earth and the hosts of heaven, we praise your name and join their unending hymn," proclaims the presiding minister in the eucharistic prayer. On the festival of All Saints we remember with thanksgiving those who have lived and died in the faith, among them John Christian Frederick Heyer, the first missionary sent out by Lutherans in North America, serving in India as a medical doctor and evangelist. All of God's saints are the sign of our hope and an image of the glory we shall inherit. Even more, they are worshipers with us this day as we sing the praises of the God who brings life out of death.

344

PRAYER OF THE DAY

Almighty God, whose people are knit together in one holy Church, the body of Christ our Lord: Grant us grace to follow your blessed saints in lives of faith and commitment, and to know the inexpressible joys you have prepared for those who love you; through your Son, Jesus Christ our Lord, who lives and reigns with you and the Holy Spirit, one God, now and forever.

VERSE

Alleluia. They are before the throne of God, and the one seated on the throne will shelter them. Alleluia.
(Rev. 7:15)

READINGS

Daniel 7:1-3, 15-18

During the second century before the birth of Jesus, the people of Israel suffered severe persecution at the hands of the Syrian king, Antiochus Epiphanes. The book of Daniel was written to support God's people during these dark and difficult days. His vision of the four beasts was meant to remind God's people that history was ultimately controlled by God and that this time of severe trial would pass.

Psalm 149

Sing the praise of the LORD in the congregation of the faithful. (Ps. 149:1)

Ephesians 1:11-23

After giving thanks for the faith of the Ephesians, Paul prays that they might also see the power of God, who has now enthroned Jesus as head of the church, which is his body.

Luke 6:20-31

Luke's recounting of Jesus' blessings and warnings suggests that God's standards and values may be quite different from those with which we are most familiar. They are the hallmark of the new life lived by God's saints.

COLOR   White

THE PRAYERS

Encouraged by the company of the saints of every time and place, let us pray for the church, the world, and all people according to their needs.

A BRIEF SILENCE.

That the church, the body of Christ, will acknowledge Christ as head over all and will live in unity with Christ and with all the members of Christ's body, let us pray to the Lord:

Lord, have mercy.

That the leaders of the world, and this nation, (including those newly elected), will exercise proper care and stewardship of the earth, all its resources, and all its people, let us pray to the Lord:

Lord, have mercy.

That all may live in accord with Christ's teaching, looking for the blessings of God and not the rewards of this world, let us pray to the Lord:

Lord, have mercy.

That the poor will be blessed with the kingdom of God, the hungry will be filled, the sick will be healed *(especially)*, so that the faithful may rejoice in triumph, let us pray to the Lord:

Lord, have mercy.

That God will enlighten the eyes of the hearts of those in our congregation, so that we will know the hope to which God has called us, let us pray to the Lord:

Lord, have mercy.

345

HERE OTHER INTERCESSIONS MAY BE OFFERED.

Let us give thanks for John Heyer and all the holy ones of the Most High who have obtained their glorious inheritance in Christ *(especially)*. That having hoped in Christ, at the end we too will sing our praise with the faithful gathered before the throne of God, let us pray to the Lord:

Lord, have mercy.

Holy God, enthroned in glory and surrounded by saints and angels, we bring before you these petitions and all else that you know we need. Hear our prayers for the sake of our Savior and King, Jesus Christ our Lord.

Amen

IMAGES FOR PREACHING

Would we know a saint if we saw one? They manifest godliness and the fullness of Christian virtue, say the church's tomes. Frederick Buechner offers a more poetic definition. "In his holy flirtation with the world, God occasionally drops a handkerchief. These handkerchiefs are called saints" *(Wishful Thinking,* New York: Harper & Row, 1973, p. 83).

Here we see God as a shy and proper lover who seeks the world's attention, and ultimately its affection, by dropping into our world something that carries a whiff of God's perfume. From the beginning God has planned a marriage. "Someday," dreams God, "a new Jerusalem will appear, dressed for a wedding, and the dance will be on."

This quaint image takes on a different look when a signer for deaf people interprets Buechner. The sign for "handkerchief" is passing a hand across the face as though wiping one's nose. Given the lives and fates of most saints, this rendering proves all too true. Saints have proved disposable as the tissues we soil and toss away. Their lives are stained with the tears God sheds over the rivers of blood we have spilled. Of them Jesus said, "Blessed are you who weep."

God also shares the starving of children whose eyes grow vacant and can't even cry. When God drops a cloth wrung ragged in a vigil over these little ones, there appears one like old Amos, or Mother Teresa, whose heartbreak bears dimensions of God's own. Of them Jesus said, "Blessed are you poor."

We easily overlook the saints God drops along our way. When we do see them we avert our eyes. They embarrass us.

We'd rather God offered other signs, not these tear-stained rags that tell the truth of our terribly fragile humanity.

But in picking up God's soiled handkerchiefs to lift them gratefully before God, we offer ourselves in grateful thanks. Which, of course, is precisely what God has hoped for all along, as we witness most clearly in the life of Jesus, from whose cross God tries so desperately to woo the world back into God's outstretched arms.

WORSHIP MATTERS

The dead bear witness to the resurrection. In Christ their graves become the gate to heaven. Does your congregation have a cemetery outside, nearby, or perhaps a columbarium? Today is the day to be there. Take the cross in procession to the cemetery. Make tombstone rubbings that witness to the faith of the dead and bring them into your narthex or foyer for the Sundays of November. Is the climate such that the liturgy might begin among the dead, or perhaps conclude there, or continue for those who wish to follow there for a blessing of the graves? Gather among the departed to remember their witness in these days of November, their ministries and their vocations, the dates of their baptisms and of their deaths. See the witness they have left behind. Have a picnic in the cemetery. Celebrate the memory of those who have come before us in faith, thanking God for their continued witness.

LET THE CHILDREN COME

Invite each family to bring a photo of a saint in their lives, living or dead. Set up a big bulletin board in the narthex where families can display their photos before worship begins. Notice how God has richly blessed us with people who surround us with God's love. Invite the congregation to dip hands in the font and mark their foreheads with the sign of the cross as a reminder that we all are saints, the baptized people of God. Before the prayers are offered, explain that during one petition you will pause to let all children name out loud in unison a saint—someone who shares God's love with them.

HYMNS FOR WORSHIP
GATHERING

For all the saints   LBW 174

Come, we that love the Lord   WOV 742, TFF 135

HYMN OF THE DAY

Ye watchers and ye holy ones   LBW 175

ALTERNATE HYMN OF THE DAY

Blest are they   WOV 764
Hallelujah! Sing to our God   HFW

COMMUNION

Behold a host   RWI 13, LBW 314
Shall we gather at the river   WOV 690

SENDING

Oh, happy day when we shall stand   LBW 351
Rejoice in God's saints   WOV 689
The trees of the field   W&P 138

ADDITIONAL HYMNS AND SONGS

Give thanks for saints   RWSB
In our days of thanksgiving   RWSB
Oh, when the saints go marching in   TFF 180
Who are these like stars appearing   H82 286

MUSIC FOR THE DAY

PSALMODY

Cherwien, David. PW , Cycle C.

Hopson, Hal H. *Psalm Refrains and Tones.* HOP 425.

Hopson, Hal H. "Sing a New Song to the Lord." U, opt hb, kybd. CG CGA204.

Wagner, Douglas E. "Dance, Sing, Clap Your Hands." U, kybd. BEC BP1266.

Psalms for Praise and Worship: A Complete Liturgical Psalter. ABI 0687093260.

CHORAL

Bach, Johann Christoph Friedrich. "In the Resurrection Glorious" in the *Chantry Choirbook.* SATB, org. AFP 0800657772.

Harris, William. "Faire Is the Heaven" in *Anthems for Choirs 4.* SATB, dbl chorus. OXF 353018X.

Marchant, Stanley. "The Souls of the Righteous" in *The Oxford Easy Anthem Book.* SATB. OXF 3533219.

Nelson, Ronald A. "The Vision of John." SATB, org, hp/pno. KJO 8866.

Pavlechko, Thomas. "The Souls of the Righteous." SATB, org. AFP 0800653327. OP.

Rachmaninoff, Sergei. "Blessed Is the Man" from *All Night Vigil* in *Songs of the Church.* SSAATTBB div. HWG GB 640.

Schulz-Widmar, Russell. "Give Rest, O Christ." SATB, org. GIA G-3819.

Shute, Linda Cable. "Who Are These Like Stars Appearing." SATB, org. AFP 0800658507.

Spencer, Williamette. "At the Round Earth's Imagined Corners." SATB. SHW A-986.

Vaughan Williams, Ralph. "Let Us Now Praise Famous Men." SATB, org. GSCH 11070.

CHILDREN'S CHOIR

Hopson, Hal H. "We Are the Children of Light." U, pno, opt desc, tamb, 2 oct hb. HOP C5080.

Page, Anna Laura. "A New Song." (Ps. 149) 2 pt trbl, kybd, opt fl. AFP 0800674499.

KEYBOARD/INSTRUMENTAL

Ferguson, John. "Behold a Host" in *Augsburg Organ Library: November.* Org. AFP 0800658965.

Sowash, Bradley. "Deep River" in *We Gather Together,* vol. 2. Pno. AFP 0800675630.

Vierne, Louis. "Requiem aeternam" in *Augsburg Organ Library: November.* Org. AFP 0800658965.

Wold, Wayne L. "For All the Saints" in *A November to Remember.* Org. AFP 080065983X.

HANDBELL

Dobrinski, Cynthia. "O God, Our Help in Ages Past." 3-5 oct. AG 2117.

McChesney, Kevin. "Symphonia on Hyfrydol." 3-5 oct. JEF JHS9300.

Moklebust, Cathy. "Behold a Host." 3-4 oct. CPH 97-6377.

Tucker, Sondra. "Meditation on Hyfrydol." 3 oct. CG CGB182.

Wagner, Douglas E. "Sine Nomine." 3-5 oct. AG 1271.

PRAISE ENSEMBLE

Fabing, S. J., Robert, arr. Dan Goeller. "Bread of Angels." SATB, pno, opt str. AFP 0800674367.

Hiebert, Lamont. "Sing for Joy!" in *Sing for Joy Songbook Hosanna!* HOS 21377.

Sadler, Gary and Jamie Harvill. "Ancient of Days" in *Best of the Best.* FEL 1891062018.

346

November 7, 2004

Twenty-third Sunday after Pentecost
Proper 27

INTRODUCTION

In these final weeks of the liturgical year, the church cries out, "Come, Lord Jesus!" We are always awaiting God's coming, and God does not disappoint us, making the divine presence known in water, bread, wine, and in this human community of faith.

The church today celebrates the life and work of John Christian Frederick Heyer, a pastor and medical doctor who was the first missionary sent out by North American Lutherans, serving in India.

PRAYER OF THE DAY

Lord, when the day of wrath comes we have no hope except in your grace. Make us so to watch for the last days that the consummation of our hope may be the joy of the marriage feast of your Son, Jesus Christ our Lord.

VERSE

Alleluia. Keep awake therefore, for you do not know on what day your Lord is coming. Alleluia. (Matt. 24:42)

READINGS

Job 19:23-27a

The dialogues of this book present Job in the midst of a tormenting problem. Job suffers the loss of family, physical health, and understanding friends, yet knows himself to be innocent. Here, in the midst of his suffering, Job clings to the hope that one day he will be vindicated.

Psalm 17:1-9

Keep me as the apple of your eye; hide me under the shadow of your wings. (Ps. 17:8)

2 Thessalonians 2:1-5, 13-17

Paul writes to encourage the church at Thessalonica in a time of confusion and opposition. Here, the confusion concerned the return of Christ. Paul speaks to those who were allowing their concern over Jesus' imminent return to divert them from the central teachings of the gospel, advising them to remember their identity as people chosen by God.

Luke 20:27-38

The Sadducees, who do not believe in the resurrection of the dead, try to trap Jesus. They ask him about the marital status of a resurrected woman who had been married to a succession of seven brothers. The real issue, says Jesus, is not "Whose wife is she?" but rather "What is your relationship with God?"

Alternate First Reading/Psalm

Haggai 1:15b—2:9

When Cyrus the Great defeated the Babylonians, his decree that exiles might return to Jerusalem and rebuild their temple brought an end to their homelessness. Upon returning, however, the people were more interested in rebuilding their own homes. The rebuilt temple paled in comparison with that of Solomon's. Haggai's message of encouragement and promise of future splendor invigorated the people and their leaders, Zerubbabel and Joshua.

Psalm 145:1-5, 18-22 (Psalm 145:1-5, 17-21 NRSV)

Great is the LORD and greatly to be praised. (Ps. 145:3)

or Psalm 98

In righteousness shall the LORD judge the world. (Ps. 98:10)

COLOR   Green

THE PRAYERS

Encouraged by the company of the saints of every time and place, let us pray for the church, the world, and all people according to their needs.

A BRIEF SILENCE.

That all bishops and pastors of the church will stand fast and hold firm to the truth of the gospel, and will work to gather all people to Christ, let us pray to the Lord.

Lord, have mercy.

That those who have been elected to office this week may serve wisely, honorably, and with a commitment for the well-being of this nation and its citizens, let us pray to the Lord.

Lord, have mercy.

That God will watch over and protect those serving in

347

the armed forces of our nation, and care for the veterans among us, let us pray to the Lord.

Lord, have mercy.

That the dying and their families will find strength in the hope of the resurrection, and that God will show marvelous lovingkindness to the sick (*especially*), let us pray to the Lord.

Lord, have mercy.

That our congregation will yearn to hear the word of God and to share the meal that unites all into the one body of Christ, let us pray to the Lord.

Lord, have mercy.

HERE OTHER INTERCESSIONS MAY BE OFFERED.

That the saints (*especially*) would inspire us also to be faithful children of the resurrection and to long for the day when in our flesh we will see God, let us pray to the Lord.

Lord, have mercy.

Holy God, enthroned in glory and surrounded by saints and angels, we bring before you these petitions and all else that you know we need. Hear our prayers for the sake of our Savior and King, Jesus Christ our Lord.

Amen

IMAGES FOR PREACHING

Even our most cherished descriptions of eternal life eventually prove absurd. Many a child has come to dread heaven, given the prospect of playing a harp for eternity. With good reason we make jokes about arrival scenes at the "pearly gates," thereby tweaking our habit of mistaking eternity for time and defining the infinite with finite words and images.

Have you heard the one about a man granted extraordinary permission to bring along some of his possessions to heaven, only to find a baggage-checker at the gates? When St. Peter spies gold bricks in the luggage, he asks incredulously, "Why would anyone come all this way with paving stones?"

There we glimpse momentarily the chasm between our thoughts and God's, between the tools of our limited minds and objects of consideration that remain for now unfathomable.

The Sadducees thought their story about the woman with seven husbands was joke enough to make the whole notion of resurrection and eternal life look foolish. They were right in one sense, of course. Resurrection from the dead could only mean mass confusion if it merely granted an endless extension of what comes before. As a modern heir of the Sadducees once observed, "Millions long for immortality who don't know what to do on a rainy Sunday afternoon."

Jesus responds with a rare comment about what lies beyond the boundary of death. Children of this world marry, he said, but not the children of resurrection. Resurrected life bears no resemblance, finally, to what we know here in space and time.

Despite all our assurances that yes, our dogs will be in heaven, we can't take anything through the "pearly gates"—not our gold, our metaphors, our virtues, or even our theology. We pass through the birth canal into eternity with the same thing Christ did—a simple trust that whatever comes next rests with God.

Whatever is, or isn't, beyond the gates, belongs to God alone. Whether we live or die, we belong to God. Even now we are children of the resurrection.

WORSHIP MATTERS

In Holy Communion, Jesus invites us to remember him by taking the simple things of the earth, giving thanks for them as part of the bounty of God's creation, and sharing them as the body and blood of Christ given for each of us. We are not about the business of historical reenactment, however, and so we do not break the bread at the moment in the institution narrative where that action of Jesus is recounted because it is not yet time to distribute the bread and wine that has been blessed for us. Rather, the bread is broken following the Lord's Prayer, when it is time to share this meal of the kingdom and to receive from Christ the forgiveness, life, and salvation won for us at so great a price.

LET THE CHILDREN COME

Psalm 17 includes the poignant verse, "Keep me as the apple of your eye; hide me under the shadow of your wings." All children long to feel secure, protected, and loved. Strive to make your church home a place of warmth and hospitality for children. Exchange hugs and handshakes with them during the passing of the peace. If they are too young for communion, find ways to help them feel included and blessed during this special meal. Provide busy books and children's bulletins. Teach greeters to welcome each child with a smile and a handshake. Display children's artwork throughout your church

building. These are all ways children will sense that
God's house is their home.

HYMNS FOR WORSHIP

GATHERING

Oh, what their joy   LBW 337
Blessed be the God of Israel   WOV 725

HYMN OF THE DAY

Jesus Christ, my sure defense   LBW 340

ALTERNATE HYMN OF THE DAY

Sing with all the saints in glory   WOV 691
I know that my Redeemer lives!   LBW 352

COMMUNION

For the bread which you have broken   LBW 200
I am the Bread of life   WOV 702

SENDING

Lord of all hopefulness   LBW 469
Alleluia, alleluia, give thanks   WOV 671
Baptized and set free   W&P 14

ADDITIONAL HYMNS AND SONGS

Neither death nor life   RWSB
To go to heaven   TFF 181
There is a Redeemer   W&P 140

MUSIC FOR THE DAY

PSALMODY

Cherwien, David. PW, Cycle C.

Haas, David. "I Call to You, God" in PCY, vol. 8.

Honoré, Jeffrey. "Lord, Bend Your Ear" in *Sing Out! A Children's Psalter*. WLP 7191.

Kogut, Malcolm. "Lord, When Your Glory Appears" in PCY, vol. 10.

Stewart, Roy James. "Lord, When Your Glory Appears" in PCY, vol. 5.

CHORAL

Gerike, Henry V. "Sing with All the Saints in Glory." SATB, org, french hrn/other inst. AFP 0800675835.

Handel, G. F. "I Know That My Redeemer Liveth" in *Messiah*. S solo, kybd. Various ed.

Handel, G. F. "Since by Man Came Death" in *Messiah*. SATB, kybd. Various ed.

Helgen, John. "That Priceless Grace." SATB, pno. AFP 0800658590.

Hopp, Roy. "From the Apple in the Garden." SATB, org. AFP 0800674138.

MacFarlane, Will C. "Christ Our Passover." SATB, org. PRE 322.35139.

Morley, Thomas. "Lamb of God." SATB. KJO 8948.

CHILDREN'S CHOIR

Collins, Dori Erwin. "God Will Always Be With Me." U, kybd, opt inst. AFP 0800675193.

Kosche, Kenneth. "Keep Me as the Apple of Your Eye." (Ps. 17:1-2) U/2 pt, kybd. CG CGA800.

Marshall, Jane. "Psalm 17:8" in *Psalms Together*. U, kybd, cong. CG CGCI8.

KEYBOARD/INSTRUMENTAL

Kolander, Keith. "Sing with All the Saints in Glory" in *Organ Music for the Seasons*, vol. 3. Org. AFP 0800675649.

Leupold, Anton Wilhelm. "Jesus, meine Zuversicht" in *Augsburg Organ Library: Easter*. Org. AFP 0800659368.

Moore, David W. "Dona nobis pacem" in *Dona Nobis Pacem: Three for Piano and Solo Instrument*. Pno, inst. AFP 0800659392.

HANDBELL

Behnke, John A. "When Morning Gilds the Skies." 3-5 oct. AFP 0800674863.

Page, Anna Laura. "Jerusalem, My Happy Home." 3-5 oct, opt hc. AGEHR AG35201.

PRAISE ENSEMBLE

Dufford, Bob. "Songs of the Angels" in *Glory and Praise*. OCP 5910GC.

Jernigan, Dennis. "We Will Worship the Lamb of Glory" in *The Dennis Jernigan Songbook*. Shepherd's Heart Music 3010380496.

Sunday, November 7

JOHN CHRISTIAN FREDERICK HEYER, MISSIONARY TO INDIA, 1873

Heyer was the first missionary sent out by American
Lutherans. He was born in Germany and came to the
United States after his confirmation. He was ordained in
1820, established Sunday schools, and taught at Gettys-
burg College and Seminary. Heyer became a missionary
in the Andhra region of India. During a break in his
mission work he received the M.D. degree from what

349

would later be Johns Hopkins University. He later served as chaplain of the Lutheran seminary at Philadelphia until his death.

Because of his work as a pastor, missionary, and medical doctor, his commemoration can lead us to be mindful of all who work for healing of both body and spirit.

Thursday, November 11

MARTIN, BISHOP OF TOURS, 397

Martin's pagan father enlisted him in the army at age fifteen. One winter day, a beggar approached Martin for aid, and he cut his cloak in half and gave a portion to the beggar. Later, Martin understood that he had seen the presence of Christ in that beggar, and this ended his uncertainty about Christianity. He soon asked for his release from his military duties, but he was imprisoned instead. After his release from prison he began preaching, particularly against the Arians. In 371 he was elected bishop of Tours. As bishop he developed a reputation for intervening on behalf of prisoners and heretics who had been sentenced to death.

Today, at the same time as we remember this soldier turned peacemaker, we remember the end of World War I and veterans of all U.S. wars. Let these commemorations together move us to pray and work for peace in our families, congregations, and nation.

Thursday, November 11

SØREN AABYE KIERKEGAARD, TEACHER, 1855

Kierkegaard, a nineteenth-century Danish theologian whose writings reflect his Lutheran heritage, was the founder of modern existentialism. Though he was engaged to a woman he deeply loved, he ended the relationship because he believed he was called to search the hidden side of life. Many of his works were published under a variety of names, so that he could reply to arguments from his own previous works. Kierkegaard's work attacked the established church of his day. He attacked the church's complacency, its tendency to intellectualize faith, and its desire to be accepted by polite society.

Kierkegaard's work makes room for doubt in the life of faith. He also served as a prophetic challenge to churches that may want to set aside paradox for an easy faith and the gospel for cultural acceptability.

350

November 14, 2004

Twenty-fourth Sunday after Pentecost
Proper 28

INTRODUCTION

Signs of the end time fill today's gospel. Christ will come again "to judge the living and the dead," we confess in the creed. How, then, shall we live, knowing that everything around us will one day pass away? We can live with hope if we know that history is heading toward the God who loves us. Yet we also live in the present moment ready for action, making the most of the time given to us as a gift.

PRAYER OF THE DAY

Lord God, so rule and govern our hearts and minds by your Holy Spirit that, always keeping in mind the end of all things and the day of judgment, we may be stirred up to holiness of life here and may live with you forever in the world to come, through your Son, Jesus Christ our Lord.

or

Almighty and ever-living God, before the earth was formed and even after it ceases to be, you are God. Break into our short span of life and let us see the signs of your final will and purpose, through your Son, Jesus Christ our Lord.

VERSE

Alleluia. The Lord says, "Surely I am coming soon." Amen. Come, Lord Jesus! Alleluia. (Rev. 22:20)

READINGS

Malachi 4:1-2a

Malachi, whose name means "my messenger," warns that the day of the Lord is coming and that it will bring doom to the evil but vindication to those who fear God.

Psalm 98

In righteousness shall the LORD judge the world. (Ps. 98:10)

2 Thessalonians 3:6-13

Some members of the Thessalonian community, because of their belief in the nearness of Christ's return, had ceased to work, preferring to live on the generosity of other members of the community. Paul warns them that if they want to eat, they need to work.

Luke 21:5-19

Luke's presentation of Jesus' teaching about the last days emphasizes the necessity for responsible behavior in the time between Jesus' ascension and the second coming.

Alternate First Reading/Psalmody

Isaiah 65:17-25

Isaiah 56–66 addresses the exiles who have returned to Jerusalem from exile in Babylon. The conditions in Jerusalem were discouraging, and the people were disillusioned. Into this gloomy situation the prophet proclaims a joyful message about a world fashioned in the designs of God's peace.

Isaiah 12

In your midst is the Holy One of Israel. (Is. 12:6)

COLOR   Green

THE PRAYERS

Encouraged by the company of the saints of every time and place, let us pray for the church, the world, and all people according to their needs.

A BRIEF SILENCE.

That God, the righteous one, would give to the church the wisdom and courage to testify of the faith that fills us, so that more may be brought from terror and uncertainty to faith, let us pray to the Lord.

Lord, have mercy.

That people everywhere may be awakened to the urgent need for proper care of God's creation, so that the seas, lands, rivers, and hills may thrive and proclaim God's praise, let us pray to the Lord.

Lord, have mercy.

That God would protect those suffering from persecution of any kind: for political beliefs, for differences from accepted norms, and especially for those suffering because of their faith, let us pray to the Lord.

Lord, have mercy.

351

That the God of love might rise up with healing for those who are sick and dying (*especially*), let us pray to the Lord.
Lord, have mercy.

That our congregation might be strengthened through word and sacrament so that we will not be weary in doing what is right, let us pray to the Lord.
Lord, have mercy.

HERE OTHER INTERCESSIONS MAY BE OFFERED.

In thanksgiving for the saints and martyrs who were granted the opportunity to testify to Christ and who endured suffering on account of their faith, that their witness may inspire us also to testify to Christ with words and wisdom from the Holy Spirit, let us pray to the Lord.
Lord, have mercy.

Holy God, enthroned in glory and surrounded by saints and angels, we bring before you these petitions and all else that you know we need. Hear our prayers for the sake of our Savior and King, Jesus Christ our Lord.
Amen

352

IMAGES FOR PREACHING

Charles Schulz once depicted two of his "Peanuts" characters building an elaborate sandcastle on a beach. Admiring their handiwork, Lucy says to Linus, "A thousand years from now people will look at what we have built here today, and be totally amazed" (United Features Syndicate, Inc., July 22, 1991). Though we chuckle at such naivete, we invariably think and behave similarly. From sandcastles to the World Trade Center towers, our temples prove surprisingly vulnerable and often crush us in their fall.

As we eavesdrop on Jesus and his disciples conversing about their doomed temple, we recall what immediately preceded their interchange. A widow, whose generosity Jesus extolled, had just put her last coins in the treasury of the very temple over which Jesus laments. Bad enough that rich folks and big donors should see their tax deductions disappear. The treasury to which this woman entrusted everything proved bankrupt.

We, too, spend all we have in the building of temples, nations, careers, and relationships with parents, siblings, relatives, and friends. All will fail us in the end, Jesus promises. Inevitably, we end up crushed, betrayed, and dead.

The good news? We hear two words of promise. First, Jesus says, "Not a hair of your head will perish." (To some, this resembles talk of permanent sand castles.) But Jesus adds, "By your endurance you will gain your souls."

Endurance here means "sticking our ground, staying low." It's not something we must find, like tokens for the last subway ride to Paradise. It's a gift—the gift of being held in the one place that will not crumble and fall, the place into which Jesus laid himself when friends betrayed him and his hair got tangled with thorns. In God's hands he rested himself.

In baptism, we lie low in that same place. No matter what else falls around us, there we find our temple. Here, too, in these hands we call the body of Christ, we find a sanctuary that will not crumble.

WORSHIP MATTERS

"I believe in the Holy Spirit, the holy catholic church, the communion of saints, the forgiveness of sins, the resurrection of the body, and life everlasting. Amen." So we say in the Apostles' Creed. The communion of saints is an article of faith for Christians. It points to scripture's promise that those who have been buried with Christ in a death like his shall surely be raised with him in a resurrection like his (Rom. 6:5). When we give thanks for the dead or the "faithful departed," we are affirming this article of our faith and trusting God in Christ to lose none that are his own but to raise them up at the last day (John 6:39-40). This prayer of thanks also points our eyes to the hope of the fulfillment when Christ will be all in all and when every tear shall be wiped from our eyes. The writer of Hebrews reminds us that we are surrounded by a great cloud of witnesses (Heb. 12:1). The faithful departed are those witnesses who finally cannot be separated from us because of the promise of Christ. It is for his resurrection and their witness that we give thanks.

LET THE CHILDREN COME

Psalm 98, which many congregations will be using today, is filled with rich images of all creation praising the Lord. Distribute a variety of rhythm instruments to older children as they enter the worship space. Teach them a signal. During various parts of the reading of the psalm, children will play their instruments in response to the signal. (Suggestions: Signal after verses 1, 4, 5, 6, 7, and 9.)

With advance preparation, older elementary children may
play a three- to five-note response on brass, woodwind,
and strings. At the close of the worship service, give
young children film canisters with a few pebbles inside.
Encourage children to shake their rhythm instruments
whenever they sing and praise God at home.

HYMNS FOR WORSHIP
GATHERING
Christ, whose glory fills the skies   LBW 265
O day of peace   WOV 762

HYMN OF THE DAY
Through the night of doubt and sorrow   LBW 355

ALTERNATE HYMN OF THE DAY
Judge eternal, throned in splendor   LBW 418
Come, Lord Jesus   RW1 20

COMMUNION
Let all mortal flesh keep silence   LBW 198
Once he came in blessing   LBW 312, W&P 78

SENDING
Son of God, eternal Savior   LBW 364
Great is thy faithfulness   WOV 771, TFF 283
We shall overcome   TFF 213

ADDITIONAL HYMNS AND SONGS
On Jordan's stormy banks   RWSB, TFF 49
Lord, it belongs not to my care   RWSB
Beauty for brokenness   W&P 17
O day of God, draw nigh   H82 601

MUSIC FOR THE DAY
PSALMODY
Cherwien, David. PW, Cycle C.
Haugen, Marty, and David Haas. "All the Ends of the Earth" in
PCY, vol. 1.
Howard, Julie. *Sing for Joy: Psalm Settings for God's Children.*
LP 0814620787.
Marshall, Jane. "Psalm 98." U, kybd. CG CGA427.
Proulx, Richard. "The Lord Has Revealed to the Nations."
GIA G-2306.
Smith, Timothy R. "The Lord Has Revealed" in STP, vol. 4.

CHORAL
Dupré, Marcel. "O salutaris." SATB, org. LED AL 15973.
Ellingboe, Bradley. "Soul, Adorn Yourself with Gladness." SATB.
AFP 0800658477.
Handel, G. F. "Why Do the Nations?" in *Messiah.* B solo, kybd. Various ed.
Johnson, Ralph. "Be Still, and Know That I Am God." SATB, org,
eng hrn/cl. KJO 8961.
Nicholson, Sydney. "O salutaris hostia" in *Two Anthems for Communion.*
SATB, S/A solo, org. Royal School of Church Music 255.
Shute, Linda Cable. "Stir Up Your Power" in *The Augsburg Easy Choirbook.* 2 pt, kybd. AFP 0800676025.
Tye, Christopher. "Sing to the Lord." SATB, org. CFI CM8216.

CHILDREN'S CHOIR
Mahnke, Allen. "We Praise You for the Sun." (Malachi 4:2) U, kybd,
opt Orff. CG CGA153.
Page, Sue Ellen. "Children of the Covenant." U, org. CG CGA495.

KEYBOARD/INSTRUMENTAL
353
Cornell, Garry. *Procesión Alegre.* Org. Celebrations Unlimited CU 801.
Manz, Paul. "Now Thank We All Our God" in *Five Hymn Interpretations for Weddings and General Use.* Org. MSM 10-850.
Miller, Aaron David. "Ebenezer" in *Augsburg Organ Library: Epiphany.*
Org. AFP 0800659341.
Organ, Anne Krentz. "Christ, Mighty Savior" in *Christ, Mighty Savior:
Piano Reflections.* Kybd. AFP 0800656806.

HANDBELL
Helman, Michael. "Nocturne in C Minor." 3-5 oct, opt hc. AGEHR
AG35120.
Kinyon, Barbar Baltzer. "Let All Mortal Flesh Keep Silence." 2 oct.
AG 1659.
Nelson, Susan. "Give Me Jesus." 3-4 oct. AFP 0800658132.

PRAISE ENSEMBLE
Gordon, Nancy, and Jamie Harvill. "Firm Foundation" in *Best of the
Best.* FEL 1891062018.
Haas. David. "God Has Done Marvelous Things" in W&P.
Kogut, Malcolm. "Lord, in Your Great Love." SATB, solo, kybd, opt
cong, gtr. GIA G-5001.

Wednesday, November 17

ELIZABETH OF THURINGIA, PRINCESS OF HUNGARY, 1231

This Hungarian princess gave away large sums of money, including her dowry, for relief of the poor and sick. She founded hospitals, cared for orphans, and used the royal food supplies to feed the hungry. Though she had the support of her husband, her generosity and charity did not earn her friends within the royal court. At the death of her husband, she was driven out. She joined a Franciscan order and continued her charitable work, though she suffered abuse at the hands of her confessor and spiritual guide. Her lifetime of charity is particularly remarkable when one remembers that she died at the age of twenty-four. She founded two hospitals and many more are named for her.

November 21, 2004

Christ the King
Proper 29

INTRODUCTION

On this last Sunday of the church year, we honor Christ, who reigns as king from the cross. The effusive descriptions of Christ in the letter to the Colossians remind us of the absolutely central and vital role he rightfully claims in our life. All space and all time belong to the one who offers paradise to those who live and die with him.

PRAYER OF THE DAY

Almighty and everlasting God, whose will it is to restore all things to your beloved Son, whom you anointed priest forever and king of all creation: Grant that all the people of the earth, now divided by the power of sin, may be united under the glorious and gentle rule of your Son, our Lord Jesus Christ, who lives and reigns with you and the Holy Spirit, one God, now and forever.

VERSE

Alleluia. I am the Alpha and the Omega, the first and the last, the beginning and the end. Alleluia. (Rev. 22:13)

READINGS

Jeremiah 23:1-6

Today's reading builds on the common ancient Near Eastern metaphor of the king as shepherd. The influence of an unjust ruler is about to bring disaster. Nevertheless, the Lord will raise up a new and righteous shepherd who will rule a restored Judah.

Psalm 46

I will be exalted among the nations. (Ps. 46:11)

Colossians 1:11-20

An early Christian hymn praises Christ as one who reigns in heaven and on earth.

Luke 23:33-43

On the cross, Jesus is revealed to be a type of ruler different from what many had anticipated. He has the power to welcome others to paradise but will not use that power to save himself from death.

Alternate Psalmody

Luke 1:68-79

God has raised up for us a mighty savior. (Luke 1:69)

COLOR White

THE PRAYERS

Encouraged by the company of the saints of every time and place, let us pray for the church, the world, and all people according to their needs.

A BRIEF SILENCE.

That God who sent Christ to be our king would also raise up shepherds of integrity to gather the church in safety and to preach the gospel message of redemption and forgiveness, let us pray to the Lord.

Lord, have mercy.

That the kingdoms and nations of the world might be shaken from complacency and so raise up honorable

354

leaders who will promote peace and justice for all people, let us pray to the Lord.

Lord, have mercy.

That God would rescue those captive to the power of darkness: those living with addictions, those who are victims of abuse, those suffering from depression, and bring them into the kingdom of light, let us pray to the Lord.

Lord, have mercy.

That God our healer would remember those who are sick *(especially)*, those who are growing older and facing declining health, and those who live with chronic illness, and be their stronghold and help in trouble, let us pray to the Lord.

Lord, have mercy.

That our congregation might become ever more a place of reconciliation and forgiveness for those who are estranged from God, let us pray to the Lord.

Lord, have mercy.

HERE OTHER INTERCESSIONS MAY BE OFFERED.

As we remember and give thanks to God for *(names, and)* all the saints in light, that we might be enabled also to share in God's promised inheritance, let us pray to the Lord.

Lord, have mercy.

Holy God, enthroned in glory and surrounded by saints and angels, we bring before you these petitions and all else that you know we need. Hear our prayers for the sake of our Savior and King, Jesus Christ our Lord.

Amen

IMAGES FOR PREACHING

Rome invented crucifixion as a way to make a cruel, public spectacle of anyone fool enough to defy the empire. When Pilate fixed over Jesus the title, "King of the Jews," he meant to ridicule the Jewish people as well. Pilate considered them laughable, and partly to annoy them he proclaimed this battered man their king.

Maybe the two fellows crucified with Jesus also spoke in jest that day. They saw the title and caught Pilate's sorry joke. So, there they hung together, a strange, royal court, a king with his advisors left and right. "Hey, King Jesus, remember me now that you've finally come to power!" says one. Perhaps he chuckled at his own feeble gallows humor. To bystanders, Jesus' response also sounded like comedy. "Right on, my friend. We'll meet in Paradise." "In your dreams," the others must have thought. "Hmph. Paradise!"

Only the empty tomb allows hindsight enough to learn who gets the last laugh. Would Pilate ever know how true his sarcastic words became, or hear the laughter in Abraham's bosom when all the folks Jesus gathered to his kingdom, including the dying thief, would celebrate and share their stories?

Quite a collection they would make, according to Luke, most of them the little people, the powerless, the world's laughingstock—shepherds, tax collectors, outcasts, fishermen; Lazarus, son of the gutter; and now a dying thief who maybe couldn't tell a final joke from a last hope. We find our place among such simple folk and sinners. Jesus' words to the dying thief address us also, especially when our lives seem a cruel joke and our faith little more than gallows humor.

In baptism, we too have been crucified with Christ. We're in on the joke. Now we hang here together, a king and his people. To others this seems a foolish spectacle. To us, it's the deepest truth we know about the church. We are nothing more, or less, than a bunch of crucified people hanging around asking, "What's next? Where do we go from here?"

The good news is, we've a reason to ask.

WORSHIP MATTERS

We know Jesus as king in metaphor in the light of his crucifixion and resurrection. Jesus never called himself a king. He presented himself as teacher and as servant of all. Those whom he called to follow him, to care for his people, to lead them in prayer are not called to set themselves up as kings in their midst, but to lead the assembly into deeper experience of the reign of Christ through their teaching, their preaching, and their servant leadership. It is a service—to serve in the way our Lord served the disciples. As he was among them, a servant of all, so we are called to be among his people today. It is the exercise of power turned upside down. To follow Jesus' leadership style in the liturgy suggests a shared ministry among pastor and lay leaders. Who proclaims the readings? Who leads the prayers? Who makes the announcements? Who distributes the bread and wine? How is ministry shared in the worship life of your congregation?

LET THE CHILDREN COME

This is the last Sunday of the church year. To mark this celebration of Christ as our King, have children process

355

holding long narrow dowels with nylon fabric streamers in all of the colors of the church year. Include at least three of each color. An older child carrying the cross leads the procession. The second child follows with streamers of gold and silver, the colors in a king's crown. Place the streamers in a large, sturdy decorative holder, creating a vase of streamers. At the end of the service, the children will process out, leaving the deep blues and purples of Advent behind.

HYMNS FOR WORSHIP

GATHERING

O Savior, precious Savior   LBW 514
Glory to God, we give you thanks   WOV 787
He is exalted   W&P 55

HYMN OF THE DAY

Lord, enthroned in heavenly splendor   LBW 172

ALTERNATE HYMN OF THE DAY

All hail the power of Jesus' name!   LBW 328, TFF 267
To God be the glory   TFF 264

COMMUNION

O Savior, precious Savior   LBW 514
Jesus, remember me   WOV 740, W&P 78

SENDING

Beautiful Savior   LBW 518
Soon and very soon   WOV 744, W&P 128, TFF 38

ADDITIONAL HYMNS AND SONGS

Christ is the king!   RWI 17, RWSB
O Christ, what can it mean for us   RWSB
Strange king   DH 61
Mighty God, while angels bless thee   REJ 348

MUSIC FOR THE DAY

PSALMODY

Burkhardt, Michael. *Three Psalm Settings.* U, cong, perc, org. MSM 80-705.
Cherwien, David. PW, Cycle C.
Cherwien, David. "Psalm 46: God Is Our Refuge." U, cong, org. MSM 80-800.
Folkening, John. *Six Psalm Settings with Antiphons.* SATB, U, cong, kybd. MSM 80-700.

Wood, Dale. PW, Cycle C.
Ziegenhals, Harriet Ilse. "God Is Our Help in Time of Trouble" in *Sing Out! A Children's Psalter.* WLP 7191.

CHORAL

Bainton, Edgar L. "And I Saw a New Heaven." SATB, org. NOV 29 0342 03.
Benson, Robert A. "O Lord Most High, Eternal King." SATB, org. AFP 0800674200.
Cherwien, David. "Beautiful Savior." SATB, org, fl, opt cong. AFP 0800675088.
Dawson, William. "Ain'a That Good News!" SATB. KJO T103A.
Fauré, Gabriel. "In paradisum" in *Requiem.* SATB, org, opt orch. HIN HMB 147A.
Handel, G. F. "He Shall Feed His Flock" in *Messiah.* S solo, kybd. Various ed.
Handel, G. F. "The King Shall Rejoice" in *Coronation Anthems,* SAATBB, opt soli, kybd, opt orch. Dover 40627.
Helgen, John. "Soon and Very Soon." SATB, pno. KJO 8889.
Schulz-Widmar, Russell. "Jerusalem, Jerusalem." 2 pt mxd, kybd. AFP 0800655214.

CHILDREN'S CHOIR

Bertalot, John. "God Is Our Hope." (Ps. 46) 2 pt, kybd. CG CGA444.
Leaf, Robert. "To the Glory of Our King." U, pno/org. CG CGA173.

KEYBOARD/INSTRUMENTAL

Fruhauf, Ennis. "Fantasy on King's Weston" in *Organ Music for the Seasons,* vol. 3. Org. AFP 0800675649.
Linker, Janet. "Variations on 'All Hail the Power of Jesus' Name.'" Org. CPH 97-6856.
Organ, Anne Krentz. "The King of Glory" in *Advent Reflections for Piano and Solo Instrument.* Kybd, inst. AFP 0800657284.
Powell, Robert. "King's Weston" in *Augsburg Organ Library: November.* Org. AFP 0800658965.

HANDBELL

Kinyon, Barbara Baltzer. "All Hail the Power of Jesus' Name." 2-3 oct. AG 1658.
Sherman, Arnold B. "Rejoice, the Lord Is King." 3-5 oct. AG 1613.

PRAISE ENSEMBLE

Hayford, Jack. "Majesty" in W&P.
Paris, Twila. "He Is Exalted" in W&P.

Tuesday, November 23

CLEMENT, BISHOP OF ROME, C. 100

Clement was the third bishop of Rome and served at the end of the first century. He is best remembered for a letter he wrote to the Corinthian congregation still having difficulty with divisions in spite of Paul's canonical letters. Clement's writing echoes Paul's. "Love . . . has no limits to its endurance, bears everything patiently. Love is neither servile nor arrogant. It does not provoke schisms or form cliques, but always acts in harmony with others." Clement's letter is also a witness to early understandings of church government and the way each office in the church works for the good of the whole.

Clement's letter reminds us that divisions within the church are a sad part of our history and that pastoral love for people must be present amid our differing views of authority, scripture, and ministry.

Tuesday, November 23

MIGUEL AGUSTÍN PRO, PRIEST, MARTYR, 1927

Miguel Pro grew up among oppression in Mexico, where revolutionaries accused the church of siding with the rich. He was a Jesuit priest who served during a time of intense anticlericalism, and therefore he carried out much of his ministry in private settings. He worked on behalf of the poor and homeless. Miguel and his two brothers were arrested, falsely accused of throwing a bomb at the car of a government official, and assassinated by a firing squad. Just before the guns fired he yelled, "¡Viva Christo Rey!" which means "Long live Christ the king!"

Make plans for work that can be done on behalf of the poor in the upcoming weeks. Raise questions about what long-term solutions may bridge the gap between rich and poor.

Thursday, November 25

ISAAC WATTS, HYMNWRITER, 1748

Isaac Watts was born in England to a nonconformist family, people who thought the Church of England had not carried its reforms far enough. As a youth, Watts complained to his father about the quality of hymnody in the metrical psalter of his day. That was the start of his hymnwriting career. He wrote about six hundred hymns, many of them in a two-year period beginning when he was twenty years old. Some of Watts's hymns are based on psalms, a nonconformist tradition, but others are not. When criticized for writing hymns not taken from scripture, he responded that if we can pray prayers that are not from scripture but written by us, then surely we can sing hymns that we have made up ourselves.

357

November 25, 2004

Day of Thanksgiving (U.S.A.)

INTRODUCTION

One of the names for holy communion is *eucharist*. It comes from a Greek word meaning "to give thanks." Food and thanksgiving always go together, for life is a precious gift from God. Every meal, every harvest, is an occasion for giving thanks and for acknowledging that all God's gifts are on loan for us to use in acts of praise.

PRAYER OF THE DAY

Almighty God our Father, your generous goodness comes to us new every day. By the work of your Spirit lead us to acknowledge your goodness, give thanks for your benefits, and serve you in willing obedience; through your Son, Jesus Christ our Lord.

VERSE

Alleluia. God is able to provide you with every blessing in abundance, so that by always having enough of everything, you may share abundantly in every good work. Alleluia. (2 Cor. 9:8)

READINGS

Deuteronomy 26:1-11

The annual harvest festival called the feast of Weeks provides the setting for today's reading. This festival celebrates the first fruits of the produce of the land offered back to God in thanks. In this text, worshipers announce God's gracious acts on behalf of Israel.

Psalm 100

Enter the gates of the LORD with thanksgiving. (Ps. 100:3)

Philippians 4:4-9

Because the Lord is near, Paul urges the Philippians to rejoice, include thanksgiving in their prayers, and take to heart whatever is worthy of praise.

John 6:25-35

The day after the feeding of the five thousand found the people still clamoring for bread. Jesus tells them that he is the bread of life and that faith in him will lead to eternal life.

COLOR White

THE PRAYERS

Encouraged by the company of the saints of every time and place, let us pray for the church, the world, and all people according to their needs.

A BRIEF SILENCE.

In thanksgiving that God has rescued us from the bondage of sin with a mighty hand and redeemed us through the outstretched arms of the crucified one, let us pray to the Lord.

Lord, have mercy.

In thanksgiving that God has given a bountiful harvest to those who work the land and blessed our country with an abundance of the fruits of the earth, let us pray to the Lord.

Lord, have mercy.

In awareness of all those who go to sleep hungry while others of us live in abundance, that God will give us generous hearts and will move us to work for justice and peace until no one suffers from hunger, let us pray to the Lord.

Lord, have mercy.

In prayer for all who are weak and sick *(especially)*, that God will be near to them and grant them healing and wholeness, let us pray to the Lord.

Lord, have mercy.

In thanksgiving for the Bread of life shared among us when we gather to hear God's word and participate in the holy meal Jesus gave us, let us pray to the Lord.

Lord, have mercy.

HERE OTHER INTERCESSIONS MAY BE OFFERED.

In thanksgiving for saints whose lives point us to the faithfulness of God that endures from age to age, let us pray to the Lord.

Lord, have mercy.

Holy God, enthroned in glory and surrounded by saints and angels, we bring before you these petitions and all else that you know we need. Hear our prayers for the sake of our Savior and King, Jesus Christ our Lord.

Amen

IMAGES FOR PREACHING

The creed today's children learn most universally declares, "I can succeed at anything I truly work to accomplish." By means of this belief we instill self-confidence that leads to persistence in the face of life's challenges.

This doctrine also lays the groundwork for plenty of mischief. Among other things, it implies that those who fail have only themselves to blame—and why should we care about slackers who fall behind? Moreover, those who succeed can mostly thank themselves. They've earned everything they have.

Little wonder that our age finds so many suffering from stress-related disorders. Only hard work and tenacity proves us worthy of our creed and the respect of our neighbors, not to mention ourselves. A few will make it to the top, though of *what* we can't be sure. The rest of us will fail, and though tempted even now to throw up our hands in defeat and surrender, we press on.

St. Paul gives us a good name for this harried state when he writes, "Do not worry about anything" (Phil. 4:6). His word for "worry" means literally to have a dissected mind. Think of your brain like a globe divided into 24 separate time zones marked off by all your worries. When Jesus once warned about the folly of worrying, he used a word that means to launch oneself like a meteorite (Luke 12:29). Apparently our age holds no patent on the quick burnout syndrome.

The alternative? Hand things over to God in prayer and thanksgiving, says Paul (Phil. 4:6). We still use the ancient gestures of prayer and thanksgiving when we lift up our hands. It looks like surrender. It also looks like crucifixion. In a way it's both, for giving thanks removes us—rescues us!—from the role of becoming self-made heroes through hard work.

With hands held high in thanks, we receive life as a gift. We receive as well the bread of life and the peace of God that surpasses understanding. In place of frenzy we know joy.

WORSHIP MATTERS

Worship planners may want to pay careful attention to the texts that are sung on this day. *Lutheran Book of Worship* and *With One Voice* have a number of hymn texts that closely link harvest, eucharist, and service to those in need. If you celebrate a non-eucharistic, perhaps ecumenical service on Thanksgiving Eve or Day, the hymns,

prayers, and preaching can still point the worshiping assembly toward the eucharist and care for the hungry.

LET THE CHILDREN COME

During Thanksgiving we remember that the earth's abundance is for all people. God wants no one to go hungry. Place an empty cornucopia on the altar. Place several large empty baskets nearby. These will remind the congregation of all of the hungry people in the world. In advance, invite the congregation to bring nonperishable food items and one fruit or vegetable suitable to place in the cornucopia. The congregation will hold onto their gifts until the offertory. At that time invite children to process, filling the cornucopia and the baskets with their offerings of food. Sing "Come, you thankful people, come" (LBW 407) during the procession.

HYMNS FOR WORSHIP
GATHERING

Sing to the Lord of harvest   LBW 412
O God beyond all praising   WOV 797
Oh, come, let us sing   W&P 107

HYMN OF THE DAY

All creatures of our God and King   LBW 527
All creatures, worship God most high!   RWI 8

ALTERNATE HYMN OF THE DAY

Let us talents and tongues employ   WOV 754, TFF 232
Praise and thanksgiving   LBW 409

COMMUNION

Now thank we all our God   LBW 533, 534
O living Bread from heaven   LBW 197

SENDING

God, whose giving knows no ending   LBW 408
Praise to you, O God of mercy   WOV 790

ADDITIONAL HYMNS AND SONGS

Make a joyful noise   RWSB
Sing unto the Lord   RWSB
Come, you thankful people, come   LBW 407
I will enter his gates   TFF 291
Let there be praise   W&P 87

359

MUSIC FOR THE DAY

PSALMODY

Cherwien, David. PW, Cycle C.

Gelineau, S. J., Joseph. "Psalm 100: Cry Out with Joy" in *Forty-one Grail/Gelineau Psalms*. GIA G-4402.

Haas, David. "Psalm 100: We Are His People" in PCY, vol I.

Howard, Julie. *Sing for Joy: Psalm Settings for God's Children*. LP 0814620787.

Marshall, Jane. *Sing Out! A Children's Psalter*. WLP 7191.

All people that on earth do dwell   LBW 245

Oh, sing jubilee to the Lord   LBW 256

Before Jehovah's awesome throne   LBW 531

CHORAL

Bach, J. S. "Now Thank We All Our God" in *Bach for All Seasons*. SATB, org. AFP 080065854X.

Biery, James. "Now Join We to Praise the Creator." SATB, org, opt inst, cong. AFP 0800675878.

Ferguson, John. "A Song of Thanksgiving" in *The Augsburg Choirbook*. AFP 0800656784.

Hopson, Hal H. "Sing Forth God's Glory." SAB, kybd. AFP 0800675444.

Jennings, Carolyn. "We Praise You, O God." SATB, org, opt tpt. AFP 0800658485.

Nelson, Bradley. "All Good Gifts." SATB, pno. KJO 8813.

Pachelbel, Johann. "Now Thank We All Our God." SATB, cont. CPH 98-1944.

Proulx, Richard. "What Shall We Offer." 2 pt mxd, org. KJO 6294.

Sweelinck, Jan Pieterszoon. "Sing to the Lord, New Songs Be Raising" in *Chantry Choirbook*. SATB. AFP 0800657772.

CHILDREN'S CHOIR

Bedford, Michael. "Jubilate Deo." (Ps. 100) U, kybd. CG CGA647.

Patterson, Mark. "Let Praise Be the First Word." U/2 pt, kybd. AFP 0800675347.

Sleeth, Natalie. "Blessing." (Philippians 4:7) U, kybd, opt fl/vln. CG CGA145.

KEYBOARD/INSTRUMENTAL

Cherwien, David. "Nun danket alle Gott" in *Augsburg Organ Library: November*. Org. AFP 0800658965.

Held, Wilbur. "We Gather Together" (Kremser) in *Hymn Preludes for Autumn Festivals*. Org. CPH 97-5360.

Peeters, Flor. "Kremser" in *Augsburg Organ Library: November*. Org. AFP 0800658965.

HANDBELL

Afdahl, Lee J. "Round Me Rings." 3-5 oct, fl. LOR 20/1221L.

Dobrinski, Cynthia. "We Praise Thee, O God, Our Redeemer." 3-5 oct. AG 1699.

Kinyon, Barbara Baltzer. "All Things Bright and Beautiful." 2-3 oct. AG 1733.

Linker, Janet and Jane McFadden. "Now Thank We All Our God." 3-5 oct, org/brass. AG 2125 (handbells); AG 2126 (full score).

Rogers, Sharon Elery. "Now Thankful People, Come." 2-3 oct. AFP 0800656652.

PRAISE ENSEMBLE

Smith, Henry. "Give Thanks" in W&P.

Talbot, John Michael. "Bread of Life" in *Best of the Best*. FEL 1891062018.

Tuesday, November 30

ST. ANDREW, APOSTLE

Andrew was the first of the twelve. He is known as a fisherman who left his net to follow Jesus. As a part of his calling, he brought other people, including Simon Peter, to meet Jesus. The Byzantine church honors Andrew as its patron and points out that because he was the first of Jesus' followers, he was, in the words of John Chrysostom, "the Peter before Peter." Together with Philip, Andrew leads a number of Greeks to speak with Jesus, and it is Andrew who shows Jesus a boy with five barley loaves and two fish. Andrew is said to have died on a cross saltire, an X-shaped cross.

We too are called to invite others to the life of Christ that we will celebrate during Advent and Christmas. In what ways will the church that bears the light of Christ lead others to meet Jesus?

360

Bibliography

CHOIRBOOKS

Augsburg Choirbook, The. Minneapolis: Augsburg Fortress, 1998. Kenneth Jennings, ed. Sixty-seven anthems primarily from twentieth-century North American composers.

Augsburg Easy Choirbook, Volume One. Minneapolis: Augsburg Fortress, 2003. Fourteen unison and two-part mixed anthems for the church year.

Bach for All Seasons. Minneapolis: Augsburg Fortress, 1999. Richard Erickson and Mark Bighley, eds. Offers movements from cantatas and oratorios presented with carefully reconstructed keyboard parts and fresh English texts. Instrumental parts available.

Chantry Choirbook. Minneapolis: Augsburg Fortress, 2000. Choral masterworks of European composers spanning five centuries, many with new English translations, and indexed for use in the liturgical assembly throughout the year.

100 Carols for Choirs. Oxford and New York: Oxford University Press, 1987. David Willcocks and John Rutter, eds. One hundred classic choral settings of traditional Christmas carols.

COMPUTER RESOURCES

Icon: Visual Images for Every Sunday. Minneapolis: Augsburg Fortress, 2000. More than 600 images by liturgical artist Tanja Butler that are based on the church year and lectionary gospel readings for use in congregational bulletins and other self-published materials.

Lutheran Resources for Worship Computer Series. Lutheran Book of Worship Liturgies; With One Voice Liturgies; Words for Worship: 2004, Year C; *Graphics for Worship; Hymns for Worship.* Minneapolis: Augsburg Fortress, 1997–2001. Hymns for Worship contains more than 1,400 hymn texts and music graphics with multiple search functions.

DAILY PRAYER RESOURCES

Book of Common Worship: Daily Prayer. Louisville, Ky.: Westminster John Knox Press, 1993. Presbyterian.

Cherwien, David. *Stay with Us, Lord: Liturgies for Evening.* Minneapolis: Augsburg Fortress, 2001. Settings for Evening Prayer and Holy Communion, available in full music and congregational editions.

For All the Saints. 4 vols. Frederick Schumacher, ed. Delhi, N.Y.: American Lutheran Publicity Bureau, 1994.

Haugen, Marty. *Holden Evening Prayer.* Chicago: GIA Publications, Inc., 1990.

Makeever, Ray. *Joyous Light Evening Prayer.* Minneapolis: Augsburg Fortress, 2000.

Ramshaw, Gail. *Between Sundays: Daily Bible Readings Based on the Revised Common Lectionary.* Minneapolis: Augsburg Fortress, 1997. Readings, indexes, and other helps for daily prayer.

Weber, Paul. *Music for Morning Prayer.* Minneapolis: Augsburg Fortress, 1999. Setting of liturgical music for morning prayer.

Welcome Home: Year of Luke. Minneapolis: Augsburg Fortress, 1997. Scripture, prayers, and blessings for the household.

ENVIRONMENT AND ART

Chinn, Nancy. *Spaces for Spirit: Adorning the Church.* Chicago: Liturgy Training Publications, 1998. Imaginative thinking about ways to treat visual elements in the worship space.

Clothed in Glory: Vesting the Church. David Philippart, ed. Chicago: Liturgy Training Publications, 1997. Photos and essays about liturgical paraments and vestments.

Huffman, Walter C., S. Anita Stauffer, and Ralph R. Van Loon. *Where We Worship.* Minneapolis: Augsburg Publishing House, 1987. Written by three Lutheran worship leaders, this volume sets forth the central principles for understanding and organizing space for worship. Study book and leader guide.

Mauck, Marchita. *Shaping a House for the Church.* Chicago: Liturgy Training Publications, 1990. The author presents basic design principles for worship space and the ways in which the worship space both forms and expresses the faith of the worshiping assembly.

Mazar, Peter. *To Crown the Year: Decorating the Church through the Seasons.* Chicago: Liturgy Training Publications, 1995. A contemporary guide for decorating the worship space throughout the seasons of the year.

Stauffer, S. Anita. *Altar Guild and Sacristy Handbook.* Minneapolis: Augsburg Fortress, 2000. Revised and expanded edition of this classic on preparing the table and the worship environment.

HYMN AND SONG COLLECTIONS

As Sunshine to a Garden: Hymns and Songs. Rusty Edwards. Minneapolis: Augsburg Fortress, 1999. Forty-six collected hymns from the author of "We all are one in mission."

Bread of Life: Mass and Songs for the Assembly. Minneapolis: Augsburg Fortress, 2000. Jeremy Young's complete eucharistic music based on *With One Voice* setting 5 and twelve of his worship songs.

Congregational Song: Proposals for Renewal (Renewing Worship 1). Minneapolis: Augsburg Fortress, 2001. More than 80 hymns and songs demonstrating possible strategies for revision of present collections.

Dancing at the Harvest: Songs by Ray Makeever. Minneapolis: Augsburg Fortress, 1997. More than 100 songs and service music items.

Earth and All Stars: Hymns and Songs for Young and Old. Herbert F. Brokering. Minneapolis: Augsburg Fortress, 2003. A collection of hymn texts by the popular writer.

O Blessed Spring: Hymns of Susan Palo Cherwien. Minneapolis: Augsburg Fortress, 1997. New hymn texts set to both new and familiar hymn tunes.

Renewing Worship Songbook. Minneapolis: Augsburg Fortress, 2003. About 200 hymns and songs in a variety of styles, not included in *LBW* or *WOV*. Full accompaniments in *Renewing Worship*, vol. 5.

Worship & Praise. Minneapolis: Augsburg Fortress, 1999. A collection of songs in various contemporary and popular styles, with helps for using them in Lutheran worship.

LEADING WORSHIP

Adams, William Seth. *Shaped by Images: One Who Presides*. New York: Church Hymnal Corporation, 1995. An excellent review of the ministry of presiding at worship.

Huck, Gabe. *Liturgy with Style and Grace*, rev. ed. Chicago: Liturgy Training Publications, 1984. The first three chapters offer a practical, well-written overview of the purpose of worship, the elements of worship, and liturgical leadership.

Huffman, Walter C. *Prayer of the Faithful: Understanding and Creatively Leading Corporate Intercessory Prayer*, rev. ed. Minneapolis: Augsburg Fortress, 1992. A helpful treatment of communal prayer, the Lord's Prayer, and the prayers of the people.

Singing the Liturgy: Building Confidence for Worship Leaders. Chicago: Evangelical Lutheran Church in America, 1996. A demonstration recording of the chants assigned to leaders in *LBW* and *WOV*.

See also Worship Handbook Series under Worship Studies.

LECTIONARIES

Lectionary for Worship (C). Minneapolis: Augsburg Fortress, 1997. The Revised Common Lectionary. Includes first reading, psalm citation, second reading, and gospel for each Sunday and lesser festival. Each reading is "sense-lined" for clearer proclamation of the scriptural texts. New Revised Standard Version.

Readings and Prayers: The Revised Common Lectionary. Minneapolis: Augsburg Fortress, 1995. Scripture citations for the Revised Common Lectionary in use within the Evangelical Lutheran Church in America.

Readings for the Assembly (C). Gordon Lathrop and Gail Ramshaw, eds. Minneapolis: Augsburg Fortress, 1997. The Revised Common Lectionary. Emended NRSV with inclusive language.

LECTIONARY-BASED RESOURCES

Life Together. Minneapolis: Augsburg Fortress. A comprehensive series of Revised Common Lectionary resources that integrates the primary activities of congregational life: worship, proclamation, and learning.

Faith Life Weekly. Reproducible weekly handouts to guide conversations, prayer, and activities in the home.

Kids Celebrate. Reproducible children's bulletins.

LifeSongs (children's songbook, leader book, and audio CDs). A well-rounded selection of age-appropriate songs, hymns, and liturgical music that builds a foundation for a lifetime of singing the faith.

Life Together: Faith Nurturing Resources for Children. Quarterly teaching and learning resources for three age levels: pre-elementary, lower elementary, upper elementary.

Living and Learning. A quarterly (except summer) guide for educational planning using the resources of Life Together.

Word of Life. Weekly devotional studies for adults based on the lectionary texts.

Share Your Bread: World Hunger and Worship. A Lectionary-Based Planning Guide. Chicago: Evangelical Lutheran Church in America, 2000. Worship materials, activity ideas, and devotional reflections that relate worship and the three-year lectionary to the church's mission in the areas of world hunger and social justice.

PERIODICALS

Assembly. Notre Dame Center for Pastoral Liturgy. Chicago: Liturgy Training Publications. Published five times a year. Each issue examines a particular aspect of worship. (800) 933-1800.

Catechumenate: A Journal of Christian Initiation. Chicago: Liturgy Training Publications. Published bimonthly with articles on congregational preparation of older children and adults for the celebration of baptism and eucharist. (800) 933-1800.

CrossAccent. Journal of the Association of Lutheran Church Musicians. Publication for church musicians and worship leaders in North America. (800) 624-ALCM.

Faith & Form. Journal of the Interfaith Forum on Religion, Art and Architecture. Editorial office. (617) 965-3018.

Grace Notes. Newsletter of the Association of Lutheran Church Musicians. (800) 624-ALCM.

Liturgy. Quarterly journal of The Liturgical Conference, Washington, D.C. Each issue explores a worship-related issue from an ecumenical perspective. (800) 394-0885.

Plenty Good Room. Chicago: Liturgy Training Publications. Published bimonthly. A magazine devoted to African American worship within a Roman Catholic context. Helpful articles on the enculturation of worship. (800) 933-1800.

Procession. Published periodically by the Office of Worship of the Evangelical Lutheran Church in America. Articles and annotated bibliographies on a range of worship topics. (800) 638-3522.

Worship. Collegeville, Mn: The Order of St. Benedict, published through The Liturgical Press six times a year. One of the primary journals of liturgical renewal among the churches. (800) 858-5450.

PLANNING TOOLS

Calendar of Word and Season 2004: Liturgical Wall Calendar. Minneapolis: Augsburg Fortress, 2003. Art by Br. Michael O'Neill McGrath. Date blocks identify seasonal or festival color. Includes Revised Common Lectionary readings for Sundays and festivals. A reference tool for home, sacristy, office.

Church Year Calendar 2004. Minneapolis: Augsburg Fortress, 2003. A one-sheet calendar of lectionary citations and liturgical colors for each Sunday and festival of the liturgical year. Appropriate for bulk purchase and distribution.

Choosing Contemporary Music: Seasonal, Topical, Lectionary Indexes. Minneapolis: Augsburg Fortress, 2000. Provides references to multiple collections of contemporary praise and liturgical songs. Includes extensive scripture and topic indexes.

Indexes for Worship Planning: Revised Common Lectionary, Lutheran Book of Worship, With One Voice. Minneapolis: Augsburg Fortress, 1996. Indexes the hymns and songs in *Lutheran Book of Worship* and *With One Voice.* Includes extensive scripture and topic indexes.

Worship Planning Calendar 2004. Minneapolis: Augsburg Fortress, 2003. A two-page per week calendar helpful for worship planners, with space to record appointments and notes for each day. Specially designed to complement Sundays and Seasons.

PREPARING MUSIC FOR WORSHIP

Cherwien, David. *Let the People Sing! A Keyboardist's Creative and Practical Guide to Engaging God's People in Meaningful Song.* St. Louis: Concordia Publishing House, 1997. Emphasis on the organ.

Farlee, Robert Buckley, gen. ed. *Leading the Church's Song.* Minneapolis: Augsburg Fortress, 1998. Articles by various contributors, with musical examples and audio CD, giving guidance on the interpretation and leadership of various genres of congregational song.

Handbells in the Liturgy: A Practical Guide for the Use of Handbells in Liturgical Worship Traditions. St. Louis: Concordia Publishing House, 1996.

Haugen, Marty. *Instrumentation and the Liturgical Ensemble.* Chicago: GIA Publications, Inc., 1991.

Hopson, Hal H. *The Creative Use of Handbells in Worship; The Creative Use of Choir in Worship; The Creative Use of Instruments in Worship; The Creative Use of Descants in Worship; The Creative Use of Organ in Worship.* Carol Stream: Hope Publishing Co.

Let It Rip! at the Piano (vol. 1 & 2) and *Pull Out the Stops.* Minneapolis: Augsburg Fortress, 2000–2003. Collections for piano and organ respectively, each containing introductions and varied musical accompaniments by various composers for more than 100 widely used hymns and songs. Emphasis on current musical styles including blues, gospel, new age, jazz, and rolling contemporary.

Rotermund, Donald. *Intonations and Alternative Accompaniments for Psalm Tones.* St. Louis: Concordia Publishing House, 1997. (*LBW* and *LW* versions available separately.)

Weidler, Scott, and Dori Collins. *Sound Decisions.* Chicago: Evangelical Lutheran Church in America, 1997. Theological principles for the evaluation of contemporary worship music.

Westermeyer, Paul. *The Church Musician,* rev. ed. Minneapolis: Augsburg Fortress, 1997. Foundational introduction to the role and task of the church musician as the leader of the people's song.

———. *Te Deum: The Church and Music.* Minneapolis: Fortress Press, 1998. A historical and theological introduction to the music of the church.

Wold, Wayne. *Preaching to the Choir: The Care and Nurture of the Church Choir.* Minneapolis: Augsburg Fortress, 2003. Practical helps for the choir director.

———. *Tune My Heart to Sing.* Minneapolis: Augsburg Fortress, 1997. Devotions for choirs based on the lectionary.

PROCLAIMING THE WORD

Brueggemann, Walter, et al. *Texts for Preaching: A Lectionary Commentary Based on the NRSV.* Cycles A, B, C. Louisville, Ky.: Westminster John Knox Press, 1993–95.

Craddock, Fred, et al. *Preaching through the Christian Year.* Three volumes for Cycles A, B, C. Valley Forge, Pa.: Trinity Press International, 1992, 1993. In three volumes, various authors comment on the Sunday readings and psalms as well as various festival readings.

Days of the Lord: The Liturgical Year. 7 vols. Collegeville, Mn.: The Liturgical Press, 1991–94. Written by French biblical and liturgical experts, this series provides helpful commentary useful also with the Revised Common Lectionary.

Homily Service: An Ecumenical Resource for Sharing the Word. Silver Spring, Md.: The Liturgical Conference. A monthly publication with commentary on Sunday readings (exegesis, ideas and illustrations, healing aspects of the word, a preacher's reflection on the readings).

New Proclamation, Year C. Minneapolis: Augsburg Fortress, 2003–2004. Various authors. A sound and useful series of commentaries on year C readings. In two volumes, Advent–Holy Week and Easter–Pentecost.

Ramshaw, Gail. *Treasures Old and New: Images in the Lectionary.* Minneapolis: Fortress Press, 2002. A creative unfolding of forty images drawn from the lectionary readings.

See also Worship Handbook Series under Worship Studies.

PSALM COLLECTIONS

Anglican Chant Psalter, The. Alec Wyton, ed. New York: Church Hymnal Corporation, 1987.

Daw, Carl P., and Kevin R. Hackett. *A Hymn Tune Psalter.* New York: Church Publishing, 1999.

Grail Gelineau Psalter, The. Chicago: GIA Publications, Inc., 1972. 150 psalms and eighteen canticles.

Guimont, Michel. *Lectionary Psalms.* Chicago: GIA Publications, Inc., 1998. Responsorial psalm settings for the three-year Roman Catholic lectionary.

Plainsong Psalter, The. James Litton, ed. New York: Church Hymnal Corporation, 1988.

Psalm Songs. David Ogden and Alan Smith, eds. Minneapolis: Augsburg Fortress, 1998. Three volumes of responsorial psalm settings by various composers.

Psalms for the Church Year. Ten volumes by different composers. Chicago: GIA Publications, Inc., 1983–1998.

Psalter, The. International Commission on English in the Liturgy (ICEL). Chicago: Liturgy Training Publications, 1995.

Psalter for Worship (A, B, C). Martin Seltz, ed. Minneapolis: Augsburg Fortress, 1995–97. Settings of psalm antiphons by various composers with LBW and other psalm tones. Psalm texts included. Revised Common Lectionary. Volume C includes all lesser festivals.

The Psalter: Psalms and Canticles for Singing. Louisville, Ky.: Westminster John Knox Press, 1993. Various composers.

Selah Psalter, The. Richard Leach and David P. Schaap, eds. Kingston, N.Y.: Selah Publishing Co., 2001. Sixty-six psalms in a variety of styles.

Singing the Psalms. Five volumes with various composers represented. Portland: Oregon Catholic Press, 1995–1999.

REFERENCE WORKS

Foley, Edward. *Worship Music: A Concise Dictionary.* Collegeville, Minn.: The Liturgical Press, 2000.

Praying Together. English Language Liturgical Consultation. Nashville: Abingdon Press, 1988. Core ecumenical liturgical texts with annotation and commentary.

Pfatteicher, Philip. *Festivals and Commemorations.* Minneapolis: Augsburg Publishing House, 1980.

———. *Commentary on Occasional Services.* Philadelphia: Fortress Press, 1983.

———. *Commentary on Lutheran Book of Worship.* Minneapolis: Augsburg Fortress, 1990.

Pfatteicher, Philip, and Carlos Messerli. *Manual on the Liturgy: Lutheran Book of Worship.* Minneapolis: Augsburg Publishing House, 1979.

Stulken, Marilyn Kay. *Hymnal Companion to the Lutheran Book of Worship.* Philadelphia: Fortress Press, 1981.

———. *With One Voice Reference Companion.* Minneapolis: Augsburg Fortress, 2000.

Van Loon, Ralph, and S. Anita Stauffer. *Worship Wordbook.* Minneapolis: Augsburg Fortress, 1995.

SEASONS AND LITURGICAL YEAR

Huck, Gabe. *The Three Days: Parish Prayer in the Paschal Triduum,* rev. ed. Chicago: Liturgy Training Publications, 1992. For worship committees, an excellent introduction to worship during the Three Days.

Hynes, Mary Ellen. *Companion to the Calendar.* Chicago: Liturgy Training Publications, 1993. An excellent overview of the seasons, festivals and lesser festivals, and many commemorations. Written from an ecumenical/Roman Catholic perspective, including commemorations unique to the Lutheran calendar.

WORSHIP BOOKS

Libro de Liturgia y Cántico. Minneapolis: Augsburg Fortress, 1998. A complete Spanish-language worship resource including liturgies and hymns, some with English translations. Leader edition (2001) with complete psalter.

Lutheran Book of Worship. Minneapolis: Augsburg Publishing House; Philadelphia: Board of Publication, Lutheran Church in America, 1978.

Occasional Services: A Companion to Lutheran Book of Worship. Minneapolis: Augsburg Publishing House; Philadelphia: Board of Publication, Lutheran Church in America, 1982.

Ritos Ocasionales. Minneapolis: Augsburg Fortress, 2000. Spanish language translation of rites from Occasional Services.

This Far by Faith: An African American Resource for Worship. Minneapolis: Augsburg Fortress, 1999. A supplement of worship orders, psalms, service music, and hymns representing African American traditions and developed by African American Lutherans.

With One Voice: A Lutheran Resource for Worship. Minneapolis: Augsburg Fortress, 1995. Pew, leader, and accompaniment editions; instrumental parts, organ accompaniment for the liturgy, cassette/CD (selections).

WORSHIP STUDIES

Gathered and Sent: An Introduction to Worship. Participant book by Karen Bockelman. Leader guide by Roger Prehn. Minneapolis: Augsburg Fortress, 1999. Basic worship study course for inquirers and general adult instruction in congregations.

Inside Out: Worship in an Age of Mission. Thomas Schattauer, gen. ed. Minneapolis: Fortress Press, 1999. Lutheran seminary teachers address the mission of the church as it pertains to various aspects of worship.

Open Questions in Worship. Gordon Lathrop, gen. ed. Minneapolis: Augsburg Fortress, 1994–96. Eight volumes on matters of current conversation and concern regarding Christian worship.

> *What are the essentials of Christian worship?* vol. 1 (1994).
>
> *What is "contemporary" worship?* vol. 2 (1995).
>
> *How does worship evangelize?* vol. 3 (1995).
>
> *What is changing in baptismal practice?* vol. 4 (1995).
>
> *What is changing in eucharistic practice?* vol. 5 (1995).
>
> *What are the ethical implications of worship?* vol. 6 (1996).
>
> *What does "multicultural" worship look like?* vol. 7 (1996).
>
> *How does the liturgy speak of God?* vol. 8 (1996).

Ramshaw, Gail. *Every Day and Sunday, Too.* Minneapolis: Augsburg Fortress, 1996. An illustrated book for parents and children. Daily life is related to the central actions of the liturgy.

———. *Sunday Morning.* Chicago: Liturgy Training Publications, 1993. A book for children and adults on the primary words of Sunday worship.

Renewing Worship. Minneapolis: Augsburg Fortress, 2001–. A continuing series of provisional resources prepared by the Evangelical Lutheran Church in America.

> *Congregational Song: Proposals for Renewal* vol. 1 (2001).
>
> *Holy Baptism and Related Rites* vol. 2 (2002).
>
> *Principles for Worship* vol. 3 (2002).
>
> *Life Passages: Marriage, Healing, Funeral* vol. 4 (2002).
>
> *New Hymns and Songs* vol. 5 (2003).
>
> *Holy Communion and Related Rites* vol. 6 (Spring 2004).
>
> *Daily Prayer* vol. 7 (Autumn 2004).
>
> *The Church's Year: Propers and Seasonal Rites* vol. 8 (Autumn 2004).
>
> *Ministry and the Church's Life* vol. 9 (Spring 2005).

Revised Common Lectionary Prayers. Proposed by the Consultation on Common Texts. Minneapolis: Augsburg Fortress, 2002. Thematic, intercessory, and scripture prayers for each Sunday and holy day in the three-year cycle.

Senn, Frank. *Christian Liturgy: Catholic and Evangelical.* Minneapolis: Fortress Press, 1997. A comprehensive historical introduction to the liturgy of the Western church with particular emphasis on Lutheran traditions.

Use of the Means of Grace: A Statement on the Practice of Word and Sacrament, The. Chicago: Evangelical Lutheran Church in America, 1997. Also available in Spanish and Mandarin versions.

Welcome to Christ. Minneapolis: Augsburg Fortress, 1997–2003. A Lutheran approach to incorporating adult catechumens.

> *A Lutheran Catechetical Guide.*
>
> *A Lutheran Introduction to the Catechumenate.*
>
> *Lutheran Rites for the Catechumenate.*
>
> *Sponsors Guide.*

What Do You Seek? Welcoming the Adult Inquirer. Minneapolis: Augsburg Fortress, 2000. An introduction to a congregational process for welcoming Christians through affirmation of their baptism.

Worship Handbook Series. Minneapolis: Augsburg Fortress, 2001–. Brief guides to liturgical ministries and celebrations for those who lead and participate in worship.

> *Acolytes and Servers.* Gerald Spice.
>
> *Assisting Ministers and Readers.* Gerald Spice.
>
> *Building the Worship Folder.* Scott Weidler.
>
> *Christian Burial.* Karen Bockelman.
>
> *Marriage.* Karen Bockelman.
>
> *Ministers of Communion from the Assembly.* Donald Luther.
>
> *Musicians in the Assembly.* Robert Buckley Farlee.
>
> *Preparing the Assembly's Worship.* Craig Mueller.
>
> *Presiding in the Assembly.* Craig Satterlee.
>
> *Sponsors and Baptism.* Elaine Ramshaw.
>
> *Ushers and Greeters.* Gerald Spice.
>
> *Welcome to Worship.* Karen Bockelman.

The Art

Sundays and Seasons presents image selections from *Icon: Visual Images for Every Sunday,* an electronic library of illustrations for all three cycles of the liturgical year. The Icon artwork, sampled here, is a series of papercuttings, a technique associated with folk art that employs incisive lines and bold contrasts.

Tanja Butler is a painter and printmaker whose work has been displayed in many solo and group exhibitions across the United States. Her artwork is included in the collection of the Vatican Museum of Contemporary Religious Art and the Armand Hammer Collection of Art. Her illustrations have been published in a variety of publications and worship resource materials. She currently teaches art at Gordon College in Wenham, Massachusetts, and lives in Lynn, Massachusetts, and Averill Park, New York.

The Design

The design elements of *Sundays and Seasons* are elemental in form and structure, expressing a simplicity of means. Silver metallic ink, chosen to fill the intimately sized icons, reflects the precious nature of both image and word. The cover's striped and solid fields of color provide a sense of serenity and order. The typeface Centaur, modeled on letters cut by the fifteenth-century printer Nicolas Jenson, expresses a beauty of line and proportion that has been widely acclaimed since its release in 1929. The book's contents use a combination of the typefaces Centaur (body text) and Univers (subtexts).

The Kantor Group, based in Minneapolis, provides communication design solutions to its clients nationwide.